Peru

a Lonely Planet travel survival kit

Rob Rachowiecki

Peru

3rd edition

Published by
Lonely Planet Publications
Head Office: PO Box 617, Hawthorn, Vic 3122, Australia
Branches: 150 Linden St, Oakland, CA 94607, USA
                 10a Spring Place, London NW5 3BH, UK
                 1 rue du Dahomey, 75011 Paris, France

Printed by
SNP Printing Pte Ltd, Singapore

Photographs by
Dave Houser   Michael Pettypool   Tony Wheeler
Richard I'Anson   Rob Rachowiecki

Front cover: Train to Machu Picchu, Tony Wheeler

Published
June 1996

Although the author and publisher have tried to make the information as accurate as possible, they accept no responsibility for any loss, injury or inconvenience sustained by any person using this book.

National Library of Australia Cataloguing in Publication Data

Rachowiecki, Rob, 1954-.
Peru.

3rd ed.
Includes index.
ISBN 0 86442 332 2.

1. Peru – Guidebooks.
I. Title. (Series: Lonely Planet travel survival kit).

918.504633

text & map keys © Rob Rachowiecki 1996
maps © Lonely Planet 1996
photos © photographers as indicated 1996
climate charts compiled from information supplied by Patrick J Tyson, © Patrick J Tyson, 1996

Rob Rachowiecki

Rob was born near London and became an avid traveler while still a teenager. He has visited countries as diverse as Greenland and Thailand. He spent most of the 1980s in Latin America – traveling, mountaineering and teaching English – and he now works in Peru and Ecuador part time as a leader for Wilderness Travel, an adventure travel company. He is the author of Lonely Planet's travel survival kits to Ecuador, Costa Rica and Southwest USA and has contributed to Lonely Planet's shoestring guides to South America and Central America as well as books by other publishers. When not traveling, he lives in Arizona with his wife Cathy and their three children: Julia (age 8), Alison (age 6) and Davy (age 3).

Dedication

For Cathy, whom I met in Peru.

From the Author

During several visits to Peru over the past year, several people provided invaluable assistance in updating this book. South American Explorers Club managers Richard Elgar and Jane Letham, along with club member Lluis Dalmau Gutsens, provided copious information about their various trips around the country. Richard and Lluis also made themselves available for last minute updates by fax as the book was being written, as did new manager Bill Glick, assisted by Ofelia.

I am especially grateful to Dr Richard Ryel of the ACEER Foundation for facilitating a very quick visit to the ACEER canopy walkway near Iquitos – a trip which remains one of my personal highlights in Peru. Barry Walker of Expediciones Manu (and the Cross Keys Pub) was charming, informative and a great source of Manu information. T'ai Roulston and Marsha Morrow of the Explorers Inn were very helpful in Puerto Maldonado.

Paul Cripps, freelance adventure guide and operator of Amazonas Explorer in Cuzco, provided much of the information about river-running, mountain-biking, and kayaking in the Cuzco area. Holber Tito Vizcarra, a student of tourism at the university in Cuzco, provided me with his detailed research on Cuzco's hotels. Carlos Milla Vidal, of Milla Turismo, was also a valuable source of Cuzco information. My good friends José Correa and Victor helped me rest and recuperate in Cuzco.

In Trujillo, Clara Luz Bravo and Michael White proved very knowledgeable and helpful, as did Lucho Hurtado and Beverly Stuart de Hurtado in Huancayo. I thank Lucho for an introduction to mountain-biking in Peru. Juan Carlos Godinez Ibarra, local cultural expert and cab driver, provided fine extra insights into Tacna. I very much enjoyed the company of Pablo Morales and chef Alfonso of Pyramid Adventures in Huaraz during a two week sojourn in the Cordillera Blanca. César Moreno Sanchez helped with recent notes from Iquitos. I also thank the Huarmey Tourist Authority.

I appreciate written and verbal input on archaeology from my colleague, Wayne

Bernhardson, who made me rethink my earlier section on this subject. Scores of readers of the last edition wrote with ideas, suggestions and updates; their names are listed in the back of the book. I particularly acknowledge the following writers: Frances Osborn (UK) sent a paper which she co-authored on changes caused by new roads in Peru's southern rainforests; José Luis Orihuela Salazar, a guide and writer from Tarma, sent me information about that city; Mary Anna Prentice (USA) contributed useful insights from the perspective of a middle-aged solo female traveler (and clearly enjoyed Peru's off-the-beaten-track archaeological wonders); John Graveley (USA) described his recent trip to Bolivia via the little-used northern route; Alberto Cafferata of Caraz sent detailed information on that town and others in the Callejón de Huaylas.

Finally, as always, my family provided a supportive and undisturbed environment in which to write this book and I thank them for their love and understanding during long sessions at the computer.

You can contact me via electronic mail at robrachow@aol.com.

From the Publisher

This edition of Peru is brought to you by the publishing professionals at Lonely Planet's US office. These editors worked nonstop and under backbreaking pressure and finished the job on time: Tom Downs, Carolyn Hubbard, Don Gates, Jeff Campbell and Laini Taylor.

Most of the maps were updated by Blake Summers. Cyndy Johnsen, Scott Noren, Beca Lafore, Paul Clifton, Chris Salcedo and Alex Guilbert finished off the stragglers.

Hayden Foell drew the pre-Columbian water vessel on the title page. Original illustrations were provided by Hayden, Hugh D'Andrade, Mark Butler and Ann Jeffree.

Hugh was responsible for cover design, while Cyndy Johnsen and Scott Summers handled layout.

Warning & Request

Things change – prices go up, schedules change, good places go bad and bad places go bankrupt – nothing stays the same. So if you find things better or worse, recently opened or long since closed, please write and tell us and help make the next edition better.

Your letters will be used to help update future editions and, where possible, important changes will also be included in a Stop Press section in reprints.

We greatly appreciate all information that is sent to us by travelers. Back at Lonely Planet we employ a hard-working readers' letters team to sort through the many letters we receive. The best ones will be rewarded with a free copy of the next edition or another Lonely Planet guide if you prefer. We give away a lot of books, but unfortunately not every letter/postcard receives one.

Contents

Map Legend

BOUNDARIES

—··—··—··— International Boundary

—··—··—··— Provincial/Department Boundary

AREA FEATURES

Park

NATIONAL PARK — National Park

HYDROGRAPHIC FEATURES

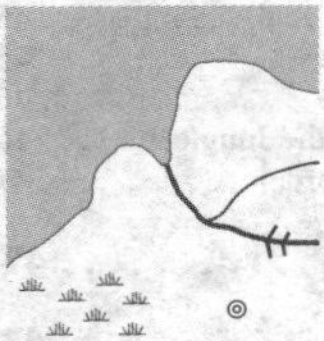

Water

Coastline

Creek

River, Waterfall

Swamp, Spring

ROUTES

Freeway

Major Road

Minor Road

Unpaved Road

Trail

Ferry Route

Railway, Railway Station

Ⓜ Metro, Metro Station

ROUTE SHIELDS

① Carreteras Sistema Nacional

⑬ Carreteras Sistema Departmental

SYMBOLS

❂ **NATIONAL CAPITAL**	✚ Airfield	⌐ Golf Course
◉ **Provincial/ Department Capital**	✈ Airport	❂ Hospital, Clinic
	∴ Archaeological Site, Ruins	⚲ Lighthouse
• **City**	⑤ Bank, ATM	⚑ Mission
• **Town**	▯ Baseball Diamond	⚑ Monument
	⊖ Bus Depot, Bus Stop	▲ Mountain
	⊞ Cathedral	🏛 Museum
▪ Hotel, B&B	⌒ Cave	♪ Music, Live
▲ Campground	† Church	← One-Way Street
⌂ Hostel	⊖ Embassy	⊜ Observatory
⊡ RV Park	⚓ Fishing, Fish Hatchery	Ⓟ Parking
▾ Restaurant	⤬ Foot Bridge	▴ Park
☕ Bar (Place to Drink)	✼ Garden	)(Pass
☕ Café	⛽ Gas Station	⋊ Picnic Area

★ Police Station
⌷ Pool
✉ Post Office
⛷ Skiing, Alpine
⛷ Skiing, Nordic
⌇ Shipwreck
❖ Shopping Mall
🏛 Stately Home
☎ Telephone
▣ Tomb, Mausoleum
⚑ Trailhead
⚶ Winery
🐘 Zoo

Note: not all symbols displayed above appear in this book.

Introduction

Peru is a wonderful country! It will fascinate the tourist, the anthropologist and the zoologist equally, for the discerning visitor cannot fail to be impressed by its cultural and geographical variety or be excited by the travel possibilities this country offers.

Peru is frequently referred to as the 'land of the Incas,' yet it could equally be called the 'land of the Moche' (or the Chavín or the Wari). It is true that the Incas formed the greatest empire on the continent and left mysterious cities such as Machu Picchu, the magnificent ruins that can still be visited today. Less well known, but equally true, is that the Incas were the last in a long series of Peruvian civilizations spanning thousands of years and that the ruins of many of these earlier civilizations can also be visited.

The Peruvian Andean mountains are arguably the most beautiful and accessible on the continent and the Cordillera Blanca has become world famous among trekkers, hikers and mountaineers. There are several other ranges in Peru which are less visited but no less magnificent. Many of the precipitous glacier-clad mountains have peaks of over 6000 meters and the high valleys between are the haunts of a host of rarely seen animals.

Visitors may glimpse mammals such as the graceful vicuña or the inquisitive viscacha, and birds ranging from the tiny Andean hummingbird to the giant Andean condor. Soaring effortlessly on a wingspan that can exceed three meters and with a weight of more than 10 kg, the condor is the largest flying bird in the world.

But the Peruvian Andes are not just the scene of remote wilderness. They are also home to millions of highland Indians who still speak their ancient tongue of Quechua (or Aymara) and preserve much of their traditional way of life. Town and village markets are thronged with herds of produce-laden llamas led by Indians

wearing distinctive ponchos that protect against the climatic extremes of this environment. The larger cities also preserve the legacy of the Spanish conquistadors, and colonial churches and mansions covered with dazzling ornamentation can also be seen.

The traveler could easily spend weeks or months among the Peruvian highlands and yet would only be visiting a small portion of the country. More than half of Peru's area lies in the verdant Amazon Basin where air or river is often the only means of transportation. Exotic plants and animals amaze and intrigue the observant visitor. The dense tropical rainforest on the eastern edges of the Andes houses the greatest variety of birds on earth – Peru, although less than twice the size of Texas, is home to

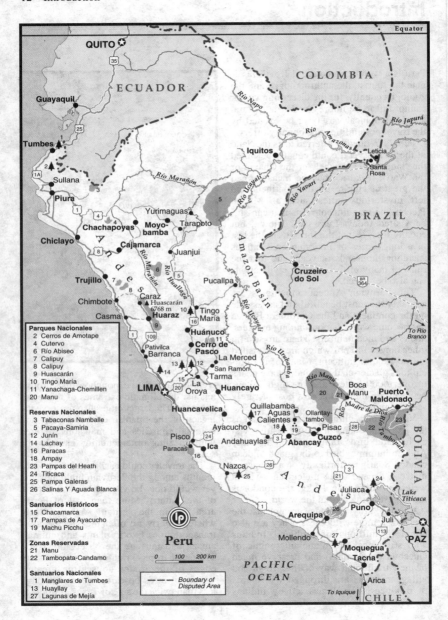

Parques Nacionales
2 Cerros de Amotape
5 Cutervo
6 Río Abiseo
7 Calipuy
8 Calipuy
9 Huascarán
10 Tingo María
11 Yanachaga-Chemillen
20 Manu

Reservas Nacionales
3 Tabaconas Namballe
5 Pacaya-Samiria
12 Junín
14 Lachay
16 Paracas
18 Ampay
23 Pampas del Heath
24 Titicaca
25 Pampa Galeras
26 Salinas Y Aguada Blanca

Santuarios Históricos
15 Chacamarca
17 Pampas de Ayacucho
19 Machu Picchu

Zonas Reservadas
21 Manu
22 Tambopata-Candamo

Santuarios Nacionales
1 Manglares de Tumbes
13 Huayllay
27 Lagunas de Mejía

Peru

0   100   200 km

----- Boundary of
       Disputed Area

PACIFIC
OCEAN

more than twice the number of bird species in the entire North American continent. It is a naturalist's paradise and, because it has been so little studied, a giant natural laboratory as well.

The Andes and the Amazon are but two of Peru's diverse geographical regions. The third is totally different, for the entire coastal strip of Peru is desert. Lima, the capital, is totally surrounded by bare rock and sand. Rivers from the Andes flow through this desert to the Pacific Ocean, creating small oases that have supported a variety of civilizations through the ages. To the north lie the ruins of Chan Chan, the greatest adobe city in the world and capital of the Chimu Empire. To the south are the mysterious Nazca Lines – giant stylized animal shapes etched into the desert many hundreds of years before the Spanish conquest. The etchings, as big as football fields, are visible only from the air. How and why the Nazca Lines were made remains shrouded in mystery – just one of the many fascinating features to encounter on a journey to that most intriguing of all Andean countries, Peru!

Facts about the Country

ARCHAEOLOGY & HISTORY

For many travelers, the first word that comes to mind when thinking of Peruvian history is Inca. Certainly, the Inca civilization is the best known and most studied of all the pre-Columbian cultures of South America and the one that most travelers will experience more than any other. But the Incas are merely the tip of the archaeological iceberg. Peru had many pre-Columbian cultures, some preceding the Incas by many centuries. Peru's pre-Columbian history is the subject of debate and disagreement amongst scholars, so after reading the outline given here you may want to do additional research and reach your own conclusions.

The concept that the numerous archaeological sites of Peru date from different eras and belonged to distinct cultures was first seriously proposed by Mr EG Squier, an Englishman who traveled throughout Peru in the 1870s. Since then, archaeologists have slowly pieced together a chronological framework for the cultures of the Peruvian area. But it has been a difficult task since none of the cultures are known to have had any written language and so their records lie entirely in archaeological excavation. Furthermore, as one culture succeeded another, they tended to introduce new values and to erode the old, as the Spanish did after defeating the Inca nation. The one difference with the Spanish conquest is that they did produce a written record of their exploits that gives some insight into the Incas.

Peru is unequaled in South America for its archaeological wealth and many archaeologists find Peru's ancient sites and cultures as exciting as those of Mexico, Egypt or the Mediterranean. For many travelers, learning about and visiting these centuries-old ruins is one of the highlights of their journey and even visitors with little interest in archaeology usually enjoy visiting one

or two of the main sites. With this in mind, this section provides a brief overview of archaeology in Peru.

Without written records, one of the main sources of information for archaeologists has been the realistic and expressive decoration found on the ceramics, textiles and other artifacts of Peru's pre-Columbian inhabitants. These relics often depict everyday life in detail and so it is well worth your while to inspect many of these artifacts in Peru's museums. One of the best ways to visualize the overall cultural history is to visit the Museo de la Nación in Lima, where exhibits are labeled and displayed chronologically. Archaeologists have found that, with intensive study, they can differentiate between ceramic styles and date them to within the length of about a human lifetime, which is more precise than using radiocarbon dating.

The following names of sites and cultures set in italic type are described in greater detail in the travel sections. The sub-headings below refer to periods named by some and recognized by many leading archaeologists. There are many texts, particularly older ones, which have different names for essentially the same time frame.

Preceramic Period

Humans are relatively recent arrivals in the New World. Not long ago it was thought that people spread throughout the Americas after migrating across the Bering Strait about 20,000 years ago. However, in 1986 there was a report in the British journal *Nature* claiming the discovery of human fossils in Brazil that dated back 32,000 years – still recent compared to the Old World but nevertheless a major discovery if substantiated (few archaeologists believe this date). All human remains found in the Americas belong to *Homo sapiens sapiens*; there is no evidence of the presence of more primitive hominids such as are known to belong to the Old World.

The first inhabitants of Peru were nomadic hunters and gatherers who roamed the country in loose-knit bands. They lived in caves, the oldest known of which is at Pikimachay in the department of Ayacucho. Human remains here date from about 14,000 years ago. They hunted fearsome animals which are long since extinct, such as giant sloths, saber-toothed tigers and mastodons. The discovery of Paiján projectile points indicates that the mastodons survived as late as about 5000 BC.

From the earliest arrivals until about 4000 BC, cultural development mainly meant improving stone implements for hunting. People knew how to make fires, wore animal skins, and made simple tools and weapons from stone and bone. As their prey became extinct they began hunting the animals we know today, such as deer, vicuña, guanaco and llamas. Hunting scenes were recorded in cave paintings at Lauricocha near Huánuco and Toquepala near Tacna. Domestication of the llama, alpaca and guinea pig began by 4000 BC, though some sources claim that cameloid domestication may have begun as early as 7000 BC.

By about 4000 BC (again, some sources claim earlier) people began planting seeds and learning how to improve crops by simple horticultural methods such as weeding. The coastal strip of Peru was then wetter than today's desert and a number of small settlements were established, thus changing the status of the people from nomadic hunters and gatherers to settled agriculturalists and fishermen. Several of these settlements have been excavated, with garbage mounds yielding the best information about life at that time. Although these places can be visited, there are no on-site museums or explanations and so looking at ancient garbage mounds is an activity with little to recommend it unless you're a professional archaeologist.

Some of the best known sites are Huaca Prieta in the Chicama Valley near *Trujillo*, Chilca and Asia, south of Lima. Chilca was inhabited about 4000 BC and the other two sites about 2000 BC. The inhabitants fished with nets or with bone hooks, sometimes using rafts, and collected seafood such as crabs and other shellfish, sea urchins, seabird eggs and even sea lions. Various crops were cultivated, including beans and cotton which appeared early (at least 3000 BC, though some sources claim earlier) as well as chili peppers, beans, squashes and, about 1400 BC, corn. The cotton was used to make clothing, mainly with the simple techniques of twining and later by weaving. Manioc (also called cassava) and sweet potatoes appeared on the coast early on, indicating trade links with the Amazon basin. The coastal people lived in simple one-room dwellings, lined with stone in Huaca Prieta, or made from branches and reeds in Asia. Ceramics and metalwork were still unknown although jewelry made of bone and shell have been found.

These early Peruvians built many structures for ceremonial or ritual purposes. One of the oldest, a raised platform facing the ocean and containing human burials, dates from about 4000 BC. It was found in the Supe Valley near *Barranca* on the north central coast. More such temple platforms appeared on the coast in the third millennium BC, indicating a prosperity based on the rich marine life of the coast. Some of these platforms were decorated with painted mud friezes. Trade with Andean and Amazonian regions was occurring as evidenced by the use of the coca leaf for ritual purposes and the introduction of exotic rainforest bird feathers.

Roughly contemporary with the later preceramic period coastal settlements was the enigmatic site of *Kotosh* near Huánuco – one of the earliest ruins in highland Peru. Little is known about the people who lived here, but their buildings were the most developed for that period, and pottery fragments found here predate by several hundred years those found in other parts of

Peru. Various forms of the Andean staple, the potato, began to be domesticated around 3000 BC.

Initial Period

Also called the Lower Formative Period, this extends very roughly from 2000 to 1000 BC and is known originally from remains found in the Virú Valley and Guañape area, about 50 km south of Trujillo on the north coast. More recently, large ceremonial temples from this period have been discovered in the Rimac Valley above Lima and various other coastal sites. Funerary offerings were associated with many of them. During this time, ceramics developed from basic undecorated pots to sculpted, incised and simply colored pots of high quality. Weaving, fishing and horticulture also improved, the latter particularly through the development of irrigation. Towards the end of this time, agricultural terraces appeared in the highlands.

Early Horizon

Lasting roughly from 1000 to 300 BC (archaeologists differ by several centuries as to the earlier date), this period has also been called the Chavín Horizon, after the site of *Chavín de Huantar*, 40 km east of Huaraz. It is termed a 'horizon' because artistic and religious phenomena appeared, perhaps independently, within several cultures in different places at about the same time, indicating some kind of interchange of ideas and increasing cultural complexity. This horizon extended throughout much of the northern and central highlands and the northern and southern coast.

The salient feature of the Chavín influence is the repeated representation of a stylized jaguar face with clearly religious overtones and so the Chavín is often termed a jaguar worshiping cult. Other animal faces, some mythical, as well as human faces are also found. Most importantly, this period represents the greatest early development in weaving, pottery, agriculture, religion and architecture – in a word, culture. During this time goldworking developed for the first time on the northern

coast. Many archaeologists see the Early Horizon as the most important cultural development of pre-Columbian Peru.

Early Intermediate Period

Around 300 BC the Chavín style gradually and inexplicably began to lose its unifying influence. Over the next 500 years several cultures became locally important, but none were individually outstanding or widespread. The best known are the Salinar culture of the Chicama Valley area near Trujillo and the *Paracas Necropolis* south of Lima. Salinar ceramics show advanced firing techniques, while the textiles of the Paracas Necropolis are markedly improved and different from the earlier Paracas Cavernas; these cotton and wool textiles are considered the finest pre-Columbian textiles to have been produced anywhere in the Americas.

From about 100 AD to 700 AD – formerly known as either the Florescent or Classic Period – pottery, metalwork and weaving reached a pinnacle of technological development in several regions throughout Peru. Two distinct cultures of this period are particularly noted for their exceptional pottery. The *Moche* from the Trujillo area produced pottery from molds and the *Nazca* people from the south coast introduced polychrome techniques. These cultures recorded their ways of life in intricate detail on their ceramics, providing archaeologists with an invaluable reference tool. Many of Peru's main museums have good collections of Nazca and Moche pottery.

These two cultures also left some interesting sites which are worth visiting. The Moche built massive platform mounds (popularly called 'pyramids') such as the *Temples of the Sun & Moon* near Trujillo and at *Sipán* near Chiclayo. This last was discovered to contain a series of tombs which have been under excavation since 1987 and are considered the most important archaeological discovery in South America in many decades. The Nazca made their enigmatic giant designs in the desert which are known as the *Nazca Lines* and are best appreciated from one of the many overflights in small airplanes available in the town of Nazca.

Other cultures of importance during this period include the Lima culture, with its main site 30 km south of Lima at *Pachaca-mac*; the Recuay culture, whose ceramics can be seen in the regional museum at *Huaraz*; and the *Cajamarca, Kuélap*, Galli-nazo and Tiahuanaco cultures.

Middle Horizon

Most of the latter half of the sixth century was marked by a catastrophic drought along the coast, contributing to the demise of the Moche. From 600 to about 1000 AD the Wari emerged as the first expansion-ist peoples known in the Andes. The ruin of their capital is the highland city of *Wari* (also spelled Huari), found about 25 km north of *Ayacucho*. Unlike the earlier Chavín, expansion was not limited to the diffusion of artistic and religious influence. The Wari were vigorous military con-querors who built and maintained impor-tant outposts throughout much of Peru. These included *Pikillacta* near Cuzco, *Cajamarquilla* near Lima, *Wilcahuaín* near Huaraz, Wariwillka near Huancayo, Wira-cochapampa near Huamachuco and Los Paredones near Cajamarca. The Wari was the first strongly militaristic and urban culture of Peru. Also, it was influenced by the Tiahuanaco religion from the Lake Titicaca region.

The Wari attempted to subdue the cul-tures they conquered by emphasizing their own values and suppressing local oral tra-ditions and regional self-expression. Thus from about 700 AD to 1100 AD, Wari influence is noted in the art, technology and architecture of most areas in Peru. More significantly, from an archaeologist's point of view, any local oral traditions which may have existed were discouraged by the con-querors and slowly forgotten. With no written language and no oral traditions, archaeologists must rely entirely on the examination of excavated artifacts to gain an idea of what life was like in the early Peruvian cultures. The Wari too, in their turn, were replaced by other cultures.

Late Intermediate Period

Because of their cultural dominance and oppression, it is not surprising that the Wari were generally not welcomed, despite their improvements in urban development and organization. By about 1000 AD they had been replaced, not by a new conquering force, but by individual groups in their local areas. These separate regional states thrived for the next 400 years, the best known being the *Chimu* kingdom in the Trujillo area. Its capital was the huge adobe city of *Chan Chan*, often referred to as the largest adobe city in the world. Chan Chan can easily be visited from Trujillo.

Roughly contemporary with the Chimu was the *Chachapoyas* culture of the Utcu-bamba River basin in the department of Amazonas. Its people built *Kuélap*, one of the most intriguing and significant of the highland ruins, which is reasonably acces-sible to the traveler (a few hours walk from the nearest dirt road). Also contemporary with the Chimu were the *Chancay* people from the Chancay Valley just north of Lima. The best collection of Chancay arti-facts is at the excellent Museo Amano in Lima. Further south was the Ica-Chincha culture whose artifacts can be seen in the Ica's Museo Regional. There were also several small altiplano kingdoms that lived near Lake Titicaca and frequently warred with one another. They left impressive *chullpas* (circular funerary towers) dotting the bleak landscape – the best are to be seen at *Sillustani*. Other groups included the Chanka who lived in the Ayacucho-Apurímac area and, of course, the early Incas, predecessors of the greatest pre-Columbian empire on the continent.

The Inca Empire

The Inca Empire, for all its greatness, existed for barely a century. Prior to 1430, the Incas, whose emperor was believed to have descended from the sun, ruled over only the valley of *Cuzco*. The Cuzqueños and the Chankas were at war for some time, eventually culminating in the 1430s with a major victory for the Cuzqueños. This marked the beginning of a remarkably rapid military expansion. The Inca Empire, known as Tahuantinsuyo (the four corners), conquered and incorporated the cultures mentioned in the preceding section as well as most of the cultures in the area stretching from southern Colombia to central Chile (including also the Andean regions of Bolivia and northern Argentina). Like the Wari before them, the Incas imposed their way of life on the peoples they conquered. Thus when the Spanish arrived, most of the Andean area had been politically unified by Inca rule. This unification did not extend completely to many everyday facets of life of the peoples of the Inca Empire and many of them felt some resentment to the Inca leaders. This was a significant factor in the success of the Spaniards during their invasion of the New World.

The Spanish Invasion

After Columbus' first landfall in 1492, the Spanish rapidly invaded and conquered the Caribbean islands and the Aztec and Mayan cultures of Mexico and Central America. By the 1520s, the conquistadors were ready to turn their attentions to the South American continent. In 1522 Pascual de Andagoya sailed as far as the Río San Juan in Colombia. Two years later Francisco Pizarro headed south but was unable to reach even the San Juan. In November 1526 Pizarro again headed south and by 1528 he had explored as far as the Río Santa in Peru. He noted several coastal Inca settlements, became aware of the richness of the Inca Empire, and returned to Spain to raise money and recruit men. Pizarro's third expedition left Panama in late 1530. He landed on the Ecuadorian coast and began to march overland towards Peru. In September 1532 Pizarro founded the first Spanish town in Peru, naming it San Miguel de Piura. He then marched inland into the heart of the Inca Empire. In November 1532 he reached Cajamarca, captured the Inca emperor, Atahualpa, and effectively put an end to the Inca Empire. (See Cuzco for more details.)

Colonial Peru

The Inca capital of Cuzco was of little use to the Spaniards who were a seafaring people and needed a coastal capital to maintain communication with Spain. Accordingly, Pizarro founded Lima in 1535 and this became the capital of the Viceroyship of Peru, as the colony was named.

The next 30 years were a period of turmoil, with the Incas still fighting against their conquerors and the conquistadors fighting among themselves for control of the rich colony. The conquistador Almagro was assassinated in 1538 and Francisco Pizarro suffered the same fate three years later. Manco Inca tried to regain control of the highlands and was almost successful in 1536, but a year later he was forced to retreat to Vilcabamba in the jungle, where he was killed in 1544. Succeeding Incas were less defiant until 1572, when the Inca Tupac Amaru organized a rebellion in which he was defeated and executed by the Spaniards.

The next 200 years were relatively peaceful. Lima became the main political, social and commercial center of the Andean nations. Cuzco became a backwater, its main mark on the colonial period being the development of a school of art called the Escuela Cuzqueña, which uniquely blended Spanish and highland Indian influences. Escuela Cuzqueña canvases can be admired now in Lima's museums and in the many colonial churches that were built in Lima and the highlands during the 17th and 18th centuries.

The rulers of the colony were the Spanish-born viceroys appointed by the Spanish crown. Immigrants from Spain had the most prestigious positions while Spaniards born in the colony were generally less important. This is how the Spanish crown was able to control its colonies. *Mestizos* (people of mixed Indian-Spanish descent) came still further down the social scale. Lowest of all were the Indians themselves who were exploited and treated as *peóns* or expendable laborers under the *encomienda* system. This resulted in the 1780 Indian uprising led by the self-styled Inca, Tupac Amaru II. The uprising was quelled and its leaders cruelly executed.

Independence

By the early 19th century, the inhabitants of Spain's Latin American colonies were dissatisfied with the lack of freedom and high taxation imposed upon them by Spain. All South America was ripe for revolt and independence. In Peru's case, important factors in the support of independence were the discovery and exploitation of a variety of rich mineral deposits beginning with the seemingly inauspicious *guano* (seabird droppings) used for fertilizer.

For Peru the change came from two directions. José de San Martín liberated Argentina and Chile and in 1821 entered Lima. That year he formally proclaimed Independence (in *Huacho*, a couple of hours drive north of Lima). Meanwhile, Simón Bolívar had freed Venezuela and Colombia and in 1822 sent Field Marshall Sucre to defeat the Ecuadorian royalists at the battle of Pichincha, near Quito, Ecuador. San Martín and Bolívar met privately in Guayaquil, Ecuador. What tran-

Simón Bolívar

spired during that meeting still remains unknown, but as a result San Martín left Latin America to live in France and Bolívar and Sucre continued with the liberation of Peru. The two decisive battles for Peruvian independence were fought at Junín on August 6, 1824, and at Ayacucho on December 9. Peru became essentially an independent state, in spite of a few royalists who managed to hold out for more than a year in the Real Felipe fortress near Lima.

Unfortunately, independence didn't spell the end of warfare for Peru: A brief war broke out with Spain in 1866, which Peru won, and was followed shortly by a longer war with Chile from 1879 to 1883, which Peru lost. The latter was over the nitrate rich areas of the northern Atacama Desert and, as a result of the war, Chile annexed a large portion of coastal southern Peru. The area around Tacna was returned in 1929.

Peru went to war with Ecuador over a border dispute in 1941. A treaty drawn up at Rio de Janeiro in 1942 gave Peru jurisdiction over what are now the northern sections of the departments of Amazonas and Loreto, but Ecuador disputes this border and armed skirmishes occur between the two countries every few years. The brief

José de San Martín

war of 1995 was the worst in a couple of decades and cost the lives of several dozen soldiers on both sides, but made no change in the recognized boundaries. Both Peru and Ecuador claimed that the other country had started the conflict.

Peru's turbulence hasn't always been restricted to warfare. The world's worst soccer disaster on record occurred on May 24, 1964, in Lima. Over 300 soccer fans were killed and hundreds more were injured in a riot following a disputed referee call during an international match between Peru and Argentina. On May 31, 1971, a 7.7 magnitude earthquake in northern Peru killed about 70,000 people, the most deadly natural disaster ever to occur in the New World.

Over the last 30 years Peru's government of has been marked by a series of military dictatorships and coups, followed by a period of civilian rule beginning in 1980 with the election of President Belaúnde Terry. He was replaced in the 1985 elections by Alán García Pérez. After two years of relative economic and political stability under García, the country began experiencing some of its worst economic and guerrilla problems in years.

The biggest economic problems of the late 1980s and early '90s were inflation, which exceeded an astonishing 10,000% at one stage, and the foreign debt, which totals about US$24 billion. In 1985 the García government placed severe restrictions on the amount Peru would pay on its foreign debt, leaving the country isolated temporarily from the international banking community and the IMF. By the end of García's five-year term, the country was in economic and political chaos. García went into exile and is now (according to a recent Peruvian newspaper report) living in a luxurious apartment in Paris. His return is sought by Peruvian authorities who accuse him of embezzling millions of dollars.

Recent politics in Peru haven't been affected strictly by government. The Maoist group *Sendero Luminoso* (Shining Path) waged a terrorist campaign against the central government from 1980 until the early '90s and the struggle claimed over 23,000 lives. The group was linked to drug cartels and was active mainly in the central part of the country, but with effects that were often felt in Lima. Another, unrelated, and small guerrilla group, the Movimiento Revolucionario Túpac Amaru (MRTA), also waged a war against the government but this conflict was more localized, mainly in the department of San Martín.

The socio-economic situation began to improve after the 1990 elections when Alberto Fujimori, the 52-year-old son of Japanese immigrants, was elected president. He defeated the well-known novelist Mario Vargas Llosa, a right-winger who advocated 'shock treatment' for Peru's ailing economy. Fujimori capitalized on fears that such treatment would mean more poverty and increased unemployment, and though his campaign promises of 'honesty and hard work' were vague, he was seen by many disillusioned voters as an alternative to the established parties and policies.

Fujimori took office on Peru's Independence Day, July 28, 1990, for a five year

President Alberto Fujimori

term. His immediate program of severe economic austerity resulted in unheard of rises in the cost of food and other essentials, but also allowed a liberal reformation of import/export, tax and foreign investment regulations leading to international financial support. He favored gradual reforms, deregulation of government controls on prices and state monopolies, and a new currency pegged to the US dollar. Much of this was, in fact, similar to Vargas Llosa's proposed 'shock treatment.'

Hampered by the disastrous economic situation left by his predecessor, as well as terrorism, drug-trafficking and corruption at most levels of government, Fujimori took dramatic – and for many alarming – action. In April 1992 he suspended the constitution and dissolved congress in an *auto-golpe* (self-coup). The perceived dictatorial anti-democratic stance lead to a suspension of foreign aid as well as outcry within Peruvian government circles. Nevertheless, Fujimori had the backing of the majority of the population and proceeded to catalyze the greatest improvements Peru had seen in many years.

Fortunately for Fujimori, the primary terrorist leaders were arrested during his presidency. In June 1992, the leader of the MRTA was captured and imprisoned. More importantly, Sendero Luminoso founder and leader, Abimael Guzmán, and several of his top lieutenants, were captured in September 1992. This certainly helped keep Fujimori's huge popular support intact during the difficult months following the auto-golpe. In November 1992, a new 80-seat unicameral congress was democratically elected (before the auto-golpe it was a bicameral congress of 60 senators and 180 deputies) and Fujimori's party (Cambio 90/Nueva Mayoría) won a majority of the seats, paving the way to renewed international support and the opportunity to radically change Peru's political, economic and social problems.

In October 1993, a new constitution was approved. Among other things, it changed the law that a president could not run for two successive terms of office, allowing Fujimori to run for re-election if he chose to do so. Other changes were the approval of a new 120-member unicameral congress and the institution of the death penalty for terrorists. In June 1994, the arrest of the new acting head of the Sendero Luminoso, Moises Simon Limaco, was announced. This culminated in a series of arrests of top-level Senderistas and by 1995 Sendero leaders were calling for an end to hostilities with the government. Certainly, terrorist activity had ceased to be a leading problem soon after Guzmán's arrest in 1992 and now only a few remote areas are considered dangerous because of guerrilla warfare.

Meanwhile, inflation dropped from over 10,000% to under 20%, and the Peruvian currency has begun a period of stability that has not been seen in decades. Previously prohibitive import taxes were restructured, allowing the easy import of items such as buses and cars. Tourists who visited before 1993 often commented on the old buses and cars; in 1996 visitors can see new bus fleets and taxis taking over the old boneshakers. Nevertheless, there are still severe socio-economic problems faced by much of the population. A census in 1993 indicates that over 60% of the population lives at or below the poverty level. Malnutrition and diseases such as cholera and dengue among the poor classes have been increasing because sanitation and health care programs are unable to keep up with population growth among the poorest people.

In 1995, Fujimori ran for an unprecedented second term against former UN Secretary General, Javier Pérez de Cuellar. Fujimori won handily, with 64% of the votes, and was reinaugurated on July 28, 1995. In his inauguration speech, Fujimori stated that with stabilization of the economy, his next objective was to combat poverty. He favors birth control and family planning, placing him at odds with the traditional Catholic Church, which wields significant power in the country. Despite this, the immediate future of Peru looks more promising than it has in years.

GEOGRAPHY

Peru covers 1,285,215 sq km, is the third largest country in South America, and the 18th largest in the world. It is more than five times the size of Great Britain. Bounded on the north by Ecuador and Colombia, to the east by Brazil and Bolivia, to the south by Chile and to the west by the Pacific Ocean, Peru lies entirely within the tropics. Its northernmost point is only a few km below the equator and its southernmost point just over 18° south.

Geographically, Peru is divided into three main regions – a narrow coastal belt, followed to the east by the wide Andean mountain range, which, further east, drops to the Amazon rainforest.

The narrow coastal strip is mainly desert, merging at the southern end into the Atacama Desert, one of the driest places on earth, and at the northern end, near Ecuador, into a mangrove swamp. This coastal desert contains Peru's major cities and its best highway, the Panamericana, which runs the entire length of Peru and is asphalted for most of the way. The desert is crossed by rivers running down the western slopes of the Andes; about 40 oases are formed in this way and are agricultural centers. Irrigation plays an essential role in

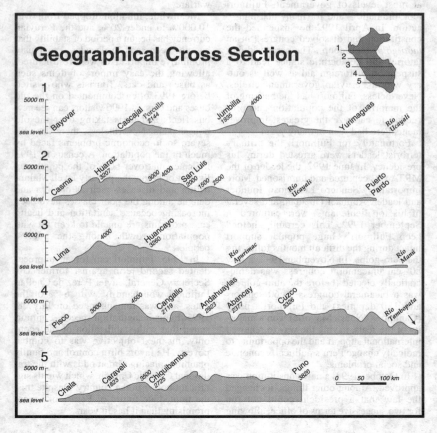

Geographical Cross Section

1
5000 m · Bayovar · Cascajal · Porculla 2144 · Jumbilla 1935 · 4000 · Yurimaguas · Río Ucayali · sea level

2
5000 m · Casma · Huaraz 3207 · 3000 4000 · San Luis 2000 1500 2500 · Río Ucayali · Puerto Pardo · sea level

3
5000 m · Lima · 4000 · Huancayo 3260 · Río Apurímac · Río Manú · sea level

4
5000 m · Pisco · 3000 4500 · Cangallo 2119 · Andahuaylas 2923 · Abancay 2377 · Cuzco 3326 · Río Tambopata · sea level

5
5000 m · Chala · Caraveli 1823 · 3500 · Chiquibamba 2725 · Puno 3820 · sea level

0   50   100 km

supporting the coastal cities and creating valuable agricultural land. The river valleys have good soil formed by the deposit of silt from the highlands but the intervalley areas are sandy or rocky desert.

The Andes, the second greatest mountain chain in the world after the Himalayas, jut rapidly up from the coast. Heights of 6000 meters are reached just 100 km inland. It's a young range still in the process of being uplifted as the Nazca plate (under the Pacific) slides under the South American plate. The Andes don't stop at the coast; 100 km offshore there is an ocean trench which is as deep as the Andes are high. The ongoing process of uplift contributes to the geological instability of the range and earthquakes are common. Active volcanoes are found in Peru's southern Andes. The mountains contain several types of mineral ores of which copper is the most important. The soils, with the exception of a few montane basins, are of poor quality.

Huascarán, at 6768 meters above sea level, is Peru's highest mountain and the world's highest mountain in the tropics. Most of Peru's Andes lie between 3000 and 4000 meters above sea level and support half the country's population. It is a rugged and difficult landscape with jagged ranges separated by extremely deep and vertiginous canyons. Although the roads are often in terrible condition, the traveler is rewarded by spectacular scenery.

The eastern slopes of the Andes are less precipitous, though no less rugged. They receive much more rainfall than the dry western slopes and so are clothed in a mantle of green cloud forest. As elevation is lost, the cloud forest becomes the rainforest of the Amazon Basin. This region has been penetrated by few roads and those which do exist go in for a short distance only. The traveler wishing to continue through the Amazon Basin to Colombia or Brazil must do so by river or air. Comparatively few people live in the Amazon Basin although it covers well over half of the country's area. Oil is extracted from the rainforests of northeastern Peru. Soil quality is poor.

CLIMATE

Peru's climate can be divided into two seasons – wet and dry – though the weather varies greatly depending on the geographical region. See the climate charts in the back of the book for specifics.

The desert coast is – as you'd expect – arid. During summer (January to March) the sky is often clear and the weather tends to be hot and sticky. This is the time Peruvians go to the beach. During the rest of the year the gray coastal mist known as the *garúa* moves in and the sun is rarely seen. I find the weather on the coast rather depressing during most of the year. It doesn't feel like the tropics! The garúa is caused by the cold Humboldt current from the south Pacific moving up the coast and causing what little moisture there is to condense into a mist, rather like the condensation on the cold faucet in a warm bathtub. During the summer, warmer central Pacific currents come down from Ecuador and temporarily push back the colder Humboldt current, providing warmer temperatures for swimming and less mist.

Moving inland, you soon rise above the coastal mist. Nazca, for example, is about 60 km inland and 600 meters above sea level – high enough to avoid the garúa, so it's hot and sunny for most of the year. Generally, the western slopes of the Andes have weather like that of Nazca.

Entering the Andes proper, you begin experiencing the wet and dry seasons. If you're interested in trekking or hiking the Inca Trail to Machu Picchu, you'll probably want to go in the dry season, from May to September. At that altitude nights can be cold, with occasional freezing temperatures in Cuzco (3326 meters), but days are filled with beautiful sunshine in the dry season. Because of this, the dry season in the Andes is known as summer and the warmer wet season is called winter. This leads to general confusion, for when it's summer on the coast it's winter in the highlands and vice versa. Confused? It gets even worse when you listen to a *Limeño* (inhabitant of Lima) arguing with a *serrano* (sierra or mountain dweller) about whether

El Niño
Every few years or so, the warm central Pacific currents of January through March are more pronounced and may flow for a longer period, causing the phenomenon *El Niño*. This is characterized by abnormally high oceanic temperatures in which much marine life (seaweeds, fishes) are unable to survive. This in turn creates problems for species, ranging from seabirds to human beings, that rely on the marine life. In addition, floods in both the coastal areas and highlands can be devastating, while other areas experience drought. A particularly intense El Niño in 1982-83 flooded much of Peru's north coast and washed out many kilometers of the Carretera Panamericana.

The climatological phenomenon is named El Niño (the baby boy) because it usually gets underway at year's end, or about the time the Christ child was born. Although very disruptive, it is still far from being fully understood by climatologists. ■

it's summer or winter. More important is whether it is the wet or dry season. The wet season in the mountains is from October to May but it usually doesn't get really wet until late January. Still, you can never tell for sure until you go!

Heading down the eastern slopes of the Andes it gets wetter. The driest months are the same as in the highlands, but the wet season tends to be more pronounced. The wettest months are from January until April, during which time roads on the eastern slopes of the Andes are often closed due to landslides or flooding. A similar weather pattern exists in the Amazon lowlands.

ECOLOGY & ENVIRONMENT
The physiographic division of Peru into coastal desert, Andean highlands and Amazon Basin clearly defines the ecological habitats of the country. The most important are the highland shrub forests and grasslands (called *páramos* in the north and *punas* in the central and south), the various kinds of cloudforests and rainforests in the Amazon Basin and the many rivers which are found flowing down both the Pacific and Atlantic slopes of the Andes.

Major economic activities include farming, grazing and logging, all of which cause serious environmental problems. Deforestation – of the highlands for firewood and of the rainforests for valuable hardwood and of both to clear land for agricultural use – has led to severe erosion. Although the problem of rainforest deforestation has currently caught the attention of the environmentally aware public, deforestation and overgrazing in the highlands, where many people live, is also a severe problem. The soil needs it's protective cover of Andean woodlands and puna grasslands. With the ongoing removal of its protective cover, the soil's quality, never very high to begin with, is rapidly deteriorating as soil gets blown off the mountains or washed down the rivers. This has also led to decreased water quality, particularly in the Amazon basin, where silt-laden water is unable to support the microorganisms that are the basis of the food chain.

Other water-related problems are pollution from mine tailings in the highlands and from industrial waste and sewage along the coast. Because of sewage contamination, many of the beaches around Lima and other coastal cities have been declared unfit for swimming. Coastal pollution combined with overfishing is a serious threat to Peru's rich marine resources.

Why Conserve the Rainforest?
The loss of tropical forests is a problem which has become acute in recent years. Deforestation is happening at such a rate that most of the world's tropical forests will have disappeared early in the 21st century. With this in mind, two important questions arise: Why are habitats such as the tropical rainforests so important and what can be done to prevent their loss?

Roughly half of the 1.6 million known species on earth live in tropical rainforests such as those found in the Amazon basin.

Scientists predict that millions more species remain to be discovered, principally in the world's remaining rainforests which have the greatest biodiversity of all the habitats known on the planet. This incredible array of plants and animals cannot exist unless the rainforest that they inhabit is protected – deforestation will result not only in the loss of rainforest but in countless extinctions as well.

The value of tropical plants is more than simply providing habitat and food for animals; it is more than the esthetic value of the plants themselves. Many types of medicines have been extracted from forest trees, shrubs and flowers. These range from anesthetics to antibiotics, from contraceptives to cures for heart diseases, malaria and various other illnesses. Countless medicinal uses of plants are known only to the indigenous inhabitants of the forest. Much of this knowledge is being lost as the various indigenous cultures are assimilated into the Western way of life, or when tribal groups are destroyed by disease or genocide. Other pharmaceutical treasures remain locked up in tropical forests, unknown to anybody. They may never be discovered if the forests are destroyed.

Many tropical crops are monocultures that suffer from a lack of genetic diversity. In other words, all the plants are almost identical because agriculturalists have bred strains which are high yielding, easy to harvest, taste good, etc. If these monocultures are attacked by a new disease or pest epidemic they could be wiped out because the resistant strains may have been bred out of the population. Plants such as bananas are also found in the wild in tropical forests. In the event of an epidemic scientists could look for disease-resistant wild strains to breed into the commercially raised crops. Deforestation leads not only to species extinction, but also to loss of the genetic diversity which may help species adapt to a changing world.

While biodiversity for esthetic, medicinal and genetic reasons may be important to us, it is even more important to the local indigenous peoples who still survive in tropical rainforests. These peoples rely on the rainforest to maintain their cultural identity and a way of life that has lasted for centuries. The accelerated pace of deforestation leads to a loss of tribal groups who are as unable to survive in a Western world as we would be if forced to survive in the jungle.

Rainforests are important on a global scale because they moderate climatic patterns worldwide. Scientists have recently determined that destruction of the rainforests is a major contributing factor to global warming which, if left unchecked, would lead to disastrous changes to our world. These changes include melting of ice caps causing rising ocean levels and flooding of major coastal cities, many of which are only a scant few meters above present sea level. Global warming would also make many of the world's 'bread-basket' regions unsuitable for crop production.

All these are good reasons why the rainforest and other habitats should be preserved and protected, but the reality of the economic importance of forest exploitation by the developing nations that own tropical forests must also be considered. It is undeniably true that the rainforest provides resources in the way of lumber, pastureland and possible mineral wealth, but this is a short-sighted view.

The long term importance of the rainforest both from a global view and as a resource of biodiversity, genetic variation and pharmaceutical wealth is recognized both by countries that contain forest as well as the other nations of the world which will be affected by destruction of these rainforests. Efforts are now underway to show that the economic value of the standing rainforest is greater than wealth realized by deforestation.

One important way of making the tropical forest an economically productive resource without cutting it down is by protecting it in national parks and reserves and making it accessible to tourists and travelers from all over the world. This type of ecotourism is becoming increasingly important for the economy of many tropical countries.

More people are likely to visit the Amazon to see monkeys in the forest than to see cows on pasture. The visitors spend money on hotels, transport, tours, food and souvenirs. In addition, many people who spend time in the tropics become more understanding of the natural beauty within the forests and of the importance of preserving them. As a result, visitors return home and become goodwill ambassadors for tropical forests.

Other innovative projects for sustainable development of tropical forests are being developed. The tagua nut is being harvested sustainably – this South American rainforest product is as hard as ivory and is used to carve ornaments and even to make buttons which are bought by North American clothing manufacturers. Brazil nuts are harvested for Ben & Jerry's 'Rainforest Crunch' ice cream. Debt for nature swaps have been initiated by conservation organizations. Iguana farms, orchid plantations, wicker work from aerial roots and harvesting seeds of ornamental plants are some of the other projects which are being explored. Whatever the methods used to preserve the rainforest, it is essential that they are protected.

FLORA & FAUNA

Peru's flora and fauna is some of the most diverse on earth. The western Amazonian uplands (eastern Andean foothills falling into the upper Amazon Basin) is one of the world's most species-rich areas. It has been labeled as one of the world's 10 biodiversity 'hot spots,' where there is an unusually high number of different species combined with a particularly large risk of destruction and extinction. Ecologist Norman Myers estimates that only a third of the western Amazonian uplands remain in their original state, and more is disappearing daily. Of Peru's 30,000 known species of vascular plants, over 20,000 have been identified in this region alone, and 25% are endemic. Thousands of more species remain to be identified. The incredible variety of plants is correlated with the high biodiversity of the animals that live within the forests.

Terry Erwin of the Smithsonian Institution has spent much time in Amazonian rainforests and reports that 3000 species of beetles were found in five different areas of rainforest – but each area was only 12 meters square! Erwin estimates that each species of tree in the rainforest supports over 400 unique species of animals – given the thousands of known tree species, this means that there are millions of species of animals living in the rainforest, many of them insects and most unknown to science. Higher animals are also found in great numbers. Peru has about 1700 species of birds, the second highest number for any country in the world. This is over twice the number found in any one of the continents of Europe, North America or Australia. Almost 400 species of mammals, almost 500 species of reptiles and amphibians, and about 2000 species of fish have been identified.

Given this incredible diversity, I can no more than give a brief overview here. The flora and fauna is most conveniently described according to Peru's three main physiographic regions.

It's true you won't see much wildlife on the coastal desert compared to the Amazon basin, but look out to sea and there is a wealth of birds and marine mammals. The single best place to see these is La Reserva Natural de Paracas (see The South Coast), although this wildlife is by no means limited to that particular reserve! A variety of small marine life and fish support huge populations of seabirds, such as pelicans, boobies, cormorants, gulls and frigatebirds, as well as small populations of rare Humboldt penguins and Inca terns. Sea lion colonies are also found.

An ascent from the coast through Peru's western Andes takes you through dry and barren slopes. Except in the river valleys, which tend to be cultivated, there is not enough moisture for much wildlife. Occasional forests of cacti are seen, and birds of prey make a living off the lizards found in the dry areas and the rodents and small birds living near the rivers. It is not until the high Andes are reached that there is enough moisture to support much flora and, in turn, fauna.

The páramo and puna are characteristic highland habitats. They are high altitude shrubland and grasslands that act as the natural 'sponge' of the Andes, catching and gradually releasing much of the water that is eventually used by city dwellers in the highlands. The páramo covers much of Peru's northern highlands continuing into Ecuador and beyond. It is characterized by a harsh climate, high levels of ultra-violet light and wet peaty soils. In the Huaraz area and on into southern Peru, the soil and weather tend to be drier and the highland areas are more grassy – this is the puna.

These highland habitats have a fairly limited flora dominated by hard grasses, cushion plants, small herbaceous plants, shrubs and dwarf trees. These have adapted well to the harsh environment and consequently the vegetation looks strange and interesting. Major adaptations include the development of small, thick leaves which are less susceptible to frost; the development of curved leaves with heavy, waxy skins to reflect extreme solar radiation during cloudless days; the growth of a fine, hairy down as insulation on the plant's surface; the arrangement of leaves into a rosette to prevent them shading one another during photosynthesis and to protect the delicate center of the plant; and the compacting of the plant so it grows close to the ground where the temperature is more constant and the wind less strong. Thus many highland plants are characteristically small and compact, sometimes resembling a hard, waxy, green carpet, called *Laretta*. Beware the small, compact and hairy Andean cacti. They look like innocuous pads of cotton wool, but have very sharp spines!

Not all highland plants are so compacted, however. The giant *Espeletia*, members of the daisy family, are a weird sight as their loosely arranged stands float into view in a typical páramo mist. Further south in the drier puna the bromeliads called *puyas* are found – plants with a rosette of spiky leaves growing out of a short trunk (see The Huaraz Area for a description).

There are dense thickets of small trees, often *Polylepis* species, or *quinua* in Spanish, members of the rose family. With the Himalayan pines, they share the world altitudinal record for trees. They were once considerably more extensive but fire and grazing have pushed them back into small pockets. Instead, spiky, resistant tussock grasses, locally called *ichu*, are commonly encountered. In order to manage the land for cattle, burning is carried out to encourage the growth of succulent young shoots. This does not favor older growth and, combined with erosion caused by overgrazing, poses considerable threats to these fragile habitats.

Animals of the highlands include members of the South American cameloids, the llama, alpaca, guanaco and vicuña. The first two have been domesticated for thousands of years while the latter two are found only in the wild state. The llama is the largest of the four; used as a pack animal, it's capable of carrying up to 25 kg. In remote areas, it is also used for meat, but you won't find llama served in any Peruvian restaurants. Also, in remote areas, llamas are sometimes sheared for their coarse wool, of which they yield about four kg every two years. The alpaca, a little

Llama

smaller, is domesticated almost exclusively for its wool, which is finer than sheep's wool and is used preferentially for clothing in the highlands. An alpaca yields about 5 kg of wool during shearings done every two years. Alpaca wool can be a variety of colors – white, brown, grey or black. The llama and alpaca can interbreed and are sometimes hard to distinguish. Generally, the alpaca has longer hair and the llama has longer ears and a tail that sticks out. The guanaco looks like a smaller version of the llama but is rarely seen. It is usually an orange-brown color with a whitish belly.

The rare vicuña is the smallest of all and, though it has never been domesticated, is sometimes caught and sheared for its wool which is the finest in the world. In Inca times, it was used solely for making the Inca's clothes. In recent years, shearing this endangered animal was illegal, although since 1995 small numbers are again being legally sheared. It produces just 250 grams of wool per shearing, which happens every three or four years, or about five times during the life of the animal. Although vicuña wool is not yet produced commercially, a 1995 report estimated that a coat made of vicuña wool will cost about US$5000. Because of this high value, vicuñas are both endangered and protected.

Other animals of the Peruvian Andean highlands include foxes, pumas, white-tailed deer and vizcachas. This last is the most commonly spotted highland mammal. It looks like a cross between a large squirrel and a rabbit. They live among boulders on rocky slopes and I've seen them right next to the Machu Picchu ruins.

Of the birds, the most well known, but not necessarily frequently sighted, is the Andean condor, often called the largest flying bird in the world. With its three-meter wing span and 10 kg weight it is certainly magnificent. Condors are best recognized by their flat, gliding flight with fingered wing tips (formed by spread primary feathers), silvery patches on the upper wing surface (best seen when the bird wheels in the sun), and a white neck ruff and unfeathered, flesh-colored

head (binoculars help). Otherwise, the bird is black.

Other birds of the highlands include the carunculated caracara, a large member of the falcon family. It has bright orange-red facial skin, yellowish bill and legs, white thighs and underparts, and is otherwise black. The Andean lapwing is common and is unmistakable with its harsh and noisy call, reddish eyes, legs and bill, and brown-white-black striped wing pattern particularly noticeable in flight.

Most towns, both in the highlands and the lowlands, are host to the ubiquitous rufous-collared sparrow. The well-known house sparrow of Europe, Asia, Australia and North America is not found in Peru – the similarly sized rufous-collared sparrow, readily identified by the chestnut collar on the back of the neck, replaces the house sparrow in Peru.

Other noteworthy birds in the Andean highlands include the torrent duck, which lives only in the whitewater areas of rivers,

Hummingbirds

For many visitors to Peru, the diminutive hummingbirds are the most delightful birds to observe. About 120 species have been recorded from Peru, and their exquisite beauty is matched by extravagant names such as 'green-tailed goldenthroat,' 'spangled coquette,' 'fawn-breasted brilliant' and 'amethyst-throated sunangel.' Hummingbirds can beat their wings in a figure-of-eight pattern up to 80 times a second, thus producing the typical hum for which they are named. This exceptionally rapid wingbeat enables them to hover in place when feeding on nectar, or even to fly backwards. These tiny birds must feed frequently to gain the energy needed to keep them flying. Species like the Andean hillstar, living in the páramo, have evolved an amazing strategy to survive a cold night. They go into a state of torpor, which is like a nightly hibernation, by lowering their body temperature by about 25°C, thus lowering their metabolism drastically. ∎

swimming submerged with just its head poking out of the water. Three species of flamingo inhabit puna lakes, especially in the south of the country. The Andean flicker is a ground-dwelling puna woodpecker – there aren't any trees to peck! For the interested observer, there are many, many other birds in Peru.

Descending the eastern Andean slopes into western Amazonian uplands, the scenery is rugged and remote. Here you will find the little-known tropical cloud forests. They are so named because they trap (and help create) clouds that drench the forest in a fine mist, allowing some particularly delicate forms of plant life to survive. Cloud forest trees are adapted to steep rocky soils and a harsh climate. They are characterized by low, gnarled growth, dense small-leafed canopies and moss-covered branches supporting a host of plants such as orchids, ferns, bromeliads and many others. These aerial plants, which gather their moisture, and some nutrients without ground roots, are collectively termed epiphytes.

The dense vegetation at all levels of this forest gives it a mysterious and delicate fairy tale appearance. It is the home of such rare species as the woolly tapir, Andean spectacled bear and puma. Many of Peru's endemic birds are found here and new species of birds are regularly discovered every few years. Who knows what other creatures new to science might dwell here? Apart from being part of a biodiversity hotspot, as discussed above, this habitat is important as a source of fresh water and for controlling erosion.

Finally, the Amazon rainforest is reached with its untold wealth of flora and fauna. A short walk into a tropical forest will reveal that it is very different from the temperate forests that many North Americans and Europeans may be used to. Temperate forests have little variety. It's pines, pines, and more pines, or interminable acres of oaks, beech and birch. Tropical forests, on the other hand, have great variety. If you stand in one spot and look around, you see scores of different species of trees, but you often have to walk several hundred meters to find another example of any particular species.

Visitors to the rainforest are often bewildered by the huge variety of plants and animals found there. With the exception of mammals and birds, there are few useful field-guides to what you might see there. If you are particularly interested in learning about the fantastic flora and fauna, it is worth investing in a guided tour – not that any guide will be able to answer all your questions!

One thing that often astounds visitors is the sheer immensity of some trees. A good example is the ceiba tree (also called the kapok), which has huge flattened supports, or buttresses, around its base and may easily reach five or more meters across. The smooth gray trunk often grows straight up for 50 meters before the branches are reached. These spread out into a huge crown with a slightly flattened appearance – the shape is distinctive and the tree is often the last to be logged in a ranching area. When you see a huge, buttressed, and flattened looking tree in a pasture in the Amazonian lowlands, it very often is a ceiba.

Some rainforest trees have strange roots – looking like props or stilts – supporting them. These trees are most frequently found where periodic floods occur – the stilt roots are thought to play a role in keeping the tree upright during the inundations. Rainforest palms, in particular, are among the trees that have these kinds of roots.

In areas that have been cleared (often naturally, as by a flash flood or by a gap created by an ancient forest giant falling during a storm) various fast-growing pioneer species appear. These may grow several meters a year in areas where abundant sunlight is suddenly available. Some of the most common and easily recognized of these are in the genus *Cecropia*, which has a number of species. Look for them in recently cleared areas, such as riverbanks. Their gray trunks are often circled by ridges at intervals of a few centimeters, but are otherwise fairly smooth, and their

Sloths & their Toilet Habits

In the Amazonian Rainforest, the diurnal three-toed sloth is quite often sighted whereas the two-toed sloth is nocturnal and therefore rarely seen. Sloths are often found hanging motionless from tree limbs, or progressing at a painfully slow speed along a branch towards a particularly succulent bunch of leaves, which are their primary food source. Leaf digestion takes several days and sloths defecate about once a week.

Sloths are most fastidious with their toilet habits, always climbing down from their tree to deposit their weekly bowel movement on the ground. Biologists do not know why sloths do this; one suggested hypothesis is that by consistently defecating at the base of a particular tree, the sloths provide a natural fertilizer which increases the quality of the leaves of that tree, thus improving the sloth's diet. You are welcome to come up with your own explanation as you travel through this fascinating region. ∎

branches tend to form a canopy at the top of, rather than all along, the trunk. The leaves are very large and palmate (like a human hand with spread fingers), with the underside a much lighter green than the top surface. This is particularly noticeable when strong winds make the leaves display alternately light and dark green shades in a chaotic manner.

Visitors to protected areas of the Amazonian lowlands may see several species of monkeys, including the howler, spider, woolly, titi, capuchin and squirrel monkeys, as well as tamarins and marmosets. The monkeys of the new world (the Platyrrhini) differ markedly from the monkeys of the old world (the Catarrhini), which include humans. New world monkeys have, comparatively, been little studied and their names are still under constant revision.

The male howler monkeys are heard as often as they are seen; their eerie vocalizations carry long distances and have been likened to a baby crying or the wind moaning through the trees. Many visitors are unable to believe they are hearing a monkey when they first listen to the mournful sound.

National Parks

Peru has many protected areas. Recently, there were seven *parques nacionales* (national parks), nine *reservas nacionales* (national reserves), seven *santuarios nacionales* and three *santuarios historicos* (national and historical sanctuaries) and

two *zonas reservadas* (reserve zones). There are also an increasing number of *reservas forestales* (forest reserves). Together these cover about 7% of the country.

With a few exceptions, the parks (and other areas) are not geared towards tourism. There are very few information centers, park guards, camping areas or lodges. Those that do exist are often privately run. Many of the parks are very remote and hard to get to, which makes them effectively off-limits to ordinary tourism. Others can be reached but require a long trip by land and boat, or chartered light aircraft, and are expensive to get to. Some areas are closed to travel in order to fully protect the flora, fauna and people living in them. Large parts of Manú, for example, are closed to all travel and are home to several Indian tribes which have had almost no contact with outsiders.

Easily and frequently visited parks include the following: Santuario Historico Machu Picchu, with its famed Inca ruins, costs US$10 to visit; Parque Nacional Huascarán has wonderful trekking in the Cordillera Blanca; and Reserva Nacional de Paracas is the best place to see coastal and marine wildlife. The latter two cost US$1 to enter. All three are easily reached by public transport and offer nearby lodging. Other places require more time, money and effort to reach. More details are given in the appropriate parts of the text.

Conservation Protected areas often lack the fundamental infrastructure needed to

Facts about the Country – Economy   31

conserve them fully and are subject to illegal hunting, fishing, logging or mining. The government simply doesn't have the money to hire enough rangers and buy necessary equipment to patrol the parks. Nevertheless, they do receive some measure of protection and various international agencies, notably The Nature Conservancy (TNC), Latin American Program, 1815 North Lynn St, Arlington, VA 22209, USA, and the many affiliates of the Worldwide Fund for Nature (called the World Wildlife Fund, WWF, in the USA), contribute money and resources to help in conservation and local education projects. They work closely with Peruvian organizations such as Fundación Peruana para la Conservación de la Naturaleza (Pro Naturaleza), Apartado 18-1393, Lima (☎ 241-2269, 446-3801, fax 446-9178). Readers who are interested in helping with conservation efforts can donate directly to Pro Naturaleza or through TNC or WWF, designating their money specifically for use in Peru. Several other conservation organizations in Peru have a more grass-roots approach, including the Asociación de Conservación para la Selva Sur, Avenida Sol 582, Cuzco, and Asociación Peruana para La Conservación de la Naturaleza (☎ 461-6316), Parque José de Acosta 187, Magdalena del Mar, Lima.

GOVERNMENT

Under the new constitution (see History), presidents hold office for five years and are permitted to run for re-election. The president has two vice presidents and a cabinet of 12 members. The congress is a unicameral and consists of 120 members. Voting is

compulsory for all citizens aged between 18 and 70 and optional for older people.

Peru is politically divided into 24 departments (states) and the constitutional province of Callao. In 1993, this system was reorganized into 11 regions, two departments and the constitutional province, but the reorganization has met with confusion and non-acceptance. At this writing, the older departmental system seems to be more adhered to than the new regional system, but that may change. The departments are further divided into provinces, of which there are 155, and the provinces subdivided into 1586 districts.

ECONOMY

Peru's gross national product in 1993 was almost US$34 billion, or US$1490 per capita. The largest sector of the working population (about 33%) is involved in agriculture and fishing, but this produces only 13% of the value of the gross domestic product (GDP). Conversely, mining employs only 2.4% of the labor force yet produces almost 11% of the GDP. Agriculture, fishing and mining have been the traditional jobs. In recent decades, however, manufacturing has played an increasing role and now employs about 10% of the labor force, producing over 21% of the GDP. The greatest part of the GDP (nearly 36%) is raised in the service industries which employ over 27% of workers.

The main food crops are rice, corn and potatoes. The main cash crop is officially coffee, which accounts for about 2% of the export earnings. However, unreported revenue from coca (exported for the production of cocaine) is far higher, and some sources suggest it is roughly comparable in value to all legal exports combined. In 1992 exports were worth a total of US$3484 million, with minerals being the most important. Copper is by far the largest single export (23.1% of the total) and other significant mineral exports include zinc (9.6%), gold (5.6%), petroleum products (5.6%), lead (4.6%) and silver (2.2%).

Fishing, particularly for anchoveta and pilchard, yields fishmeal that accounted for 12.6% of 1992 exports. In the 1960s, Peru was catching more tons of fish than any other country in the world. Overfishing, combined with a disastrous El Niño in 1971-72, caused the fishing industry to collapse in one season. Recovery did not begin until the late 1970s and today the industry is still well below the levels of the 1960s, partly because of recurring El Niños. There is, however, more effort to manage the overfishing problem.

Imports, which during 1992 and 1993 have exceeded exports by about 8%, are mainly basic foodstuffs (particularly cereals), machinery, transportation equipment and manufactured goods. By far the biggest trading partner is the USA (27.2% of imports and 21.4% of exports) followed by Japan (7.7% of imports and 9.8% of exports). Colombia, Argentina, Brazil, Germany and Venezuela are also important sources of imports and China, UK, Italy, Brazil, Germany and Venezuela are important export destinations.

The domestic economic situation was a disaster at the end of the García administration in 1990. The current government, under the leadership of President Fujimori, has made sweeping economic reforms, beginning with an austerity package that raised prices of food and gasoline manyfold. Tax and import laws were eased, many state-run industries privatized, and monopolies eliminated. This led to renewed international confidence in Peru, significant foreign investment and the beginning of the repayment of parts of Peru's foreign debt. Inflation, at an annual rate of over 10,000% in the early 1990s, has dropped to the low teens and, in 1994, Peru had the strongest economic growth of any Latin American country. (I even went as far as to buy stocks in Telefónica del Peru – there's a hot insider tip for you which is worth much more than the price of this book!)

POPULATION & PEOPLE
Peru's population in 1994 was 23.4 million, almost half of which is concentrated in the narrow coastal desert. The population is predicted to double by 2022. Lima (including Callao) has a population of over seven million and the second and third cities, Arequipa and Trujillo, also in the coastal region, have populations of about 750,000 each.

About half the population is found in the highlands – mostly rural Indians or mestizos who practice subsistence agriculture. There are few large cities in the highlands but many small towns. The highlanders prefer to be called *campesinos* (country people or peasants) rather than Indians, which is considered insulting. Because of the very poor standard of living in the highlands, many campesinos have migrated to the coast but overpopulation problems in the cities mean their lot rarely improves.

More than 60% of Peru lies in the Amazon Basin east of the Andes. This region is slowly becoming colonized but as yet only 5% of the population lives there.

Over half of Peru's population is Indian. Quechua-speaking Indians are the majority (about 47% of the total) and are mainly found in the highlands, although a significant number have been driven down to the coast in recent years following the political unrest caused by the Sendero Luminoso. Aymara-speaking highlanders come a distant second (over 5%) and other groups, mainly Amazon Indians, comprise almost 2%. About 32% is mestizo, 12% is white and the remaining less than 2% is black, Asian or other groups.

EDUCATION
Primary education for 6- to 12-year-olds is compulsory, although this is difficult to enforce in remote rural areas. Nevertheless, primary school enrollment is about 95% and there are about 29,000 schools with over 4 million students. Secondary school for ages 12 to 16 is not compulsory and there is only about 42% enrollment. Almost 7000 schools provide for about two million students. Many schools offer two sessions, morning and afternoon, in order to accommodate more students. Facilities

ROB RACHOWIECKI

TONY WHEELER

ROB RACHOWIECKI

MICHAEL PETTYPOOL

MICHAEL PETTYPOOL

RICHARD I'ANSON

Llama at Machu Picchu

An ocelot (an endangered species) for sale in a grocery store in an Amazonian village

Tamandua (a species of anteater) on the banks of the Río Manu

Giant anteater along the Río Manu

Alpacas in the Cordillera Blanca

Blue-and-yellow macaws

are basic and the quality of education is low. Parents who can afford it send their children to private schools.

Higher education is carried out in vocational and teacher training schools, pre-universities and universities, of which there are 46. Some 40% of these are private and the rest are state-run. Higher education used to be free in state run colleges but, since 1993, this is no longer the case.

According to UNESCO, adult illiteracy figures in 1990 were 14.9% of the population (8.5% of males and 21.3% of females). This is an improvement over the 27.5% illiteracy level of 1972 and illiteracy continues to decline gradually. There are adult literacy programs as well as bilingual schools for students for whom Quechua or other Indian tongues are the first language. The government allocated about 16% of the 1994 budget to education.

ARTS
Traditional
The heritage of the Andean Indians is best seen in the many folk art forms that are still common today and which serve as much to preserve an ancient culture as to entertain. For the visitor, the most obvious of these art forms will be music, dance and crafts.

Both pre-Columbian and colonial architecture are also of great interest to the visitor.

Andean Music & Dance Pre-Columbian Andean music was based on the pentatonic scale of D-F-G-A-C and used wind and percussion instruments. Some of these are found in archaeological museums and date as far back as 5000 BC. The string instruments used today are based on instruments introduced by the Spanish. Traditional Andean music is popularly called *música folklórica* and is frequently heard at fiestas as well as being performed in bars and restaurants. Bars which specifically cater to musical entertainment are called *peñas*.

There are many different forms of wind instruments, based on regional differences. The most representative are *quenas* and *zampoñas*. The quena (or kena) is a flute usually made of bamboo of varying lengths, depending on the pitch desired. In the past it could have been made of bone, clay or wood. A *mohseno* is a large bamboo flute producing the deepest bass notes. The zampoña is the Spanish name for what is referred to as a *siku* in Quechua. It is a set of panpipes with two rows of bamboo canes, seven in one and six in the other. Zampoñas come in sizes ranging from the tiny, high-pitched *chuli* to the meter-long, bass *toyo*. Other forms of panpipes have different names. Also seen are *ocarinas*, small oval clay instruments with up to 12 holes. Occasionally, horns made of animal horns or sea shells are heard.

Percussion instruments include the inevitable drum, called a *bombo*, usually made from a hollowed out segment of cedar, walnut or other tree, and using stretched goat skin for the pounding surface. Rattles, called *shajshas*, are made of polished goat hooves tied together.

Almost all of today's música folklórica groups also use string instruments. The guitar is sometimes seen, but the most typical is the *charango*, which is based on a small, five-stringed Spanish guitar but modified by the Andean people to the extent that the charango can now be considered an original Andean instrument in its own right. It is a tiny guitar with the resonance box traditionally made of an armadillo shell, though they are mostly wooden these days. It has five pairs of strings usually tuned to E-A-E-C-G. The music produced by folklórica groups varies from melancholy and soulful to upbeat and festive. Música folklórica bands have toured North America and Europe in the '80s and '90s, spreading the popularity of their music far beyond the Andes. Perhaps the best known example of Andean music is *El Cóndor Pasa*, adapted by Paul Simon.

More recent additions to the instruments used in the Andes include harps, violins and a variety of brass instruments. These are most often seen in large outdoor bands strolling around towns and villages on fiesta days, producing a cacophony of sound and surrounded by masked and elaborately costumed dancers.

The many forms of música folklórica change from region to region. The most representative is a *huayno* which is associated with a dance of the same name. Hundreds of other kinds of dances are known and performed in the highlands. Many have a religious and ceremonial as well as social significance. Although dance performances can be seen in theaters and restaurants in the highlands, nowhere are they as colorful and authentic as those performed communally during the many fiestas.

Coastal Music & Dance On the coast, music and associated dances are quite different. The coastal *música criolla* has its roots in Spain and Africa. The main instrumentation is guitars and a *cajón*, a wooden box on which the player sits and pounds out a rhythm with his hands. The guitar is, obviously, Spanish but the cajón is attributed to black slaves brought by the Spanish. The most popular of the coastal dances is the *marinera*, a graceful romantic dance employing much waving of handkerchiefs. This is a performance to be watched rather than a dance with audience participation. Marinera dance competitions are frequently held on the coast with the most important being in Trujillo, on the north coast.

In the last few decades, Afro-Peruvian music has enjoyed a comeback, especially in the Chincha area on the south coast. This music and its accompanying dance has grown increasingly popular on TV shows and as a performance art, though certainly Peruvians will go to clubs and dance it as well. A popular performance dance is the *alcatraz* during which one dancer carrying a candle attempts to light a paper flag tucked into the back of the partners waist. This leads to plenty of fast and rhythmic moving of the hips in an attempt to avoid getting burned!

Just as in the highlands, coastal music can be heard at peñas in the main towns.

Crafts Handicrafts made in the Andes are based on pre-Columbian necessities such as weaving (for clothes), pottery and metallurgy. Today, woven cloth is still seen in the traditional ponchos, belts and other clothes worn by Andean Indians. Also, weaving has extended to cover a variety of rugs and tapestries which are popular souvenirs. The traditionally worked alpaca wool is also in great demand for sweaters and other items. Pottery, very important and well developed by many pre-Columbian cultures in Peru, is still important today as a popular souvenir item. The best are often based on ancient designs, shapes and motifs. Jewelry, especially the gold and silver pieces which are a direct link back to ancient rituals and heritage, are also in demand as a craft today.

Architecture The Inca architecture of Machu Picchu is, perhaps, the single greatest attraction in Peru. But there is much more in the way of Inca architecture, especially in (but not limited too) the Cuzco area. Various other pre-Columbian cultures have left us with magnificent examples of their architecture – see Visiting Archaeological Sites under Activities in the next chapter.

Colonial architecture is most importantly represented by the many imposing cathedrals, churches, monasteries and convents built during the 16th, 17th and 18th centuries. These are extremely ornate, both outside and inside. Altars are often gold leafed. The religious statues and paintings found inside churches were often carved or painted by early Indian artists with strong Spanish influence. These gave rise to the so-called *Escuela Cuzqueña* art form – colonial art blending Andean and Spanish ideas.

Modern

Music & Dance Traditional music plays a major part of Peru's musical scene. Although there is a national symphony orchestra and ballet company, and touring companies from other countries often visit, classical music is enjoyed by relatively few people.

Modern popular music includes rock, pop, reggae, punk and blues, all usually imported though there are a few Peruvian rock bands. Chilean-style protest songs and jazz also enjoy a limited popularity. Much more popular are other forms of Latin American dance music such as the omnipresent salsa, and *cumbia* and *chicha*, both from Colombia. *Salsatecas* cram in hundreds of Peruvians for all-night dance fests.

Film The film industry is still in its infancy. Few Peruvian films have been produced and most of them are short documentaries. Going to the movies is a popular pastime, however, and major cities have cinemas screening imported films with Spanish subtitles. In recent years, however, many cinemas have shut down to be replaced by video pubs or video clubs where you can rent a film and take it home to watch, or watch it right there at the club along with a drink or snack.

Theater Drama is quite popular in Lima, less so outside of the capital. It is of little interest to the visitor, however, unless you speak good Spanish. If you do, look for theater bars in the Miraflores and San Isidro districts of Lima, where you can see a play while enjoying a drink and light snack.

Literature Peru's most famous novelist is the internationally recognized Mario Vargas Llosa (born 1936), who ran in the Peruvian presidential election of 1990, coming second. Most of his books have been translated into various languages including English. As is common among Peruvian authors, his novels often delve deeply into Peruvian society, politics and culture. His first novel, *The Time of the Hero*, was publicly burned because of its detailed exposé of life in a Peruvian military academy. Vargas Llosa's work is very complex, with multiple plots and changing time sequences or flashbacks.

Two Peruvian writers are particularly noted for their portrayals of the difficulties facing Peruvian Indian communities. José María Arguedas (1911-1969) wrote *Deep Rivers* and *Yawar Fiesta* among others. Ciro Alegría (1909-1967) was the author of *The Golden Serpent*, about life in a jungle village on the Río Marañón, and *Broad and Alien is the World*, about repression among Andean Indians. These have all been translated into English. Other writers who are considered important but await translation include Julio Ramón Ribeyro (born 1929) and Alfredo Bryce Echenique (born 1939).

César Vallejo (1892-1938) wrote *Trilce*, a book of 77 avant-garde poems touted by some critics as one of the best books of poetry ever written in Spanish. Vallejo is considered Peru's greatest poet. Pablo Neruda, a Chilean poet, describes Machu Picchu as 'Mother of stone and sperm of condors' which is only one of the many powerful images he uses in his epic poem, *The Heights of Machu Picchu*, available in English. Anthologized modern Peruvian poetry is available in English in *Peru: The New Poetry* (London Magazine Editions, 1970; Red Dust, New York, 1977) and *The Newest Peruvian Poetry in Translation* (Studia Hispanica Editions, Texas, 1979).

CULTURE & SOCIETY

Essentially, Peru is a bicultural society. The whites are the rich middle and upper classes and the Indians are poor peasants, *campesinos*. Indians may also be called *indígenas* (natives) but never *indios*, which is considered insulting. What may be acceptable in middle-upper class society might not be acceptable in Indian society, and vice versa. In between, of course, are the mestizo people (of mixed Spanish/Indian heritage) whose customs and attitudes lean either towards white or Indian manners, depending on the individuals and their socio-economic status. The same comments apply to other, very small, minority groups.

Generally speaking, Peruvians are more formal than, say, North Americans. Hands are shaken on meeting and leaving a person on most occasions and verbal greetings are exchanged. *Buenos días* is a good start in a conversation with anyone ranging from a cab driver to a shop assistant. In more involved situations, this may be followed by a lengthier exchange of pleasantries. Women also kiss one another on the cheek and men, if they know the woman, may do so as well. Men may use an *abrazo*, a sort of back-slapping hug, between themselves if they are friends. Indians, on the other hand, don't kiss and their handshakes, when offered, are a light touch rather than a firm grip. In all situations, politeness is a valued habit.

Peruvians are used to less personal space than many North Americans and Europeans may be used to. Conversations tend to take place face to face, streets and public transport are very crowded, and homes have little individual space. Frequent kissing and hugging on a non-sexual basis, such as described above, is another example of this. Noise seems part of the way of life. Radios and TVs in hotel rooms are turned on early in the morning and late at night without thought of whether neighboring rooms can hear.

If you ask someone if they would like to have a drink or meal with you, you are expected to pay for it. Because of economic constraints, most Peruvians are unable to invite you to their homes or a restaurant for a meal on a casual basis. If you are invited, it is a semi-formal occasion so you should wear nice clothes and bring a small gift (flowers, chocolates, wine). Dinner conversation can run the gamut of sports, religion, politics and the arts, but discussion of personal finances is considered in poor taste.

In poor areas, however, campesinos will often ask you about your lifestyle and how much money you make. They are amazed at your apparently incredible wealth. You can tone this down a bit by talking a little about the higher costs of living in your country and getting onto another subject. A popular topic is the family. Women, especially, can expect to be asked how many children they have. This can become tiresome for single women who by Peruvian standards appear to be long past the marriageable age. This is, however, less a sexist attitude and more a friendly conversational gambit. Family life is important in Peru. Machismo, however, is also part of the culture. For more information on these attitudes, see the section for Women Travelers and Gay & Lesbian Travelers in the next chapter.

Peruvian (indeed, Latin American) attitudes towards time are not very precise. If invited to dinner or to meet someone, being up to an hour late is socially acceptable and expected. However, if you are told *Hora Inglesa* (English time), you are expected to be more or less punctual. In business situations, however, punctuality is more likely to occur than in social settings. In all cases, delays because of anything ranging from a flat tire to a late flight are to be expected, long lines are the norm, and patience is a virtue worth acquiring.

Clothing in the highland regions is fairly sedate. Men don't wear shorts and women don't wear halter tops or shorts. If trekking, shorts are usually viewed as acceptable on the popular tourist hikes, though the locals rarely wear them. Men shouldn't hike barechested through villages. In the lowland regions, particularly the jungle, men and women do wear shorts.

Men may be seen urinating and spitting in public. Campesino women also urinate in public by simply squatting down with their voluminous skirts around them. While public urinating and spitting cannot be considered a Peruvian custom, they are not heavily frowned upon. Belching or burping, on the other hand, is considered the height of impoliteness. Spit if you must but never belch.

When calling someone over to you, don't crook your finger up and beckon, as people may do in North America or Europe. This is considered very rude. A better way to call someone over from a distance is to give a flat, downward swipe of the open hand. Body language using hands and facial expressions is hard to describe but an important part of interpersonal communications. Watch to see how Peruvians do it.

Andean Indians have used coca leaves for centuries. The most frequent use is by chewing. Leaves are placed in the mouth one by one and moistened with saliva until a wad of wet leaves is produced. A small amount of *llipta* (a mixture of mineral lime and wood ashes – gringos have used baking soda reasonably successfully) is added to the moistened leaves and the entire mass is kept in the cheek and chewed occasionally. Although this gives some relief from hunger and fatigue, it is by no means equivalent to using cocaine, which Andean people do not do. Cocaine use is illegal, but coca use is legal and normal among Andean Indians. Coca leaves are freely sold at highland markets. Other traditional uses for coca leaf are as offerings to the *apus* (mountain gods), particularly when going on a long trip; as social exchanges between people meeting on a trip; and for medicinal and mystical purposes.

When using alcohol, be it the local *chicha* or fermented corn drink, or stronger aguardiente or other drink, Andean Indians invariably spill a few drops on the ground for *Pachamama* (Mother Earth). This is done both outdoors and inside their houses (which usually have earthen floors).

RELIGION

In common with most Latin American countries, the religion of Peru is predominantly Roman Catholic; over 90% of the population at least nominally professes that faith. Some of the older towns have splendid colonial Catholic churches. The Indians, while outwardly Roman Catholic, tend to blend Catholicism with their traditional beliefs. Thus offerings to the Pachamama or apus, as described in the preceding section, are an essential part of Indian life.

Although Roman Catholicism is the official religion, the constitution allows citizens to practice any religion they choose. Some churches of other faiths can be found, but these form a small minority. In recent years, there has been an increase of small Protestant groups and cults of many kinds.

LANGUAGE

For the traveler, Spanish is the main language. In the highlands, most Indians are bilingual, with Quechua being the preferred language in most areas except around Lake Titicaca where Aymara is spoken. For most Indians, Spanish is a second tongue and between one and two million do not to speak Spanish at all. These people live in very remote areas, so it is rare for the traveler to encounter Indians who speak no Spanish. Although English is understood in the best hotels, airline offices and tourist agencies, it is of little use elsewhere.

If you don't speak Spanish, take heart. It is an easy language to learn. Courses are available in Lima (see the Lima chapter) or you can study books, records and tapes while you are still at home and planning your trip. These study aids are often available free at public libraries – or you might consider taking an evening or college course. Once having learned the basics, you'll be able to talk with people from all over Latin America – apart from Brazilians, who are predominantly Portuguese-speaking.

Spanish is easy to learn for several reasons. Firstly, it uses Roman script. Secondly, with few exceptions, it is spoken as it is written and vice versa. Imagine trying to explain to someone learning English that there are seven different ways of pronouncing 'ough'. This isn't a problem in Spanish. Thirdly, many words are so similar to English that you can figure them out – *Instituto Geográfico Nacional* means the National Geographical Institute.

Even if you don't have time to take a Spanish course, at least bring a phrasebook and dictionary. Lonely Planet's *Quechua Phrasebook* and *Latin-American Spanish Phrasebook* are recommended. Don't dispense with the dictionary, because the phrasebook won't help you translate the local newspaper.

Although the Spanish alphabet looks like the English one, there are minor differences. 'Ch' is considered a separate letter, so *champú* (which means shampoo) will be listed in a dictionary after all the words beginning with just 'c'. Similarly, 'll' is a separate letter, so a *llama* is listed after all the words beginning with a single 'l'. The letter 'ñ' is listed after the ordinary 'n'. Bear this in mind also when using telephone directories or other reference works. Vowels with an accent are accented for stress and are not considered separate letters. Recently, however, the Academia Real de la Lengua Española (in Spain) has decided to eliminate 'ch' and 'll' as separate letters, which means that new Spanish dictionaries will list champú and llama in the same word order that English speakers are used to. Whether this will spread to Latin American Spanish remains to be seen.

Pronunciation is generally more straightforward than it is in English. If you say a word the way it looks like it should be said, the chances are that it will be close enough to be understood. You will get better with practice of course. A few notable exceptions are 'll' which is always pronounced 'y' as in 'yacht,' the 'j' which is always pronounced 'h' as in 'happy,' and the 'h' which isn't pronounced at all. Thus the phrase *hojas en la calle* (leaves in the street) would be pronounced 'o-has en la ka-yea.' Finally, the letter 'ñ' is pronounced as the 'ny' sound in 'canyon.'

Grammar

Word order in Spanish is generally similar to English sentence construction with one notable exception. Adjectives follow the nouns they qualify instead of preceding them as they do in English. Thus 'the white house' becomes *la casa blanca*.

Articles, adjectives and demonstrative pronouns must agree with the noun in both gender and number. Nouns ending in *a* are generally feminine and the corresponding articles are *la* (singular) and *las* (plural). Those ending in *o* are usually masculine and require the articles *el* (singular) and *los* (plural). Common exceptions to this rule are *el mapa, el problema, el dentista, el idioma* and *la mano*.

There are hundreds of other exceptions to these guidelines that can only be memorized or deduced by the meaning of the word. Plurals are formed by adding *s* to words ending in a vowel and *es* to those ending in a consonant.

In addition to using all the familiar English tenses, Spanish also uses the imperfect tense and two subjunctive tenses (past and present). Tenses are formed either by adding a myriad of endings to the root verb or preceding the participle form by some variation of the auxiliary verb *haber* (to have – as in I have been).

There are verb endings for first, second and third person singular and plural. Second person singular and plural are divided into formal and familiar modes. If that's not enough, there are three types of verbs – those ending in 'ar', 'er' and 'ir' – which are all conjugated differently. There are also a whole slough of stem-changing rules and irregularities which must be memorized.

Greetings & Civilities

good morning	*buenos días*
good afternoon	*buenas tardes*
good evening	*buenas tardes*
yes	*sí*
no	*no*
hello	*hola*
See you later.	*Hasta luego.*
Good bye!	*Adios!* (formal)
	Chao! (informal and very popular)

How are you?
  ¿Cómo estás? (familiar)
  ¿Cómo está? (formal)

please	*por favor*
thank you	*gracias*
It's a pleasure.	*Con mucho gusto.*

Some Useful Phrases

Do you speak Spanish?
  ¿Habla usted castellano?
Where (which country) do you come from?
  ¿De dónde (qué país) es usted?
Where are you staying?
  ¿Dónde estás alojado?
What is your profession?
  ¿Cuál es su profesión?

What time do you have?
¿Qué hora tiene?
Don't you have smaller change?
¿No tiene sencillo?
Do you understand? (casual)
¿Me entiende?
Where can I change money/traveler's checks?
¿Dónde se cambia monedas/cheques de viajeros?
Where is the … ?
¿Dónde está el/la … ?
How much is this?
¿A cómo?, ¿Cuánto cuesta esto?,
¿Cuánto vale esto?

too expensive	demasiado caro
cheaper	más barato
I'll take it.	Lo llevo.

What's the weather like?
¿Qué tiempo hace?

Buy from me!	Cómprame!
to the right	a la derecha
to the left	a la izquierda

Continue straight ahead.
Siga derecho

I don't understand.	No entiendo
more or less	más o menos
when?	¿Cuándo?
how?	¿Cómo?
How's that again?	¿Cómo?
where?	¿Dónde?

What time does the next plane/bus/train leave for … ?
¿A qué hora sale el próximo avión/ómnibus/tren para … ?

where from?	¿de dónde?
there	allí
around there	por allá
here	aquí
around here	por aquí
It's hot/cold.	Hace calor/frío

Some Useful Words

airport	aeropuerto
altitude sickness	soroche
bank	banco
block	cuadra
bus station	terminal terrestre
cathedral, church	catedral, iglesia
city	ciudad
downhill	por abajo

exchange house	casa de cambio
friend	amigo/a
husband/wife	marido/esposa
Indian/peasant	campesino (never indio)
mother/father	madre/padre
people	la gente
police	policía
post office	correo
rain	lluvia
snow	nieve
town square	plaza
train station	estación de ferro carril
uphill	por arriba
wind	viento

Time

What time is it?	¿Qué hora es?
It is one o'clock.	Es la una
It is two o'clock.	Son las dos
midnight	medianoche
noon	mediodía
in the afternoon	de la tarde
in the morning	de la mañana
at night	de la noche
half past two	dos y media
quarter past two	dos y cuarto
two ten	dos con diez minutos
twenty to two	veinte para las dos
Sunday	domingo
Monday	lunes
Tuesday	martes
Wednesday	miércoles
Thursday	jueves
Friday	viernes
Saturday	sábado
rainy season (winter)	el invierno
dry season (summer)	el verano
today	hoy
tomorrow	mañana
yesterday	ayer

Numbers

1	uno	5	cinco
2	dos	6	seis
3	tres	7	siete
4	cuatro	8	ocho

9	*nueve*	19	*diecinueve*	90	*noventa*	700	*setecientos*
10	*diez*	20	*veinte*	100	*cien*	800	*ochocientos*
11	*once*	21	*veintiuno*	101	*ciento uno*	900	*novecientos*
12	*doce*	30	*treinta*	200	*doscientos*	1000	*mil*
13	*trece*	31	*treinta y uno*	201	*doscientos*	50,000	
14	*catorce*	40	*cuarenta*		*uno*		*cincuenta mil*
15	*quince*	50	*cincuenta*	300	*trescientos*	100,000	
16	*dieciseis*	60	*sesenta*	400	*cuatrocientos*		*cien mil*
17	*diecisiete*	70	*setenta*	500	*quinientos*	1,000,000	
18	*dieciocho*	80	*ochenta*	600	*seiscientos*		*un millón*

Facts for the Visitor

PLANNING
When to Go
Peru's high tourist season is from June to August, which coincides both with the dry season in the highlands and summer vacation in North America and Europe. Certainly, this is the best time to go if you are interested in hiking the Inca Trail to Machu Picchu, or climbing and trekking elsewhere. People can and do visit the highlands year round, though the wettest months of January to April make trekking and backpacking a wet and muddy proposition. If you aren't planning on spending any time in a tent, however, you shouldn't have any major problems in the rainy season. Many of the major fiestas such as Virgen de la Candelaria, Carnaval and Semana Santa occur in the wettest months and continue undiminished even during heavy rain.

On the coast, Peruvians visit the beaches during the sunny weather from late December through March, although none of the beaches are particularly enticing. The rest of the year the coast is clothed in the *garúa* (coastal mist) and, although the beaches don't attract visitors, the coastal cities can be visited at any time.

In the eastern rainforests it rains, of course. The wettest months are December through April, as in the highlands, but tourism continues undiminished for two reasons. One is that it rarely rains for more than a few hours at a time and so there are plenty of bright sunny periods to enjoy. The second is that it can rain year round and locals are used to briefly taking cover during the heaviest downpours. It's not a big deal.

What Kind of Trip?
Whether you take a guided tour or travel independently (or with a friend or family member) is entirely up to you – both guided and independent travel are good options. Independent travelers, however, should rely on public transport rather than rent a car (see the Getting Around chapter).

What to Bring
As an inveterate traveler and guidebook writer, I've naturally read many guidebooks. I always find the What to Bring section depressing, as I'm always told to bring as little as possible. I look around at my huge backpack, my two beat-up duffel bags bursting at the seams, and I wonder sadly where I went wrong.

I enjoy camping and climbing, so I carry a tent, ice axe, heavy boots, etc. I'm an avid bird-watcher and I'd feel naked without my binoculars and field guides. And of course I want to photograph these mountains and birds which adds a camera, lenses, a tripod and other paraphernalia. In addition, I enjoy relaxing just as much as I enjoy mountain climbing and taking photographs of birds, so I always have at least two books to read in addition to all my indispensable guides and maps. Luckily, I'm not a music addict, so I'm able to live without a guitar, a portable tape player or a short-wave radio.

I'm not the only one afflicted with the kitchen sink disease. In Latin America alone, I've met an Australian surfer who traveled the length of the Pacific coast with his board, looking for the world's longest left-handed wave; a couple of Canadian skiers complete with those skinny boards; a black man from Chicago who traveled with a pair of meter-high bongo drums; an Italian with a saxophone (a memorable night when those two got together); a Danish journalist with a portable typewriter; a French guy with a boom box and (by my count) 32 tapes; and an American woman with several hundred weavings that she planned to sell. All of these were budget travelers staying for at least six weeks and using public transport.

After confessing to the amount of stuff I travel with, I can't very well give the time honored advice of 'travel as lightly as possible.' I suggest you bring anything that is important to you. If you're interested in photography you'll only curse every time you see a good shot (if only you'd brought your telephoto lens) and if you're a musician you won't enjoy the trip if you constantly worry about how out of practice you're getting.

There's no denying, however, that traveling light is much less of a hassle, so don't bring things you can do without. Traveling on buses and trains is bound to make you slightly grubby, so bring one change of dark clothes that don't show the dirt, rather than seven changes of nice clothes for a four week trip. Many people go overboard with changes of clothes, but one change to wash and the other to wear is the best idea. Bring clothes that wash and dry easily (jeans take forever to dry). Polypropylene clothing dries quickly.

The highlands are often cold, so bring a windproof jacket and a warm layer to wear beneath, or plan on buying a thick sweater in Cuzco or one of the other Andean towns frequented by tourists. A down jacket (bought at home) is well worth the investment if you get cold easily. A hat is indispensable; it'll keep you warm when it's cold, shade your eyes when it's sunny and keep your head dry when it rains. A great deal! A collapsible umbrella is great protection against sun and rain.

You can buy clothes of almost any size if you need them, but shoes are limited to size 43 Peruvian which is about 10½ North American. If you are planning on doing a lot of hiking, I suggest you wear your hiking boots on your flight to Peru – of all your luggage, a comfortable, broken-in pair of boots will be one of the hardest things to replace in Peru.

For light traveling, I often divide my trip into segments and take what I need for that segment and leave my other gear in storage. Most hotels will do this for you and if you're a member of the South American Explorers Club (SAEC, see Useful Organi-

zations) you can leave your gear in their Lima clubhouse for as long as you want.

The following is a checklist of small, useful items that you will probably need:

- Pocket torch (flashlight) with spare bulb and batteries
- Travel alarm clock
- Swiss Army style penknife
- Sewing and repairs kit (dental floss makes excellent, strong and colorless emergency thread)
- A few meters of cord (useful as a clothesline or for spare shoelaces)
- Sunglasses
- Plastic bags
- Soap and dish, shampoo, toothbrush and paste, shaving gear, towel
- Toilet paper (rarely found in cheaper hotels and restaurants)
- Ear plugs for sleeping in noisy hotels or buses
- Insect repellent
- Sun Block
- Address book
- Notebook
- Pens and pencils
- Paperback book (easily exchanged with other travelers when you've finished)
- Spanish-English dictionary
- Small padlock
- Large folding nylon bag to leave goods in storage
- Water bottle
- First-aid kit (see Health section)

Tampons are available in Peru, but only in the major cities and in regular sizes, so make sure you stock up with an adequate supply before visiting smaller towns and villages. If you use contraceptives, these are available in the major cities. The choice of contraceptives is limited, however, so if you use a preferred type you should bring it from home; they don't weigh much.

A sleeping bag is useful if you plan to travel on a budget (or for camping) because some of the cheaper hotels don't supply enough blankets and it can get cold at night. However, most hotels will give you another blanket if you ask

Insect repellant is rarely needed unless you are planning a trip into the Amazon Basin in which case you should bring repellant from home, because that sold in Peru does not work effectively. The most effective brands have a high percentage of DEET (N,N-diethyl-m-toluamide) – look at the label.

You need something to carry everything around in. A backpack is recommended because it is less tiring than carrying baggage by hand and your hands are left free. On the other hand, it's often more difficult to get at things inside a pack and so some travelers prefer a duffel bag with a full-length zipper, or the traditional suitcase. Whichever you choose, ensure that it is a strong, well-made piece of luggage or you may find yourself wasting time replacing zippers, straps and buckles. If you bring a backpack, make it one with an internal frame. External frames snag on bus doors, luggage racks and airline baggage belts and are liable to be twisted, cracked or broken.

If you wish to go trekking or backpacking, you'll find that Cuzco and Huaraz have gear for rent, including tents, stoves, sleeping pads and bags, and backpacks.

Maps

Road maps of Peru are available in advance from the South American Explorers Club (see Useful Organizations) or from specialty map stores in major cities in North America and Europe. The SAEC and map stores have a limited number of detailed topographical or trekking maps. These are expensive in Peru and more expensive elsewhere. I have also found good selections of topographical maps in the reference departments of some major universities.

In Peru the Instituto Geográfico Nacional (see Lima) has the most complete selection of maps. Few city maps are published. Except for perhaps a detailed map of the whole of Lima, the city maps in this book are among the best available. Road maps can be a little optimistic – some of the roads marked, particularly in the jungle, haven't been built yet or are no more than very rough tracks.

TOURIST OFFICES

The decline of tourism in the early 1990s caused by terrorism led to the closing down of FOPTUR government tourist offices in Peru and abroad. Now that Peru has stabilized and is safe to travel in, tourist offices are slowly reopening, although they are not found in every town and tend to change addresses frequently. Not all are government operated, though some operate under the aegis of the newly formed Ministerio de Industria, Comercio, Turismo y Integración (MICTI). The most recent addresses are listed in the text of each town in the book.

Getting reliable, recent, and useful tourist information ahead of your trip is not easy – the SAEC, a Peruvian embassy, or this book are your best options. The US Department of State issues travel advisories about every country, including Peru, but their statements tend to be overly cautious.

VISAS & DOCUMENTS

Citizens of most Western European nations and of the USA and Canada who are entering Peru as tourists do not require visas and can enter Peru with a valid passport. Australians, New Zealanders, Spanish citizens and some other nationals do require visas. Travelers who require visas can normally obtain them from Peruvian embassies or consulates in the capital cities of neighboring countries if they are traveling around South America. Alternatively, apply for one at a Peruvian embassy before you leave home.

Your passport should be valid for at least six months after your arrival date, so check your passport's expiration date if you haven't done so recently. A tourist card (a sheet of paper in duplicate) is given to everyone on arrival in Peru. After you fill it out, the immigration official retains one copy and you keep the other. There is no charge for this card, but don't lose it as you will need it to extend your stay, for passport checks, and to leave the country. If you lose it, another can be obtained at the *migraciones* (immigration office) in Lima and other major cities, or at the exit point from the country. It's best to get a new tourist card in a major city because the immigration officials hassle you if you try to exit without one and a bribe is sometimes necessary to obtain one when leaving the country.

On arrival you are normally asked how long you want to stay. The maximum allowed is 90 days, but less is often given unless you insist that you need the full 90 days. You are given an identical stamp in both your passport and tourist card which indicates how long you can stay. If you have a ticket out of the country you can usually get enough days to last until you leave, but make sure you show your ticket to the duty officer as soon as you start dealing with him and before your passport is stamped, as he won't want to change it afterwards.

If you want to stay in Peru for longer than the 90 days (or whatever) you are given on arrival, it is not difficult to renew your tourist card. The only hassle is that this costs US$20 for each 30 day extension and takes a few hours of your time. You are allowed a maximum of three renewals to a maximum of 180 days in Peru. If you wish to stay longer than this, you must leave the country then return to begin the process over. It is relatively straightforward to leave the country overland to Ecuador, Chile or Bolivia. The easiest place for tourist card renewals is the migraciones office in Lima, where the process can take less than an hour. In other cities you may have to leave your passport overnight. The addresses of the many migraciones offices are given under the cities which have them.

In addition to a passport and tourist card, you officially need a ticket out of the country. Evidence of sufficient funds for your stay is not normally required. It's rare to be asked to show an onward ticket, unless you're one of those travelers for whom a visa is required. One traveler has reported that the requirement to show an onward ticket was waived when he produced a typed travel itinerary (which you don't have to stick to). If you buy an airline ticket for use as an exit ticket it can normally be refunded if you don't want to use it. Alternatively, buy an MCO (Miscellaneous Charges Order) from an airline belonging to IATA (International Air Transport Association). This can be used for any flight on an IATA airline or can be refunded if it hasn't expired. Airline departure desks outside Peru might not let you fly to Peru on a one-way ticket and may insist that you buy an onward ticket or an MCO before you can board the aircraft. (I saw this happen at the AeroPerú desk in Miami to a Japanese woman traveling on a Japanese passport but who was a resident of Peru.)

Bus tickets can be bought at land borders but these are not transferable or refundable. If you don't have an exit ticket it's best not to worry, as you probably won't be asked to show one anyway.

Always carry your passport and tourist card when you are out of your hotel (or at least a photocopy of the passport pages with your photo and passport number) as there are occasional document checks on public transport and you can be arrested if you don't have identification. Another document which is useful for identification is a drivers' license (as long as it has a photo) or any official looking document that has a recent photo of you. When traveling between towns, always carry your passport because there are occasional passport controls at the entrance and exit points of main towns, whether you arrive by bus, taxi, air, rail or boat.

International vaccination certificates are not required by law, but vaccinations are advisable. See the Health section.

Student cards are occasionally useful. These save you money at some archaeological sites and museums (entrance fee discounts of up to 50% are possible) but aren't honored everywhere. They must have a photo on them to be honored at all.

EMBASSIES
Peruvian Embassies Abroad
Australia
   Qantas House, Suite 1, 9th floor, 97 London Circuit, Canberra, ACT 2601 (☎ (06) 257-2953, fax (06) 257-5198)
   Postal address: PO Box 971, Civic Square, ACT 2608
Bolivia
   Avenida 6 de Agosto y Guachalla, Edificio Alianza, La Paz (☎ (2) 35-3550, fax (2) 36-7640)

Brazil
SES, Av das Nações, Lote 43, 70428-900, Brasília, DF (☎ (61) 242-9435, fax (61) 243-5677)

Canada
170 Laurier Ave West, Suite 1007, Ottawa K1P 5V5 (☎ (613) 238-1777, fax (613) 232-3062)

Chile
Avenida Andrés Bello 1751, Providencia 9, Casilla 16277, Santiago (☎ (2) 235-2356, fax (2) 235-8139)
San Martín 220, Arica (☎ 23-1020)

Colombia
Carrera 10 bis, No 93-48, Santa Fe de Bogotá, DC (☎ (1) 257-6292, fax (1) 257-3753)

Ecuador
Edificio España, Penthouse, Amazonas 1429 y Colón, Quito (☎ (2) 554-161, (2) 562-134, fax (2) 562-349)

France
50 ave Kléber, 75116 Paris (☎ (1) 47 04 34 53, fax (1) 47 55 98 30)

Germany
53175 Bonn 1, Godesberger Allee 127 (☎ (228) 373045, fax (228) 379475)

Israel
52 Rehov Pinkas, Apt 31, 8th floor, Tel Aviv 62261 (☎ (3) 544-2081, fax (3) 546-5532)

New Zealand
Level 8, Cigna House, 40 Mercer St, POB 2566, Wellington (☎ (4) 499-8087, fax (4) 499-8057)

Spain
Príncipe de Vergara 36, 5D, 28001 Madrid (☎ (1) 431-4242, fax (1) 577-6861)

UK
52 Sloane St, London SW1X 9SP (☎ (171) 235-1917, fax (171) 235-4463)

USA
1700 Massachusetts Ave, NW, Washington DC 20036 (☎ 202-833-9860, fax 202-659-8124)

Foreign Embassies in Peru

All the following are in Lima or the suburbs and are open weekdays. There are other embassies or consulates listed under the major cities, particularly Arequipa.

Argentina
Pablo Bermúdez 143, Jesus Mariá (☎ 4633-5847, 433-5704), 9 am to 2 pm

Austria
Avenida Central 643, San Isidro (☎ 442-0503, 442-1807), 9 am to noon

Belgium
Angamos 380, Miraflores (☎ 446-3335), 8.30 am to noon

Bolivia
Los Castaños 235, San Isidro (☎ 422-8231), 9 am to 1 pm

Brazil
José Pardo 850, Miraflores (☎ 446-2635, ext 131, 132), 9.30 am to 1 pm

Canada
Frederico Gerdes 130, Miraflores (☎ 444-4015), 8.30 to 11 am

Chile
Javier Prado Oeste 790, San Isidro (☎ 440-7965, 440-3280), 9 am to 1 pm

Colombia
Natalio Sanchez 125, 4th floor, Lima (☎ 433-8922, 433-8923), 9 am to noon

Denmark
Bernardo Monteagudo 201, Magdalena (☎ 462-1090), 9.30 am to 12.30 pm, 3.30 to 4.30 pm

Ecuador
Las Palmeras 356, San Isidro (☎ 442-4184), 9 am to 1 pm

Finland
Bolognesi 125, office 1004, Miraflores (☎ 446-9294, 444-0860), 9 am to 1 pm

France
Arequipa 3415, San Isidro (☎ 442-0702, 442-9578), 9 am to noon

Germany
Arequipa 4210, Miraflores (☎ 445-7033), 9 am to noon

Israel
Natalio Sánchez 125, 6th floor, Lima (☎ 433-4431, 10 am to 1 pm

Italy
Gregorio Escobedo 298, Jesús Mariá (☎ 463-2727/8/9), 9 am to noon

Japan
San Felipé 356, Jesús Mariá (☎ 463-0000), 9 am to 1 pm and 3 to 6 pm

The Netherlands
Principal 190, Santa Catalina (☎ 475-6537, 476-1069), 9 am to noon

New Zealand
Natalio Sánchez 125, 11th floor, Lima (☎ 433-4738, 433-5032) 8.30 am to 12.30 pm

Norway
Canaval Moreyra 595, San Isidro (☎ 440-4048), 9 am to noon

South Africa
Natalio Sánchez 125, Lima (new embassy, ☎ not available)

Spain
  Jorge Basadre 498, San Isidro (☎ 470-5600, 470-5678), 9 am to 1.30 pm
Sweden
  Camino Real 348, Torre El Pilar, 9th floor, San Isidro (☎ 440-6700, 440-6750), 10 am to noon
Switzerland
  Salaverry 3240, San Isidro (☎ 462-4090), 9 am to 12.30 pm
UK
  Natalio Sánchez 125, 11th floor, Lima (☎ 433-4738, 433-5032), 9 am to 1 pm
USA
  Grimaldo del Solar 346, Miraflores (☎ 444-3621, 434-3000), 8 am to noon
Venezuela
  Manuel Corpancho 193, Lima (☎ 433-4511), 8.30 am to noon

CUSTOMS

You can bring two liters of alcohol and 400 cigarettes into Peru duty free. You can bring items for personal use but are allowed only US$200 worth of gifts. If bringing in a valuable item for personal use (eg, bicycle, laptop computer) you may be asked to pay a bond of 25% of the value of the item, which is supposedly refundable when you leave. Unfortunately, it can be problematical to get a refund in the short period of time that you are at the airport leaving the country. It's the usual run-around: 'The officer isn't here; Come back tomorrow; Get your refund at the office downtown,' etc, etc. If asked to pay a bond, resist as much as you can by insisting that the item is for personal use and that you will not be selling it in Peru. If you absolutely cannot make any headway, undervalue the item as much as you dare to minimize your potential loss, and check with customs a day or two before you leave. If you are traveling on a tour, ask your inbound tour operator for assistance.

It is illegal to take any pre-Colombian artifacts out of Peru and it is illegal to bring them into most countries. Bringing animal products from endangered species home is also illegal. Coca leaves are legal in Peru but not in most other countries. Coca leaves in the form of tea bags are freely available in Peruvian shops, but these, too, are illegal in most countries (even though it would be impossible to produce any significant amount of cocaine from a small box of coca tea bags!)

People who have jobs where random urine testing for drugs occurs should note that (I've been told) drinking coca tea may leave trace amounts of chemical in your urine.

MONEY

Peruvian currency is the nuevo sol (S/). Bills of S/10, S/20, S/50 and S/100 are circulating. In addition, the I/5,000,000 bill from the old inti currency (see sidebar The Ups & Downs of the Sol) is still considered legal tender and worth the equivalent of S/5. No other inti bills are legal tender. The nuevo sol is divided into 100 céntimos and there are copper-colored coins of S/0.05, S/0.10 and S/0.20 and silver-colored coins worth S/0.50 and S/1. In addition, there are rather odd but not unattractive bimetallic coins with a copper

---

The Ups & Downs of the Sol

When I first visited Peru in 1982, I received about 500 soles for US$1. By the end of 1985, the Peruvian currency was valued at 17,300 soles to the US dollar. In 1986 a new currency was introduced by the simple (and, in Latin America, common) expedient of slashing the last three digits. The new currency was called the *inti*, and was worth I/17.30 to the US dollar when introduced. (Sol is the Spanish word for sun and inti means the same thing in Quechua, the Andean Indian language.)

By 1991, the value of the US dollar had reached about I/1,000,000 and the government introduced yet another currency, the nuevo sol, worth 1,000,000 intis. At this writing, the nuevo sol (written S/) is worth S/2.25 against the US dollar. (Once in a while I figure out how many of the old soles I would get for a US$1 if the currency had not been changed. Today it works out at a staggering 2,250,000,000 old soles – quite a wad in the old wallet!) ■

center surrounded by silver; these are worth S/2 and S/5. Note that there are plenty of worthless old coins out there that vendors occasionally try and slip into your change, so inspect them carefully.

Costs

Costs in Peru are lower, on average, than in most first world countries but higher than in neighboring Ecuador and Bolivia, and a little higher than Chile. Costs are higher in Lima and Cuzco than anywhere else on the coast or highlands. If you're on a very tight budget, you can get by on a bare bones budget of US$10 to US$15 per day, but that means staying in the most basic of hotels and traveling very slowly. Most budget travelers spend closer to an average of US$20 per day mainly because of the large distances that have to be covered to properly visit Peru. The best ways to save money are to share a hotel room and to eat the standard set lunch menu in cheap restaurants.

If you can afford to spend a little more, however, you'll probably enjoy yourself more too. The luxury of a simple room with a private hot shower and a table and chair to write letters home can be had for as little as US$10 or US$15 for a double if you know where to go – this book will show you where. Saving time and energy by flying back from a remote destination which took you several days of land travel to reach is also recommended if you can afford to spend a bit more.

I sometimes meet travelers who spend most of their time worrying how to make every penny stretch further. It seems to me that they spend more time looking at their finances than looking at the places they're visiting. Of course, many travelers are on a grand tour of South America and want to make their money last, but you can get so burned out on squalid hotels and bad food that the grand tour becomes an endurance test. Traveling comfortably and enjoyably for six months can be more rewarding than a full year of strain and sacrifice.

Due to violent swings in the exchange rate and various political or economic

problems, costs in both dollars and nuevos soles has changed rapidly in the past. Costs of many services tripled in dollar terms and went up astronomically in local currency within a few months during 1991, for example. By the same token, prices can fall equally rapidly. Bear this in mind when reading prices in these pages – they are a guideline only. Although dollar costs tend to stay comparatively stable, you can still experience a noticeable change in prices within a month. However, during the economic and political stability of the past two years, prices in dollar terms have remained fairly stable.

Some current costs to give you a guideline are as follows. Hotel rooms, double occupancy, can be well over US$100 for a luxury hotel in those few cities that have them; about US$50 for a 1st-class hotel; about US$20 for an economy hotel; and about US$6 in a basic budget place. Air fares within Peru are about US$50 to US$100. Bus fares average about US$1 per hour of travel on the regular buses, US$2 on the luxury buses. A beer will be from US$1 to US$3, depending on where you drink it. A cheap set lunch in a simple restaurant is under US$2; a good meal in a nice restaurant is US$10 to US$20; a superb meal in a fancy restaurant could go over US$50. A local telephone call is US25¢, a local bus ride is US35¢, an international airmail letter is US$1, and a major newspaper is US60¢.

Changing Money

Cash & Traveler's Checks The easiest currency to exchange is the US dollar. Other hard currencies are exchangeable only in the main cities and, with the possible exception of the German mark, at a high commission. The US dollar is always preferable and often the only currency you can change in the smaller towns. Visitors from countries other than the US would do best to buy US dollars (cash or traveler's checks) at their home bank.

It is most important to examine dollars carefully. Banks in Peru will not accept dollar bills with even the smallest tears or other damage. Heavily worn or written-on bills aren't accepted either. False dollar bills circulate in Peru occasionally, so examine any that you may obtain there.

The following information is meant as a guide only. Peruvian currency exchange regulations can change at any time and your best source of information when you arrive is probably to ask a fellow traveler who has been in Peru for a while.

Money can be changed in banks, *casas de cambio* (exchange houses), or with street changers. First-class hotels and restaurants will also accept dollars. Exchange rates vary a little from place to place, but not a lot (they are often within 1% or 2% of each other for cash dollars) so it's not worth spending too long in shopping around for the best deal. The exception is your hotel which may have a high commission. Traveler's checks are changed at a lower rate than cash – a commission of a few percent is often charged, depending on the bank and the town. People changing traveler's checks should shop around a little bit.

Banks are good for changing traveler's checks and giving cash advances on credit cards, but can be rather slow and bureaucratic. Casas de cambio are often faster and give about the same rates as the banks for cash dollars, but rarely take traveler's checks. These also have the advantage of longer business hours. For changing traveler's checks in smaller towns, the Banco de Crédito is often your only choice. In larger towns, Interbanc and Banco Mercantil have both been recommended. The Banco de Crédito will sometimes change traveler's checks into US dollars at a small commission. This depends on the availability of cash dollars and so is more likely to occur in larger cities. The most widely accepted traveler's checks are American Express and Thomas Cook, though I have also used other brands with no problem.

Street changers hang out near the banks and casas de cambio. There is no real advantage to using them – their rates are never better than the best rates in banks or casas de cambio and travelers have reported being cheated. If you do use street changers, count your money very carefully *before* handing over the dollars and use your own calculator, as some changers have 'fixed' ones. Street changers are useful at times when you need to change money outside of business hours or at land borders. Read the Dangers & Annoyances section later in this chapter for suggestions about keeping your money safe.

If you are arriving at Lima airport you'll find several banks, some of which are open 24 hours a day. Exchange rates at the airport are almost the same as in Lima, but count your money carefully, as the tellers have been known to short-change tired travelers arriving late at night. This happened to me but I counted the money before I left the window and was quickly given the balance when I politely informed the teller of his 'mistake.' Departing travelers can usually change their remaining Peruvian currency back into cash dollars but, as this can be unreliable, try not to be left with a huge wad of nuevos soles when you leave. On one occasion (in the early 1990s) I was told, when leaving Peru through Lima's International Airport, that the Peruvian government had suspended trading on Peruvian currency and I couldn't change my excess back to dollars!

Banking hours are erratic. From January to March banks on the coast are open only from 8.30 to 11.30 am. During the rest of the year they are open longer – sometimes into the afternoon and on Saturdays, but don't count on it. Expect long lines and delays in banks and try to go early in the morning for the most efficient service. Casas de cambio are often open from 9 am to 6 pm, or later in tourist areas such as Cuzco, but tend to close at lunch for a couple of hours.

Credit Cards These can be used but an 8% commission is added to the bill so you are better off bringing cash and traveler's checks for purchases. The exception to this is using your credit card for a cash withdrawal (in Peruvian money) where the commission is lower. Visa has been recommended by several travelers as being by far the most widely accepted. Visa cards can be used in Unicard ATMs and at Banco de Crédito, Interbanc and Banco Mercantil. MasterCard can be used at Banco Wiese and Banco Mercantil. Amex cards can be used at Interbanc. Credit cards approaching their expiration date may not be accepted in many places.

International Transfers If you run out of money, it is a simple matter to have more sent to you, assuming that you have someone at home kind enough to send you money. A bank transfer is fastest by fax, although this will take a couple of days to arrange. Ask at a Peruvian bank how to arrange this, what the commission is, and whether you can receive the money in US dollars or Peruvian currency. Only some banks will provide this service (at a small commission). Again, the Banco de Crédito is recommended.

Tipping & Bargaining
The cheapest restaurants do not include a tip in the bill. If you want to tip waiters, make sure you give it directly to them and don't leave it lying on the table. Tipping is not expected in very basic restaurants. In better restaurants, tip the waiter up to 15%. In many better restaurants a 10% service charge is included, but you can give the waiter an extra 5% if the service is good.

Taxi drivers are not tipped – bargain a fare beforehand and stick to it. Tip bell hops or porters about US50¢ per bag in the better establishments. If hiring a local guide, tip them about US$3 to US$5 per client for each full day's work if they are good, professional, multilingual guides – less if they aren't. If there's a large group of you, tip about US$2 per client per day. These are minimal recommendations; you can, of course, tip more. If going on a trek it is customary also to tip the cook and porters. Tip them at least as much as the guide and split it between them.

Bargaining is accepted and expected in markets when buying crafts and occasionally in other situations. If you're not sure whether bargaining is appropriate, just ask

for a *descuento*, discount. These are often given in hotels, at tour agencies, in souvenir shops and other places where tourists spend money.

Taxes
A combination of taxes and service charges is added to bills in the best hotels and restaurants – this can reach as much as 28% so you should prepare for this. The cheapest hotels and restaurants don't add a tax. Some better restaurants that do may include it in the prices on the menu (*Impuestos Incluidos*). Ask if you aren't sure. If 28% is added, 10% is for service so you take this into account when tipping.

Souvenirs and food are not taxed in stores.

Change
Don't expect to be able to pay for inexpensive services with large bills, because change is often not available. Cab drivers may say they don't have change simply to try and make a bit of extra money. It's worth first asking drivers *¿Tiene cambio de diez soles?* – Do you have change for ten soles (or whatever the size of your bill) – to make sure you're not stuck with overpaying later. If traveling to small towns, bring a supply of small denomination bills.

POST & TELECOMMUNICATIONS
Post
Sending Mail The Peruvian postal service has recently improved substantially but letters are more expensive to send than in more developed countries. Airmail postcards or letters are about US$1 to most foreign destinations. For a few cents more they can be registered (*certificado*), which gives you peace of mind but isn't really necessary. Letters from Peru to the USA (as an example) can take from one to two weeks, depending where you mail from. Lima is the best place for the fastest service.

The post office in each town is marked on the town maps provided in this book. Opening hours are very convenient. In many towns the post office is open from

9 am to 8 pm on weekdays, and a half day on Saturday or Sunday.

Mailing parcels is best done from the main post office in Lima. Large parcels (up to 10 kg) need to be checked by customs, so bring your parcel open and then sew it up in a cloth sack. Parcels weighing more than 10 kg have to go from the special Correos, on Calle Toma Valle (no number), a street which runs perpendicular to the airport entrance. Small packages weighing less than 1 kg (2 kg to some destinations) can be sent in an openable (drawstring) bag by *pequeños paquetes* service, which goes by certified airmail. There is no surface mail outside Lima, meaning there's no alternative to very expensive airmail. Regulations change from year to year. I don't recommend sending parcels from Peru because of the high cost.

There are international express services such as DHL but these are even more expensive. If you buy a huge amount of souvenirs, you'll find it cheaper and easier to pay excess luggage charges rather than mailing large parcels home.

Receiving Mail There are several places where you can receive mail but most travelers use either the post office or American Express. Although some embassies will hold mail for you, others may refuse to do so and will return it to the sender. Ask before using your embassy. You can also have mail sent to you care of your hotel, but it's liable to get lost. The best place to receive mail is care of the South American Explorers Club, Casilla 3714, Lima 100 (for club members only). It will hold your mail for months, help you recover packages from customs if necessary and return or forward mail according to your instructions if you leave the country.

If you have mail sent to the post office, remember that it is filed alphabetically, so if it's addressed to John Gillis Payson Esq, it could well be filed under G or E instead of the correct P. It should be addressed, for example, to John PAYSON, Lista de Correos, Correos Central, Lima, Peru. Ask your loved ones to clearly print your last name and avoid witticisms such as 'World Traveler Extraordinaire' appended to it. American Express also holds mail for clients. As an example, address mail: John PAYSON, c/o American Express, Lima Tours, Casilla 4340, Belén 1040, Lima. (Thanks to my father-in-law for allowing me to use his name.)

Telephone

The government-run telephone system was privatized in 1994 and is now the Spanish-owned Telefónica del Peru. (In addition, Lima has a local telephone company called La Compañía Peruana de Teléfonos.) Service with Telefónica is being expanded and modernized and is improving, although the downside is that telephone numbers may have changed by the time you read this. Call ☎ 103 for directory enquiries. Also, with the new system expanding all the time, be prepared for changes in the information given below.

Telefónica offices are marked on all street plans in this book. The bigger towns have fax services there as well; the smaller towns have only the phone. Most towns of any size will have several smaller Telefónica offices in addition to the main one marked on the map. Ask locally about this before going all the way across town to the main office. Even the most remote villages can often communicate with a major city and so connect you into an international call.

Since the recent modernization, telephone booths or little green pay phones (available in some stores and restaurants) are becoming widespread in the major cities. To make long distance or international calls, you can dial direct from coin telephones if you have a pile of one nuevo sol coins (machines don't yet take two or five nuevo soles coins, but may in the future). Alternatively, go to one of the many Telefónica del Peru offices and buy a telephone card. A card for S/30 (about US$13) will last about 4½ minutes to the USA or a little shorter to Europe. These are the cheapest way to call. In some smaller towns, you may have to go through the operator in the Telefónica office until new equipment is installed. Rates are cheaper on Sunday and in the evening after 9 pm.

Telefónica offices are usually open from 8 am to 10 pm or sometimes later in the major cities. The best hotels can connect international calls to your room at almost any time, though these are operator assisted and so more expensive. Collect or reverse-charge phone calls are possible to those countries that have reciprocal agreements with Peru.

In the early 1990s, you needed to buy tokens, called fiches RIN, to use local phones. These are now being phased out; you can now expect to find coin or card-operated phones just about everywhere. Telefónica offices usually have public phones available for local calls.

Telephone numbers are six digits in most of Peru and (since late 1994) seven digits in Lima. Area codes are three digits in most towns, always beginning with 0. (The main exception is Lima, with a two digit code – 01). To make a long distance call to a Peruvian number from within Peru, dial the area code first, including the 0. Area codes for Peruvian cities are given in the text under each city.

The country code for Peru is 51. To call a Peruvian number from overseas, dial your international access code, followed by the country code, followed by the area code *without* the 0, followed by the six or seven digit number.

Fax

Fax services are available at many locations, including better hotels and most of the Telefónica del Peru offices. It costs about US$3 to US$7 (higher rates outside of Lima) to send a page to the USA and a few cents to receive a page. Telefónica offices will hold faxes clearly marked ATENCIÓN (your name).

Many hotels and other offices have fax machines which double as telephones. Thus you may try to send a fax to a hotel, only to have a Spanish-speaking hotel receptionist come on the line. Some of these receptionists haven't a clue about

faxes and won't respond to the fax signal. You hear them saying 'Halo! Buenos dias.' Then they hang up, which has cost you a long distance phone call with no fax sent. You try again (assuming you speak Spanish) and explain to the receptionist that you want to send a fax, and you are then put on hold for several minutes while a manager or someone who knows how to turn the fax switch on is called over. In addition to this, fax communications are the most likely to cut out because of problems on the line. It can be time-consuming, frustrating and expensive to send a fax to Peru. I recently had to make seven attempts, including a six minute phone call, before I could send a one page fax from the USA to Peru, so be prepared for this.

BOOKS

There are a few good bookstores in Lima that sell books in English but they are expensive. The best place for guidebooks is the South American Explorers Club. Outside of Lima, books in English are not easily available, except in Cuzco. It's best to buy the books you want at home.

Travel Guides

There are few books on Peru but several on South America with useful chapters on Peru, suitable for travelers visiting several countries in the continent. For the budget traveler, Lonely Planet's *South America on a Shoestring* is recommended for its many maps and money-saving information.

A broader approach is available in *The South American Handbook*, published annually by Trade & Travel Publications, UK, and at Passport Books, USA. Now in its 70-somethingieth edition, it is called the South American Bible by some travelers. It is suitable for everyone from budget travelers spending a year in Latin America to businesspeople on expense accounts visiting the major capitals.

A general guidebook is *The Real Guide to Peru* by Dilwyn Jenkins (Prentice Hall, 1989). Although its maps and hard travel information are not very detailed, it has some interesting background on Peru.

The Sierra Club's *Adventuring in the Andes* by Charles Frazier, 1985, also has some interesting background but lacks good maps and tries to cover too much in too few pages.

One of my favorite guidebooks covers only the Cuzco area but does that entertainingly and in some detail. *Exploring Cusco* by Peter Frost (Nuevas Imagenes, Lima, 4th Ed 1989) is highly recommended for anyone planning to spend any length of time in the Cuzco area – all the main sites are described. The book is available in Lima and Cuzco.

For general advice read *The Tropical Traveller* by John Hatt (Penguin, 3rd ed 1993). This is an excellent compilation of information on all aspects of travel in the tropics (not just Peru) and is entertainingly written.

Archaeology & History
A host of books deal with the Incas. Going back to the arrival of the Spanish conquistadors, the best book is undoubtedly John Hemming's lucid and well-written *The Conquest of the Incas* (Harcourt, Brace, Jovanovich, 1970), available as a Penguin paperback. If you read only one book on the Incas and the conquest, make this it. Also there is Hemming's *Monuments of the Incas* (Little, Brown & Co, 1982), which is magnificently illustrated with Edward Ranney's B&W photographs of the major Inca ruins.

The Royal Commentary of the Incas was written in the early 1600s by Garcilazo de la Vega. This historian was born in Cuzco in 1539 of an Inca princess and a Spanish soldier. His book is the most widely translated, easily available and readable of the contemporary accounts of Inca life.

A newer text, particularly recommended for readers more seriously interested in Peruvian archaeology, is *The Incas and Their Ancestors: The Archaeology of Peru* (Thames & Hudson, 1992), by Michael E Moseley. Another recommended recent book is Richard L Burger's *Chavín and the Origins of Andean Civilizations* (Thames & Hudson, 1993).

Natural History
There are no comprehensive guides to the flora and fauna of Peru. Bird-watchers are best served by various helpful books.

An Annotated Checklist of Peruvian Birds by Parker III, Parker and Plenge (Buteo Books, 1982) is a checklist plus information on bird-watching in Peru and costs US$20.

For field guides try *The Birds of the Department of Lima, Peru* by Maria Koepcke, translated by Erma J Fiske (Harrowood Books, 2nd ed 1983, US$17). Although the book covers only a relatively small area of Peru and uses simple black and white sketches, it is useful for bird-watching along most of the desert coast and the western and central parts of the Andean highlands.

For the eastern slopes of the Andes and the Amazonian lowlands the best book is *A Guide to the Birds of Colombia* by S L Hilty & W L Brown (Princeton University Press, 1986, US$45). This is a comprehensive guide book with professional color plates. Because Colombia has a land border with Peru, many of the rainforest species are the same. Dedicated birders will buy the excellent *Birds of the High Andes* (Apollo Books, Denmark, 1990), by Jon Fjeldså & Niels Krabbe. It's in English and covers all the Andes (not just Peru), is very comprehensive, but costs US$150.

Even more detailed is *The Birds of South America* by R S Ridgely & G Tudor. This is a new four-volume set for the specialist and is expensive. The first volume, *The Oscine Passerines* (University of Texas Press, 1989), costs US$70. Volume two is *The Suboscine Passerines* (1994), and costs US$85. The remaining two volumes will appear in due course. A cheaper (US$45) and far less detailed guide to South American birds is *South American Land Birds: A Photographic Guide to Identification* (Harrowood Books, 2nd ed 1989) by John S Dunning. A good source for these and other bird books is the American Birding Association (☎ (719) 578-0607, 1 (800) 634-7736, fax (719) 578-9705), PO Box 6599, Colorado Springs, CO 80934, USA.

Neotropical Rainforest Mammals – A Field Guide by Louise H Emmons (University of Chicago Press, 1990) describes and illustrates almost 300 species from Peru's and other Latin American countries' rainforests. Good general books on South American natural history which contain information on Peru include Michael Andrews' *Flight of the Condor* (Little, Brown & Co, 1982) and David Attenborough's *The Living Planet* (Little, Brown & Co, 1984).

For the layperson interested in rainforest biology, I recommend the entertaining and readable *Tropical Nature* by Adrian Forsyth & Ken Miyata (Scribner's & Sons, 1984). Forsyth is also the author of a children's book *Journey Through a Tropical Jungle* (Simon & Schuster, 1988). Other good natural history books include *A Neotropical Companion* by John C Kricher (Princeton University Press, 1989). This book is subtitled 'An Introduction to the Animals, Plants, and Ecosystems of the New World Tropics.' Another good choice is Catherine Caulfield's *In the Rainforest* (University of Chicago Press, 1989), which emphasizes the problems of the loss of the rainforest.

Hiking & Climbing

The best all-round book is *Backpacking & Trekking in Peru & Bolivia* by Hilary Bradt (Bradt Publications, 6th ed 1995). It has a wealth of fascinating background information as well as entertaining descriptions and maps of more than a dozen good backpacking trips in Peru and Bolivia. These include classic treks such as the Inca Trail to Machu Picchu and the Llanganuco/Santa Cruz loop in the Cordillera Blanca, as well as some little known hikes in less visited areas.

The Peruvian Andes by Philippe Beaud, (Cordee in the UK and Cloudcap Press in the US, 1988) combines climbs and treks in the Cordilleras Blanca and Huayhuash. This paperback is trilingual (French, English and Spanish).

Pure & Perpetual Snow by David Mazel (FreeSolo Press, 1987), is an account of an expedition to climb Ausangate and Alpamayo – not a guide, but presenting an idea of what climbing in Peru is like. What climbing is not normally like is described in *Touching the Void* (Jonathan Cape, 1988), by Joe Simpson. This is the true story of a deadly climbing accident in the Cordillera Huayhuash – and a climber who, despite desperate odds, didn't die.

Travel & Adventure

A fine travel book about Peru is Ronald Wright's *Cut Stones & Crossroads: A Journey in the Two Worlds of Peru* (Viking Press, 1984), now available in Penguin paperback. It gives a good idea of what Peru and traveling around it are really like. Also excellent is *Journey Along the Spine of the Andes* by Christopher Portway (Oxford Illustrated Press, 1984). This book describes the author's travels from Bolivia to Colombia and, again, is a realistic introduction to independent travel in the Andes.

Of the many good books about Amazon travel, the following are recommended. As with the others, they don't deal with Peru alone but with the Amazon region as a whole. They are *The Rivers Amazon* by Alex Shoumatoff (Sierra Club Books, 1978) and *Passage Through El Dorado* by Jonathan Kandell (William Morrow, 1984). Peter Matthiessen's *The Cloud Forest* (Penguin, 1987; first published in 1961) describes his journey from the rivers of Peru to the mountains of Tierra del Fuego; his experience in Peru led to his novel *At Play in the Fields of the Lord*, a superb and believable story of the conflict betwen the forces of 'development' and indigenous peoples. A recent, slightly disconcerting and haunting extended essay of an artist's journey to the Peruvian Amazon is Roberta Allen's *Amazon Deam* (City Lights, 1993).

MEDIA
Newspapers & Magazines

There are dozens of newspapers available in Peru. Most towns of any size publish a local newspaper which is useful for finding out what's playing in the town cinemas and reading the local gossip, but has little national news and even less international news. The best newspapers are available in Lima, although many of these are sensationalist rags that luridly portray murder victims or women's buttocks on the front page while relegating world affairs to a few columns behind the sports section.

One of the best papers is *El Comercio*, published in Lima. It is a dry, conservative newspaper which comes in several sections and keeps up to date with cultural and artistic events in the capital as well as national and international news. It often has interesting travel articles about Peruvian destinations. A shorter version (missing the events sections) is available in other cities but is more expensive than in Lima. Other OK newspapers are the conservative *Expreso* and the moderate to left wing *La República*.

There is one English language magazine called the *Lima Times*, which is published monthly. Foreign newspapers and magazines are available at good bookshops and street stands.

The South American Explorers Club publishes a quarterly magazine, the *South American Explorer*, which has a host of articles about Peru and other parts of the continent.

Radio & Television

Peru has seven major television channels plus cable, but the local programming leaves a lot to be desired. Apart from interminable sports programs, the choice is very bad Latin American soap operas or reruns of old and equally bad North American sit-coms. The evening news broadcasts are quite good, especially for local news. Occasionally a National Geographic special makes its way to the screen. These types of programs are advertised days ahead in the better newspapers. Most hotels that offer a TV lack cable.

If you carry a portable radio, there are plenty of stations with a better variety of programs to choose from. Programs are in Quechua and Spanish. The BBC World Service and the Voice of America can be picked up in Peru on short-wave radio.

PHOTOGRAPHY & VIDEO

Definitely bring everything you'll need. Camera gear is very expensive in Peru and the choice of film is limited. Some good films are unavailable, such as Kodachrome slide film. Others are kept in hot storage cabinets and are sometimes sold outdated, so if you do buy film in Peru check its expiration date.

Don't have film developed in Peru if you can help it, as processing is often shoddy, especially for slide film, though print film is adequate if you aren't a professional. However, carrying around exposed film for months if you are on a long trip is also asking for washed-out results. It is best to send film home as soon as possible after it's exposed. The mail service is expensive, so try to send film home with a friend.

I always buy either process-paid film or prepaid film mailers. The last thing you want on your return from a long trip is to worry about how you're going to find the money to develop a few dozen rolls of film.

The heat and humidity of the tropics can wreak havoc on delicate electronic cameras. If you like to use a gee-whiz camera with electronic auto-iris and atom-splitting view finder, I suggest you carry a simple mechanical body as a back-up.

Tropical shadows are very strong and come out almost black on photographs. Often a bright but hazy day gives better photographs than a very sunny one. Taking photographs in open shade or using fill-in flash will help. The best time for shooting is when the sun is low – the first and last two hours of the day. If you are heading into the Amazon lowlands you will need high-speed film, flash, a tripod or a combination of these to take photographs in the jungle. The amount of light penetrating the layers of vegetation is surprisingly low.

The Peruvian people are highly photogenic. From a charmingly grubby Indian child to the handsomely uniformed presidential guard, the possibilities for people pictures are endless. However, most people resent having a camera thrust in their faces and people in markets will often proudly turn their backs on pushy photographers.

Ask for permission with a smile or a joke and if this is refused don't become offended. Some people believe that bad luck can be brought upon them by the 'evil eye' of the camera. Sometimes a tip is asked for. This is especially true in the highly visited Cuzco area. Here, locals will dress up in their traditional finery and pose against Andean backdrops. Some entrepreneurs even bring their llamas into Cuzco's main square. These people consider themselves to be posing for a living and become angry if you try to take their picture without giving them a tip. Be aware of people's feelings – it is not worth upsetting someone just to get a photograph.

The video system is the same as in the US and not compatible with systems used in Europe.

TIME

Peru is five hours behind Greenwich Mean Time. Although Peru is almost on the equator (from roughly 0° to 18°S) and the days are roughly of equal length year round, in the mid-1980s Peru introduced daylight-saving time to operate from December to March. When this occurred there was utter chaos in the airports with no one knowing when the flights were taking off! Peru no longer uses daylight-saving time.

It is appropriate here to mention that punctuality is not one of the things that Latin America is famous for.

ELECTRICITY

Peru uses 220 volts, 60 cycles AC, except Arequipa which is on 50 cycles. Plugs are of the flat, two-pronged type found in the USA.

WEIGHTS & MEASURES

Peru uses the metric system, as I have throughout this book. For reasons which I haven't figured out, gasoline is sold in gallons (I think US gallons) but everything else is metric. A conversion table is at the back of the book.

LAUNDRY

There are no self-service laundry machines in Peru. This means that you have to find someone to wash your clothes or else wash them yourself. There are laundromats (lavanderías) in the main cities but you still must leave the clothes for at least 24 hours. Rates are from about US$1 a kilo, including drying and folding, though many places charge closer to US$2. Some lavanderías only do dry-cleaning so check.

If you wash clothes yourself, ask the hotel staff where to do this. Some of the cheaper hotels will show you a huge cement sink and scrubbing board which is much easier to use than a bathroom washbasin. Often there is a well-like section full of clean water next to the scrubbing board. Don't dunk your clothes in this water to soak or rinse them as it is used as an emergency water supply in case of water failure. Use a bowl or bucket to scoop water out instead, or run water from a tap. Some towns suffer from water shortages and prohibit clothes washing in hotel rooms.

HEALTH

Travel health depends on your predeparture preparations, your day-to-day health care while traveling and how you handle any medical problem or emergency that does develop. While the list of potential dangers can seem quite frightening, with a little luck, some basic precautions and adequate information, few travelers experience more than upset stomachs.

Travel Health Guides

There are a number of books on travel health including:

Staying Healthy in Asia, Africa & Latin America, Moon Publications. Probably the best allround guide to carry, as it's compact but very detailed and well organized.

Travelers' Health, Dr Richard Dawood, Random House. Comprehensive, easy to read, authoritative and also highly recommended, although it's rather large to lug around.

Where There is No Doctor, David Werner, Macmillan. A very detailed guide intended for someone, like a Peace Corps worker, going to work in an underdeveloped country, rather than for the average traveler.

Travel with Children, Maureen Wheeler, Lonely
  Planet Publications. Includes basic advice on
  travel health for younger children.

Predeparture Preparations

Health Insurance A travel insurance
policy to cover theft, loss and medical
problems is a wise idea. There are a wide
variety of policies and your travel agent
will have recommendations. The international student travel policies handled
by STA Travel or other student travel organizations are usually good value. Some
policies offer lower and higher medical-
expense options, but the higher coverage is
chiefly for countries like the USA where
medical costs are extremely high. Check
the small print on your insurance form:

- Some policies specifically exclude 'dangerous
  activities,' which can include scuba diving,
  motorcycling, even trekking. If such activities
  are on your agenda you don't want that sort of
  policy.
- A locally acquired motorcycle license may not
  be valid under your policy.
- You may prefer a policy that pays doctors or
  hospitals direct rather than you having to pay
  on the spot and claim later. If you have to claim
  later make sure you keep all documentation.
  Some policies ask you to call back (reverse
  charges) to a center in your home country
  where an immediate assessment of your problem is made.
- Check if the policy covers ambulances or an
  emergency flight home. If you have to stretch
  out you will need two seats and somebody has
  to pay for them! Some policies are designed
  specifically to cover the cost of emergency
  medical evacuation in the case of serious injury
  or illness.

Medical Kit A small, straightforward
medical kit is a wise thing to carry. A kit
should include:

- Aspirin, Panadol, Ibuprofen, or similar drugs,
  for pain or fever.
- Antihistamine (such as Benadryl), useful as a
  decongestant for colds and allergies, to ease the
  itch from insect bites or stings, and to help
  prevent motion sickness.
- Antibiotics, useful if you're traveling well off
  the beaten track, but they must be prescribed
  and you should carry the prescription with

you. See the paragraph below about using
antibiotics.
- Kaolin preparation (Pepto-Bismol), Imodium
  or Lomotil, for stomach upsets.
- Rehydration mixture, for treatment of severe
  diarrhea. This is particularly important for children, but is recommended for everyone.
- Antiseptic such as Betadine, which comes as
  impregnated swabs or ointment, and an antibiotic powder or similar 'dry' spray, for cuts
  and grazes.
- Calamine lotion, to ease irritation from bites or
  stings.
- Bandages, for minor injuries.
- Scissors, tweezers and a thermometer (note
  that mercury thermometers are prohibited by
  airlines).
- Insect repellent, sunscreen, suntan lotion, chap
  stick and water purification tablets.
- A couple of syringes, in case you need injections in a country with medical hygiene problems. Ask your doctor for a note explaining
  why they have been prescribed.
- Motion sickness medication.
- Throat lozenges.
- First aid booklet.

Ideally antibiotics should be administered
only under medical supervision and should
never be taken indiscriminately. Take only
the recommended dose at the prescribed
intervals and continue using the antibiotic
for the prescribed period, even if the illness
seems to be cured earlier. Antibiotics are
quite specific to the infections they can
treat. Stop immediately if there are any
serious reactions and don't use the antibiotic at all if you are unsure that you have
the correct one.

In Peru, if a medicine is available at all it
will generally be available over the counter
and the price will be much cheaper than in
the West. It is possible that drugs that are
no longer recommended or have even been
banned in the West are still being dispensed
in Peru.

It may be a good idea to leave unwanted
medicines and syringes with a local clinic,
rather than carry them home.

Health Preparations Make sure you're
healthy before you start traveling. If you
are embarking on a long trip make sure
your teeth are OK; there are lots of places

where a visit to the dentist would be the last thing you'd want.

If you wear glasses take a spare pair and your prescription. Losing your glasses can be a real problem, although in many places you can get new spectacles made up quickly, cheaply and competently.

If you require a particular medication take an adequate supply, as it may not be available locally. Take the prescription or, better still, part of the packaging that shows the generic rather than the brand name (which may not be locally available), as it will make getting replacements easier. It's a wise idea to have a legible prescription with you to show you legally use the medication – it's surprising how often over-the-counter drugs from one place are illegal without a prescription or even banned in another.

Immunizations Vaccinations provide protection against diseases you might meet along the way. Although no immunizations are currently necessary to enter Peru, the further off the beaten track you go the more sensible it is to take precautions.

It is important to understand the distinction between vaccines recommended for travel in certain areas and those required by law. Essentially the number of vaccines subject to international health regulations has been dramatically reduced over the last 10 years. Currently yellow fever is the only vaccine subject to international health regulations. Vaccination as an entry requirement is usually only enforced when coming from an infected area.

On the other hand a number of vaccines are recommended for travel in certain areas. These may not be required by law but are recommended for your own personal protection.

All vaccinations should be recorded on an International Health Certificate, which is available from your physician or government health department.

Plan ahead for getting your vaccinations: some of them require an initial shot followed by a booster, while some vaccinations should not be given together.

It is recommended you seek medical advice at least six weeks prior to travel. Be prepared for some soreness and other side effects from immunizations – don't leave them for the day you are packing for the trip. Ask your doctor about your choice of vaccines and their various possible side effects.

Most travelers from developed countries will have been immunized against various diseases during childhood but your doctor may still recommend booster shots against diptheria-tetanus, measles or polio. The period of protection offered by vaccinations differs widely and some are contraindicated if you are pregnant.

In some countries immunizations are available from airport or government health centers. Travel agents or airline offices will tell you where. Vaccinations include:

Cholera Not required by law but occasionally travelers face bureaucratic problems on some border crossings. Protection is poor and it lasts only six months. It is contraindicated in pregnancy. The cholera epidemic which occurred in Peru in 1991 was bought quickly under control and does not pose any special threat to travelers.

Infectious Hepatitis The most common travel-acquired illness which can be prevented by vaccination. Protection can be provided in two ways – either with the antibody gamma globulin or with a new vaccine called Havrix. In the US this is called Hepatitis A vaccine. Havrix is more expensive and must be taken at least three weeks before departure but is recommended because it provides up to 10 years of immunity. Gamma globulin lasts only six months and may interfere with the development of immunity to other diseases, so careful timing is important with it's use.

Tetanus & Diphtheria Boosters are necessary every 10 years and protection is highly recommended.

Typhoid Available either as an injection or oral capsules. Protection lasts from one to three years and is useful if you are traveling for long in rural, tropical areas.

Yellow Fever Travelers to Peru should get this vaccination if planning a trip to the Amazon, but it is not necessary for visits to the coast or Andean highlands. Protection lasts 10 years. You usually have to go to a special yellow fever vaccination center. Vaccination is contraindicated during pregnancy but if you must travel to a high-risk area it is probably advisable.

Basic Rules

Care in what you eat and drink is the most important health rule; stomach upsets are the most likely travel health problem (between 30% and 50% of travelers in a two-week stay experience this) but the majority of these upsets will be relatively minor. Don't become paranoid; after all, trying the local food is part of the experience of travel.

Water The number one rule is *don't drink the water* and that includes ice. If you don't know for certain that the water is safe always assume the worst. Reputable brands of bottled water or soft drinks are generally fine. Take care with fruit juice, particularly if water may have been added. Tea or coffee should be OK, since the water should have been boiled.

Water Purification The simplest way of purifying water is to boil it thoroughly. Vigorously boiling for five minutes should be satisfactory; however, at high altitude water boils at a lower temperature, so germs are less likely to be killed.

Water filters may or may not remove all dangerous organisms, so read the manufacturers literature carefully before purchasing one. If you cannot boil water, chemical treatment may be more reliable than a filter. Chlorine tablets (Puritabs, Steritabs or other brands) will kill many but not all pathogens, including giardia and amoebic cysts. Iodine is very effective in purifying water and is available in tablet form (such as Potable Aqua), but follow the directions carefully and remember that too much iodine can be harmful.

If you can't find tablets, tincture of iodine (2%) or iodine crystals can be used. Four drops of tincture of iodine per liter or quart of clear water is the recommended dosage; the treated water should be left to stand for 20 to 30 minutes before drinking.

Food Salads and fruit should be washed with purified water or peeled when possible. Ice cream is usually OK if it is a reputable brand name, but beware of street vendors and of ice cream that has melted and been refrozen. Thoroughly cooked food is safest but not if it has been left to cool or if it has been reheated. Shellfish such as mussels, oysters and clams should be avoided, as should undercooked meat, particularly in the form of mince or ground beef. Steaming does not make bad shellfish safe for eating. Having said that, it is difficult to resist Peruvian seafood dishes like *ceviche*, which is marinaded but not cooked. I have had no problems with this as long as it is served in a reputable restaurant.

If a place looks clean and well run and if the vendor also looks clean and healthy, then the food is probably safe. In general, places that are packed with travelers or locals will be fine, while empty restaurants are questionable. The food in busy restaurants is cooked and eaten quite quickly with little standing around and is probably not reheated.

Nutrition If your food is poor or limited in availability, if you're traveling hard and fast and therefore missing meals, or if you simply lose your appetite, you can soon start to lose weight and place your health at risk.

Make sure your diet is well balanced. Eggs, beans, lentils and nuts are all safe ways to get protein. Fruits you can peel (bananas, oranges or mandarins for example) are always safe and a good source of vitamins. Try to eat plenty of grains (rice) and bread. Remember that although food is generally safer if it is cooked well, overcooked food loses much of its nutritional value. If your diet isn't well balanced or if your food intake is insufficient, it's a good idea to take vitamin and iron pills on a long trip.

In hot climates make sure you drink enough – don't rely on feeling thirsty to indicate when you should drink. Not needing to urinate or very dark yellow urine is a danger sign. Always carry a water bottle with you on long trips. Excessive sweating can lead to loss of salt and therefore muscle cramping. Salt tablets are not a good idea as a preventative, but in places where salt is not already used adding some to your food can help.

Everyday Health Normal body temperature is 98.6°F or 37°C; more than 4°F or 2°C higher indicates a 'high' fever. The normal adult pulse rate is 60 to 80 per minute (children 80 to 100, babies 100 to 140). You should know how to take a temperature and a pulse rate. As a general rule the pulse increases about 20 beats per minute for each degree Celcius rise in fever.

Respiration (breathing) rate is also an indicator of illness. Count the number of breaths per minute: between 12 and 20 is normal for adults and older children (up to 30 for younger children, 40 for babies). People with a high fever or serious respiratory illness (like pneumonia) breathe more quickly than normal. More than 40 shallow breaths a minute usually means pneumonia.

Illnesses ranging from the common cold to cholera have been proven to be easily transmitted through manual contact. Try not to put your hand to your mouth and wash your hands before meals. Clean your teeth with purified water rather than straight from the tap. Avoid climatic extremes: Keep out of the sun when it's hot, dress warmly when it's cold. Avoid potential diseases by dressing sensibly. You can get worm infections by walking barefoot. You can avoid insect bites by covering bare skin when insects are around, by screening windows or beds and by using insect repellents. Seek local advice: If you're told the water is unsafe due to jellyfish, piranhas or schistosomiasis, don't go in. In situations where there is no information, discretion is good practice.

Medical Problems & Treatment
Self-diagnosis and treatment can be risky, so wherever possible seek qualified help. Drug dosages given in this section are for emergency use only.

An embassy or consulate can usually recommend a good place to go for such advice. So can the best hotels, although they often recommend doctors with the highest prices. (This is when that medical insurance really comes in useful!) Generally speaking, though, Peruvian doctors charge less than their counterparts in North America or Europe. In some places standards of medical attention are so low that for some ailments the best advice is to get on a plane and go somewhere else. Adequate medical care is available in the major cities and the best places are mentioned in the city chapters of this book.

Climatic & Geographical Considerations
Sunburn In the tropics, the desert, or at high altitude you can get sunburnt surprisingly quickly, even through cloud. Use a sunscreen (SPF 15 minimum) and take extra care to cover areas which don't normally see sun – eg, your feet. A hat provides added protection, and you should also use zinc cream or some other barrier cream for your nose and lips. Calamine lotion is good for mild sunburn.

Prickly Heat Prickly heat is an itchy rash caused by excessive perspiration trapped under the skin. It usually strikes people who have just arrived in a hot climate and whose pores have not yet opened sufficiently to cope with greater sweating. Keeping cool but bathing often, using a mild talcum powder or even resorting to air-conditioning, may help until you acclimatize.

Heat Exhaustion Dehydration or salt deficiency can cause heat exhaustion. Take time to acclimatize to high temperatures and make sure you get sufficient liquids. Wear loose clothing and a broad-brimmed hat. Do not do anything too physically demanding.

Salt deficiency is characterized by fatigue, lethargy, headaches, giddiness and muscle cramps and in this case salt tablets may help. Vomiting or diarrhea can deplete your liquid and salt levels.

Heat Stroke This serious – sometimes fatal – condition can occur if the body's heat-regulating mechanism breaks down and the body temperature rises to dangerous levels. Long, continuous periods of exposure to high temperatures can leave you vulnerable to heat stroke. You should avoid excessive alcohol or strenuous activity when you first arrive in a hot climate.

The symptoms of heat stroke are feeling unwell, not sweating very much or at all, and a high body temperature (39°C to 41°C). Where sweating has ceased the skin becomes flushed and red. Severe, throbbing headaches and lack of coordination will also occur, and the sufferer may be confused or aggressive. Eventually the victim will become delirious or convulse. Hospitalization is essential, but meanwhile get the victim out of the sun, remove their clothing, cover them with a wet sheet or towel and then fan continually.

Fungal Infections Hot weather fungal infections are most likely to occur on the scalp, between the toes or fingers (athlete's foot), in the groin (jock itch or crotch rot) and on the body (ringworm). You get ringworm (which is a fungal infection, not a worm) from infected animals or by walking on damp areas, like shower floors.

To prevent fungal infections wear loose, comfortable clothes, avoid artificial fibers, wash frequently and dry carefully. If you do get an infection, wash the infected area daily with a disinfectant or medicated soap and water, and rinse and dry well. Apply an antifungal powder like the widely available Tinaderm or Tinactin. Try to expose the infected area to air or sunlight as much as possible and wash all towels and underwear in hot water as well as changing them often.

Cold Too much cold is just as dangerous as too much heat, as it may cause hypothermia. If you are trekking at high altitudes or simply taking a long bus trip over mountains, particularly at night, be prepared. In the high Andes you should always be prepared for cold, wet or windy conditions, particularly when walking, backpacking or trekking.

Hypothermia occurs when the body loses heat faster than it can produce it and the core temperature of the body falls. It is surprisingly easy to progress from very cold to dangerously cold due to a combination of wind, wet clothing, fatigue and hunger, even if the air temperature is above freezing. It is best to dress in layers; silk, wool and some of the new artificial fibers are all good insulating materials. A hat is important, as a lot of heat is lost through the head. A strong, waterproof outer layer is essential, because keeping dry is vital. Carry basic supplies, including food containing simple sugars to generate heat quickly, and lots of fluid to drink. A space blanket is something all travelers in cold environments should carry.

Symptoms of hypothermia are exhaustion, numb skin (particularly toes and fingers), shivering, slurred speech, irrational or violent behavior, lethargy, stumbling, dizzy spells, muscle cramps and violent bursts of energy. Irrationality may take the form of sufferers claiming they are warm and trying to take off their clothes.

To treat mild hypothermia, first get the person out of the wind and/or rain, remove their clothing if it's wet and replace it with dry, warm clothing. Give them hot liquids – no alcohol – and some high-calorie, easily digestible food. Do not rub victims, instead allow them to slowly warm themselves. This should be enough to treat the early stages of hypothermia. The early recognition and treatment of mild hypothermia is the only way to prevent severe hypothermia, which is a critical condition.

Altitude Sickness Acute Mountain Sickness or AMS occurs at high altitude and can be fatal. The lack of oxygen at high altitudes affects most people to some extent.

A number of measures can be adopted to prevent acute mountain sickness:

- Ascend slowly – have frequent rest days, spending two to three nights at each rise of 1000 meters. When you first arrive at high altitude try not to over exert yourself.
- Drink extra fluids. The mountain air is dry and cold and moisture is lost as you breathe.
- Eat light, high-carbohydrate meals for more energy.
- Avoid alcohol as it may increase the risk of dehydration.
- Avoid sedatives.
- Drink the coca tea *(mate de coca)* available in most Andean hotels and restaurants.

Even with acclimatization you may still have trouble adjusting. Breathlessness; a dry, irritative cough (which may progress to the production of pink, frothy sputum); severe headache; loss of appetite; nausea; and sometimes vomiting are all danger signs. Increasing tiredness, confusion and lack of coordination and balance are real danger signs. Any of these symptoms individually, even just a persistent headache, can be a warning. Mild altitude sickness *(soroche)* will generally abate after a day or so but if the symptoms persist, or become worse, the only treatment is to descend – even 500 meters can help.

There is no hard and fast rule as to how high is too high: AMS has been fatal at altitudes of 3000 meters, although 3500 to 4500 meters is the usual range. It is always wise to sleep at a lower altitude than the greatest height reached during the day.

The prescription drug Diamox (acetazolamide) has been shown to help with acclimatization if taken the day before the ascent and during the first few days at high altitude. There are some mild side effects, such as increased urination, tingling sensations in the extremities and making fizzy drinks taste funny. If you are interested in trying Diamox, talk to your doctor.

Motion Sickness Eating lightly before and during a trip will reduce the chances of motion sickness. If you are prone to motion sickness try to find a place that minimizes disturbance – near the wing on aircraft, close to midships on boats and near the center on buses. Fresh air usually helps; reading and cigarette smoke don't. Commercial motion-sickness preparations, which can cause drowsiness, have to be taken before the trip commences; when you're feeling sick it's too late. Ginger is a natural preventative and is available in capsule form.

Jet Lag Jet lag is experienced when a person travels by air across more than three time zones. It occurs because many of the functions of the human body are regulated by internal 24-hour cycles called circadian rhythms. When we travel long distances rapidly, our bodies take time to adjust to the 'new time' of our destination, and we may experience fatigue, disorientation, insomnia, anxiety, impaired concentration and loss of appetite. These effects will usually be gone within three days of arrival, but there are ways of minimizing the impact of jet lag:

- Rest for a couple of days prior to departure; try to avoid late nights and last-minute dashes for traveler's checks, passport, etc.
- Try to select flight schedules that minimize sleep deprivation; arriving late in the day means you can go to sleep soon after you arrive. For very long flights, try to organize a stopover.
- Make yourself comfortable by wearing loose-fitting clothes and perhaps bringing an eye mask and ear plugs to help you sleep.
- Avoid excessive eating and alcohol during the flight. Drink plenty of non-carbonated, non-alcoholic drinks such as fruit juice or water.
- Avoid smoking – it causes greater fatigue.

Diseases of Poor Sanitation
Diarrhea A change of water, food or climate can all cause the runs; diarrhea caused by contaminated food or water is more serious. Despite all your precautions you may still have a mild bout of traveler's diarrhea but a few rushed toilet trips with no other symptoms is not indicative of a serious problem. Moderate diarrhea, involving half a dozen loose bowel movements in a day, is more of a nuisance.

Dehydration is the main danger with any

diarrhea – children dehydrate particularly quickly. Fluid replacement remains the mainstay of management. Weak black tea with a little sugar, soda water, or soft drinks allowed to go flat and diluted 50% with water are all good. With severe diarrhea a rehydrating solution is necessary to replace minerals and salts. Commercially available ORS (oral rehydration salts) are very useful; add the contents of one sachet to a liter of boiled or bottled water. In an emergency you can make up a solution of eight teaspoons of sugar to a liter of boiled water and provide salted cracker biscuits at the same time. You should stick to a bland diet as you recover.

Lomotil or Imodium can be used to bring relief from the symptoms, although they do not actually cure the problem. Only use these drugs if absolutely necessary – that is, if you *must* travel. For children Imodium is preferable, but under all circumstances fluid replacement is the most important thing to remember. Do not use these drugs if the person has a high fever or is severely dehydrated.

Antibiotics may be needed for diarrhea that lasts for more than five days, or that is severe, or for watery diarrhea with fever and lethargy or with blood and mucus (gut-paralyzing drugs like Imodium or Lomotil should be avoided in this situation).

The recommended drugs (adults only) would be either norfloxacin 400 mg or ciprofloxacin 500 mg twice daily for three days. Bismuth subsalicylate may be useful but is not available in Australia. Two tablets for adults and one for children can be taken every hour up to eight times a day. Recommended drugs for children are co-trimoxazole (Bactrim, Septrin, Resprim) with dosage dependent on weight.

Giardiasis The parasite causing this intestinal disorder is present in contaminated water. The symptoms are stomach cramps, nausea, a bloated stomach, watery, foul-smelling diarrhea and frequent gas. Giardiasis can appear several weeks after you have been exposed to the parasite. The symptoms may disappear for a few days and then return; this can go on for several weeks. Tinidazole, known as Fasigyn, or metronidazole (Flagyl) are the recommended drugs for treatment. Either can be used in a single treatment dose. Antibiotics are of no use.

Dysentery This serious illness is caused by contaminated food or water and is characterized by severe diarrhea, often with blood or mucus in the stool. There are two kinds of dysentery. Bacillary dysentery is characterized by a high fever and rapid onset; headache, vomiting and stomach pains are also symptoms. It generally does not last longer than a week, but it is highly contagious.

Amoebic dysentery is often more gradual in the onset of symptoms, with cramping abdominal pain and vomiting less likely; fever may not be present. It is not a self-limiting disease: It will persist until treated and can recur and cause long-term health problems.

A stool test is necessary to diagnose which kind of dysentery you have, so you should seek medical help urgently. In an emergency the recommended drugs for bacillary dysentry are norfloxacin 400 mg, ciprofloxacin 500 mg or co-trimoxazole 160/800 mg (Bactrim, Septrin, Resprim) twice daily for seven days. Co-trimoxazole is also the recommended drug for children.

For amoebic dysentery, the recommended adult dosage of metronidazole (Flagyl) is one 750-mg to 800-mg capsule three times daily for five days. Children aged between 8 and 12 years should have half the adult dose; the dosage for younger children is one-third the adult dose. An alternative to Flagyl is Fasigyn, taken as a two-gram daily dose for three days. Alcohol must be avoided during treatment and for 48 hours afterwards.

Cholera Cholera vaccination is not very effective. The bacteria responsible for this disease are waterborne, so attention to the rules of eating and drinking should protect the traveler.

Outbreaks of cholera are generally

widely reported, so you can avoid such problem areas. The 1991 epidemic in Peru was confined to extremely poor neighborhoods which, for the most part, lacked running water and a proper sewage system. These are not places where the traveler would normally go.

The disease is characterized by a sudden onset of acute diarrhea with 'rice water' stools, vomiting, muscular cramps and extreme weakness. You need medical help – but first begin treatment for dehydration, which can be extreme, and if there is considerable delay in getting to a hospital then begin taking 250 mg of tetracycline four times daily. It is not recommended for children aged eight years or under nor for pregnant women. An alternative drug is Ampicillin. Remember that while antibiotics might kill the bacteria, it is a toxin produced by the bacteria that causes the massive fluid loss. Fluid replacement is by far the most important aspect of treatment.

Viral Gastroenteritis This is caused not by bacteria but, as the name suggests, by a virus. It is characterized by stomach cramps, diarrhea and sometimes by vomiting or a slight fever. All you can do is rest and drink lots of fluids.

Hepatitis Hepatitis A is a very common problem among travelers to areas with poor sanitation. With good water and adequate sewage disposal in most industrialized countries since the 1940s, very few young adults now have any natural immunity and must be protected. Protection is through the new vaccine Havrix (Hepatitis A vaccine) or the antibody gamma globulin.

The disease is spread by contaminated food or water. The symptoms are fever, chills, headache, fatigue, feelings of weakness and aches and pains, followed by loss of appetite, nausea, vomiting, abdominal pain, dark urine, light colored feces, jaundiced skin and the whites of the eyes possibly turning yellow. In some cases you may feel tired, have no appetite, experience aches and pains and be jaundiced. You

should seek medical advice, but in general there is not much you can do apart from resting, drinking lots of fluids, eating lightly and avoiding fatty foods. People who have had hepatitis must forego alcohol for six months after the illness, as hepatitis attacks the liver and it needs that amount of time to recover.

Hepatitis B, which used to be called serum hepatitis, is spread through contact with infected blood, blood products or bodily fluids – especially through sexual contact, unsterilized needles and blood transfusions. Other risk situations include having a shave or tattoo in a local shop, or having your ears pierced. The symptoms of type B are much the same as type A except that they are more severe and may lead to irreparable liver damage or even liver cancer. Although there is no treatment for hepatitis B, an effective prophylactic vaccine is readily available in most countries. The immunization schedule requires two injections at least a month apart followed by a third dose five months after the second. Persons who should receive a hepatitis B vaccination include anyone who anticipates contact with blood or other bodily secretions, either as a health care worker or through sexual contact with the local population, particularly those who intend to stay in the country for a long period of time.

Hepatitis Non-A Non-B is a blanket term formerly used for several different strains of hepatitis, which have now been separately identified. Hepatitis C is similar to B but is less common. Hepatitis D (the 'delta particle') is also similar to B and always occurs in concert with it; its occurrence is currently limited to IV drug users. Hepatitis E, however, is similar to A and is spread in the same manner, by water or food contamination.

Tests are available for these strains, but are very expensive. Travelers shouldn't be too paranoid about this apparent proliferation of hepatitis strains; they are fairly rare (so far) and following the same precautions as for A and B should be all that's necessary to avoid them.

Typhoid Typhoid fever is another gut infection that travels the fecal-oral route – contaminated water and food are responsible. Vaccination against typhoid is not totally effective and it is one of the most dangerous infections, so medical help must be sought.

In its early stages typhoid resembles many other illnesses: Sufferers may feel like they have a bad cold or the initial stages of a flu, as early symptoms are a headache, a sore throat and a fever which rises a little each day until it is around 40°C or more. The victim's pulse is often slow relative to the degree of fever present and gets slower as the fever rises – unlike a normal fever where the pulse increases. There may also be vomiting, diarrhea or constipation.

In the second week the high fever and slow pulse continue and a few pink spots may appear on the body; trembling, delirium, weakness, weight loss and dehydration are other symptoms. If there are no further complications, the fever and other symptoms will slowly diminish during the third week. Still, you must get medical help since pneumonia (acute infection of the lungs) or peritonitis (perforated bowel) are common complications, and typhoid is very infectious. The fever should be treated by keeping the victim cool and dehydration should also be watched for.

The drug of choice is ciprofloxacin at a dose of one gram daily for 14 days. It is quite expensive and may not be available. The alternative, chloramphenicol, has been the mainstay of treatment for many years. In many countries it is still the recommended antibiotic but there are fewer side affects with Ampicillin. The adult dosage is two 250-mg capsules, four times a day. Children aged between 8 and 12 years should have half the adult dose; younger children should have one-third the adult dose. People who are allergic to penicillin should not be given Ampicillin.

Worms These parasites are most common in rural, tropical areas and a stool test when you return home is not a bad idea. They can be present on unwashed vegetables or in undercooked meat and you can pick them up through your skin by walking in bare feet. Infestations may not show up for some time, and although they are generally not serious, if left untreated they can cause severe health problems. A stool test is necessary to pinpoint the problem and medication is often available over the counter.

Diseases Spread by Animals & People

Tetanus This potentially fatal disease is found in undeveloped tropical areas. It is difficult to treat but is preventable with immunization. Tetanus occurs when a wound becomes infected by a germ that lives in the feces of animals or people, so clean all cuts, punctures or animal bites. Tetanus is also known as lockjaw, and the first symptom may be discomfort in swallowing, or stiffening of the jaw and neck; this is followed by painful convulsions of the jaw and whole body.

Rabies Rabies is caused by a bite or scratch by an infected animal. Dogs are noted carriers as are monkeys and cats. Any bite, scratch or even lick should be cleaned immediately and thoroughly. Scrub with soap and running water, and then clean with an alcohol solution. If there is any possibility that the animal is infected medical help should be sought immediately. Rabies takes at least five days and sometimes several weeks to develop, but once it develops it is always fatal. A vaccination after the bite occurs but before rabies appears generally results in complete recovery. Even if the animal is not rabid, all bites should be treated seriously as they can become infected or can result in tetanus. A rabies vaccination is now available and should be considered if you are in a high-risk category – particularly if you intend to explore caves (bat bites can be dangerous) or work with animals.

Meningococcal Meningitis This rare (in Peru) but very serious disease attacks the brain and can be fatal. A scattered, blotchy rash, fever, severe headache, sensitivity to light and neck stiffness which prevents

ROB RACHOWIECKI

ROB RACHOWIECKI

TONY WHEELER

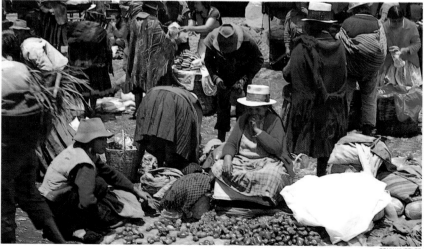
TONY WHEELER

Peruvian market scenes

MICHAEL PETTYPOOL

ROB RACHOWIECKI

ROB RACHOWIECKI

forward bending of the head are the first symptoms. Death can occur within a few hours, so immediate treatment is important. Treatment is large doses of penicillin given intravenously, or, if that is not possible, intramuscularly (in the buttocks). Vaccination offers good protection for over a year, but you should also check for reports of current epidemics.

Tuberculosis (TB) Although this disease is widespread in many developing countries, it is not a serious risk to travelers. Young children are more susceptible than adults and vaccination is a sensible precaution for children under 12 traveling in endemic areas. TB is commonly spread by coughing or by unpasteurized dairy products from infected cows.

Schistosomiasis Also known as bilharzia, this disease is carried in slow-moving water (especially behind dams) by minute worms. It is quite common in the Brazilian Amazon, less so in Peru.

The worms attach themselves to your intestines or bladder, then produce large numbers of eggs. The worm enters through the skin, and the first symptom may be a tingling and sometimes a light rash around the area where it entered. Weeks later, when the worm is busy producing eggs, a high fever may develop. A general ill feeling may be the first symptom; once the disease is established abdominal pain and blood in the urine are other signs.

Don't swim in fresh water where bilharzia is present. Even deep water can be infected. If you do get wet, towel off quickly as the worms supposedly burrow into the skin as the water evaporates. Dry your clothes as well. Seek medical attention if you have been exposed to the disease and tell the doctor your suspicions, as schistosomiasis in the early stages can be confused with malaria or typhoid. If you cannot get medical help immediately, praziquantel (Biltricide) is the recommended treatment. The recommended dosage is 40 mg/kg in divided doses over one day. Niridazole is an alternative drug.

Diphtheria Diphtheria can be a skin infection or a more dangerous throat infection. It is spread by contaminated dust contacting the skin or by the inhalation of infected cough or sneeze vapor. Frequent washing and keeping the skin dry will help prevent skin infection. A vaccination is available to prevent the throat infection.

Sexually Transmitted Diseases STDs are spread through sexual contact with an infected partner. Abstinence is the only 100% preventative, but monogamous sexual relations is safe as long as both partners are healthy and remain trustworthy. Using condoms is also effective. Gonorrhea and syphilis are common STDs; sores, blisters or rashes around the genitals, discharges or pain when urinating are common symptoms. Symptoms may be less marked or not observed at all in women. Syphilis symptoms eventually disappear completely but the disease continues and can cause severe problems in later years. The treatment of gonorrhea and syphilis is by antibiotics. There is no cure for herpes (which causes blisters but is not normally very dangerous) or for AIDS.

HIV/AIDS HIV, the Human Immunodeficiency Virus, may develop into AIDS, Acquired Immune Deficiency Syndrome (SIDA in Spanish). HIV is a significant problem in neighboring Brazil and the virus is spreading to the Peruvian population, particularly among prostitutes of both sexes. Any exposure to blood, blood products or bodily fluids may put an individual at risk. Transmission is predominantly through heterosexual sexual activity. This is quite different from industrialized countries where transmission is mostly through sexual contact with homosexual or bisexual males, or via contaminated needles shared by IV drug users. Apart from abstinence, the most effective preventative is to practice safe sex using condoms. Condoms (*preservativos*) are available in some Peruvian pharmacies, though they are expensive and of low-quality (I'm told it's worth wearing two). It is impossible to detect the HIV-positive status of an otherwise healthy-looking person without a blood test.

HIV/AIDS can also be spread through infected blood transfusions; if you need a blood transfusion go to the best clinic which normally will screen blood for transfusions. It can also be spread by dirty needles – vaccinations, acupuncture, tattooing and ear or nose piercing can potentially be as dangerous as intravenous drug use if the equipment is not clean. If you do need an injection, ask to see the syringe unwrapped in front of you, or better still, take a needle and syringe pack with you overseas – it is a cheap insurance package against infection with HIV.

Fear of HIV infection should never preclude treatment for serious medical conditions. The risk of infection remains very small.

Insect-Borne Diseases
Malaria This serious disease is spread by mosquito bites. If you are traveling in endemic areas it is extremely important to take malarial prophylactics. Symptoms include headaches, fever, chills and sweating which may subside and recur. Without treatment malaria can develop more serious, potentially fatal effects.

Antimalarial drugs do not prevent you from being infected but kill the parasites during a stage in their development.

There are several types of malaria. The problem in recent years has been the emergence of increasing resistance to commonly used antimalarials like chloroquine, maloprim and proguanil. Newer drugs such as mefloquine (Lariam) and doxycycline (Vibramycin, Doryx) are often recommended for chloroquine and multidrug-resistant areas. In Peru, chloroquine is still considered effective, but it is only a matter of time until chloroquine-resistant strains begin to establish themselves, as they already have in neighboring Ecuador.

Expert advice should be sought, as there are many factors to consider when deciding on the type of antimalarial medication, including the area to be visited, the risk of exposure to malaria-carrying mosquitoes,

your current medical condition, and your age and pregnancy status. It is also important to discuss the side-effect profile of the medication, so you can work out some level of risk versus benefit ratio. It is also very important to be sure of the correct dosage of the medication prescribed to you. Some people have inadvertently taken weekly medication (chloroquine) on a daily basis, with disastrous effects. While discussing dosages for prevention of malaria, it is often advisable to pack the dosages required for treatment, especially if your trip is through a high-risk area that would isolate you from medical care.

Note that, in Peru, malaria occurs only in the Amazon basin and parts of the far north coast and so you needn't worry about the disease if you aren't spending time in those regions.

The main messages are:

- The mosquitoes that transmit malaria bite from dusk to dawn so during this period wear light colored clothing; wear long pants and long sleeved shirts; use mosquito repellents containing DEET on exposed areas; avoid perfumes or scented aftershave; use a mosquito net – it may be worth carrying your own.
- While no antimalarial is 100% effective, taking the most appropriate drug significantly reduces the risk of contracting the disease.
- No one should ever die from malaria. It can be diagnosed by a simple blood test. Contrary to popular belief, once a traveler contracts malaria he or she does not have it for life. Malaria is curable, as long as the traveler seeks medical help when symptoms occur.

Dengue Fever There is no prophylactic available for this mosquito-spread disease; the main preventative measure is to avoid mosquito bites. A sudden onset of fever, headaches and severe joint and muscle pains are the first signs before a rash starts on the trunk of the body and spreads to the limbs and face. After a further few days, the fever will subside and recovery will begin. Serious complications are not common but full recovery can take up to a month or more. Quite common in neighboring Brazil, it is rare in Peru.

Yellow Fever This disease is endemic in the Amazon basin. It is a viral disease transmitted to humans by mosquitoes; the initial symptoms are fever, headache, abdominal pain and vomiting. There may appear to be a brief recovery before the disease progresses to more severe complications, including liver failure. There is no medical treatment apart from keeping the fever down and avoiding dehydration, but yellow fever vaccination gives good protection for 10 years.

Chagas' Disease In remote rural areas of South and Central America this parasitic disease is transmitted by a bug that hides in crevices and palm fronds and often takes up residence in the thatched roofs of huts. It comes out to feed at night. A hard, violet-colored swelling appears at the site of the bite in about a week. Usually the body overcomes the disease unaided, but sometimes it continues and can eventually lead to death years later. Chagas' disease can be treated in its early stages, but it is best to avoid thatched-roof huts, sleep under a mosquito net, use insecticides and insect repellents. Always check bedding for hidden insects.

Typhus Typhus is spread by ticks, mites or lice. It begins as a bad cold, followed by a fever, chills, headache, muscle pains and a body rash. There is often a large painful sore at the site of the bite and nearby lymph nodes are swollen and painful.

Tick typhus is spread by ticks. Seek local advice on areas where ticks pose a danger and always check your skin carefully for ticks after walking in a high-risk area such as a tropical forest. A strong insect repellent can help, and serious walkers in tick areas should consider having their boots and trousers impregnated with benzyl benzoate and dibutylphthalate. Typhus is present but not very common in Peru.

Cuts, Bites & Stings
Cuts & Scratches Skin punctures can easily become infected in hot climates and

may be difficult to heal. Treat any cut with an antiseptic such as Betadine. Where possible avoid bandages and Band-aids, which can keep wounds wet.

Bites & Stings Bee and wasp stings are usually painful rather than dangerous. Calamine lotion will give relief and ice packs will reduce the pain and swelling. There are some spiders with dangerous bites but these are not usually fatal and antivenins are usually available. Scorpion stings are notoriously painful but are very rarely fatal. Scorpions, spiders, ants and other biting creatures often shelter in shoes or clothing. Develop the habit of shaking out your clothing before putting it on, especially in the lowlands. Check your bedding before going to sleep. Don't walk barefoot and look where you place your hands when reaching to a shelf or branch.

Snakes To minimize your chances of being bitten always wear boots, socks and long trousers when walking through undergrowth where snakes may be present. Don't put your hands into holes and crevices, and be careful when collecting firewood.

Snake bites do not cause instantaneous death and antivenins are usually available. If bitten, keep calm and still, wrap the bitten limb tightly, as you would for a sprained ankle, and then attach a splint to immobilize it. Then seek medical help, if possible with the dead snake for identification. Don't attempt to catch the snake if there is even a remote possibility of being bitten again. Tourniquets and sucking out the poison are now widely discredited as treatment for snake bites.

Jellyfish Local advice is the best way of avoiding contact with these sea creatures which have stinging tentacles. The stings from most jellyfish are rather painful but not lethal. Dousing in vinegar will deactivate any stingers that have not 'fired.' Calamine lotion, antihistamines and analgesics may reduce the reaction and relieve the pain.

Bedbugs & Lice Bedbugs live in various places, but particularly in dirty mattresses and bedding. Spots of blood on bedclothes or on the wall around the bed can be read as a suggestion to find another hotel. Bedbugs leave itchy bites in neat rows. Calamine lotion may help.

All lice cause itching and discomfort. They make themselves at home in your hair (head lice), your clothing (body lice) or in your pubic hair (crabs). You catch lice through direct contact with infected people or by sharing combs, clothing and the like. Powder or shampoo treatment will kill the lice and infected clothing should then be washed in very hot water.

Other Creatures Scabies are mites that burrow into your skin and cause it to become red and itchy. To kill scabies, wash yourself with a benzene benzoate solution, and wash your clothes too. Both benzene hexachloride and benzoate are obtainable from pharmacies in Peru.

Ticks (see Typhus) are best removed by gripping them gently with tweezers and working them back and forth. Don't leave the head stuck in your skin. Chiggers are tiny mite larvae that burrow under the skin and feed on you for several days. They itch like crazy and are best avoided by not walking through long grass without long trousers and insect repellant.

Botfly eggs are deposited under the skin. When they hatch, the larvae burrow deeper and you can feel them moving around – disconcerting and uncomfortable but not dangerous. It is hard to remove them, though various suggestions are offered. Try putting Vaseline or nail polish over the hole in the skin, thus suffocating the beasts and causing them to stick their heads out at which time they can be pulled out with tweezers. Many travelers have concluded, however, that botflies have to be removed surgically.

Sandflies can cause the disfiguring disease leishmaniasis, and are small enough to crawl through mosquito nets. Use insect repellants, particularly when sleeping on the ground in the lowlands.

Your worst nightmare might be the candirú fish (also known as the orifish), a nasty little bugger that can swim up your urethra, supposedly when you are urinating, and then become embedded in the urinary tract. Surgical removal is the best 'cure.' A better option is not to pee in the river and not to swim naked in the Amazon basin.

Women's Health

Gynecological Problems Poor diet, lowered resistance due to the use of antibiotics for stomach upsets and even contraceptive pills can lead to vaginal infections when traveling in hot climates. Wearing skirts or loose-fitting trousers and cotton underwear will help to prevent infections.

Yeast infections, characterized by a rash, itch and discharge, can be treated with a vinegar or lemon-juice douche, or with yogurt. Nystatin suppositories are the usual medical prescription. Trichomoniasis is a more serious infection; symptoms are a discharge and a burning sensation when urinating. Male sexual partners must also be treated, and if a vinegar-water douche is not effective medical attention should be sought. Metronidazole (Flagyl) is the prescribed drug.

Pregnancy Most miscarriages occur during the first three months of pregnancy, so this is the most risky time to travel as far as your own health is concerned. Miscarriage is not uncommon, and can occasionally lead to severe bleeding. The last three months should also be spent within reasonable distance of good medical care. A baby born as early as 24 weeks stands a chance of survival, but only in a good modern hospital. Pregnant women should avoid all unnecessary medication, but vaccinations and malarial prophylactics should still be taken where possible. Take additional care to prevent illness and pay particular attention to diet and nutrition. Alcohol and nicotine, for example, should be avoided.

Women travelers often find that their periods become irregular or even cease while they're on the road. Remember that a missed period in these circumstances doesn't necessarily indicate pregnancy. There are health posts or family planning clinics in many urban centers, where you can seek advice and have a urine test to determine whether or not you are pregnant.

TOILETS

Peruvian plumbing leaves something to be desired. Flushing a toilet can lead to an overflow. This problem is ameliorated by not putting anything other than human waste into the toilet. Even putting toilet paper into the bowl can clog up the system and so a waste receptacle is routinely provided for the paper. This may not seem particularly sanitary, but it is much better than clogged bowls and water on the floor. A well-run hotel or restaurant, even if it is cheap, will ensure that the receptacle is emptied and the toilet cleaned every day.

Public toilets are almost non-existent outside of transportation terminals and restaurants. Those in transportation terminals are often dirty. It is not unusual to see men urinating against walls on side streets. Both men and women can ask to use the bathroom in a restaurant even if they are not patrons. Occasionally, permission isn't granted because, you're told, the facility isn't functioning properly, in which case you should simply try a second restaurant. Toilet paper is provided only in the better hotels and restaurants and most people carry a supply of their own.

WOMEN TRAVELERS

Generally, women travelers will find Peru safe and pleasant to visit.

That is not to say, however, that machismo is a thing of the past. On the contrary, it is very much alive and practiced. Peruvian men generally consider *gringas* to be more liberated (and therefore to be easier sexual conquests) than their Peruvian counterparts. Local men will often make flirtatious comments, whistles and hisses to single women – both Peruvian and foreign. Women traveling with another woman are not exempt from this attention. Peruvian women usually deal with this by looking away and completely ignoring the man – this works reasonably well for gringas too. Women who firmly ignore unwanted verbal advances are normally treated with respect. Wearing a ring on the wedding finger (whether married or not) acts as a good deterrent.

Traveling with another woman may give you some measure of psychological support. Traveling with a man tends to minimize the attention that Peruvian men may direct towards women travelers. Increasing numbers of Peruvian men are becoming sensitive to the issue of machismo – they may practice it with their buddies, but won't hassle every gringa they see.

Occasionally, you hear of a woman traveler being raped. A rape prevention counselor who worked with women in the US Peace Corps suggests that a lone woman should never wander around poorly lit areas at night or remote places at any time. Other suggestions include carrying a metal whistle (in your hand – not in your backpack). This produces a piercing blast and will startle off most would-be rapists long enough for a woman to get away.

I have met many women who have traveled safely, and alone, throughout Peru. Many have made friends with Peruvian men and found them charming and friendly. However, unless you are attracted to a local man, you should avoid going somewhere with him alone, as that indicates that you are interested in sleeping with him and you will be pressured to do so. Friendships are best developed in public group settings.

There is not much in the way of local resources for women travelers. The South American Explorers Club in Lima and Quito is often staffed by women – these friendly and wonderful people can offer straightforward advice.

Two books I have seen and which appear to be useful are *Women Travel – Adventures, Advice & Experience* by Natania Jansz & Miranda Davies (Prentice Hall) and *Handbook for Women Travelers* by Maggie & Jemma Moss (Piatkus Publishers).

I would be very pleased to receive practical advice for women from women travelers. Send letters to the Lonely Planet office in Oakland, CA.

GAY & LESBIAN TRAVELERS
Gay rights in a political or legal context don't even exist as an issue for most Peruvians. Sexuality is more stereotyped in Peru (and in many Latin countries) than it is in Europe and North America, with the man playing a dominant macho role and the woman tagging along with that. This attitude spills over into homosexuality, with straight-acting macho men not considered to be gay, even if they are, while an effeminate man, even if he is straight, will be called a *maricón* – a mildly derogatory term for homosexual men. Relatively few gay men in Peru are exclusively homosexual, and bisexuality is the norm. This means that AIDS is often transmitted heterosexually and is a growing problem in Peru. (See Health.)

Lesbians are an almost ignored segment of the population. I have heard that there is one organization in Lima which is supportive to gays and lesbians, but I have been unable to track it down. The various gay-oriented travel guides that are available (not in Peru) rarely have much information about Peru.

DISABLED TRAVELERS
Unfortunately, Peru's infrastructure offers little convenience for disabled travelers, as is the case in most third world countries. Wheelchair ramps are few and far between and pavements are often badly potholed and cracked. Bathrooms and toilets are often barely large enough for an able-bodied person to walk into, so very few indeed are accessible to wheelchairs. Features such as signs in Braille or telephones for the hearing-impaired are virtually unknown. Nevertheless, there are disabled Peruvians who get around, mainly through the help of others. It is not particularly unusual to see disabled travelers being carried bodily to a seat on a bus, for example. For some general advice, a good starting point might be *Nothing Ventured: Disabled People Travel the World* (Rough Guides, 1991).

TRAVEL WITH CHILDREN
Children pay full fare on buses if they occupy a seat, but often ride for free if they sit on a parent's knee. Children under 12 pay half fare on domestic airline flights and get a seat while infants under two pay 10% of the fare but don't get a seat.

In hotels, the general rule is simply to bargain. Children should never have to pay as much as an adult, but whether they stay for half price or free is open to discussion.

While 'kids' meals' (small portions at small prices) are not normally offered in restaurants, it is perfectly acceptable to order a meal to split between two children or an adult and a child.

Foreigners traveling with children are still a curiosity in Peru and will meet with extra, generally friendly, attention and interest.

For more suggestions, see Lonely Planet's *Travel With Children* (3rd ed, 1995).

USEFUL ORGANIZATIONS
The single most useful organization is the recommended South American Explorers Club. They have three offices – in the USA, Ecuador and Lima. Full details are given in the Lima chapter.

You can get up-to-date information on safety, political and economic situations, health risks and costs for all the Latin American countries (including Peru) from *The Latin American Travel Advisor*. This is an impartial, 16-page, quarterly newsletter published in Ecuador. Four issues are US$39, the most recent issue is US$15 and back issues are US$7.50 sent by airmail from LATA, PO Box 17-17-908, Quito, Ecuador (fax (2) 562-566, email lata@pi.pro.ec).

DANGERS & ANNOYANCES
Theft
Peru has a reputation for thievery and, unfortunately, it is fully warranted. There's no denying that many travelers do get

ripped off. On the other hand, by taking some basic precautions and exercising a reasonable amount of vigilance, you probably won't be robbed. What normally happens is that travelers are so involved in their new surroundings and experiences that they forget to stay alert and that's when something is stolen. It's good to know that armed theft is not as frequent as sneak theft. Remember that crowded places are the haunts of pickpockets. This means badly lit bus and train stations or bustling markets and fiestas.

Thieves look for easy targets. Tourists who carry a wallet or passport in a hip pocket are asking for trouble. Leave your wallet at home; it's an easy mark for a pickpocket. A small roll of bills loosely wadded under a handkerchief in your front pocket is as safe a way as any of carrying your daily spending money. The rest should be hidden. Always use at least a closable inside pocket or preferably a body pouch, money belt or leg pouch to protect your money and passport.

You can carry the greater portion of your money in the form of traveler's checks. These can be refunded if lost or stolen, often within a few days. However, exchange rates for traveler's checks is a few percent less than cash dollars, depending on the exchange regulations at the time you visit. Some airlines will also reissue your ticket if it is lost. You must give details such as where and when you got it, the ticket number and which flight was involved. Usually a reissuing fee (about US$20) is charged, but that's much better than buying a new ticket. Stolen passports can be reissued at your embassy. For this you need a police report of the theft and positive identification.

Pickpockets are not the only problem. Snatch theft is also common, so don't wear gold necklaces and expensive wristwatches or you're liable to have them snatched from your body. I've seen it happen to someone walking with me and by the time I realized that something had been stolen the thief was 20 meters away and jumping on to a friend's motorcycle. Snatch theft can also

occur if you carry a camera loosely over your shoulder or place a bag on the ground for just a second.

Thieves often work in pairs or groups. While your attention is being distracted by one partner, another is robbing you. The distraction can take the form of a bunch of kids fighting in front of you, an old lady 'accidentally' bumping into you, someone dropping something in your path or spilling something on your clothes – the possibilities go on and on. The only thing you can do is try, as much as possible, to avoid being in very tight crowds and to stay alert, especially when something out of the ordinary occurs.

To worry you further, there are the razor blade artists. No, they don't wave a blade in your face and demand 'Your money or your life!' They are much too gutless for that kind of confrontation. They simply slit open your luggage with a razor blade when you're not looking. A pack on your back or luggage in the rack of a bus or train – even your trouser pocket – are all vulnerable. Many travelers carry their day packs on their chests to avoid having them slashed during day trips to markets and other crowded public spaces. When walking with my large pack, I move fast and avoid stopping, which makes it difficult for anyone intent on cutting the bag. If I have to stop, at a street crossing for example, I tend to gently swing from side to side so I can feel if anyone is touching my pack and I look around a lot. I never place a bag on the ground unless I have my foot on it. I don't feel paranoid – walking fast and looking around on my way from bus station to hotel has become second nature to me. It is always a good idea to walk purposefully wherever you are going, even if you are lost.

One of the best solutions to the rip-off problem is to travel with a friend and to watch one another. An extra pair of eyes makes a big difference. I often see shifty-looking types eyeing luggage at bus stations, but they notice if you are alert and are less likely to bother you. If you see a suspicious looking character, look them directly in the eye and point them out to your traveling companions. They'd much rather steal something from the tired and unalert traveler who has put their bag on a chair while buying a coffee, and who, 10 seconds later, has their coffee but no bag!

It is a good idea to carry an emergency kit somewhere separate from all your other valuables. This kit could be sewn into a jacket (don't lose the jacket!) or even carried in your shoe. It should contain a photocopy of the important pages of your passport in case it's lost or stolen. On the back of the photocopy you should list important numbers such as all your traveler's check serial numbers, airline ticket numbers, credit card or bank account numbers, telephone numbers, etc. Also keep one high denomination bill with this emergency stash. You will probably never have to use it, but it's a good idea not to put all your eggs into one basket.

Take out traveler's insurance, but don't get paranoid. Stay alert and you can spend months in Peru without anything being stolen.

Drugs
Definitely avoid any conversation with someone who offers you drugs. In fact, talking to any stranger on the street can hold risks. It has happened that travelers who have talked to strangers have been stopped soon after by plainclothes police officers and accused of talking to a drug dealer. In such a situation, never get into a vehicle with the 'police,' but insist on going to a bona fide police station on foot. Be wary of false or crooked police who prey on tourists.

Be aware that there are draconian penalties for the possession of even a small amount of drugs for personal use. There's no chance of a fine and probation – minimum sentences are several years in jail.

Altitude Sickness
Cuzco and Lake Titicaca are both high on the list of many travelers' destinations, and they are high in the mountains too. Many

visitors fly in from Lima, at sea level, and usually experience some mild altitude sickness during the first day or two. Make sure that you allow for a rest day at the beginning of your visit to the highlands to allow you to acclimatize. See the Health section for more details.

Terrorism
There are two guerrilla groups in Peru, the small MRTA and the larger and better known Sendero Luminoso. As described in the previous chapter, the main leaders of both groups were captured and imprisoned in 1992 and, since then, travel safety has improved dramatically. Occasional bombings and shootings by a few remaining Senderistas are still reported, but these are infrequent and not generally aimed at tourists. The chances of being subject to terrorist attack are probably no greater than in most other countries.

Earthquakes
Peru is in an earthquake zone and small tremors are frequent. Every few years a large earthquake results in loss of life and property damage. Should you be caught in an earthquake the best advice is to take shelter under a solid object such as a desk or doorframe. Do not stand near windows or heavy objects. Do not run out of the building. If you are outside, attempt to stay clear of falling wires, bricks, telephone poles and other hazards. Avoid crowds in the aftermath.

Dangerous Travel Areas
Peru is generally safe to travel in but I would avoid two routes at this time. One is the Río Huallaga valley between Tingo María and Tarapoto. This is where the majority of Peru's illegal drug growing takes place and the area is somewhat dangerous. Also, in the aftermath of terrorism, isolated groups of bandits hijack or rob buses in remote areas. The most dangerous area of late is the mountains above Puquio on the Nazca to Abancay road. This route should be avoided.

It is always safer (and more scenic!) to

take buses during the day as night buses are occasionally held up in remote areas of the country. This doesn't happen very often and, in some cases, you have no choice but to travel at night. The situation can change so you should seek local advice.

BUSINESS HOURS

Hours are variable and liable to change. Some places may have posted hours and not adhere to them. Many shops and offices close for an extended lunch break. Be flexible and patient when needing to get things done.

HOLIDAYS & SPECIAL EVENTS

Many of Peru's main festivals favor the Roman Catholic liturgical calendar. These are often celebrated with great pageantry, especially in highland Indian villages where the Catholic feast day may well be linked with some traditional agricultural festival (such as spring or harvest) and be the excuse for a traditional Indian fiesta with much drinking, dancing, rituals and processions. Other holidays are of historical or political interest, such as *Fiestas Patrias* (National Independence) on July 28 and 29. On major holidays, banks, offices and other services are closed and transportation tends to be very crowded, so book ahead if possible.

The following list describes the major holidays, which may well be celebrated for several days around the actual date. Those marked by an asterisk (*) are official public holidays when banks and other businesses are closed; others are more local holidays. If an official public holiday falls on a weekend, offices close on the following Monday. If an official holiday falls midweek, it may or may not be moved to the nearest Monday to create a long weekend.

January 1*
  Año Nuevo (New Year's Day) – particularly important in Huancayo where a fiesta continues until January 6.
February 2
  La Virgen de la Candelaria (Candlemas) is a colorful fiesta in the highlands, particularly in the Puno area.

February-March
  Carnaval – held on the last few days before Lent, it's often celebrated with water fights, so be warned. It's a particularly popular feast in the highlands with the Carnaval de Cajamarca being one of the biggest.
March-April*
  Semana Santa (Holy Week) – This is the week before Easter. Maundy Thursday afternoon and all of Good Friday are public holidays. Holy Week is celebrated with spectacular religious processions almost daily, with Ayacucho being recognized as having the best in Peru. Cuzco is also good for Easter processions.
May 1*
  Labor Day
June
  Corpus Christi – the 9th Thursday after Easter. The Cuzco processions are especially dramatic.
June 24*
  Inti Raymi – also St John the Baptist and Peasant's Day. This is a public half day holiday. Inti Raymi celebrates the winter solstice and is the greatest of the Inca festivals. It's certainly the spectacle of the year in Cuzco and attracts many thousands of Peruvian and foreign visitors. Despite its commercialization, it's still worth seeing the street dances and parades as well as the pageant held in Sacsayhuaman. It's also a big holiday in many of the jungle towns.
June 29*
  San Pedro y San Pablo (St Peter & St Paul)
July 16
  La Virgen del Carmen – mainly celebrated in the southern sierra, with Paucartambo and Pisac near Cuzco and Pucara near Lake Titicaca being especially important.
July 28-29*
  Fiestas Patrias (Peru's Independence) – while celebrated throughout the country, in the southern sierra festivities can begin three days ahead with the feast of St James on July 25. This is perhaps the biggest national holiday and the whole nation seems to be on the move. Buses and hotels are booked long in advance. Hotel prices can triple.
August 30*
  Santa Rosa de Lima – patron saint of Lima and of the Americas. Major processions in Lima.
October 8*
  Battle of Angamos
October 18
  El Señor de los Milagros (the Lord of the

Miracles) – celebrated with major religious processions in Lima; people wear purple.

November 1*
Todos Santos (All Saint's Day) – an official public holiday.

November 2
Diá de los Muertos (All Soul's Day) – celebrated with gifts of food, drink and flowers taken to family graves; especially colorful in the sierra. The food and drink is consumed and the atmosphere is festive rather than somber.

November 5
Puno Day – spectacular costumes and street dancing in Puno celebrate the legendary emergence of the first Inca, Manco Capac, from Lake Titicaca. Celebrated for several days.

December 8*
Fiesta de la Purísima Concepción (Feast of the Immaculate Conception)

December 25*
Navidad (Christmas Day)

Local fiestas and festivals are held somewhere in Peru every week. Many are mentioned in the individual town descriptions.

ACTIVITIES
Visiting Archaeological Sites
Visiting Peru without seeing the Inca ruins in the Cuzco area (especially Machu Picchu) is a bit like visiting Egypt without seeing the pyramids. If you're interested in more than just the Inca Empire, however, I recommend the following.

Trujillo is an excellent base for seeing Chan Chan (the huge adobe capital of the Chimu) as well as Moche pyramids and good museums. If you have any spare time in Huaraz, the 2500-year-old ruins of the Chavín are worth a day trip. The artifacts of Paracas are best seen in museums and the Nazca Lines can only be appreciated properly from the air. The newly excavated site of El Señor del Sipán near Chiclayo is interesting if you want to see archaeology in action but the highlight is the display in the nearby Bruning Museum. The funerary towers at Sillustani, near Lake Titicaca, are worth seeing if you have a spare day in Puno. Kuélap is great if you have the energy to go to such a remote area. Other sites, while worthwhile for someone who is

particularly interested in archaeology or has plenty of time in Peru, don't offer as many rewards as those mentioned.

Outdoor Activities
Trekking, backpacking and mountaineering are very rewarding during the May to September dry season in the Andes. Cuzco, for the Inca Trail, and Huaraz, for the Cordillera Blanca, are the biggest centers and details are given under those towns.

River running is a popular activity year round, with higher water levels in the rainy season. See Cuzco and Huaraz in the highlands and Cañete on the South Coast for details.

Mountain biking is a fledgling sport in Peru. See Cuzco, Huaraz and Huancayo for options.

Swimming and surfing is an activity enjoyed mainly by a few middle and upper class young people along the coast. The water is cold from April to December, when locals wear wet suits to surf. Indeed, surfers wear wet suits year round, even though they could get away with not using them in the January to March period when the water is a little warmer. The surfing is quite good but available facilities and equipment are very basic. Swimming is locally popular from January to March, although the beaches are very contaminated near the major coastal cities and there are many dangerous currents. The beaches are not very attractive and I wouldn't come to Peru to swim!

WORK
Officially you need a work visa to work in Peru. You can, however, possibly get a job teaching English in language schools without a work visa, usually in Lima. Schools occasionally advertise for teachers in the newspapers, but more often jobs are found by word of mouth. They expect you to be a native English speaker and the pay is usually low – US$100 per week is quite good. See Lima and Cuzco for schools which might hire you.

If, in addition to speaking English like a native, you actually have a bona fide teaching credential, so much the better. American and British schools in Lima will sometimes hire teachers of maths, biology and other subjects and often help you get a work visa if you want to stay. They also pay much better than the language schools. Members of the South American Explorers Club may find that their Lima office has contacts with schools that are looking for teachers. Some enterprising travelers make money selling jewelery or art in crafts markets. Most other jobs are obtained by word of mouth and the possibilities are limited.

ACCOMMODATION

There is a lot of variety and no shortage of places to stay in Peru. These come under various names such as *pensión, residencial, hospedaje* and *hostal*, as well as simply hotel. In most cases, a *pensión* or a *hospedaje* offers cheap and basic lodging. A *residencial* is usually cheap but perhaps a little better. *Hostal* and *hotel* are catch-all terms which can be applied to both the cheapest and most expensive hotels in town.

It is rare to arrive in a town and not be able to find someplace to sleep, but during major fiestas or the high tourist season, accommodations can be tight. This is especially true around Christmas and New Year, and for several days around the Fiestas Patrias (Peru's Independence) on July 28. You may find yourself paying 10 times more than your normal budget – or, instead, sleeping on someone's floor in a sleeping bag – at these times! Plan ahead for both accommodations and public transport during major fiestas.

Because of lack of rooms during fiestas, as many hotels as possible are marked on the town maps. The fact that a hotel is marked on a map does not necessarily imply that it is recommended, particularly the cheapest and very basic accommodations described, but they are there if everywhere else is full. See the Places to Stay sections for descriptions of the hotels. If you are going to a town specifically for a market or fiesta, try to arrive a day or so early if possible.

Sometimes it's a little difficult to find single rooms (particularly in cheap hotels) and you may get a room with two or even three beds. In most cases, though, you are charged for one bed and don't have to share, unless the hotel is full. Ensure in advance that you won't be asked to pay for all the beds or share with a stranger if you don't want to. This is no problem 90% of the time.

Most of the following comments apply particularly to budget travelers staying at bottom end hotels. However, these comments often apply to middle range hotels and even to top end places.

If you are traveling as a couple or in a group, don't assume that a room with two or three beds will always be cheaper per person than a room with one bed. Usually it is, but sometimes it isn't. If I give a price per person, a double or triple room will usually cost two or three times a single, though you should always try and bargain in these situations. If more than one price is given, this indicates that doubles and triples are cheaper per person than singles. I give prices for one or two people as a guideline. Travelers on a tight budget should know that rooms with four or more beds are available in many cheap hotels and these work out cheaper per person if you're traveling in a group. Couples sharing one bed *(cama matrimonial)* are usually, though not always, charged a little less than a double room with people in separate beds.

Remember to look around a hotel if possible. The same prices are often charged for rooms of widely differing quality. If you are on a tight budget and are shown into a horrible airless box with just a bed and a bare light bulb, you can ask to see a better room without giving offense simply by asking if they have a room with a window, or explaining that you have to write some letters home and is there a room with a table and chair. You'll often be amazed at the results. If the bathrooms are shared, ask to see them and make sure that the toilet flushes and the water runs. If the shower looks and smells as if someone vomited in it, the staff obviously doesn't do a very good job of looking after the place. There's probably a better hotel at the same price a few blocks away.

Cheap hotels don't always have hot water. Even if they do, it might not work or might be turned on only at certain hours of the day. Ask about this if you're planning on a hot shower before going out to dinner – often there's only hot water in the morning. Another intriguing device you should know about is the electric shower. This consists of a cold water showerhead hooked up to an electric heating element that is switched on when you want a hot (more likely tepid) shower. Don't touch anything metal while you're in the shower or you may discover what an electric shock feels like. Some hotels charge extra for hot showers and a few simply don't have any showers at all. You can always use the public hot baths which are available in most towns.

If you're not a shoestring traveler, most towns have pricier hotels with clean, private bathrooms.

Most hotels will provide a key to lock your room and theft is not very frequent. Nevertheless, carrying your own padlock is a good idea if you plan on staying in the cheapest hotels. Once in a while you'll find that a room doesn't look very secure – perhaps there's a window that doesn't close or the wall doesn't come to the ceiling and can be climbed over. In such cases it's worth looking for another room – assuming you're not in some tiny jungle town where there's nothing else. This is another good reason to look at a room before you rent it. You should never leave valuables lying around the room – they can be too tempting for a maid who earns just US$4 a day.

Money and your passport should be in a secure body pouch while other valuables can usually be kept in the hotel strongbox. (Some cheaper hotels might not want to take this responsibility.) If you leave valuables in a hotel, place them in a carefully sealed package so that it will be obvious if it has been tampered with. Always get a receipt. If you leave valuables in your room

(eg, camera gear), pack them out of sight at the bottom of a locked bag or closed pack. Don't become paranoid though. In 15 years of traveling in Peru, I have rarely had something taken from my hotel room. Usually, it was partly my fault. I left my camera on the bed instead of at the bottom of a closed pack and it was gone when I got back. I rarely hear of people who have been ripped off from their hotel rooms, particularly if they take basic precautions.

If you're really traveling off the beaten track, you may end up in a village that doesn't even have a basic pensión. You can usually find somewhere to sleep by asking around, but it might be just a roof over your head rather than a bed, so carry a sleeping bag or at least a blanket. The place to ask at first is probably a village store – the store owner usually knows everyone in the village and will know who is in the habit of renting rooms or floor space. If that fails, you may be offered floor space by the mayor *(alcalde)* or at the *policía* and allowed to sleep on the floor of the school house, the jail or the village community center.

Bottom end hotels are the cheapest, but not necessarily the worst. Although these are usually quite basic, with just a bed and four walls, they can nevertheless be well looked after and very clean. They are often good places to meet other travelers, both Peruvian and foreign. Prices in this section range from about US$3 to US$10 per person. Hotels are usually arranged in roughly ascending order of price.

Often I include some hotels for the sake of completeness, but a listing does not imply a recommendation – if a hotel has something more than a roof and a bed to recommend it, this is mentioned in the brief descriptions. Every town has hotels in the bottom end price range and in smaller towns that's all there is. Although you'll usually have to use communal bathrooms in the cheapest hotels, rooms with a private bathroom can sometimes be found for under US$6 per person.

Youth hostels as we know them in other

parts of the world are not common in Peru, but the cheaper hotels make up for this deficiency. There are almost no camp sites in the towns; again, the constant availability of cheap hotels make town camp sites unnecessary for travelers on a budget.

Hotels in the middle price range usually cost from about US$8 or US$10 per person, and are also arranged in roughly ascending order of price. They are not always better than the best hotels in the bottom group. However, you can find some very good bargains here. Even if you're traveling on a budget, there are always special occasions (your birthday?) when you can indulge in comparative luxury for a day or two.

FOOD

It is worth remembering that the main meal of the day is usually lunch *(almuerzo)*. Breakfast is often minimal, although *desayuno Americano* (American breakfast) is always available at better hotels and restaurants. Dinner *(cena)* is usually served late – don't expect much dinner action before 8 pm.

If you're on a tight budget, food is undoubtedly the most important part of your trip expenses. You can stay in rock bottom hotels, travel 2nd class and never consider buying a souvenir, but you've got to eat well. This doesn't mean expensively, but it does mean that you want to avoid spending half your trip sitting on the toilet.

The worst culprits for causing illness are salads and unpeeled fruit. Stick to fruit which can be peeled such as bananas, oranges and pineapples. With unpeeled fruit or salads, wash the ingredients yourself in purified water. It can be a lot of fun getting a group together and heading out to the market to buy salad veggies and preparing a huge salad. You can often persuade someone in the hotel to lend you a suitable bowl, or you could buy a large plastic bowl quite inexpensively and sell or give it away later.

As long as you take heed of the salad warning, you'll find plenty of good things to eat at reasonable prices. You certainly don't have to eat at a fancy restaurant (where kitchen facilities may not be as clean as the white tablecloths). If a restaurant is full of locals, it's usually a good sign.

If you're on a tight budget you can eat from street and market stalls if the food is hot and freshly cooked, though watch to see if your plate is going to be dunked in a bowl of cold greasy water and wiped with a filthy rag.

Also worth remembering (if you're trying to stretch your money) is that *chifas* (Chinese restaurants) can offer good value. The key word here is *tallarines*, which are noodles. Most chifas will offer a tallarines dish with chopped chicken, beef, pork or shrimp for under US$2. Other dishes are also good but not quite as cheap. Many restaurants offer an inexpensive set meal of the day (especially at lunch time) which is usually soup and a second course. This is called simply *el menú*. If you want to read a menu, ask for *la carta*. Some menus have English translations, though these are often amusingly garbled. 'Fred Chicken' and 'Gordon Blue' may play starring roles.

If you aren't on a tight budget, you'll find plenty to choose from in the major cities. Most average restaurants will have meals in the US$4 to US$10; only the big cities have fancy restaurants charging more. The really luxurious places with food and ambiance to rival a good restaurant anywhere in the world may have meals as high as US$50 a person, including wine, taxes and tip. Errors on bills (usually in the restaurant's favor) are not uncommon. Check the bill carefully. (See Taxes & Tipping.)

Typical Peruvian dishes are tasty, varied and regional. This stands to reason – seafood is best on the coast while the Inca delicacy, roast guinea pig, can still be sampled in the highlands. A description of some regional dishes is given in the Places to Eat sections of the major cities. Spicy foods are often described by the term *a la criolla*. Here is a brief overview of some of Peru's most typical dishes:

Lomo Saltado – chopped steak fried with onions, tomatoes and potatoes, served with rice; a standard dish served everywhere, especially at long distance bus meal stops.

Ceviche de Corvina – white sea bass marinated in lemon, chili and onions and served cold with a boiled potato or yam. It's delicious. If any one dish is to be singled out as most typical of Peru, it is this.

Ceviche de Camarones – the same thing made with shrimps. These dishes are large appetizers or small meals.

Sopa a la Criolla – a lightly spiced noodle soup with beef, egg, milk and vegetables. It's hearty and filling.

Palta a la Jardinera – avocado stuffed with cold vegetable salad.

Palta a la Reyna – avocado stuffed with chicken salad. This is one of my favorite appetizers and it can make a light meal.

Most foodstuffs available at home are available in one form or another in Peru. The following basic glossary will help in translating Peruvian menus:

almuerzo	lunch
anticucho	shish kebab
arroz	rice
azúcar	sugar
cabro, cabrito	goat
calamares	squid
camarones	shrimp
cangrejo	crab
carne	meat
cena	supper
cerdo, chancho	pork
chaufa, chaulafan	fried rice (Chinese style)
cordero	mutton
choclo	corn on the cob
churrasco	steak
desayuno	breakfast
empanadas	meat/cheese pastries
ensalada	salad
estofado	stew
frutas	fruit
helado	ice cream
huevos fritos	fried eggs
huevos revueltos	scrambled eggs
langosta	lobster
lomo	beef
lomo apanado	breaded beef cutlet
lomo a la chorrillana	steak with onions
mantequilla	butter
mariscos	seafood
pan	bread
papas fritas	french fried potatoes
parrillada	mixed grill
pescado	fish
pollo	chicken
postre	dessert
queso	cheese
sopa, chupe	soup
torta	cake
tortilla	omelet
trucha	trout
verduras	vegetables

Camote (Sweet Potato)

Guanábana (Soursop)

Jícama

Granadilla (Passionfruit)

Apilla (Oca)

Guayaba (Guava)

Chayote

Añú

Some native fruits and vegetables

Culinary No-Nos

In some areas of Peru – especially in the jungle – meals are prepared from endangered or protected species. Recent Peruvian TV reports have denounced the availability of dolphin *(chancho marino* or *muchame)* in some coastal restaurants. In the jungle, you occasionally may be offered tortoise eggs *(huevos de charapa)*, turtles *(motelo)*, paca or agouti *(majas)*, monkey *(mono)*, armadillo and others.

Also, a jungle radio broadcast claims that poor people are hunting some animals with rat poison, because it is cheaper than shotgun shells, and that the meat can be dangerous for humans. Readers are advised to avoid eating protected wildlife and perhaps to discuss conservation issues with jungle guides or restaurant owners. ■

DRINKS

Tea & Coffee

Tea *(té)* is served black with lemon and sugar. If you ask for tea with milk, British style, you'll get a cup of hot milk with a tea bag to dunk in it. *Maté* or *té de hierbas* are herb teas. *Maté de coca* is a tea made from coca leaves and served in many restaurants in the highlands. It's supposed to help the newly arrived visitor in acclimatization.

Coffee is available almost everywhere but is often disappointing. Sometimes it is served in cruets as a liquid concentrate which is diluted with milk or water. It doesn't taste that great and it looks very much like soy sauce, so always check before pouring it into your milk (or over your rice)! Instant coffee is also served. Espresso and cappuccino is sometimes available but only in the bigger towns. *Café con leche* is milk with coffee, and *café con agua* or *café negro* is black coffee. Hot chocolate is also popular.

Water

I don't recommend drinking tap water anywhere in Latin America. *Agua potable* means that the water comes from the tap but it's not necessarily healthy. Even if it comes from a chlorination or filtration plant, the plumbing is often old, cracked and full of crud. (Salads washed in this water aren't necessarily clean.) One possibility is to carry a water bottle and purify your own water (see the Health section). If you don't want to go through the hassle of constantly purifying water, bottled mineral water, *agua mineral*, is available in bottles ranging up to two liters in size. *Agua con gas* and *agua sin gas* is carbonated and non-carbonated mineral water.

Soft Drinks

Many of the usual soft drinks are available, as are some local ones with such tongue twisting names as Socosani or the ubiquitous Inca Cola, which is appropriately gold colored and tastes like fizzy bubble gum. Soft drinks are collectively known as *gaseosas* and the local brands are very sweet. You can also buy Coca-Cola, Pepsi Cola, Fanta or orange Crush (called *croosh)* and Sprite – the latter pronounced 'essprite.' Ask for your drink *helada* if you want it out of the refrigerator, *al clima* if you don't. Remember to say *sin hielo* (without ice) unless you really trust the water supply. Diet soft drinks have recently become available.

Fruit Juice

Juices *(jugos)* are available everywhere and to my taste are usually better than gaseosas, but cost more. Make sure you get jugo *puro* and not con agua. The most common kinds are:

blackberry	*mora*
grapefruit	*toronja*
orange	*naranja*
passionfruit	*maracuya*
papaya	*papaya*
pineapple	*piña*
watermelon	*sandiá*
local fruit	*naranjilla*
(tasting like bitter orange)	

Alcohol

Finally we come to those beverages which can loosely be labelled 'libations.' The selection of beers is limited to about a dozen types, but these are quite palatable and inexpensive. Beer comes in various sizes – 355 ml, 620 ml, one liter and the recently introduced 'litro cien' (1100 ml), locally nicknamed a 'margarito.' Light lager-type beers *(cerveza)* and sweet dark beers *(malta* or *cerveza negra)* are available.

On the coast there is Pilsen, which is made in Callao and Trujillo. Experts claim that Pilsen Trujillo is better made than Pilsen Callao but they taste quite similar and are the strongest of the coastal beers. Slightly lighter and less strong is Cristal. Another light coastal beer is Garza Real found on the north coast.

Two highland towns known for their beer are Cuzco and Arequipa which make Cuzqueña and Arequipeña respectively. Both are available in lager and dark. Cuzqueña is Peru's best beer, according to many drinkers. Arequipeña tastes slightly sweet. In the jungle there is San Juan, which is brewed in Pucallpa and advertises itself as 'the only beer brewed on the Amazon.' It's not a bad light beer. Imported beers are usually expensive with the exception of the light Paceña from La Paz which is occasionally available.

Peru has a thriving wine industry and produces acceptable wines, though not as good as Chilean or Argentine varieties. The best wines are from the Tacama and Ocucaje wineries and begin at about US\$4 a bottle (more in restaurants). The usual selection of reds, whites and rosés is available – I'm afraid I'm not a connoisseur, so experts will have to experiment themselves.

Spirits are expensive if imported and not very good if made locally, though there are some notable exceptions. Rum is cheap and quite good; a white grape brandy called *pisco* (the national drink) is usually served as a pisco sour – a tasty cocktail made from pisco, egg white, lemon juice, sugar, syrup, crushed ice and bitters; *guinda* is a sweet cherry brandy and the local firewater,

aguardiente or sugar cane alcohol, is an acquired taste and very cheap.

Bottles

The advantage of buying a bottled drink in a store is that it is usually cheaper than in a restaurant; the disadvantage is that you have to drink it at the store because the glass bottle is usually worth more than the drink inside. You can pay a deposit, but you have to return bottles to the store you bought them from; a different store won't pay for it. Large, plastic, disposable bottles are now popular and you can take these with you. Canned drinks cost a lot more than bottles.

SPECTATOR SPORTS

Soccer (called *fútbol)* and bullfighting are the best attended of spectator sports. Basketball is also quite popular. Although tennis is not especially popular in Peru, the Peruvian tennis player Jaime Yzaga is one of the few athletes whose name might be recognized by non-Peruvians.

The soccer season is late March to November. There are many teams though their abilities on the whole are fairly indifferent. The best teams are from Lima and the traditional *clásico* is the match-up between Alianza Lima and Universitario (La U). These matches are played in the Estadio Nacional in Lima and entrance ranges from about US\$2.50 in the popular section (not recommended as most of the fan violence happens here) to US\$7 in the better *oriente* (eastern) section to US\$15 to US\$30 for the best seats in the *occidente* (western) section. Weekend matches are often double-headers (two games, four teams). The 1994 Peruvian soccer champions were Sporting Cristal of Lima.

The bullfighting season in Lima is from early October through early December and attracts internationally famous matadors. See Lima for more details. Outside of Lima, bullfights may occur at a variety of fiestas but are not of an international level. Animal rights activists do not enjoy much prominence or even tolerance in Peru.

THINGS TO BUY

Souvenirs are good, varied and cheap. Although going to villages and markets is fun, you won't necessarily save a great deal of money – similar items for sale in shops are often not much more expensive. In markets and smaller stores, bargaining is acceptable, indeed expected. In tourist stores in the major cities prices are sometimes fixed. Some of the best stores are quite expensive, but the quality of their products is often superior.

You can buy everything in Lima, be it a blow-pipe from the jungle or a woven poncho from the highlands. Although it is usually a little more expensive to buy handicrafts in Lima, the choice is varied, the quality is high and it's worth looking around some of Lima's gift shops and markets to get an idea of the items you'd like to buy. Then you might go to the areas where the items you're interested in are made – but often the best pieces are in Lima.

Cuzco also has a great selection of craft shops but the quality is no higher than in Lima. Old and new weavings, ceramics, paintings, woolen clothing and jewelry are all found here. Cuzco has a good selection of the more traditional weavings.

The Puno-Juliaca area is good for knitted alpaca sweaters and knickknacks made from the totora reed which grows on Lake Titicaca. The Huancayo area is good for carved gourds as well as for excellent weavings and clothing in the cooperative market. The Ayacucho area is famous for modern weavings and stylized ceramic churches. San Pedro de Cajas is known for its peculiar weavings which are made of rolls of yarn stuffed with wool (you'll recognize the style instantly when you see it). The Shipibo pottery sold in Yarinacocha near Pucallpa is the best of the jungle artifacts available. Superb reproductions of Moche and Mochica pottery are available in Trujillo. Shopping for these is described in more detail under the appropriate towns.

Crafts as souvenirs or gifts are relatively cheap by Western standards. A good rule of thumb is if you like something very much, buy it (assuming you can afford it). You may not find exactly the same thing again and if you do find a better example, you can always give the first one away as a gift.

Souvenirs made from animal products are not normally allowed into most Western nations. Objects made from skins, feathers, turtle shells and so forth should not be bought because their purchase contributes to the degradation of the wildlife in the rainforests.

Getting There & Away

There are four ways of getting to Peru: by air from anywhere in the world; by land from the neighboring South American countries; by river boat up the Amazon from Brazil (or, very rarely, up the Madre de Dios from Bolivia); and by sea (also a rare option).

AIR

Jorge Chávez International Airport in Lima is the main hub for flights to the Andean countries from Europe and North America, so it is easy to fly to Peru from those continents. There are also some international flights to Iquitos in Peru's Amazon region. Cuzco has international flights from Bolivia.

The ordinary tourist or economy class fare is not the most economical way to go. It is convenient, however, because it enables you to fly on the next plane out, which you can't do when you buy an advance purchase excursion (APEX) ticket (see below). Also, an economy class ticket is valid for 12 months. If you want to economize further, there are several options.

Students with valid international student cards and those under 26 can get discounts with most airlines. Whatever age you are, if you purchase your ticket well in advance and stay a minimum length of time you can buy an APEX ticket, which is usually about one-third cheaper than the full economy fare based on a roundtrip purchase. Several restrictions normally apply. You must purchase your ticket at least 21 days (sometimes more) in advance and you must stay away a minimum period (this varies from 7 to 21 days) and return within 180 days (sometimes less, occasionally more). APEX tickets normally do not allow stopovers and there are extra charges if you change your dates of travel or destinations. Individual airlines have different restrictions and these change from time to time. A good travel agent can tell you about this. Stand-by fares are another possibility.

The cheapest way to go is with a ticket sold by companies specializing in AIR (the so-called 'bucket shops,' although this term is little used these days) that are legally allowed to sell discounted tickets to help airlines and charter companies fill their flights. These tickets often sell out fast and you may be limited to only a few available dates and have other restrictions. While APEX, economy and student tickets are available direct from the airlines or from a travel agent, discounted tickets are available only from the discount ticket agencies themselves. Most of them are good, reputable, legalized and bonded companies but, once in a while, a fly-by-night operator comes along and takes your money for a supercheap flight and gives you an invalid or unusable ticket, so check what you are buying carefully before handing over your money.

Discount ticket agencies often advertise in newspapers and magazines; there is much competition and a variety of fares and schedules are available. Fares to South America have traditionally been relatively expensive, but ticket agencies have recently been able to offer increasingly economical fares to that continent.

Courier travel is another possibility, if you are flexible with dates and can manage with only carry-on luggage. Couriers are hired by companies who need to have packages delivered to Peru (and other countries) and will give the courier exceptionally cheap tickets in return for using his or her baggage allowance. These are legitimate operations – all baggage that you are to deliver is completely legal. And it is amazing how much you can bring in your carry-on luggage. I have heard of couriers boarding an aircraft wearing two pairs of trousers and two shirts under a sweater and rain jacket and stuffing the pockets with travel essentials. Bring a folded plastic shopping bag and, once you have boarded the aircraft, you can remove the extra clothes and place them in the plastic bag! (Try not to have metal objects in inside pockets when you go through the metal detector at the airport! Also bear in mind that most courier companies want their couriers to look reasonably neat, so you can't overdo the 'bag lady' routine.) Remember, you can buy things like T-shirts, a towel and soap after you arrive at your destination, so traveling with just carry-on is certainly feasible. Courier flights are more common from the USA than Europe. This is a good option for people flying from New York or Miami. For up-to-date information, contact Travel Unlimited, PO Box 1058, Allston, MA 02134, USA, which publishes monthly listings of courier and cheap flights to Peru and many other countries – this newsletter is recommended for cheap fare hunters. A year's subscription costs US$25 in the USA, US$35 elsewhere. You can get a single issue for US$5. For a general overview there are several books, including the *Courier Air Travel Handbook* by Mark Field (Thunderbird Press).

The high season for air travel to and within Peru is June through early September and December through mid-January. Lower fares may be offered at other times.

It is worth bearing in mind that roundtrip fares are always much cheaper than two one-way tickets. They are also cheaper than an 'open jaws' fare, which enables you to fly into one city (say Lima) and leave via another (say Rio de Janeiro).

From North America

From Canada, American Airlines and United have connections from Calgary, Montreal, Toronto and Vancouver to Miami, and on to Lima.

From the USA, there are direct flights to Lima from Los Angeles, New York and Miami. Again, American Airlines and United are the main carriers, but AeroPerú and Faucett are Peruvian airlines that also

have satisfactory service. Faucett is the only airline offering weekly (Saturday) flights to Iquitos from Miami. Also, you can arrange internal flight discounts if you travel with a Peruvian airline. The drawbacks are that Peruvian airlines have fewer international flights and have a worse on-time record. However, I have found that their in-flight service is of an international standard and their late departures are not much worse than anybody else.

Generally speaking, the USA does not have such a strong discount ticket agency as Europe or Asia, so it's harder getting heavily discounted flights from the USA to South America. In recent years, however, 'consolidators' (as discount ticket agencies in the US are called) have begun to appear. Sometimes the Sunday travel sections in the major newspapers (the *Los Angeles Times* on the west coast and the *New York Times* on the east coast) advertise cheap fares to South America, although these are sometimes no cheaper than APEX fares. A useful book about this is *Consolidators: Air Travelers' Bargain Basement* by Kelly Monaghan.

A travel agent that can find you the best deal to Peru (and anywhere else in the world) is Council Travel Services, a subsidiary of the Council on International Educational Exchange (CIEE). You can find their address and telephone numbers in the telephone directories of many North American cities, particularly those with universities. Contact their headquarters at ☎ 212-661-1414, fax 212-972-231 or write to them at 205 E 42nd St, New York, NY 10017. Also good for cheap air is STA Travel (☎ 1-800-777-0112, 213-937-8722, fax 213-937-2739), 5900 Wiltshire Blvd, Los Angeles, CA 90036. They also have many subsidiaries in other towns. Both are good for student, youth and budget fares. In Canada, a similar company is Travel CUTS (☎ 416-977-3703; fax 416-977-4796), 171 College St, Toronto, Ontario, M5T 1P7.

Typical APEX fares are US$499 to US$599 from Miami, US$620 to US$670 from New York and US$699 to US$870 from Los Angeles. Low season discounts can knock the Miami fare down to US$419. These fares are all roundtrip fares and may include an internal flight from Lima to a city of your choice if you fly with a Peruvian airline. Fares may be more expensive if you want to stay a few months. People are often surprised that fares from Los Angeles in southern California are so much higher than from northerly New York. A glance at the world map soon shows why. New York at 74° west is almost due north of Miami at 80° and Lima at 77°. Thus planes can fly a shorter, faster and cheaper north-south route. Los Angeles, on the other hand, is 118° west and therefore much further away from Lima than New York.

AeroPerú and Faucett have various deals available if you fly from Miami to Lima with them. Faucett is the best bet for discounted tickets within Peru while Aero-Perú offers attractive 'Visit South America' tickets which give good discounts if you wish to see several countries in South America in a short time. Americana (not American Airlines!) have recently offered discounts on around Peru passes (see Getting Around). These tickets change on a frequent basis so you should talk to the airlines or your travel agent about their current offerings.

From Europe

Discount ticket agencies generally provide the cheapest fares from Europe to South America. Fares from London are often cheaper than from other European cities, even though your flight route may take you from London through a European city! Don't ask me why. Many European (especially Scandinavian) budget travelers buy from London ticket agencies as cheap fares are difficult to find in their own countries. Discounted tickets available from these ticket agencies are often several hundred dollars cheaper than official fares and usually carry certain restrictions but they are valid and legal.

In London competition is fierce. Discount flights are often advertised in the classifieds of newspapers ranging from the *Times* to *Time Out*. I have heard consistently good reports about Journey Latin America (JLA) (☎ 0181 747 3108 for flights, 0181 747 8315 for tours, fax 0181 742 1312), 16 Devonshire Rd, Chiswick, London W4 2HD, England. They specialize in cheap fares to Peru and the entire continent as well as arranging itineraries for both independent and escorted travel. They will make arrangements for you over the phone or fax. Ask for their free magazine *Papagaio* with helpful information. Another reputable budget travel agency is Trailfinders (☎ (171) 938-3366) 42-50 Earl's Court Rd, London W8 6EJ. The useful travel newspaper *Trailfinder* is available from them for free. Also worth a try are STA Travel (☎ (171) 938-4711), Priory House, 6 Wrights Lane, London W8 6TA, who specialize in fares for students and those under 26, and Passage to South America (☎ (171) 602-9889, fax (171) 602-4251), 113 Shepherd's Bush Rd, London, W6 7LP. The cheapest fares from London may start at UK£495, which is an incredible deal considering the distance. Restrictions are usually that they may leave only on certain days, they may be valid for only 90 days, and there may be penalties for changing your return date. A UK£10 departure tax is added.

There are few direct flights from Europe to Peru; many involve a change of plane and carrier in Miami or a South American capital other than Lima. The following direct flights are available at this writing (no change of planes is required at the stops):

Aeroflot – from Moscow via Luxembourg, Shannon (Eire) and Cuba.
AOM – from Paris via French Guiana and Quito.
Iberia – from Madrid via the Dominican Republic.
KLM – from Amsterdam via Aruba or Curacao.
Lufthansa – from Frankfurt via Caracas and Bogotá.

From Latin America

AeroPerú has offices in Buenos Aires, Argentina; La Paz, Bolivia; Rio de Janeiro and São Paolo, Brazil; Santiago, Chile; Bogotá, Colombia; Quito and Guayaquil, Ecuador; Asunción, Paraguay; Caracas, Venezuela; Panama City, Panama; and Mexico City, Mexico. International passengers with AeroPerú can include a free round trip from Lima to a Peruvian city in the price of their international ticket. Flights from Latin American countries are usually subject to high tax and good deals are not often available.

Many Latin American airlines fly to Lima, including Aerolineas Argentinas; Avensa, Servavensa and Viasa of Venezuela; Avianca of Colombia; Copa of Panama; Lacsa of Costa Rica; LanChile; Lloyd Aereo Boliviano; Saeta of Ecuador; and Varig of Brazil. In addition, the US companies American Airlines and United have flights between several Latin American cities and Lima.

From Australia & New Zealand
There is no real choice of routes between Australia and South America and there are certainly no bargain fares available. Qantas flies from Sydney to Papeete, Tahiti, where you stay overnight, then continue to Santiago, Chile, and Lima with LanChile. Both Qantas and American Airlines fly from Sydney or Melbourne to Honolulu and onto Los Angeles, where Lima connections are made. Aerolineas Argentinas flies from Sydney to Buenos Aires, where connections to Lima are made. Fares are about US$1700 on these routes. Similar routes are available from New Zealand for about US$1900.

From Asia
Increasing numbers of Japanese tourists are visiting Peru. Several airlines offer flights from Tokyo which connect with flights to Lima. All Nippon Airways flies from Tokyo to Los Angeles and New York, American Airlines flies to Miami, United Airlines to Newark, Varig to São Paulo. These flights plus connecting flights to Lima are about US$2700 to US$3100, though Asian discount ticket agencies may have better offers.

Korean Air flies from Seoul via Tokyo to Los Angeles and then connects to Lima. Philippine Airlines flies Manila-Los Angeles.

LAND
Car
If you live in the Americas, it is possible to travel overland. However, if you want to start from North or Central America, the Carretera Panamericana stops in Panama and begins again in Colombia, leaving a 200 km roadless section of jungle known as the Darien Gap. This takes about a week to cross on foot and by canoe in the dry season (January to mid-April) but is much heavier going in the wet season. This overland route has become increasingly dangerous because of banditry and drug-related problems, especially on the Colombian side. Most overland travelers fly or take a boat around the Darien Gap. Recently, a car-ferry began operating from Panama to Colombia, which is the cheapest way to go. This is the *Crucero Express* sailing from Colón, Panama, to Cartagena, Colombia, three times a week. The voyage takes about 18 hours and goes overnight. Fares are about US$80 for a person in a shared cabin, and US$130 for a car. Duty-free attractions such as gambling and cheap alcohol are available.

Bus
Once you are in South America it is relatively straightforward to travel by public bus from the Andean countries (Colombia, Ecuador, Chile and Bolivia) although this is a fairly slow option. See Lonely Planet Guides to those countries for full details.

Some companies offer international buses to other countries. Ormeño Internacional has weekly buses from Quito, Ecuador (US$60, 38 hours), Bogota, Colombia (US$145, three days), Caracas, Venezuela (US$195, four days and four hours), Santiago, Chile (US$70), and Buenos Aires, Argentina (US$140). Cruz del Sur has buses from La Paz, Bolivia (US$33 to US$41). Caracol, a subsidiary of Cruz del Sur, has slightly cheaper buses to the northern countries and more expensive buses to the south which include meals (from Santiago for US$91, Buenos Aires for US$180, Montevideo, Uruguay, for US$190, Asunción, Paraguay, for US$218, and Río de Janeiro, Brazil, for US$248). Other major South American cities are served if they are on the way.

In the past, international bus services were problematical, with passengers being dropped at the border and told to continue on another bus that left hours later, but I'm told that these new services are much more reliable. You should check carefully with the company about what is included and whether the service is direct or you have to change. It is almost always cheaper to buy tickets to the border, cross, and buy tickets on the other side.

RIVER

It is possible to travel by river boat all the way from the mouth of the Amazon at Belém in Brazil to Iquitos in Peru. Travelers will need to break the journey up into several stages because rarely will a single boat do the entire trip.

The easiest way is to take one boat from Belém to Manaus in central Brazil and then a second boat from Manaus to Benjamin Constant on the Brazilian side of the Peruvian-Brazilian-Colombian border. At this point you can take local motor boats across the border to the small Colombian port of Leticia, from where you can easily find boats into Peru.

From Belém to Leticia will take about two weeks, depending on the currents and which boat you are on. From Leticia on to Iquitos takes a further one to three days. The entire trip will cost roughly US$100 or less if traveling on the lower decks. Further information about river travel in Peru is found in the Getting Around and Amazon Basin chapters.

SEA

It is possible to arrive in Lima's port of Callao by both expensive ocean liners and cheaper freight vessels. Few people arrive by sea, however, because services are infrequent and are normally more expensive and less convenient than flying.

DEPARTURE TAXES

Airport departure tax is US$17.70, payable in either US dollars or nuevos soles.

TOURS

From North America

Because of the easy flight connection to Peru, the USA has far more companies offering tours than the rest of the world put together! There must be well over a hundred companies that offer tours to Peru. You can find their addresses in advertisements in outdoor and travel magazines such as *Outside, Escape* and *Ecotraveler* as well as more general magazines such as *Natural History, Audubon* and *Smithsonian*. Another way of finding tour companies to Peru (or anywhere else) is through Adventure Source (☎ 1-800-249-2885, 206-328-4426), 1111 E Madison Suite 302, Seattle, WA 98122. They will send you brochures from a variety of companies which meet your travel dates and interests. They also publish a *Tour Shopper* catalog (US$6) which lists and describes hundreds of companies. The following are some of the best and longest established companies.

Wilderness Travel (☎ 1-800-368-2794, 510-548-0420, fax 510-548-0347, email info@wildernesstravel.com), 801 Allston Way, Berkeley, CA 94710, has been sending small groups (4 to 15 participants) to Peru (and many other countries) since the 1970s, and is one of the best in the business. They offer a good variety of treks (ranging from four nights on the Inca Trail to over two weeks in the remote Cordillera Huayhuash) combined with hotel portions in the Cuzco-Machu Picchu area. They also offer comfortable hotel-based tours visiting the most interesting areas of Peru.

International Expeditions (☎ 1-800-633-4734, 205-428-1700, fax 205-428-1714), One Environs Park, Helena, AL 35080, offers the best variety of tours in the Amazon. They visit both the northern and southern Peruvian rainforests, including stays at the ACEER lab and canopy walkway, stays in jungle lodges, and river boat and camping options. More details are given in the Amazon chapter. They can combine Amazon trips with visits to other parts of Peru. Other companies going to the Amazon tend to specialize in one area and are mentioned in the appropriate parts of the text.

Wildland Adventures (☎ 1-800-345-4453, 206-365-0686, fax 206-363-6615), 3516 NE 155th St, Seattle, WA 98155, has a variety of treks, including Inca Trail clean-up campaigns, and general tours with an emphasis on ecology and local culture. They come well-recommended. Mountain Travel-Sobek (☎ 1-800-227-2384, 510-527-8100, fax 510-525-7710), 6420 Fairmont Ave, El Cerrito, CA 94530, is good for trekking and river-running tours.

Climbers can contact American Alpine Institute (☎ 206-671-1505), 1515 12th St, Bellingham, WA 98225, or Colorado Mountain School (☎ 303-567-5758, 303-596-6677), PO Box 2062, Estes Park, CO 80517. Both companies are recommended and have lessons and workshops in the USA to prepare clients for their annual guided climbs in the Cordillera Blanca.

From the UK
Because of the greater distances involved, there are far fewer companies offering tours to Peru from the UK. Some British travelers even prefer to book through a US company and travel with a bunch of Yanks! The best choice in the UK is to look at companies specializing in South America. The companies listed above under 'Air' all offer a variety of tours to Peru.

WARNING
The information in this chapter is particularly vulnerable to change: Prices for international travel are volatile, routes are introduced and cancelled, schedules change, special deals come and go, and rules and visa requirements are amended. Airlines and governments seem to take a perverse pleasure in making price structures and regulations as complicated as possible. You should check directly with the airline or a travel agent to make sure you understand how a fare (and ticket you may buy) works. In addition, the travel industry is highly competitive and there a re many lurks and perks.

The upshot of this is that you should get opinions, quotes and advice from as many airlines and travel agents as possible before you part with your hard-earned cash. The details given in the chapter should be regarded as pointers and are not a substitute for your own careful, up-to-date research.

Getting Around

Peru is a big country so you'll need several months to visit it all overland. If your time is limited, you'll have to choose the areas that are the most important to you. Public buses are frequent and reasonably comfortable on the major routes and are the normal form of transport for most Peruvians and many travelers on a budget. Less traveled routes are served by older and less comfortable vehicles. There are two railway systems which can make an interesting change from bus travel. Those in a hurry or desiring greater comfort or privacy can hire a car with a driver, which is often not much more expensive than renting a self-drive car. Air services are widespread and particularly recommended for those short on time. In the jungle regions, travel by river boat or by air is normally the only choice.

Whichever form of transport you use, remember to have your passport on your person and not packed in your luggage or left in the hotel safe. You may need to show your passport to board a plane. Buses may have to go through a transit police check upon entering and leaving major towns; in the past, passports had to be shown, but this rarely occurred on my last trip. Regulations change frequently so be prepared. If your passport is in order, these procedures are no more than cursory. If you're traveling anywhere near the borders you can expect more frequent passport controls.

AIR

If you are arriving in Lima (or Iquitos) with one of Peru's two international airlines – Faucett or AeroPerú – remember to ask about their internal flights before making your reservation. They may include a free trip from Lima to the city of your choice, but the ticket must be bought outside of Peru. They also sometimes offer Air Passes which give you discounted air travel within Peru. Again, the ticket must be bought outside the country and you may have to

decide upon an itinerary in advance. Faucett and AeroPerú only fly to and from countries in the Americas.

Domestic Airports

The main airports are shown on the accompanying Internal Air Flights map, but there are many others that are often no more than a grass strip in the jungle. They can be reached on some of the smallest airlines or by chartered light aircraft. The main airports charge a US$4 domestic departure tax, payable at the time you get your boarding pass.

Domestic Airlines

Once you have arrived in Peru, you'll find that international carriers AeroPerú and Faucett also serve many of the major domestic routes. Faucett serves more towns than AeroPerú and is more reliable. In addition, several new companies have been created in the last few years. Americana's service is almost as widespread as the first two, and has a good reputation for reasonable punctuality. Aero Continente is smaller but also quite good and serves more of the smaller towns. These main four carriers normally have similar prices to one another. Imperial Air is the smallest of the jet airlines and also is the cheapest, but offers more limited service. They have downsized over the past few months – perhaps a sign that they are going to close down?

Expresso Aéreo flies to the more remote towns and often uses older propeller aircraft. The company frequently changes its itineraries and its flights are subject to cancellation more often than other companies. AeroCóndor has small 20 seater aircraft to a few towns (currently Chimbote, Cajamarca, Huánuco, Tingo María) and tour flights to Nazca (to see the Nazca Lines). There are also a handful of small airlines flying to remote destinations in light

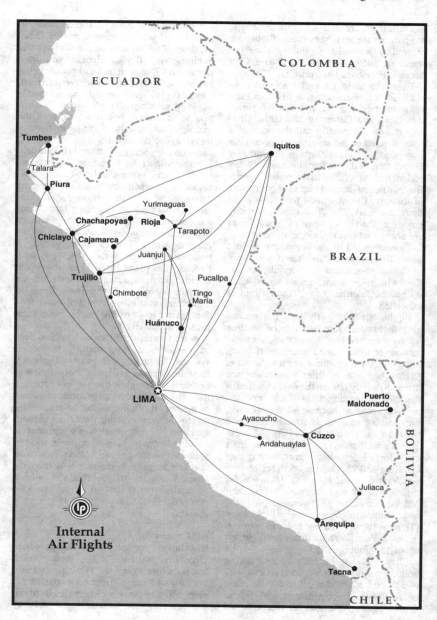

**Internal
Air Flights**

aircraft; these are detailed in the appropriate parts of the text. Very cheap flights are offered by Grupo 8, the military airline, but these are infrequent and hard to get on because Peruvians have priority.

Even the budget traveler should consider an occasional internal flight in Peru because they are inexpensive by North American and European standards. One-way tickets are usually half the price of a roundtrip ticket and so you can travel one-way overland and save time by returning by air. All tickets sold in Peru have an 18% tax added; this is included in the prices I quote. Buying tickets abroad can save you some of this tax. Chile is good for this – taxes there are only 2%. You can easily buy tickets in the border town of Arica. Fares are always subject to change, of course.

Tickets issued by one company are not normally usable on another if you want to change your schedule. Normally, an airline will allow their tickets to be used on another airline only if their flight is cancelled.

Flights are frequently late. Early morning flights are more likely to be on time but by the afternoon flights may have slid an hour or more behind schedule. If flying in or out of Cuzco, there are no afternoon flights because weather conditions are often too windy later in the day. This means that the last morning flight, if it is very late, may be canceled because of the weather, thus leaving passengers stranded. Try and book an early flight to and from Cuzco. You should show up at least an hour early for all domestic flights, as baggage handling and check-in procedures tend to be chaotic. Also, it is not unknown for flights to leave up to an hour *before* their official departure time because predicted bad weather might cancel the flight later. (This has happened to me twice in over 100 flights in Peru and both times the flight left about 15 minutes early.)

Flights tend to be fully booked during holiday periods so make reservations well in advance. Make sure all reservations are confirmed and reconfirmed and reconfirmed again. As a general rule I would reconfirm flights both 72 and 24 hours in advance, as well as a week or two ahead of time. The airlines are notorious for bumping you off your flights if you don't reconfirm – I've even heard of people being bumped off after they had reconfirmed. Cuzco flights are especially notorious for booking problems. If it's impossible for you to reconfirm because you're in the middle of nowhere, have a reliable friend or travel agent do this for you. And don't show up for your flight at the last minute.

Some flights have seating assignments while others are on a first-come, first-seated basis when you board the airplane. There are no separate sections for smokers and nonsmokers on internal flights; nonsmokers have to suffer. Many flights have extraordinarily good views of the snow-capped Andes – it is worth getting a window seat even if the weather is bad, because the plane often rises above the clouds giving spectacular views of the mountains. When flying from Lima to Cuzco try and sit on the left-hand side for great views of the 6271-meter-high peak of Salcantay.

A maximum of 20 kg of checked luggage is allowed on internal flights (though you can frequently get away with more). Lost luggage is a depressingly frequent problem (although it has yet to happen to me). Normally the luggage turns up on one of the next day's flights, but be prepared – try to include valuables such as camera gear and essentials such as a warm coat (if heading to the highlands) or medication in your carry-on luggage. Always lock your checked luggage, make sure it is properly labeled and try to see that the correct destination tag is tied on by the check-in personnel. Unlocked luggage is routinely pilfered.

Air Passes

Regulations for air passes change often. Generally, you have to buy them abroad, but sometimes they are available in Peru, but only to foreign visitors. Overland travelers will find that travel agencies in Arica, Chile, and Quito, Ecuador – and probably in other towns – will sell air passes. They are also available in other countries through travel agents that specialize in Latin American travel. Americana recently offered tickets flying to any one city for US$55 and on up in decreasing increments to US$215 for five cities or US$275 for unlimited cities in a 30 day period. Similar deals are often offered by Faucett and AeroPerú, particularly to travelers flying to Peru with them internationally from the USA or another Latin American country.

The main drawback is that not every city is served by each of these airlines. Currently, all three airlines serve Lima, Arequipa, Chiclayo, Cuzco, Iquitos, Juliaca, Piura, Pucallpa, Tacna and Trujillo. Only Americana and Faucett serve Ayacucho and Tumbes. Only Americana and Aero-Perú serve Puerto Maldonado. Only Faucett serves Yurimaguas, Tarapoto, Talara, Rioja and Ilo. This changes every few months.

BUS
Long Distance
Without a doubt, buses are the most frequently used form of public transport in Peru. This is hardly surprising when one considers that most Peruvians are too poor to afford a car. Fares are relatively cheap because the cost of labor (booking office clerks, drivers and mechanics) is very low and because buses tend to run full and sell all their seats. They go just about everywhere except for the deep jungle (reached by air or river) and Machu Picchu (accessible by train or foot only).

Bus Companies The following are the major bus companies – there are scores of others. Ormeño has many buses, frequent departures and average prices; their service is quite good. Cruz del Sur also has extensive services and is OK. Both companies have several subsidiary companies that leave from the same terminal as the mother company in the main cities. Other large companies include Expreso Sudamericano which is one of the cheapest and slowest, with more frequent delays, but they get there. Civa Cial is usually OK as well.

TEPSA has a poor reputation for driving too fast using old buses and is among the most expensive. The bigger companies often have luxury buses charging 30% to 50% more and providing express service, with toilets, snacks, videos and air-conditioning.

General Information The scores of competing bus companies all have their own offices; there are almost no central bus terminals (with recent exceptions in Tacna and Arequipa). In some towns, the different bus companies have their offices clustered around a few city blocks while elsewhere the terminals may be scattered all over town. I have tried to mark as many companies as possible on my city maps and the accompanying text will tell you which destinations are served by which companies.

It is always a good idea to buy your ticket in advance. This guarantees you a seat and also means that you can check out the schedules and prices of different companies without being encumbered by your luggage. There is sometimes a separate 'express' ticket window for people buying tickets for another day. Schedules and fares change frequently and vary from company to company; because of this I only give an approximate idea of how frequently buses leave and the average fares. Exact fares and schedules would be obsolete within weeks. Students with international student cards may be able to get a 10% discount. Travelers on a tight budget can shop around for the best fares. Prices vary substantially but so does the quality of the buses. At low travel periods, some companies try to sell more seats by offering discounted bus fares – watch for these if you are on a tight budget. Conversely, fares can double during peak periods or around holidays such as Christmas or Independence (July 28), when tickets may be sold out several days ahead of time. Buses can be much delayed during the rainy season, especially in the highlands and jungles. From January to April, journey times can double or even triple because of landslides and bad road conditions.

When you buy your ticket, try and avoid the seats at the back of the bus because the ride is nearly always bumpier. On some of the rougher mountain roads you can literally be thrown out of your seat in the back of the bus. Also try to avoid the seats over the wheel wells because you'll lose leg space. Always ask where the bus is leaving from because the ticket office and bus stop are sometimes on different streets.

When waiting in bus terminals, watch your luggage very carefully. Snatch theft is common and thieves work in pairs – one may distract you while the other grabs your bag. Razor blade artists abound, too. While you're dozing off, leaning against your pack, somebody may try to slash through the pockets. Keep luggage where you can see it and stay alert. I hear depressingly frequent stories of theft in bus stations. Thieves are looking for an easy rip off and won't bother you if you appear to be on top of things. They will bother you, however, if you leave your pack leaning against the wall for 15 seconds when you're buying a bar of chocolate. Turn around with your chocolate and – no pack! See Dangers & Annoyances in Facts for the Visitor for more information on playing it safe.

During the journey, your luggage will travel in the luggage compartment unless it is small enough to carry on board. This is normally reasonably safe. You are given a baggage tag in exchange for your bag, which should be securely closed or locked if possible. I like to watch my pack getting loaded onto the bus and I usually exchange a few friendly words with the loader (who is often the driver's assistant) just to make sure that my bag is properly loaded and going to the right destination. During a long trip I get off and check my bag at stops and generally maintain a high profile. If you're on a night bus you'll want to sleep, but I've not had any problem with anyone claiming my luggage in the middle of the night. Your hand luggage is a different matter. If you're asleep with a camera around your neck you may well wake up with a neatly razored strap and no camera at the end of it. I sleep with my carry-on

bag (usually a day pack) strapped on to my person and with my arms around it.

Some travelers prefer to bring their luggage on the bus with them because there are occasional reports of theft from the luggage compartment. This works if your pack is reasonably sized (luggage racks are either non-existent or just big enough for a briefcase) so you have to be able to shove it between your legs or on your lap. Of course, you can't go to sleep unless the pack is securely strapped to you.

Distances are great in Peru and you'll probably take some trips at night. In some cases, night trips are impossible to avoid because all buses travel at night. On the whole, day travel is the best, both to be able to see the scenery and because night trips are (rarely) subject to banditry (details are given in appropriate chapters). It takes roughly 20 to 24 hours to get from either the Ecuadorian or Chilean border to Lima along the (mainly) paved Carretera Panamericana (Pan-American Hwy) which is the best long distance highway in Peru.

Buses using the Panamericana are reasonably comfortable and have reclining seats. The same kinds of buses may be used on the rougher roads into the mountains but they are generally less comfortable because the constant bumping and jarring has often broken the reclining mechanism on some of the seats. How good a seat you get is largely a matter of luck. On the more remote highways, the buses are often of the uncomfortable 'school bus' type. An irritating habit that bus companies have is to shift all the rows of seats forward so that they can get another row or two in the bus. This is fine if you're short or medium-sized, but can be a real pain if you're six-foot-one. The heating in buses rarely works and it can literally get down to freezing inside the bus when traveling in the mountains at night, so bring a blanket, sleeping bag or warm clothes as hand luggage. Conversely, the air-conditioning rarely works and so it can get very hot and sweaty on some of the lowland trips, especially if the windows can't be opened.

Long-distance buses stop for at least

three meals a day (unless you travel on one of the luxury buses which serve snacks and don't stop). The driver will announce how long the stop will be but it's usually worth asking again unless you're sure you heard right. 'Diez minutos' and 'treinta minutos' sound very much alike when the driver mumbles the words while stifling a yawn. And it's your responsibility to be on the bus when it leaves. Many companies have their own special rest areas and these are sometimes in the middle of the desert so you don't have any choice but to eat there. The food is generally inexpensive but not particularly appetizing. I generally eat the lomo saltado (chopped beef fried with vegetables and served with rice) and find it's one of the standard, more edible dishes. Some travelers prefer to bring their own food.

These rest stops double as lavatory stops. Some of the better long-distance buses do have toilet cubicles aboard but don't rely on them. Sometimes they don't work and are locked, at other times they are used as an extra luggage compartment and, if they do work, somebody invariably vomits over the whole thing just before you go to use it. Rule number one of travel in Peru is to always carry your own roll of toilet paper because you will never find any in the toilets. Most rest stop areas have a place that sells essentials like toilet paper, toothpaste, chocolate and other snacks.

If you're traveling during long holiday weekends or special fiestas, you may find that buses are booked up for several days in advance, so *book as early as you can* for these periods.

Whenever you travel, be prepared for delays and don't plan on making important connections after a bus journey. Innumerable flat tires, a landslide, or engine trouble can lengthen the two-day journey from Lima to Cuzco to a five-day odyssey. Such lengthy delays are not very common, but a delay of several hours can be expected quite frequently.

If you want to travel immediately, remember that you can often flag down a bus almost anywhere, even if it is a long distance one. Once, my wife Cathy and I decided to go to Huaraz from Lima and as we were walking towards the Ormeño bus terminal, I saw a bus marked Huaraz standing at a traffic light. We quickly crossed the street, waving at the driver as we ran, and he let us onto the bus, thus saving us a walk to the terminal and a wait for the next bus. Of course, long-distance buses are less likely to stop if they are full or traveling at high speed.

A useful thing to carry on an overnight bus is a flashlight, because the driver nearly always shuts off the interior lights when the bus is underway. Being so close to the equator, it is dark for 12 hours and a flashlight enables you to read a book for a few hours before going to sleep. And when you do decide to sleep, ear plugs are a good idea.

Dangerous Routes In the mid-1980s, I traveled all over Peru by long-distance bus with no problems. From 1989 to 1993, some routes were dangerous because of guerrilla activity by the Sendero Luminoso. Since the 1992 capture of the Sendero leader, this problem has dissipated and bus travel is now generally safe throughout the country. The major exceptions are the bus route from Cuzco to Nazca via Abancay, which has been subject to banditry between Abancay and Nazca, particularly around Puquio. The Río Huallaga Valley north of Tingo María is dangerous because of intensive drug trafficking. I wouldn't take a bus on these routes. Other, less severe, warnings are mentioned in the text where appropriate.

The situation may have changed by the time you read this. Ask at a tourist office, South American Explorers Club, travel agents, or other travelers what the current situation is in these and other areas.

TRUCK

In remote areas, trucks may double as buses. Sometimes they are pick-up trucks with rudimentary wooden benches and at other times they are ordinary trucks; you just climb in the back, often with the cargo.

I once had a ride on top of a truck carrying two bulls – for 12 hours my feet dangled just centimeters away from a pair of impressively large horns. If the weather is OK, you can get fabulous views as you travel in the refreshing wind (dress warmly). If the weather is bad, you hunker down underneath a dark tarpaulin with the other passengers – unless the cargo happens to be two bulls in which case you stay on top and get soaked to the bone. It certainly isn't the height of luxury, but it may be the only way of getting to some areas, and if you're open minded about the minor discomforts, you may find these rides among the most interesting in Peru.

Payment for these rides is usually determined by the driver and is a standard fare depending on the distance. You can ask other passengers how much they are paying; usually you'll find that because the trucks double as buses they charge almost as much as buses.

TRAIN

The Peruvian railways go from the coast to the highlands and were major communication links between the *sierra* and the coast before the advent of roads and later air travel. Trains are less used today but nevertheless still play a part in Peru's transport system.

The central railroad runs from Lima to the mining town of La Oroya, where it branches north and south. The northbound line goes to Cerro de Pasco but has been closed to all but freight trains since the early 1980s. The southbound line goes to Huancayo but only freight trains go there. A 1995 World Bank investment to the tune of US\$35 million is aimed at making this route operational again for passenger trains. If it is open again when you visit Peru, you'll find that the trip takes a whole day and passes through the station of Galera, which is 4781 meters above sea level and the highest standard-gauge train station in the world. In Huancayo you can change train stations and then continue to Huancavelica. The Huancayo to Huancavelica section is running at this time.

The southern railroad runs from the coast at Mollendo through Arequipa to Lake Titicaca and Cuzco. With the decline of Mollendo's importance as a shipping port and the construction of the asphalted Carretera Panamericana from Arequipa to Lima, the short Mollendo-Arequipa section is now closed to passenger traffic. The Arequipa-Lake Titicaca-Cuzco section is, however, the longest and busiest section of Peru's railways. Trains from Arequipa to Puno, on the shores of Lake Titicaca, run three nights a week (they were nightly in the past). You can change at Juliaca, about 40 km before Puno, for trains to Cuzco. The Arequipa-Juliaca (or Puno) service takes a whole night; the Puno-Cuzco service takes a whole day. In Cuzco there are two train stations; one for the service described above and the other for services to Machu Picchu. You cannot go directly from Arequipa or Lake Titicaca to Machu Picchu at this time; there are plans afoot to extend the track and make this possible in the future. Meanwhile, you have to take a taxi (or walk a few km) between the two stations in Cuzco. There are several trains from Cuzco to Machu Picchu every day.

The last segment of Peru's southern railway is found in the extreme south of the country. It is a border train which runs daily between Tacna in Peru and Arica in Chile.

There are several classes. Second class is the cheapest, very crowded, uncomfortable and highly prone to theft. First class is about 25% more expensive, much more comfortable and safer. Then there are Pullman cars (also called Tourist Class) which require a surcharge. They are heated and give access to food service.

In addition to the normal train *(tren)*, there is a faster electric train called an *autovagón*. This is smaller and more expensive than the ordinary train and runs on only a few routes.

The main drawback to traveling by train is thievery. The night train from Arequipa to Puno is especially notorious, particularly in the crowded and poorly-lit 2nd class carriages where a dozing traveler is almost certain to get robbed. Dark train stations are also the haunts of thieves, who often work in pairs or small groups. The answer to the problem is to travel by day and stay alert, to travel with a friend or group, and to travel 1st class. Above all, stay alert. The Pullman classes have a surcharge and are the safest carriages to ride in because only ticket holders are allowed aboard.

For all services it is advisable to buy tickets in advance – the day before is usually best. This way you don't have to worry about looking after your luggage while lining up to buy a ticket at a crowded booking office window. Often, advance tickets are hard to buy at the train stations because travel agencies buy them up in bulk and sell them at a US$2 or US$3 surcharge – convenient if you can afford it but very irritating if you are traveling on a budget.

BOAT

Although Peru has a long coastline, travel along the coast is almost entirely by road or air and there are no coastal passenger steamer services, although international cruise ships arrive at the port in Callao once in a while.

In the highlands there are boat services on Lake Titicaca which, at just over 3800 meters, is the highest navigable lake in the world. Boats are usually small motorized vessels that take about 20 passengers from Puno to visit the various islands on the lake. There are departures every day and costs are low. There used to be a couple of larger steamships crossing the lake from Puno to Bolivia but this service no longer exists. Instead there is a hydrofoil which is very expensive and can be booked through travel agents (details are given under Puno). It is much cheaper to take a bus from Puno to La Paz, Bolivia, which gives you the opportunity to 'cross' Lake Titicaca by a ferry over the narrow Estrecho de Tiquina.

In Peru's eastern lowlands, however, boat travel is of major importance. Boats are mainly of two types – small dugout canoes or larger cargo boats. The dugout canoes are usually powered by an outboard engine and act as a water taxi or bus on some of the smaller rivers. Sometimes they are powered by a strange arrangement which looks like an inboard motorcycle engine attached to a tiny propeller by a three-meter-long propeller shaft. Called *peki-pekis*, these canoes are a slow and rather noisy method of transportation but are OK for short trips; they are especially common on Yarinacocha (a lake near Pucallpa). In some places, modern aluminum launches are found, but dugouts are still more common. As one gets further inland and the rivers widen, larger cargo boats are normally available.

Dugout Canoe

Dugout canoes often carry as many as 24 passengers and are the only way to get around many roadless areas. Hiring one yourself is expensive. Taking one with other passengers is much cheaper but not as cheap as bus travel over a similar distance. This is because an outboard engine uses more fuel per passenger/km than a bus engine, and because a boat travels slower than a bus.

Many of the boats used are literally dugouts, with maybe a splashboard added to the gunwales. They are long in shape but short on comfort. Seating is normally on hard, low, uncomfortable wooden benches accommodating two people each. Luggage is stashed forward under a tarpaulin, so carry hand baggage containing essentials for the journey.

If it is a long journey you will be miserable if you don't take the following advice, advice which is worth the cost of this book! BRING SEAT PADDING. A folded sweater or towel will make a world of difference to your trip. Pelting rain or glaring sun are major hazards and an umbrella is excellent defense against both. Bring sunblock lotion and wear long sleeves, long pants and a sun hat – I have seen people unable to walk because of second degree burns on their legs from a six-hour exposure to the tropical sun. As the boat motors along, the breeze tends to keep insects away and it also tends to cool you down so you don't notice the burning effects of the sun. If the sun should disappear or the rain begin, you can get quite chilled, so bring a light jacket. Insect repellent is useful during stops along the river. A water bottle and food will complete your hand luggage. Remember to stash your spare clothes in plastic bags or they'll get soaked by rain or spray.

A final word about dugout canoes – they feel very unstable! Until you get used to the motion, you might worry about the whole thing just rolling over and tipping everybody into the piranha, electric eel, or boa constrictor infested waters. Clenching the side of the canoe and wondering what madness possessed you to board the flimsy contraption in the first place doesn't seem to help. But dugouts feel much less stable than they really are, so don't worry about a disaster; it almost never happens. I've ridden many dugouts without any problems, even in rapids. Nor have I met anyone who was actually dunked in.

River Boat

This is the classic way to travel down the Amazon – swinging in your hammock aboard a banana boat piloted by a grizzled old captain who knows the waters better than the back of his hand. You can travel from Pucallpa to the mouth of the Amazon this way, although boats don't do the entire trip. Instead you'll spend a few days getting to Iquitos where you'll board another, slightly larger boat and continue for a few more days to the border with Brazil and Colombia. From there, more boats can be found for the week-long passage to Manaus (Brazil) in the heart of the Amazon Basin.

Although cargo boats ply the Ucayali from Pucallpa to Iquitos, and the Marañon from Yurimaguas to Iquitos, they tend to leave only once or twice a week. The boats are small, but have two decks. The lower deck is normally for cargo and the upper for passengers and crew. Bring your own hammock. Food is usually provided, but it is basic and not necessarily very hygienic; you may want to bring some of your own.

To arrange a passage, ask around at the docks until you hear of a boat going where you want to go then find out who the captain is. It's usually worth asking around about the approximate cost to avoid being overcharged, though some captains will charge you the same as anybody else. Departure time often depends on a full cargo and *mañana* may go on for several days if the hold is only half full. Usually you can sleep on the boat while you are waiting for departure, if you want to save on hotel bills. At no time should you leave your luggage unattended.

Boats to Iquitos are relatively infrequent and rather small, slow and uncomfortable. Beyond Iquitos, however, services are more frequent and comfortable. Things are generally more organized too; there are chalk boards at the docks with ship's names, destinations and departure times displayed reasonably clearly and accurately. You can look over a boat for your prospective destination and wait for a better vessel if you don't like what you see. Some boats even have cabins, though these tend to be rather grubby airless boxes and you have to supply your own bedding. I prefer to use a hammock. Try to hang it away from the engine room and not directly under a light, as these are often lit far into the evening, precluding sleep and attracting insects. Food is usually included in the price of the passage, and may be marginally better on some of the bigger and better ships. If you like rice and beans – or rice and fish, or rice and tough meat, or rice and fried bananas – you'll be OK. If you don't like rice, you'll have a problem. Bottled soft drinks and beers are usually available and priced very reasonably – ask about this before the boat leaves because you definitely don't want to drink the water. Sanitary facilities are basic but adequate, and there's usually a pump shower on board.

Boats from Iquitos used to go all the way to the mouth of the Amazon, though this is almost unheard of these days. However, the very fact that ocean-going vessels are capable of reaching Iquitos indicates how vast this river is. Many

A Week on the Amazon

Once I traveled by boat from Iquitos all the way to Manaus and had a great time. I was already aware of the lack of wildlife so I brought a couple of very thick books. Yet I found I barely had the time to read them, there was so much to do. The views of the great river stretching all around were often very beautiful, particularly during the misty dawns and the searing sunsets.

Quarters were close on the passenger deck, and my elbows literally touched my neighbor's when I was in my hammock. Friendliness and an easy-going attitude are essential ingredients for a river trip. Most of the passengers are friendly and fun, and you can have a great time getting to know them.

On the first evening of a seven day trip, I was sitting in the bow enjoying the cooling breeze and watching the sun go down. Soon, a small crowd of Peruvian and Brazilian passengers and crew gathered, and a rum bottle and guitar appeared. Within minutes, we had a first-rate party going with singing, dancing, hand clapping and an incredible impromptu orchestra. One of the crew bent a metal rod into a rough triangle which he pounded rhythmically, someone else threw a handful of beans into a can and started shaking, a couple of pieces of polished wood were clapped together to interweave yet another rhythm, a mouth harp was produced, I blew bass notes across the top of my beer bottle and everyone had a great time. A couple of hours of rhythmic music as the sun went down became a standard part of the ship's routine and gave me some of my most unforgettable moments of South American travel.

Once or twice a day, the boat would pull into some tiny Amazonian port to load or off-load passengers and cargo. The arrival of a big boat was often the main event of the day in one of these small river villages, and the entire population might come down to the riverbank to swap gossip and watch the goings on. This, too, added to the interest of the trip. ■

people have misconceptions about sailing down the Amazon, watching monkeys swinging in the tree tops, snakes gliding among the branches, and parrots and macaws flying across the river in front of you. In reality, most of the banks have been colonized and there is little wildlife there. Also, the boats often navigate the midstream, and the shoreline is seen only as a rather distant green line. In fact, some people find the monotonous diet and long days of sitting in their hammocks to be boring and they don't enjoy the trip. For others it's a great experience – I hope my descriptions help you decide whether this is something you'd like to attempt or want to avoid. See the sidebar 'A Week on the Amazon,' above, for more on Amazon travel. If you'd like to do it in greater comfort, there are much more expensive boats with air-conditioned cabins available which are for tourists rather than cargo and river passengers. See Exploring the Jungle in the Amazon Basin chapter for details.

CAR & MOTORCYCLE
Car Rental

The major car rental companies (Budget, Avis, National and Hertz) are found in Lima and a few are found in the other major cities. In general, car rental is not cheap (averaging US$50 a day for a car). There are plenty of hidden charges for mileage (per km), insurance and so on, so make sure you understand the rental agreement before renting a car. A deposit by credit card is usually required and renters normally need to be over 25. Your own driver's license should be accepted for driving in Peru.

If you really want to drive, bear in mind that it is a long way from Lima to most major tourist destinations and it is suggested that you use bus or air to wherever you want to go and rent a car when you get there. Also bear in mind that the condition of the rental vehicles is often not very good, roads are badly potholed (even the paved Panamericana) and drivers extremely aggressive. Road signs, where they exist, are often small and unclear. Gas stations are few and far between. Vehicles such as 4WD jeeps are very expensive and many companies are reluctant to rent ordinary cars for anything but short coastal runs. Theft is all too common so you should not leave your vehicle parked in the street or you'll lose your hubcaps, windscreen wipers, or even your wheels. When stopping overnight, park the car in a guarded lot (the better hotels have them). Generally, I do not recommend self-drive car rental.

Buying a Car

I don't recommend trying to buy, drive and then resell a car unless you are planning on a long stay and are prepared to put up with a lot of red tape. Using public transport is generally more efficient given the negative points outlined above.

Taxis

Taxis can be rented for long distance trips, which takes care of many of the problems outlined above. This costs little more than renting a car. Not all taxi drivers will agree to drive long distance, but if one does you should check his credentials before hiring him for several days.

Motorcycle Rental

Motorcycle rental seems to be an option mainly in jungle towns like Iquitos and Puerto Maldonado, where bikers can go for short runs around town and into the surroundings but not much further.

BICYCLE

Each year there are a handful of cyclists who attempt to cycle from Alaska to Argentina, or shorter long-distance rides, and they manage to get through Peru OK. They report that the Panamericana is incredibly long, boring, windy, sandy, miserable, and there is a good chance that you will be knocked off by kamikaze truck and bus drivers who will not stop to see if you're OK. Cycling in the Andes is more fun and visually rewarding, though hard

work. Mountain bikes are recommended, road bikes won't stand up to the poor roads.

Renting bikes is only a recent option in Peru and is described under the towns of Huaraz, Huancayo and Cuzco. These are rented to people who want to stay in the general area of those towns, not travel all over the country. The bicycles that are available aren't bad, but if you're a dedicated biker you're probably better off bringing your own. Most airlines will fly them at no extra cost if you box them. However, boxing the bike gives baggage handlers little clue to the contents and the box is liable to be roughly handled, possibly damaging the bike. An alternative is wrapping it in heavy duty plastic – baggage handlers are less likely to drop or throw the bike in this case. Airlines' bicycle carrying policies do vary a lot, so shop around.

Be wary at Peruvian Customs, where agents may try and sting you for a '25% of value, fully refundable bond.' It's not clear if this is legal or not but if you are insistent enough you may persuade the customs agent that it's your personal baggage, not for resale in the country. If you can't get around the bond, undervalue you bike as much as you dare, because it will be difficult and time-consuming to get your bond back when you leave.

Bicycle shops are few and far between in Peru and used to carry a completely inadequate selection of parts. This has improved recently with the lifting of prohibitive taxes on bike parts.

HITCHHIKING

Hitching is never entirely safe in any country in the world, and is not recommended. Travelers who decide to hitch should understand that they are taking a small but potentially serious risk. People who do choose to hitch will be safer if they travel in pairs and let someone know where they are planning to go.

Hitchhiking is not very practical in Peru for three reasons: There are few private cars, public transport is relatively cheap, and trucks are used as public transport in remote areas, so trying to hitch a free ride on one is the same as trying to hitch a free ride on a bus. Many drivers of *any* vehicle will pick you up but will also expect payment. If the driver is stopping to drop off and pick up other passengers, ask them what the going rate is. If you are the only passenger, the driver may have picked you up just to talk with a foreigner, and he may wave aside your offer of payment. If you do decide to try hitching, make sure in advance of your ride that you and the driver agree on the subject of payment.

WALKING
Peru is certainly a good destination for adventurous treks in the Andes. Both the Inca Trail to Machu Picchu and the Cordillera Blanca have justly become world famous for hiking and backpacking. Some excellent guidebooks have been published specifically for foot travelers – see Books in the Facts for the Visitor chapter.

Walking around cities is generally safe, even at night, if you stick to the well-lit areas. Always be on the alert for pickpockets, though, and make inquiries before venturing into an area you don't know.

LOCAL TRANSPORTATION
There are no underground or surface trains in any city in Peru. Local transportation is therefore limited to bus or taxi.

Local Bus
Local buses are usually slow and crowded, but cheap. Local buses often go out to a nearby village and this is a good way to see an area. Just stay on the bus to the end of the line, pay another fare and head back again, usually sitting in the best seat on the bus. If you make friends with the driver, you may end up with an entertaining tour as he points out the local sights, in between collecting other passengers' fares.

When you want to get off a local bus, yell *Baja!*, which means 'Down!' (as in 'The passenger is getting down'). Telling the driver to stop will make him think you're trying to be a back seat driver, and

you will be ignored. He's only interested if you're getting off, or down from the bus. Another way of getting him to stop is to yell *Esquina!*, which means 'Corner!' He'll stop at the next one. A *por favor* doesn't hurt and makes everyone think you speak excellent Spanish. If you don't actually speak Spanish and someone tries to converse after your display of linguistic brilliance, a smile and a sage nod should suffice until you get down from the bus.

Taxi
For short hops around a city, just flag down one of the many taxis that seem to be everywhere. They are recognizable by the small red taxi sticker in the windshield. The cars themselves can be of almost any model and color. Taxis called by telephone are available in Lima and some of the other major cities and are listed in applicable chapters. These are more expensive than taxis flagged down on the street but are also safer and more reliable. Those flagged down on the street are not regulated and, although I've never had a problem with one, I would avoid taking one of those if carrying a large amount of money or going to the airport with all my luggage.

The black *remisse* taxis outside the expensive hotels are usually the most convenient, comfortable and reliable, and some of their drivers speak English. They do a brisk trade in taking well-heeled tourists to the airport or Gold Museum. They are also the most expensive and have set rates which are often two or three times the rate of a taxi flagged down on the street.

Shared taxis or *colectivos* do set runs and are especially found in Lima and between Huancayo and Lima. In Lima, the driver drives along with one hand out of the window holding up as many fingers as the number of seats available. You can flag them down on any corner and get off wherever you like. There used to be more *comites* or shared intercity taxis but these are now disappearing with the main exception of Huancayo to Lima. They have been displaced by improved bus and plane services. Note that the term colectivo is also used to denote a bus, especially a minibus or van.

Whatever kind of taxi you take, there are two things to remember: Fares are invariably cheaper than in North America or Europe and you must always ask the fare in advance because there are no meters. It is quite acceptable to haggle over a taxi fare – drivers often double or triple the standard rate for an unsuspecting foreigner. Try to find out what the going rate is before taking a cab. About $1 is the fare for the cheapest and shortest run in most cities.

Finally, you can hire a taxi with a driver for several hours or even days. The cost varies depending on how far you expect to drive in a day and on how luxurious a vehicle you get. If you speak Spanish and make your own arrangements with a driver you could start around $40 per day, if you are driving on better roads and making occasional stops, more if driving a long way or on poor roads. On the other hand, a tourist agency could arrange a comfortable car with an English-speaking driver for about twice as much. Often, your hotel can help arrange a taxi for you. If you hire one for several days, make sure that you discuss eating and sleeping arrangements. Some drivers will charge enough to be able to make their own arrangements, while others will expect you to provide a room and three meals.

Tipping is not the norm, especially for short hops within the city. If you hire a driver for the day and he is particularly helpful or friendly, you may want to tip.

TOURS

Most people who take tours in Peru either arrange them in their home countries with a reputable outfitter (some of which are mentioned in the Getting There & Away chapter) or take local tours in Peru. Not many travelers come to Lima to buy a tour covering much of Peru and most agencies in Lima aren't set up for this kind of travel. Instead, agencies will book your flights and hotels and arrange to have you met by a local tour representative in the towns you wish to visit, in effect combining a series of local tours. The best known and most experienced of these agencies in Lima is Lima Tours (☎ 427-6624, 432-1765, fax 432-3383), Belén 1040, which is recommended for package tours although they are also among the most expensive. Travelers will find it cheaper to make their own travel and hotel arrangements to the towns of their choice and then take local tours with one of the agencies available in the most popular destinations. The better agencies are listed under the appropriate city.

Lima

If, like me, you read the *Paddington Bear* books in your youth, Lima in 'darkest Peru' may conjure up images of an exotic city in the heart of a lush tropical jungle. Unfortunately, this is far from the reality. The city, sprawled untidily on the edge of the coastal desert, is mainly modern and not particularly exotic. Despite its many urban problems, most visitors find Lima an interesting, if nerve racking, place to visit.

Lima is the capital of Peru. Almost a third of Peru's 24 million inhabitants now live in Lima, making most of the city overcrowded, polluted and noisy. Much of the city's population growth can be attributed to the influx of very poor people from other areas of Peru, especially the highlands. They come searching for a better life with a job and, perhaps, opportunities for their children. Most end up living in the *pueblos jovenes*, or 'young towns.' These shanty towns, which surround the capital, lack electricity, water and adequate sanitation. Jobs are scarce; most work as *ambulantes* or street vendors selling anything from chocolates to clothes pins and earning barely enough for food. Their chances of improving their lot are very slim.

Lima's location in the center of Peru's desert coastline gives it a climate and environment that can only be described as dismal. From April to December, the coastal fog, known as garúa, blots out the sun and blankets the city's buildings in a fine gray mist. Unless they are repainted annually, the buildings soon take on a ghostly pallor from the incessant mist that coats the rooftops with a thin, concrete-like layer of hardened gray sludge. The situation is not much better during the few months of Lima's short summer – although the sun does come out, smog makes walking the city streets a sticky and unpleasant activity. As the waste products of nearly eight million Lima residents mostly end up in the Pacific, the beaches are overcrowded cesspools and the newspapers carry daily health warnings during summer.

Having read this far, you might well be wondering how to avoid Lima. However, if you're planning any kind of extensive traveling in Peru, you will find it virtually impossible to avoid the desert coastline and, in turn, Lima. Despite the city's drawbacks, having no choice is not the only reason to visit Lima. Its people are generally friendly and hospitable, there are plenty of opportunities for dining, nightlife and other entertainment and, perhaps most important of all, the great selection of museums includes some of the best in Peru. So it's worth trying to ignore the traffic jams and the crowds and getting to know something of the people and the culture of Peru.

History
Because it was founded by Francisco Pizarro on January 6, 1535, the Catholic feast of Epiphany, or the Day of the Kings, its first name was the City of the Kings. A university opened in 1551 and Lima became the seat of the Spanish Inquisition in 1569. The city grew quickly and was the continent's richest and most important town during early colonial times.

This changed in 1746 when a disastrous earthquake wiped out most of the city, leaving only a few churches and houses standing, some of which can still be visited. Because of Lima's importance, rebuilding was rapid and most of the old colonial buildings that can still be seen here date from after the earthquake. After the wars of independence from Spain in the 1820s, other cities became increasingly important as capitals of the newly independent states and Lima's importance as a colonial center vanished.

Unfortunately, much of Lima's original

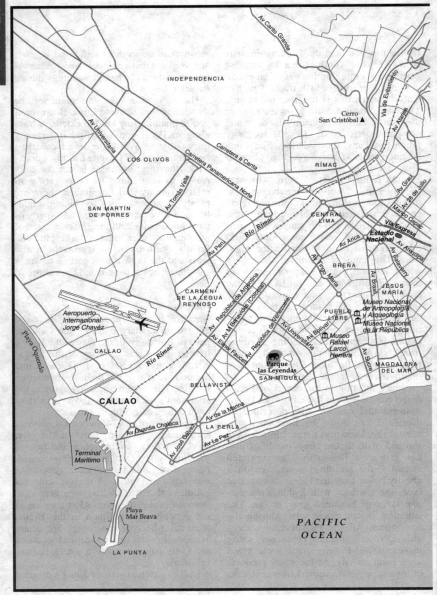

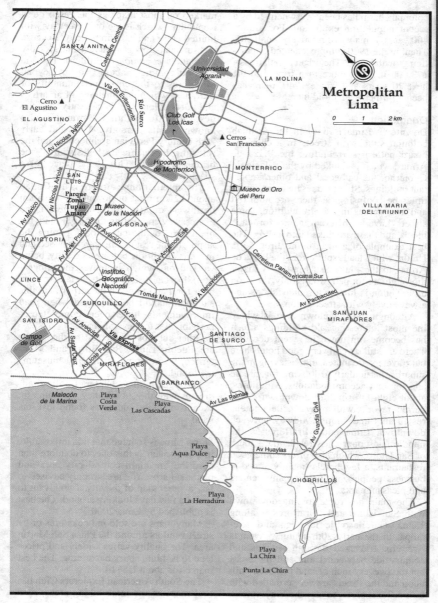

Metropolitan
Lima

0   1   2 km

SANTA ANITA

Universidad
Agraria

LA MOLINA

Cerro
El Agustino

EL AGUSTINO

Carretera Central

Vía de Evitamiento

Río Surco

Club Golf
Los Icas

Cerros
San Francisco

MONTERRICO

Av Nicolás Ayllón

SAN
LUIS

Av Nicolás Arriola

Av Canadá

Hipódromo
de Monterrico

Museo de Oro
del Peru

VILLA MARIA
DEL TRIUNFO

Parque
Zonal
Tupau
Amaru

Museo
de la Nación

Av México

Av Javier Prado Este

SAN BORJA

Av Aviación

LA VICTORIA

Av Angamos Este

Carretera Panamericana Sur

LINCE

Instituto
Geográfico
Nacional

Av Benavides

Av Pachacutec

SAN JUAN
MIRAFLORES

Tomás Marsano

SURQUILLO

Av Panamericana

SAN ISIDRO

Av Arequipa

Vía Expresa

SANTIAGO
DE SURCO

Campo
de Golf

Av Saga Cruz

Av José Pardo

MIRAFLORES

BARRANCO

Malecón
de la Marina

Playa
Costa
Verde

Playa
Las Cascadas

Av Las Palmas

Av Guardia Civil

Playa
Aqua Dulce

Av Huaylas

CHORRILLOS

Playa
La Herradura

Playa
La Chira

Punta La Chira

colonial charm has been overwhelmed by a recent population explosion. For almost 400 years, Lima was a relatively small city. Then, in the 1920s, unprecedented population growth began. The urban population of 173,000 in 1919 more than tripled in the next 20 years and, since 1940, there has been a further twelvefold increase.

Orientation

Downtown Lima is built in the Spanish colonial style with streets in a checkerboard pattern surrounding the Plaza de Armas, which is flanked by the Palacio de Gobierno, the cathedral and other important buildings. Street names here can sometimes be confusing, as there are both old and new names in use. In addition, some streets have a different name for each block, and these are linked into a *jirón*. The best example of a jirón is the Jirón de la Unión, which leads south from the Plaza de Armas to the Plaza San Martín. A major thoroughfare for pedestrians only, the Jirón de la Unión is lined with many shops and always lively with street action.

Although the downtown area is where the most interesting old buildings are, it has become run down in recent decades. There are still several very good hotels here but travelers are increasingly staying in the suburbs, particularly if looking for middle and top end accommodations. Miraflores, about eight km south of downtown, is the current favorite with many excellent hotels, restaurants and shops. Midway between downtown Lima and Miraflores is the middle and upper class residential suburb of San Isidro, which also offers some good restaurants, a few hotels (mainly aimed at business people), major shopping centers and pleasant parks.

The main bus route joining downtown with San Isidro and Miraflores is along Tacna, Garcilaso de la Vega and Arequipa. In the early 20th century, Avenida Arequipa traversed through ranches and countryside between Lima and the coast but today every inch of land has been built upon and the streets are very crowded with traffic. Taxis prefer to take the Via Expresa,

marked on most maps as the Paseo de la República, which is the only freeway with limited entry and exits in the city. Because it is sunken below ground level, it is locally nicknamed *el zanjón* (the ditch). The Via Expresa continues about two km beyond Miraflores to the cliff-top community of Barranco, which is something of an artists and poets colony and is currently the liveliest suburb for nightlife. Barranco is also known for its attractive 19th and early 20th century Peruvian architecture and the romantic El Puente de los Suspiros (the bridge of sighs). This is the place for a special date.

The international airport is in Callao about 12 km west of downtown or 16 km northwest of Miraflores, but there is no expressway connecting the airport with the main parts of the city. Roads joining the airport to the rest of Lima are crowded and in poor condition but are currently being worked on (which increases the congestion). During rush hours it can take over an hour for a taxi to reach the airport, but this situation should be alleviated when road improvements have been completed – probably not for several years.

Other suburbs of interest to the visitor are Pueblo Libre, San Borja and Monterrico, where some of the best museums are found.

Throughout this chapter, I follow addresses with the suburb they are found in, except for those addresses found in Lima itself.

Maps Lima is so huge that it is impossible, in a book such as this one, to do more than describe the main central city area and major suburbs. You are strongly advised to buy a street map of the city if you want to spend a few days looking around. The best is published by Lima 2000.

Many maps are sold in bookstores or by street vendors around the Plaza San Martín area. The quality varies widely and prices tend to be high, so try bargaining. The best map costs about US$14.

The South American Explorers Club has trail maps of the main hiking areas, road maps of Peru and detailed street and bus maps of Lima. If they don't have the maps you want, they'll know where you can get them.

For topographical maps, go to the Instituto Geográfico Nacional (IGN, ☎ 475-9960) at Aramburu 1198, Surquillo. It's open from 9 am to 4 pm on weekdays; you need your passport to get in. Don't arrive after 3 pm because you won't have enough time to do your business before 4 pm and they are reluctant to let you in. In January, they close around lunch time. The Servicio Aerofotográfico Nacional at Las Palmeras Air Force base in Chorrillos can sell you aerial photographs from 8.30 am to noon and 2 to 4 pm on weekdays. Some of these aerial photos are available from the IGN.

Information
Tourist Offices Infotur (☎ 424-5131, 431-0117), Jirón de la Unión 1066 (also known as Jirón Belén), about half a block from the Plaza San Martín, has a wealth of up-to-date information about transport, hotels and sightseeing throughout the more frequently visited parts of Peru. Hours are 9.30 am to 6 pm, Monday to Friday, and 10 am to 2 pm on Saturday. There is also a tourist information office at the airport. It's not as good but will help you find a hotel by phone. The Municipalidad, just off Lima's Plaza de Armas, has a tourism office for local information (☎ 427-6080), Jirón de la Unión 300, open 8.30 am to 1.30 pm weekdays. In Miraflores there is a municipal tourist information booth in Parque Kennedy near the artists' market open from 9 am to 8 pm daily. Also there is a Centro de Información y Promoción Turística (☎ 444-3915, 447-9539), San Martín 537, Miraflores. This is open from 9 am to 5 pm on weekdays. These places change their hours frequently.

A most useful source of general information is the *Peru Guide*. This free booklet is published monthly by Lima Editora and can be found at some of the better hotels, restaurants and tourist spots in Lima, as well as at the South American Explorers Club. A new free booklet called *Golden Guide* appeared in April 1995 with plans to publish every two months.

South American Explorers Club For many long-term travelers and expatriate residents, this club has become something of a legend. Since it was founded by Don Montague and Linda Rojas in 1977, the club has been involved in activities ranging from the 1980 cleanup of the Inca Trail to the cleanup of erroneous media reports about discoveries of 'lost' Peruvian cities in 1985. Primarily, however, it functions as an information center for travelers, adventurers and scientific expeditions and the club's headquarters in Lima can provide excellent advice about travel anywhere in Latin America, with an emphasis on Peru.

The club has an extensive library of books, maps (some published by the club) and the trip reports of other travelers. A variety of the most useful books and maps are for sale and there are trail maps for the Inca Trail, the Mt Ausangate area, the Cordilleras Blanca and Huayhuash, as well as general maps of South America. You can also get useful current information on travel conditions, currency regulations, weather and so on.

The club is an entirely member-supported, nonprofit organization. Annual membership costs US$40 per person (US$60 for a couple), which covers four issues of their excellent and informative *South American Explorer* magazine. (Membership dues are US tax-deductible. Members outside the USA have to add US$7 for postage). In the past, the magazine came out at irregular intervals but it is now published quarterly. Members also receive full use of the clubhouse and its facilities. These include an information service and library, introductions to other travelers and notification of expedition opportunities, storage of excess luggage (anything from small valuables to a kayak), storage or forwarding of mail addressed to you at the club, a relaxing place to read, research or just have a cup of tea and a chat with the friendly staff, a book exchange, buying and selling of used equipment,

LIMA

discounts on the books, maps and gear sold at the club and other services. The storage facilities are particularly useful if you plan on returning to Peru – I leave climbing gear and other heavy stuff here from year to year. Nonmembers are welcome but are asked to limit their visits to the club to about half an hour and are not eligible for membership privileges. Paid-up members can stay all day – a welcome relief from the madhouse bustle of Lima. The club is highly recommended.

If you're in Lima, you can simply go to the clubhouse (☎ /fax 425-0142) and sign up. Otherwise, mail your US$40 (and any questions you have) direct to the club at Casilla 3714, Lima 100. The street address is República de Portugal 146, on the 13th block of Alfonso Ugarte in the Breña district of Lima, about a 10 or 15 minute walk from the Plaza San Martín. The club is open from 9.30 am to 5 pm on weekdays. Although the club has been at the same address since it was founded, it may move to Miraflores some time this century. Check with one of the other offices if you can't find them in Breña.

The club's US office (☎ 607-277-0488) is at 126 Indian Creek Rd, Ithaca, NY 14850. The magazine is published there and if you're not sure whether or not you want to join, send them US$6 for a sample copy of the *Explorer* and further information. Non-member subscriptions are US$22 for four issues and US$35 for eight issues.

In 1989 the club's Quito office (☎ /fax 566-076) at Toledo 1254 was opened. The postal address is Apartado 21-431, Eloy Alfaro, Quito, Ecuador. Travelers to Ecuador will find the same range of services here as is offered by the Lima office and access to these is included in the annual membership fee.

Foreign Consulates See the Facts for the Visitor chapter for a list of embassies in Lima.

Visas Lima is one of the easiest places in Peru to have your tourist permit extended. Most foreign visitors receive a 90-day permit on arrival that can be extended for a further 90 at a cost of US$20 per 30 days. Sometimes you can get 60 days for US$20 on your first visit or you may get only 30 days and have to return for further extensions. Foreigners requiring tourist visas can also renew. Once your maximum of 180 days is up, you must leave the country. However, there is no law against crossing the border to a neighboring country and returning the next day to start the process over again.

The Lima immigration office *(migraciones)* was, for many years, on the 500 block of Paseo de la República and 28 de Julio. In late 1995 (just as I was finishing this book) they suddenly moved to a building on España at Huaraz, about four blocks west of Alfonso Ugarte (just off the west edge of my map). They open at about 9 am on weekdays and it's best to go first thing in the morning if you want to get your extension the same day. Specially stamped paperwork is required which can be bought at the Banco de la Nación (it costs almost US$3). You will need your passport and the white immigration slip you received on entry (it's not a disaster if you lose it but the process becomes more time consuming and expensive). These documents are presented with a fee of US$20 (payable in cash dollars or nuevos soles). Sometimes (especially on your last 30-day extension), you may be asked for a ticket out of the country, though you can get around this by showing enough money. The more affluent you look, the less hassle you'll have. Remember that regulations change frequently in Latin America and Lima is no exception! (The new office is close to the South American Explorers Club and members should stop by to ask about the latest regulations.)

A bus ticket from Lima to the Ecuadorian, Bolivian or Chilean border will cost you about the same as the US$20 visa renewal fee so, if you're on a tight budget, you might want to spend your money traveling to a convenient border and reentering the country instead.

A final word about student visas. You can get one if you're studying in Peru but, as they're usually more hassle than they're worth, many foreign students prefer to use tourist permits if they are taking a Spanish course.

Money Interbanc (☎ 433-4200), Jirón de la Unión 600, or Larco 690, Miraflores (and many other branches) is one of the easiest places to change traveler's checks at the lowest commissions. They are open from 9.45 am to 3 pm on weekdays and 9.45 am to 12.45 pm on Saturday.

The American Express office will not cash their own checks. Good rates for Amex checks are given at the Banco Mercantil (☎ 428-8060), Carabaya at Ucayali; (☎ 442-8000), Ricardo Rivera Navarette 641, San Isidro; (☎ 447-8914), Larco 467, Miraflores. They are open from 9 am to 5 pm on weekdays and 10 am to noon on Saturday. If you have Citicorp traveler's checks, the Citibank (☎ 442-0909), Dean Valdivia 423 at Begonias, San Isidro, will cash them at no commission. Banco de Crédito (☎ 427-5775), Jirón Lampa 499, also changes Amex checks and gives cash advances on Visa cards. It is better to cash traveler's checks into nuevos soles rather than into US dollars to get the best rates.

Note that during the Lima summer, from January to March, some banks are open only in the morning. The government tried to introduce afternoon banking in 1986 but popular opinion didn't allow this to happen – everyone wants to go to the beach on hot summer afternoons. During the rest of the year, most banks are open in the afternoons but hours vary from bank to bank. Expect long lines in banks, especially on Monday mornings.

Casas de cambio, or exchange houses, usually give the same rate as banks for cash, tend to be quicker, and are open longer. Traveler's checks are harder to cash at casas de cambio. There are several casas de cambio downtown on Ocoña (behind the Hotel Bolívar) and on Camaná between Nicolás de Pierola (also called Colmena) and Ocoña. They are also found along Larco in Miraflores. One casa de cambio, P&P, exchange traveler's checks at either of their two locations: Nicolás de Pierola 805 at Camaná (☎ 428-8653); and Benavides 735, Miraflores (☎ 444-2404). LAC Dolar (☎ 428-8127, fax 427-3906), Camana 779 office 201, is safe, reliable, and changes cash and traveler's checks at reasonable rates. Hours are 8.30 am to 7.30 pm Monday to Saturday and 9 am to 2 pm on Sundays and some holidays. Casas de cambio are open for longer hours than banks but shop around, particularly when exchanging a large amount of money.

Street changers often hang around the casas de cambio. The corner of Plaza San Martín and Ocoña is a favorite spot – on some days every person on the block seems to be buying or selling dollars.

If you need to receive money from home, the Banco de Crédito has been recommended. Check with the main office for instructions on how to have the money sent.

Report lost or stolen Amex traveler's checks to the Amex office at Lima Tours (☎ 427-6624), Belén 1040. These are the easiest to deal with. Report lost Citicorp checks to Citibank and Visa checks to Banco de Crédito (see above). The Thomas Cook representative is Viajes Laser (☎ 47-9499, fax 47-8717), Comandante Espinar 331, but they don't replace stolen checks. Other traveler's checks are less easy to negotiate so you are advised to stick with these mentioned here.

Visa cards can be used in Unicard ATMs and at Banco de Crédito, Interbanc and Banco Mercantil. For more information on Visa, call ☎ 472-7076 (Spanish) or 442-8966 (English). MasterCard can be used at Banco Wiese (☎ 428 3400), Cuzco 245, and (☎ 445 2290), Diagonal 176, Miraflores. The Banco Mercantil also gives cash advances on Mastercard. Amex cards can be used at Interbanc.

Post The main post office (☎ 427-5592) is inside the city block on the northwest corner of the Plaza de Armas. Mail sent to you at Lista de Correo, Correos Central, Lima, should be collected here. The main office is open from 8 am to 8 pm Monday to Saturday and from 8 am to 2 pm on

Sunday. There are also branch post offices in various districts of Lima. The Miraflores branch post office (☎ 445-0697), Petit Thouars 5201, is open from 8 am to 8 pm Monday to Saturday. The post office at the airport is open from 8 am to 6 pm Monday to Saturday.

American Express clients can have mail held for them at Amex, c/o Lima Tours, Belén 1040, Lima. You can pick up mail between 9 am and noon and from 3 to 5 pm on weekdays.

Bring identification when collecting mail from either Amex or a post office.

Members of the South American Explorers Club can have mail held for them at Casilla 3714, Lima 100, Peru.

Sending parcels abroad is reasonably safe if you send them certificado. Lima is the best city to send parcels from. Further details of international parcel post are given in the Post section of the Facts for the Visitor chapter.

Private companies such as DHL (☎ 451-8587), Los Castaños 225, San Isidro, provide overnight mail service to the USA and other destinations; this is very expensive.

Telecommunications There are two telephone systems. The main one is Telefónica del Peru, for service nationwide. In addition, Companía Peruana de Telefonos (CPT) is in Lima only. The telephone system changed ownership in 1994 and is being expanded and modernized in Lima during 1995 and '96. This will lead to possible changes in phone numbers and better services. Call ☎ 103 for directory inquiries.

The area code for Lima is 01 when calling from outside Bolivia but within Peru. From outside Peru drop the 0.

Fax Fax services are available at many locations, including most of the Telefónica del Peru offices. One place providing late service is on Avenida Bolivia 347 (☎ 424-5261). They'll hold faxes clearly marked ATENCIÓN before your name at fax 430-0614. They are open from 7 am to 11 pm.

Cultural Centers The Instituto Cultural Peruano-Norteamericano (☎ 446-0381), Arequipa 4798, Miraflores, and (☎ 428-3530), Cuzco 446, Lima, offers US newspapers, a library and Spanish courses. You can read British newspapers at the Peruvian British Cultural Association (☎ 470-5577), Arequipa 3495, San Isidro, or at the British Council (☎ 470-4350), Alberto Lynch 110, San Isidro. Germans can head over to the Goethe Institut (☎ 433-3180), Jirón Nazca 722, Jesús María, and the French have the Alliance Française (☎ 446-8511), Arequipa 4598, Miraflores. All of these present a variety of cultural programs (plays, film screenings, art shows, lectures, etc) at irregular intervals.

Travel Agencies The many travel agencies in Lima can sell airline tickets, make hotel reservations and provide tour services. Tours bought in Lima which visit other parts of Peru will normally be cheaper than tours bought in your home country but more expensive than tours bought in the nearest major town to the area you wish to visit.

For guided tours of Lima (the city, the churches, the museums, Lima by night, the nearby archaeological sites such as Pachacamac, and so on), Lima Tours (☎ 427-6624, 432-1765, fax 432-3383), Belén 1040, is one of the best, though their tours aren't particularly cheap, starting at US$15 to US$20 per person. Comfortable transport and English-speaking guides are provided.

For specialized tours for individuals or small groups, I suggest you ask the South American Explorers Club for a recommendation of a reliable private guide. You can hire a guide for about US$25 a day plus expenses.

For adventure tourists, several companies have offices in Lima. Aventours (☎ 444-1067) at Avenida La Paz 442, Miraflores, specializes in river running and trekking in the Cuzco area. Explorandes (☎ 445-0542, fax 445-4686), San Fernando 320, Miraflores, also specializes in trekking and river-running adventures. These tours tend more towards the top end of the market; cheaper tours can be joined by traveling to the area in which you're interested and making contact there.

The Río Cañete, a three or four hour drive south of Lima (see Cañete in South of Lima), has river running opportunities. The following companies run trips there: Apumayo Expediciones (☎ 442-3886, fax 422-5246), Emilio Cavencia 160, Oficina 201, San Isidro (they also do trips on the Río Tampobata and Río Colca); Cano Andes (☎ 477-0188), San Martín 455, Barranco; TrekAndes (☎ 445-8078), Benavides 212, Miraflores; Cascada Expediciones (☎ /fax 446-6022), San Lorenzo 219; Miraflores; Peruvian River & Mountain (☎ 448-2168); Aventura Peru (☎ 440-5584).

Bookstores The best selection of English-language guidebooks can be found at the South American Explorers Club. The club also has a paperback book exchange for members only. The ABC bookstore (☎ 444-0372), under the Cine El Pacífico at the Ovalo in Miraflores, has a good but expensive selection of English, German and French newspapers, magazines, coffee-table books and guidebooks. They have a few other branches. There is a good selection of paperback novels at the Librería El Pacífico, also under Cine El Pacífico. Bear in mind that most English-language books about Peru are much cheaper in Britain or the US than in Peru.

Libraries The Biblioteca Nacional (☎ 428-7690), Abancay at Miró Quesada, has books in Spanish. For books in English, German and French, contact one of the cultural centers discussed above.

Laundry Many hotels can have your laundry done for you – the more expensive the hotel, the more expensive the laundry. Peru does not have self-service coin-operated laundries. Instead, you must leave your clothes with a lavandería, or laundry, and pick them up the following day, though same-day service can be arranged at extra cost.

Many lavanderías only do dry cleaning and others charge by the item rather than by the load. The lavandería I use is LavaQuick at Benavides 604 and La Paz in Miraflores. Here, you'll pay about US$5 for a 4 kg load, washed, dried and folded. They offer 24-hour service, or same-day service if you pay a tip, and are open from 9 am to 6 pm Monday to Saturday, closing at 1 pm on Thursday. Others offering similar service are Bubijitas (☎ 444-9506), Porta 293, Miraflores, open from 9 am to 7 pm, Monday to Saturday; Lavavelos, Atahualpa 175, Miraflores, open 8 am to 6 pm, Monday to Saturday; and Lavacenter (☎ 440-3600), Victor Maurtua 140, San Isidro, open from 9.30 am to 6.30 pm on weekdays and 9 am to 3 pm on Saturday. I couldn't find a lavandería in downtown Lima. Ask at your hotel for directions to the nearest lavandería.

Medical Services Considered to be the best, but also the most expensive general clinic is the Clínica Anglo-American (☎ 221-3656), on the 3rd block of Salazar, San Isidro. A consultation will cost up to about US$45 and a gamma globulin shot costs US$35. This is one of the few places that stocks gamma globulin.

In San Borja, try the Clínica San Borja (☎ 441-3141) at Avenida del Aire 333. In Lima, there's the Clínica Internacional (☎ 428-8060) at Washington 1475. All of these clinics have 24-hour service and some English-speaking staff. A little cheaper, and also good, is the Clínica Adventista (☎ 445-9040) at Malecón Balta 956, in Miraflores. Here a consultation costs about US$23.

For the cheapest yellow fever, tetanus and typhoid shots, try the Hospital de Niños (☎ 424-6045), Brasil 600. For tropical diseases, try Instituto de Medicina Tropical (☎ 482-3903, 482-3910), at the Universidad Particular Cayetano Heredia, Avenida Honorio Delgado, San Martín de Porres. There are many other hospitals and clinics.

If you are bitten by a dog or other animal and need a rabies shot, call the Centro Antirrábico (☎ 431-4047).

A recommended English-speaking doctor is Dr Alejandro Bussalle Rivera (☎ 471-2238), León Velarde 221, Lince.

Well-recommended dentists are Dr Gerardo Aste and son (☎ 441-7502), Antero Aspillaga 415, office 101, San Isidro. Dr Aste speaks excellent English and did a very thorough and painless job of replacing a filling I broke in Peru.

If you have a spectacle prescription with you, you can have a spare pair of glasses made up cheaply by one of Lima's numerous opticians. There are several along Cailloma in the city center and around Schell and Larco in Miraflores. Having your eyes examined for a new prescription is also cheap but some ophthalmologists practicing in Peru have archaic equipment and don't do a very good job. If you need a new prescription, ask at your embassy for a recommended ophthalmologist.

Emergency For emergencies ranging from robbery to rabies you can contact the tourist police for advice and assistance. They have been recommended to me by several people for their courtesy and helpfulness. English-speaking police are usually available and they can cut down on a lot of red tape if you need a police report to make an insurance claim or get a traveler's check refund. The policía de turismo (☎ 437-8171, 435-1342, 437-8262), Museo de la Nación building, Javier Prado Este 2465, San Borja, is open from 8 am to 8 pm.

Other emergency telephone numbers are for the police (☎ 105) and fire (☎ 116).

A 24-hour hotline (☎ 471-2994, 471-2809, fax 471-1617) is available to answer questions and give advice in the case of emergencies. Both English and Spanish speaking operators are available. The hotline also helps travelers who feel they have been cheated or overcharged by travel agencies, tour operators, hotels, restaurants, etc.

Visiting Prisoners People wishing to visit foreign (English-speaking) prisoners (mainly in jail on drug charges) can contact the Foreign Prisoners' Fellowship (☎ 445-7908), Church of the Good Shepherd, Avenida Santa Cruz 491, Lima, or write to Apartado 5152, Lima 18.

Dangers & Annoyances With literally millions of very poor and unemployed people, it is hardly surprising that Lima has a crime problem. Don't be overly worried – you are unlikely to be mugged or otherwise physically hurt but many travelers do have their belongings stolen. Please reread the Dangers & Annoyances section of the Facts for the Visitor chapter before arriving in Lima.

Occasionally, there are reports in the foreign press of bombings, blackouts and demonstrations in Lima. While these undeniably occur, I've traveled in Peru almost every year since 1981 (with four visits in 1994 and 1995) and have come to the conclusion that Lima is as safe as any other major city if you take the necessary precautions outlined in the Facts for the Visitor chapter. If you don't take those precautions, you can expect to have that Rolex ripped off your wrist.

Downtown Lima has many pickpockets. Be especially careful here. But don't assume that ritzy Miraflores is free of thieves. Take proper precautions throughout Lima and Peru.

Things to See
The numerous museums, churches and colonial houses in Lima are enough to keep the sightseer occupied for several days. Most are described below. Unfortunately, opening hours are subject to frequent change; call the museum or check with a tourist office or at the South American Explorers Club for up-to-date times. Entrance fees may also vary noticeably from those given here; if you are on a tight budget you should check before you go. Hours are often shortened drastically during the coastal summer season (January to March), with January one of the most difficult months to find places open all day. Mornings are generally the best time to go anywhere during summer.

Lima's museums are described first, followed by religious buildings and other sights. Lima's many churches, monasteries and convents are a very welcome break from the city's noisy traffic and incessant crowds. Opening hours tend to be even more erratic than those of the museums – churches are often closed for restoration, religious services or because the caretaker is having an extended lunch – so you have to take your chances. While the museums and religious buildings will undoubtedly take up most of the visitor's sightseeing time, Lima also has many plazas, buildings and other sites of interest.

Museo de la Nación The new, state-run Museo de la Nación (☎ 437-7797, 476-9875), Javier Prado Oeste 2466, San Borja, has excellent models of Peru's major ruins as well as exhibits about Peruvian archaeology. This museum now offers the nation's best overview of its archaeological heritage at a much more affordable price than some of the private collections. Chavín stone carvings, Nazca ceramics and Paracas weavings are all displayed here, along with collections of the best artifacts from all major Peruvian cultures. There are also exhibits from the now defunct Museo de Ciencias de la Salud, describing medical practices in pre-Columbian times as well as 18th and 19th century medical instruments. Besides the permanent collections there are often special shows on the ground floor as well as lectures and other events.

Hours are 9 am to 7 pm, Tuesday to Friday, and 10 am to 7 pm, Saturday and Sunday. Adults/students pay US$1.50/75¢.

Museo de Oro del Peru This museum (☎ 435-0791, 435-2917), Alonso de Molina 100, Monterrico, is two separate collections in the same private building, owned by the Mujica Gallo family. The incredibly rich Gold Museum is in a huge basement vault. The thousands of gold pieces range from ear plugs to ponchos embroidered with hundreds of solid gold plates. In addition, there are numerous other artifacts made of silver and precious stones and gems such as lapis lazuli, emeralds and pearls.

The Arms Museum, housed in the top half of the building, is reputed to be one of the world's best. Even if, like me, you have no interest in guns, you'll probably be fascinated by the thousands of ancient and bizarre firearms from all over the world that are displayed here. One of my favorite exhibits is a huge, ornately decorated blunderbuss. It's about two meters long, with a five cm bore and a flaring, trumpet-like muzzle, and dates from the 19th century. Although it looks more suitable for hunting elephants, it's labeled as a duck-hunting rifle!

The Gold Museum's private collection is high on the 'must see' list for many tourists visiting Peru on guided tours and admission is correspondingly high at US$5 per person. This covers entry to both the Gold and Arms museums; separate tickets are

At rest with ear-plugs: water vessel from the Moche culture

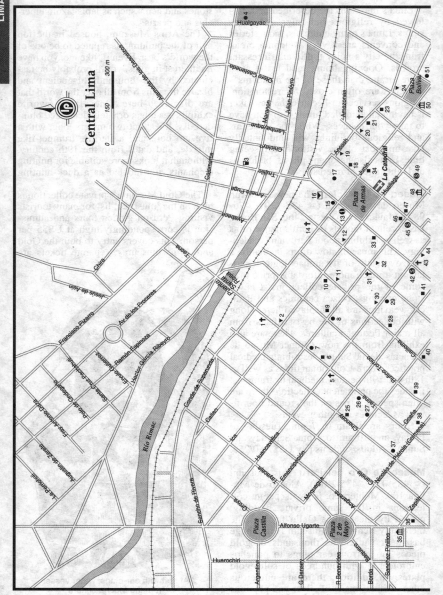

Central Lima

0   150   300 m

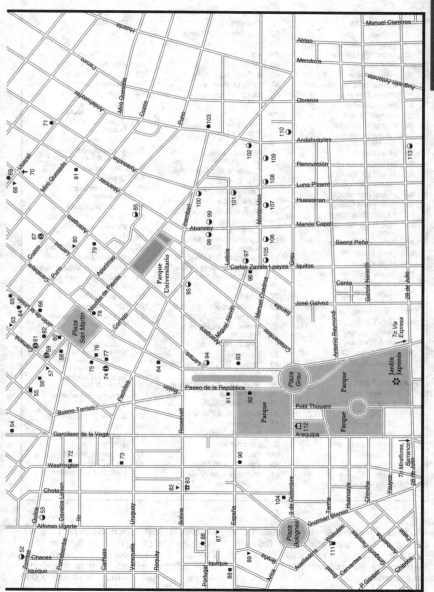

PLACES TO STAY

6	Pensión Ibarra
9	Hotel Residencial Roma
10	Gran Hotel Savoy
18	Hostal Lima
21	Hotel Europa
23	Hostal España
25	Wilson Hotel
28	Hotel Claridge
33	Pensión Unión
34	Hostal Wiracocha
36	Hostal Residencial Los Virreyes
38	Hotel Crillón
39	Hostal del Sol
40	Hotel La Casona
41	Hostal Samaniego
46	Hostal Damascus
47	Gran Hotel Maury
56	Familia Rodríguez
58	Hostal San Martín & Hotel El Plaza
60	Gran Hotel Bolívar
65	Hotel Richmond
72	Hotel Eiffel
73	Hostal Kori Wasi II
76	Hostal Belén
77	Hostal La Estrella de Belén
79	Hostal Universo
81	Gran Hotel
88	Hostal Iquique
91	Lima Sheraton
96	Hotel Grand Castle
104	Hostal de las Artes

PLACES TO EAT

2	Govinda
11	Manhattan Restaurant
12	Tic Tac Chifa
19	El Cordano
20	Restaurant Machu Picchu
24	Las Trece Monedas
30	La Casera
32	El Pan Nuestro
44	Raimondi
55	Pastelería Kudani
57	Casa Vasca
58	Parrilladas San Martín
63	Natur
68	L'Eau Vive
80	Heydi
82	El Capricho
87	Chifa La Paisana
89	La Choza Nautica

OTHER

1	Santuario de Santa Rosa de Lima
3	Hatuchay
4	Plaza de Acho & Museo Taurino
5	Church of Las Nazarenas
7	Cine Central
8	Teatro Municipal
13	Municipalidad
14	Church of Santo Domingo
15	Monumento de Francisco Pizarro
16	Correos Central & Museo Filatélico
17	Palacio de Gobierno
22	Church of San Francisco & Catacombs
26	Cine Tacna
27	Cine Lido
29	Teatro Segura
31	Church of San Agustín
35	Museo de la Cultura Peruana
37	Cine Portofino
42	Interbanc
43	Church of La Merced
45	Banco Mercantil
48	Museo del Banco Central de Reserva
49	Banco de Crédito
50	Museo de la Inquisición
51	Congreso
52	Turismo Chimbote
53	Cruz del Sur
54	Faucett Airline
59	P&P Casa de Cambio
61	McDollar & other casas de cambio
62	Cine Plaza
64	Cine Excelsior
66	Cine Adan y Eva
67	Banco Wiese
69	Palacio Torre Tagle
70	Church of San Pedro
71	Mercado Central
74	Infotur
75	Lima Tours & American Express
78	Cine Metro & CPT International Telephone Office
83	Telefónica del Peru 24-Hour Fax location
84	Cine República
85	Olano
86	South American Explorers Club
90	Cine Conquistador
92	Museo de Arte Italiano
93	Palacio de Justicia
94	TEPSA
95	Transportes Rodríguez
97	Ormeño & subsidiaries
98	Transportes Vista Alegre
99	Movil Tours, Paradise Tours
100	Buses to Chosica
101	Empresa Huaraz
102	Buses to Pachacámac & Pucusana
103	Santa Catalina Convent
105	Colectivos to Chosica; Cruz del Sur ticket office, Civa Cial; Mariscal Caceres, Soyuz
106	Buses to Cañete, Chincha, Ica
107	Expreso Sudamericano
108	Transfysa
109	Comité 12 to Huancayo
110	Olano
111	Las Brisas del Lago Titicaca
112	Museo de Arte, Filmoteca
113	Transportes León de Huánuco & Transmar

not sold. Photography is prohibited but postcards and color slides are for sale. Hours are noon to 7 pm daily. There are high quality (but expensive) gift shops on the grounds.

Museo Rafael Larco Herrera This private museum (☎ 461-1312), Bolívar 1515, Pueblo Libre, has one of the most incredible ceramics collections to be found anywhere. It is said to include about 55,000 pots. Many of the items were collected in the 1920s by a former vice president of Peru. Entering the first rooms is like walking into a museum store – one is overwhelmed by shelf after shelf stacked to the high ceilings with thousands of ceramics grouped roughly into categories such as animals, people and medical practices.

Further into the museum, the best pieces are displayed in the uncluttered manner they deserve. The museum also has mummies, a gold room, a small cactus garden, textiles made from feathers and a Paracas weaving that contains 398 threads to the linear inch – a world record. In a separate building is the famous collection of pre-Columbian erotic pots that illustrate, with remarkable explicitness, the sexual practices of several Peruvian cultures. All in all, this museum is highly recommended to everyone and certainly should not be missed by the ceramicist.

Hours are 9 am to 6 pm daily, except Sunday when it closes at 1 pm. (At this writing the museum stays open during lunch hours, thought they have closed for lunch in the past.) Adults/students pay US$5/2.50. Photography is not allowed.

Museo de Arte Lima's art museum (☎ 423-4732) is housed in a very handsome building at Paseo de Colón 125 (the popular name for 9 de Diciembre). It exhibits far more than art and its collection ranges from colonial furniture to pre-Columbian artifacts as well as canvases spanning 400 years of Peruvian art. It's well worth a visit.

Hours are 10 am to 1 pm and 2 to 5 pm, Tuesday to Sunday. Admission is about US$1 and photography is not allowed. On some evenings the museum has a 'Filmoteca' showing a diverse range of films (see Entertainment).

Museo de Arte Italiano Housed in a fairytale neoclassical building in a park on the 2nd block of the Paseo de la República, the Museum of Italian Art (☎ 423-9932) exhibits paintings, sculptures and prints mainly from the early 20th century. Italian and other European art is represented. The detailed mosaic murals on the outside walls should be looked out for. Hours are 8.30 am to 2 pm from Monday to Friday. Adults/students pay US50¢/25¢.

Museo Amano Those interested in Peruvian archaeology will want to visit this museum (☎ 441-2909), Retiro 160, off the 11th block of Angamos in Miraflores. Its fine private ceramics collection is arranged chronologically to show the development of pottery through Peru's various pre-Columbian cultures. The museum specializes in the little-known Chancay culture, of which it has a remarkable collection of textiles.

Entry is free and in small groups (you have to form your own group), by advance appointment only. The tours are available on weekdays at 2, 3, 4 and 5 pm. All groups are met punctually at the door by a guide who will show you around for exactly one hour – it's best if you understand Spanish or have someone along to translate. You cannot wander the museum's halls at will but, by listening to the guide, you'll learn a good deal about the development of pottery in Peru and about the Chancay culture.

Museo Pedro de Osma This private museum (☎ 467-0915, 467-0019), Pedro de Osma 421, Barranco, has a fine collection of Colonial art, furniture, sculpture, metalwork and much more from all over Peru. Admission is limited to 10 persons and is by appointment only. Call the day before to arrange a visit. A guided tour costing US$3 lasts about 90 minutes and leaves at either 11 am or 4 pm on weekdays.

Museo Nacional de Antropología y Arqueología This used to be the best collection tracing the prehistory of Peru chronologically from the earliest archaeological sites to the arrival of the Spaniards. Some of the pieces formerly exhibited here have been moved to the new Museo de la Nación, but a worthwhile collection remains. Look for enlightening scale models of Machu Picchu and other sites, as well as some of the original stelae and obelisks from Chavín. The museum building and grounds are attractive and quiet and there is a simple café.

The museum (☎ 463-5070, 463-2909) is at Plaza Bolívar, at the intersection of Avenida San Martín and Vivanco in Pueblo Libre. Hours are 9 am to 6 pm Tuesday to Saturday and 9 am to 5 pm on Sunday. Admission is US$1.50.

Museo Nacional de la República Also known as the Museo Nacional de Historia (☎ 463-2009), this building once was the home of the revolutionary heroes San Martín (from 1821 to 1822) and Bolívar (from 1823 to 1826). The museum contains late colonial and early republican paintings, furnishings and independence artifacts and is mainly of interest to students of the Peruvian revolution. The building is next to the Museo Nacional de Antropología y Arqueología and entrance details are the same.

Museo del Banco Central de Reserva This archaeological museum (☎ 427-6250), in the Banco Central de Reserva at the corner of Ucayali and Lampa, specializes in ceramics from the Vicus culture, as well as housing a small collection of other pre-Columbian artifacts and 19th and 20th century Peruvian art. In the heart of the city center, it represents a welcome haven from the hustle and bustle of changing money or reconfirming airline tickets but is also worth visiting in its own right.

Hours are 10 am to 4 pm Tuesday to Friday and 10 am to 1 pm on weekends. Admission is free but you need to show a passport or national ID card to get in.

Museo de la Inquisición The building housing this museum (☎ 428-7980), Junín 548, was used by the Spanish Inquisition from 1570 to 1820 and subsequently became the senate building. It is now a university library. Visitors can walk around the basement in which prisoners were tortured

and there's a rather ghoulish waxwork exhibit of life-size unfortunates on the rack or having their feet roasted. In the library upstairs is a remarkable wood ceiling.

Hours are 9 am to 1 pm and 2.30 to 5 pm on weekdays. Admission is free and guided tours in Spanish are offered about every half hour.

Museo de la Cultura Peruana This small museum (☎ 423-5892), Alfonso Ugarte 650, specializes in items more closely allied to popular art and handicrafts than to archaeology and history. Exhibits include ceramics, carved gourds, recent art, traditional folk art and costumes from various periods and places.

Hours are 10 am to 2 pm, Tuesday to Saturday. Adults/students pay US50¢/25¢ and there is a US$2.50 fee for photography.

Museo de Historia Natural The Natural History Museum (☎ 471-0117), Arenales 1256 (one block west of the 12th block of Arequipa near the dividing line of Jesús María and Lima), has only a modest collection of stuffed animals but, if you want to familiarize yourself with the fauna of Peru, it warrants a visit. Mammals, birds, reptiles, fish and insects are all represented.

Hours are 9 am to 6 pm weekdays, 9 am to 1 pm on Saturday. Adults/students pay US$1/50¢.

Museo Numismático del Banco Wiese If you collect, study or have an interest in coins, this place is for you. The museum (☎ 427-5060, ext 553) is on the 2nd floor of the Banco Wiese, Cuzco 245, and exhibits Peruvian coins, bills and medals from colonial days to the present. Hours are 9.15 am to 12.45 pm weekdays and admission is free.

Museo Filatélico Appropriately housed in the main post office, on the corner of the Plaza de Armas in Lima, the Philatelic Museum (☎ 428-7931) gives you the chance to examine, buy and trade Peruvian stamps. (The collection of Peruvian stamps is incomplete.) Hours are 9 am to 2 pm weekdays, and 10 am to noon on weekends. Entry is free.

If you want to buy stamps for your collection, you'll find the museum shop open from 8 am to noon and 2 to 3 pm weekdays. Collectors and dealers meet at the museum on the last Sunday of each month to buy, sell and trade stamps.

Museo Taurino The Bullfight Museum (☎ 482-3360) is at the Plaza de Acho, Lima's bullring, at Hualgayoc 332, Rimac. Even if you oppose bullfighting, you might want to visit the museum just to see the matadors' relics. These include a holed and bloodstained costume worn by a famous matador who was gored and killed in the Lima bullring some years ago. (Score one for the bulls!) Also worth seeing are some very good paintings and engravings of bullfighting scenes by various artists, notably Goya. Hours are 8 am to 4 pm, Monday to Saturday. Adults/students pay US50¢/25¢.

La Catedral Completed in 1555, the original cathedral, on the southeast side of the Plaza de Armas, was soon deemed too small and another planned in its place. Work on the new cathedral began in 1564 and the building was still unfinished when it was consecrated in 1625. It was more or less complete by 1649 but was badly damaged in the 1687 earthquake and almost totally destroyed by another earthquake in 1746. The present reconstruction is based on the early plans.

The interior is stark compared to many Latin American churches. Of particular

TONY WHEELER

interest are the coffin and remains of Francisco Pizarro in the mosaic-covered chapel just to the right of the main door. For many years, there was debate over whether the remains were actually those of Pizarro. Recent investigations revealed that the remains previously on display were, in fact, those of an unknown conquistador. Since the transfer to the chapel of Pizarro's real remains, discovered in the crypt in the early 1980s, most authorities agree that the exhibit is now authentic. Also of interest is the well-carved choir and the small religious museum in the rear of the cathedral.

The cathedral's opening hours have changed regularly over the years. At last check, they were 10 am to 1 pm and 2 to 5 pm on weekdays, 10 am to 3.30 pm on Saturday and closed Sunday. Adults/students pay US$1.50/75¢, including entry to the religious museum. Tours in English are available. Some photography is allowed and color slides and postcards are on sale.

San Francisco This Franciscan church and monastery is famous for its catacombs. It is less well known for its remarkable library where you can see thousands of antique texts, some dating back to the time of the conquistadors.

The church is one of the best preserved of Lima's early colonial churches. Finished before the earthquake of 1687, which badly damaged most of Lima's churches, San Francisco withstood both this and the earthquake of 1746 better than the others. However, the 1970 earthquake caused considerable damage. Much of the church has been well restored in its original baroque style with Moorish influence.

Tours are available with English- or Spanish-speaking guides. Joining a tour is strongly recommended because it will enable you to see the catacombs, library, cloister and a very fine museum of religious art off-limits to unguided visitors. The underground catacombs are the site of an estimated 70,000 burials and the fainthearted may find the bone-filled crypts slightly unnerving.

The monastery is at the corner of Lampa

and Ancash and hours are 9.30 am to 5.30 pm. The US$2 admission includes the guided tour. Spanish-speaking tours leave several times an hour and there are also tours led by English-speaking guides at least once an hour. The church only is open from 6 am to noon and 5 to 8.30 pm.

Convento de los Descalzos This infrequently visited convent and museum lies at the end of the Alameda de los Descalzos, an attractive if somewhat forgotten avenue in the Rimac district, north of central Lima across the Río Rimac. (Though one of the poorer areas of Lima, Rimac is safe to visit during the day.) Visitors can see old winemaking equipment in the 17th century kitchen, the refectory, the infirmary, typical cells of the Descalzos, or 'the barefooted' (a reference to the Franciscan friars), and some 300 colonial paintings of the Quito and Cuzco schools.

Hours are 9.30 am to 1 pm and 3 to 5.45 pm daily except Tuesday. Admission is US50¢ and Spanish-speaking guides will show you around. A tour lasts about 40 minutes.

Santuario de Santa Rosa de Lima Saint Rose, the first saint of the Western Hemisphere, is particularly venerated in Lima, where she lived, and a peaceful garden and small church have been built on the 1st block of Tacna, roughly at the site of her birth. The sanctuary itself is a small adobe hut, built by Saint Rose in the early 1600s as a private room for prayer and meditation.

Hours are 9.30 am to 1 pm and 3 to 6 pm. Admission is free.

Santo Domingo This church is on the first block of Camaná, across from the post office. It is one of Lima's most historic churches because it was built on the land granted by Francisco Pizarro to the Dominican Friar Vicente Valverde in 1535. The friar accompanied Pizarro throughout the conquest and was instrumental in persuading him to execute Atahualpa after the Inca had been captured and ransomed in Cajamarca.

Construction of the church of Santo Domingo began in 1540 and was finished in 1599. Although the structure survived the earthquakes reasonably well, much of the interior was modernized late in the 18th century. The church contains the tombs of Saint Rose and the black Saint Martín de Porras (also of Lima), as well as an alabaster statue of Saint Rose that was presented to the church by Pope Clement in 1669. There is also fine tile work showing the life of Saint Dominic and pleasantly quiet cloisters in which you can walk and relax.

Hours are 7 am to 1 pm and 4 to 8 pm daily. The monastery and tombs are open from 9 am to 12.30 pm and 3 to 6 pm Monday to Saturday and 9 am to 1 pm on Sunday and holy days. Admission is US$1.

La Merced On the busy pedestrian street of Jirón de la Unión at Miró Quesada, La Merced is another historic church with a long and colorful history. The church was built on the site of the first mass celebrated in Lima in 1534, before Pizarro's official founding of the city in 1535. The original building, a temporary affair, was soon replaced by a larger church. This, in turn, was torn down and construction of a third building began in 1628. The structure was seriously damaged by the 1687 earthquake but, once again, rebuilding was soon underway. Work started on a new facade after damage in the 1746 earthquake, and in 1773, the church suffered further damage when a fire destroyed all the paintings and vestments in the sacristy. Thus, most of today's church dates to the 1700s. An attempt was made to modernize the facade early this century, but in 1936 it was restored to its original appearance. Inside the church is an ornately carved chancel and an attractively decorated cloister.

Hours are 8 am to 12.30 pm and 4 to 8 pm daily. The cloister is open from 9 am to noon and 3 to 5 pm on weekdays. A museum is planned to open in 1995.

San Pedro Many experts consider this small baroque church to be one of the finest examples of early colonial architecture in Lima. It's on the corner of Azangaro and Ucayali in the old center. It was consecrated by the Jesuits in 1638 and has changed little since. The interior, sumptuously decorated with gilded altars, Moorish-influenced carvings and an abundance of beautiful glazed tile work, is well worth seeing. Hours are 7 am to 12.30 pm and 4.45 to 8 pm daily and admission is free.

San Agustín This church is on the corner of Ica and Camaná. In contrast to San Pedro, the church of San Agustín has been altered much more than Lima's other early churches. The churrigueresque (an elaborate and intricately decorated Spanish style, named for the architect José Churriguera and common in colonial Latin America) facade dates from the early 1700s and is the oldest part of the church to have remained intact. Much of the church was reconstructed at the end of the 19th century and again after the extensive damage of the 1970 earthquake.

Hours are 9 am to noon on weekdays and at various other hours.

Las Nazarenas This church on the corner of Huancavelica and Tacna was built in the 18th century and is not, in itself, of great interest. The site on which it is built, however, plays a part in one of the most passionate of Lima's traditional religious feasts.

The site used to be a shanty town inhabited mainly by liberated black slaves. Early in the 17th century, an ex-slave painted one of the walls of the shanty town with an image of the crucifixion of Christ. Although the area was destroyed by an earthquake in 1655, the wall with the mural survived. This was considered a miracle and the church of the Nazarene was later built around the wall. On 18 October each year, a copy of the mural, known as the Lord of the Miracles, is carried around in a huge procession of many thousands of the faithful. The procession continues for two or three days, with the holy image being

taken from church to church before being returned to Las Nazarenas.

Hours are 6 to 11.30 am and 4.30 to 8.30 pm daily. Admission is free.

Plaza de Armas The central and most important plaza in any Peruvian town is called the Plaza de Armas and Lima is no exception. This large plaza (140 sq meters) was once the heart of Lima but not one original building remains. The oldest surviving part, the impressive bronze fountain in the center, was erected in 1650 and the oldest building on the plaza, the cathedral, was reconstructed after the 1746 earthquake.

The exquisitely balconied Archbishop's palace to the left of the cathedral is a relatively modern building dating to 1924. The Palacio de Gobierno on the northeast side of the plaza was built in the same period. Here, a handsomely uniformed presidential guard is on duty all day and the daily ceremonial changing of the guard takes place at noon (get there by 11.45 am). The other buildings around the plaza are also modern: the municipalidad (town hall) built in 1945, the Unión Club and various stores and cafés.

On the corner of the plaza, opposite the cathedral, there is an impressive statue of Francisco Pizarro on horseback (actually, he was a mediocre horseman). Apparently, the equestrian statue was once in the center of the plaza but, as the clergy took a dim view of the fact that the horse's rear end faced the cathedral, the statue was moved to its present position. I'm told that there is an identical statue in Pizarro's home town of Trujillo, Spain.

Plaza San Martín Dating from the early 1900s, the Plaza San Martín is one of the major plazas in central Lima. The bronze equestrian statue of the liberator, General San Martín, was erected in 1921.

Jirón de la Unión Five blocks of this street join the Plaza de Armas and the Plaza San Martín. These five blocks are a pedestrian precinct and contain several good jewelry stores, bookstores and movie theaters as well as the church of La Merced. Consequently, it is always very crowded with shoppers, sightseers, street performers, ambulantes and, inevitably, pickpockets. Few visitors to Lima miss this street but it is essential to keep your valuables in an inside pocket or money belt.

Palacio Torre Tagle The palace is at Ucayali 363. Built in 1735, this mansion is considered to be the best surviving colonial house in Lima. It now contains the offices of the Foreign Ministry, so entry on weekdays is either prohibited or restricted to the patio. On Saturday, you can enter the building between about 9 am and 5 pm; a tip to the caretaker may allow you access to the fine rooms and balconies upstairs.

Casa Aliaga The Aliaga house is at Jirón de la Unión 224. This is one of Lima's most historic houses and is furnished completely in the colonial style. It stands on land given to Jerónimo de Aliaga by Pizarro in 1535 and has been occupied by the Aliaga family ever since. The house can be visited only with Lima Tours, who charge US$22 for a half-day city tour that includes the Aliaga house.

Other Colonial Houses Other colonial houses are easier to visit though they are not as important as those already mentioned. The Casa Pilatos, Ancash 390, now houses the National Culture Institute, and is easiest to visit outside of office hours, especially from 2 to 6 pm weekdays or 9 am to 5 pm weekends. If you knock on the closed door a guard will usually let you in for a look around. The Casa de la Riva, Ica 426, is run by the Entre Nous Society, and is open from 10 am to 1 pm and 2 to 4 pm. Admission is US$1. The Casa de Riva-Aguero (☎ 427-9275), Camaná 459, houses a small folk art collection. Hours for the collection are 1 to 8 pm weekdays and 9 am to 1 pm on Saturday. The rest of the house is shown only by appointment. The Casa de Ricardo Palma (☎ 445-5836), Gral Suarez 189, Miraflores, was the home of the Peruvian author of that name from 1913 until his death in 1919. Hours are 9.30 am to 12.30 pm and 1.30 to 6 pm on weekdays. Adults/students pay US$1/25¢. The Casa de Oquendo (☎ 428-7919), Conde de Superunda 298, is a 19th century house with an art gallery open from 9 am to 1 pm.

Zoo The zoo (☎ 452-6913), in the Parque de las Leyendas between Lima and Callao, is divided into three areas representing the three major geographical divisions of Peru: the coast, the sierra (or Andes) and the Amazon basin. Peruvian animals make up most of the exhibits, though there are a few more typical zoo animals such as elephants. The zoo has recently been modernized and hours are 9 am to 5 pm daily *(usually* – it may close on Monday). Admission is US$1.

Archaeological Sites There are a few minor pre-Incan ruins in the Lima metro area. The Huaca Huallamarca is a restored Maranga temple dating from about 200 AD to 500 AD. It is at the corner of El Rosario and Nicolas de Riviera in San Isidro. Hours are 9 am to 2 pm daily except Tuesday and there is a small on-site museum. Admission is US50¢.

The Huaca Juliana (also called the Huaca Pucllana ☎ 445-8695), is a recently excavated pre-Incan temple, three blocks west off the 45th block of Arequipa in Miraflores. It dates to about the 4th century AD. Local guides say it was built in the shape of a frog (use your imagination!) and a communication passage has been found in the frog's mouth that was supposedly an oracle. There is an on-site museum and a restaurant that has live folkloric music at 1 pm on weekends. Hours are 9 am to 4 pm daily except Tuesday. Admission is US50¢.

There is also a Maranga pyramid at the Zoo which can be seen by paying admission to the Zoo (see above).

Street Markets There are several street markets ranging from the incredibly crowded general market in central Lima to the leisurely and relaxed artists' market in Miraflores.

Lima's Mercado Central (main market) is at Ayacucho and Ucayali to the southeast of Abancay. The market officially occupies a whole city block but, as this area is not nearly large enough, the stalls and vendors congest the streets for several blocks around. You can buy almost anything here, but be prepared for extreme crowding and watch your valuables. Many people enjoy this eye-opening experience, despite the discomfort.

The streets behind the post office are the center of a black market known as Polvos Azules, or 'blue powders.' Since the last edition, two readers have sent me explanations of this name. Either it's because gunpowder used to be sold here or because *añil* or indigo, a dye in blue-powdered form, was sold here. Take your pick. Either way, Polvos Azules is as crowded as the Mercado Central, so watch your wallet just as closely. This is the place to find smuggled (or stolen) luxuries such as ghetto blasters and perfume, as well as a remarkable variety of other consumer goods and a few handicrafts.

Lima's main flower market, at the south end of the National Stadium (9th block of Paseo de la República), is a kaleidoscopic scene of beautiful flowers at bargain prices. The selection is best in the morning. Since 1990, many of the flower sellers have moved to the Santa Rosa bridge (where Avenida Tacna crosses the Río Rimac). This area is just as colorful.

The Indian Artisans' Market is along the north side of Avenida de la Marina on the 600 to 1000 blocks. in the Pueblo Libre. The selection of handicrafts here is extremely varied, as are prices, so shop carefully. This is, perhaps, one of the less tourist-oriented handicraft markets but, obviously, any handicraft market relies on tourist consumption. Better quality at much higher prices can be found at various handicraft stores in Miraflores (see the Things to Buy section).

An artists' and artisans' market functions on Parque Kennedy, in the heart of Miraflores, in the afternoons and evenings from Thursday through Sunday. It is a good place to see local artists' work, which ranges from garish 'painting by number' monstrosities in oil to some good watercolors.

Miraflores

Miraflores is the Lima suburb visited most frequently by tourists. Until the 1940s, it was a beachfront community separated from the capital by countryside and haciendas. Lima's recent population boom has made this countryside the fashionably elegant residential district of San Isidro while Miraflores has become one of Lima's most important shopping, entertainment and residential areas.

Many of the capital's best restaurants and night spots are found here and the pavement cafés are great places to see and be seen. As you'd expect, the prices and quality of everything ranging from sweaters to steaks will be higher in Miraflores than in other parts of the city. Miraflores is linked to Lima by the tree-lined Avenida Arequipa, along which run frequent colectivos and buses.

There are many beaches (see Activities, below) and a good point from which to view them is from the Mirador (Lookout) de Miraflores at the end of Malecón 28 de Julio and the nearby Parque del Amor, with its huge new statue of a couple kissing (inaugurated St Valentine's Day 1993). Another spot is the Parque Salazar at the end of Larco where there is also an outdoor amphitheater with performances in summer (late December to April).

Activities

Swimming and surfing are popular with Limeños during the summer months of January, February and March. Playa Costa Verde in Miraflores (also called Waikiki) is a favorite of local surfers and they can be seen here year round, wearing wet suits. There are seven other beaches in Miraflores and four more in Barranco. However, the water is heavily polluted at all of Lima's beaches and newspapers warn of the serious health hazard posed by swimming and surfing. In addition, there are plenty of thieves and so you can't leave anything unattended for a second. Despite the health warnings, Limeños visit the beaches in large numbers in summer and it's very crowded on weekends. It's best to go in a sizable group – if you want to go at all. Cleaner beaches are found south of Lima (see Around Lima at the end of this chapter).

Lima has several tennis and golf clubs and the 1st class hotels and tour agencies can help organize a game for you. Sudex Agency (☎ 442-2737, 442-3684) may be able to help with tennis and golf in Lima. El Pueblo Inn, a country club 11 km east of Lima on the Carretera Central, has tennis (US$3), swimming (US$2.50), riding, golf and bowling. You can go tenpin bowling (US$3) and play pool at the Brunswick Bowl (☎ 445-5683), Balta 135, Miraflores. Hours are 9 am to 3 am. Lima Cricket and Football Club (☎ 461-1270), Justo Amadeo Vigil 200, Magdalena, may allow (at their discretion) English-speaking visitors with passports temporary membership for a small fee. This club is popular with expats and offers many sports activities beyond the obligatory cricket and football and has a reasonably priced bar and restaurant.

Several hotels (see Places to Stay) have casinos. Betting is in US dollars and rules are similar to Nevada rules, with minor differences. One is that Blackjack (21) players must bet in exact multiples of the table minimum so that on a US$2 minimum table, you can bet US$4 or US$6, but not US$5. Slot machines at these casinos have a reputation for being very tight.

Language Courses
Perhaps because Lima is not as attractive a city as, say, Quito in Ecuador, fewer people stay here to learn Spanish. Nevertheless, courses are offered. The Centro de Idiomas (☎ 435-0601, 435-5970, fax 449-6437), Manuel Olguin 215, Monterrico, has recommended one on one classes for US$10 per hour and also small group classes. The

Instituto Cultural Peruano-Norteamericano (see Cultural Centers, above) has four-week classes for about US$100. These meet for two hours each weekday morning and have about 10 to 15 students per class. Another cheap alternative is the Instituto de Idiomas de La Universidad Católica (☎ 441-5962), Camino Real 1037, San Isidro.

Work
Most job opportunities are for English teachers. Pay is usually low and you're doing well if you make US$500 a month. Native English speakers can try Fermath Inglés, Tudela y Varela 215, Miraflores, or TRANSLEX on the Paseo de la República in Miraflores. Instituto de Inglés William Shakespeare (☎ 422-1313) is fairly well organized but they pay low and have been known not to pay on time. Foster and Fosters (☎ 442-7520, 422-6893) hires people with no qualifications but they don't have a great reputation. Also try the Asociación Cultural Peruano/Britanico at Arequipa 3495.

If you actually have a teaching qualification, you might do better. The American school, the Colegio Roosevelt (☎ 435-0590) in Monterrico, hires substitute teachers on a daily basis as needed. Bona fide teachers sometimes hang out in Brenchley's Pub (see Places to Eat) so you might make further contacts there. American a nd British oil workers also drink there, though oil-related jobs are not easy to find unless you have some experience and qualifications.

Writers and photographers should pick up a copy of the *Lima Times*. You might be able to sell your work to this monthly magazine – it won't make you rich but it will help pay the bills.

Special Events
There are major processions in Lima on August 30 in honor of Saint Rose, patron saint of Lima and the Americas. October 18 sees huge religious processions in the capital in honor of the Lord of the Miracles.

See Public Holidays & Special Events in the Facts for the Visitor chapter for details of national holidays.

Places to Stay

Lima offers literally scores of hotels ranging from US$3 per night cheapies to luxury hotels costing well over US$100. It is impossible and unnecessary to list them all, but this selection should include something that suits you.

Generally speaking, hotels are more expensive in Lima than in other Peruvian cities (except the tourist mecca of Cuzco). Most of the cheapest are in central Lima, with some well-known budget hotels to be found within a few blocks of the Plaza de Armas. At night, the city center is not as safe as some of the more upmarket neighborhoods (such as Miraflores) and is also dirtier and noisier. However, there's no real problem as long as you don't parade around with a gold chain on your neck and a wallet peeking out of your hip pocket.

Mid-range and expensive hotels are all over Lima; there are some excellent luxury hotels both in the heart of the city and in Miraflores.

Whether you are staying in cheap or expensive accommodations, always ask about discounts if you plan to spend some time in Lima. Most places will offer cheaper weekly rates and may give you a discount for a stay of just a few days.

Places to Stay – bottom end

Lima *Hostal España* (☎ 428-5546), Azangaro 105 (no sign), is a rambling old mansion full of plants, birds and paintings and is the favorite place for gringo budget travelers. Accommodations are basic, but clean, safe and friendly, and costs about US$3 per person in shared rooms and US$6/9 for singles/doubles. There are hot showers, laundry facilities, a small café and a roof-top terrace (that is spoiled somewhat by animals kept in too-small cages). Nearby is the equally cheap but shabbier and less pleasant *Hotel Europa* (☎ 427-3351), Ancash 376. The communal

showers sometimes have hot water. The dingy old *Hostal Lima* (☎ 428-5782), Carabaya 145 (right next to the Presidential Palace!), charges US$8 for a double or US$5 for a couple (one bed) and claims to have a hot shower.

Another cheapie is the *Hotel Richmond* (☎ 427-9270), at the intersection of Jirón de la Unión and Cuzco. It has a reasonably attractive old-fashioned lobby with marble stairs and stained glass windows, but the rooms are grimy, the water erratic and it doesn't feel too secure, which is too bad because the property holds promise. Rooms are US$4/6 for singles/doubles, some with private bath. Further along the same street is the cleaner, friendly *Pensión Unión* (☎ 428-4136), Unión 442, on the 3rd floor (go through the bookshop). It costs US$4 per person (US$3 for students with ID) and sometimes has hot water in the evenings.

The reasonably clean *Hostal Belén* (☎ 427-8995), Jirón Belén 1049, is in a large old building, has very hot water, is popular with young Europeans and has received recommendations. Rooms cost US$7/10. The *Hostal Universo* (☎ 428-0619), Azangaro 754, is quite close to several bus terminals and is basic though safe. Rooms with private bath and tepid water are US$7/10, a little less with communal baths.

The friendly *Familia Rodríguez* (☎ 423-6465), Nicolás de Piérola 730, 2nd floor, Apartment 3, is very popular and recommended. Dormitory style rooms are US$5 per person including breakfast. They are helpful to their visitors. The *Hostal Samaniego*, Emancipación 184, Apartment 801, is also friendly and has dorm rooms for US$5 per person.

The friendly and recommended *Pensión Ibarra*, Tacna 359, 16th floor, is run by some interesting women who make a real effort to keep this place safe, comfortable and clean. Kitchen facilities are available. Rates are $7 per person including breakfast.

The *Hostal Damascus* (☎ 427-6029), Ucayali 199, is fairly clean and friendly although the rooms are musty. A double room with private hot shower is US$10 or a little less without bath. The old *Gran Hotel* (☎ 428-5160, 427-1611), Abancay 546, has spacious rooms that are clean but have seen better days. (One report describes 'some rather damp smelling, friendly staff.') Rooms with private bath are US$9/12 for one/two beds, US$2 less in a room with communal bath, and there is occasional hot water.

The *Hotel Claridge* (☎ 428-3680), Cailloma 437, has adequate rooms for US$7.50/10 with bath and hot water. The friendly *Hostal Wiracocha* (☎ 427-1178), Junín 270, has rooms with bath and hot water for US$10/12. Rooms without bath are cheaper, but the communal showers lack hot water. The *Hotel La Casona* (☎ 427-6273 or 75), Moquegua 289, has a very pleasant plant-filled lobby that hints at an elegant past. The carpeted rooms are shabby but not too bad and the hot water is reliable. Singles/doubles with bath cost about US$10/12.50, but discounts can be arranged if you're staying for a few days. The *Wilson Hotel* (☎ 424-8924), Chancay 633, has double rooms with private bath and hot water for US$12.

The *Hostal Iquique* (☎ 433-4724), Iquique 758, is clean, friendly and has hot water. Rooms with shared bath are US$7.50/11 for one/two beds and US$11/12.50 with private bath. *Hostal Kori Wasi II* (☎ 433-8127), Washington 1139, is clean and has rooms with private bath, mini fridge and TV for about $13 a double (one bed). The *Hostal Del Sol* (☎ 428-1353, 428-0546), Rufino Torrico 773, charges US$10/15 with private bath. Rooms are clean but very worn and the management is indifferent. The clean *Hotel Eiffel* (☎ 424-0188), Washington 949, offers double rooms with plenty of hot water for US$15. The management speaks English but the place had a 'For Sale' sign up recently. The friendly *Hotel Residencial Roma* (☎ 427-7576, fax 427-7572), Ica 326, is clean, central and attractive and has rooms with bath and hot water for US$15/20 and rooms with shared bath for US$10/15. An inexpensive travel

agent is in the same building. The *Hostal de las Artes* (☎ 433-0031), Chota 1454, has a small art gallery and café. Rooms with private bath and slightly erratic hot water are US$9/11. A few cheaper rooms (shared bath) and a more expensive larger room (with TV) are also available.

Miraflores The *Youth Hostel* (☎ 446-5488), Casimiro Ulloa 328, charges US$8 or US$10 per person, which is the cheapest accommodation you'll find in Miraflores. The hostel offers laundry facilities, travel information, minimal kitchen facilities and a swimming pool that lacks water – maybe they'll fix it. Also in this price range is the clean *Pensión José Luis* (☎ 444-1015), F Paula Ugarriza 727 (no sign), on a quiet residential street. You must make a reservation at this popular pensión that has rooms of various sizes, some with kitchenettes.

If you want to stay with a family, try calling the following to see if space is available. *M Luisa Chávez* (☎ 447-3996), Genero Castro Iglesias 273, charges US$8/15 for singles/doubles or US$10/17 with breakfast. *Señora Jordan* (☎ 445-9840), Porta 724, is friendly and charges US$12 per person, including breakfast. The house is quiet. *Pensión Yolanda*, run by the friendly English-speaking Yolanda Escobar (☎ 445-7565), Domingo Elías 230, charges US$12/20 for singles/doubles including breakfast and allows use of her kitchen. Rosa Alonso (☎ 423-7463), Larraboren 231, Jesús María, charges US$10 per person.

The *Pensión San Antonio* (☎ 447-5830), Paseo de la República 5809, is friendly and often full. They charge about $10 per person or $12.50 with private bath and hot water.

Places to Stay – middle

Lima The *Hostal Renacimiento* (☎ 433-2806), Parque Hernán Velarde 52, is a lovely house on a quiet cul-de-sac just off the 1st block of Arequipa (just off the south end of the map). Rooms with private bath are US$16 per person, less with shared bath. Another good choice at this price is

Hostal La Estrella de Belén (☎ 428-6462), Belén 1051, which is clean and safe. Similarly priced is the clean *Hostal Residencial Los Virreyes* (☎ 432-2612, 431-2733), Cañete 826, near Plaza Dos de Mayo (which makes it rather noisy). The friendly *Residencial Los Pettirrojos* (☎ 433-8685), José Díaz 400 and Saco de Oliveros, is three blocks off the map near the Estadio Nacional. Rooms with private bath, some with balconies, are US$25/30, or US$5 less with shared bath. There are tea and coffee making facilities.

The *Hostal San Martín* (☎ 428-5337, fax 423-5744), Nicolás de Piérola 882 (on the Plaza San Martín), is pretty friendly and helpful and boasts air-conditioned rooms with private bath, hot water, TV, minibar, telephone and a decent restaurant. Rooms are US$30/42 for singles/doubles, including breakfast, and it's a decent value. Next door is the clean and modern *Hotel El Plaza* (☎ 428-6270, 428 6278, fax 428-6274), Nicolás de Piérola 850. Rooms lack air-conditioning and the restaurant isn't great, but it's OK otherwise. They have been known to overcharge foreigners, though.

The *Gran Hotel Savoy* (☎ 428-3520, fax 433-0840), Cailloma 224, is not all that grand but is OK for US$32/45 with private bath, hot water and TV. Breakfast is included. Slightly cheaper but also OK is the *Hotel Grand Castle* (☎ 428-3181, 428-3185, fax 428-6241), Carlos Zavala Loayza 218, opposite the Ormeño bus terminal. This is not a very good area but it is convenient for the bus. Rooms all have private bath, hot water and phone, there is a decent restaurant and a small breakfast is included in the rates. Slightly pricier is the *Gran Hotel Maury* (☎ 427-6210), Ucayali 201, only one block from the Plaza de Armas and reputedly the hotel where the pisco sour was invented.

Miraflores There are plenty of good, small, mid-range hotels in Miraflores. All the following have private baths and hot water. The *Hostal El Patio* (☎ 444-2107, 444-4884), Diez Canseco 341a, is friendly,

good value and recommended. Rooms are US$27/33 with breakfast or a few dollars more with a kitchenette. *Hostal San Antonio Abad* (☎ 447-6766, 444-5475, fax 446-4208), Ramón Ribeyro 301, is popular and pleasant. Rooms with TV and telephone are US$25/35, including breakfast. The friendly *La Castellana* (☎ 444-3530, fax 446-8030), Grimaldo del Solar 222, is in an attractive colonial-style house with pleasant rooms for US$37/47 including continental breakfast. Outside is a grassy garden. Also good is the *Hostal Señorial* (☎ 445-9724, 445-7306), José González 567, which has a nice garden with outdoor eating area. Good-sized rooms with TV are US$30/40 including breakfast.

The comfortable *Hostal Lucerna* (☎ 445-7321), Las Dalias 276, has rooms with TV for US$30/37. The clean *Hostal Inca Palace* (☎ 444-3714), Shell 547, is $28/38 including continental breakfast. The *Residencial Huaychulo* (☎ 445-1195), Dos de Mayo 494, is safe and friendly. Rooms are $35/42. The *Hostal Esperanza* (☎ 444-2411, fax 444-0834), Esperanza 350, is safe and spotless. Rooms with TV and phone are US$36/40. The friendly *Hostal El Ejecutivo* (☎ 447-6310, fax 444-2222), 28 de Julio 245, offers good clean rooms with phone and TV for US$27/35 including breakfast.

The very clean *Hostal Residencial Alemana* (☎ 445-6999), Arequipa 4707, charges US$30/46 for spacious rooms with TV, including an excellent breakfast. Light snacks are available during the day. The *Hostal Torreblanca* (☎ 447-9998, fax 447-3363), José Pardo 1543, offers singles/doubles for US$28/40 including continental breakfast. Three rooms at the back are smaller and poorer than others so ask for a room in the main building. Another reasonable choice is the *Hostal Palace* (☎ 447-6305), Miraflores 1088, which is US$32/40 with breakfast.

Also recommended is the comfortable and friendly *Hostal Miramar Ischia* (☎ 446-6969), Malecón Cisneros 1244, near José Gálvez. Some of the rooms have an ocean view and rates are US$42/56 including

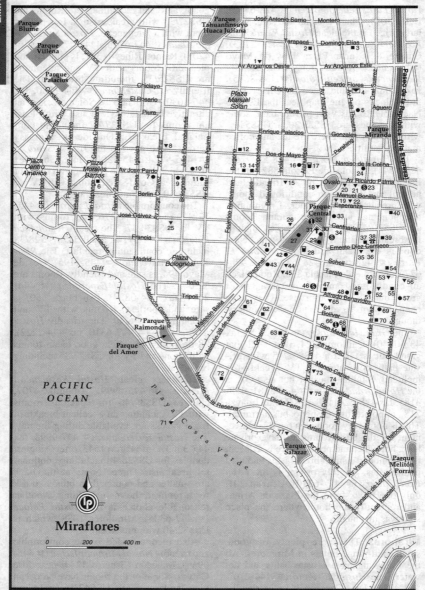

Parque
Blume

Parque
Villena

Parque
Palacios

Parque
Centro
America

Plaza
Morales
Barros

PACIFIC
OCEAN

Parque
Raimondi

Parque
del Amor

Playa Costa Verde

Miraflores

0   200   400 m

Parque
Tahuantinsuyo
Huaca Juliana

José Antonio Sarrio   Montero

Terapacá
2

Domingo Elías

3

Av Angamos Oeste   Av Angamos Este

1

Chiclayo

El Rosario

Piura

Plaza
Manuel
Solan

Chiclayo

Piura

Ricardo Flores

Av Petit Thouars
4

Aguero

5

Parque
Miranda

Enrique Palacios   Gonzales   Pershing

8

10

7

9

11

Av José Pardo

Berlin

José Gálvez

Francia

Madrid

Plaza
Bolognesi

Italia

Tripoli

Venecia

12

13 14

Dos de Mayo

16   17

15

Av Ricardo Palma

Ovalo

18   20 21   23
19   22
24

Manuel Bonilla
Esperanza

40

26

27

32

33

31   30

29   34

28

Centenarias

Ernesto Diez Canseco

37 38   39
35 36

Parque
Central

41

42

43   44
45

Schell

Tarata

54

46   47

48   49

50   53
52
51   55   57

56

Alfredo Benavides

65

64

Bolivar

66   68
San Martin

69

70

67

28 de Julio

61

62

63

Manco Cápac

73
74

José Gonzáles

75

72

Juan Fanning

Diego Ferré

76

Las Dalias

Alcanfores

San Fernando

Santa Isabel

71

77

Aristides Aljovin

Parque
Salazar

Av Armendáriz

Av Vasco Núñez de Balboa

Ignacio de Loyola

Carolina

Las Acacias

Parque
Meliton
Porras

Paseo de la Republica (Via Expresa)

PLACES TO STAY	PLACES TO EAT
2 Hostal Residencial Alemana	1 Quattro D
3 Pensión Yolanda	8 Pizza Hut
6 Hostal Torreblanca	15 La Tranquera
12 Residencial Huaychulo	18 Haiti
13 Hotel El Doral	19 Burger King
14 El Pardo	20 La Tiendecita Blanca (Café Suisse)
37 Hostal El Patio	21 Liverpool & Vivaldis
39 Miraflores César	22 La Trattoria
40 Hostal Esperanza	25 Cebichería Don Beta
47 Hotel Las Américas	26 La Pizzería & other Italian restaurants
49 El Condado	35 Las Tejas
50 Hotel María Angola	36 La Huerta del Sol
54 Hostal Inca Palace	44 Super Rueda II
55 La Castellana	45 Nonno Rossi and others
58 Pensión San Antonio	48 Tomas
59 Youth Hostel	51 Carlin
60 Hostal San Antonio Abad	52 El Mono Verde, La Creperie
61 Grand Hotel Miraflores	53 Bircher Berner
62 Hostal El Ejecutivo	56 Govinda
63 Hotel José Antonio	64 La Sueca
67 La Hacienda	65 Fragola & Pasta Subito
70 Hostal Ariosto	71 La Rosa Nautica
72 Señora Jordan	73 El Trapiche
74 Hostal Señorial	75 New York Pizza Company
76 Hostal Lucerna	77 El Rincón Gaucho
	OTHER
	4 Post Office
	5 Handicraft Market
	7 LAB, Lan Chile, Viasa, American Airlines
	9 Santa Isabel Supermarket
	10 Aero Continente Airline
	11 AeroPerú Airline
	16 Lavavelos
	17 Brenchley Arms
	18 Cine Pacífico, ABC Bookstore
	23 Banco Financiero
	24 Casa de Ricardo Palma
	27 Handicraft Market
	28 Bizarro
	29 Centro Cultural de Miraflores
	30 Municipalidad
	31 Church (La Virgen Milagrosa)
	32 Tourist Information Booth, Artists' Market
	33 Alpamayo Store
	34 Banco Mercantil
	36 El Alamo Shopping Arcade
	38 Telefónica del Peru
	41 Faucett
	42 Cine Romeo & Cine Julieta
	43 Bowling Alley
	46 Interbanc
	48 MASS Supermarket (24 hours)
	51 El Suche Shopping Arcade
	57 Taller de Fotografía Profesional
	66 Centro de Información y Promoción Turístico
	68 El Sargento Pimienta
	69 LavaQuick

Map labels: Parque Tradiciones, Mariano Odicio, Oscar Bartolme, Pedro Silva, Castellano, Juan Fanning, 58, Alfaro, 59, 60, Alfredo Benavides, Ramón Ribeyro, Paseo de la República (Vía Expresa), Parque Reducto, Juan de la Fuente, Francisco de Osollo, Av. Reducto, Parque Confraternidad

breakfast. The similarly priced *Hotel El Doral* (☎ 447-6305, fax 446-8344), José Pardo 486, has a swimming pool and rooms with TV, minibar and small sitting room. Also good is the *Grand Hotel Miraflores* (☎ 447-9641, 447-9490, fax 446-5518), 28 de Julio 151, with rooms for US$45/58. They have a casino.

Places to Stay – top end

Lima The venerable *Gran Hotel Bolívar* (☎ 427-2305, 427-6400, fax 428-7674, 433-8626), Jirón de la Unión 958, Plaza San Martín, is the oldest top-class hotel in town and a delightful place in which to wander. The hotel reputedly serves one of the better pisco sours in town and, if you can't afford a room, you can still luxuriate with an (expensive) drink in the bar. A string quartet plays light classical pieces in the beautiful, domed, stained-glass rotunda during afternoon tea (pricey but charming). If you stay here, try to get rooms on the 2nd or 3rd floor – the upper floors seem less used and slightly musty. Rooms are spacious and comfortable, with luxurious bathrooms, and go for US$76/90.

A few blocks away the modern and excellent *Hotel Crillón* (☎ 428-3290/1/2/3, fax 432-5920), Nicolás de Piérola 589, has a Sky Room restaurant and bar on the top floor with stupendous views of Lima and occasional live music. There is also a 24-hour restaurant and casino. Large comfortable rooms are well-appointed with writing desks, plenty of storage space and big bathrooms. Rates are US$88/112. The *Lima Sheraton* (☎ 433-3320, fax 433-6344), Paseo de la República 170, charges US$140 for a typical Sheraton room – clean, modern, comfortable and spacious.

Miraflores The helpful *Hostal Ariosto* (☎ 444-1414, 444-1416, fax 444-3955), La Paz 769, seems to attract famous people such as jazz musicians and writers, as well as a fair sprinkling of international business people and tourists. There is 24-hour restaurant service and a small but attractive plant-filled courtyard. Rooms cost about US$70/84, including continental breakfast,

LIMA

but discounted rates can be arranged for large groups and long stays. Also recommended in this price range are the *Hotel José Antonio* (☎ 445-7743, 445-6870, 446-6056, fax 446-8295), 28 de Julio 398, and the *La Hacienda* (☎ 444-4346, fax 444-1942), 28 de Julio 511. Both have decent restaurants and the Hacienda has a casino.

The *Miraflores César* (☎ 444-1212, fax 444-4440), La Paz 463, has for two decades held the dubious distinction of being the most expensive hotel in Miraflores (although it's now getting some challengers) at US$198/224 for some of the most luxurious rooms in town. There's a great view-bar on the 18th floor, a swimming pool, sauna, exercise room, three restaurants (one open 24 hours) and plenty of antiques to set off the essentially modern quality of the place. Service is excellent.

Other luxury hotels include the *El Pardo* (☎ 447-0283, 447-0558, fax 444-2171), Pardo 420, which charges US$166/185. They have a pool, sauna, exercise room and 24-hour room service. The *Hotel Las Américas* (☎ 445-9494, 446-9944, fax 444-1137), Benavides 415, has 1st-class rooms for US$192/218 as well as suites ranging from US$280 to US$590. It's one of Miraflores' newest hotels and has many modern conveniences including a pool and gym, as well as restaurants and bars. The smaller and relatively low key *Hotel María Angola* (☎ 444-1280, fax 446-2860), La Paz 610, has one of Lima's fanciest and best regarded French restaurants, a small pool, a casino and excellent rooms catering to business travelers. Rates are about US$100/120. *El Condado* (☎ 444-3614, fax 444-1981), Alcanfores 465, has very comfortable and spacious rooms (some with whirlpool), a fine restaurant and piano bar, and a roof-top terrace. Rates are US$130/140.

Business people can often get corporate discounts at these top end places.

Places to Eat

As with hotels, Lima has a vast selection of restaurants of every price range and quality. Note that taxes and service charges on meals can be exorbitant. Cheap restaurants rarely charge extra, but check first if you're on a tight budget. The fancier restaurants can add up to 31% to your bill in combined taxes and service charges. (The waiter then discreetly whispers 'This is the legal tax, señor – it doesn't include a tip.' Add up to 5% of the pre-tax bill if the service really is excellent.)

Places to Eat – budget

Lima The cheapest set lunch menus cost under US$2 in the cheaper restaurants. Try the unnamed chifa at Ancash 306 for large, inexpensive portions of tallarines (noodle dinners). A few doors away, the *Restaurant Machu Picchu*, Ancash 312, is popular with gringos while *El Capricho*, Bolivia 328, is popular with locals. Both are good and cheap.

The *Tic Tac Chifa*, Callao 184 near the Plaza de Armas, is cheap and clean with set lunches for US$1.25. *Chifa La Paisana*, on the 1300 block of Alfonso Ugarte, has cheap, large portions of good food.

The friendly, family-run *Natur*, Moquegua 132, is inexpensive and recommended for vegetarian meals. Also serving vegetarian food is *Govinda*, Callao 480; it's cheaper but not as good as the one in Miraflores. *Heydi*, Puno 367, is a very popular cevichería open only for lunch.

El Cordano, Ancash 202, is a little more expensive but has an interesting 1920s decor, a varied menu of typical Peruvian snacks and meals, and a great selection of Peruvian beers, wines and piscos. Hours here are 9.30 am to 9 pm, but it's often dead at night. *La Casera*, Huancavelica 244, also has a good range of typical Peruvian food at reasonable prices. The *Manhattan Restaurant*, Cailloma 225, has a pleasant atmosphere and good set lunch menu for US$2. *El Pan Nuestro*, Ica 129, is open from 8 am to 9 pm, Monday to Saturday, and has a US$2.50 set lunch in very nice surroundings. The *Pastelería Kudani*, Nicolás de Piérola 716, serves good cakes and pastries.

On Quilca, between the Plaza San Martín and Avenida Garcilazo de la Vega, there are several inexpensive restaurants. Other cheap restaurants can be found all over Lima.

Miraflores Here, restaurants are more expensive. The vegetarian places are among the cheapest. These include *Govinda*, Schell 630, run by the Hare Krishnas and, a block away, the *Bircher Berner* (☎ 444-4250), Schell 598. This restaurant gets my special award for the slowest service in Lima, but the food is good and there is a nice garden in which to sit while you wait for it. They are closed on Sunday. The lunch menu here is US$3. Another choice is *Restaurant Vegetariano*, Manuel Bonilla 178, which also has breads and products to take out.

Also fairly cheap are US-style fast food joints like *Burger King*, Larco 235, and *Whatta Burger*, Grau 120. Inexpensive Peruvian-style fast food is available 24 hours at *Tomas*, above the Mass Supermarket, Benavides 486. The trendy *La Huerta del Sol* (☎ 444-2900), La Paz 522, upstairs in the pricey El Alamo shopping plaza, has a surprisingly reasonable US$3 set lunch and other plates for about US$5. Many meals here are vegetarian. *Super Rueda II*, Porta 133, is good for tacos and sandwiches.

Barranco Try the *anticucho stands* by El Puente de los Suspiros. Although food sold on the street is generally suspect, the delicious beef heart shish kebabs served up here come right off the grill and so won't make you sick. A *porción* of four small sticks is just under US$3. Or grab a you-know-what at *Sandwiches Monstrous* on Piérola near Grau or a reasonably-priced pizza around the corner at *Tío Dan*.

Places to Eat – middle
Lima My favorite seafood restaurant is *La Choza Nautica* (☎ 424-1766), Breña 204 at Pasaje Río Bravo. Very good ceviches and other seafood dishes are about US$5 or US$6. They are closed Sunday and Monday evenings.

The *Raimondi*, Miró Quesada 110, is a good lunchtime restaurant popular with Lima's businessmen. There's no sign and the exterior gives no indication of the spacious comfort within. A set lunch is US$3.50 and there is a wide variety of other, more expensive, options.

Another favorite is the *L'Eau Vive* (☎ 427-5712), Ucayali 370, where the food, prepared and served by a French order of nuns, features dishes from all over the world as well as some exotic cocktails. It's in an extremely quiet colonial-style house and a welcome relief from the Lima madhouse. Set lunches are about US$6 and evening dinners run close to US$20 but profits go to charity. Hours are 12.30 to 2.45 pm and 7.30 to 9 pm daily except Sunday. The nuns sing an *Ave María* at the end of dinner.

Miraflores A good seafood restaurant is *Cebichería Don Beta* (☎ 446-9465), José Gálvez 667. Don't be put off by the tiny exterior – it opens up inside. This place is very popular among Peruvians for lunch but is quiet in the evenings. Ceviches start around US$7. There are several other seafood restaurants on this street.

For a good variety of standard Peruvian fare, try *Las Tejas* (☎ 444-4360), Diez Canseco 340. Most meals here are about US$10. *El Trapiche*, Larco 1031, is a locally popular place serving good seafood and meat in the US$15 to US$20 range. They are closed on Monday.

Lovers of Italian food will find several pizzerias by the Parque Kennedy in Miraflores. *La Pizzería* (☎ 446-7793), Diagonal 322, is (too) expensive but quite good and a very popular place at night; other places are cheaper but none is outstanding. Some people say that the *Pizza Hut* (☎ 440-7473), Comandante Espinar 202, has the best pizza. *New York Pizza Company*, Larco 1145, has been recommended for vegetarian pizza.

La Trattoria (☎ 446-7002), Bonilla 106, is recommended for tasty, home-made pasta (that you can watch them make). Meals here are about US$8 to US$15. Much cheaper but still pretty good is *Nonno Rossi*, Porta 185a. Also cheap is

Pasta Subito, which serves Italian fast food almost next door to *Fragola*, Benavides 468, which has good Italian ice cream. Perhaps the best Italian ice cream, as well as delicious cakes and good coffee, is found at *Quattro D* (☎ 447-1523), Angamos Oeste 408.

Miraflores has many pavement cafés that are great for people watching. The *Haiti* (☎ 445-0539), on the traffic circle (*óvalo*) next to El Pacífico cinema, is an excellent place to watch the world go by while you have a coffee. The waiters are very suave with their black bow ties but the food receives mixed reviews ranging from mediocre to very good. *La Tiendecita Blanca* (☎ 445-9797), Larco 111 on the other side of the traffic circle, has been a Miraflores landmark for over half a century and has a superb pastry selection. Nearby, *Vivaldis* (☎ 447-1636), Ricardo Palma 258, is one of the more 'in' places for rich young Mibrafloreños. The *Liverpool*, on the same block, is a similar café but always seems to be less crowded and more expensive. Of the several pavement cafés along Larco, *La Sueca*, Larco 759, has excellent pastries.

The Brenchley Arms (☎ 445-9680), Atahualpa 176, is, as its name suggests, a British pub. It's as genuine as you'll find in Peru and is run by Englishman Mike Ella and his Peruvian wife, Martha. (The couple bought the pub from the original owners, the Brenchleys, in 1990). The small but excellent dinner menu offers such delights as pork or lamb chops, liver and onions, hot pies and curries. Prices are in the US$5 to US$12 range. Beer consumption is high – British beer is not imported into Peru but the local Pilsen and Cristal seem to do the trick. There is a dart board and you can read the British newspapers. This is the haunt of many foreigners as well as Limeñps. British and American expatriates who work for oil companies, schools or embassies will be delighted to tell you about Peru's 'problems.' Hours are from 6 pm to closing time (anywhere from 11 pm to . . . ?). Meals are served until 10 pm. They are closed on Sunday.

Barranco *La Canta Rana* 'the singing frog,' (☎ 445-0498), Génova 101, is a great cevichería with ceviches starting around US$5 and all manner of other seafood also available. It's open for lunch only and has a great weekend ambiance. *Abdala*, Grau 340, is a good place for falafel and Arabic food. *D'Puccio*, San Pedro de Osma at Lavalle, has a cozy atmosphere and serves a range of seafood and meat dishes averaging around US$8. Carnivores can chow down at *La Ponderosa Parrillada*, Grau near Peña, where a meal is about US$10.

San Isidro *Cafe Ole* (☎ 440-1186), Pancho Fierro 115, is a Spanish style café with excellent cappuccinos and good snacks. *Lung Fung* (☎ 441-8817, 440-7635), República de Panamá 3165, is Lima's most elegant Chinese restaurant with an indoor Oriental garden.

Places to Eat – top end

Lima Another colonial mansion turned into a fancy restaurant is *Las Trece Monedas* (☎ 427-6547), Jirón Ancash 536. Both Peruvian and French items appear on the menu. A set lunch menu is about US$9 and à la carte items run from US$12 to US$26. They open from noon to 4 pm and 7 to 10 pm, Monday to Saturday. Also good, and less expensive, is the *Casa Vasca* (☎ 423-6690), Nicolás de Piérola 734, which serves Spanish cuisine from 11 am to 10 pm daily. The top end hotels all have fine restaurants.

Miraflores *La Creperie* (☎ 444-1800), La Paz 635, serves an exceptional array of crepes as well as other food. *El Mono Verde* (☎ 444-0518), La Paz 651, has a good selection of steaks, seafoods, Peruvian and international food. *El Señorio de Sulco* (☎ 446-6911), Malecón Cisneros 1470 (at the end of Pardo overlooking sea) is known for its excellent *criollo* (coastal Peruvian) seafood and meats. Meals here run around US$25. The cozy, elegant and delightful *Carlin* (☎ 444-4134), La Paz 646, is one of the capital's best (and priciest) international restaurants. They close on Sunday.

El Rincón Gaucho (☎ 447-4778), Parque Salazar (at end of Larco overlooking the sea) is the best place for Argentine steaks for around US$20. They close on Monday. Another recommendation for meat eaters is *La Tranquera* (☎ 447-5111), Pardo 285. They serve a US$70 parrillada (mixed grill) that supposedly serves five, though the waiter claims it will serve 10 people. They also have a special selection of meats such as *cuy* (a US$30 guinea pig), rabbit and game.

For a special meal (seafood is their speciality), I enjoy *La Rosa Nautica* (☎ 447-0057). It's in a fabulous building at the end of a pier at Costa Verde in Miraflores. The ocean is floodlit and surfers sometimes skim through the pilings. To get there, take a taxi to the pier and then ride a bicycle rickshaw the last 100 meters along the boardwalk to the restaurant door. A meal for two à la carte will easily go over US$100 here, but they have several very good set menus for around US$25 to US$35 (including wine and perhaps a pisco sour) that are better value.

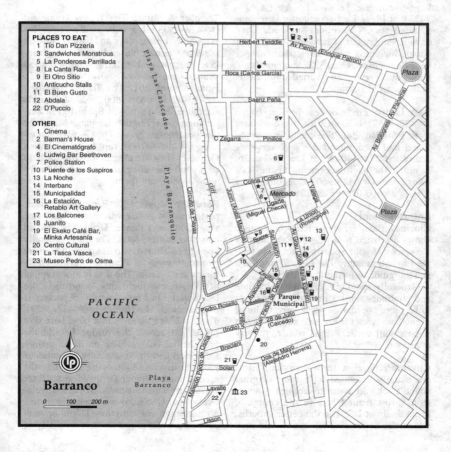

LIMA

Chorrillos Limeños recommend a newer, oceanfront restaurant which rivals La Rosa Nautica for seafood at lower prices. It's *El Salto De Fraile* (☎ 467-1355), or 'the priest's leap' – you can guess the story. It's at the Herradura beach; take a taxi.

Barranco *El Otro Sitio* (☎ 477-2413), Sucre 317, has been recommended for its romantic location next to El Puente de los Suspiros, and for its good Peruvian food and live music in the evenings. It also offers an 'all you can eat' criollo buffet with some 15 dishes for about US$18. They often have live music. *La Costa Verde* (☎ 477-2424), at Playa La Barranquito, is recommended for its excellent seafood. They have a Sunday buffet for about US$35 per person including wine. Somewhat cheaper is *El Buen Gusto*, Grau 323, an elegant café with good service and varied light meals in the heart of Barranco.

San Isidro *Los Condes de San Isidro* (☎ 422-2557), is in an attractive old house at Paz Soldán 290. The menu is international and recommended. *La Reserve de Jean Patrick* (☎ 440-0952), Las Flores 326, is noted for its fine French cuisine. *Los Años Locos* (☎ 442-4960), Conquistadores 430, is a good bet for excellent steaks.

Entertainment

Cinemas, theaters, art galleries and music shows are listed in a newspaper called *El Comercio*. If your Spanish is not up to this, the English monthly *The Lima Times* has a general guide to forthcoming events.

Generally speaking, nightlife starts late and continues until 3 or 4 am, so it tends to be more popular on weekends. Cultural events, such as the theater and the symphony, start earlier; films run from early afternoon.

Cinemas Foreign (non-Peruvian) films are usually screened with their original sound track and Spanish subtitles. Admission varies from US$2 in the center of Lima to about US$4 in the better suburbs, where the better cinemas are. Some may offer a half-price night (currently Tuesdays). You can often see the latest Oscar nominees or Cannes winners along with the usual selection of horror, porn and kung fu.

Some cinema clubs show better films – these are listed in the newspapers' cultural events section, separately from the ordinary cinema listings. The *Filmoteca* at Lima's Museo de Arte shows a wide range of films, often with particular themes for a week. Admission is only US$1. The *Cinematógrafo* (☎ 477-1961), Pérez Roca 196, Barranco, screens excellent films with good sound quality for about US$3.50.

Theater & Music The *Teatro Municipal* (☎ 428-2303), Ica 300, is the venue for symphony, opera, plays and ballet. The best seats are expensive and even cheap tickets cost several dollars. Another good venue is the *Teatro Segura* (☎ 427-7437), Huancavelica 261. The *Teatro Arequipa* (☎ 433-6919), on the 800 block of Avenida Arequipa, has revues in Spanish. For surprisingly good English-language plays, see the local theater group *The Good Companions* (☎ 447-9760) run by the British Council. They are always looking for help so if you're planning on staying in Lima for a few weeks, call them.

Peruvian Music Live Peruvian music is performed at *peñas* where you can often sing along and dance. Drinks are served and, sometimes, food. They are generally open from Thursday to Saturday. There are two main types of Peruvian music – *folklórico* and *criolla*. The first is more typical of the Andean highlands – and therefore less popular in Lima – while the second is more coastal. The *Hatuchay* (☎ 427-2827), Trujillo 228, Rimac, is in a huge barn of a place just across the bridge behind the presidential palace. The music is mainly folklórico and there is plenty of audience participation and dancing during the second half. Typical Peruvian snacks are served, as well as drinks. There's a (relatively low) US$3 cover charge and there's no minimum consumption. Doors open at about 9 pm and music starts around 10 pm.

Get there early or make advance reservations to ensure a good seat. A taxi to get there isn't a bad idea.

A well-recommended folklórico peña that is very popular with Limeños is *Las Brisas del Lago Titicaca* (☎ 423-7405), Wakulski 168. Cover charge is about US$5 and they open about 9.30 pm. Other, not as good, peñas include the reasonably priced *Wifala*, Cailloma 633, where folklórico music is played; the *Peña Machu Picchu*, Azangaro 142, is a cheap, boozy, seedy local place; and *Peña El Ayllu*, Moquegua 247, open most nights and free.

For criolla music, there are good places in Barranco. *La Estación* (☎ 467-8804), Pedro de Osma 112, and *Los Balcones* (☎ 495-1149), Grau 294, are among the best but their cover charge can be as high as US$15. There are several others. In Miraflores, *Sachun Peña* (☎ 441-0123, 441-4465), Avenida del Ejército 657 (away from the center), has been recommended for a variety of acts that get underway around midnight. The cover is about US$10.

Bars Lima has plenty of cheap but drab places to drink – almost any cheap restaurant will sell you a cheap beer. These aren't described here. The bars listed below have some local color, character, or class (not necessarily concomitantly) and they charge accordingly.

The *Brenchley Arms* in Miraflores is a good pub to meet English-speaking locals and has a happy hour for spirits from 6 to 9 pm on Fridays and Saturdays – see the Places to Eat section for more information.

Also good in Miraflores is *El Sargento Pimienta* (Sergeant Pepper) (☎ 445-6033), San Martín 587, which has reasonably priced food and recorded '60s and '70s rock and salsa during the day and good live music (about a US$7 cover) on Friday nights. *Satchmo's*, La Paz 538, features international jazz musicians and cover charges can be high.

At night, Barranco is the most happening place. Friday and Saturday nights are like big, crowded parties. It's quieter midweek. People can start the night at the politically incorrect *Barman's House*, Piérola 109 at Grau, which is a drive-in cocktail bar with possibly the cheapest good drinks in Barranco. Flashy cars driven by flushed drivers are lined up outside. You can arrive on foot (or by cab), hang out on the sidewalk with your plastic bottle of piña colada, then saunter down Grau to the more elegant places a few minutes' stroll away.

Juanito, Grau 274, is one of the oldest haunts, a leftist peña of the 1960s that retains its early simple decor and is a popular hang-out now for expats. The party crowd are often to be found in *La Noche* (☎ 477-4154), Bolognesi 317, which nestles snugly at the end of a street crammed with trendy bars. A lot of these have happy hours during the week, but not during the crowded weekends. *Ludwig Bar Beethoven*, Grau 687, has classical music, often live. *El Ekeko Cafe Bar* (☎ 467-1729), Grau 266, is another popular choice.

Nightclubs There are several nightclubs that tend to be dark and expensive with many kissing couples. Many have a members- or couples-only policy, but you can often get around this by showing your passport and telling the doorman you're a tourist. Miraflores has several danceclubs, including *La Nueva Miel* (☎ 445-3699), José Pardo 120, and the *Rosa Nautica* above the Rosa Nautica restaurant. These play fairly standard disco, salsa and rock music. For more alternative fare, try *Bizarro* (☎ 446-2895), Lima 417 (upstairs), Miraflores. There is a US$5 cover including the first drink (Thursday is 'Ladies'

LIMA

Night' when women get in free) and they have indie-rock music during the week but tend towards techno music at weekends (one correspondent writes 'Good for rave heads but not normal people'). They also have a lively pool table and a dart board dangerously perched right above the pool table.

Spectator Sports
Soccer, called *fútbol*, is the national sport but is closely rivaled by volleyball, which is of a high standard. Peru's Estadio Nacional, off the 7th, 8th and 9th blocks of the Paseo de la República, is the venue for the most important soccer matches and other events. Sometimes you can watch two 1st Division games in one afternoon for the cost of one seat (about US$10).

Horse racing is also popular. Meetings are held most weekends and some weekday evenings at the Monterrico Racetrack, at the junction between the Pan-American Hwy South and Avenida Javier Prado. I understand that, if you're reasonably well dressed and take your passport, you can use the members' stand.

Bullfighting has a good following in Lima. The bullfighting season is from mid-October to the beginning of December and there is also a short season in March. Famous foreign matadors fight in the bull-ring at Acho in Rimac and in 1993 Spanish matador Cristina Sanchez was the first woman to fight in Lima. Bullfights are widely advertised in the major newspapers and tickets are sold well in advance. Prices are expensive ranging from US$5 to US$80 for one event and up to US$600 for season tickets. Cockfighting is also popular and events are advertized locally.

Things to Buy
A wide variety of handicrafts from all over Peru is available in Lima. Jewelry – including gold, silver and turquoise – is also popular and reasonably priced. The best selections of top quality arts and crafts are found in shops and shopping arcades. Shopping hours are generally 10 am to 8 pm, Monday to Saturday, with variable lunchtime closing. Shop prices tend to be high but they vary so it pays to shop around. Cheaper crafts are found in the markets. Prices are fixed in some stores but you can bargain in others. If you're buying several items in a place, it's always worth asking for a discount. Remember: carry cash in a safe inside pocket or money belt when shopping. Cash dollars or traveler's checks can be used in some of the better stores and exchange rates are often within 1% of the best rates in town.

Miraflores has some very nice shops and although they tend to be expensive, the quality and shopping atmosphere are as good as or better than you'll find anywhere. Highly exclusive jewelry and handicrafts stores are to be found in the very attractive El Suche arcade, off the 6th block of La Paz in Miraflores. The 5th block of La Paz is also good – the El Alamo shopping arcade is recommended. The fact that Peru's most expensive hotel, Césars, is on this block will give you an idea of what to expect. Also recommended in Miraflores is Anti-suyo (☎ 447-2557), Tacna 460, a coopera-tive of Indian work from all over Peru. There are many other stores in this area.

In Barranco, Minka (☎ 442-7740), Grau 266, is a not-for-profit handicrafts store with profits going directly to artisans' cooperatives. They are closed on Sunday and Monday. Also good in Barranco is Las Pallas (☎ 477-4629), Cajamarca 212 at Grau. La Casa de la Mujer Artesana Manuela Ramos (☎ 423-8840), Perú 1550 at Brasil, Pueblo Libre, is a cooperative with good quality work from the surround-ing shanty towns. Artesanias del Peru (☎ 440-1925), Jorge Basadre 610, San Isidro, has also been recommended. The several stores in the gardens of the Museo de Oro have high quality crafts and jewelry.

If you're looking for less expensive stuff, try these markets. The largest Indian arti-sans' market is along the northern side of Avenida de la Marina, on the 600 to 1000 blocks. There is a great selection of handi-crafts here, but the quality and prices vary a good deal, so shop carefully. There is also an Indian crafts market, in Miraflores, on the 52nd block of Petit Thouars 1½ blocks south of Angamos.

The streets west of the Palacio de Gobierno and behind the Correos Central (central post office) are the focus of the Polvos Azules black market. There is a remarkable variety of consumer goods. This is the place to come if you're looking for smuggled or stolen luxuries such as portable stereos or cameras. They have a small handicrafts market.

For camping gear, try the expensive Alpamayo, Larco 345, Miraflores. Ursus (☎ 422-6678), Avenida del Ejército 1982, San Isidro, manufactures and sells backpacks and climbing gear. Todo Camping (☎ 447-6279), Angamos Oeste 350, sells camping gas cartidges for about US$3.

Slide and print film developing tends to be poor. One place that has been recommended is Taller de Fotografía Profesional (☎ 444-2304), Grimaldo del Solar 275, Miraflores. Frankitec (☎ 428-4331), Lampa 1115, has been recommended for repair of mechanical cameras.

There are many supermarkets loaded with both local and imported food, drink, toiletries, medicines, etc. One of the best is the 24-hour Supermercado Mass on Benavides at Alcanfores in Miraflores. On a Saturday night this place is packed with young Mirafloreños buying six-packs of beer or grabbing a sandwich while they hang out with their friends. It's quite a scene which easily rivals any North American mall hangout.

Getting There & Away

Air Lima's Aeropuerto Internacional Jorge Chávez is divided into two sections. As you look at the building from the parking area, the national arrivals and departures section is to your right. To the left is the international section. If your international flight arrives during the day, look for a tourist information booth before going through immigration. They can advise you about current exchange rates and transport from the airport.

At immigration, request as many days as you need; otherwise, you'll get the standard 30 days. Make sure you receive and keep the entry slip because you need to surrender it when leaving Peru. In the baggage claim area you'll find a bank where you can change money (see Money). After passing through customs, it's only a few meters to taxis and other transportation so avoid porters in the baggage claim area, unless you want to have your luggage trundled 20 meters outside the door and dumped into the most expensive taxi available. When several flights arrive at once, it can be a real zoo, so keep your wits and your luggage about you!

The usual airport facilities are available in the terminal. Local, long distance, and international phone offices, banks, and a post office are on the ground floor and restaurants are upstairs. A Diners Club Lounge that is free to Diners Club credit card holders and US$6 for other travelers makes a good place to wait if you arrive in the wee hours and have an early morning connection. A 24-hour left-luggage room charges about US$2 per piece per day.

Well over 30 international airlines have offices in Lima. Check the yellow pages under 'Aviación' for telephone numbers, and call before you go, as offices change address frequently.

If departing internationally, check in at least two hours early, as many flights are overbooked. There is a US$17.70 international departure tax, payable in cash dollars or nuevos soles.

There is a domestic departure tax of about US$4 (payable in nuevos soles) at Lima airport.

Airlines offering domestic flights include:

Aero Continente
   Francisco Masías 544, San Isidro (☎ 442-6458, 442-7829)
   Reservations (☎ 451-8280, 442-8770)
   Central Switchboard (☎ 221-3069, 221-3099, fax 221-0835)
   Miami, FL USA (☎ 1-800-249-4733, fax 1-305-346-0430)
AeroCóndor
   Juan de Arona 781, San Isidro (☎ 442-5215, 442-5663, fax 442-9487)
   Airport (☎ 452-3254)

136   Lima – Getting There & Away

LIMA

AeroPerú
  Garcilazo de la Vega 870 (☎ 433-1341)
  José Pardo 601, Miraflores (☎ 447-8900, 447-8255)
  24-hour reservations (☎ 447-8333)
Americana
  Larco 345, Miraflores (☎ 447-1902)
  Benavides 439, Miraflores (☎ 444-1246, 444-0027, fax 444-3950)
  24-hour reservations (☎ 447-1919)
  Airport (☎ /fax 452-5408)
Expresso Aéreo
  Edificio Caracol, Larco 101, 3rd floor (☎ 447-4631, 241-2547)
Faucett
  Garcilaso de la Vega 865 (☎ 433-6364, fax 433-7137)
  Diagonal 592, Miraflores (☎ 446-3444, fax 445-7649)
  Reservations (☎ 464-3322, 452-6641, 451-9711, fax 464-3510)
Imperial Air
  Avenida Javier Prado Este 1372, San Isidro (☎ 476-0775, 476-4305, 476-4542, fax 476-7799)
  Airport (☎ /fax 464-9460)
Transportes Aereos Andahuaylas (TAA)
  Camaná 828, office 102, Lima (☎ 427-0986, fax 427-2975)

Domestic flight schedules and ticket prices change frequently. Recent one-way fares from Lima were US$60 to US$110 to most towns. For destinations reached from Lima, see the Air Flights map in Getting Around. AeroCóndor does flights over the Nazca lines in light aircraft on a daily basis, and has a few inter-city flights. A day tour over the Nazca lines from Lima, including lunch, is over US$340. (It's much cheaper to take a bus to Nazca and fly from there.)

More remote towns require connecting flights, and smaller towns are not served every day. Getting flight information, buying tickets and reconfirming flights are best done at the airline offices (or a reputable travel agent) rather than at the airport counters, where things can be chaotic. You can buy tickets at the airport on a space-available basis, however, if you're in a hurry to leave for somewhere.

Grupo Ocho (the military airline) has weekly flights to Cuzco, Puerto Maldonado, Pucallpa and some small jungle towns.

Go to their airport counter early in the day of the flight, get your name on the waiting list and be prepared for a long wait. Grupo Ocho has flights to Cuzco on Thursday mornings – get your name on the list by 6 am and hope. Flights are half the price of commercial airlines but are subject to over-booking and cancellation. You might try to get on the list a day or two early, but this is problematical because Peruvians are given priority over foreigners. It is easier to fly with Grupo Ocho from an airport other than Lima.

Overbooking is the norm on domestic flights, so be there at least an hour early. Officially, you should reconfirm 24 to 72 hours in advance, but it's best to reconfirm upon arrival, then both 72 and 24 hours in advance and perhaps a couple of other times as well. Flights are changed or canceled with depressing frequency, so it's worth phoning the airport or airline just before leaving for the airport.

If you're going to be traveling in a remote part of Peru, try to find a responsible travel agent or other person to reconfirm for you 72 hours before your flight. (Members of the South American Explorers Club can have the club reconfirm for them.) Passengers may be stranded for days because, having failed to reconfirm, they were bumped off their flight and found that all flights for several days were full. This is especially true during the busy months of July and August when tourists trying to get on flights, particularly to and from Cuzco, are literally driven to tears. *Reconfirm!* – then reconfirm again. Get to the airport at least an hour before the scheduled departure of your flight and, obnoxious as this may sound, push if you have to – it can get very crowded.

Bus Both national and foreign destinations are served from Lima. For foreign destinations, see the Getting There & Away chapter.

The most important road out of Lima is the Carretera Panamericana (Pan-American Hwy), which runs northwest and southeast roughly parallel to the coast. Long-distance north and southbound buses leave Lima every few minutes; it takes about 24 hours to drive to either the Ecuadorian or the Chilean border. Other buses ply the much rougher roads inland into the Andes and across into the eastern jungles.

There is no central bus terminal; each bus company runs its own office and terminal. Lima's bus stations are notorious for theft so it makes sense to find the station and buy your tickets in advance, unencumbered by luggage.

For a description of the various bus companies and general bus info, see the Bus section in the Getting Around chapter. The biggest bus company in Lima is Ormeño (☎ 427-5679, 428-8453), Carlos Zavala 177 (it is supposedly the biggest privately owned bus company on the continent, if not the world). There are various subsidiaries at the same address such as Expreso Ancash (to the Huaraz area), Expreso Continental (to North Coast cities), Expreso Chinchano (to Cañete and Chincha), Expreso Ormeño (to South Coast cities, Arequipa, and connections to Cuzco), San Cristóbal (to Juliaca and Puno), and Costa Sierra (to Huancayo). Fast, more comfortable, more expensive long distance services are offered to Trujillo, Tumbes, Ica and Tacna.

Cruz del Sur (☎ 424-1005, 427-1311, 423-1570), Quilca 531, serves the entire coast plus Huaraz, Huancayo, Arequipa, Puno and Cuzco. Cruz del Sur also sells tickets from a new terminal at the corner of Zavala and Montevideo, where there are several other companies. The buses depart from the Quilca depot but you should check in case this changes in the future. Cruz del Sur has normal service, ideal service (slightly better bus with video and fewer stops), and imperial service (includes food and videos and doesn't stop very often). Imperial service goes less often and you get a discount by buying a roundtrip bus ticket. Fares are almost twice that of the normal service, but it's worth it to Peruvian passengers who want to sleep on the bus and not be bothered by innumerable stops. Foreign travelers may find the cheaper

normal service to be more interesting, if not as efficient and comfortable. Cities with imperial service include Chimbote, Trujillo, Chiclayo, Arequipa, Tacna and Huaraz. Ask about others.

Expreso Sudamericano (☎ 427-6540, 427-1077), Montevideo 618, also has buses to most of these destinations as does TEPSA (☎ 473-1233, 427-6077), Paseo de la República 129.

Olano (☎ 428-2370, 427-3519), Grau 617, also has an office at Apurímac 567, and has buses to the north and south coast, as well as inland to Chachapoyas and Moyobamba. Olano features (on some routes) 'bus-camas' which are buses with fully reclining seats you can stretch out and sleep in.

For the Huaraz area, several newer companies are competing with the traditional companies by offering new buses and reasonable prices. Cruz del Sur's imperial service is about US$10 and has both overnight and day services. To see the views, use Civa Cial (☎ 428-5649, 432-4926), Zavala and Montevideo, or Transportes Rodríguez (☎ 428-0506), Roosevelt 354. (Problems have been reported with the latter company's luggage storage.) Also try Empresa Huaraz (☎ 427-5260), Leticia 655, or Movil Tours (☎ 428-1414) and Paradise Tours (☎ 427-5369, 428-0740), both at Abancay 947. If going to Chiquian, the best bet is Transfysa (☎ 428-0412), Montevideo 724, with departures at 8 am every other day, or TUBSA (☎ 428-4510), Leticia 633.

Civa Cial also goes to Chachapoyas, Cajamarca and Cuzco.

For the Huancayo area, apart from Cruz del Sur there's the recommended Mariscal Cáceres (☎ 427-2844, 474-7850), which has offices both at the corner of Zavala and Montevideo and at 28 de Julio 2195, La Víctoria. For the Tarma/Chanchamayo area, there's Transportes Chanchamayo (☎ 432-4517), Luna Pizarro 453, La Víctoria. Note that La Víctoria is a poor neighborhood – use a taxi to get there if laden with luggage. It's OK to walk there to get a ticket unencumbered by gear.

Transportes León de Huánuco (☎ 432-9088), on the 1500 block of 28 de Julio, La Víctoria, go to Pucallpa (via Huánuco and Tingo María). They also go to La Merced. Transmar (☎ 433-7440), on the same block, also goes to Pucallpa as well as Ayacucho (via Pisco).

Transportes Vista Alegre (☎ 427-6110, 427-4155), Abancay 900, has decent buses to Trujillo, Chimbote and Casma. Turismo Chimbote (☎ 424-0501), Huarochiri 785 just off Zorritos, has good new buses to Chimbote. Soyuz, in the terminal at Zavala and Montevideo, goes to Cañete, Chincha and Ica. Buses for these towns also leave from further down the block on Montevideo.

For approximate fares and journey times, see the respective cities.

Colectivo This is an alternative to buses for long-distance overland drives. The colectivo taxis cost almost twice as much as buses but, as they're generally about 20% faster, speed is their main advantage. After six or seven passengers and a driver have squeezed inside, they're not much more comfortable than the buses and departures are less frequent. If you want to pay for all the seats, you can get an *expreso* and, often, can leave right away.

Companies operating colectivo taxis are called comités. Their popularity is declining as buses get more comfortable and the number of airlines increase. The main one in Lima is Comité 12 (☎ 427-1283, 427-3327), Montevideo 736, which goes to Huancayo (US$15) and Ayacucho (US$37) but allows only 10 kg of luggage (extra is US50¢ a kg) and requires a minimum of five passengers.

Train The train from Lima goes inland to Huancayo but is for freight only at this time, although it did provide daily passenger service in the 1980s and may do so again in the future. In 1995, the World Bank reportedly invested US$35 million into getting the Lima-Huancayo passenger train running again, so maybe there'll be a service again by the time you read this.

Meanwhile, you can get a taste of what it used to be like to leave Lima by rail on Sundays at 8 am when a train does an excursion to San Bartolomé, 1600 meters above sea level and about 70 km inland. The train returns at 4 pm and the fare is US$3.50.

Lima's train station, Desamparados, is on Avenida Ancash, behind the Presidential Palace.

Car Rental The major car rental companies are all represented in Lima and have desks at the airport. But renting a car in Lima is not necessarily convenient. Lima itself is a mess to drive around and parking is difficult so you are better off taking a taxi. See Car Rental in the Getting Around chapter.

Boat Lima's port is Callao, only 15 km from the city center. Very few travelers arrive in Peru by ship and most of the vessels docking at Callao carry freight rather than passengers. The docks area is not particularly attractive and has a reputation for being somewhat dangerous for the unwary.

Getting Around

To/From the Airport Taxis directly outside the airport terminal charge about US$12 to US$15 for trips to Lima and Miraflores. (They may try to charge more but anything over US$15 is way out of line.) If you don't have a lot of luggage, speak Spanish, and are used to travel in Latin America, turn left outside the terminal and walk about 100 meters to a gate, turn right and walk another 100 meters to the road outside the airport. Here, you can get a cab for US$3.50 to US$7 to Lima, a bit more to Miraflores, depending on how well you bargain and what time of day (or night) it is.

There are colectivo taxis and hotel buses available that charge about US$5 per person and drop you off at your chosen hotel.

The cheapest way to get to or from the airport is by city bus Nos 35 or 11, which run from Plaza Dos de Mayo along Alfonso Ugarte, past the airport, and cost US30¢. If you have a pile of luggage, this isn't recommended.

Getting to the airport by taxi is cheapest if you just flag one down and bargain. If you want to pay the full US$15, you can call a taxi in advance (see the list under Taxi, below). During daylight hours, there is a colectivo taxi service from Nicolás de Piérola and Tacna. They charge just under US$1 per passenger (five person minimum). Taxis entering the airport have to pay a parking fee of about US$1.50. If you ask to be dropped off outside and walk in the last 200 meters, you can save that cost.

Recent road construction around the airport has led to lengthy delays. Allow at least an hour to the airport if you are traveling during the week, more during rush hours.

Bus Taking the local buses around Lima is something of a challenge. They're often slow and crowded, but they will get you to your destination very cheaply (fares are generally about US30¢), along with the millions of Lima commuters who rely on the capital's bus service every day. Bus lines are identifiable by their destination cards, numbers and color schemes.

The *Guía de Transportes de Lima Metropolitana*, published by Lima 2000, is now out of date and out of print. If it is ever updated and reprinted, it will show you where every bus line goes, tell you whether a route is serviced by a large omnibus or a small minibus and describe the bus' color schemes and route numbers. They are reluctant to reprint, however, because routes change so quickly. At last count, there were over 180 bus lines listed in the old guide, so it's beyond the scope of this book to list them all. If you want to travel on the local buses, get more specific information from a tourist office, the South American Explorers Club, or local people.

It takes a certain sense of adventure to use Lima's bus system but, if you can put up with the crush and bustle, it's a lot of fun. Several readers have written that they enjoyed the cheap and often interesting rides. Don't forget to keep your money in a safe place – pickpockets haunt the crowded buses and theft is common.

There are a few colectivo lines that operate minibuses that drive up and down the same streets all day long. The most useful goes from Lima to Miraflores along Avenidas Tacna, Garcilaso de la Vega and Arequipa. You can flag them down and get off anywhere. The fare is about US50¢.

Taxi If you can't face the crowded buses, you'll find that taxis are generally reasonably priced and efficient. If there are three or four of you, they can be quite cheap. You'll pay less if you speak some Spanish and are prepared to bargain – taxis don't have meters so you have to agree on a price with the driver before you get in. As a rough guide, a trip from the city center to Miraflores will be about US$3 to US$4. Gringos are often, though not always, charged more.

Taxis can be identified by the (usually) red-and-white taxi sticker on the windshield. Taxis can be any make or color, Volkswagen Beetles being the most common. Those few that are actually licensed usually have a blue and yellow paint job, are often parked outside the best hotels and restaurants and always charge two or three times more than other cabs. The following all work 24 hours and accept advance reservations. Asterisked (*) companies are recommended by the South American Explorers Club.

Lady's Taxi	☎ 470-8526*
Lima Driver	☎ 476-2121
Nova Taxi	☎ 444-0336
Taxi Amigo	☎ 436-7475*
Taxi Distinguido	☎ 435-7458
Taxi Frecuente	☎ 442-7514
Taxi Gol	☎ 477-0664
Taxi Kar	☎ 445-7159
Taxi Ligero	☎ 441-4490
Taxi Noche Buena	☎ 468-2359
Taxi Miraflores	☎ 446-3953
Taxi Móvil	☎ 422-6890
Taxi Seguro	☎ 448-7226*
Taxi USA	☎ 437-7686

Around Lima

The following day or weekend trips can all be done using public transport.

PACHACAMAC

The Pachacamac ruins are the closest major archaeological site to Lima and the most frequently visited. They are about 31 km south of the capital and are easily accessible by public transport.

Although Pachacamac was an important Incan site and a major city when the Spanish arrived, it predated the Incas by roughly 1000 years and had been a major ceremonial center on the central coast long before the expansion of the Inca Empire. Most of the buildings are now little more than walls of piled rubble, except for the main temples that are huge pyramids. These have been excavated but, to the untrained eye, they look like huge mounds with rough steps cut into them. One of the most recent of the complexes, the Mamacuña, or 'House of the Chosen Women,' was built by the Incas. It has been excavated and rebuilt, giving some idea of Inca construction. The complex is surrounded by a garden and, as the roof beams are home to innumerable swallows' nests, it is of interest to ornithologists as well as archaeologists.

The site is extensive and a thorough visit takes some hours. Near the entrance is a visitor's center with a small museum and a cafeteria. From there, a dirt road leads around the site. Those with a vehicle can drive from complex to complex, leaving their car in various parking spots to visit each section. Those on foot can walk around the site. This takes about an hour at a leisurely pace but without stopping for long at any of the sections. Although the pyramids are badly preserved, their size is impressive. You can climb the stairs to the top of some of them – on a clear day, they offer excellent views of the coast.

Lima Tours operates guided tours to Pachacamac daily except Monday for about US$21 per person (six people needed), including roundtrip transport and an English-speaking guide. Smaller groups pay more per person (US$30 for four, US$36 for two).

Those wishing to visit Pachacamac without a guided tour can do so by catching a minibus – bus No 120 – from the corner of Colmena and Andahuaylas, near the Santa Catalina convent, in Lima. The bus is light blue in color with orange trim, and leaves every 20 or 30 minutes, as soon as they have a load. The fare is about US50¢. The journey takes roughly an hour – tell the driver to let you off near the *ruinas* or you'll end up at Pachacamac village, about 1 km beyond the entrance. Alternatively, use the colectivo to Lurín, which leaves from the 900 block of Montevideo.

The ruins are open daily, except Monday, from 9 am to 5 pm. Entry costs US$3.50 and a bilingual booklet describing the ruins is available for US$1. When you're ready to leave, flag down any bus outside the gate. Some of the passing buses are full, but you can usually get onto one within 30 minutes or so. It's advisable not to wait until late in the afternoon as buses are likely to be full and you don't want to be stuck in the dark trying to get on a bus.

You can hire a taxi from Lima that will wait for you at the ruins for two or three hours. Expect to pay about US$25 to US$30.

BEACHES

There are several beaches south of Lima. These include El Silencio, Las Señoritas, Los Caballeros, Punta Hermosa, Punta Negra, San Bartolo, Santa María, Napolo and Pucusana. They are crowded with Limeños during the January to March summer. Many beaches have a strong current and there are drownings every year so inquire locally before swimming. Some beaches have private clubs used by Limeños and camping is possible on most beaches outside of the metro Lima area, although facilities are minimal or nonexistent. Theft is a real problem so you should go with a large group and watch your belongings. Punta Hermosa, San Bartolo and Santa María, about 30 to 45 km from Lima, have good hotels charging around US$60 for a double room during the busy summer. Pucusana (68 km from Lima) has several cheaper hotels (see The South Coast chapter).

To get to the beaches, take a Pucusana-bound bus. Colectivos 97 (red and blue with white trim) leave from near the corner of Colmena and Andahuaylas in Lima (US$1, two hours). You can get off where you want and hike down to the beach, which is often one or two km away from the highway.

Although the beaches are popular with Limeños, the problems with currents, thieves, access, lack of facilities and shade-less desert landscape make them unattractive to me. If you have friends in Lima with a car, you may enjoy the beaches more, but travelers on their own should realize that these are not beautiful tropical beach resorts.

THE CENTRAL HWY
This road heads directly east from Lima, following the Rimac River valley into the foothills of the Andes. You'll find several places of interest along the first 80 km of the road east of Lima. Various confusing systems of highway markers and distances are used in different guidebooks but bus drivers usually know where you need to get off. The road continues to La Oroya (see the Central Highlands chapter).

Puruchuco
Puruchuco consists of a reconstructed Incan chief's house with one room identified as a guinea pig ranch. Although this is only a minor site, the small museum here is quite good and the drive out gives you a look at some of Lima's surroundings. Puruchuco is about 5 km from Lima along the Central Hwy (using the highway distance markers) and 13 km from central Lima. It is in the suburb of Ate, just before the village of Vitarte, and is marked by a clear signpost on the highway. The site, several hundred meters along a road to the

right, is open from 9 am to 5 pm Tuesday to Sunday. Admission is US50¢. Information on how to get there is given later in this section.

Cajamarquilla
This large site dates to the Wari culture of 700 to 1100 AD and consists mainly of adobe mud walls, some sections of which have been restored. Admission is from 9 am to 5 pm Tuesday to Sunday and costs US50¢. A road to the left at about Km 10 (18 km from central Lima) goes to the Cajamarquilla zinc refinery, almost five km from the highway. The ruins are about halfway along the refinery road and then to the right along a short, rough road. They aren't very clearly marked, though there are some signs, so ask.

Santa Clara
This village, at about Km 12 (20 km from central Lima), is the site of two well-known resorts, the *Granja Azul* and *El Pueblo* (☎ 494-1616, 494-2607, 446-6427). The first is more of a restaurant with dancing on the weekends; the second resembles a country club and features a swimming pool, golf course, tennis courts and so on. El Pueblo is also used for conventions and rooms are US$70/85.

Chaclacayo
The village of Chaclacayo is at Km 27, about 660 meters above sea level – just high enough to rise above Lima's coastal garúa, or sea mist. Normally, you can bask in sunshine here while about seven million people in the capital below languish in the gray fog. A double cabin at one of the several vacation hotels such as *Centro Vacacional Huampani* and *Centro Vacacional Los Cóndores* will cost about US$45. There are pleasant dining, swimming and horse riding facilities.

Chosica
The resort town of Chosica, 860 meters above sea level and almost 40 km along the Central Hwy, was very popular with Limeños early in the 20th century. Today,

LIMA

its popularity has declined somewhat, though escapees from Lima's garúa will still find it the most convenient place to take advantage of the numerous variously priced hotels in the sun.

Getting There & Away

Buses to Chosica leave frequently from Lima and can be used to get to the intermediate places mentioned above. The majority of buses leave from near the intersection of Colmena and Ayacucho. The No 200a green-and-red bus to Chosica leaves from the 15th block of Colmena. The No 200b silver bus with red trim leaves from the 15th block of Colmena and continues to the village of Ricardo Palma, a few km past Chosica. The No 200c dark green bus with white trim leaves from the 15th block of Colmena and continues beyond Chosica to the fruit-growing area of Santa Eulalia. The No 201 cream-and-red bus leaves from

the 15th block of Colmena for the village of San Fernando, passing through all points to Chaclacayo but not going to Chosica.

Bus No 202a leaves from the 8th block of Ayacucho for Santa Clara. The No 202b green-and-blue bus leaves from the 12th block of Colmena (Parque Universitario) for Santa Clara, and stops at the Granja Azul. The No 202c bus leaves from the 8th block of Ayacucho for Jicamarca via Vitarte and Huachipa, and takes you near Cajamarquilla. The No 202d bus leaves from the 8th block of Ayacucho for the Cajamarquilla refinery. The No 204 bus goes from the 10th block of Ayacucho to Chosica. Fares are about US$0.50 to Chosica.

Alternatively, take a colectivo from the 100 block of Montevideo. They leave when full, between 6 am and 10 pm, go direct to Chosica, are much faster and charge US80¢.

The South Coast

The entire coastal lowlands of Peru are a desert interspersed with oases clustered around the rivers which flow down the western slopes of the Andes. Running through these desert lowlands is the Carretera Panamericana, which joins the Ecuadorian border in the north with the Chilean border in the south – a driving distance of about 2675 km. Most of this is paved and it is the best highway in the country. Lima lies roughly in the middle of the Peruvian coastline.

The south coast generally has more travelers than the north. This is because the Carretera Panamericana south of Lima goes through many places of interest and is the overland route (through Arequipa) to those hugely popular destinations for the traveler in South America, Lake Titicaca and Cuzco.

The main towns of interest for travelers along the south coast are: Pisco for the nearby wildlife, Ica for its museum and wine industry, Nazca for the famous Nazca Lines, the beautiful colonial city of Arequipa (see the Arequipa chapter) nestling under a perfect cone-shaped volcano, and Tacna for travelers heading to Chile. There are many other places worth visiting if you have the time.

PUCUSANA
This small fishing village, 68 km south of Lima, is a popular beach resort. From January to April it can get very crowded, especially at weekends, but for the rest of the year you can often have the place to yourself.

Beaches
There are four beaches in this area. Pucusana and Las Ninfas beaches are small and on the town's seafront, so they tend to be the most crowded. La Isla, a beach on an island in front of the town, can be waded out to at very low tide. Boats frequently go

there from the small harbor. The most isolated beach is Naplo which lies almost 1 km away and is reached by walking through a tunnel. There are good views from the cliffs around the town.

Places to Stay & Eat
There are four hotels, none of which are very fancy. The best is the new *Salón Blanco*. There is also an old *Salón Blanco* which is not so good. The *Hotel Bahía* is quite good and its restaurant is recommended. The cheapest place to stay is the *Hotel Delicias*. All of these can be found on or within a block of the seafront, as can several seafood restaurants. Hotel prices are around US$10 for a double, but are usually higher during the busy summer weekends which are best avoided.

Getting There & Away
Because Pucusana is about 8 km off the Carretera Panamericana, the main bus companies running along the coast don't normally stop there. From Lima you must take the Pucusana colectivo 97 (US$1, 2 hours) which frequently departs from the corner of Colmena and Andahuaylas near the Plaza Santa Catalina. The colectivos are red and blue with white trim.

CAÑETE
The full name of the small town of Cañete, about 144 km south of Lima, is San Vicente de Cañete. About 15 km north of town along the Panamericana is Cerro Azul, where there is a locally popular beach with surfing, and a small Inca ruin. The road to Lunahuaná (see below) leaves from Cañete.

Places to Stay & Eat
There are a couple fairly basic but clean and adequate hotels on the Plaza de Armas charging about US$8 to US$12 for a double with bath and cold water. There are several inexpensive restaurants on or close

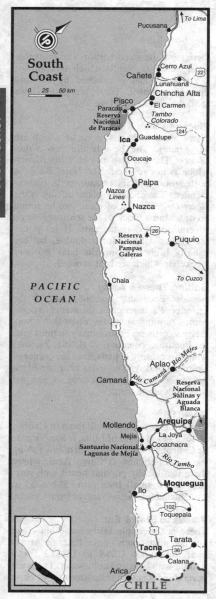

South Coast

0   25   50 km

PACIFIC
OCEAN

to the plaza. The best restaurant is *El Piloto* on the Panamericana.

Getting There & Away

Expreso Chinchano, which is part of the Ormeño bus company in Lima, has six or eight daily buses for US$3. The journey to Cañete takes about 2½ hours from Lima.

LUNAHUANÁ

From Cañete, a road goes inland up the Río Cañete valley to the pleasant village of Lunahuaná, about 40 km away. From here river runners sometimes take inflatable rafts or kayaks back down the Río Cañete. Near Lunahuaná are three wineries which can be visited. The best time to go for wine is in March, when there is a *Fiesta de la Vendimia* harvest festival, though wine tasting is offered year round.

The local *níspero* tree is a member of the rose family and produces a small yellow fruit used in making preserves. The *Fiesta del Níspero* is held in late September. The Cañete valley also has several ruins which are under investigation. Near Lunahuaná is the Ruina Incawasi and near Imperial, a village about 8 km east of Cañete, is the Ruina Ungara, and there are others.

River Running

The season for river running is December to April – the rainy months in the Andes – when the Río Cañete runs high enough. February is the best month, when the rapids may reach Class 3. This trip is suitable for beginners. Outfitters in Lima often take groups at weekends for a cost of about US$20 per person. Call Javier Bello or Fernando Parodi of Aventura Peru (☎ 440-5584) who speak English and have all necessary equipment. Javier has a house in the Cañete valley where you can camp if you want to make a full weekend of it. Other outfitters to try are Cascada Expediciones (☎ 446-6022), Peruvian River & Mountain (☎ 448-2168), Trek Peru (☎ 442-0594) and Trek Andes (☎ 447-8078). These are all Lima telephone numbers (dial 1 before the numbers). There are no outfitters based in Lunahuaná.

Places to Stay & Eat

There are a two or three good hotels in this town, including the *Hostal Río Alto* and *Hotel Campestre Embassy*, both of which have a swimming pool, restaurant, disco and rooms with private hot showers. Rates are about US$30 or US$40 a double. There are also a few cheaper hotels in the town center such as the *Hostal Candela* and *Hostal Lunuhuaná* where a double room is roughly US$10.

There are several restaurants serving seafood and meat. The local specialty is crawfish – a type of small, freshwater lobster.

Getting There & Away

Minibuses go to Lunahuaná from near the Plaza de Armas in Cañete.

CHINCHA

The small town of Chincha Alta is the next landmark, some 55 km beyond Cañete. The small Chincha Empire flourished in this area during the regional states period around the 13th century and was conquered by the Incas in the late 14th century. They retained importance within the Inca Empire and the Lord of Chincha was present at Cajamarca in 1532 when the Incan Atahualpa was captured by the Spaniards. If you have a passionate interest in archaeology, you'll find the best of the surviving ruins are at Tambo de Mora on the coast, about 10 km west of Chincha, and at the nearby temple of La Centinela.

Chincha has a large black population and the area is known for its Afro-Peruvian music. The best place to hear and dance to this is at a peña in the district of El Carmen, which is a 30 minute minibus ride from the Plaza de Armas in Chincha. The best times to go are during Fiestas Patrias in late July, Verano Negro at the end of February, Christmas and during a local fiesta in late October. During these times, minibuses run from Chincha to El Carmen all night long and the peña is full of Limeños and local blacks dancing all night long – it's quite a scene. There's a cover charge of about US$5.

Places to Stay

During the festivals mentioned above, the hotels often double or triple their prices and are completely full. Some people avoid this problem by dancing all night and then taking an early morning bus back to Lima!

A few simple hotels in town include the basic *Hostal Residencial San Francisco*, Callao 154, and the *Hotel Sotelo*, Benavides 260. Each charge about US$7 for a double. Better is the *Hostal Residencial Majestic*, Diego del Almagro 114, with rooms for about US$5/8 or rooms with bath and cold shower for US$7/10. There are a few other places with rooms in this price range. The best one in the town center is the *Hotel Seville*, Callao 155, which charges US$18/25 for singles/doubles with private hot shower.

Outside the town is the 200-year-old *Hacienda San José* (take a taxi) which has great buffet lunches, a pool, a pleasant garden and a private chapel with catacombs. Rooms with full board are about US$60 a double.

PISCO-PARACAS AREA

Pisco shares its name with the white grape brandy produced in this region and is the first town south of Lima frequently visited by travelers. It is a fairly important port of about 90,000 people and lies about 235 km south of the capital. Nearby fish processing factories can create a noticeably unpleasant smell if the wind is blowing the wrong way. Most visitors use Pisco as a base to see the wildlife of the nearby Islas Ballestas and Península de Paracas, but the area is also of considerable historical and archaeological interest.

The resort village of Paracas is about 15 km south of Pisco and is full of private seaside villas which are empty for most of the year. Because accommodations are expensive and limited, most travelers stay in Pisco and make day trips from there to the Península de Paracas and Islas Ballestas.

SOUTH COAST

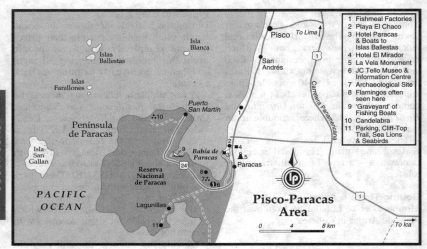

Map legend:

1 Fishmeal Factories
2 Playa El Chaco
3 Hotel Paracas & Boats to Islas Ballestas
4 Hotel El Mirador
5 La Vela Monument
6 JC Tello Museo & Information Centre
7 Archaeological Site
8 Flamingos often seen here
9 'Graveyard' of Fishing Boats
10 Candelabra
11 Parking, Cliff-Top Trail, Sea Lions & Seabirds

Pisco-Paracas Area

0   4   8 km

Information

The hotels and the Ballestas Travel Service on the Plaza de Armas in Pisco provide tourist information with a bias!

You can usually pay for tours with cash dollars. The Banco de Crédito, also on the Plaza de Armas, will change cash dollars, but traveler's checks are less easily negotiated.

The area code for Pisco is 034; drop the 0 when calling from another country.

Flora & Fauna

The Península de Paracas and the nearby Islas Ballestas make up La Reserva Nacional de Paracas, the most important wildlife sanctuary on the Peruvian coast. The area is particularly known for its bird and marine life. The birds nest on the offshore islands in such numbers that their nitrogen-rich droppings (guano) collect in quantities large enough to be commercially exploited for fertilizer. This practice dates from at least Incan times. Large sea lion colonies are also found on the islands.

The most common guano-producing birds are the guanay cormorant, the Peruvian booby and the Peruvian pelican. These are seen in colonies of several thousand birds. Less frequently seen, but of particular interest, are the Humboldt penguins on the Islas Ballestas and the Chilean flamingos in the Bahía de Paracas. The Andean condor occasionally descends to the coast and may be seen gliding majestically on the cliff thermals of the peninsula. The most useful guidebook to the coastal birds is *The Birds of the Department of Lima, Peru* by Maria Koepke. It is available from Harrowood Books, Newtown Square, Pennsylvania, USA, and sometimes from bookstores in Lima or at the Hotel Paracas.

Apart from the birds and sea lions, other seashore life is evident. The most obvious are the jellyfish, some reaching about 70 cm in diameter and with stinging tentacles trailing one meter or more behind them. One calm day when the sea was glassy smooth I was crossing the Bahía de Paracas and saw a huge flotilla of jellyfish gently floating in the upper layers of the ocean. There must have been hundreds of them. Often they are washed up on the shore where they will quickly dry out in the hot sun and form beautiful mandalic patterns on the sand. Sea hares, ghost crabs and seashells are also found by beach-combers strolling along the shore. Swimmers should be wary of jellyfish.

Islas Ballestas

Except for the people collecting guano, it is prohibited to land on the islands, so the only way to visit the bird and sea lion colonies is to go on an organized boat tour. If you're the sort of person who shudders at the thought of an organized tour, take heart. These trips are fun, inexpensive and definitely worthwhile.

Various places in Pisco offer tours, but basically they are all the same. Everyone is put into one group irrespective of where they sign up (except those who take the more expensive Hotel Paracas tour). Ballestas Travel Service (☎ 53-3095), San Francisco 249 on the corner of the Plaza de Armas, represents a number of agencies which take turns running trips.

The tours leave daily at about 7 am and cost about US$7 to US$20 per person – depending on the season, your ability to bargain and the quality of the boat. Usually they leave from the plaza or will pick you up from your hotel in a minibus. When everyone has been collected you will be driven to Paracas to board the boats for the excursion. The cheapest are ancient and

slow and may lack life jackets. There's no cabin so dress appropriately to protect against the wind and spray and carry sun protection. People who suffer from motion sickness should take medication about an hour before they board the boat. Taking the stuff after you begin to feel nauseous doesn't help.

The outward boat journey takes about one to two hours and en route you will see the so-called Candelabra, which is a giant figure etched into the coastal hills rather like the figures of the Nazca Lines. No one knows who made the hill drawing or what it signifies, although you'll hear plenty of theories.

About an hour is spent cruising around the islands (some reports say 30 minutes, which is too short. Ask about this.) You can't fail to see plenty of sea lions on the rocks and swimming around your boat, so try to bring a camera and binoculars. Although you can get close enough to the wildlife for a good look, some species, especially the penguins, are a little less visible. If you show some interest the boat operator will usually try to point out and name (in Spanish) some of the species. Wear a hat as there are lots of birds in the air and it's unusual for someone to receive a direct hit! Some boat drivers reportedly bring their boats in too close and harass the wildlife; don't let your driver do this.

On your return trip ask to see the flamingos. These are usually found in the southern part of the bay and not on the direct boat route. Sometimes the boat operator will ask for a small tip to pay for the extra fuel and time needed to do this. The flamingos aren't always there. The best times are supposedly in June to August, but I've seen them in October and January too.

On your return to the mainland, a minibus will take you back to Pisco in time for lunch. If you want to stay longer in Paracas, you'll have to make your own way back.

Warning A reader reports that one of the guides on this tour offered her drugs. Beware of crooked guides.

ROB RACHOWIECKI

Peruvian Boobies on Islas Ballestas

SOUTH COAST

Archaeology in the Paracas Area

Pisco is an oasis watered by the river of the same name, but the surrounding countryside is barren and sandy desert typical of Peru's coast. Early in the 20th century, no one suspected that the drifting dunes of this arid area had covered the site of a well-developed culture which predated the Incas by more than a thousand years. It was not until 1925 that the Peruvian archaeologist JC Tello discovered burial sites of the Paracas culture which existed in the area from about 1300 BC until 200 AD. These people are considered to have produced the finest textiles known in the pre-Columbian Americas.

Little is known about the early Paracas culture, Paracas Antiguo, except that it was influenced by the Chavín Horizon. Most of our knowledge is about the middle and later Paracas culture from about 500 BC to 200 AD. This is divided into two periods known as Paracas Cavernas and Paracas Necropolis, named after the main burial sites discovered.

Cavernas is the middle period (500 BC to 300 BC) and is characterized by communal bottle-shaped tombs which were dug into the ground at the bottom of a vertical shaft which was often to a depth of six meters or more. Several dozen bodies of varying ages and both sexes – possibly family groups – were buried in some of these tombs. They were wrapped in relatively coarse cloth and accompanied by funereal offerings of bone and clay musical instruments, decorated gourds and well-made ceramics.

Paracas Necropolis (300 BC to 100 AD) is the site that yielded the treasure trove of exquisite textiles for which the Paracas culture is now known. This burial site is about 20 km south of Pisco and can still be seen, despite the coverage of drifting sands. It is near the Museo JC Tello on the north side of Cerro Colorado on the isthmus joining the Península de Paracas with the mainland.

The Necropolis consisted of a roughly rectangular walled enclosure in which more than 400 funerary bundles were found. Each consisted of an older mummified man (who was probably a nobleman or priest) wrapped in many layers of weavings. It is these textiles which are marveled at by visitors now. They average about 1 by 2½ meters in size, although one measuring 4 by 26 meters has been found. This size is in itself remarkable because weavings wider than the span of the weaver's arms (a bit over a meter) are rarely found in Peru. The textiles consist of a wool or cotton background embroidered with multicolored and

Garments from Paracas

Península de Paracas

Tours to the Península de Paracas from Pisco are not quite so frequent. They can be combined with an Islas Ballestas Tour to make a full day excursion. Costs of this tour are about the same as the Islas Ballestas Tour, and a discount for combining them can normally be arranged. A tour to the peninsula will often include a chance to view a flamingo colony from land. The Hotel Paracas will organize an expensive tour. Alternatively, hire your own taxi in Pisco and try to get a group together. A half-day taxi hire will cost about US$25. Another option is to catch the colectivo into Paracas village and walk, but allow yourself plenty of time. Bring food and, more importantly, plenty of drinking water.

Near the entrance to Paracas village is an obelisk commemorating the landing of the liberator San Martín. (See the sidebar Of Flags and Flamingos.) The bus continues further in and will drop you in front of the Hotel Paracas if you ask the driver. It's

Detail of a Paracas Necropolis textile

exceptionally detailed small figures. These are repeated again and again until often the entire weaving is covered by a pattern of embroidered designs. Motifs such as fish and seabirds, reflecting the proximity to the ocean, are popular, as are other zoomorphic and geometric designs.

It is best to visit the Lima museums to view the Paracas mummies, textiles and other artifacts. The Museo Nacional and the Museo Rafael Larco Herrera are particularly recommended. In the Pisco-Paracas region, visit the Museo JC Tello in the Península de Paracas and the excellent Museo Regional in the departmental capital of Ica.

Our knowledge is vague about what happened in the area during the thousand years after the Paracas culture disintegrated. A short distance to the southeast, the Nazca culture became important for several centuries after the disappearance of the Paracas culture. This in turn gave way to Wari influence from the mountains. After the sudden disappearance of the Wari Empire, the area became dominated by the Ica culture which was similar to and perhaps part of the Chincha Empire. They in turn were conquered by the Incas.

About this time a remarkable settlement was built by the expanding Incas, one which is perhaps the best preserved early Inca site to be found in the desert lowlands today. This is Tambo Colorado, so called for the red-painted walls of some of the buildings. Hallmarks of Inca architecture such as trapezoid-shaped niches, windows and doorways are evident, although the buildings were made not from rock but from adobe bricks. It is about 50 km inland from Pisco and although not as spectacular as the Inca ruins in the Cuzco area, archaeology enthusiasts or travelers with the time will find it worth a visit. ■

worth going into the hotel to look at the large-scale wall map and the books for sale in its gift shop.

Continue on foot either along the tarmac road south of Paracas or, better still, walk along the beach from the hotel and look for seashore life.

About 3 km south of the hotel on the road is a park entry point where a US$1 fee may be charged, though it's not always open. You can see it from the beach. A park complex is about 2 km beyond the

entrance. Here you'll find an information center and the Museo JC Tello. The information center is free and the museum charges about US$1 for entry. Unfortunately, the museum's best pieces were stolen a few years ago, but a small collection of weavings and other artifacts remains. A few hundred meters behind this complex is the Paracas Necropolis, though there's not much to see. Flamingos are often seen in the bay in front of the complex.

Beyond the park complex the tarmac road continues around the peninsula, past a graveyard of old fishing boats, to Puerto San Martín, which is a smelly and uninteresting fish meal plant and port on the northern tip of the peninsula. It's best to forget the tarmac road and head out on one of the dirt roads crossing the peninsula.

The first dirt road branches left from the tarmac, a few hundred meters beyond the park complex. after 6 km it reaches the little fishing village of Lagunillas where you'll probably find someone to cook fresh fish for you. The road continues about 5 km more, roughly keeping parallel to the coast, then comes to a parking lot from where a footpath leads to a cliff-top lookout. Here there are grand views of the ocean with a sea lion colony on the rocks below and plenty of seabirds gliding by. Continue further in if you're adventurous.

You can also take a rough track to the Candelabra, but it's a long way. Shortly before Puerto San Martín a dirt road branches from the tarmac and heads for the site, about 7 km away. If you want to spend a lot of time exploring the Península de Paracas, obtain topographic map 28-K from the Instituto Geográfico Nacional in Lima.

Tambo Colorado
The easiest way to visit this early Incan coastal site is to hire a taxi in Pisco for half a day, which will cost about US$30 if you bargain. Otherwise you can take a Pisco-Ayacucho bus. The road goes through the middle of the site, so you can't miss it. Once you get to the site, ask the locals about when to expect a return bus from the mountains – there's usually one every afternoon. An on-site caretaker will answer your questions and collect a fee of about US$1.

Places to Stay
Due to the nearby fishing industry, Pisco is occasionally full of fishing folk, hotels are booked out and prices rise. This is unpredictable because in order to avoid overfishing, short seasons are periodically declared. These last a few days every few months and are the times to avoid – but no one knows for sure when an open season will be declared.

Pisco is a popular destination during national holidays, especially the Fiestas Patrias (July 28) when every hotel is full and prices reportedly triple for beds and tours.

Places to Stay – bottom end
The *Hostal Pisco*, on the plaza, charges about US$4 per person in rooms with shared and not very clean baths, and their prices tend to fluctuate. They have hot water. Rooms with private bath are about US$10 double. This place is popular with budget travelers, but mixed reports have been received. Various readers have described it as friendly, dirty, helpful, a hassle for single women, good, run down, clean, short on single rooms, having plenty of hot water, overpriced, the cheapest . . . Take your pick. They have a business card which (illegally) reproduces my Pisco map on the back. My lawyer advises me to wait until the Hotel Pisco gets bought by the Hilton chain, then I can sue and retire.

The *Hotel Colonial*, on the Plaza Belén, charges US$9/13 for a double/triple with shared bath. There aren't any singles but the showers are hot and the place is clean.

Of Flags & Flamingos
Local guides tell a perhaps apocryphal story of how the liberator, General José de San Martín, landed on the beaches of Paracas on September 8, 1820. Tired after a long journey, the general dozed off on the beach. When he awoke, he was dazzled by the view of a flamboyance of flamingos flying by. The outstretched wings in the setting sun gave San Martín the inspiration for the red outer panels of what is now the Peruvian flag. ■

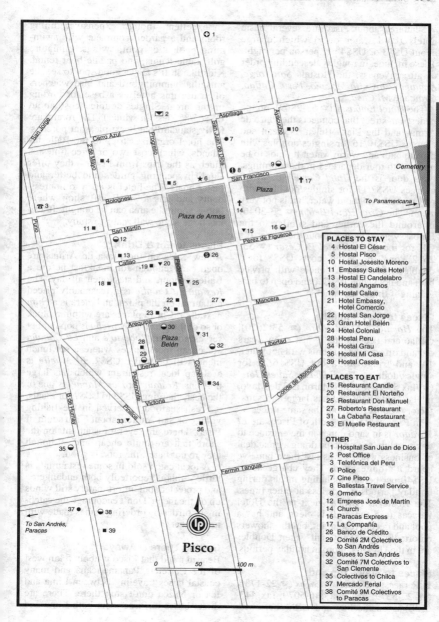

To Panamericana →

To San Andrés,
Paracas ←

Pisco

0   50   100 m

PLACES TO STAY
4 Hostal El César
5 Hostal Pisco
10 Hostal Josesito Moreno
11 Embassy Suites Hotel
13 Hostal El Candelabro
18 Hostal Angamos
19 Hostal Callao
21 Hotel Embassy,
    Hotel Comercio
22 Hostal San Jorge
23 Gran Hotel Belén
24 Hotel Colonial
28 Hostal Peru
34 Hostal Grau
36 Hostal Mi Casa
39 Hostal Cassia

PLACES TO EAT
15 Restaurant Candie
20 Restaurant El Norteño
25 Restaurant Don Manuel
27 Roberto's Restaurant
31 La Cabaña Restaurant
33 El Muelle Restaurant

OTHER
1 Hospital San Juan de Dios
2 Post Office
3 Telefónica del Peru
6 Police
7 Cine Pisco
8 Ballestas Travel Service
9 Ormeño
12 Empresa José de Martín
14 Church
16 Paracas Express
26 Banco de Crédito
29 Comité 2M Colectivos
    to San Andrés
30 Buses to San Andrés
32 Comité 7M Colectivos to
    San Clemente
35 Colectivos to Chilca
37 Mercado Ferial
38 Comité 9M Colectivos
    to Paracas

Scattered about Pisco are several basic hotels (cold water only) which charge about US$3 or US$4 per person per night. These include, in roughly descending order of attractiveness, the Hostals *San Jorge, Angamos, Josesito Moreno, Peru, Callao, Grau* and *Mi Casa*.

The *Hotel Embassy* (☎ 53-2809), on the pedestrian street that connects the Plaza de Armas and the Plaza Belén, is clean and charges US$10/16 for singles/doubles with private bath and warm water. It tends to be noisy with tour departees in the mornings. Next door is the *Hotel Comercio*, which charges US$7/11 for singles/doubles with private bath and tepid water, but is not very clean. The *Gran Hotel Belén* (☎ 53-3046) is around the corner and similar to the Embassy and charges about the same. It's OK for the price. *Hostal El César* (☎ 53-2512), on 2 de Mayo, costs US$8 for a double, US$15 for a double with private bath and hot water. It's OK and open to bargaining if things are quiet.

Places to Stay – middle
The *Hostal El Candelabro* (☎ 53-2620), Callao and Pedemonte, is just a few years old and offers decent rooms with hot water, TV and fridge for about US$16/24 for singles/doubles. The *Embassy Suites Hotel* (☎ /fax 53-2040), San Martín at 2 de Mayo, is also quite new and has large and satisfactory rooms for about the same price.

In Paracas, 15 km south of Pisco, the *El Mirador* is in sand dunes at the entrance to town. It didn't seem to be doing a great deal of business when I was last there but I've heard it's quite good. They charge about US$40 per person including meals during holiday periods, much less at other times. The *Hostería Paracas* next to the Hotel Paracas (see top end) is clean and has a pool and decent restaurant, but the showers reportedly spout only salt water. Doubles are in the US$30s, more in holiday periods.

Places to Stay – top end
In Paracas, the *Hotel Paracas* (☎ 22-1736, fax 22-5379; in Lima 446-5079, fax 447-6548) is on the bay and is the best with

an excellent, though expensive, dining room and a garden complete with swimming pool, kids pool, swings, miniature golf, table tennis, and paddle boat rental. Kids like it. It's also a good spot to see the amazilia hummingbird and bird watchers often use this hotel as a base for birding in the area. Singles/doubles cost about US$65/85 (less in winter). The rooms are fairly standard but boast pleasant porches. The hotel organizes trips to the Ballestas Islands, which cost two or three times as much as the trips from Pisco – they offer English speaking guides and better and faster boats. The hotel is open to nonresidents and has a small gift shop where books about the area can be bought. It also has large-scale wall maps to study.

Places to Eat & Drink
A few cafés on the Plaza de Armas are open early enough for breakfast before a Ballestas tour, and stay open all day. The *Restaurant Candie* is a reasonably priced restaurant on the plaza, and there is a *chifa* next door. Cheap places are within a block or so of the plaza: *El Norteño* is popular but serves no beer, *Roberto's* and *La Cabaña* are cheap local places where a set lunch menu will be under US$2. *El Muelle* is a cheap local restaurant which has large portions. *Restaurant Don Manuel* is one of the best, charging US$2 to US$7 for meals.

Fresh seafood is served in the fishing village of San Andrés, about 5 km south of Pisco. There are several restaurants on the shore that are quite cheap and, although they're not fancy, the food is good.

A local catch sold in some restaurants is turtle – this is reportedly both endangered and protected, but unfortunately still winds up on the menu. Don't encourage the catching of turtles by ordering dishes made with turtle meat.

Getting There & Away
Bear in mind that Pisco is about 5 km west of the Carretera Panamericana and many coastal buses traveling between Lima and Ica or Nazca don't stop there. There are direct buses to Pisco from both Lima and

Ica. If you're not on a direct bus make sure you ask if the bus goes into Pisco or you may be left at the turn-off with 5 km to walk. Local buses between the turn-off and Pisco stop by sporadically and charge US25¢.

The Ormeño bus company has a terminal a block away from the Plaza de Armas. Buses leave for Lima (US$4, 4 hours) and Ica (US$1, 1½ hours) roughly every hour. Ormeño also has several buses a day to Nazca (US$3.50, 3½ hours) and three buses to Arequipa (US$12, 16 hours). A couple of buses a day go up to Ayacucho (US$11) and tickets can be bought for Cuzco, but a change of bus is involved. (The bus ride between Nazca and Abancay en route to Cuzco is not recommended at this time because of bandit activity. Ask which route the bus takes.)

Other long distance bus companies include Paracas Express and Empresa José de San Martín, both with several daily buses to and from Lima.

To get to Paracas it's best to first go to Pisco and then catch a local bus, although Paracas Express will go on to Paracas from Lima if there's enough demand.

Getting Around

Comité 9M colectivos to Paracas leave from the market about every half hour and cost US50¢. Comité 2M colectivos to San Andrés leave every few minutes for US20¢. Buses usually leave when they're full, so if you go to San Andrés and then try and continue to Paracas you may wait a long time. It's often better to return to Pisco and take the Paracas bus from the market.

ICA

Ica is a pleasant colonial town of about 150,000 people. It was founded by Jerónimo Luis de Cabrera in 1563 and is the capital of the Department of Ica. It lies about 305 km south of Lima and 80 km from Pisco. The Carretera Panamericana heads inland from Pisco, rising gently to 420 meters above sea level at Ica. Because of this, the town is high enough to rise above the coastal garúa (sea mist) and the

climate is dry and sunny. The desert surrounding Ica is noted for its huge sand dunes.

Many visitors stop here. Ica is irrigated by the river of the same name and the oasis is famous for its grapes. There is a thriving wine and pisco industry and the distilleries and wineries can be visited. There are attractive colonial churches, an excellent museum and several annual fiestas.

Information

Tourist Office This is at Grau 148 and is open from 8 am to 2.30 pm Monday to Friday. The people there are helpful.

Money The Banco de Crédito on the Plaza de Armas changes traveler's checks and cash. Money changers on the street nearby will also change cash. Rates are slightly less favorable than in Lima or Arequipa.

Post & Telecommunications The post office is at the corner of San Martín and Chiclayo. The main Telefónica del Peru office is at San Martín and Huánuco but a more convenient one is on the plaza. The area code for Ica is 034.

Dangers & Annoyances I have received reports of theft in Ica. It's a quiet looking town but stay alert, particularly in the bus terminal and market areas.

Wineries

Wineries and distilleries are known as *bodegas* and can be visited year round, but the best time is during the grape harvest from late February until early April. At other times there's not much to see.

The best of Peru's wine comes from the Tacama and Ocucaje wineries. Unfortunately, these are among the most difficult to visit because they are fairly isolated. The Vista Alegre winery makes reasonable wine and is the easiest of the large commercial wineries to visit. In addition to wine, they are a large producer of pisco. Some smaller family-run wineries can also be visited.

To get to the Vista Alegre winery, walk

SOUTH COAST

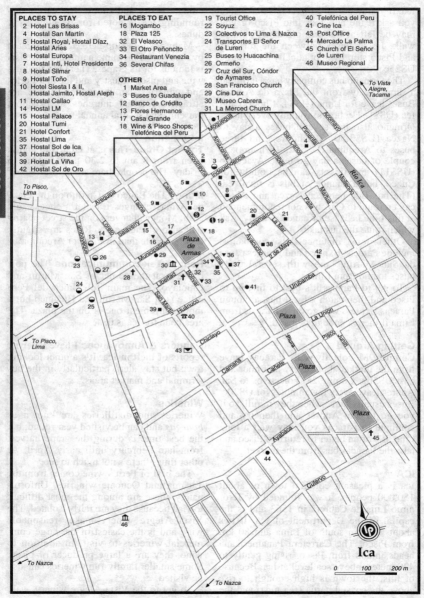

PLACES TO STAY
2 Hotel Las Brisas
4 Hostal San Martín
5 Hostal Royal, Hostal Díaz,
   Hostal Aries
6 Hostal Europa
7 Hostal Inti, Hotel Presidente
8 Hostal Silmar
9 Hostal Toño
10 Hotel Siesta I & II,
   Hostal Jaimito, Hostal Aleph
11 Hostal Callao
14 Hostal LM
15 Hostal Palace
20 Hostal Tumi
21 Hotel Confort
35 Hostal Lima
37 Hostal Sol de Ica
38 Hostal Libertad
39 Hostal La Viña
42 Hostal Sol de Oro

PLACES TO EAT
16 Mogambo
18 Plaza 125
32 El Velasco
33 El Otro Peñoncito
34 Restaurant Venezia
36 Several Chifas

OTHER
1 Market Area
3 Buses to Guadalupe
12 Banco de Crédito
13 Flores Hermanos
17 Casa Grande
18 Wine & Pisco Shops;
   Telefónica del Peru

19 Tourist Office
22 Soyuz
23 Colectivos to Lima & Nazca
24 Transportes El Señor
   de Luren
25 Buses to Huacachina
26 Ormeño
27 Cruz del Sur, Cóndor
   de Aymares
28 San Francisco Church
29 Cine Dux
30 Museo Cabrera
31 La Merced Church

40 Telefónica del Peru
41 Cine Ica
43 Post Office
44 Mercado La Palma
45 Church of El Señor
   de Luren
46 Museo Regional

Ica

0   100   200 m

across the Grau bridge and take the second left turnoff. It's about a 3 km walk and all the locals know it. However, this walk goes through a rough neighborhood so you may want to take a taxi or bus. The Nos 8 or 13 city buses go near there via the main plaza. The entrance to the winery is a large yellow-brick arch. It's open from 9 am to 5 pm on weekdays, but it's best to go in the morning as they often close in the afternoon, despite a sign to the contrary. Reportedly, it closes completely in November. About 8 km farther is the Tacama winery, but no buses go there so you'll have to hire a taxi or walk. The Ocucaje winery is about 36 km south of Ica and a short distance off the Carretera Panamericana. Again, you need to hire a taxi to get there although it might be possible to take a bus bound for Nazca and get off at the Ocucaje turnoff.

The easiest of the small local bodegas to visit are in the suburbs of Guadalupe, about 3 km before Ica on the road from Lima. City buses frequently depart for here from opposite the Hostal Europa in Ica. In Guadalupe you'll find the Bodegas Peña, Lovera and El Carmel within a block or two of the plaza. These are very small operations compared to the larger wineries. There are many stalls selling huge bottles of various kinds of piscos and wines. Also recommended, the Bodega Catador is 7 or 8 km south of Ica and can be reached by the blue and white R6 bus leaving from Lambayeque and Grau. Apart from wine and pisco, they have a gift shop and a restaurant with dancing in the evenings during the harvest.

Museo Regional de Ica
Don't miss this museum in the southwestern suburbs; it's about 1½ km from the city center and can be reached by taking bus No 17 from the Plaza de Armas. It's also a pleasant walk. The museum is open from 8 am to 6 pm on weekdays, 9 am to 6 pm on Saturdays and 9 am to 1 pm on Sunday. Admission is US$1.20 or US50¢ for students with ID. There is an extra US$1.50 or US$2 fee for cameras or video recorders.

This is one of the best small regional museums in Peru. It is very informative and well laid out and because it's fairly small you don't feel overwhelmed and can learn a great deal. Interesting maps and paintings can be bought as souvenirs.

There are excellent collections of artifacts from the Paracas, Nazca and Inca cultures and some superb examples of Paracas weavings as well as textiles made from feathers. There are beautiful Nazca ceramics, well-preserved mummies, trepanned skulls and trophy heads, *quipus* (the knotted strings used by the Incas as mnemonic devices) and many other objects.

Museo Cabrera
The Cabrera stone museum is on the Plaza de Armas. There's no sign but you'll find it at Bolívar 170. It's one of the strangest museums you'll ever see, consisting of a collection of 11,000 carved stones and boulders that depict pre-Columbian surgical techniques and day-to-day living. The owner, Dr Javier Cabreras (who is descended from the city founder) claims that these stones are hundreds of years old, but most authorities don't believe him. You can see some of the stones in the museum entrance, but for a proper look at them and a guided tour you must shell out US$5! The museum is open from 9 am to 1 pm and from 4 to 8 pm, but may close on Sunday.

Churches
The rather bare church of **San Francisco** has some fine stained-glass windows. The church of **La Merced** was rebuilt in 1874 and contains finely carved wooden altars. The **cathedral** contains the tomb of a local priest, Padre Guatemala, to whom miracles have been attributed. The church of **El Señor de Luren** boasts an image of the Lord which is venerated by pilgrims biannually.

Nazca Lines
It's much cheaper to fly over the lines from Nazca (see Nazca, later in this chapter) but if you're in a hurry you can do it from Ica

for about US$100 per person. A minimum of three is required. Ask at the Hotel Las Dunas, which has an airstrip.

Special Events

Ica has more than its share of fiestas. The most famous is the wine harvest festival held every March. It's called the Festival Internacional de Vendimia. There are processions and beauty contests, cockfights and horse shows, arts and crafts fairs, music and dancing, and of course the pisco and wine flow freely. It usually begins the first (or second) Friday in March and continues for 10 days. The festival site is the Campo Feriado on the outskirts and it costs US$1.20 to enter. During the weekday, tasting and buying wine, honey and other food seems to be the thing to do. Most of the other events are held in the evenings or weekends.

In October the religious pilgrimage of El Señor de Lurén culminates in a traditional all-night procession on the third Monday of the month. This festival is repeated in March and sometimes coincides with Holy Week celebrations.

The Carnaval de Yunza takes place in February. Participants dress in beautiful costumes and there is public dancing. One dance involves circling a tree until it is pulled down. There is also the water-throwing typical of any Latin American carnival.

The founding of the city on June 17, 1563 is celebrated every June during Ica week. The more important Ica Tourist Festival is held in the latter half of September.

Places to Stay

All hotels raise their prices substantially during the festivals, especially the March harvest festival when hotels are often fully booked and rates double or even triple in the cheapest hotels. The prices below are average non-festival rates. The lowest rates are usually during April, May, June, September, November and December. Other months coincide with the Peruvian coastal summer or northern hemisphere vacation periods.

Places to Stay – bottom end

The area around Independencia and Castro-virreyna has cheap hotels. Some of the hotels in the area are busy with short stay couples, but they aren't especially sleazy or dangerous.

The *Hostal Europa*, Independencia 258, is about US$4/6 for singles/doubles. The rooms are basic but the beds are clean and there's a wash basin in each room. Similarly priced cold-water cheapies include *Hostal Díaz* (☎ 23-1601), Independencia 167, which is clean and has some rooms with private bath for an extra couple of dollars. Others on the same block are *Hostal Royal* which is OK, the *Hostal Aries* which is friendly but charges a little more, the *Hostal Jaimito* which looks run-down and the *Hostal Aleph* (☎ 22-1332), which charges US$4.50 a person. The nearby *Hostal Toño* is OK for US$5/6.50. The *Hostal Callao* (☎ 23-5976), on Callao south of Independencia, has rooms for US$5/7 and rooms with private bath for US$7/9 and hot water is available. The *Hostal Lima*, Lima 262, and the *Hostal LM*, Salaverry at Loreto, are other reasonable cold water cheapies at about US$5/8. The *Hostal Inti* (☎ 23-3141), Amazonas 235, charges US$5/9 in basic rooms with private cold showers. If all of these are full and you're on a tight budget, you can try the cheap and very basic hostals *San Martín, Titos* and *Libertad*.

The popular *Hostal La Viña* (☎ 22-1043), at San Martín and Huánuco, charges about US$5/7, or US$7/9 for rooms with private bath and hot water (although I hear it has been renovated and prices have doubled). The *Hotel Presidente* (☎ 22-5977), Amazonas 223, is good and clean at US$7/9 with bath and hot water. The *Hostal Sol de Oro* (☎ 23-3735), La Mar 371, is very clean and friendly and charges US$8/10 in rooms with private bath and hot water. The *Hotel Confort* (☎ 23-3072), La Mar 257, is clean and good at US$9/13 with private bath and tepid showers. Others to try are *Hostal Palace* and *Hostal Tumi* which I didn't check out.

Places to Stay – middle

The clean *Hotel Las Brisas* (☎ 23-2737), Castrovirreyna 246, is secure and has airy rooms with good beds and hot showers for US$11/16. You may need to ask at the desk to have the hot water turned on. The *Hotel Siesta I* (☎ 23-3249), Independencia 194, and the *Hotel Siesta II* (☎ 23-1045), Independencia 160, both have adequate rooms with hot showers for US$14/19. The Siesta II has a decent restaurant. The *Hostal Silmar* (☎ 23-5089, 22-5251), Castrovirreyna 110, has clean carpeted rooms with private bath and TV for US$20/23. They also have one of the town's better restaurants. The clean *Hostal Sol de Ica* (☎ 23-6165, fax 23-6168), Lima 265, is one of the best in the town center. Carpeted rooms with private bath, TV and phone are US$27/32 including breakfast in the hotel restaurant.

Some way out of town is the *Hostal Medanos* (☎ 23-1666) at the 300 km marker on the Carretera Panamericana. It has a swimming pool and costs about US$30 per double.

Places to Stay – top end

There are no really good hotels in the town center, though the *Grand Hotel Ica* (☎/fax 23-3320; in Lima 241-2202, fax 241-6149) comes fairly close. They have suites and bungalows for US$90 a double. About 2 km from the Plaza de Armas, it's a very modern building with a swimming pool and restaurant. Singles/doubles cost about US$50/65, which includes a continental breakfast, and discounts are often offered during the low season.

Out on the Panamericana are more good hotels. The pleasant, colonial-style *Hostal El Carmelo* (☎ 23-2191, in Lima 444-9500), at the 301 km marker, has a swimming pool and a small winery on the premises. Nice rooms are about US$32/40. The fairly luxurious *Hotel Las Dunas Sun Resort* (☎ 23-1031, in Lima 442-3090, 442-3091, fax 442-4180) at the 300 km marker has comfortable rooms with TV at US$65/77 (a few dollars less midweek). More expensive are suites with a whirlpool bath. Rooms lack air-conditioning.

The resort offers a swimming pool with water slide, two tennis courts, a small golf course, children's playground, sandboard rental, other games, a sauna, horse riding, Nazca Lines overflights and other excursions. A new recommendation is the *Hotel Ocucaje Sun & Wine Resort* (☎ in Lima 440-7977, 428-7145), near the Ocucaje winery by km 336 of the Panamericana. Rates are US$50/60.

Places to Eat

The *Restaurant Venezia*, on Lima just off the Plaza de Armas, serves good pizza, pasta, desserts and coffee at reasonable prices and has been recommended. There are also several chifas and other inexpensive restaurants along Calle Lima. Also try the cheap *Mogambo*, on Tacna just north of the plaza, and the *Plaza 125*, on the plaza, which serves inexpensive chicken. Also on the plaza is *El Velasco*, which serves good snacks and cakes.

El Otro Peñoncito, Bolívar 255, is very clean and serves good sandwiches and meals at medium prices. A reader recommends the clean, medium-priced *Huaranga* but I don't know where it is! Ask around. The restaurants in the *Hostal Silmar* and *Hotel Siesta II* are among the best in town.

Entertainment

There's not much happening in Ica outside of fiesta times. Of the two cinemas shown on the map, the *Cine Dux* has the better of a poor movie selection. The *Casa Grande Snack Bar* on the north side of the plaza is a bar and pool hall catering mainly to men.

Things to Buy

If you just want to buy some local wine or pisco without going to the source, a good place to go is the east side of the Plaza de Armas, where you'll find several wine shops.

Getting There & Away

Air A small local airport used to have scheduled flights from Lima but doesn't at this time. AeroCóndor flies from Lima or

Nazca on tourist trips over the Nazca Lines and charters aircraft here.

Bus Ica is a main bus destination on the Carretera Panamericana and is easy to get to from Lima, Nazca and Arequipa.

Most of the bus companies are clustered around a little park at the west end of Salaverry, so it's easy to wander around comparing prices and schedules. Several companies run frequent buses up and down the Panamericana and Ormeño seems to have the greatest number of departures, though other smaller companies may be cheaper. Cruz del Sur is OK for southbound buses but they don't sell tickets to Lima and they board on a space available basis. If going to Pisco, make sure your bus is entering town and not dropping you on the Panamericana 5 km from Pisco.

There are many departures for Lima (US$4.50, five hours, or US$10 with Ormeño's deluxe service, four hours), Pisco (US$1, one hour), Nazca (US$2.50, three hours) and Arequipa (US$12 to US$16, 15 hours). Some continue to Tacna or a few to Cuzco.

Colectivo Taxi colectivos for Lima (five passengers) and Nazca (seven passengers) leave from opposite Ormeño as soon as they are full. Fares are US$12 to Lima (3½ hours) and US$3 to Nazca (2½ hours).

Getting Around
Buses for Huacachina leave from the corner of Lambayeque and Municipalidad. Buses for Guadalupe leave from Independencia and Castrovirreyna.

HUACACHINA
This is a tiny resort village nestled in huge sand dunes about 5 km west of Ica. There's a small lagoon which Peruvians swim in because it's supposed to have curative properties, though it looks murky and uninviting. The surroundings are pretty – graceful palm trees, colorful flowers, attractive buildings in pastel shades and the backdrop of giant sand dunes. It's a

pleasant side trip from Ica and a very quiet place to rest.

The sand dunes invite hiking and playing. You can rent sandboards for US$1.50 an hour if you want to slide, surf, ski or whatever down the dunes and get sand into various body nooks and crannies that you probably didn't even want to know about.

Places to Stay & Eat
There are two hotels and both are around the lagoon. To the right of the bus stop is the attractive pink *Hotel Mossone* (☎ 23-1651, 23-6136, fax 23-6137; or in Lima 442-6718, 442-8365, fax 442-3468), which has been recently renovated and has simple but stylish rooms around a pleasant courtyard. There is a nice restaurant and an elegant bar, both overlooking the lagoon and a swimming pool. The rooms all have private hot shower and a TV (one channel!) and rates are US$30/50. Suites are US$70 to US$90. One reader reports that the hotel was built in the 1940s by Nazis who escaped from Europe – I don't know if that's true or not.

A little further around the lagoon is the blue *Gran Hotel Salvatierra*, which is much cheaper but didn't seem to be doing much business when I walked in – I couldn't find a receptionist. Some people have not been able to resist sleeping in the sand dunes. Beware of thieves.

The Mossone is the best place to eat. There are several inexpensive restaurants and food vendors by the lagoon or you could bring a picnic lunch.

Getting There & Away
A bus marked Huacachina leaves two or three times an hour from Ica (see above), takes 20 minutes and costs US25¢.

NAZCA
From Ica, the Carretera Panamericana heads roughly southeast, passing through the small oasis of Palpa, famous for its orange groves, then rises slowly to Nazca at 598 meters above sea level, around 450 km south of Lima. Although only a small town of about 30,000 people, it is

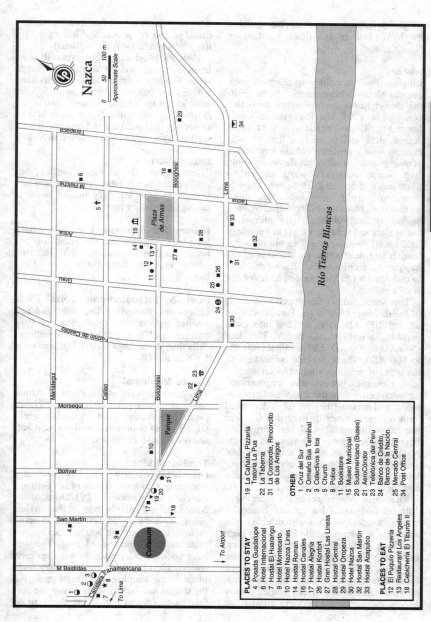

Nazca

0   50   100 m
Approximate Scale

Plaza de Armas

Río Tierras Blancas

SOUTH COAST

To Airport

To Lima

Carretera Panamericana

Coliseum

PLACES TO STAY

4   Posada Guadalupe
6   Hotel Internacional
7   Hostal El Huarango
9   Hotel Montecarlo
10 Hotel Nazca Lines
14 Hotel Roman
16 Hostal Canales
17 Hostal Alegria
26 Hostal Konfort
27 Gran Hostal Las Lineas
28 Hostal Central
29 Hostal Oropeza
30 Hotel Nazca
32 Hostal San Martín
33 Hostal Acapulco

PLACES TO EAT

12 El Puquio Pizzeria
13 Restaurant Los Angeles
18 Cebichería El Tiburón II
19 La Cañada, Pizzeria
     Tratoria La Pua
22 La Taberna
31 La Concordia, Rinconcito
     de Los Amigos

OTHER

1   Cruz del Sur
2   Ormeño Bus Terminal
3   Colectivos to Ica
5   Church
8   Police
11 Bookstore
15 Museo Municipal
20 Sudamericano (Buses)
21 AeroCóndor
23 Telefónica del Peru
24 Banco de Crédito,
     Banco de la Nación
25 Mercado Central
34 Post Office

frequently visited by travelers interested in the Nazca culture and the world famous Nazca Lines.

History

Like the Paracas culture to the north, the ancient Nazca culture was lost in the drifting desert sands and forgotten until this century. In 1901, the Peruvian archaeologist Max Uhle was the first to excavate Nazca sites and to realize that he was dealing with a separate culture from other coastal peoples. Before his discovery, only five Nazca ceramics were known in museums and no one knew how to classify them. After 1901, thousands of ceramics were found. Most were discovered by *huaqueros* (grave robbers) who plundered burial sites and sold their finds to interested individuals or museums. Despite the amateurish and destructive excavations of the huaqueros, archaeologists have been able to construct a fairly accurate picture of the Nazca culture.

The Nazca culture developed as a result of the disintegration of the Paracas culture around 200 AD. It is divided into three periods: early (200 AD to 500 AD), late (500 AD to 700 AD) and terminal (700 AD to 800 AD). These periods coincide with the types of ceramics studied by archaeologists. Ceramics, because they are preserved so much better than items made of cloth or wood, and because they are often decorated with representations of everyday life, are the most important tool for unraveling Peru's ancient past. The designs on the Nazca ceramics show us their plants and animals, their fetishes and divinities, their musical instruments and household items and the people themselves.

The early Nazca ceramics were very colorful and showed a greater variety of naturalistic designs. Pots with double necks joined by a stirrup handle have often been found, as well as shallow cups and plates. In the late period, the decoration was more stylized. (The decorations were, in all cases, much more stylized than the rigorously natural styles of the contemporary Moche culture of the northern coast.) The designs painted on the ceramics of the terminal period are poorer and influenced by the Wari culture from the highlands.

Even the most casual observer will soon learn to recognize the distinctive Nazca style. The colors are vivid and the stylized designs are painted directly onto the ceramic rather than being molded. The effect is strong and attractive. Nazca ceramics can be seen in the museums of Lima and Ica, as well as in the small local museum in Nazca.

Information

There is no official tourist office, but information is available from the hotels – usually they're strongly biased towards taking one of their tours!

Money The Banco de Crédito changes traveler's checks, as do some of the hotels geared to international tourists. Money changers hang out in front of the bank.

Post & Telecommunications These offices are marked on the map. I've had several reports that Telefónica del Peru charges much higher rates for international calls than in the large cities. The area code for Nazca is 034.

Museo Municipal

This local museum on the Plaza de Armas has a small but good collection of Nazca ceramics and other stuff. Hours are weekdays 9 am to noon and 4 to 6 pm, and Saturdays 9 am to 12.30 pm.

The Nazca Lines

Once, while traveling on a bus to Nazca, I was amazed to find that one of my (gringo) traveling companions hadn't heard of the Nazca Lines. I naively thought that anyone going to Nazca would have heard all about them. So, what are the Nazca Lines?

Actually, no one really knows. They are huge geometric designs drawn in the desert and visible only from the air. They were made by the simple expedient of removing the darker sun-baked stones from the surface of the desert and piling them up on

Two Inca skulls, one deformed by tying flat boards around the forehead in childhood, considered a sign of prestige and beauty

ROB RACHOWIECKI

ROB RACHOWIECKI

Excavating a tomb at Sipán, near Chiclayo

ROB RACHOWIECKI

José Correa, Chinchero ruins

ROB RACHOWIECKI

Mummies, Cemetery of Chauchilla, near Nazca

ROB RACHOWIECKI

Inca experimental agricultural terraces at Moray

ROB RACHOWIECKI

Salt pans dating from Inca times, still in use

TONY WHEELER

Sillustani

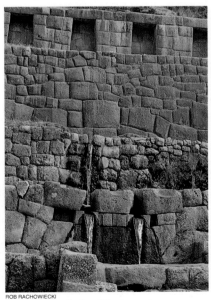

ROB RACHOWIECKI

Inca baths at Tambomachay

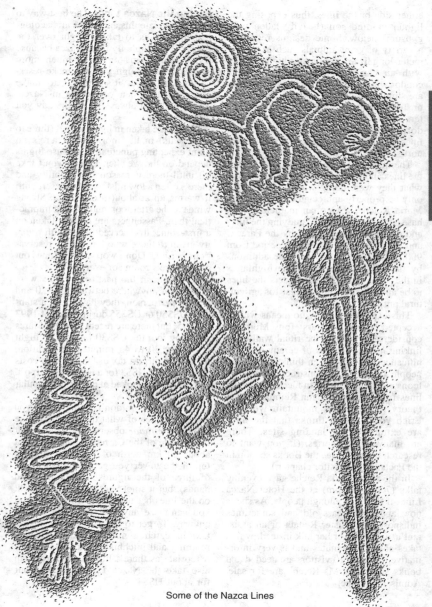

Some of the Nazca Lines

either side of the lines, thus exposing the lighter colored soil (heavily laden with gypsum) below. Some designs represent a variety of giant animals such as a 180-meter-long lizard, a 90-meter-high monkey with an extravagantly curled tail or a condor with a 130-meter wingspan. Others are simple but perfect triangles, rectangles or straight lines running for several kilometers across the desert. There are several dozen different figures. The best-known lines are found in the desert about 20 km north of Nazca.

The questions remain: Who constructed the lines and why? And how did they know what they were doing when the lines can only be properly appreciated from the air? Maria Reiche, a German mathematician, has spent most of her life studying the lines and thinks they were made by the Paracas and Nazca cultures during the period from 900 BC to 600 AD, with some additions by the Wari settlers from the highlands in the 7th century. She considers the lines to be an astronomical calendar for agricultural purposes.

This explanation is by no means widely accepted by other writers. Tony Morrison considers the lines to be ritual walkways linking *huacas* or sites of ceremonial significance. Jim Woodman thinks the Nazca people knew how to construct hot-air balloons and that they did, in fact, observe the lines from the air. Johann Reinhard has a theory that involves mountain worship. Erich von Daniken thinks that the lines are extraterrestrial landing sites. There are many other theories. (If you want to research the topic, see the Books section in the Facts for the Visitor chapter.)

In the past, Maria Reiche gave evening talks (7 or 7.30 pm) at the Hotel Nazca Lines if there are enough people. As she is now about 90 years old and sometimes indisposed, her sister Renata or an assistant usually deliver her talk instead, which takes about 30 minutes and is very informative. Usually, 10 visitors are needed and books signed by Ms Reiche are for sale. Admission is free.

Seeing the Nazca Lines The best way to fully appreciate this enormous archaeological mystery is to take a flight over the lines. Most people fly from Nazca because flying from Lima or Ica is much more expensive. Although you can make reservations in Lima, it's cheaper to make arrangements when you arrive in Nazca. You can almost always fly on the day you want.

Flights are taken in light aircraft (three to nine seats) in the mornings. There's no point expecting punctuality because flights depend on the weather. Planes won't take off until there is reasonable visibility and there's often a low mist over the desert until it warms up at about 9 or 10 am. Strong winds in the afternoon make flying impractical then. Passengers are usually taken on a first-come, first-served basis, with priority given to those who have made reservations in Lima. Don't worry – nine times out of 10 there's room for everyone.

Although, in the past, overflights were offered for anywhere between US$20 and US$60 per person, they have been a standard US$50 or US$55 during most of 1993 to 1995, but there are recent reports of fares dropping into the US$30 range. The flight is usually 30 to 45 minutes. In addition, there is an airport tax of US$2 and it costs about another US$3 for a taxi to the airport. Flights can be booked at any of the popular tourist hotels.

If you can't or don't want to fly, you can get an idea of what the lines look like from the *mirador* observation tower, built on the side of the Carretera Panamericana about 20 km north of Nazca. From the top of the tower you get an oblique view of three of the figures (lizard, tree and hands), but it's not very good. Don't walk on the lines because it damages them and you can't see anything from the ground anyway. To get to the tower either take a taxi or catch a northbound bus in the morning and hitchhike back. Don't leave it too late as there's little traffic. You can also take the Nazca Lines mirador tour for about US$4.

Other Excursions

Many people come to Nazca, take an over-flight, and go on, but there's a lot more to see. The Nazca and Alegría hotels organize inexpensive guided tours. There are also plenty of taxi drivers and guides on the streets. Always ask to see an official guides card. Don't go on a tour with an unlicensed guide – the tours visit uninhabited areas, and some unlicensed guides/drivers are in cahoots with armed, masked robbers who will show up and steal your camera and valuables.

Some of the destinations mentioned below can be combined, but there must be a minimum of three people on a tour. One or two people are OK so long as three are paid for. Most tours will include a stop at a potter's or goldsmith's shop for a demonstration and shopping.

Cemetery of Chauchilla One of the most interesting tours is to this cemetery, 30 km away. Here you'll see bones, skulls, mummies, pottery shards and fragments of cloth dating back to the late Nazca period. Although everything of value has gone, it's quite amazing to stand in the desert and see tombs surrounded by bleached skulls and bones that stretch off into the distance. The tour takes about 2½ hours and costs US$7 per person, with a minimum of three passengers.

Paredones Ruins & Cantallo Aqueduct

The ruins are not very well preserved but the underground aqueducts, built by the Nazcas, are still in working order and provide irrigation to the nearby fields. The stone work is quite fine and it is possible to enter the aqueducts through the *ventanas* (windows) which the local people use when they clean the aqueducts annually. A caretaker here will charge you US50¢.

These sites are closer to Nazca and within walking distance if you have several hours spare. Cross the river on the Arica Bridge and go straight on for a couple of kilometers to the Paredones and a further couple of kilometers to the Cantallo aqueduct, which is found in the grounds of the Hacienda Cantallo. I haven't done this walk, so check locally first. Tours are available for about US$5 per person (three passenger minimum).

Cahuachi West of the lines is Cahuachi, the most important known Nazca center. There are several pyramids and a site called El Estaquería, which consists of rows of logs half buried vertically in the ground – one report suggests that their function is as some kind of calendar. The site is being excavated (during two or three months a year) and it may be closed to visitors then. Inexpensive three-hour tours are available.

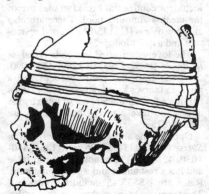 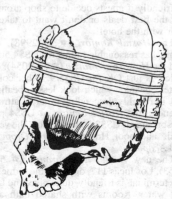

Pre-Incan method of beautifying skulls

Sacaco A more expensive six-hour tour goes to Sacaco to look for fossils, though I don't know anyone who has done it.

Reserva Nacional Pampas Galeras
This vicuña sanctuary is high in the mountains 90 km east of Nazca, and is the best place to see these animals in Peru. It takes about 2½ hours through wild mountain scenery and a taxi charges about US$60 roundtrip (up to four passengers).

Places to Stay – bottom end
The two hotels most used by budget travelers are the *Hotel Nazca* (☎ 52-2085), Lima 438, and the *Hostal Alegría* (☎ /fax 52-2444), Lima 168. The Nazca is run by the Fernández family. Basic, clean rooms are US$5/8 and there is tepid water in the communal showers. The Alegría is run by Ephraín Alegría who speaks several languages. They charge about US$3.50 per person in basic, clean rooms. There are tepid showers in the communal bathroom, though one reader points out that there can be a line for them because only two showers serve 15 rooms. Rooms with private bath and ceiling fan are US$14 double and new rooms are being built. Both of these hotels have received several recommendations for their cheap tours and helpful service. Both have also had reports that the service becomes decidedly unfriendly if guests decide to shop around for the best deals or don't want to take a tour with the hotel!

The *Hostal Konfort* (☎ 52-2998), on Lima, has reasonable rooms for US$4.50/8 and the *Hostal San Martín* (☎ 52-2054), on Arica, is just OK for US$5/9. Other cold-water cheapies which look less appealing are, in roughly descending order of attractiveness, the *Hostal Central* at US$4 per person and, at US$3.50 per person, the very basic and poor Hostals *Roman, Oropeza* and *Acapulco*.

The new *Hostal El Huarango* (☎ 55-2053), Los Incas 117, opposite the Ormeño bus terminal, is friendly, quite nice, and has hot water. Rooms with shared bath are US$8/11 and one room with a double bed and private bath is US$16. The small, family-run *Posada Guadalupe* (☎ 52-2249), San Martín 225, is clean, quiet and friendly with a little garden. Rooms are US$6/10 or US$9/15 with private bath and electric hot showers.

Places to Stay – middle
The *Hotel Internacional* (☎ 55-2166), Maria Reiche 112, looks quite good. Simple but clean rooms with private bath and hot water cost US$11/13; bigger bungalows with patios cost US$13/17. It also has a secure parking lot. The *Hotel Montecarlo* (phone out of order), on Lima, has a swimming pool (summer only), bar and cafeteria. Rooms are US$13/20 with private bath and hot water from 7 pm to 8 am. A good clean hotel on the plaza is the *Gran Hostal Las Lineas* (☎ 52-2488) where carpeted rooms with private hot showers cost US$16/22. There is a decent-looking restaurant. The *Hostal Canales* (☎ 52-2099), on Bolognesi just off the Plaza, is new, clean and friendly. Rooms are US$11/16 with shared bath or US$16/22 with private bath, including breakfast.

Places to Stay – top end
The best hotel in Nazca is the *Hotel Nazca Lines* (☎ 52-2293), on Bolognesi, where the most attractive rooms are US$80 and include a continental breakfast and use of the clean swimming pool. There are also cheaper rooms (US$45/51), a good restaurant and a quiet lounge.

The lovely converted hacienda *Hotel de la Borda* (☎ 52-2293; in Lima 442-3090, fax 442-4180), has pretty gardens and a pool, and serves knockout pisco sours in its bar. It's a few kilometers out of town by the airport, so take a taxi. Double suites are US$64/82.

Opposite the airport is the *Hostal Maison Suisse* (☎ 52-2434, 52-0639, in Lima 440-1030, 421-0335). The hotel is comfortable and has a restaurant and a swimming pool. Rates are US$35/45 including breakfast. They sometimes do packages with AeroIca (☎ in Lima 421-6653) where the combined stay/overflight is cheaper than if you buy them separately.

Places to Eat

The best hotels serve good food, but are expensive. (The Hotel Nazca Lines has a cheap restaurant.) Cheap meals can be found all over Nazca; there seems to be a restaurant on every block. Cheap restaurants around the market area include *La Concordia* and, next to it, *Rinconcito de los Amigos* for chicken. The friendly *Restaurant Los Angeles*, just off the plaza, has a cheap set lunch, good reasonably priced other meals, nice chocolate cake, and decent pisco sours. *El Puquío Pizzería* nearby is a small friendly pizza place, run by a charming old couple. On Lima, near the Hostal Alegría, are two restaurants with nice atmosphere. *La Cañada* has good Peruvian food at reasonable prices and the *Pizzería Tratoria La Pua* has a limited and rather pricey menu, but is quite good.

Cebichería El Tiburón II, on San Martín, is a typical coastal fish restaurant with good cheap ceviches but overpriced juices. At night it transforms into *El Huakero Discotec* with music and strange-tasting piña coladas. *La Taberna*, on Calle Lima, is a bit more upmarket – perhaps overpriced – but sometimes has live music on Saturday night.

Entertainment

The Hotel Nazca Lines will allow travelers to use its pool for about US$2.50 (no charge if you are a guest). They have free lectures given by Maria Reiche's staff in the evenings.

Nazca sometimes has music in the restaurants on weekends (see above).

Getting There & Away

Air You can fly here from Lima with AeroCóndor or AeroIca; people who do that normally fly over the Nazca Lines and return the same day.

Bus Nazca is a major destination for buses on the Carretera Panamericana and is easy to get to from Lima, Ica or Arequipa.

Ormeño has the most frequent departures, with several buses a day to Lima (US$7, eight hours) as well as intermediate points. It also has two or three buses a day to Arequipa (US$9, 10 hours) and Tacna (US$12, 14 hours).

Ormeño buses to Cuzco leave every two days and take 30 to 40 hours. The trip is best broken in Arequipa. The route used to go via Abancay but now takes the safer Arequipa route. A few companies still go via Abancay but this route is not recommended because of bandit activities. Other companies are along the main street and have similar destinations and slightly differing prices. Cruz del Sur is quite good, while Sudamericano is cheaper and not as good.

Colectivo Fast colectivo taxis to Ica leave when they are full (usually at least hourly during the day) from the intersection of the Panamericana with Lima (US$3, 2½ hours).

CHALA

The first town of any importance on the Carretera Panamericana southeast of Nazca is the fishing village of Chala about 170 km away. In Inca times, fresh fish was sent by runners from near here to Cuzco – an amazing effort. Chala's main attractions are fresh seafood and the opportunity to break the long journey to Arequipa, but most travelers just tough it out and keep going. Maybe that's a good reason to stop, as you won't see too many tourists.

The Incan ruins at Puerto Inca, 10 km north of town, can be visited. Get there by heading north for 6 km on the Panamericana, then turning left near Km 603 and following a dirt road 4 km to the coastal ruins.

The area code is 064.

Places to Stay & Eat

The best place is the *Hotel de Turistas*, Comercio 601, at the south end of the beach. The verandah faces the ocean but the bedrooms don't. It's a nice place for a coffee stop. Rooms are about US$20/30. Opposite is the cheaper *Hostal Otero*.

Further along the beach is the basic *Hostal Grau*, which is clean and friendly with shared cold showers. Rates are US$9 for a double – ask for a room at the back with ocean views. There are also the cheap *Hostal Everyt* and *Hostal Viña*.

The *Puerto Inca Hostal* (☎ 21-0224, leave message), on the beach near the ruins, has a few simple but clean rooms with food available. Camping is allowed. The owner, Mitzi Perales, will pick guests up at Chala on request.

CAMANÁ

From Chala, the Carretera Panamericana runs close to the coast until it reaches Camaná, about 220 km away. The views of the ocean are often very good as the highway tortuously clings to sand dunes dropping down to the sea.

Camaná is 175 km from Arequipa and the road is paved, so it's a popular summer beach resort with Arequipeños. The beaches are good but are 5 km from the center, so you must take the local bus to La Punta to visit them. At La Punta there are private holiday bungalows but no tourist facilities.

Places to Stay

Hotels tend to be full during summer weekends (January to March). The reasonably priced *Hotel de Turistas* at Calle Lima 138 has a garden. It's about four blocks from the Ormeño bus terminal. Closer to the terminal is the OK *Hostal Lider*, and the basic *Hostal Lima*, which is clean and charges US$4 per person. The *Hostal Victoria* and the *Gran Hostal Premier* are two of several other basic places.

Getting There & Away

The Ormeño terminal is on the 300 block of Lima and the Tepsa terminal is on the 500 block.

MOLLENDO

The Carretera Panamericana leaves the coast at Camaná and heads inland for 135 km to the junction of Repartición. Here, a major branch road heads east into the Andes for 42 km to Arequipa. The Panamericana turns south towards the coast and, after a further 15 km, divides again. The southeastern branch goes on towards the Chilean border while the southwestern road heads to Mollendo.

This small port of 15,000 people is about 110 km southwest of Arequipa and is a popular beach resort for Arequipeños during the January to March summer season but is very quiet for the rest of the year. Mollendo is normally reached by road from Arequipa after traveling through interesting desert with delicate brown, pink and gray colors, particularly attractive in the oblique light of early morning. Near La Joya are some extraordinary crescent-shaped gray sand dunes which look as if they have been deliberately poured in unlikely positions on the pinkish rock. Beyond, the desert becomes very rocky with tortured-looking cacti eking out an existence in the salt-laden soil.

Mollendo is a pleasant town with several plazas, attractive hilly streets and a beach. There are customs agencies and shipping offices but most ships now dock in Matarani, 15 km to the northwest. One of the best reasons to visit Mollendo is to go to the nearby nature sanctuary at Mejía (see below).

Information

The Banco de Crédito changes dollars. The area code is 054.

Places to Stay

Single rooms are difficult to obtain during weekends in the high season, when prices go up. Bargain in the low season. There are several cheap and basic cold-water hotels charging about US$4 or US$5 per person. These include *Hostal Fory Foy*, Arequipa 681, which is clean and good and has some rooms with a private bath for a couple of dollars more. (The hostal's name was the Hostal 45, which Peruvians pronounce 'fory foy' – hence the odd name!) Others in this price range include the clean and friendly *Hotel San Martín*, the *La Posada Inn* and *Hostal Willy*.

For a little more money, a good clean hotel is the *Hostal La Cabaña* (☎ 53-3833), Comercio 240, which charges US$6/10 (communal bathrooms) or US$8/12 in rooms with private bath. There is hot water in the mornings and/or evenings. The *Hostal Paraiso* (☎ 53-2126) has decent rooms for US$10/14 with private bath and TV. Next door is the similarly priced *Hostal Sol y Mar*. A little more expensive is the good *Hostal Belmar* and the best in town is reputedly the *Mollendo Hotel* (☎ 53-3104), Arequipa 100, with doubles for about US$20. All these have hot water some or all of the time.

Places to Eat
The *Marco Antonio*, Comercio 254 next to the Hostal La Cabaña, is a good and reasonably priced restaurant. Nearby, *El Barril* is another good choice and the *Toldo Pizzería* serves Italian and other food. These three are probably the best.

Cheap restaurants are found along Calle Arequipa near the market. The *Restaurant Faisano* by the Hostal Paraiso is a reasonably cheap place. The *Chifa Tun Fung* and the *Chifa San Wha* are OK for Chinese food. For ice cream and snacks try the *Heladería Venecia*. The Hostal Belmar has a restaurant.

Getting There & Away
The passenger train from Mollendo to Arequipa hasn't run for years, though freight trains keep this route open.

Buses to Arequipa (almost three hours) cost US$2. Empresa Aragón has seven buses daily to Arequipa, Flores Hermanos has eight daily, and Ormeño has four daily. TEPSA runs four buses a week direct to Lima.

Minibuses go to the beach resort of Mejía for US30¢. They leave from the corner of Tacna and Arequipa. Some continue through Mejía to the Río Tambo valley, La Curva, and Cocachacra to El Fiscal (US$1.50, two hours).

Comité 1 has shared colectivo taxis leaving for Arequipa once or twice a day. The fare is US$2.50 for the two hour trip.

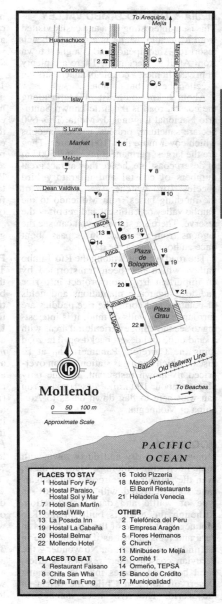

Mollendo

0   50   100 m
Approximate Scale

PACIFIC OCEAN

PLACES TO STAY
1 Hostal Fory Foy
4 Hostal Paraiso, Hostal Sol y Mar
7 Hotel San Martín
10 Hostal Willy
13 La Posada Inn
19 Hostal La Cabaña
20 Hostal Belmar
22 Mollendo Hotel

PLACES TO EAT
4 Restaurant Faisano
8 Chifa San Wha
9 Chifa Tun Fung

16 Toldo Pizzería
18 Marco Antonio, El Barril Restaurants
21 Heladería Venecia

OTHER
2 Telefónica del Peru
3 Empresa Aragón
5 Flores Hermanos
6 Church
11 Minibuses to Mejía
12 Comité 1
14 Ormeño, TEPSA
15 Banco de Crédito
17 Municipalidad

MEJÍA & THE RÍO TAMBO VALLEY

This is an interesting area and easily visited from Mollendo. Mejía is a summer beach resort for Arequipeños and is a ghost town from April to December. There are plenty of private homes, a couple of snack bars, an excellent beach, but no hotels.

About 6 km southeast of Mejía along the coastal road is the little-known Santuario Nacional Lagunas de Mejía. This 690 hectare sanctuary protects coastal lagoons which cover more than 100 hectares. They are the largest permanent lakes in 1500 km of desert coastline, hence they attract great numbers of coastal and migratory bird species. Bird watchers can take one of the morning buses from Mollendo to the Tambo valley or El Fiscal and get off at the reserve. There's a sign and you can see the lagoons from the road. Buses pass about once an hour during the day.

The road continues along the Río Tambo valley, which has been transformed by an important irrigation project into rice paddies, sugarcane plantations and fields of potatoes and corn. The rice paddies are surrounded by walls of mud. It is interesting to see these huge agricultural areas with a sand dune and desert backdrop. The road joins the Carretera Panamericana at El Fiscal, which has a gas station and an overpriced fly-blown restaurant. It's the only place in about 100 km of desert road. You can wait here to flag down buses to Arequipa or Moquegua.

MOQUEGUA

Moquegua is a dry and dusty town with some interesting buildings. Many of these, even the cathedral, are roofed with sugarcane stalks covered with dried mud – a type of wattle and daub construction. Although the town is built on the Río Moquegua, it is one of the driest towns in Peru and feels almost as if it should be in the middle of the Sahara. No wonder – the Peruvian coastal desert reaches its driest point here and merges into the Atacama Desert of northern Chile, the driest in the world. The river does manage to provide enough moisture for some agriculture (mainly grapes and avocados), but a couple of kilometers from the river you would never believe that agriculture is possible anywhere nearby.

Moquegua has a population of about 10,000 and is the capital of the small department of the same name. It is 1412 meters above sea level and 220 km southeast of Arequipa. At the northeastern end of town is a small hill which you can climb easily for an excellent view of the mud roofs of Moquegua and the surrounding arid mountains. The pleasant and shady Plaza de Armas, with a wrought iron fountain and topiary hedges, is a welcome relief from the desert. A small Museo Regional is on the plaza.

There really isn't much to do in Moquegua, but I found it . . . different.

Places to Stay

There are about a dozen hotels, most of them quite basic with cold water in shared bathrooms. The city suffers from an erratic water supply, which is reflected in the hotels. One that is clean and OK at US$4 per person is the *Hostal Cornejo*. A cheaper one is the acceptable *Hostal Comercio*. A better one is the *Hostal Arequipa* at US$7/11 or the similarly priced, pleasant and quiet *Hostal Carrera*. The cheapest and most basic are around the market (always the most prone to theft but the area doesn't seem too dangerous, at least in daylight when I walked around) and include the Hostals *El Ovalo, Sparto, La Paz, Libertad* and *Los Angeles*. Others to try away from the market are the *Hostal Torata* and *Central*.

The *Hostal Los Limoneros* has a pleasant garden and simple, clean singles/doubles with private bath for US$15/22, or US$8/14 with shared bath. There's hot water occasionally. The *Hotel El Mirador de Moquegua* (☎ 76-1765; in Lima 442-3090, fax 442-4180) has hot water but is about 3 km from the town center. There is a swimming pool and restaurant. Rooms with bath cost about US$34/49, and bungalows are US$56/69.

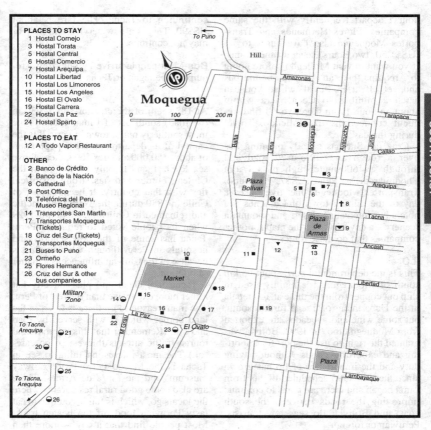

PLACES TO STAY
1 Hostal Cornejo
3 Hostal Torata
5 Hostal Central
6 Hostal Comercio
7 Hostal Arequipa
10 Hostal Libertad
11 Hostal Los Limoneros
15 Hostal Los Angeles
16 Hostal El Ovalo
19 Hostal Carrera
22 Hostal La Paz
24 Hostal Sparto

PLACES TO EAT
12 A Todo Vapor Restaurant

OTHER
2 Banco de Crédito
4 Banco de la Nación
8 Cathedral
9 Post Office
13 Telefónica del Peru, Museo Regional
14 Transportes San Martín
17 Transportes Moquegua (Tickets)
18 Cruz del Sur (Tickets)
20 Transportes Moquegua
21 Buses to Puno
23 Ormeño
25 Flores Hermanos
26 Cruz del Sur & other bus companies

SOUTH COAST

Places to Eat

The cheapest places are, as usual, around the market, but there are better restaurants on Avenida Moquegua, northeast of the plaza. One that is in an older building with character is *A Todo Vapor*, which means 'full steam ahead!'

Getting There & Away

The easiest way to get to Moquegua is by bus from either Arequipa or Tacna. Some bus offices are by the market but they only sell tickets. The buses leave from small terminals down a hill west of the market, so make sure that you know where the departure point is when buying a ticket. Buses to Lima (about US$13, 19 to 24 hours) leave several times daily with Ormeño, Cruz del Sur and Angelitos Negros. These buses make intermediate stops at Camaná, Chala, Nazca and Ica.

Buses to Arequipa (US$2.50, up to four hours) leave with either Cruz del Sur, Ormeño, Transportes Moquegua, Flores Hermanos or Angelitos Negros about every hour. Buses to Tacna (US$2, 2½ hours) depart frequently with the same companies. Flores Hermanos and Transportes Moquegua also have buses to Ilo (US$1.50, two hours) several times a day. If you want to visit Mollendo before going to Arequipa, take an Arequipa-bound bus and get off at El Fiscal, where you can catch a minibus to Cocachacra within about an hour. From there, you'll find frequent connections to Mollendo. Travel during the day.

Cruz del Sur has a daily morning bus over a rough and little-used road and through a 4600-meter-high pass (Abra Choquijarani) to Puno (US$7, 10 hours). Transportes Moquegua has five buses a day to the mining town of Cuajones (no hotels but interesting desert and mountain scenery – a day trip). See the map for other companies that do these routes.

ILO
This is the departmental port, about 95 km south of Moquegua. It's mainly used to ship out copper from the mine at Toquepala in the Department of Tacna further south, but some wine and avocados are exported from Moquegua too. In 1992, Bolivia was granted the right to use the port for importing and exporting goods without paying duty and the importance of Ilo has grown since then. In 1995 scheduled flights from Lima began and there are plans to continue improving the roads between the south coast and Bolivia. Ilo sees few tourists, Peruvian or foreign.

The area code is 054.

Places to Stay
Hotels are often full with mining engineers and Bolivian businesspeople. The *Gran Hotel Ilo* (☎ 78-2411, 78-2311, fax 78-2421), Cáceres 3007, has singles/doubles with a private bath for US$30/40. There are a few cheaper hotels. Try the *Hostal Karina* (☎ 78-1397), *Hostal Paraiso* (☎ 78-1432), or *Hotel Grau* (☎ 78-1752).

Getting There & Away
Air In 1995, Faucett began flying from Lima on Monday, Wednesday and Friday,

continuing to Tacna. The fare is about US$90. This is a new service and may or may not continue.

Bus Most people arrive by bus from Arequipa, Moquegua or Tacna.

TACNA
At 18° south of the equator and 1293 km (by road) southeast of Lima, Tacna is the most southerly major town in Peru. It is the capital of its department, has a population of about 150,000 and lies 560 meters above sea level. Tacna is only 36 km from the Chilean border and has strong historical ties with that country. It became part of Chile in 1880 during the War of the Pacific and remained in Chilean hands until 1929 when its people voted to return to Peru. Tacna has some of the best schools and hospitals in Peru, though whether this is because of the Chilean influence is a matter of opinion.

Tacna is a clean and pleasant city but rather more expensive than the rest of Peru. The main reason to go there is to cross the land border which is well served by road and rail. (Remember that this international tourist traffic attracts thieves, so be careful.) The most interesting thing to see in Tacna is the Museo Ferroviario (railway museum) and the Plaza de Armas. There are also some good rural restaurants where the locals go, which is fun if you like to eat tasty Peruvian food off the beaten track. Most people find that a day is more than enough to stay in Tacna.

Information
The tourist office has closed.

Consulates The Chilean Consulate is near the railway station and is open weekdays from 8 am to 12.30 pm. Most travelers just need a tourist card, freely available at the border. French and a few other nationals need a visa.

The Bolivian Consulate is at the southeast end of town, on Avenida Piura. A taxi costs about US$1. Hours are weekdays from 9 to 11 am and 4 to 5 pm.

The Most Helpful Bolivian Consul

Few travelers enter Bolivia from Tacna without stopping at Puno, but it is possible to do so via a little-used road to Juli on the south shore of Lake Titicaca. For this reason there is a Bolivian consul in Tacna but he doesn't get much business. One year I went to the consulate just to check on opening times and was almost dragged in by a very excited man who grabbed my passport and peered at it, all the while telling me there was 'No problema, no problema.' He scurried around his huge desk and agitatedly dug through a drawer overflowing with impressive looking rubber stamps and ink pads. He carefully selected an immaculate page in my passport and covered it with five different stamps, all the while continuing his chattering litany, 'No problema, no problema.' The stamps were carefully numbered, dated and signed with a flourish. Finally, wielding a large wooden stamp, he delivered the coup de grace – an imprint reading GRATIS to show the world that he, at least, would not consider accepting a bribe. With a benign smile my passport was returned to me complete with Tourist Visa No 027-85 – the 27th visa he had issued that year. It was December. I hadn't the heart to tell him that I wasn't going to Bolivia. ■

Money Banks and street money changers are found at the southeast end of the Plaza de Armas. Banco de Crédito is the best bet for traveler's checks.

When crossing the border it doesn't make much difference if you change your Peruvian nuevos soles to dollars before changing them to Chilean pesos or going direct from nuevos soles to pesos. If you have a large amount of nuevos soles left you may gain about 1% or 2% if you change them to dollars in Peru before crossing the border. As can be expected, the situation changes from month to month so try and talk to travelers coming the other way to check that there haven't been any major changes.

Telecommunications The area code for Tacna is 054; drop the 0 when dialing from overseas.

Travel Agencies There are a dozen in town. The best is Tacna Tours (☎ 71-1791, fax 72-4767), 28 de Julio 102. They can put you in touch with Juan Carlos Godinez Ibarra, a local cab driver who knows Tacna well.

Museo Ferroviario

This is at the train station and is open weekdays from 9 am to 3 pm. Admission is about US10¢. It's a 'must' for railway enthusiasts and even if you're not crazy about trains there is an interesting display of turn of the century engines and other rolling stock. It also has a philatelic section displaying stamps with railway themes from all over the world.

Parque de la Locomotora

A British locomotive built in 1859 and used as a troop train in the War of the Pacific is the centerpiece of this pleasant downtown park.

Museo de Instituto Nacional de Cultura

This small museum is in the Casa de Cultura and is officially open weekdays from 8 am to noon. If it's closed, you can often find someone to open it if you ask at the office. The main exhibit deals with the War of the Pacific which is explained by paintings and maps. There is also a small collection of archaeological pieces and local art. Admission is free.

Museo de Zela

This small museum is housed in a colonial house on the 500 block of Zela and gives a look at the interior of one of Tacna's oldest buildings. Hours are 10 am to 1 pm and 3 to 5 pm daily; free.

Plaza de Armas

The main feature of the plaza is the huge arch – a monument to the heroes of the

SOUTH COAST

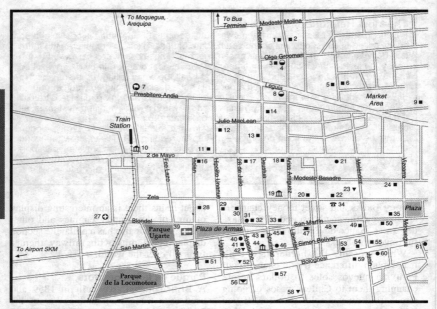

PLACES TO STAY

1   Hostal Napoli
2   Hostal Portal
3   Hostal El Oscar
5   Hostal Don Abel
6   Hostal Cuzco
9   Hotel Don Quijote
11 Hostal Florida
12 Hostal Unanue
13 Hostal Pacífico
14 Pensión Alojamiento Genova
16 Hostal 2 de Mayo
17 Hostal Bon Ami, Alojamiento Betito
18 Hotel Copacabana
20 Hotel San Cristóbal
22 Hostal Lider, H & C Pensión
24 Hostal Angi
25 Holiday Suites Hotel
28 Hostal Inclan
29 Hostal El Mesón
30 Hostal Hogar
32 Hotel Lima
33 Hotel Emperador
35 Lido Hostal

36 Hostal El Inca
41 Hostal Virrey
43 Plaza Hotel
45 Gran Hotel Central
49 Garden Hostal, Hostal Alborada
50 Hotel Camino Real
51 Hostal Alcazar
54 Hostal Alameda
55 Hostal Premier
57 Gran Hotel Tacna
59 Hostal Avenida, Hostal Zapata

PLACES TO EAT

23 Paladar Restaurant
26 El Remanso Restaurant
37 El Gaucho Restaurant
42 Restaurant Sur Peruano
45 El Viejo Almacén
47 Café Genova
48 Chifa Say Wa
52 El Pollo Pechugon, Chifa Kenny
58 Rancho San Antonio Restaurant

OTHER

4   Ormeño
7   Chilean Consulate
8   Colectivos to Moquegua
10 Museo Ferroviario
15 Productos Pelipor
19 Museo de Zela
21 Teatro Municipal
27 Hospital
31 Americana Airlines
33 Banco de Crédito
34 Telefónica del Peru
38 Bolivian Consul
39 La Catedral
40 AeroPerú Airlines
44 Casa de Cultura
46 Faucett Airlines
53 Aero Continente
56 Post Office
60 Mercado Central
61 Peña Brundun

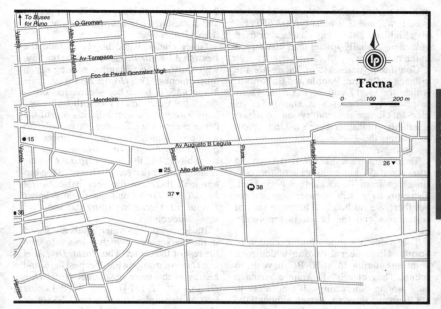

War of the Pacific. It is flanked by larger-than-life bronze statues of Admiral Grau and Colonel Bolognesi. Nearby, the six-meter-high bronze fountain was designed by the French engineer Alexandre Gustave Eiffel. The fountain supposedly represents the four seasons. Eiffel also designed the cathedral which is noted for its clean lines, fine stained-glass windows and onyx high altar. The plaza is a popular meeting place for Tacneños in the evenings and has a patriotic flag-raising ceremony every Sunday at 10 am.

Around Tacna

The countryside around the city is popularly called *la campiña*. The area is known for vineyards, olive groves and orchards set in the desert and irrigated by the Río Caplina, which runs under Avenida Bolognesi in Tacna and provides water for the city. Wine is locally made in small bodegas which typically produce a few thousand liters of *vino de chacra* – a rough but pleasing table wine with a high alcohol content, sometimes reaching 18%. March and April are the main production times. Local bodegas can be visited but none are tourist attractions per se. Ask a cab driver if he knows of one. Several suburbs and small villages have good rural restaurants which attract locals and tourists. They often have live bands at weekends, particularly for lunch.

Pocollay is a suburb 5 km from Tacna and can be reached by walking east on Avenida Bolognesi or taking a bus along that street. It is popular with Tacneños for its restaurants, which are especially busy on Sundays. Dishes served include patasca à la tacneña, which is a thick spicy vegetable and meat soup; picante de guatita or hot peppered tripe (better than it sounds!); cazuela de ave or a thick chicken and vegetable soup; choclo con queso or hot corn on the cob with cheese; chicharrones de chancho or deep-fried chunks of pork, usually served with popcorn; asado de chancho or roast pork; cordero a la parilla or barbecued lamb; and that most typical of Peruvian highland dishes, cuy chactado or fried guinea pig, usually spicier than that served in the mountains.

Continuing northeast of Tacna are the villages of **Calana**, **Pachía** and **Calientes**, which are 15, 17 and 24 km from Tacna respectively. The area is known for its pleasant climate and countryside (by desert standards). In Pachía there's a good typical restaurant, the *Bochio*, and Calientes has hot springs.

Tacna's main seaside resort is Boca del Río, about 55 km southwest of the city. Buses go from Tacna along a good road. Tacneños have built summer homes there but there are no hotels. There are several restaurants and the beach is reportedly good.

The modern copper-mining center of **Toquepala** is near a cave in which rock paintings dating to 8000 BC have been found. They clearly illustrate a guanaco hunt among other things. It's not easy to get there and there's no hotel, although the people at the mine may be able to help with floor space.

Places to Stay – bottom end

Hotels in Tacna, especially the cheapest ones, sometimes suffer from water shortages and showers are not always available. Despite this, hotel prices are relatively high, particularly in the center. Many travelers opt to stay in Arica, Chile, where hotels are better, though not cheaper.

The *Hotel San Cristóbal*, Zela 660, is a basic, clean hotel charging US$4 per person. They keep water running most of the time. Nearby, the *Hostal Unión* is cheap, basic and dirty. The *Hostal Alameda* (☎ 72-3071), Bolognesi 780, charges US$4 per person, US$5 with private bath, but had no water when I was there in the afternoon. Mornings are reportedly better. The similarly priced *Hostal Pacífico* is reasonably clean. Buckets of water are available in the event of a shortage. Convenient for the railway station is the basic but clean *Hostal 2 de Mayo*, which charges US$5 per person and sometimes has hot water in the communal bathrooms.

Other cheap, basic hotels include the *Pensión Alojamiento Genova*, Deustua 559, which also has a restaurant serving cheap lunch menus. The *Hostal Bon Ami*, 2 de Mayo 445, is basic but secure, has occasional hot water and is clean, though problems with water occur. Still, it's one of the better cheapies at US$4 per person or US$6 with private bath. The similarly priced but more basic *Alojamiento Betito* is on the same block, and the nearby *Hostal Unanue* is also in this price range. Closer to the bus terminal, there are the very basic *Hostal Napoli* and *Portal* and the slightly better *Hostal El Oscar* charging US$6/9 for singles/doubles.

Basic cheap cold-water hotels are found in the market area, which is less safe than the rest of the center. The *Hostal Don Abel* and *Cuzco* are among the cheapest here, and nearby is the more up-market *Hotel Don Quijote* (☎ 72-1514), Augusto B Leguía 940, with singles/doubles for US$5/8 or US$6/10 with private bath.

Several hotels charge about US$10/15 for rooms with private bath and hot water. The *H & C Pensión* (☎ 71-2391), Zela 734, is clean and quite good but the single rooms have shared hot showers. The *Lido Hostal* (☎ 72-1184), San Martín 876A, is another decent option. The *Hostal Copacabana* (☎ 72-1721), Arias Araguez 370, has clean rooms which may be noisy at weekends because of the loud disco next door. The *Hostal Inclan* (☎ 72-3701), Inclan 171, isn't bad and also has some decent budget rooms (US$4 per person) with shared baths. The *Hostal Alcazar* is small and not very friendly but has clean rooms. Other choices in the US$10/15 range include the reasonable *Hostal Angi* (☎ 71-3502), Modesto Basadre 893, the fairly basic but conveniently located *Hostal Virrey* (☎ 72-3061), Ayacucho 88, and the rather grimy *Hostal Florida* (☎ 71-1204), 2 de Mayo 382, which has hot water but only in the mornings.

Places to Stay – middle

All the rooms in this section have private bath and hot water. Some of the more expensive ones may have a dual pricing system whereby foreigners are charged more. The highest prices are charged before Christmas and at weekends when shoppers from Chile come to town. Prices may drop when hotels are not busy.

The clean and friendly *Hostal Lider* (☎ 71-5441, 71-1176), Zela 724, has some rooms with TV and phone and charges about US$12/20. The *Hostal Avenida* (☎ 72-4582, 72-4531), Bolognesi 699, and *Garden Hostal* (☎ 71-1825), Junín 78, both charge about US$14/21 and look OK. The *Hotel Lima* (☎ 71-1912, fax 71 3781), San Martín 442, is about US$16/23 and has been praised for its decent restaurant and central location but criticized for its water supply (hot water from 6 to 10 am and 6 to 10 pm).

The *Hostal Zapata* (☎ 72-1921, fax 72-4101), Bolognesi 701, charges US$18/25 for adequate rooms with a telephone. Also in this price range is the friendly *Hostal Hogar* (☎ 71-1352), 28 de Julio 146, which has TVs in the rooms and is run by women who are nice but is otherwise fairly simple. The *Hostal El Inca* (☎ 72-1141), San Martín 982, is currently an adequate hotel in this price range but there are plans to make it the Americana hotel for passengers on that airline. Anything could happen with the prices then.

The *Hostal Premier* (☎ 71-5943, fax 71-5110), has rather small simple rooms that do offer TVs and telephones. It also has a snack bar. Rates are about US$23/33. The *Hostal Alborada* (☎ 71-2621), is an overpriced couple place charging US$30 for a double with TV. The *Hotel Emperador* (☎ 71-4291), San Martín 558, has rooms with telephone for US$30/40 but doesn't seem like anything special aside from being right by the Plaza de Armas. Opposite, the *Gran Hotel Central* (☎ 71-2281, 71-4841, fax 72-6031), San Martín 561, has nicer rooms for US$33/45. The clean, modern and friendly *Hostal El Mesón*

(☎ 72-5841, fax 72-1832), Unanue 175, is also close to the plaza and has a cafeteria. They charge US$35/48. Also in this price range but away from the center is the *Holiday Suites Hotel* (☎ 71-5371, 72-2662), Alto de Lima 1476, offering large rooms (but no suites) and a pool. These last three have parking garages.

Places to Stay – top end

The *Plaza Hotel* (☎ 72-2101, fax 72-6952), San Martín 421, is on the plaza and offers reasonable carpeted rooms with TV and phone for US$40/50. They have a cafeteria. The *Hotel Camino Real* (☎ 72-6212, 72-1891, fax 72-6433), San Martín 855, has nice rooms with minibar, TV and phone for US$45/60 as well as suites for US$90. They have a restaurant, bar with dancing, and cafeteria. The best in town is the *Gran Hotel Tacna* (☎ 72-4193, fax 72-2015; in Lima 442-3090, fax 442-4180), Bolognesi 300. Rooms are about US$58/77 and may include breakfast; bungalows and suites are US$115 a double. They have a pool, tennis court, pleasant grounds, a restaurant and a bar with dancing.

Places to Eat

One of the best and most popular restaurants in town is the Italian-style *El Viejo Almacén*, San Martín 577. It charges between US$3 and US$6 for a meal and has good steaks, pasta, ice cream, espresso coffee, cheap local wine and desserts. Nearby is the cheaper *Café Genova* with pavement tables and good coffee.

If you don't want Italian food, try the *Restaurant Sur Peruano* at Ayacucho 80. It's inexpensive and popular with the locals, especially at lunch time, Monday to Saturday. Another local favorite is the very clean *Paladar*, Meléndez 228, where a set lunch menu is under US$2 and the food is good.

Good Chinese food is to be had at the popular *Chifa Say Wa*. For chicken, try *El Pollo Pechugon*, Bolognesi 378, where half a grilled chicken and French fries will cost you about US$3.50. Locals say it's the best chicken in Tacna. Next door, the *Chifa Kenny* has good cheap set lunch menus starting at US$1.50. There are several other budget restaurants along Bolognesi between the post office and Junín.

The fairly new *El Gaucho* (☎ 72-6522), Pinto 100, specializes in Argentine-style parrilladas (mixed grills) which cost about US$15 but are very good. They also serve other international foods. The lively *Cevichería El Corsario* (☎ 72-4506), Avenida Arica at San José, is in the southwest corner of town along an unpaved road near the Ciudad Universitaria. Take a taxi to find it. They open at 6 am and serve some of the best ceviches and seafood in town. Ceviches start around US$5. Nearby is another recommended seafood restaurant, the *Silvia* (☎ 72-4345), Miraflores 702. It is quieter than the Corsario.

The *Helados Piamonte*, on Bolognesi a block from the Gran Hotel Tacna, is recommended for ice cream. The restaurant at the Hotel Lima is quite good and not expensive, while those at the Hotel de Turistas and Hotel Camino Real are good but pricey.

The *Rancho San Antonio* (☎ 72-4471), Coronel Bustios 298, serves good Peruvian and international food in a garden setting and has entertainment at weekends (see below). *El Remanso* (☎ 71-2034, 72-1722), Lima 2069, also has international food and entertainment.

In the campiña are several rustic restaurants that really come alive for weekend lunches with good typical food and live music. In Pocollay, 5 km northeast of Tacna, there's *Restaurant Don Manuel* on the Plaza de Armas, with reasonably priced good local food and a loud but fun band. A few blocks beyond the plaza, *La Huerta* is a nice quiet outdoor place with no music. *Restaurant Campestre El Hueco* (☎ 71-3901), on the outskirts of Pocollay on the way to Pacchia, has good meals (including cuy) in the US$8 to US$15 range. They have a variety of live music for weekend lunches.

Entertainment

The *Rancho San Antonio* restaurant has peñas on Friday or Saturday nights. Several acts may be featured with a variety of Latin American music, including merengue, salsa, nueva ola and folklórica. Shows get underway around 10 pm and a cover is charged. The *El Remanso* restaurant has a video pub and live music from about 10 pm on Saturdays. Rock, reggae, etc, is often featured. Cover is about US$3. *Peña Brundun* on Bolognesi at Herrera is another weekend nightspot that doesn't charge a cover. Nightspots with dancing are found at the Hotel de Turistas and Hotel Camino Real. The local newspaer *El Correos* can tell you what's going on.

Things to Buy

Although there is a semi duty-free area and markets with international goods, these are of more interest to locals than to most readers. There are no real bargains here.

A local product is *damascos macerados* – a damson plum which is marinaded for two years in locally produced pisco. You can then buy either the fruit-flavored liquor or jars of the pisco-soaked fruit. Both are good. A store selling this is Pelipor, at Varela 409.

Getting There & Away

Air There are several flights every day to and from Arequipa. There are also several flights a day to and from Lima, some of which stop in Arequipa and others which are direct. Faucett has three flights a week to Ilo, a service which began only recently. You can make same day connections via Arequipa to Juliaca, Cuzco and Puerto Maldonado, and via Lima to most major northern Peruvian cities. Aero Continente, AeroPerú, Americana, Imperial Air and Faucett all serve Tacna (see map for locations). Fares (including tax) are about US$108 to Lima with most of them, though Faucett may be more expensive unless you buy the ticket several days in advance. Imperial Air is cheaper but flew to and from Arequipa and Lima only on three evenings a week in early 1995 and recently suspended that itinerary, so check with them. Fares to Arequipa are US$26. Additional domestic departure tax of US$4 is charged at the airport.

Air tickets are subject to a 18% tax if the ticket is bought in Peru. Several Peruvian airlines have offices in Arica, Chile, where the tax on the same ticket is 2%. If you buy airline tickets in Arica, be sure to ask about discounts and air passes (see Getting There & Away).

If you fly from Lima to Tacna, cross to Arica by land, then fly from Arica to Santiago – it will cost you about US$100 less than the international Lima-Santiago fare bought in Peru.

In the past, there were international flights (with AeroPerú) from Arica to Lima which were no more expensive than flying from Tacna. These have been discontinued but you should ask to see if they have been started again.

Various international flights leave intermittently from Tacna. AeroPerú recently had international flights between Tacna and La Paz, Bolivia, on Friday evenings. Americana advertised weekly flights to/from Salta, Argentina, during December 1994, for Christmas shopping sprees.

Bus There is now a new (since the last edition) Terminal Terrestre on Unanue, at the northeast end of town. A US45¢ terminal use tax is levied from all passengers. It's normally well-organized, but sometimes gets a bit crazy when there are large groups of locals going home after shopping sprees.

Flores Hermanos (☎ 72-6691) is the biggest local company, with about 14 buses a day to Arequipa, seven to Moquegua, 10 to Ilo, and a daily 3.45 pm bus (additional departures at weekends) to Toquepala. Several companies run frequent buses to Lima (US$17 to US$35, 21 to 28 hours). Some companies run luxury services (with aircon, videos, on-board toilet, snacks, etc).

Most buses leave in the evening. Arequipa (US$4 to US$7, seven hours) is frequently served, as are other destinations south of Lima. Cruz del Sur has buses to Cuzco in the evening.

Most buses leave from the terminal, but there are exceptions (which may change in the future). Ormeño (☎ 72-4401), with several buses a day to Arequipa and Lima, has offices at Arias Araguez 700. Buses to Puno (US$8, 12 hours) and the Lake Titicaca area leave, usually in the evenings, from the jumble of various bus companies on Avenida Circumvalación, north of the city and east of the main terminal. Local buses to Boca del Río (the beach) and to Calientes leave from outside but close to the terminal.

Buses (US$2) and colectivo taxis (US$4) to Arica, Chile, leave frequently from the terminal. Taxi drivers help you through the border formalities (if your papers are in order). However, a new bus/taxi terminal for Arica is being planned on the Panamericana, about 2 km south of town en route to the airport. If this becomes a reality, things will change yet again. Write and let me know.

Finally, note that northbound buses are frequently stopped and searched by immigration and/or customs officials not far north of Tacna. Have your passport handy and beware of passengers asking you to hold a package for them while they go to the bathroom! The road to Moquegua is often a dead straight run through red-hued desert, but several passport and customs checks can slow the trip.

Colectivo Most colectivo services have now stopped with the exception of those from the bus terminal to Arica and from the corner of Leguia and Arias Araguez to Moquegua. This last may also stop soon.

Train Trains between Tacna and Arica are the cheapest but slowest way to cross the border. Turn of the century locomotives can be seen in the Tacna train station while you wait for the train. Supposedly, there are trains from Tacna at 5 am and 1 pm daily but travelers report that they don't always leave, despite the timetable at the train station. The morning departure is the most likely but you can't rely on it. The trip takes 1½ hours. Your passport is stamped at the train station, there is no stop at the actual border and you receive your entry stamp when you arrive. There are no money changers at the station.

Getting Around

The airport is 5 km south of town. A taxi charges about US$4 to Tacna or you can go direct from the airport to Arica, with the appropriate stop at the border, for US$40. There is no airport bus.

A Taxi from downtown to the bus terminal is about US$1.50.

GOING TO CHILE

Border crossing formalities are relatively straightforward in both directions. Taxis are the quickest way of crossing while trains are the cheapest. The border closes at 10 pm. Chile is an hour ahead of Péru (2 hours if daylight saving time is in effect). A casa de cambio in Arica is at 18 de Septiembre 330, where you can change both soles and dollars into pesos and vice versa.

From Arica you can continue south into Chile by air or bus or northeast into Bolivia by air or one of the two trains a week (currently Tuesday and Saturday mornings, often full from December to March). There are plenty of hotels and restaurants; Arica is quite a lively place. For information about travel in Chile, go to the Chilean tourist office (☎ 23-2101), Avenida Prat 305, or consult Lonely Planet's *Chile & Easter Island*.

The Arequipa Area

At 2325 meters above sea level in the mountainous desert of the western Andes, Arequipa is a city of the highlands rather than one of the coastal lowlands. It is, however, better connected with the coastal transportation network than it is with the highlands and is therefore often included with the south coast in many guidebooks.

The Panamericana leaves the coast at Camaná and heads east into the Andes. At Repartición, 135 km beyond Camaná, the Panamericana swings south, but a major highway continues climbing eastward for a further 40 km to Arequipa, capital of its department and the main city of southern Peru. Arequipeños claim that with a population of about a million the city is Peru's second largest, but it vies with Trujillo for this honor.

It certainly is a beautiful city surrounded by spectacular mountains. The most famous of these is the volcano El Misti (5822 meters), which has a beautiful conical peak topped by snow. It rises majestically behind Arequipa's cathedral and is clearly visible from the Plaza de Armas. To the left of El Misti is the higher and more ragged Chachani (6075 meters), and to the right is the lower peak of Pichu Pichu.

Many of the city's buildings date to colonial times, and many are built from a very light-colored volcanic rock called *sillar*. The buildings dazzle in the sun, which shines almost every day, earning Arequipa the nickname 'the white city.' Locals, however, sometimes say that 'When the moon separated from the earth, it forgot to take Arequipa.'

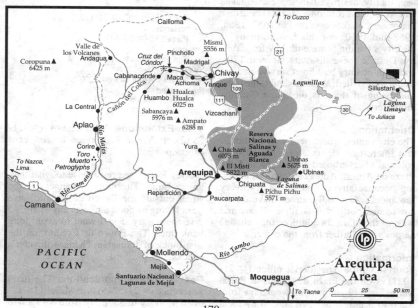

History

Arequipa has a long history. There is archaeological evidence of pre-Inca settlement by Aymara Indians from the Lake Titicaca area. Some scholars think the Aymaras named the city – *ari* means 'peak' and *quipa* means 'lying behind' in Aymara; hence Arequipa is 'the place lying behind the peak' (probably referring to the conical peak of Misti). Other people claim that it is a Quechua name. An oft-heard legend says that the fourth Inca, Mayta Capac, was traveling through the valley and became enchanted by it. He ordered his retinue to stop, saying, '*Ari, quipay*,' which translates to 'Yes, stay.'

The Spaniards refounded the city on August 15, 1540, and the date is remembered with a week-long fair in Arequipa. The fireworks show in the Plaza de Armas on August 14 is particularly spectacular.

Unfortunately, the city is built in an area highly prone to earthquakes, and none of the original buildings remain. Arequipa was totally destroyed in the earthquakes and volcanic eruptions of 1600. Further major earthquakes occurred in 1687, 1868, 1958 and 1960. For this reason, many of the city's buildings are built low for stability. Despite these disasters, several 17th- and 18th-century buildings survive and are frequently visited. Without doubt, the most interesting of these is the Santa Catalina monastery.

Orientation

The city center, where nearly all the hotels and interesting sights are, is based on a colonial checkerboard pattern around the Plaza de Armas. Addresses can be confusing because streets change names every few blocks. Generally, streets have different names north and south and east and west of the plaza. In addition, they change names again farther from the center.

Information

Tourist Office The tourist office (☎ 21-1021) is on the Plaza de Armas at Portal Municipal 112 and is open weekdays from 8 am to 5 pm. It is often staffed by local tour guide students, so information varies in quality and quantity. The Policía de Turismo (see Emergency below) also provides information.

Visiting hours for churches in Arequipa are erratic. They vary every time I visit the city. The tourist office usually knows when specific churches are open to visitors, but even they can't keep up with the changes. Most churches are normally open from 7 to 9 am and from 6 to 8 pm for worship, and extended hours for tourism.

Foreign Consulates

Argentina
    Mercaderes 212, office 704 (☎ 21-5004)
Austria
    Jerusalén 201 B (☎ 21-1507)
Bolivia
    Piérola 209, office 321 (☎ 21-3391)
Britain
    Quezada 107 (☎ 21-1961)
Chile
    Mercaderes 202, office 401 (☎ 22-6787)
Finland
    Emmel 109 (☎ 22-3708)
Japan
    San Camilo 102 (☎ 21-1223)
Netherlands
    Parra 218 (☎ 24-3073)
Panama
    San José 214 (☎ 21-5123)
Sweden
    Tacna y Arica 145 (☎ 22-0751)
Switzerland
    Piérola 114 (☎ 21-2291)

Visa Extensions Migraciones (☎ 21-2552), P Viejo 216, does tourist card extensions.

Money Rates are pretty close to what they are in Lima. The money changers in the street outside the Banco de Crédito have been giving as good a rate as anywhere, so give them a try if you want to avoid long bank lines. The Banco de Crédito, on the first block of Jerusalén, changes traveler's checks.

Post & Telecommunications The main post office (☎ 21-5245) is at Moral 118. It's open Monday to Saturday from 8.45 am to

6.45 pm. There are several Telefónica del Peru offices that provide local and international phone and fax service. The main one (☎ 21-1111) is at A Thomas 201. The area code for Arequipa (and the surrounding area) is 054; drop the 0 when dialing from overseas.

Cultural Centers There are several cultural centers that are very active with art shows, concerts, film festivals, etc. They have libraries and cafés and welcome travelers. The main ones are the Instituto Cultural Peruano-NorteAmericano (☎ 24-3201, 24-3841), Melgar 109; Alianza Francesa (☎ 21-5579), Santa Catalina 208; Instituto Cultural Peruano-Alemán (☎ 21-8567), Ugarte 207; and Complejo Cultural Chaves de la Rosa, Santa Catalina 101.

Newspapers Three local newspapers have cinema and entertainment listings and abbreviated versions of international news. They are *El Pueblo, Arequipa Al Dia* and *Correo.*

Travel Agencies There are several travel agencies offering tours to the Cañón del Colca and other nearby areas described in the Around Arequipa section. The Colca trip goes almost every day, but other advertised daily trips go infrequently due to lack of passengers.

I have received mixed reports about all travel agencies, and none stand out as much better than others except for the expensive outfits like Coltur (☎ 25-1510, fax 23-9159), San Francísco 206, and the local branch of Lima Tours at Santa Catalina and Moral. These charge several times more than the many cheaper agencies who will often pool their clients.

Conresa (☎ 21-1847, 21-5820), Jerusalén 409, or Continental, Jerusalén 402, often provide the vehicle for the cheaper agencies' pool. Although large, comfortable buses are often offered, minibuses are usually provided unless there are plenty of travelers. Unfortunately, the minibuses get overcrowded and don't have adequate leg room for tall people. It may be better to go in a smaller group with a car. Catalina Tours has been criticized for using minibuses, but most agencies will if the group is small. Trips may be cancelled or postponed if there are not enough clients, but you aren't told this until the time of departure, when some poor excuse like 'vehicle trouble' is given. If possible, avoid paying until you are actually on the vehicle. Expeandes (☎ 21-2888, fax 22-8814), La Merced 408, has been recommended for more adventurous tours and has equipment for rent. There are many other agencies – shop around.

Guides often speak English and/or other languages, but not all of them do. Some can spout a garbled explanation in poor English but don't really speak the language fluently. Guides should be able to produce a Tourist Guide card. Multilingual guides who have been recommended include Dante Fernandez (☎ 23-1657) and the Manrique family (☎ 22-4238).

Laundry There are a couple of lavanderías on A Thomas near Garcí Carbajal.

Medical Services There are several hospitals and clinics, of which the best is Clínica Arequipa (☎ 25-3408, 25-3424), at Avenida Bolognesi and Puente Grau.

Emergency The Policía de Turismo (☎ 23-9888), Jerusalén 317, provides basic tourist information and helps in the event of emergencies. They are friendly and open 24 hours.

Dangers & Annoyances Pickpockets abound on the busy street of San Juan de Dios, where many bus companies have offices. Also take care around the market and train station areas, particularly at night, but watch your belongings carefully anywhere in town. There have been several reports of belongings being stolen from restaurants, so keep your stuff in sight. Thieves work in groups, some distracting you while another snatches your bag. For further information, see the Dangers & Annoyances section in Facts for the Visitor.

Monastery of Santa Catalina

The Monasterio de Santa Catalina, Santa Catalina 300, wins my 'most fascinating colonial religious building in Peru' award, so even if you've overdosed on churches, you should try to see it. Actually, it's not a monastery, as the name suggests; it's a convent. Nor is it just a religious building; it's a good-sized complex of about 20,000 sq meters, covering an entire city block – almost a city within a city. For more description, see the sidebar 'Monasterio Misterioso.'

There are two ways of visiting Santa Catalina. One is to wander around slowly, discovering the intricate architecture of the complex; the other is to get slightly lost and then find your way again, revisiting the areas you enjoyed the best. This is the way I recommend as being the most fun. Alternatively, you can hire a guide. Ask for a guide when you buy your entrance ticket and you'll be given the next available one. Between them, they speak English, French, German and Italian, and there are plans to add a Japanese-speaking guide. The tours last about 90 minutes, and there is no set cost. A tip is appreciated and well deserved.

Entrance costs US$3.50, and it's open daily from 9 am to 5 pm (last tickets sold at 4 pm). There is a small cafeteria that sells delicious homemade snacks cooked by the nuns.

The Cathedral

The imposing cathedral stands on the Plaza de Armas. The original structure, dating from 1656, was destroyed by fire in 1844. It was rebuilt over the next few years, but badly damaged by the earthquake of 1868, and so most of what you see has been rebuilt since then. The outside is impressive, but the inside is surprisingly bare. As

Monasterio Misterioso

The Monasterio de Santa Catalina was built in 1580 and enlarged in the 17th century. The founder was a rich widow, María de Guzmán, who only accepted nuns from the best Spanish families. All the nuns had to pay a dowry. Traditionally, the second daughter of upper-class families entered a nunnery, supposedly to live in poverty and renounce the material world. In fact, each nun had between one and four servants or slaves (usually black), and they were able to invite musicians to perform in the convent, have parties and generally live in the style to which they had become accustomed while growing up.

After about three centuries of these goings on, the pope complained that Santa Catalina was more like an exclusive club than a convent, and he sent Sister Josefa Cadena, a strict Dominican nun, to straighten things out. She arrived in 1871, sent all the rich dowries back to Europe, and freed all the servants and slaves, giving them the choice of staying on as nuns or leaving.

The convent is surrounded by imposing high walls, and the approximately 450 people (about a third of them nuns and the rest servants) who once lived here never ventured outside the convent. Accordingly, the place was shrouded in mystery for almost 400 years. It finally opened to the public in 1970, when the mayor of Arequipa forced the convent to comply with laws requiring it to install electricity and running water. The nuns, now too poor to do this, opened their doors to tourism to pay for the modernization.

Today, the approximately 20 remaining nuns continue to live a cloistered life, but only in the northern corner of the complex. The rest is open to the public, who are free to wander around. It's like stepping back in time to a forgotten world of narrow twisting streets and tiny plazas, beautiful courtyards and simple living quarters.

Much of Santa Catalina has been excellently restored, and the delicate pastel colors of the buildings are attractively contrasted with bright flowers, period furnishings and religious art. It is a paradise for photographers, who often spend all day capturing the subtle changes in light as the sun moves across the sky. It's a wonderful place to just relax and wind down, write your journal and perhaps reflect upon your trip. ■

with many of Arequipa's churches, the interior emphasizes an airy spaciousness and luminosity, and the high vaults are much less cluttered than churches in other parts of Peru.

The cathedral stretches the entire length of one side of the plaza, the only one that does in Peru. The interior has a distinctly international flair. This cathedral is one of 70 basilicas in the world that are entitled to display the Vatican flag (on the right side of the altar). Both the altar and the 12 columns carved into the 12 apostles are from Italian marble. The huge Byzantine-style brass lamp hanging in front of the altar is from Seville, Spain. The pulpit was carved in France from European cedar. In 1870, Belgium provided the very impressive organ, which is reputedly the largest in South America. For over a century it played very poorly because of damage during shipping. The Belgian authorities sent a specialist over to restore it in the 1980s, and now concerts are given on it two or three times a month.

The cathedral is supposedly open from 7 to 10.30 am and 4.30 to 8 pm, but this changes frequently. Entrance is free.

La Compañía

Just off the southeastern corner of the Plaza de Armas, this church is one of the oldest in Arequipa and noted for its ornate main facade, which bears the inscription 'Año 1698' although the side porch dates from 1654. This Jesuit church was so solidly built that it withstood the earthquakes that toppled the cathedral and other buildings.

The main altar is of Central American cedar carved in churrigueresque style and completely covered in 18 kt gold leaf. To the left of the main altar is the San Ignacio chapel with a wonderful polychrome cupola. Unfortunately, many of the other original murals were covered with plaster and white paint by 19th-century restorers.

Attached to the church are two attractive cloisters, which are now used commercially. There are several stores selling high-quality alpaca goods, locally produced liquors, antiques and other products.

Opening times vary from year to year. Recently the church was open from 9 am to 1 pm and from 3 to 8 pm, with free admission. To see the San Ignacio chapel costs US45¢. The chapel is open from 9 am to noon and 3 to 6 pm. The cloisters function from 7 am to 8 pm.

San Francisco

This church was originally built in the 16th century and has been damaged by earthquakes. It still stands, and visitors can see a large crack in the cupola – testimony to the power of the quakes. There is an impressive silver altar, but by Peruvian standards the rest of the church has a relatively simple interior.

Hours are 5.30 to 8.30 pm. Admission is free.

La Recoleta

A short walk from the city center is the monastery of La Recoleta, built on the west side of the Río Chili in 1648 by the Franciscans and now completely rebuilt. This is the most interesting place to visit in Arequipa after Santa Catalina. The Franciscans were among the most active of the Catholic missionaries, and study and education played a large part in their activities.

I was fascinated by their huge library of more than 20,000 books, many of which are centuries old. They have several *incunables*, or books dating from before 1501, and their oldest volume dates from 1494. The library also has several 19th-century Peruvian maps, printed in Lima, and showing Iquitos and the territory north of the Río Marañón as part of Ecuador, which it was until the Ecuadorian-Peruvian war of 1941.

There is also a museum of Amazonian exhibits collected by the missionaries. These include a large collection of stuffed birds and animals, as well as objects made by the Indians. They have an extensive collection of preconquest artifacts and religious art of the Cuzqueño school. You can visit the cloisters and monks' cells.

AREQUIPA AREA

The monastery, at La Recoleta 100, is open Monday to Saturday from 9 am to noon and from 3 to 5 pm. Admission is US$2. A Spanish-speaking guide is available (tip expected). Make sure that you don't miss the library, especially if you're a bibliophile.

Other Churches
If you're particularly interested in churches from the colonial era, then you might also want to visit the churches of San Agustín, Santo Domingo, Santa Teresa and La Merced.

Museums
For a city of its size, Arequipa doesn't have a good selection of museums. One of the best is in the monastery of La Recoleta. The Museo Histórico Municipal has a few paintings, historical documents, photographs, maps and other paraphernalia pertaining to the city's history. It is open weekdays from 8 am to 6 pm. Admission is US50¢. There is an archaeological collection at the University of San Agustín on Avenida Ayacucho about a kilometer east of the center, but it was recently closed for maintenance.

Colonial Houses
Many beautiful colonial houses, now being used as art galleries, banks or offices, can be visited. One of the best is Casa Ricketts, built in 1738. It was first a seminary, then the archbishop's palace, and then a school before passing into the hands of one of Arequipa's upper-crust families, who finally sold it to the Banco Central. It now houses a small art gallery and museum, as well as bank offices. It's open weekdays from 8 am to noon and from 3 to 6 pm; entry is free.

The Casona Iriberry, housing the Complejo Cultural Chaves de la Rosa, is a pleasant colonial house with several patios. It dates from the late 1700s. Also worth seeing are the Casa de Moral, now owned by the Banco Industrial, and the Goyeneche Palace.

Yanahuara
The suburb of Yanahuara is within walking distance of the town center and makes a good excursion. Go west on Avenida Puente Grau over the bridge and continue on Avenida Ejército for about six or seven blocks. Turn right on Avenida Lima and walk five blocks to a small plaza where you'll find the church of Yanahuara, which dates from 1750. There's a *mirador* (viewing platform) at the end of the plaza from where there are excellent views of Arequipa and El Misti.

Head back along Avenida Jerusalén (in Yanahuara), which is the next street parallel to Avenida Lima, and just before reaching Avenida Ejército you'll see the well-known Picantería Sol de Mayo, where you can stop for a good lunch of typical Arequipeño food. The roundtrip should take about 1½ hours, starting from the town center, but if you get tired, there's the green city bus, with a Yanahuara sign, that leaves Arequipa along Puente Grau and returns from Yanahuara Plaza to the city every few minutes.

Cayma
A little way beyond Yanahuara is Cayma, another suburb with an oft-visited church. To get there, continue along Avenida Ejército about three blocks beyond Avenida Jerusalén and then turn right on Avenida Cayma and climb up this road for about a kilometer. Alternately, from Yanahuara, take Calle San Vicente and then Avenida Leon Velarde to Cayma. The church of San Miguel Arcángel is open from 9 am to 4 pm, and the church warden will take you up the small tower for a tip, where you'll have excellent views, particularly in the afternoon. Buses marked Cayma go there from Arequipa along Avenida Grau.

Tingo
Tingo is another of the frequently visited suburbs of Arequipa, 5 km south of the city. There's a small lake, swimming pools and typical restaurants, which are popular with Arequipeños on Sundays, but it's pretty

quiet during the rest of the week. Catch a Tiabaya bus from the corner of Avenidas Parra and Salaverry.

Paucarpata

This suburb is about 7 km southeast of town and features an attractive colonial church on the main plaza as well as a great local restaurant (see Places to Eat). Gray buses along Socabaya in Arequipa go there, or take a cab. From Paucarpata, El Molino de Sabandía is about a 2 km walk away; this mill was built in 1621, fell into disrepair and was restored in 1973. As you walk there, note the Inca terracing en route, particularly around the village of Yumina. You can visit the mill for US$1, and they'll make it work for you. The pleasant surrounding gardens with grazing llamas are a nice place for a picnic in the country.

Spanish Courses

The Instituto Cultural Peruano-NorteAmericano (☎ 24-3201, 24-3841), Melgar 109, offers Spanish courses. Individual teachers also offer classes. Ask at the instituto or the tourist office.

Special Events

Arequipeños claim that their Holy Week (before Easter) celebrations are similar to the solemn and traditional Spanish observances from Seville. Maundy Thursday, Good Friday and Holy Saturday processions are particularly colorful and, in some districts, end with the burning of an effigy of Judas. Arequipa fills up for the Fiesta de la Virgen de Chapi on May 1, which, if it coincides with Easter, makes hotel rooms very difficult to find. The fiesta itself takes place at the Santuario de la Virgen de Chapi, 45 km from Arequipa. Pilgrims walk there, camping en route.

The founding of the city, August 15, is celebrated with parades, fireworks, dancing, beauty pageants and other events over the course of several days. There are several other minor fiestas throughout the year.

Places to Stay – bottom end

Some of the cheapest hotels are near the train station and market, where you should be careful, especially at night.

One of the best of the really cheap and basic hotels is the clean *Hotel Crillon Serrano* (☎ 21-2392), Peru 109, which is friendly and sometimes has warm water in the morning. They charge about US$3 per person or US$4 with private bath. Next door, the *Pensión Tito* (☎ 23-4424), Peru 105B, is a few cents more and also a good deal. The *Hotel Regis* (☎ 22-3612), Ugarte 202, is a good budget hotel. It's clean, safe and friendly, and has 24-hour hot water, a rooftop terrace and rooms for US$4.50 per person. The *Hostal Colca Tours* (☎ 21-1679), Victor Lira 105, is also recommended as clean, safe and friendly. It's an excellent deal at US$5.50/10 for rooms with private warm showers, but it's near the market – not a very good location.

Travelers on a very tight budget will find cheaper hotels, but they are not as good. *Hostal Comercio* (☎ 21-2186), on San Camilo, is probably the cheapest place in town: very basic, not very clean and supposedly with hot water at times. Rates are US$2.50/4.50 for singles/doubles. The *Gran Hotel* (☎ 21-2001), A Thomas 451, is among the cheapest at US$3/5, but it's dirty and only has cold water. The *Hostal Granada*, on Peru near the market, is even worse and more expensive. The basic *Hostal America* (☎ 24-3141), Peral 202, has erratic hot water and is US$3 per person or US$8 for a double with bath. For the same price, the *Hotel San Francisco* (☎ 23-4006), San Juan de Dios 314A, has hot water in the morning, but it isn't very clean. The *Hostal Lider Inn* (☎ 23-8210), Consuelo 429, charges US$5.50 for reasonably clean double rooms with private hot showers; it's popular with young Arequipeño couples. The *Hostal Europa* (☎ 23-9787) and *Hostal Paris* (☎ 23-6250) are next to each other and close to the train station, but they are fairly basic and only have hot water in the morning. The Europa charges US$3 per person and the

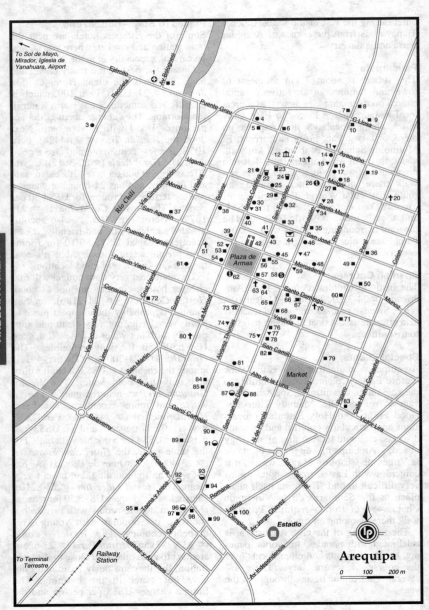

To Sol de Mayo,
Mirador, Iglesia de
Yanahuara, Airport

To Terminal
Terrestre

Railway
Station

Plaza de
Armas

Market

Estadio

Arequipa

0   100   200 m

PLACES TO STAY

2	La Posada del Puente Grau
5	Hostal Wilson
6	Hostal Santa Catalina
7	Hotel Jerusalén
8	La Casa de Mi Abuela
9	Hostal Latino
10	Hostal Núñez
16	La Boveda Inn
19	Residencial Rivero
27	La Casa de Melgar
29	Hotel Regis
33	Hotel Crismar
35	Hotel La Fontana
36	Hostal America
37	Hostal Tumi de Oro
49	Hostal Mercaderes
50	Hotel Conquistador
53	Hotel Maison Plaza
55	Hostal Nikos
56	Hostal Mirador
57	Hotel El Portal
60	Hotel Crillon Serrano, Pensión Tito
65	Hostal V Lira
66	Hostal Hugo, Jorge's
68	Hostal Imperial
69	Hotel La Condesa
71	Hotel Viza
72	Hostal Lider Inn
76	Hostal Royal
78	Hotel San Francisco
79	Hostal Granada
82	Hostal Comercio
83	Hostal Colca Tours
84	Hostal Americano
85	Gran Hotel
86	Hostal San Juan
89	Hotel San Gregory
90	Hostal Virrey
94	Hostal Florida
95	Hostals Europa, Paris
97	Hostal Grace
98	Hostal Premier
99	Hostal Colonia
100	Hostal Extra

PLACES TO EAT

2	La Posada del Puente Grau
11	Govinda Vegetarian Restaurant, Other Budget Places
15	Pizzería Los Leños
16	Lakshimivan Vegetarian Restaurant
28	Lluvia de Oro
31	Café Peña Anuschka
34	Pizzería San Antonio
41	Central Garden Restaurant
47	Restaurant Bonanza
52	Restaurant Cuzco, Balcony Restaurant, Others
59	La Rueda Parrilladas
67	Monzas
74	Cevichería 45
75	Restaurant América
77	Restaurant Dalmacia, Puerto Rico

OTHER

1	Clínica Arequipa
3	Monasterio de La Recoleta, Museo
4	National Car Rental
12	Museo Municipal, Crafts Shops
13	San Francisco
14	Conresa Tours
17	Continental Tours
18	Instituto Cultural Peruano-NorteAmericano
20	Santa Teresa
21	Monasterio de Santa Catalina
22	La Quenas
23	Romie's Peña
24	Blues Bar
25	Instituto Cultural Peruano-Alemán
26	Tourist Police, Information
30	Alianza Francesa
32	Coltur
35	Peña, Picantería
38	Casa de Moral
39	Complejo Cultural Chaves de la Rosa, Casona Iriberry
40	Lima Tours
42	La Catedral
43	Casa Ricketts
44	Correos Central
45	Map Store
46	Carnaby Disco
48	Cine Municipal
51	San Agustín
54	AeroPerú, Faucett, Americana, Aero Continente (Airlines)
57	Cine Portal, Imperial Air
58	Banco de Crédito
61	Casablanca Disco
62	Tourist Office
63	La Compañía
64	Cine Fenix
70	Santo Domingo
73	Telefónica del Peru
80	La Merced
81	Cine Ateneo
84	Cine Variedades
87	Bus Companies to Colca
88	Many Bus Companies
91	Cruz del Sur, Sur Peruano
92	Cruz del Sur
93	Ormeño
96	Expreso Sudamericano

AREQUIPA AREA

Paris is US$4/5, or US$6/8 in rooms with a private bath.

The *Hostal San Juan* (☎ 24-3861), San Juan de Dios 521, is a little better, though it's on a noisy street; it charges US$4/7 and has doubles with private hot shower for US$8. The *Hostal Mercaderes* (☎ 21-4830), Peral 117, is basic but OK for US$4/6 or US$6 per person with private bath and warm showers. The *Hostal Mirador* charges a little more (but beware

of overcharging; ask to see the posted rates), and it supposedly has hot water in the shared bathrooms, though reports are mixed about this. A few rooms (mainly doubles and triples) have great views over the Plaza de Armas. The small *La Boveda Inn*, Jerusalén 402, has double rooms with shared showers for US$8 and a popular vegetarian restaurant in the courtyard. The basic *Hostal V Lira* (☎ 21-3161) has hot water and is reasonably secure. Rates are

US$5/8. The equally basic *Hostal Virrey* (☎ 23-5191) sometimes has hot water and charges US$4/6, or US$6/9 with private bath.

The reasonably clean and friendly *Hostal Royal* (☎ 21-2071), San Juan de Dios 300A, has hot water and rooms for US$4.50 a person, or US$10 for a double with private bath. The popular *Hostal Santa Catalina* (☎ 22-2722), Santa Catalina 500, is basic but fairly clean, and there is hot water; it charges US$6/8, or US$7.50/10 with private bath. The rooms on the ground floor are noisier than the ones upstairs. The *Residencial Rivero* (☎ 22-9266), Rivero 420, is similarly priced, has tepid water and is not outstanding. The basic but clean and adequate *Hostal Grace* (☎ 23-5924), Quiroz 121, near the train station, charges US$7/9 in rooms with communal warm showers. Similar and in the same price range is the *Hostal Imperial* (☎ 21-2125), San Juan de Dios 210, and the *Hostal Nikos* (☎ 21-7713), Mercaderes 142, though Nikos is reportedly dirty and poorly maintained.

The *Hostal Núñez* (☎ 21-8648, 22-0111), Jerusalén 528 (no sign), is good, secure and friendly and charges US$5 per person, or US$9/15 with a private bath. There is hot water and a terrace, and the place is popular with gringos. The *Hostal Tumi de Oro*, San Agustín 311A, is clean and friendly and has hot water. They charge US$5 per person, or S$7.50/12.50 with private bath. The *Hostal Americano* (☎ 21-1752), A Thomas 435, is basic but clean and has hot water. There are beautiful red geraniums in the passageways, and it's run by a friendly, if slightly fussy, elderly couple. All rooms are US$10 for one or two people with shared bathrooms. Others in this price range include *La Casa de Melgar* (☎ 22-2459), Melgar 108A, which is friendly and in a nice building, with adequate rooms; the *Hostal Colonia* (☎ 24-2766), on Socabaya, with basic but large rooms; the *Hostal Extra* (☎ 22-1217), on Olimpica at Leticia, which is friendly and surrounded by a garden; and the decent *Hotel San Gregory* (☎ 24-5036), A

Thomas 535, whose clean rooms all come with a private bath.

Hostal Hugo/Jorge's (☎ 21-3988), Santo Domingo 110, has basic rooms for US$6/10 and rooms with private hot bath for US$11/15. The nice *Hostal Wilson* (☎ 23-8781), Grau 306, charges US$6 per person or US$7.50 per person with private bath. The *Hostal Florida* (☎ 23-8467, 22-8710), San Juan de Dios 664B, is OK and charges US$7.50/12.50 with shared bath or US$11/16 with private bath. The clean *Hostal Premier* (☎ 24-1091), Quiroz 100, charges US$9/14 or US$12/16 with private bath.

Places to Stay – middle

The very respectable and secure *La Casa de Mi Abuela* (☎ 22-3194), Jerusalén 606, is a good choice. The *abuela* (grandmother) after whom the place is named died in 1994 at the age of 100. Singles/doubles with a private shower and hot water cost US$16/23, or half this price with shared bathrooms. There's an attractive garden full of singing birds, with tables and chairs provided for breakfast. Breakfast in bed is available and is not too expensive. Each room has a radio and a stock of beer and soft drinks, which you pay for when you leave. Also, there are some bungalows. It's clean and well run and very secure – you must ring a bell to get in.

For the same price, the *Hostal Latino* (☎ 24-4770), Carlos Llosa 135, has large comfortable rooms with private hot baths, as well as a café. A new recommendation is the *Villa Baden Baden* (☎ 22-2416), Manuel Ugarteche 401, in the Selva Alegre suburb 1½ km north of the Plaza de Armas. This is a small B&B that charges about US$12 per person including breakfast.

The recommended *Hotel Conquistador* (☎ 21-2916, fax 21-8987), Mercaderes 409, is good value for US$23/31. The staff are friendly, and the manager speaks English. The lobby of the attractive colonial house is elegant, and the rooms, though fairly plain, have telephones. There is a restaurant. The similarly priced *Hotel Jerusalén* (☎ 24-4481, 24-4441, fax 24-3472), Jerusalén

601, has a restaurant, in-room telephones, and the luxury of a sit-down bathtub in some rooms – good if you're fed up with showers.

The *Hotel Maison Plaza* (☎ 21-8929, 21-8931), Portal de San Agustín 143, is right on the Plaza de Armas, though only two rooms have plaza views. They charge US$25/41, including breakfast, and have a suite (with plaza view) for US$55. The *Hotel La Fontana* (☎ 23-4161, fax 23-4171), Jerusalén 202, is a pretty good hotel with rooms for US$30/40. The similarly-priced *Hotel Viza* (☎ 23-2301, 23-2232), Peru 202, has adequate, carpeted rooms with telephones and TV. The *Hotel Crismar* (☎ 21-5290), Moral 107, has pretty good rooms with phone and TV for US$33/45. They have a decent restaurant and bar.

Places to Stay – top end

On the plaza is the very modern *Hotel El Portal* (☎ 21-5530, fax 23-4374), Portal de Flores 116. Good rooms are about US$50/65, plus a 50% surcharge if you have a plaza view. This is one of the best run and most comfortable hotels in town; it even boasts a rooftop swimming pool as well as a couple of restaurants, a bar and a disco. The similarly priced *La Posada del Puente* (☎ 25-3132, fax 25-3576), Avenida Bolognesi 101, is a small new boutique hotel with about 15 attractive rooms and a good, elegant, pricey restaurant and bar. The garden and river views make for a nice setting. More expensive is the *Libertador Arequipa* (☎ 21-5110, fax 24-1933; in Lima 442-1996, 442-1995), Plaza Bolívar in Selva Alegre, 1½ km north of the Plaza de Armas. Rooms cost US$96; suites are US$160, which is expensive for what you get. This is the grande dame of Arequipa's hotels, and the spacious rooms and public areas have a charmingly old-fashioned air. The stylish pink building is nicely set in sizable gardens with an unheated swimming pool and playground. There is a sedate restaurant and a fine Sunday brunch.

The *Hotel La Condesa* (☎ 21-3641, fax 21-3040), Piérola 201, was formerly the good *Hotel Presidente*; it changed hands in 1995. The new owners plan on making it the best hotel in town. It's already one of the most expensive at about US$65/95.

Places to Eat

In Arequipa, there are many budget restaurants around the Plaza de Armas, particularly on the Santa Catalina side. The *Balcony Restaurant* and the *Restaurant Cuzco*, on the northwest side of the plaza, 2nd floor, have fine views overlooking the plaza, the cathedral and El Misti; the food is OK and not expensive, but the service varies from slow to atrocious. Still, find your way up there (through a door to the right of the airline offices) and read, write and enjoy the views. Below the balcony are a few more cheap to middle-priced restaurants.

There are plenty of cheap chicken places; you can get half a grilled chicken for about US$2.50 in several places along San Juan de Dios, but watch for pickpockets on this street. Three good but reasonably priced restaurants in the 300 block of San Juan de Dios are the *Puerto Rico* (☎ 21-7512), the *Dalmacia* and the *América* – this last has good ice cream and snacks. There are also cheap restaurants offering set lunches for about US$1.50 or less along La Merced.

The *Govinda*, Jerusalén 505, is a vegetarian place run by the Hare Krishnas, and it's very cheap. Another popular vegetarian restaurant is *Lakshimivan* in the Boveda Inn, Jerusalén 402. There are several other cheap restaurants on these blocks, including *Lluvia de Oro*, Jerusalén 308.

Good Italian food is available at *Pizzería San Antonio* (☎ 21-3950), at Jerusalén and Santa Marta. This place is popular with young locals. Also very popular is the *Pizzería Los Leños*, Jerusalén 407, where they bake the pizza in a wood-burning oven. Recorded rock music (Rolling Stones) is interspersed with live Peruvian folklórico musicians wandering in during the evening, creating a friendly atmosphere. It's open Monday to Saturday from 5 pm till late. For some reason, they sell backpacks and camping gear. There are several other pizzerias.

For coffee drinkers, two upmarket cafés on the first block of San Francisco have good espresso, cappuccino and snacks. The best coffee, and also the most expensive, is at *Monzas*, on Santo Domingo, a block east of the plaza.

The *Bonanza*, Jerusalén 114, serves a good variety of reasonably priced dishes and is also popular with Arequipeños. Meals are in the US$3 to US$7 range.

The best ceviche (and nothing else) is served in the little *Cevichería 45* (☎ 24-2400), A Thomas 221, from 9 am to 3 pm. For Argentine-style steaks and grills, *La Rueda Parrilladas* (☎ 21-9330), Mercaderes 206, is expensive but good.

The friendly *Café Peña Anuschka*, Santa Catalina 204, serves homemade pastries, German specialities and tropical cocktails, and it occasionally has live musicians. Local art exhibited on the wall is for sale.

The best places for traditional food are outside the central area. Try the *Sol de Mayo*, Jerusalén 207 in the Yanahuara district. It is open only for lunch and serves good and reasonably priced (though not budget-priced) Peruvian food. (A luncheon visit to the Sol de Mayo should be combined with a visit to the mirador in Yanahuara.) Slightly farther afield is the excellent and locally popular *Tradición Arequipeña* (☎ 24-2385), Avenida Dolores 111, in the southeastern suburb of Paucarpata. Most taxi drivers know it (less than US$2 from the city center). Meals here are in the US$3 to US$6 range, and it is also open for lunch. A third recommendation is *La Cantarilla* (☎ 25-1515), Tahuaycani 106, in the southwestern suburb of Sachaca. Again, take a cab.

Try rocoto relleno (hot peppers stuffed with meat, rice and vegetables), cuy chactado (seared guinea pig), ocopa (potatoes with a spicy sauce and fried cheese), chupe de camarones (shrimp soup), chancho al horno (suckling pig), anticucho (shish kebab of beef or beef hearts) and ceviche (marinated seafood), and wash it down with chicha (fermented maize beer).

The alley behind the cathedral on Plaza de Armas has several popular, quaint and pricey restaurants. The names and owners of these places change often and quality varies accordingly. There are also some new mid- to high-priced places beside the Hotel El Portal. The *Central Garden Restaurant* and others on the first block of San Francisco are pricey but good. The restaurant in La Posada del Puente hotel is pretty good.

Entertainment

Things are generally pretty quiet midweek. An irritating habit of some places is to advertise a nightly peña when in fact there's rarely anything going on except from Thursday to Saturday nights. An exception is the small and rustic *Las Quenas* (☎ 21-5468), Santa Catalina 302, with live music nightly from 9 pm. Music varies, though folklórico predominates. There is a US$2.50 cover charge, and they serve food.

The *El Sillar* is a good late night weekend peña, with music getting underway around 11 pm and dancing continuing through the wee hours. The cover charge is about US$2.50, and the show has been recommended. The address has changed two or three times recently, so ask locals.

Romie's Peña (☎ 23-4465), Zela 202, has long been popular. It's a very lively but tiny

bar, so get there before 10 pm to get in – you have to ring the bell. The folklórico music is usually good. The cover charge is US$3, and the drinks are pricey. (A recent unconfirmed report indicates it has closed.) Locals recommend two good peñas in the Yanahuara district. These are *El Búho* (folklórico) and *La Piramide* (criollo). There is occasionally entertainment at the *Peña Picantería*, Jerusalén 204.

The most happening bar is the *Blues Bar*, on the last block of San Francisco, with good drinks and music. It seems to be the current gathering place for young Arequipeños.

The best disco is the *Casablanca*, on Sucre near Puente Bolognesi, which is in the basement of a garage. It has a US$4 cover charge and is locally popular for dancing. Another place is the *Carnaby*, on Jerusalén.

There's also the usual selection of cinemas, some of which show English-language movies with Spanish subtitles. Also check the various cultural centers for films and other events.

Things to Buy

High-quality souvenirs are sold in stores in the Santo Domingo cloister. For alpaca clothing and handicrafts, El Zaguan (☎ 21-8703), Santa Catalina 105, has been recommended. For sweaters, T-shirts and other clothes made of the local high-quality Pima cotton, Franky & Ricky, Mercaderes 405, is recommended. Lanificio del Perú (☎ 22-5305, 24-1373), on Argentina in the Paucarpata suburb, is a factory outlet selling high-quality alpaca cloth at good prices.

Getting There & Away

Air The airport is 9 km northwest of the center of town. There are seven or more direct flights to Lima, and about four each to Tacna, Cuzco, and Juliaca every day. All the airline offices are on the Plaza de Armas, and their fares are usually the same. Phone numbers are AeroPerú (☎ 21-2835, 21-6820), Aero Continente (☎ 21-9721, 21-7314), Americana (☎ 21-2892) and Faucett (☎ 21-2322, 21-2352). Faucett may

charge more unless you buy a ticket several days in advance and Imperial Air is cheaper but recently suspended its services to Arequipa (they may return). One-way to Lima costs about US$102, to Cuzco US$53, to Juliaca US$48 and to Tacna US$25.

Servicios Aereos AQP (☎ 25-6068, fax 24-2030, 21-6767) flies nine-passenger, twin-engined Piper Comanches to anywhere you want to go, including local sightseeing.

All non-Peruvian passengers must pay a US$4 departure tax at the airport.

Bus A new Terminal Terrestre opened in 1993 on Avenida A Avelino Caceres, about 3 km south of the center of town. Most bus and colectivo offices remain at their old locations on San Juan de Dios, mainly around the 600 block (between Alto de la Luna and Socabaya). Tickets are sold in these offices (as well as at the terminal) but most buses leave from and arrive at the terminal. Exceptions are buses that arrive late at night, which may stop first at the terminal and then continue to their office in town, or buses that leave early in the morning to some of the destinations mentioned in the Around Arequipa section, below. Make careful inquiry about where a bus will leave from when buying tickets. The terminal is modern and well organized, with shops, restaurants and a tourist information office (☎ 24-1735). As always, watch your belongings at the terminal. There is a US50¢ departure tax charged.

Lima is between 16 and 21 hours away. Ormeño, Cruz del Sur, Civa, Flores Hermanos and Expreso Sudamericano are among the companies that have several buses a day to Lima, most leaving in the afternoon. Fares range from a standard US$12 to US$25 for Cruz del Sur's Imperial Service with food.

For intermediate south coast points, most buses stop in Nazca (US$7 and up, about 9 to 12 hours) as well as Camaná, Chala and Ica, but remember that Pisco is about 5 km off the Panamericana Hwy and not all buses go there. Change in Ica if necessary. For north of Lima, change in Lima. There are also many buses a day via Moquegua to Tacna (US$4 to US$7, seven hours).

If you're going inland to Lake Titicaca, Ormeño has two night buses to Puno, Cruz del Sur has two day buses to Puno, and Transportes Jacantay has a daily bus in the afternoon going to Juliaca, Puno, Desaguadero and La Paz, Bolivia. Other companies also go to Titicaca. It's about 13 hours and US$8 to Puno, US$18 to La Paz. The road to Juliaca is in terrible shape, and many travelers prefer the train. There have been incidents of night buses to Juliaca being held up. These and other companies also have buses to Cuzco (US$10 to US$12, around 18 hours) on a poor road. The journeys to Juliaca and Cuzco can take much longer in wet weather.

Ormeño has three international buses a week to Santiago, Chile (US$80), and Buenos Aires, Argentina (US$130).

Santa Ursula has five departures daily for the coast at Mollendo. Many of its buses go on to Mejía. Cruz del Sur has afternoon departures to Mollendo and there are others. For Ilo, there are buses with Cruz del Sur and Angelitos Negros.

For sightseeing in the Department of Arequipa, try Transportes Transandino, which has daily departures at 4.15 am and 1.30 pm for Chivay (US$2.50, three hours) continuing through Yanque, Achoma and Maca to Cabanaconde (US$4, seven hours) on the upper Colca Canyon. Turismo Expres Condor also has a daily afternoon bus to Chivay, and there are others. Empresa Jacantay has a 6.30 am departure for Cabanaconde via Huambo. (A roundtrip to the Colca Canyon via Sihuas, Huambo, Cabanaconde and Chivay can therefore be done using public transport.) Other companies going to Chivay and Cabanaconde include Transportes Prado, Transportes Colca and Transportes Cristo Rey, all in the Terminal Terrestre. Between them they have departures at 4 am, 1 and 1.30 pm.

For buses to Corire (US$2.50, three hours) to visit the Toro de Muerte petroglyphs, go with Flores Hermanos, El Chasqui or Transportes del Carpio. Between them, they have

departures almost every hour from about 5.30 am. El Chasqui also goes to Valle de Majes (US$2) for river running, as do Transportes Berrios and Mendoza. Transportes Mendoza has buses to the Valle de los Volcanes.

Train The Arequipa-Juliaca route is bleak, but the views of the altiplano are interesting, and you may see flamingos, vicuñas, alpacas and llamas. Unfortunately, daylight trains do not run, so you can't see much! The journey to Juliaca (and Puno) is much more comfortable by train than by bus.

The night train leaves Arequipa at 8 pm on Tuesday, Wednesday, Friday and Sunday and arrives at Juliaca at 6 am the following day. (There has been daily service in the past and this may resume.) This train continues to Puno, an hour away, or you can connect with the day train to Cuzco, which leaves Juliaca at 9 am. Thus it is possible to buy a through ticket to Cuzco from Arequipa, arriving at 6 pm. If going to Puno, it is cheaper and quicker to buy a ticket to Juliaca and then catch one of the many minibuses to Puno waiting for the train.

A large number of people have their bags slashed or stolen or their pockets picked on the night train, particularly in the overcrowded and badly lit 2nd class and to a lesser extent in 1st class. There are also a large number of thieves mingling with the crowds, waiting for the night train in the bustling Arequipa train station or looking for tired passengers disembarking in Juliaca. Watch your baggage carefully and constantly. You are safest buying the Pullman-class tickets in addition to your 1st-class ticket.

The Pullman car has comfortable reclining seats for sleeping and heated carriages (it gets very cold on the altiplano at night, and most of the journey is at altitudes of more than 4000 meters). Attendants keep the doors locked and allow only ticket holders into the carriages and also keep an eye on luggage. Oxygen is available if you begin to suffer from altitude sickness.

Fares from Arequipa change frequently.

TONY WHEELER

TONY WHEELER

TONY WHEELER

Monastery of Santa Catalina, Arequipa

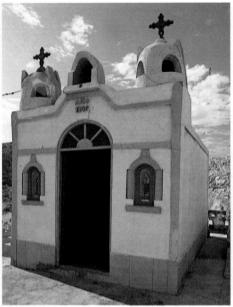

Since the 1st edition of this book you could pay anywhere between US$2 and US$13 for a 1st-class ticket to Juliaca, with fares in 2nd class at about 25% lower. There is a surcharge for Pullman class (on top of the 1st-class fare). At this time fares to Puno are US$15/12/9.50 for Pullman/1st/2nd, to Juliaca they are US$15/10/8 and to Cuzco they are US$33/21.50/17. The price of a ticket depends on fluctuating exchange rates and various regulations, so see for yourself what the going rate is when you get there.

It's best to buy tickets in advance rather than trying to do so while guarding your luggage in the predeparture crowds. Ticket office opening hours change constantly, and there are usually very long lines, which can mean you'll be waiting for several hours. You can buy tickets from various travel agencies, such as Continental Tours and Conresa Tours, on the 400 block of Jerusalén. Each charge about a 25% commission but provide a transfer from your hotel to the station. Shop around for the best deal. If the Pullman surcharge to Cuzco is too expensive, consider taking 1st class for the Juliaca-Cuzco section; it's done in daylight when it is easier to guard your luggage.

I've occasionally heard talk of starting a comfortable sleeper service on the night train, using quaint old-fashioned sleeper coaches. It sounds nice, but I doubt that anything will come of these ideas.

Getting Around

To/From the Airport There are no airport buses, although buses and minibuses marked Río Seco, Cono-Norte or Zamacola go along Puente Grau and Ejército and pass within a kilometer of the airport – ask the driver where to get off. A taxi from downtown costs about US$5. From the airport, shared colectivo taxis charge US$2.50 per person and take you to your hotel.

To/From the Bus Terminal Buses and minibuses go southbound along Bolívar and Sucre to the Terminal Terrestre. A taxi will cost about US$2.

Car National Car Rental, Bolívar 25, rents a compact car for US$71 a day, including insurance, taxes and 200 'free' km. Further distance is about US$1 per 4 km. You need to be 25 years old and have a major credit card and drivers license. You can rent a taxi with a driver for less!

Around Arequipa

Several long-distance excursions can be made from Arequipa. The most popular is the tour of the Cañón del Colca. Others include climbing the volcano El Misti and other mountains, visiting the Majes Canyon and the petroglyphs at El Toro Muerto and hiking in the Valle de los Volcanes.

Although many of these places can be visited by public transport, this is often inconvenient. So, taking a tour is sometimes worth the extra money, unless, of course, you have the time and prefer the adventure of taking infrequent ramshackle buses to remote areas. The main advantage of taking a tour is that you can stop at the most interesting points for sightseeing and photography, while on public transport the bus just keeps going. Nevertheless, many travelers have written to say that they had a great time visiting these areas using a combination of buses and hiking.

If you decide to go on a guided tour, you'll have many options, as there are about a dozen tour companies operating out of Arequipa. Some of these aren't very good, so make sure you discuss exactly what to expect before parting with your money. (See Travel Agencies above for a few recommendations.) Don't take a trip offered by a street tout. They will simply take you to a travel agency and rake in a commission without providing any extra services.

Alternatively, if there is a group of you to split the cost, you could rent a car or hire a taxi and driver. I was quoted US$110 for a taxi and driver for two days, but you could easily bargain this down.

COLCA CANYON

Controversy rages about whether or not this is the world's deepest canyon. The sections that you can see from the road on a standard guided tour are certainly very impressive but are not the deepest parts of the canyon. To see the deepest sections you have to make an overnight trip and hike in. Some measurements of the depth of the canyon are taken only from the north rim, which is higher than the south, so decide for yourself! Anyway, it certainly warrants a visit if you have the time.

Guided Tours

Guided tours are about US$20 to US$25 for a day or US$10 more for a two-day trip with the cheaper agencies. Costs depend on the size of the group and bargaining. The expensive agencies can give private tours for up to three times as much. The one-day trip lasts about 12 hours and is rushed and tiring. I would take a two-day trip. The extra cost includes lodging with breakfast in Chivay, but other meals are usually at your own expense.

Most one-day guided tours leave Arequipa (2325 meters) well before dawn and climb northwest past Chachani volcano, following the route of the railway. (The old route used to go over a pass between Chachani and El Misti. This road, although shorter, is in very bad condition and not used by tour buses anymore.) The road continues through the **Reserva Nacional Salinas y Aguada Blanca**, which covers 367,000 hectares at an average elevation of 3850 meters. Here, vicuñas are often sighted. Later in the trip domesticated alpacas and llamas are frequently seen, so it is possible to see three of the four members of the South American cameloid family in one day. Seeing the fourth member, the guanaco, is very hard as they have almost disappeared from this area.

After two to three hours a breakfast stop is made at Viscachani (4150 meters). The road continues through bleak altiplano over the high point of about 4800 meters, from where the snowcaps of Ampato (6288 meters) are seen. Then the road drops spectacularly to **Chivay**, which is about 160 km from Arequipa.

The thermal hot springs of Chivay are sometimes visited (US25¢ entrance; bring swimming gear and towel), and then the tour bus continues west following the south bank of the upper Colca Canyon. The landscape is remarkable for its Inca and pre-Inca terracing, which goes on for many kilometers and is the most extensive I've seen in Peru. The journey is worthwhile to see the terracing alone. Along the route are several villages whose inhabitants are involved in agriculture and continue using the terraces today. At **Yanque** an attractive church that dates from the early 1700s is sometimes visited.

About 20 km beyond Chivay, and about 4 km beyond **Achoma**, is the *Albergue Turístico de Achoma* where lunch may be taken either on the way in or out. Soon after leaving the lodge the bus often stops for the driver to point out a small carved boulder that is supposed to represent a pre-Columbian map of the terracing. The end point of the tour is at the lookout known as **Cruz del Cóndor**, about 60 km beyond Chivay and an hour's drive before you get to the village of Cabanaconde. As the name suggests, Andean condors are sometimes seen here; early morning or late afternoon are the best times for this, although they have been reported at various hours during the day. From the lookout the view is impressive, with the river flowing 1200 meters below. Mt Mismi, on the other side of the canyon, is about 3200 meters above the canyon and some guides will tell you that the depth measurement should be taken from Mismi's summit. In fact, deeper sections can be seen if you go farther in, but this requires leg work from **Cabanaconde** (3290 meters). Most tours don't go as far as Cabanaconde, but you can visit it by public transport (see Getting There & Away).

The people living in the Cañón del Colca region are known for their traditional clothing, worn especially by the women (who don't particularly enjoy being photographed; ask permission). Their dresses and jackets are beautifully embroidered, and their hats are distinctive. In the Chivay area at the east end of the canyon the white hats are usually woven from straw and embellished with lace, sequins and badges. At the west end of the canyon the hats are of cotton and colorfully embroidered.

Beyond the Guided Tours

Travelers doing it alone should read the Guided Tours description for background.

Pinchollo is a small village a few kilometers before the Cruz del Cóndor. From here, a trail climbs south toward Nevado Hualca Hualca (a snowcapped volcano of 6025 meters) to an active geothermal area where there is a geyser that is continuously erupting. The jet of steam shoots between 15 and 30 meters into the air, and Arequipeños say it is the only geyser in the world that is continuously active – I don't know if it's true. It takes about four hours to walk to the geyser, but you must be acclimatized as much of the trail is well over 4000 meters above sea level. The trail is fairly easy to follow, or you can find a local boy in Pinchollo to guide you for a tip. The downhill return will take less than two hours, and the views of the snowcapped mountains are good. You can stay in Pinchollo and continue on to Cruz del Cóndor on foot – about two hours.

Cabanaconde is a good base for continuing on into the deepest parts of Cañón del Colca on foot. Ask for directions or, better, hire a local guide, since there are several trails and it can be confusing. There are a couple of different long-distance walking possibilities outlined in Bradt's *Backpacking and Trekking in Peru and Bolivia*. One goes from Cabanaconde down to the canyon bottom, then up the other side over a 5000 meter pass to Andagua in the Valle de los Volcanes. This adventure takes about five to seven days.

This area is fairly popular with Peruvian tourists but is still pretty much off-the-beaten-track for international tourism. Travelers should expect basic accommodations.

Places to Stay & Eat

Chivay, at an altitude of about 3700 meters,

is the capital of the province of Caylloma and has several simple hotels. Around the main plaza you'll find the *Hostal Anita, Pensión Tierra del Fuego, Hostal Plaza* and the *Hostal Municipal*. These are basic, cold water hotels charging about US$2 a person. The *Hotel Grau* is similar and is three blocks north of the plaza on Calle Grau. Two or three blocks west of the plaza along Avenida Salaverry are the *Hostal Colca* and the *Hostal Posada del Inca*, both with restaurants and considered the best in town at this time. The Colca charges US$4.50/7.50 per person without/with private bath, and it occasionally has hot water. The Posada del Inca is US$7.50 per person with private bath and hot water. These places are favored by tour groups, but the restaurant at the Posada del Inca has been criticized as overpriced, with similar food available at half the price in several little restaurants and comedores around the plaza and market areas.

If staying in Chivay, visit the hot springs that are 4 km to the northeast of the village by road. There are minibuses or walk. Here there is a clean swimming pool, changing rooms, a basic cafeteria and an admission fee of US25¢. The mineral-laden water is said to have curative properties; one traveler writes that it does a good job of boiling eggs for a picnic lunch!

The *Albergue Turístico de Achoma*, 4 km beyond Achoma and about 25 km beyond Chivay, is the most comfortable place to stay in the Colca area. Although it is some distance from the canyon itself, it is a good center for walking and inspecting the pre-Columbian terracing. Rooms with a bath and hot water are in the US$20s. Meals are available. Reservations can be made at the travel agencies in Arequipa, though it's not often full so you could try just showing up.

In Pinchollo, there are very basic places to stay. One report tells of *El Refugio* near the main plaza with five beds at US50¢ per person, and another mentions a *hospedaje* charging US$1.25 per person. In both cases, a sleeping bag and flashlight are recommended because it is very cold and the village lacks electricity.

Cabanaconde has a couple of basic family-run pensions that charge about US$2.50 per person. These are the *Hotel Cruz del Cóndor* and *Hostal Solarex*. Bathroom facilities are poor in both places. There is electricity for a couple of hours each evening.

Getting There & Away
If you don't want a guided tour, see the Arequipa section for details on bus companies that have daily dawn departures to Chivay. Some continue from Chivay past Achoma and Pinchillo (where you can get off) and on to Cabanaconde. The section of road beyond Cabanaconde to Huambo veers away from the canyon. It is also the roughest part of the road and there is little transport.

Buses leave Cabanaconde before dawn for the return to Arequipa via Chivay. In Chivay, there are bus offices along Calle Zarumilla (one block north and west of the plaza). Buses for Arequipa leave at 3 am and 1.30 pm, and possibly at other times.

RIVER RUNNING
An excellent guide to the Cañón del Colca appears in *Kayak Through Peru* by the Polish Canoandes Expedition, 1981. It is out of print, but the South American Explorers Club has a reference copy. The Colca was first run in 1981 and is a dangerous and difficult river, not to be undertaken lightly (a friend of mine died in it). A few commercial outfitters do expensive rafting trips through portions of the river in August. See the January 1993 *National Geographic* for a description of a recent expedition.

You can also do easier trips on the Río Majes (which the Colca flows into). The *Majes River Lodge* (☎ 21-0256), in the village of La Central, 190 km by road west of Arequipa and at 820 meters above sea level, is the most convenient base. Contacts for the lodge in Arequipa are the Hotel Crismar or with river guide Carlos Zúñiga (☎ /fax 25-5819). The modern lodge has double rooms with private bath and hot water for about US$20. There is a

restaurant, bar and large garden with outdoor games areas and camping (US$2 per person). A grade III, 8 km whitewater run in inflatable rafts costs about US$10, including transportation from the lodge. The actual run lasts about an hour and is suitable for beginners. Experienced river runners can take a 25 km, grade IV run lasting three hours for US$25.

The lodge can also be used as a base to visit the Valle de Los Volcanes and Toro Muerto (see below). Transportation can be arranged from Arequipa, though it is cheaper to take one of the public buses from Arequipa's Terminal Terrestre (Berrios, Chasqui, Mendoza and Carpio all go there for about US$2).

MOUNTAIN CLIMBING
There are many high mountains in the Arequipa area that are technically not very difficult. The main problems are extreme weather conditions (carry suitable clothing and tent), altitude (solved by adequate acclimatization) and lack of water (you should carry a minimum of four liters per person per day). If you're a beginning climber, remember that people have died in these mountains, and it's not as easy a climb as it looks. Be aware of the main symptoms of altitude sickness. If in doubt, go back down.

Maps of the area can be obtained from the Instituto Geográfico Nacional and the South American Explorers Club in Lima. Also try the bookstore (formerly called San Francisco) on Mercaderes and the climbing guides in Arequipa.

The best local guide is the very experienced and highly recommended Carlos Zárate, who can be contacted at the Alianza Francesa (see Cultural Centers in Arequipa). If he is in the mountains, his wife, Olivia Mazuelos, works there and can tell you when he'll be back. Carlos Zárate is an expert climber and can provide up-to-date information, rent out equipment, arrange transportation, and guide you or put you in contact with a guide. He is busiest from January to March, when weather conditions are often cloudy and he is hired by climbers who don't want to get lost.

El Misti

This 5822-meter-high volcano looms over Arequipa and is the most popular local climb. It is technically one of the easiest ascents of any mountain of this size in the world. Nevertheless it is hard work and you normally need an ice axe and, sometimes, crampons. There are a variety of routes.

To get to the mountain by public transport, take a bus to Chiguata. Buses leave at about 6 am and 1 pm (possibly more often) from Avenida Sepulveda in the Miraflores district and take about an hour to reach Chiguata for a fare of US75¢. From Chiguata to the base camp takes about eight hours or more along rough trails. It's a hard uphill slog, and there's little if any water en route. From the base to the summit and back takes a further eight hours, and there's no water. There is a 10-meter-high metal cross at the summit. The downhill hike from the base camp to Chiguata takes three hours or less. A bus returns from Chiguata to Arequipa at 4 pm.

Another route is to take a 6 am bus to Chasqui, getting off at the Aguada Blanca hydroelectric plant. It's about a three-hour drive. From here climb five hours to Monte Blanco and a further six hours to the summit. The return can be done in as little as three hours. Although many people camp at Monte Blanco, some people hire a vehicle, leave Arequipa in the middle of the night, start climbing from Aguada Blanca before dawn and return on the same day.

It is possible to climb from Arequipa itself, on the so-called Apurimac Route. This is a long two-day climb and people have been followed and robbed on it. Thus it is suitable only for large groups who have members prepared to stay in the camp and look after the tents. This is a cheap and popular option with large local student and climbing groups.

If you hire a vehicle, you can get much higher up the mountain than by public transport, and it saves you having to hassle with your luggage on a crowded public bus.

Other Mountains

One of the easiest 6000 meter peaks in the world is **Chachani** (6075 meters), as close to Arequipa as El Misti. You need crampons, an ice axe and good equipment. There are various routes, one of which involves driving by 4WD to Campamento de Azufrera at 4950 meters. From here you can summit in about nine hours, if acclimatized, and return in under four. Alternatively, there is a good spot to camp at 5300 meters, for a two day trip. Other routes take three days and are more difficult.

Human Sacrifice in the Andes

Ampato gained recent fame when American mountaineer/archaeologist Johan Reinhard, accompanied by Miguel Zárate, climbed the peak in September 1995 and found that the eruptions of nearby Sabancaya had melted the snow off the summit, thus exposing an Inca girl who had been sacrificed there. She had been almost perfectly preserved by the icy temperatures for about 500 years. At least 10 similar Inca sacrifices have been discovered atop various Andean mountains since 1954.

A month later, Reinhard returned with more climbers and discovered two more human sacrifices, one well preserved. All three are now stored in a freezer at the Universidad Católica in Arequipa. (See *Newsweek*, November 6, 1995, for the full story.) Reinhard is no stranger to climbing the Andes in search of archaeological remains. A few years earlier, he was part of a team that discovered a human sacrifice near the summit of Pichu Pichu (5571 meters) a few kilometers east of Arequipa (see the March 1992 *National Geographic*).

The Incas considered the mountains gods – who could kill by volcanic eruption, avalanche or climatic catastrophes – and made human sacrifices to appease them. What is most amazing is the ability of the Incas to climb well over 6000 meters above sea level, and sometimes to construct ritual altars and temples at these elevations, without modern climbing equipment. ∎

Sabancaya (5976 meters) is part of a massif on the south rim of the Cañón del Colca, which includes **Hualca Hualca** (6025 meters) and **Ampato** (6288 meters). Sabancaya is currently the most active of the region's volcanoes and has been erupting in recent years. I am told that the crater can be approached in between eruptions if you have an experienced guide. Sounds like a pretty risky proposition to me! Ampato is a fairly straightforward three-day ascent, and you get good views of the active Sabancaya – this seems like a safer option.

Other nearby mountains of interest include **Ubinas** (5672 meters), which can be reached from the village of Ubinas, served by a daily morning bus from Arequipa. This is a two-day climb, and there is a lot of geothermal activity. **Mismi** (5556 meters) is a fairly easy three- or four-day climb on the north side of the Cañón del Colca. You can approach it from the villages of Cailloma and, with a guide, find the lake that is reputedly the source of the Amazon. The highest mountain in southern Peru is the more difficult **Coropuna**, which is variously labeled as 6305 or 6425 meters on maps. The Andes have many remote peaks, and altitudes have not yet been definitively measured in many cases.

LAGUNA DE SALINAS

This lake, east of Arequipa between the mountains of Pichu Pichu and Ubinas, is a salt lake that becomes a white salt flat during the dry months of May to December. Its size and the amount of water in it vary from year to year depending on the weather. During the rainy season it is a good place to see various flamingo species as well as other Andean water birds. The elevation here is about 4300 meters.

A Transportes Silva bus leaves from the 200 block of Avenida Sepulveda in Arequipa on Monday, Thursday and Saturday at 6 or 7 am. The fare is US$3.50 for the four-hour ride. You can hike around the lake, which can take about two days, then return down the Río Andamayo as far as Chiguata (a long day), from where a daily 4 pm bus returns to Arequipa. Catching a bus from the lake back to Arequipa is difficult because the bus usually begins at the village of Ubinas and is very full by the time it passes the lake.

TORO MUERTO

This is a magnificent and unusual archaeological site in the high desert. It consists of hundreds of carved boulders spread over about 2 sq km of desert. Archaeologists are uncertain of the cultural origins of this site, but it is thought that it was made by the Wari culture about 1200 years ago.

To reach the site by public transport, take a bus to Corire (US$2, three hours) and then walk for about 1½ hours. Transportes Flores Hermanos as well as the bus companies going to Majes go there. In Corire there is the basic *Hostal Willy*, which charges about US$3 per night and can provide information on reaching the site. It can get very hot and dry, so bring plenty of extra water and sun protection. If you don't want to sleep in Corire, take an early bus from Arequipa (they start at 5.30 am) and get off at a gas station 2 km before the town of Corire. Opposite the gas station is a dirt track that goes up a valley to the petroglyphs. Buses return from Corire to Arequipa once an hour, usually leaving at 30 minutes past the hour. There are several simple restaurants along the main street in Corire, some of which serve the local specialty *camarones* (river shrimp).

The Toro Muerto petroglyphs can also be visited more conveniently but expensively on full-day tours from Arequipa.

VALLE DE LOS VOLCANES

This unusual valley is covered with scores of small and medium-sized volcanic cones and craters – a veritable moonscape. The 65-km-long valley surrounds the village of Andagua near the snowcapped mountain of Coropuna. It is a weird and remote area that is seldom visited by travelers. Perhaps that's a good reason to go.

Other interesting sights in the area include *chullpas* (pre-Columbian funerary towers) at Soporo, reportedly a two hour hike from Andagua. A car can get very close to the site. En route to Soporo is a pre-Columbian city named Antaymarca. Northeast of Andagua, at a place called Izanquillay, the Río Andahua runs through a lava canyon about 50 meters deep but only five meters wide. There is a spectacular 40 meter high waterfall here.

To get to the Valle de los Volcanes, take a Mendoza bus from Arequipa through Corire on to Andagua. The bus leaves daily at 5 pm and costs about US$9 to Andagua. There are a couple of cheap and basic hostals; one is run by the Consejo Municipal de Andagua and is often full. Another is run by Señor Aguilar, and it is reportedly better. Topographical maps of the area are available at the usual places.

The Lake Titicaca Area

Generations of school children have been taught that Lake Titicaca, at 3820 meters above sea level, is the highest navigable lake in the world and this alone seems to make it a tourist attraction. In fact, there are many navigable lakes at altitudes of over 4000 meters, such as Lake Junín in Peru's central Andes, but Lake Titicaca is widely believed to be the world's highest simply because it has frequent passenger boats and is better known than other higher lakes. If you like trivia, amaze your friends with the fact that Lake Titicaca, at over 170 km in length, is the largest lake in South America and the largest lake in the world above 2000 meters. At this altitude, the air is unusually clear and the deep blue of the lake is especially inviting. Because various interesting boat trips on the lake can be taken from Puno, Peru's major port on

Lake Titicaca, many travelers spend some days in Puno en route to either Cuzco or Bolivia.

There are many other reasons to linger in the area, not the least of which is the incredibly luminescent quality of the sunlight on Peru's high plain, the altiplano. Horizons seem limitless and the earthy tones of the scenery are as deep as the lake itself. These colors are reflected in the nut-brown faces of the people of the altiplano, as well as in their colonial churches and archaeological monuments, several of which are well worth visiting. The Department of Puno is also famous for its folk dances which are the wildest and most colorful in the Peruvian highlands. And, if this isn't enough, there are fascinating Andean animals to be seen – huge herds of domesticated alpaca and llama – and sparkling

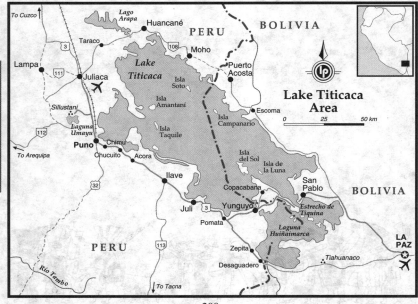

highland lakes full of water birds such as the giant Andean coot and various species of rosy-colored flamingo.

Dangers & Annoyances
The 3820 meter elevation means that travelers run a real risk of getting *soroche* (altitude sickness) if arriving directly from the coast. Rather than flying in from Lima, plan on spending time in Arequipa (2325 meters) and then Cuzco (3326 meters) for best acclimatization.

JULIACA
With a population of about 100,000, Juliaca is the largest town in the Department of Puno and has the department's only commercial airport. It is also an important railway junction with connections to Arequipa, Puno and Cuzco. At an elevation of 3822 meters, Juliaca is the first altiplano town many overland travelers visit en route from the coast to Cuzco or Lake Titicaca. Many of its inhabitants are Indians but it still remains of comparatively little interest and most people prefer to go on to Puno where there are better hotels and a view of Lake Titicaca.

The main reasons to stay here relate to making train or plane connections, taking the rarely traveled northern route into Bolivia, or visiting the Monday market. There is also a daily market along the railway tracks at which you can buy almost anything. A nice day trip (or overnight) is to the town of Lampa (see below).

Information
Money The Banco de Crédito, M Nuñez 138, changes traveler's checks and may be the only place to do so. They'll also give a cash advance on a Visa card and are open weekdays from 9.15 am to 1.15 pm and 4.30 to 6.30 pm. Casas de cambio and street changers on the block north of this bank will change cash dollars.

Post & Telecommunications These offices are shown on the map. The area code for Juliaca is 054.

Medical Services Juliaca's Clínica Adventista de Juliaca is the best hospital in the Department of Puno. Any cab driver can take you there.

Dangers & Annoyances If you arrive from the coast, especially by air, remember to take it easy for one or two days – see Altitude Sickness in the Health section of the Facts for the Visitor chapter.

The railway station has a number of thieves meeting arriving and departing passengers. Keep your eyes open, your luggage locked, and your wits about you. Taxi drivers routinely try to overcharge foreigners.

Places to Stay – bottom end
The water supply is not reliable in the bottom end hotels. You'll find several cheap, basic cold-water places near the train station. The *Hotel Don Pedro* (☎ 32-1442) and the *Hostal Loreto* have little to recommend them beyond their low prices (US$2.50/4) and proximity to the train station. The Don Pedro has a few rooms with a double bed and private bath for US$7.50. The *Hotel Centro* (☎ 32-1636), Nuñez 350, and the *Hostal Rosedal* by the post office are just OK for US$4/5. They are a little better than some really basic cheapies such as the *Hotel Ferrocarril* (☎ 32-1441) at just US$1.50 per person, *Hotel del Sur* at US$2 per person and the unfriendly *Gran Hotel Juliaca* at US$3.50 per person.

Better cheap places include the following. The *Hostal San Antonio* (☎ 32-1701), San Martín 347, is basic but fairly clean. Rooms are US$3.50/5 and some have a private toilet, though not shower. Hot showers are an extra US$1.20. They have a sauna for US$3. Hours for the sauna are 10 am to 6 pm, open for women on Thursday and Saturday, men on Friday and Sunday, and mixed on other days. The *Hostal Sakura* (☎ 32-1194), Unión 133, is OK for US$3 per person or US$5/8 with private bath and occasional hot water. Also decent is the small and friendly *Hostal Aparicio*

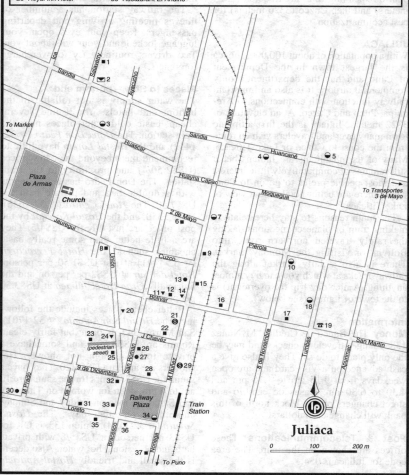

PLACES TO STAY
1 Hostal Rosedal
6 Eurobuilding Hotel
8 Karlo's Hostal
9 Hotel Yasur
12 Gran Hotel Juliaca
15 Hotel Centro
16 Hotel Ferrocarril
17 Hostal San Antonio
22 Hotel del Sur
23 Hostal Santa Elisia
25 Hostal Sakura
26 Royal Inn Hotel

28 Hostal Don Carlos
31 Hostal Aparicio
32 Hotel Don Pedro
33 Hostal Peru
35 Hostal Loreto
37 Samari Hotel

PLACES TO EAT
11 Pollería La Manja
14 Pollería Riko Riko
20 Café Dorado
24 Restaurant Trujillo
36 Restaurant El Andino

OTHER
2 Post Office
3 San Cristóbal
4 Transportes Jacantaya
   & other companies
5 Cruz del Sur
7 Local bus to airport
10 Transportes Los Angeles
   minibuses to Puno
13 Cine Centro
18 Empresa de Transportes
   San Martín
19 Telefónica del Peru

21 Money Exchange
26 AeroPerú Airline
27 Video Pub La Miel
29 Banco de Crédito
30 Faucett Airline
34 Minibuses to Puno
37 Americana Airline

LAKE TITICACA AREA

To Market

Plaza de Armas

Church

To Transportes 3 de Mayo

Railway Plaza

Train Station

Juliaca

0   100   200 m

To Puno

(☎ 32-16250), Loreto 270, which has some hot water and charges US$3.50 per person.

Slightly more expensive, and more agreeable, is the clean and friendly *Hotel Yasur* (☎ 32-1501), M Nuñez 414, also called the Yarur. Rooms are US$4.50/6.50 or US$5.50/8 with private bath. Hot water is available in the morning and evening. The Yasur fills up fast, so get there as early as you can.

The clean, comfortable and recommended *Hostal Peru* (☎ 32-1510), opposite the railway plaza, charges US$5.50/8.50, or US$7/11 with private bath, and has hot water in the evening. They have a simple but slightly pricey restaurant. The *Hostal Santa Elisia* (☎ 32-2711), Pasaje Elise 142, is about US$7.50 per person and overpriced – bargain here. The *Eurobuilding Hotel* (☎ 32-1186) is a big new hotel with seven floors of dark corridors and reasonably comfortable rooms with bath and hot water for US$10/15.

Places to Stay – middle
The *Royal Inn Hotel* (☎ 32-1561, fax 32-1572), San Roman 158, charges US$12/21 for clean, good rooms with telephone, private bath and hot water, and US$8.50 per person in rooms with communal bath. They have one of the best restaurants in town and room service is available. The friendly *Karlo's Hostal* (☎ 32-2568, 32-1817), Unión 317, has nice comfortable rooms with TV and hot water for US$12.50/20. A restaurant is attached. The new *Samari Hotel* (☎ 32-1870), near the train station, is one of the best hotels in town and has nicely decorated rooms with TV for US$20/28. They also have a restaurant. The *Hostal Don Carlos*, also near the train station, has clean, pleasant rooms with heating, TV and minibar for US$30/40. The *Cadena Hotelera Turística Juliaca* (☎ 32-1571, fax 32-2635; in Lima ☎ 224-0263, 476-2469, fax 224-8581) is at Manuel Prado 335, on the outskirts of town (take a taxi). Good rooms are US$50/77 and there is an adequate restaurant.

Places to Eat
Juliaca's town center seems to have a simple restaurant on every block – they're nothing to write home about but you certainly won't starve. There are several cheap chicken restaurants of which *Pollería Riko Riko* and *Pollería La Manja*, on the same block of Bolívar, are quite good. The *Restaurant El Andino* is a cheap, interesting looking place on the railway plaza, but one traveler reports receiving a fake S/10 bill there. The *Café Dorado* seems OK. The *Restaurant Trujillo* is locally popular, quite good, but a little pricey. The restaurant at the *Royal Inn Hotel* is the best I could find.

Entertainment
There is a definite lack of peñas – you'll find more action in Puno. The *Cine Centro* and *Video Pub La Miel* are shown on the map.

Things to Buy
Monday is market day and Juliaca has some of the cheapest prices for alpaca goods if you can bargain. The market is held west of the Plaza de Armas. On other days there is a small tourist-oriented market by the railway station.

Getting There & Away
Air Juliaca airport serves both Juliaca and Puno. There are about eight flights a day scheduled to and from Lima. Aero Continente, AeroPerú (☎ 32-2001), Americana (☎ 32-1844) and Faucett (☎ 32-2993, 32-1966) all have flights from Lima, most via Arequipa and a few via Cuzco. Americana has an evening flight to Tacna daily except Saturday. There are no flights to Bolivia. Fares are US$108 to Lima and US$49 to Arequipa or Cuzco. There is a US$4 airport tax.

Bus There are buses to most points in southern Peru with services offered by several companies so it's best to check them all out if you're on a tight budget. See the section on Puno for regional bus travel information and fares – they are about US$1 less from

Juliaca than in Puno. San Cristóbal (☎ 32-1181) has buses to Arequipa and Lima, Cruz del Sur (☎ 32-2011) to Arequipa, Lima and Cuzco, as do Jacantaya and several others. Buses all travel at night. Empresa de Transportes San Martín has night buses to Moquegua, Tacna and Ilo. Transportes 3 de Mayo to Huancané (US$1.25, two to three hours) leave from Calle Huancané three blocks east of Apurimac.

Several companies provide services to Puno by minibus. Most cruise past the railway station looking for passengers, or you can catch a Transportes Los Angeles minibus from the corner of 8 de Noviembre and Piérola. The fare is US50¢.

Train Juliaca is the busiest railway crossroad in Peru. The single train station serves Puno to the south, Cuzco to the northwest and Arequipa to the southwest. Although you can get off at intermediate points, these are of little interest to most travelers. If you want to take the train on to Machu Picchu, you have to change stations in Cuzco – there is no direct service between Juliaca and Machu Picchu.

Tickets in 2nd class are occasionally sold out in advance: for 1st class (which has numbered and reserved seats) this is almost always the case, so think ahead. Buy the ticket the day before you travel. Ticket office hours change often and lines are invariably long.

See the Puno section, below, for details about trains, times and fares. Fares from Juliaca are a few cents cheaper than from Puno and trains leave about one to two hours after the Puno departure time.

Passengers arriving on the overnight train from Arequipa and continuing on to Cuzco normally have a couple of hours between trains to wander around. Many salespeople at the station sell alpaca sweaters and ponchos so, if you prefer, you can do your shopping through the carriage window. Bargain hard – prices tend to drop just before the train leaves.

Passengers arriving at night from Cuzco and heading directly on to Puno will find

that, if they get off the train in Juliaca and continue on one of the minibuses waiting outside the train station, they'll get into Puno half an hour ahead of the train. Definitely beware of thieves in the ill-lit Juliaca station, which has a reputation for luggage-snatching and pickpocketing. Read the warnings in the Arequipa Train section and watch your belongings with an eagle eye.

Getting Around
To/From the Airport A red-and-cream colored bus with an *Aeropuerto* placard cruises around town before heading to the airport. One place to catch it is marked on the map. The fare is US30¢. Alternately, bargain for a taxi and expect to pay about US$2. At the airport, you'll find colectivos heading directly to Puno for US$2.50 a passenger.

LAMPA
This quiet and charming little town is 23 km northwest of Juliaca. It is nicknamed 'La Ciudad Rosada' because most of its buildings are painted pink. The attractive church of La Inmaculada can be visited and contains a copy of Michelangelo's famous statue La Pieta, donated by a leading local citizen named Don Enrique Torres Belón, who is buried in the church. A caretaker will show you around. A tiny museum at the back of a shop at Ugarte 462 and Ayacucho contains local pottery. There is reportedly a chinchilla farm a little way out of town that can be visited. There is a colorful Sunday market.

Places to Stay & Eat
Most visitors come on day trips but you could overnight at the very basic but friendly *Hostal Lima*, Lima 135, which charges a little over US$1 per person. A chicken restaurant on the corner of the plaza opposite the church is one of the better restaurant options.

Getting There & Away
Buses leave when full from Avenida Huáscar in Juliaca, near the market a few

blocks past where the map stops. Buses charge US75¢ and there are faster but less comfortable minibuses for a little more. Buses returning from Lampa to Juliaca stop at 2 de Mayo, near the market area.

NORTHERN ROUTE TO BOLIVIA

This little-traveled, adventurous route into Bolivia is recommended only for experienced off-the-beaten-track travelers who have little concern for time or comfort. You should first get an exit stamp from Peruvian migraciones in Puno. They'll predate the stamp by three days to give you time to do the trip if you explain which way you are going. Then head to Juliaca.

Decrepit 3 de Mayo buses full of Andean Indians travel from Juliaca to **Huancané** several times a day. The three-hour journey costs about US$1.25. The company has no office; just show up and pay on the bus. Occasionally, buses continue to Moho, on the route to Bolivia, or to Rasapata. Huancané is a small town of 5000 inhabitants. You can stay at the very basic *Hostal Santa Cruz,* M Castilla 103, next to where the bus from Juliaca terminates. Slightly better hotels are the *Hostal Huancané*, on the Plaza de Armas, and the *Hostal Grau*, Grau 108. There are a few cheap restaurants near the plaza, of which the *Pollería Lady* is locally popular.

There are two or three buses leaving every day from Huancané to **Moho** (US$1.50, two hours). Some buses originate in Juliaca so you may have to stand. Trucks also do this route. The unsigned and basic *Alojamiento Mojo* just off the main plaza is the only place to stay at this time – ask around for it. Beds are US$1.50. The town's electricity comes on at night for an hour or two only, so bring spare batteries for your flashlight. Mojo is a friendly and clean little place with cobbled streets and about 2000 people. Locals say that only about one foreign traveler a week comes through town so they enjoy chatting with them.

A truck runs from Moho to Bolivia most mornings, leaving at the cheery hour of 3 am. If you're not an early riser you could walk about five or six hours to the border and a further four to the nearest Bolivian town of **Puerto Acosta**. The first two hours are uphill but then it flattens out. A walker reports in 1995 that he saw only two vehicles all day, one of which was going from Bolivia to Moho, so don't plan on hitchhiking.

At the border is a tiny village with no hotels or restaurants. The police here are reportedly unfriendly so make sure your documents are in order. The Bolivian migraciones is in Puerto Acosta where you'll need to get your passport stamped. The office is on the main plaza and, if it's closed, you can often find someone to open it if you ask around; US$1 is charged for this service. There is a basic alojamiento on the plaza charging about US$1 and a couple of cheap restaurants nearby. There may be another hotel. Transportation out of Puerto Acosta does not leave daily, so take the first vehicle you can, be it truck or bus, heading towards La Paz.

The nearest Bolivian consul is in Puno. The Puno section contains more information about entering Bolivia.

PUNO

Puno was founded on November 4, 1668, near the site of a now-defunct silver mine called Laykakota. However, apart from the cathedral, there are few colonial buildings to see. The town itself is drab and not very interesting but it does offer a good selection of hotels and there is plenty to see in the environs.

For many travelers, Puno (at 3830 meters) is the highest place they'll spend any amount of time. The weather at this altitude can be extreme. It's very cold at night, particularly during the winter months of June, July and August when temperatures can drop well below freezing. If you're cold, buy a thick alpaca sweater from the market – they're cheap. The rainy season is October to May. During the wettest months (December to April), floods and landslides sometimes close the roads but the train

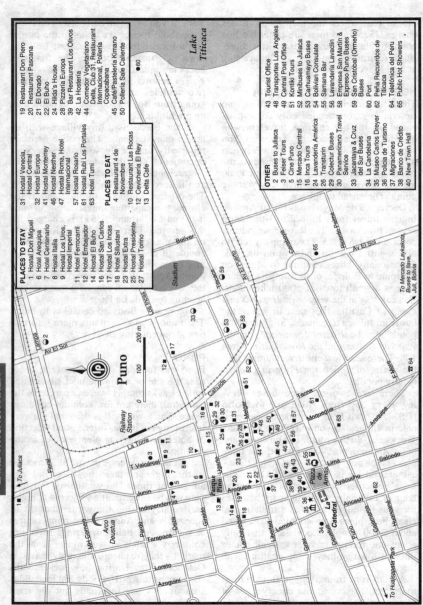

PLACES TO STAY
1 Hostal Don Miguel
6 Hotel Arequipa
7 Hotel Centenario
8 Hostal Italia
9 Hostal Los Uros,
   Hostal Imperial
11 Hotel Ferrocarril
12 Hotel Embajador
14 Hostal El Buño
16 Hostal San Carlos
17 Hostal Los Incas
18 Hostal Sillustani
23 Hostal Extra
25 Hostal Presidente
27 Hostal Torino
31 Hostal Venecia,
   Hostal Central
32 Hostal Europa
41 Hostal Monterrey
46 Hostal Nesther
47 Hostal Roma, Hotel
   Internacional
57 Hostal Rosario
61 Hotel Rubi Los Portales
63 Hotel Tumi

PLACES TO EAT
4 Restaurant 4 de
   Noviembre
10 Restaurant Las Rocas
12 Cevichería El Rey
13 Delta Cafe
19 Restaurant Don Piero
20 Restaurant Pascana
21 El Dorado
22 El Buho
24 Hilda's House
28 Pizzería Europa
39 Bar Restaurant Los Olivos
42 La Hostería
44 Comedor Vegetariano
   Delta, Club 31, Restaurant
   Internacional, Polería
   Copacabana
45 Café/Pastelería Kimano
50 Polería Sale Caliente

OTHER
2 Buses to Juliaca
3 Feiser Tours
5 Cine Puno
15 Mercado Central
16 Inca Tours
24 Lavandería América
26 Transturin
29 Colectur Buses
30 Panamericano Travel
   Service
33 Jacantaya & Cruz
   del Sur Buses
34 La Candelaria
35 Museo Carlos Dreyer
36 Policía de Turismo
37 Migraciones
38 Banco de Crédito
40 New Town Hall
43 Tourist Office
48 Transportes Los Angeles
49 Central Post Office
51 Koniki Tours
52 Minibuses to Juliaca
53 Carhuamayo Buses
54 Bolivian Consulate
55 Samana Bar
56 Lavandería Lavaclin
58 Empresa San Martín &
   Expreso Puno Buses
59 San Cristóbal (Ormeño)
   Buses
60 Port
62 Peña Recuerdos de
   Titicaca
64 Telefónica del Peru
65 Public Hot Showers

usually keeps running. Because the sun is very strong at this altitude, sunburn is a common problem; remember to wear a wide-brimmed hat and use a sunblock lotion.

Puno has about 80,000 inhabitants and is the capital of the Department of Puno, mainly because of its important position on the shores of Lake Titicaca. Nearby Juliaca is larger.

Information

Tourist Office The tourist office (☎ 35-1449, 35-3804) has moved at least six times in the last decade. The most recent location is on the northeast corner of the Plaza de Armas. Hours are 8 am to 1 pm and 2 to 6 pm, Monday to Saturday.

Bolivian Consulate This is at Puno 350 on the Plaza de Armas and is open weekdays from 8.30 am to 1 pm and 4 to 5 pm.

Citizens of the USA, UK, Israel and most western European countries don't require visas and can enter Bolivia with just a passport. Canadians, the French and many other nationals need a visa. The cost and time taken to issue a visa varies depending on the nationality but about US$20 is average. Regulations for Australians and New Zealanders have been changing so stop by the consul and ask if you're not sure.

Immigration The migraciones office (☎ 35-2801), Libertad 403, will extend Peruvian visas and tourist cards, but they are reportedly slow. It may be easier to just go to Bolivia and return.

Money Although Bolivian pesos can be exchanged in Puno, travelers to and from Bolivia are advised to buy or sell Bolivian pesos at the border for the best exchange rates.

You will find most of the banks on Calle Lima. The Banco de Crédito, at Grau and Independéncia, is the best bet for changing traveler's checks or getting money on a Visa credit card, but lines are long. Money changers hang out in front of the banks and

may give better rates and faster service, but watch carefully or you can be cheated. They normally deal just in cash US dollars or Bolivian pesos. Casas de cambio operate intermittently.

Some hotels may change money, particularly for guests.

Post & Telecommunications The Puno post office, Moquegua 267, is open from 8 am to 6 pm daily except Sunday when it closes at 1 pm.

Telefónica del Peru, Moquegua at Arequipa, is open from 7 am to 10 pm daily for national/international phone calls and faxes. The area code for Puno (and the surrounding area) is 054.

Travel Agencies There are many agencies offering local tours and services. It definitely pays to shop around and talk to other travelers about their experiences.

Beware of street touts hanging around the popular gringo hotels and restaurants. They are not always reliable. However, there are some decent guides who sometimes approach you informally when things are slow. Ask to see an official guide card. Some agencies that have been recommended include Feiser Tours (☎ 35-3112), Valcárcel 155; Panamericano Travel Service, Tacna 245; Kontiki Tours (☎ 35-2771), Melgar 188; and Inca Tours (☎ 35-1062), Ugarte 145. There are many others. Transturin (☎ 35-2771, 35-1316), Libertad 176, does expensive tours across Lake Titicaca using a catamaran (see Going to Bolivia, later in this chapter). The agencies next to the better hotels are quite good but may charge a bit more.

Laundry Lavandería América (☎ 35-1642), Moquegua 169, charges by the piece and is expensive. Lavandería Lavaclin, Deustua 223, may be cheaper.

Medical Services The best hospital is in Juliaca.

Emergency The Policia de Turismo is at Deustua 588.

Cathedral

La Catedral, on the Plaza de Armas, was
completed in 1757. The interior is more
spartan than you'd expect after seeing the
well-sculpted lower part of the main
facade, though there is a silver-plated main
altar.

Museo Carlos Dreyer

Just off the plaza at Conde de Lemos 289
is the town's main museum, formerly a
private collection that was bequeathed
to the city on the owner's death. Hours
on weekdays are 8.30 am to 1.30 pm
and admission is US$1. Opening hours
change frequently and it's best to go in the
morning.

Views

There are two good viewing spots. The
best is Huajsapata Park, a little hill about a
10-minute walk southwest of town. It is
topped by a larger-than-life white statue of
the first Inca, Manco Capac, looking out
over Lake Titicaca, the legendary site of
his birth. The view of the town and the
lake is excellent.

There are also good views from the
Arco Deustua, an arch on Calle Independencia. The arch was built in honor of
the Peruvians who died in the battles of
Junín and Ayacucho during the fight for
independence.

Mercado Central

The central market is always interesting,
especially in the morning when the salespeople are setting up their stalls. It's full of
Indian women sitting behind piles of potatoes or peanuts and is also a good place to
buy woolen clothes.

Places to Stay

Many of Puno's cheaper hotels have only
cold showers and, at this altitude, most
people find them more unpleasant than
invigorating. If you want to economize,
you can stay in a cheap hotel and use the
public hot showers. The best, on Avenida
El Sol, charges about US$1 for a 30-minute

hot shower and is open between 7 am and
7 pm daily, except holidays. You can also
try the gymnasium on Calle Deusta; it
is open from 7 am to 3 pm Tuesday to
Sunday.

The better hotels fill up quickly when the
evening trains arrive, so try to find a room
as soon as possible. The prices given may
rise (up to double) during fiestas and sometimes in the evening, though hotels are supposed to display the prices of their rooms
on a board. Many hotels in Puno have triple
and quadruple rooms which work out quite
cheaply if you are traveling with friends.

Electricity and water shortages are a
recurring problem. Keep a flashlight handy.
I have received several reports of theft from
hotel rooms. No particular hotel has this
reported as an ongoing problem but you
should minimize the risk by not leaving
your valuables in plain sight. Hide valuables in your (locked if possible) luggage,
carry money and passports in a money belt
or body pouch, and where available use the
hotel's security deposit.

Places to Stay – bottom end

There are cheap, basic hotels near the
corner of Libertad and Tacna, most of
which are none too clean and have only
cold showers. Even if they claim to have
hot water, it doesn't always work. The following charge about US$3/5 for singles/
doubles and are listed only because they
are Puno's cheapest (and most basic): The
dirty, unfriendly *Hostal Torino*, Libertad
126; the very poor and unfriendly *Hostal
Venecia*; the better *Hostal Extra* (☎ 35-
1123), Moquegua 124, which has hot water
sometimes and is the best of the super-
cheapies; the *Hotel Centenario*, Deza 211;
the *Hostal Rosario* (☎ 35-2272), Moquegua 325; the *Hostal Los Incas*, Los Incas
105, with no singles, plenty of triples and
quads, and an extra US$1 for a hot shower.
The basic *Hostal Roma* (☎ 35-1501),
Libertad 115, charges US$3/6 and has
dorm rooms for US$2 per person.

For a little more money you can have hot
water but, because of water shortages, it is

often available only at certain hours of the day, usually in the evening. The *Hostal Europa* (☎ 35-3023), Ugarte 112, has built up a reputation among budget travelers as *the* place to stay in Puno – it is often full of gringos. Double rooms are US$8. It's clean, with left-luggage facilities and hot water in the evening. It has been criticized, however, because of shower problems. As one reader writes, 'No showers were working on the upper floor and on the lower floor the only working shower burst into flames.' They also lack single rooms (though they will rent a double as a single if things are slow, which is not very often) and they take reservations but are liable to forget them. Another reader describes how she spent a couple of nights here sharing a double with a male friend. When the friend left and she wanted to stay on by herself for another night, the receptionist concluded that she was a prostitute.

The *Hotel Arequipa* (☎ 35-2071, Arequipa 153, also lacks singles and charges US$8 for a double. They are OK and have hot water sometimes. Probably the best hotel in this price range is the quiet *Hostal Los Uros* (☎ 35-2141), Valcárcel 135. It has hot water in the evening and a cafeteria, open for early simple breakfasts. There are only a few single rooms but plenty of triples and even quads. Rates are US$5.50/8.50/12.50/16.50 for one to four people with shared bath or US$7/11/16.50/22 with private bath.

The *Hostal Central* (☎ 35-2461), Tacna 269, is friendly and clean, though one reader complains that the wax used on the floor smells overpoweringly toxic. Rooms vary in price. The best are US$7.50/12 for singles/doubles with shared bathroom with some hot water. The clean *Hostal San Carlos* (☎ 35-1862), Ugarte 161, has telephones in the rooms and claims to have hot water all day. Rooms are US$8/11 or US$13/18 with private bath. They have a restaurant open for breakfast. The *Hostal Presidente* (☎ 35-1421), Tacna 248, charges US$7/10 but has hot water for only a couple of hours a day and doesn't seem too good.

The *Hostal Nesther* (☎ 35-1631), Deustua 268, has hot water from 6 to 8 am only, is clean and isn't a bad choice at US$8/13 for rooms with private baths. The *Hostal Monterrey* (☎ 35-1691), Grau 148, used to be a popular gringo hotel but seems to have fallen out of favor recently. Rooms are US$8/11 or US$10/16 with private bath but they have hot water only in the mornings. The *Hotel Tumi* (☎ 35-3270), Cajamarca 253, is another reasonable choice for US$10/14 for rooms with private bath, but they are open to bargaining.

Places to Stay – middle

The clean *Hostal Rubi Los Portales* (☎ 35-3270), Cajamarca 243, has rooms for US$13/19 with private bath and hot water. Front rooms are OK, but the rooms at the back are small and dark. The similarly priced *Hostal Imperial* (☎ 35-2386), Valcárcel 145, is clean and pleasant but has hot water only from 6.30 am to noon and 6.30 pm to midnight. They are planning to open a restaurant on the premises.

The *Hotel Ferrocarril* (☎ 35-1752, 35-2011), La Torre 145, across from the train station, has a few clean rooms for US$7/9 with cold communal showers, and better rooms for US$20/29 with private (electric) tepid showers and central heating – make sure these features are working properly before taking the room. The hotel restaurant is reasonably priced.

The recommended *Hostal El Buho* (☎ 35-1409), Lambayeque 142, is a good, clean, friendly mid-range hotel with pleasant rooms and hot showers. Rates are US$20/27 and you can rent a TV in your room for an extra US$2.50. The good, clean *Hostal Italia* (☎ 35-2521), Valcárcel 122, will provide a room heater for those who request one. Make sure your hot shower works because a few of the rooms are a long way from the water pump and may lack decent hot water. Rooms in the middle of the hotel seem the best. Rates are US$20/30 but you can bargain them down a bit if things are slow. Others in this price range include the *Hostal Don Miguel*

(☎ 35-1371, fax 35-2873), La Torre 545, which has a restaurant and seems OK, and the *Hotel Embajador* (☎ 35-2070), Los Incas 289, which is being remodelled.

The best place in Puno itself is the friendly and helpful *Hotel Sillustani* (☎ 35-1881, 35-2641, fax 35-1431), Lambayeque 195, where clean, carpeted rooms with bath and TV cost US$30/40, but there is hot water only from 5.30 to 9.30 am and 6 to 9 pm. The hotel has a reasonable restaurant and breakfast is usually included in the price of the room.

Places to Stay – top end
The well-run *Hotel Isla Esteves* (☎ 35-3870, 35-2271; in Lima ☎ 221-0822/4, fax 440-6197) is attractively located on an island in the western part of Lake Titicaca. The island is connected with Puno by a 5 km road over a causeway but, as there are no buses, access is a pain. Taxis charge about US$2 for the trip. About half of the rooms look directly out over the lake and the exceptionally beautiful views are the hotel's main attraction. The rooms themselves are clean and spacious but lack warmth and character, as does the hotel itself. There is also a decent restaurant (beware of overcharging), bar, giftshop and discotheque open when there is enough demand. Rooms are about US$70/95, but discounts can be arranged if they aren't busy.

Places to Eat
There are several restaurants on the corner of Moquegua and Libertad. The *Comedor Vegetariano Delta*, Libertad 215, is cheap and dingy, but recommended for early breakfasts and has vegetarian food. A reader recommends a new *Delta Cafe* at the Parque Pino – I don't know if it's in addition to or instead of the old one. The *Restaurant Internacional*, Libertad 161, is one of the best in town and has a wide range of good dishes at medium prices – about US$3 or US$4 for most dishes. Their International plate is huge. They often have music in the evenings, usually before 8 pm. *Club 31* is cheap and uncrowded but looks

pretty dismal. *Restaurant Las Rocas*, near the Hostal Los Uros on Valcárcel, has good food and is reasonably priced, though it lacks atmosphere.

There are other cheap restaurants along Avenida Lima – the *Restaurant Pascana* (☎ 35-1962), Lima 339, is good and has set lunches for a little over US$1 and offers vegetarian as well as fish and meat dishes. Opposite, the *Restaurant Don Piero* (☎ 35-1788), Lima 354, has local trout meals (US$4) and other, cheaper plates. *El Dorado* (☎ 35-2702), Lima 371, is good and reasonably priced. The cozy *La Hostería*, Lima 501, is popular for pizzas (about US$4.50) and other meals. They also have good apple pie and chocolate cake and an excellent selection of alcoholic concoctions. They sometimes have music in the evenings. For those on a budget, the simple *Restaurant 4 de Noviembre*, on Junín near Deza, has set lunches for about US$1 – it's popular with the locals.

The *Café/Pastelería Kimano*, Arequipa 509, has good pastries and also serves pizza. It's open from 5 to 9 pm and is popular with the locals. The *Bar Restaurant Los Olivos*, Ayacucho 237, is also fairly popular with locals. *Pollería Sale Caliente*, Tacna 381, has been described by one enthusiast as the best chicken place in Peru. *El Buho*, Libertad 386, is a cozy pizza place and *Pizzería Europa* at the corner of Tacna and Libertad is another decent choice. *Cevichería El Rey*, Los Incas 271, looks good and has ceviches from US$3.50. *Hilda's House*, Moquegua 189, is pleasant, tranquil and has reasonable prices. One reader raves that they have the best chocolate cake in western South America. They serve meals as well as desserts.

The *Quinta La Kantuta*, at Arequipa 1086 some way from the center, serves typical lunches (including cuy) daily, except Monday.

Entertainment
Cine Puno sometimes screens English-language movies with Spanish subtitles.

Musicians often do the rounds of the

Fiestas & Folklore around Lake Titicaca

The department of Puno is noted for its wealth of traditional dances – up to 300 different varieties. Some dances are rarely seen by tourists while others are performed in the streets during the various annual fiestas. Many have specific significance, which locals will explain to you if you make friends with them. Although the dances often occur during processions celebrating Catholic feast days, they usually have their roots in completely different, preconquest celebrations. These are often tied in with the agricultural calendar and may celebrate such events as planting or harvesting. Even if you have difficulty understanding the meaning of the dances, you'll be fascinated by the extremely rich, ornate and imaginative costumes that are often worth more than an entire household's ordinary clothes. Included in this show of color and design are grotesque masks, dazzling sequined uniforms and animal outfits, to mention just a few.

The elaborately outfitted dancers are accompanied by musicians playing a host of traditional instruments. Most of the brass and string instruments have obvious Spanish influences but many of the percussion and wind instruments have changed little since Inca times. These include *tinyas* (hand drums or tambourines) and *wankaras* (larger drums) as well as a host of different shakers, rattles and bells. Inca wind instruments include the very typical and well-known panpipes. These come in a variety of lengths and tones ranging from tiny, high-pitched instruments to huge base panpipes almost as tall as the musician. The pipes, often made from bamboo, are known as *antaras, sikus* or *zampoñas*, depending on their size and range. *Flautas* (flutes) are also seen at most fiestas. The most common are simple bamboo penny whistles called *quenas*, while others are large blocks that look as though they've been hollowed out of a plank of wood. The most esoteric of these flutes is the *piruru*, carved from the wing bone of an Andean condor.

Seeing a street fiesta with dancing can be planned or it can be a matter of luck. Some celebrations are held in one town and not in another; at other times, such as carnival, there are fiestas everywhere. Ask at the tourist office about any fiestas in the surrounding area.

Apart from the major Peruvian fiestas listed in the Facts about the Country chapter, the following is a selection of fiestas that are particularly important in the Lake Titicaca region. Candlemas is one of the most spectacular and is spread out for several days around the actual date, depending upon which day of the week Candlemas falls. If it falls on a Sunday to Tuesday, things get underway the previous Saturday, if it falls on a Wednesday to Friday, things normally get underway the following Saturday, but this is all subject to change. Puno week is also a big deal, celebrating the legendary birth of Manco Capac from Lake Titicaca. There are many colorful and important dances, and some wild drinking parties.

These fiestas are crowded affairs so watch your pockets.

January 6	Epiphany
February 2	Candlemas (or Virgen de la Candelaria)
March 7–8	Saint John
May 2–4	Alacitas (Puno miniature handicrafts fair)
	Holy Cross (Huancané, Taquile)
July 25	Saint James (Taquile)
September 24	Our Lady of Mercy
November 1–7	Puno week

This list is not exhaustive – there are other fiestas. Most are celebrated for several days before and after the actual day. ■

restaurants, usually playing a half hour set of folklórico music, passing the hat, and then moving on. The weekend is the best time to come across a good musical evening. The *Peña Recuerdos de Titicaca* (☎ 35-1999), Ancash 239, sometimes has a peña at weekends. *La Candelaria* (☎ 35-1562), Deustua 654, is a sort of dinner-theater with Andean dances and folklórico music, and a US$2.50 cover charge.

My favorite bar is *Samana*, Puno 334. Its fireplace, thatched roof and wooden benches provide a pleasant atmosphere and there is live music most weekends for a low cover charge. It is occasionally closed.

Things to Buy
This is one of the best towns in Peru to get good quality woolen and alpaca sweaters and other products at fair prices. These items are sold in many places but the open-air market near the railway station may have the best choices if you know how to bargain. Watch for pickpockets here.

Getting There & Away
Air The nearest airport is in Juliaca, about 44 km away. Several travel agents in Puno will sell you tickets. There is a Faucett office at Libertad 265. Travel agents have a shuttle service direct to the airport for about US$2.50 per person. See the Juliaca section for further information about flights.

Bus The roads to Cuzco and Arequipa are in bad shape and many people choose to travel in greater comfort on the train. There have been reports of hold-ups of night buses, and most buses travel at night. One reader reports that the road is better and safer since 1995, but I still prefer the train. For those who prefer to use the bus, Cruz del Sur and San Cristóbal (the Ormeño subsidiary) have the best buses.

Cruz del Sur (☎ 35-2451), Avenida El Sol 568, has buses to Arequipa (US$10, 12 hours), Cuzco (US$10, 14 hours), and Lima (US$25, 42 hours) all leaving between 4 and 5 pm. They also have a bus to La Paz, Bolivia (US$6.50, 5 hours), via

Desaguadero, at 10 am three times a week. San Cristóbal (☎ 35-2321), on the 300 block of Titicaca, has slightly cheaper overnight buses to Arequipa and Lima. Cheaper still are Jacantaya (☎ 35-1931), Avenida El Sol 594, with overnight buses to Arequipa and Lima, and Carhuamayo (☎ 35-3522), Melgar 334, with an overnight bus to Cuzco.

For Tacna (US$7.50, 15 hours), try Expreso Puno, Titicaca 258, or the nearby Empresa San Martín or 3 de Julio. All have buses leaving about 5 pm.

Buses to towns on the south side of the lake and the Bolivian border depart frequently during the day from the Avenida El Ejército side of the Mercado Laykakota.

For buses to Juliaca (US50¢, about an hour), Transportes Los Angeles leave several times an hour from the corner of Tacna and Libertad. Buses also go from the corner of Lampa and El Sol. Slightly faster but more cramped minibuses leave from the corner of Cahuide and Titicaca.

Train The first few kilometers of the journey out of Puno are along the shores of Lake Titicaca, and the views are good. Trains used to leave daily, then were cut to two a week, but departures are now four times a week and daily service during the high season may soon be resumed. Currently, the Cuzco train leaves at 7.25 am on Monday, Wednesday, Thursday and Saturday, arriving at 5.30 pm. The Arequipa train leaves at 7.45 pm on Monday, Wednesday, Friday and Saturday, arriving at 6 am the following day. Check for service changes. Be alert for thieves at the railway station and on the trains, especially the night train to Arequipa (see Arequipa for more information).

The 1st-class fare to Cuzco has varied from about US$2 to US$20 over the past decade. There has been talk of privatizing the (now government-run) train service, which could lead to heavy price increases and other changes. In 1995, Cuzco fares were about US$10.50/13.50/18 in 2nd/1st/Pullman class, while Arequipa fares are US$9.50/12/15. The Pullman fare to Cuzco has been as high as over US$30 in the past. Be careful of the ticket you buy – there have been complaints of 1st-class tickets being sold for Pullman prices, without the added safety and comfort of that class.

While the Pullman class is safest, 1st class is reasonably safe if you are traveling during the day (to Cuzco) and remain awake and alert. Some shoestring budget travelers have taken 2nd to Cuzco without incident; others have been robbed. On the night train to Arequipa, 2nd class is not recommended. Note that even in the best class, seats are not very comfortable, and the ride is pretty bouncy.

Even if you buy your Cuzco ticket the day before, sometimes the numbered 1st-class and Pullman seats get sold out. It is difficult to buy tickets earlier than the day before, though, and lines are always long. Recent reports indicate that seats sell out fast to travel agents, who often have tickets – but at a commission of about US$2 to US$4 extra. (Commissions as high as 100% have been reported, so check carefully.) This is worth it if you don't have the time or patience to stand in line for a long time but a pain if you have the time to stand in line and are trying to economize. The ticket office opens at 8 am and you should get there early. For Arequipa, tickets are sold on the day of travel. Buying tickets days in advance was not possible recently, although it has been possible in the past.

Some travelers prefer to take the bus to Juliaca and continue by train from there, especially when traveling to Cuzco, because it's quicker and cheaper. The Cuzco train between Puno and Juliaca is very slow and stops for a long time near Juliaca while connecting with the Arequipa-Juliaca-Cuzco carriages. However, you lose the attractive train ride along the shores of the lake.

Car If you want to see the wild and scenic countryside between Puno and Arequipa during the day, you can hire a taxi. There used to be colectivo taxis charging about twice as much per passenger as the buses but these seem to have been discontinued.

A taxi might charge around US$100 to go to Arequipa. Comité 1 on Plaza Pino might be a good place to start looking.

Boat The steamer service from Puno to Bolivia was discontinued in the mid-1980s. There is sporadic talk of renewing the service, but this will probably never happen. The bus with hydrofoil and catamaran services (via Juli or Copacabana, Bolivia – see Going to Bolivia later in this chapter) are very expensive compared to buses from Puno to La Paz.

Boats from the Puno dock leave for various islands in the lake (see Around Puno, below). Tickets bought directly from the boats at the dock are invariably cheaper than those bought from agencies in town. (As we go to press I have received an unconfirmed report that tour boats now leave from a dock a few kilometers north of town and taxis and minibuses go there.)

Getting Around
Tricycle taxis are a popular way of geting around Puno and are a little cheaper than ordinary taxis.

Around Puno

There are several excursions to take from Puno. Lake Titicaca trips to the floating islands of Los Uros or to Isla Taquile or Isla Amantaní are all popular. You can also visit the Isla del Sol and Isla de la Luna on the Bolivia part of the lake. Land trips visit the archaeological site of Sillustani. A drive along the southern shores of the lake takes in various small towns famous for their colonial churches and their fiestas. The Bolivian ruins at Tiahuanaco can also be visited.

Most of these excursions can be done cheaply on public transport. Tour companies will arrange guided trips, but these are more expensive and not necessarily worth the extra money. I went on a guided tour of the archaeological site of Sillustani because there is little literature about the site and I wanted to learn as much about it as I could. I was with a small group of non-Spanish-speaking travelers, who were also particularly interested in Sillustani and, like me, wanted an informative visit. I arranged an excursion with an agency that promised a private vehicle to pick us up from the hotel and an English-speaking guide to explain the ruins. The old bus that did arrive was almost an hour late and stopped to pick up two more small groups along the way, as well as a few friends of the driver. We were charged an extra fee for admission to the site and, to top it all, the guide knew very little more about the ruins than we did and spoke no English – I ended up translating for him.

Of course, anyone who has spent any time traveling in Latin America knows that these things happen and that you have to expect and accept them. However, when you're paying for it, this is more difficult. If you do take a guided tour, you might want to sign a written agreement or defer payment until the trip is underway. Try and meet the guide beforehand, if possible. Some tours are quite good and worth the money.

SILLUSTANI

The Inca Empire was known as Tahuantinsuyo, or 'The Land of Four Quarters.' The southern quarter was called Collasuyo after the Colla tribe which, along with the rival Lupaca tribe, dominated the Lake Titicaca area and later became part of the Inca Empire.

Little is known about the Colla people. They were a warlike tribe who spoke Aymara, not Quechua, and they had unusual burial customs for their nobility. Their dead were buried in funerary towers called *chullpas*, which can be seen in various places in the Puno area. The most impressive of these are the chullpas of Sillustani, the tallest of which reaches a height of about 12 meters; there are several others almost as tall. Standing on a small hilltop in the Lake Umayo peninsula, these towers look very impressive against the bleak landscape. They are either round or

square and house the remains of Colla nobility, who were buried in family groups complete with food and belongings for their journey into the next world. The only opening into the towers was a small hole facing east, just large enough for a person to crawl through. After a burial, the entrance was sealed. Nowadays, nothing remains of the burials. The chullpas, however, are well preserved and worth seeing, both for their architecture and for their impressive location.

The outside walls of the towers are made from massive coursed blocks. These are reminiscent of Inca stonework but were not built by the Incas; archaeologists consider this architecture more complicated than that of the Incas. Some of the chullpas of Sillustani are unfinished. Carved but unplaced blocks and a ramp used to raise them to the correct height are among the points of interest at the site. A few of the blocks are decorated – the carving most often noticed by visitors is that of a lizard.

Sillustani is partially encircled by Lake Umayo. This interesting Andean lake is home to a variety of plants and water birds. Ornithologists should particularly watch for the giant Andean coot, the white-tufted and silvery grebes, the puna ibis, the Andean goose, the black-crowned

Andean goose

night-heron, the speckled and puna teals, the yellow-billed pintail, the Andean lapwing, the Andean gull (strange to see a 'sea' gull so far from the ocean) and, if you're very lucky, one of the three species of flamingo found in the Andean highlands.

Getting There & Away

Tours are offered by a number of agencies and usually leave at 2.30 pm from near the Panamericano Travel service on Tacna. The cheapest tours are about US$7.50 and include the entrance to the ruins (US$2.50). Not all guides speak English. The roundtrip takes about 3½ hours and allows you about 1½ hours at the ruins. This schedule is convenient because the afternoon light is the best for photography, though the site can be pretty crowded in the afternoon. There is a small on-site museum. Dress warmly and bring sun protection.

If you prefer more time at the site, you could hire a taxi for US$15. If you can get a group together, this isn't much more expensive than the tour bus but you don't get a guide and have to pay the entrance fee of US$2.50 per person.

Camping by the lake is reportedly possible but no facilities are provided. Don't leave anything unattended and go in a group.

FLOATING ISLANDS

The floating islands (Islas Flotantes) of the Uros people are the Puno area's major tourist attraction and, as a result, have become somewhat overcommercialized. Despite this, the excursion remains popular because there is nothing quite like it anywhere else.

Intermarriage with Aymara-speaking Indians has seen the demise of the pure-blooded Uros and none exist today. They used to speak their own language but nowadays speak Aymara. Always a small tribe, they began their unusual floating existence centuries ago in an effort to isolate themselves from the Collas and the Incas. Today, about 300 people live on the islands but the attractions of shore life are slowly eroding even this small number.

The lives of the Uros are totally interwoven with the *totora* reeds that grow abundantly in the shallows of Lake Titicaca. These reeds are harvested and used to make anything from the islands themselves to little model boats for sale to tourists. The islands are constructed from many layers of reeds. The reeds rot away from the bottom and are replaced at the top, so the ground is soft and springy and you must be careful not to put your foot through a rotted-out section. The biggest of the islands contains

several buildings, including a school. The inhabitants of one island have built a small one-room museum with stuffed birds and animals inside. Admission is US50¢. They have also built an observation platform so that you can climb up about seven or eight meters and survey the surroundings from the rickety perch – another US50¢ donation. The building walls are still made of totora but some of the roofs are now tin.

From tightly bundled reeds, the Uros build canoe-shaped boats for transport and fishing. A well-constructed boat can carry a whole family for about six months before beginning to rot. You can usually persuade one of the Uros to give you a ride on a boat, but be prepared to pay and give a tip for taking photographs.

Plenty of women will try to sell you their handicrafts such as models made from totora and embroidered wall hangings. Many visitors find it annoying to be constantly pestered to buy souvenirs, give presents to the children and hand out money every time a camera is lifted. Begging and selling are more common here than in most other parts of Peru. However, on some islands the begging has improved somewhat over recent years as the villagers have come up with more satisfying ways of making some money such as the museum, observation tower and boat rides.

Getting There & Away

Getting to the Floating Islands is easy: just go down to the docks and hang around – within minutes, you'll be asked to take a trip to the islands. You can hire an expensive private boat or go with the next group. Boats generally leave several times between 7 am until early afternoon if there is enough passenger demand. The standard trip, visiting the main island and perhaps one other, takes about four or five hours and it's best to leave by about 8.30 am. Boats leave as soon as they have 15 or 20 passengers and charge a fixed price – usually around US$3.50 per person. All the boats are small, rather decrepit motorboats with no life jackets, though I've never heard of an accident.

Many tour agencies in Puno will sell you tickets for an Uros trip but they usually use the same boats as independent travelers and charge more. Unless you insist on a private tour and are prepared to pay more for it, going down to the docks and buying your own ticket is the best idea. Guided tours cost about US$7 per person if there is a large enough group, and over US$10 a person if there are only a few tourists.

En route, you may well see the Uros paddling around in their reed boats, fishing or gathering totora reeds. Various bird species live on and around the lake (see Sillustani above). Even though the Uros and their floating islands are rather sad, the ride on the lake can be beautiful in good weather.

ISLA TAQUILE

This is a real island, not a floating one, and it is less frequently visited than Uros. The long trip is best done with an overnight stay, though day trips from Puno are possible.

Taquile (Taquili on some maps) is the most fascinating of islands. The men wear tightly woven woolen caps and always seem to be walking around the island knitting them. The headgear looks like a floppy nightcap and can only be described as cute. I'm told that men wear red hats if they are single and red and white hats if they are married. The women weave the elegant-looking waistcoats which the men wear with their knitted caps, rough-spun white shirts and thick, calf-length black pants, giving them a very raffish air. The women, in their many-layered skirts and delicately embroidered blouses, also look very handsome. These garments, which are among the best-made traditional clothes that I've come across in Peru, can be bought in the island's cooperative store on the main plaza.

The people of Taquile speak Quechua, rather than the Aymara of most Titicaca Indians, and maintain a strong sense of group identity. They rarely marry non-Taquile people and their lives are untrammeled by such modernities as roads. There are no vehicles, not even bicycles, on the island and there are almost no dogs. Electricity was introduced in the 1990s, but is not available everywhere.

Although Taquile is very peaceful, the islanders are by no means content to let the world pass them by. When enterprising individuals from Puno began bringing tourists to visit the island, the islanders fought the invasion. It wasn't the tourists they objected to, it was the Puno entrepreneurs. Now the passenger boats to Taquile are owned and operated by the islanders themselves. This control enables them to keep tourism at what they consider to be reasonable levels. This may be the key to maintaining a respectful, cooperative relationship between locals and tourists – something sadly lacking on the floating islands of the Uros.

Unfortunately, there are rare instances of thieving and begging, so the place obviously isn't perfect. Perhaps tourism is beginning to have negative effects. Try to minimize the impact of your visit.

The island's scenery is beautiful. The soil is a deep, earthy, red color which, in the strong highland sunlight, contrasts magnificently with the intense blue of the lake. The backdrop of Bolivia's snow-capped Cordillera Real on the far side of the lake completes a splendid picture. The island is 6 to 7 km long with several hills, which have Inca terracing on the sides and small ruins on top. Visitors are free to wander around exploring these ruins and enjoying the peaceful scenery. You can't do this on a day trip (well, you can, but you'll miss the returning boat) so you should stay overnight if you can.

San Diego (Saint James Day, July 25) is a big feast day on Taquile. Dancing, music and general carousing go on for several days until the beginning of August, when the Indians traditionally make offerings to mother earth, Paccha Mama. New Year's Day is also festive and rowdy. Many islanders go to Puno for La Virgen de la Candelaria and Puno week (see Puno) and Taquile is liable to be somewhat deserted then.

Places to Stay & Eat
Some people elect to stay overnight on Taquile – a worthwhile decision. A steep stairway, from which there are lovely views, leads from the dock to the center of the island. The climb takes about 20 minutes, more if you're not acclimatized, and it is strongly recommended that you don't do it immediately after arriving from the coast – climbing stairs at 4000 meters is a painful, breathless and potentially dangerous experience if you're not used to it. (One reader claims that she counted over 500 steps and I'm not going to quibble with that.)

In the center, a group of the inhabitants will greet you and, if you wish, will arrange accommodations. Individuals and small groups are assigned to island families who will put you up in their rustic houses (there are no hotels as such). There is a standard charge of about US$2 per person and gifts of fresh food are appreciated. Beds are basic but clean and adequate and facilities minimal. You will be given some blankets but bring a sleeping bag as it gets very cold at night. Bathing means doing what the locals do: washing in cold water from a bucket and, in a few cases, using the fields as a latrine. If you like a little luxury, overnighting in Taquile is not for you. You can camp if you bring everything. Campers are charged about half of the cost of a bed in someone's house.

If you do decide to stay the night, remember to bring a flashlight as there is no lighting. It's also a good idea to take in the lay of the land while it's still light. Some friends of mine became completely lost on the island in the dark, couldn't find the house where they were staying, and ended up having to rough it for the night.

The few simple restaurants in the center of the island sell whatever is available: fresh lake trout much of the time but boiled potatoes and fried eggs if you're out of luck. About a 10 minute walk from the main plaza (on the main route to and from the dock) is the *Restaurant Los Amigos* in the house of local musician César Hautta Cruz. They often have good meals of fresh trout at reasonable prices, but bottled drinks are pricey.

You can usually buy bottled drinks but they have been known to run out. Boiled tea is usually safe to drink, though it's worth bringing a water bottle and purifying tablets or filter if you have them. Also bring extra food unless you're prepared to take pot luck on what's available in the restaurants. Make sure you have small bills because change is limited and there's nowhere to change dollars. Beware of overcharging in restaurants and settle the price of the meal before you eat it. Bring extra money too; many travelers are unable to resist the high quality of the unique woven and knitted clothes sold in the island's cooperative store.

Although conditions are primitive by Western standards, visiting Taquile is a wonderful experience and some travelers stay for several days. The people are friendly and the lifestyle is peaceful and relaxed. I stayed here once at the time of a full moon and watched the sunset and moonrise from a small Inca ruin atop one of the island's hills. It was windless and still and, as the mirror-like lake darkened slowly, I felt that Taquile was its own little world, completely detached from the rest of the earth. When the moon came up over the almost 7000-meter snowcaps of the Cordillera Real, it seemed twice as bright and much larger than normal in the crystalline air over the lake. An unforgettable evening.

Getting There & Away

A boat for Taquile leaves the Puno dock every day (twice a day if there's enough demand). Departure time is usually about 8 or 9 am; you can either go down to the dock the day before to check the departure time or show up by 7.30 am and see what's available. The 24-km trip takes four hours (sometimes including a brief stop at the Islas Uros) and costs about US$5, one way. Pay the captain to avoid a surcharge from a ticket tout. You then get about two hours on the island and the return trip leaves at 2.30 pm, arriving in Puno around nightfall.

This is the same boat to take back if you decide to stay overnight. Remember to bring adequate sun protection – the intensity of the tropical sun bouncing off the lake at almost 4000 meters can cause severe sunburn.

Tour agencies also offer this trip but it's cheaper and just as easy to go down to the docks and get your own ticket, unless you want a guided day trip.

ISLA AMANTANÍ

This island is similar to and a few kilometers north of the smaller Taquile. Because it is further away from Puno, Amantaní is visited less often and has fewer facilities than Taquile. Basic food and accommodations are available but tend to be limited. You can get a bed and three basic meals (not for delicate stomachs) for about US$4 per day or pay US$2 to sleep and eat in one of the few small 'restaurants.'

As with Taquile there are good views, no roads, no vehicles, no dogs, and it's very tranquil. One traveler reports that there is a post office and a telephone link. Several hills are topped by ruins, among the highest and best known of which are Pachamama and Pachatata (Earth Mother and Earth Father), which date to the Tiahuanaco culture.

Boats to Amantaní leave the Puno dock between 7.30 and 8.30 am most mornings (ask around for the next departure) and one-way fares are about US$5 if you pay the captain direct. Boats often stop at the floating islands on the way out but not on the return trip, which is a few cents cheaper. Several boats and islanders have been recommended, but transport depends on what's in town and where you stay depends on the islanders. They have a rotating system that gives everybody a fair chance to make some money. Both the Julio Borda and the Bernardo Quispe Manani families have been recommended by my readers and other families are recommended in other books, so it probably doesn't much matter whom you end up with.

From Puno, it is possible to go roundtrip to Taquile via the Islas Uros and Amantaní and back to Puno. It is more difficult to do the trip in reverse because few boats go from Taquile to Amantaní. There is a boat from Amantaní to Taquile most days for a fare of US$1.50. It's difficult to visit Amantaní on a day trip. If you plan on going to Amantaní then Taquile, ask for one-way boat tickets (otherwise, you'll usually be sold the roundtrip ticket to Amantaní as a matter of course).

Puno travel agencies charge about US$20 and up for a tour to Amantaní, with one night in Amantaní and quick visits to Taquile and the floating islands. The cheapest tours simply facilitate buying services which you could buy yourself but it's not a bad deal. They charge about 50% more to save you hassling with it and it's worth considering if you don't speak Spanish. More expensive tours may add a decent guide, some of which are English speaking. Meals may be included – check details carefully. Three day/two night tours are available with the first night at Amantaní and the second at Taquile. Check the details of a tour carefully and buy from reputable agents rather than street touts.

ISLA DEL SOL & ISLA DE LA LUNA

The most famous island on Lake Titicaca is the Isla del Sol (Island of the Sun), legendary birthplace of Manco Capac, the first Inca. Both the Isla del Sol and Isla de la Luna (Island of the Moon) have Inca ruins. They are in the Bolivian portion of the lake and you should visit them from the Bolivian port of Copacabana, about 11 km beyond the border town of Yunguyo.

SOUTH SHORE TOWNS

An interesting bus excursion can be made to the towns of Chimu, Chucuito, Ilave, Juli, Pomata and Zepita on the southern shores of Lake Titicaca, all described below. If you start early enough, you can visit all of them in a day and be back in Puno for the night. Alternatively, you could stay in one of the generally poor hotels in these towns or continue on to Bolivia.

Getting There & Away

If you're interested in visiting any of the towns along the south shore of Lake Titicaca, go to the Avenida El Ejército side of Puno's Mercado Laykakota. Cheap, very slow buses and slightly more expensive, faster minibuses leave from here for the south shore towns and the Bolivian border. Buses to the nearer towns, such as Ilave, are more frequent but, if you're patient, you should be able to leave for the town of your choice within an hour. Minibus fares to the border are about US$2 and proportionately less to closer towns.

Chimu

The road east of Puno closely follows the margins of the lake. After about 8 km, you reach the village of Chimu – hikers might find this a pleasant lakeshore walk. Chimu is famous for its totora reed industry and its inhabitants have close ties with the Uros. Bundles of reeds are piled up to dry and there are always several reed boats in various stages of construction. Although this is an interesting sight, I found the villagers not particularly friendly to sightseers (though a correspondent tells me that their initial reserve can be overcome).

Chucuito

The village of Chucuito, about 18 km east of Puno, was of some importance as a major Lupaca center and a precolonial stone sundial can be seen in the main plaza. Chucuito has two attractive colonial churches – Santo Domingo (with an Inca ruin next to it) and La Asunción. Opening hours are erratic. There is a trout hatchery east of the town.

Places to Stay The *Hostal Cabañas* (☎ 35-2108; leave a message for Alfredo Sanchez) on the outskirts of Chucuito charges about US$13/20/24 for singles/doubles/triples. Its main attraction is the superb view of the lake, but they also have table tennis and other minor amenities. There is a restaurant.

Ilave

Near Chucuito, the road turns southeast away from the lake (though the waters can usually be seen in the distance) and soon reaches Platería, a village once famous for its silverware. About 40 km from Puno, the road passes through the straggling community of Molleko. This area is noted for the great number of mortarless stone walls that snake eerily across the bleak altiplano.

Ilave is 56 km from Puno. It doesn't have the interesting colonial architecture of the other towns but its position at the crossroads gives it some importance. Ilave also has a Sunday market. A daily bus travels the little-used road to Tacna. Unfortunately, the bus leaves at 3 pm and travelers miss much of the scenery. The journey takes about 15 hours and costs US$7.50.

Juli

The road returns to the lake near the bay of Juli, where flamingos are sometimes seen. Juli is 80 km from Puno and famous for its four colonial churches. They are all in a greater or lesser state of disrepair but are slowly being restored as funds become available. The oldest, San Juan Bautista, dates from the late 1500s and contains richly framed colonial paintings depicting the lives of Saint John the Baptist and Saint Teresa. This church is now a museum open from 8 am to noon (though this varies) and admission is US50¢.

The Church of La Asunción, finished in 1620, offers excellent vistas of Lake Titicaca from its large courtyard. Its belfry was struck by lightning and shows extensive damage. The Church of Santa Cruz has lost half of its roof. The Church of San Pedro, on the main plaza, is in the best condition. It is interesting to see the churches in their unrestored state and get some idea of what the magnificent colonial churches of such popular tourist centers as Cuzco would look like had they not been carefully and extensively restored.

Hydrofoil service to Bolivia operates from Juli's port (see Going to Bolivia, below).

Market day in Juli is Thursday.

Places to Stay The very basic *Alojamiento El Rosal*, Puno 128, just off the main plaza, charges US$2.50 per person and is the only place in Juli to stay at this time.

Pomata

Beyond Juli, the road returns to the lake shore again and continues to Pomata, 106 km from Puno. As you arrive in Pomata you'll see the Dominican church, dramatically located on top of a small hill. It was founded in 1700 and is known for its many baroque carvings and for its windows made of translucent alabaster. Work on its restoration may have finished. As with the other churches in the region, you can never tell exactly when it will be open.

Just out of Pomata, the road forks. The main road continues southeast through Zepita (where there is another colonial church) to the Bolivian border town of Desaguadero, while a side road, leading to the other border crossing at Yunguyo, hugs the shore of Lake Titicaca.

Places to Stay The only place seems to be with the *Familia Rosa Pizano* at house No 30 on the main plaza.

GOING TO BOLIVIA

For many travelers, Puno and Lake Titicaca are stepping stones to Bolivia, which borders the lake to the south. For information about Bolivian entrance formalities, see the Bolivian Consulate information in Puno. Bolivian time is one hour ahead of Peruvian time.

Over Lake Titicaca

The steamer service from Puno to the Bolivian port of Guaqui was discontinued over a decade ago. There is sporadic talk of restarting this service though it seems increasingly unlikely – check with a travel agent to find out if the steamer is sailing again.

The available boats and hydrofoils from Puno to La Paz are much more expensive than a bus ride. The Transturin service, which costs about US$130, leaves Puno by bus at 6.30 am and goes to Copacabana, Bolivia, from where a catamaran sails to the Isla del Sol for a quick visit before continuing to the Bolivian port of Huatajata and on to La Paz by bus, arriving at 5 pm. This service includes hotel transfers, a visit to one or two churches in the south shore towns, lunch and a guide. Transturin has an office in Puno as well as a La Paz office (☎ 591-2-363654, 591-2-328560, fax 591-2-391162), Camacho 1321.

An irregular service to and from Bolivia operates from Juli's small port. A hydrofoil leaves most days and costs about US$150 per passenger, including bus transfers between your Puno hotel and Juli and between Huatajata and your hotel in La Paz, Bolivia. The hydrofoil stops for a brief visit to the Isla del Sol and Copacabana, both in Bolivia, and breakfast, lunch and a guide are included. Further information can be obtained in travel agencies in Puno or La Paz or from Crillon Tours (☎ 591-2-350363, fax 591-2-391039), Camacho 1223, La Paz, Bolivia.

Overland

There are two overland routes from Puno to La Paz, Bolivia: via Yunguyo or via Desaguadero. Each has its advantages, described below. Also, there is a rarely used northern route from Juliaca, described earlier in this chapter.

The Yunguyo route is the more attractive and has the added interest of the boat crossing at the Estrecho de Tiquina. Some travelers like to break the trip in the pleasant Bolivian port of Copacabana. The Desaguadero route is more direct but less attractive and the road in worse shape on the Bolivian side. This route can be combined with a visit to the Bolivian ruins at Tiahuanaco.

Via Yunguyo Buses leave from the Avenida El Ejérjito side of Mercado Laykakota in Puno for the border town of Yunguyo (2½ hours, US$2). Yunguyo has a couple of basic hotels but, as there is little of interest in Yunguyo, most people go on to Bolivia. You will find money changers in the main plaza and on the street by the border, which is about 2 km away. Change just enough to get you to La Paz and count your money carefully. The border is open from 8 am to 6 pm and formalities are fairly straightforward. Exit taxes are sometimes asked for but these are not legal. The money goes into the official's pocket.

Bolivian immigration formalities take place almost a kilometer away and taxis are available. From there, it's about 10 km more to Copacabana. Available transport ranges from trucks to buses to taxis and is more frequent on Sunday, which is market day in Yunguyo. On weekdays you may have to wait up to an hour. Copacabana is a much nicer place than Yunguyo and has several hotels in various price ranges as well as a port from where inexpensive tours to Isla del Sol are available so, if you want to break your journey, do so here. Remember that Bolivian time is one hour ahead of Peruvian time.

There are several buses a day from Copacabana to La Paz. The trip takes approximately five hours, including a boat crossing of the Estrecho de Tiquina. You have to register with the Bolivian navy to cross – a simple formality but don't miss your bus! The fare is about US$4 including the ferry.

If you leave Puno early in the morning, you can reach La Paz in a single day. For an extra few dollars, a Puno to La Paz ticket with a company such as Colectur (☎ 35-2302), Tacna 221, is the most convenient option. They will drive you to Yunguyo, stop at the money exchange, show you exactly where to go for exit and entrance formalities and drive you to Copacabana, where you are met by a Bolivian bus for the trip to La Paz. Although it's not as cheap as buying separate tickets, being guided through the border formalities and provided with a through service is attractive to some travelers.

In La Paz, you can find agents for the through service to Puno in the Residencial Rosario at Ilampu 704, and nearby at Colectur at Ilampu 626. Different international exchange rates make the La Paz to

Puno trip more expensive than the same journey in the other direction.

See Lonely Planet's *Bolivia* for more details on the Copacabana area.

Via Desaguadero Buses leave Puno's Mercado Laykakota market every hour or so for Desaguadero ($2, two hours), where there are basic hotels. The *Hotel Montes* charges about US$2 per person but is not recommended. A little better is the *Hostal Panamericano* (☎ 35-0221), Panamericano 151 near the border, where basic but clean little rooms are US$3/5 with shared cold showers. The town's best hotel is *Hostal San Carlos* (☎ 35-0240), 28 de Julio 322, charging US$5/7.50 with shared warm shower. A sauna is an extra US$2.50. On the Bolivian side next to the border is the *Hotel Bolivia* with clean double rooms for about US$9, hot water and a decent restaurant.

The border is open from 8 am to 5 pm daily, though you can cross back and forth easily enough outside these hours if, for example, you want to eat at the Hotel Bolivia. Remember that Bolivia is an hour ahead of Peru, so though you can leave Peru after 4 pm, you can't officially enter Bolivia. You will find money changers at the border and a casa de cambio around the corner. This border crossing used to be a little complicated and corrupt, but recent reports indicate that it is very straightforward.

From Desaguadero to La Paz, a bus costs under US$2 and takes about four or five hours. Buses leave several times during the day. If you leave Puno at dawn you can be in Bolivia early enough to stop at Tiahuanaco for a quick visit before continuing on to La Paz (the Desaguadero-La Paz bus passes near the ruins).

Cruz del Sur (☎ 35-2451), Avenida El Sol 568, Puno, has through services to La Paz for US$6.50 three times a week.

BOLIVIA TO PERU
There is rarely any hassle at either border and you can get 90 days in Peru without difficulty. This is good if your tourist card has almost expired – just go to La Paz for an evening and come back to Peru the next day. See the Visas & Documents section in the Facts for the Visitor chapter for more information.

The Cuzco Area

This chapter covers the Department of Cuzco, which includes the city of Cuzco, many smaller towns and villages, nearby archaeological sites and the Inca Trail to Machu Picchu. The most direct road link from here to the coast goes via Abancay, the capital of the Department of Apurimac, then on through the southern part of the Department of Ayacucho to join the Panamericana near Nazca. Unfortunately, guerrilla attacks in the past and, more recently, banditry have made this road dangerous between Puquio and Abancay. At this time, overland travelers to Cuzco are advised to take a bus from Arequipa or a train from Puno, both of which are safe. Another travel possibility, and a rough and adventurous one it is, is the road trip from Huancayo through Ayacucho and Abancay to Cuzco. The road is in poor shape, but it is now safe enough after the cessation of most of the area's Sendero Luminoso activity. However, these situations may change, so ask locally.

Although the Department of Cuzco lies in exceptionally beautiful Andean surroundings, its beauty is only a secondary attraction for tourists. Almost every visitor to Peru comes to Cuzco, the heart of the once-mighty Inca Empire, to see the most fascinating and accessible archaeological ruins on the continent.

Cuzco

Cuzco is the hub of the South American travel network and, in this respect, is reminiscent of Kathmandu in Nepal. Both cities attract thousands of travelers who come not just to visit a unique destination but also to experience an age-old culture that is very different to their 20th-century way of life.

Cuzco is the archaeological capital of the Americas and the continent's oldest continuously inhabited city. Massive Inca-built stone walls line most of Cuzco's central streets and form the foundations of colonial and modern buildings. The streets are often stepped and narrow and thronged with Quechua-speaking descendants of the Incas.

Cuzco is the capital of its department and has about 300,000 inhabitants. The city is 3326 meters above sea level, and during your first few days, you should take care not to overexert yourself, particularly if you've flown in from Lima at sea level.

History
Cuzco is a city steeped in history, tradition and legend. Indeed, it is often difficult to know where fact ends and myth begins. When Columbus arrived in the Americas, Cuzco was the thriving, powerful capital of the Inca Empire. According to legend, the city was founded in the 12th century by the first Inca, Manco Capac, the son of the sun. During his travels, Manco Capac plunged a golden rod into the ground until it disappeared. This point was *qosqo*, or 'the earth's navel' in the Quechua language, and it was here that he founded the city that was to become the center of the Western hemisphere's greatest empire.

Parts of this legend are undoubtedly based on fact – the Inca Empire did have its origins around the 12th century, Cuzco did become its capital and Manco Capac was one of the earliest Inca leaders – but the archaeological record shows that the area was occupied by other cultures for several centuries before the rise of the Incas. Very little is known about these pre-Incas except that some of them were involved in the Wari expansion of the 8th and 9th centuries.

The Incas had no written language and their history was entirely oral, passed down through the generations. The

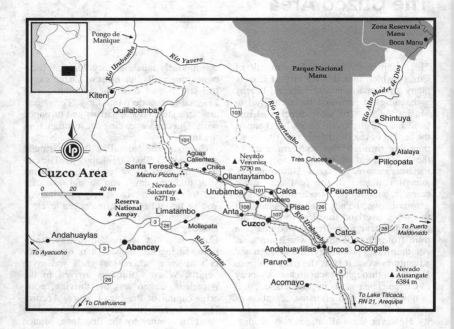

Cuzco Area

empire's main expansion occurred in the hundred years or so prior to the arrival of the conquistadors. As the oral records of that important period are relatively accurate, our knowledge of Cuzco's history dates back to about the middle of the 15th century. Led by Francisco Pizarro, the Spanish reached Cuzco in the 16th century – in 1533 – and from that point on written records (the so-called chronicles) were kept. These included accounts of Inca history as related by the Incas to the Spanish chroniclers. The most famous of these accounts was written by Garcilaso de la Vega. He was born in Peru in 1539, the son of an Inca princess and a Spanish conquistador, and lived in the Cuzco area until the age of 21. He then moved to Spain, where he died in 1616. Although neither his writings nor those of the other chroniclers can be considered entirely accurate, they do give a good overview of Inca history.

The reigns of the first eight Incas – Manco Capac and those who succeeded him – spanned a period from around the 12th century to the early 15th century. The small tribe they governed was one of several groups living in the Andean highlands during the 13th and 14th centuries. These Incas left few signs of their existence, though the remains of some of their palaces can still be seen in Cuzco. In chronological order, they were:

1. Manco Capac – The Palace of Colcampata is traditionally attributed to Manco Capac, the first Inca, but some sources claim that it was built by Huáscar shortly before the arrival of the Spaniards. The massive retaining walls with 11 niches can be seen next to the Church of San Cristóbal, on a hill on Cuzco's northwestern outskirts. The walls, at least to my untrained eye, seem too well made to be attributable to the first Inca, but the story persists.

2. Sinchi Roca – Some of the walls of his palace, the Palace of Cora Cora, can be seen in the

Lake Umayo near Sillustani, Puno

ROB RACHOWIECKI

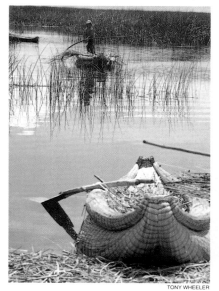

TONY WHEELER

Reed boat at Uros Islands, Lake Titicaca

ROB RACHOWIECKI

On Isla Taquile, Lake Titicaca

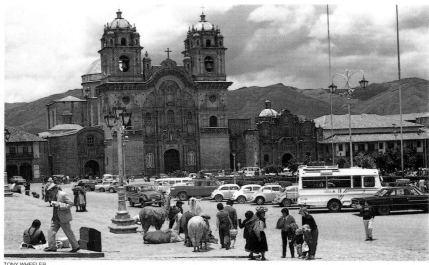

TONY WHEELER

La Compañía in Cuzco

TONY WHEELER

TONY WHEELER

The lively Plaza de Armas, Cuzco

TONY WHEELER

Truck, between Pisac and Cuzco

TONY WHEELER

Blind musician along the Inca street of Hatunrumiyoc, Cuzco

courtyards of houses to the right of Calle Suecia as you walk uphill from the Plaza de Armas.

3. Lloque Yupanqui
4. Mayta Capac
5. Capac Yupanqui
6. Inca Roca – The huge blocks of this Inca's palace now form the foundations of the Museo de Arte Religioso and include the famous 12-sided stone of Hatunrumiyoc.
7. Yahuar Huacac
8. Viracocha Inca – His palace was demolished to make way for the present cathedral on the Plaza de Armas.

The ninth Inca, Pachacutec, began the empire's great expansion. Until his time, the Incas had dominated only a small area close to Cuzco, frequently skirmishing with, but not conquering, various other highland tribes. One such tribe, the expansionist Chanka, occupied a region about 150 km east of Cuzco and, by 1438, was on the verge of conquering Cuzco. Viracocha Inca and his eldest son, Urcon, believed that their small empire was lost, but Viracocha Inca's third son refused to give up the fight. With the help of some of the older generals he rallied the Inca army and, in a desperate final battle, managed to rout the Chanka. According to legend, the unexpected victory was won because the boulders on the battlefield turned into warriors and fought on the side of the Inca.

The victorious younger son changed his name to Pachacutec and proclaimed himself the new Inca over his father and elder brother. Buoyed by his victory over the Chanka, he began the first wave of the expansion that was to eventually create the Inca Empire. During the next 25 years, he conquered most of the central Andes between the two great lakes of Titicaca and Junín.

Historians have frequently compared the mighty military figure of Pachacutec to the likes of Alexander the Great and Genghis Khan. He was also a great urban developer. Pachacutec devised the city's famous puma shape and diverted the Río Sapphi and Río Tullumayo into channels that crossed the city, keeping it clean and providing it with water. He built agricultural terraces and many buildings, including the famous Coricancha temple and his palace on what is now the western corner of the Plaza de Armas. Parts of the walls are visible to diners at the Inka Restaurant.

There was, of course, no Plaza de Armas before the arrival of the Spanish. In its place was an even greater square divided by the Sapphi Canal. The area covered by today's Plaza de Armas was known as Aucaypata or Huacaypata and on the other side of the Sapphi, the area now called the Plaza Regocijo was known as the Cusipata. Together, they formed a huge central plaza that was the focus of the city's social life.

Pachacutec was fortunate to have a son, Tupac Yupanqui, who was every bit as great a leader as his father. During the 1460s, Tupac Yupanqui helped his father subdue a great area to the north, which included the northern Peruvian and southern Ecuadorian Andes of today as well as the northern Peruvian coast. After he took over as ruler in 1471, becoming the 10th Inca, the empire continued to expand dramatically. By the time of Tupac Inca's death around 1493, the Inca Empire extended from Quito in Ecuador to south of Santiago in Chile.

Huayna Capac, the 11th Inca, was the last to rule over a united empire. When he assumed power after the death of his father, the empire was by far the greatest ever known in the Western hemisphere and there was little left to conquer. Nevertheless, Huayna Capac marched (he would, in fact, have been carried in a litter) to the northernmost limits of his empire, in the region today marked by the Ecuadorian-Colombian border. Here, using Quito as his base of operations, the Inca fought a long series of inconclusive campaigns against the tribes of Pasto and Popayán in what is now southern Colombia. He also sired a son, Atahualpa, who was born of a Quitan mother.

By this time, Europeans had discovered the New World and brought with them various Old World diseases. Epidemics, including smallpox and the common cold, swept down from Central America and the Caribbean. Huayna Capac died in such an epidemic around 1525. Shortly before his death he divided his empire, giving the northern part around Quito to Atahualpa and the southern Cuzco area to another son, Huáscar.

Both sons were well suited to the responsible position of ruling an empire, so well suited that neither wished to share power and a civil war ensued. Huáscar was the more popular contender because, having lived in Cuzco for most of his life, he had the people's support. Atahualpa, on the other hand, had lived in outposts of the empire and had few followers around Cuzco. He did, however, have the backing of the army that had been fighting the northern campaigns. In 1532, after several years of warfare, Atahualpa's battle-hardened troops won the major battle of the civil war and captured Huáscar outside Cuzco. Atahualpa, the new Inca, retired to Cajamarca to rest.

Meanwhile, Francisco Pizarro landed in northern Ecuador and marched south in the wake of Atahualpa's conquests. Although Atahualpa was undoubtedly aware of the Spanish presence, he was too busy fighting the civil war to worry about a small band of foreigners. By the autumn of 1532, however, Pizarro was in northern Peru, Atahualpa had defeated Huáscar and a fateful meeting was arranged between the Inca and Pizarro.

The meeting, which took place in Cajamarca on November 16, 1532, was to change radically the course of South American history. The Inca was ambushed by a few dozen armed conquistadors, who succeeded in capturing Atahualpa, killing thousands of unarmed Indians and routing tens of thousands more. The conquest of the Incas had begun.

The conquest succeeded for two main reasons. Firstly, Pizarro realized that the emotion of the recent civil war still ran high, and he decided to turn this to his advantage. Accordingly, after holding Atahualpa prisoner for a number of months

and then murdering him, he marched into Cuzco and was accepted by the Cuzqueños because their loyalties lay more with the defeated Huáscar than with Atahualpa. Additionally, Pizarro played on the petty intrigues within the Cuzqueño Inca factions.

The second reason was the superior Spanish weaponry. Mounted on horseback, protected by armor and swinging steel swords, the Spanish cavalry was virtually unstoppable. The Spaniards hacked dozens of unprotected Indian warriors to death during a battle. The Indians responded with their customary weapons – clubs, spears, slingshots and arrows – but these were rarely lethal against the mounted, armor-plated conquistadors. Furthermore, in the early battles, the Indians were terrified of the Spaniards' horses and primitive firearms, neither of which had been seen in the Andes before.

It took Pizarro almost a year to reach Cuzco after capturing Atahualpa. In an attempt to regain his freedom, the Inca offered a ransom of a roomful of gold and two rooms of silver. This was to be brought from Cuzco. To speed up the process, Pizarro sent three soldiers to Cuzco early in 1533 to strip Coricancha, or the 'Golden Courtyard,' of its rich ornamentation. Pizarro himself entered Cuzco on November 8, 1533, after winning a series of battles on the road from Cajamarca. By this time, Atahualpa had been killed and Pizarro appointed Manco, a half-brother of Huáscar, as a puppet Inca. For almost three years, the empire remained relatively peaceful under the rule of Manco Inca and Pizarro.

In 1536, Manco Inca realized that the Spaniards were there to stay and decided to try and drive them from his empire. He fled from the Spanish and raised a huge army, estimated at well over a hundred thousand. He laid siege to the Spaniards in Cuzco and almost succeeded in defeating them. Only a desperate, last-ditch breakout from Cuzco and a violent battle at Sacsayhuaman saved the Spanish from complete annihilation. Manco Inca retreated to

Ollantaytambo and then into the jungle at Vilcabamba.

The Inca Empire was Andean, so situating its capital in the heart of the Andes at Cuzco made a lot of sense. The Spaniards, however, were a seafaring people and needed to maintain links with Spain. Therefore, in 1535, Pizarro founded his capital on the coast at Lima. Although Cuzco remained very important during the first postconquest years, its importance declined once it had been captured, looted and settled. By the end of the 16th century, Cuzco was a quiet colonial town. All the gold and silver was gone, and many of the Inca buildings had been pulled down to make room for churches and colonial houses. Despite this, enough Inca foundations remain today to make a walk around the heart of Cuzco a veritable journey back in time.

Few events of historical significance have occurred in Cuzco since the Spanish conquest, apart from two major earthquakes and one important Indian uprising. The earthquakes, in 1650 and 1950, brought colonial and modern buildings tumbling down, yet most of the Inca walls were undamaged. The only Indian revolt that came at all close to succeeding was led by Tupac Amaru II in 1780, but he, too, was defeated by the Spaniards. The battles of Peruvian Independence in the 1820s achieved what the Inca armies had failed to do, but it was the descendants of the conquistadors who wrested power from Spain, and life in Cuzco after independence continued much as before.

The discovery of Machu Picchu in 1911 affected Cuzco more than any event since the arrival of the Spanish. With the development of international tourism in the second half of this century, Cuzco has changed from a provincial backwater to Peru's foremost tourist center. Until the 1930s, its main link with the outside world was the railway line to Lake Titicaca and Arequipa. Now, the modern international airport allows daily flights to Lima and other destinations, and roads and rail link Cuzco with the rest of the country. Going to Peru and missing Cuzco is as unthinkable as visiting Egypt and skipping the pyramids.

Orientation

The heart of the city is the Plaza de Armas, with Avenida Sol being the main business street. Walking just two or three blocks north or east of the plaza will take you to streets little changed for centuries – many are for pedestrians only. A new pedestrian street between the Plaza del Tricentenario and Huaynapata gives great views over the Plaza de Armas. Recently, the city has had a resurgence of Quechua pride and the official names of many streets have changed from Spanish to Quechua spellings. Cuzco has become Qosco (or Q'osqo or Cusco, etc), Cuichipunco has become K'uychipunko, and so on. Maps available from the tourist office retain the old spellings, however, and most people still use them.

Information

Tourist Offices The official tourist office on the east corner of the Plaza de Armas has closed, though it continues to be shown on many locally available maps and may reopen there. Information is provided at a tourist office next to the Banco de la Nación on the second block of Avenida Sol.

There's sometimes an English-speaking staff member who can give you up-to-date details of train schedules, opening hours, festivals and so on. The office sells visitor tickets to the various sites around Cuzco.

Visitor Ticket It is expensive to buy individual entrance tickets to the major sites in and around Cuzco. Instead, you have to buy the so-called Visitor Ticket. This costs US$10, gives access to 14 different sites and can be purchased from OFEC (Oficina Ejecutiva del Comité), Avenida Sol 106, or from the tourist office, a travel agent, or at some of the sites. Tickets bought at some of these places, especially travel agents, are valid for just five days, so ask around about where to get a ticket valid for 10 days (the OFEC or tourist offices are your best bets).

Cuzco

To Sacsayhuaman,
Qenko, Puca Pucara,
Tambo Machay

To Sacsayhuaman

0   100   200 m

To trucks, buses for
Mollepata, Abancay,
Ayacucho

Plaza de
Tricentenario

La Catedral

Plaza de
Armas

Plaza
Regocijo

Plaza
San Francisco

Mercado
Central

Machu Picchu
Quillabamba
Railway
Station

3 Cruces de Oro

Av del Ejercito

CUZCO AREA

Pumacurco
Choquechaca
Ataúd
Alabado
Carmen Alto
Ladrillos
Purgatorio
Resbalosa
Kiskapata
Huaynapata
Pumapaccha
Tecsecocha
Coricalle
Amargura
Ataúd
Tullumayo
Pasaje
Cuesta San Blas
Tandapata
Atoqsaycuchi
Choquechaca
Saphi
Teatro
Tecsecocha
Suecia
Procuradores
Plateros
Espaderos
Loreto
Calle Triunfo
Santa Catalina
Arequipa
Herrajes Quiñas
San Agustín
Maruri
Pampa del Castillo
Afligidos
Meloc
Arcopata
Tambo de Montero
Santa Teresa
Siete Cuartones
Arones
Teatro
Nueva Alta
Nueva Baja
Fierro
Ceniza
Tordo
Saphi
San Juan de Dios
Granada
Garcilaso
Heladeros
Mantas
Maruri
Av Sol
Marquez
San Bernardo
Meson de la Estrella
Queru
Santa Clara
Concevidayoc
Tupac Amaru
Cascaparo
Hospital San Pedro
Chaparra
Av Baja
Unión
Quera
San Andrés
Matará
Ayacucho
Cruz Verde
Teete
Pera
Belén
Lechugal
Kanchina
Puente Rosario
Culchleunos
Calle Nueva
Trinitarias
Desamparados
Quesqua

PLACES TO STAY

1 Hostal Cahuide
4 Hostal El Arqueólogo
6 Hostal Huayñapata
8 Hostal Familiar
10 Hostal Corihuasi
11 Albergue Municipal
12 Hotel Carlos V
13 Hostal Inca World
15 Hostal San Blas
16 Hostal Suecia II
17 Hostal Residencial Rojas
18 Hostal Royal Qosco
19 Hostal Suecia I, Hostal Rainbow Lodge
24 Hostal Cáceres
31 Hostal Incawasi
37 Hostal Tumi I
39 Hotel Royal Inka II
43 Picoaga Hotel
49 Espaderos Hotel
49 Hostal Chaski
52 Hostal Loreto
55 Hotel Conquistador
57 Hostal Royal
58 Korichaska Chekol
60 Hotel Royal Inka I
62 Hotel Las Marqueses
65 Hotel Cuzco
66 Hotel Espinar
68 Hotel Virrey
69 Hostal Wiracocha
75 Hostal Tumi II
76 Hotel Internacional San Agustín
77 Hotel Libertador

78 Residencial Torres
81 Hotels Garcilaso I & III
82 Hostal El Solar
87 Hostal Colonial Palace
88 Gran Hostal Machu Picchu
89 Hostal del Inca
95 Hotel del Angel
96 Hotel Cristina
98 El Dorado Inn
102 Santo Domingo Convent
108 Hostal Matará
109 Tambo Hotel
110 Hotel Los Portales
111 Hostal Chavín
114 San Agustín Plaza
125 Hotel Savoy
129 Hotel Imperio
131 Hostals Comercio & San Pedro
132 Hostal La Posada
133 Hostal Milan
134 Hostal San Martín
135 Hostals Trinitarias & Hispano
136 Hostal Tambo Real
137 Hotel Belén

PLACES TO EAT

3 Quinta Eulalia
23 Victor Victoria & Miski Wasi
25 Chez Maggy & Others
26 Pollería Haway & Kusikuy
30 El Piccolo, La Estancia Imperial, El Mesón Los Portales
32 Inka Restaurant
35 El Ayllu Café & La Yunta

40 José Antonio
42 Café Haylliy & Others
45 Pucará & other restaurants
48 Govinda Vegetarian Restaurant, Café Varayoc
48 El Mesón de los Espaderos
53 Restaurant El Paititi
61 El Truco
64 La Mamma Pizzería, other Italian restaurants
74 La Retama
79 Restaurant El Tordo
85 Trattoria Adriano
93 Chef Victor
124 La Peña de Don Luis

OTHER

2 Colcampata Ruins
5 San Cristobal Church
7 San Blas Church
9 Teatro Inti Raymi
14 San Antonio Church
20 Museo de Arqueología
21 Museo de Arte Religioso
22 Santa Teresa Church
27 Ukukus Bar
28 Cuzco Amazonico Lodge
29 Expediciones Manu & Instinct
33 American Express & Lima Tours
34 Faucett Airline
36 El Triunfo Church
38 Customs
41 Explorers Inn, Tambo Lodge Offices
44 Kamikaze Bar
47 Kerara Jazz Bar & Mama Africa Pub
50 Cross Keys Pub
51 La Compañía Church
54 El Muki Discotheque
56 Convento, Museo de Santa Catalina

59 Buses to Abancay, Andahuaylas
63 Museo de Historia Regional
67 Helicusco
70 Museo de Historia Natural
71 OFEC Office
72 Craft Market
73 Banco de Crédito
80 San Francisco Church
83 Farmacia Internacional
84 La Merced
86 Teatro Municipal
90 Inca Craft Market
91 Banco de la Nación
92 Tourist Office
94 Centro Comercial Cuzco
97 AeroPerú Airline
99 Americana, Imperial Air
100 Telefónica del Peru
101 Coricancha Ruins, Santa Domingo
103 Transportes Chican
104 Transportes Pitusiray
105 Ormeño Buses
106 Santa Clara Church
107 Excel Language Center
112 Aventours
113 Manu Nature Tours
115 Explorandes
116 Milla Turismo
117 Qosco Center of Native Dance
118 Peruvian Andean Treks, Tambopata Jungle Lodge
119 Migraciones (Immigration)
120 Central Post Office
121 Transportes Oropesa
122 Transportes Collasuyo
123 Expreso Cometa Buses
126 Waterfall Monument
127 CIVA Buses
128 Cruz del Sur Buses
130 San Pedro Church

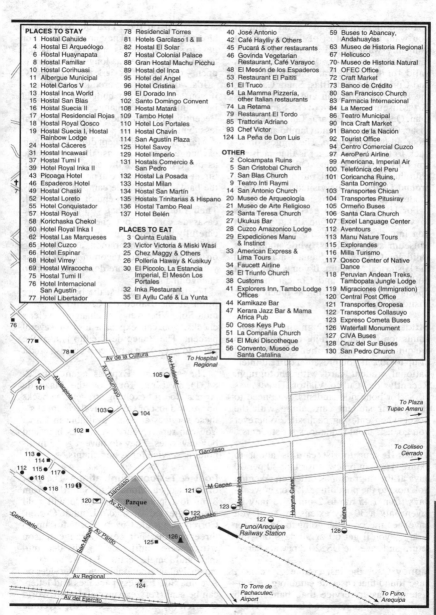

Ten dollars represents good value if you want to visit most of the sites, but if you only want to see a couple of them, the ticket is expensive. Within Cuzco, it's valid for the cathedral, Santo Domingo and Coricancha, San Blas, Santa Catalina, the Historical Museum and the Religious Art Museum. It also covers Sacsayhuaman, Qenko, Puca Pucara, Tambo Machay, Pisac, Chinchero, Ollantaytambo and Pikillacta, all outside Cuzco. The biggest drawback to the Visitor Ticket is that each site can only be visited once. Other museums, churches and colonial buildings in and around Cuzco can be visited free or for a modest individual admission charge.

For US$5, you can get partial tickets to visit some sites. One ticket will get you into the cathedral, the Religious Art Museum and San Blas, while another is valid for Coricancha, Santa Catalina and the Historical Museum. If you want to visit both the cathedral and Coricancha, this option will end up costing as much as the Visitor Ticket.

Student Cards Although many of the admission fees at the ruins and other sites are quite high, you can often get a discount of up to 50% if you present a current international student card with photograph. Recently, the Cuzco Visitor Ticket was US$5 for bona fide students, who need to show their student card along with the ticket when entering each site. Wherever you go, ask about reductions for students.

Visas If your tourist card is about to expire, you can renew it for US$20 per 30 days at the migraciones office on Avenida Sol, next to the post office. It's open weekdays from 7.45 am to 2 pm. You may be given only a 30-day extension, so if you have the time, consider going to Bolivia for a day – you'll get 60 or 90 days on your return and save the US$20 renewal charge.

Money Over the last couple of years, I have found that casas de cambio give consistently faster service than banks, with similar exchange rates and less fuss. There are several on the Plaza de Armas and along Avenida Sol. They are usually in or next to souvenir stores or travel agents and tend to remain open as long as the store is open – often till after dark and on Sunday.

It's worth shopping around, particularly if you are on a tight budget or change a large amount, as exchange rates can vary. Recently, however, the variation has been less than 1%.

Many hotels will accept dollars, but their exchange rates are not usually as favorable as those offered by the casas de cambio. Street moneychangers can be found outside the banks and casas de cambio, especially at the Plaza de Armas end of Avenida Sol. Their rates equal what you'll get at the casas de cambio, but check your money carefully before handing over your dollars. Rip-offs are not uncommon, and changing on the street is not recommended unless you know what you are doing and want to change in a hurry.

For traveler's checks, the best rates are often at the Banco de Crédito on Avenida Sol. Wherever you change traveler's checks, you can expect a loss of several percent. The Banco de Crédito is also the place to get a cash advance on a Visa credit card.

The American Express agent (☎ 22-8431), in Lima Tours on the Plaza de Armas, doesn't exchange traveler's checks nor refund lost or stolen traveler's checks – these services are only available in Lima. You can report your lost checks here and buy new ones. They do have a good mail-holding service for Amex clients.

Post & Telecommunications The post office is open Monday to Saturday from 8 am to 8 pm. The post office will hold mail addressed to you c/o Lista de Correo, Correos Central, Cuzco, Peru, for up to three months. For some strange reason letters were, until recently, divided into male and female sections! There are (very expensive) international courier services on Avenida Sol. Express packages and letters can be sent (very expensively) with World Courier (☎ 23-4051, 23-6890), Avenida

Sol 615, or DHL (☎ 22-3874, 22-8857), Portal de Harinas 177, Plaza de Armas.

Telefónica del Peru on Avenida Sol has both national and international telephone and fax services and is open from 7 am to 11.30 pm. Expect to wait up to an hour for international calls. The area code for Cuzco (and the surrounding area) is 084; drop the 0 when dialing from overseas. They will accept and hold incoming faxes for you at 24-1111.

Travel Agencies Tour agencies fall roughly into two groups; those that provide standard tours of Cuzco and the various other ruins in the area and those that offer adventure tours such as trekking, climbing, river running, kayaking, mountain biking or jungle trips.

There are many tour companies, and I have heard mixed reports about most of them. One letter will say that Top Tours was great, the next will say that they were overpriced with a lousy guide. Another traveler will say that Cheap Tours was great, and the next will say that it was cheap and terribly disorganized. The most common complaints are that the tour did not go according to schedule or as advertised and that a company overcharged.

If you decide to take a tour, ask questions before you pay. First, ask fellow travelers about their experiences, then talk to the tour agency. Is there an English-speaking guide? Will there be many tourists who don't speak English, requiring the guide to repeat everything in two or three languages? (This is a problem when doing a local ruins tour.) How big will the group be? What kind of transport is used? How long will be spent at each place, and how long will be spent eating lunch or traveling or whatever? Can you check the equipment you will be using (for a trek or rafting trip)? Can you meet the guide, particularly for a multiday trip. Be aware that agencies may merely act as an agent for another company, selling you a trip that is then run by someone else who pays a commission. Agents at the airport are notorious for charging a good deal more for a tour run by

a cheaper outfit in town. You should deal directly with the tour operator or outfitter running the tour.

Costs vary, so it's worth shopping around. Sometimes there are 'price wars' that can lead to a lot of local bad feeling as guides are underpaid and vehicles are overcrowded in order to cut corners and offer the cheapest possible trip. This is to everyone's detriment. The cheaper tours are liable to be crowded, multilingual affairs, while the more expensive ones can be tailored to the needs of the individual. The cheapest agencies change names and owners quite often and are less stable than the more expensive outfitters. Your best bet is to ask other budget travelers for reports on the cheaper agencies, then check them out yourself.

Having said all this, I cannot 100% recommend any particular agent, especially the cheaper ones. Those described below are, however, pretty reputable.

The standard tours include a half-day city tour, a half-day tour of the nearby ruins (Sacsayhuaman, Qenko, Puca Pucara and Tambo Machay), a half-day tour of the Sunday markets at either Pisac or Chinchero, a full-day trip to the Urubamba Valley (Pisac and Ollantaytambo and, perhaps, Chinchero) and a full-day visit to Machu Picchu. It is worth spending more time, if you can, in the Urubamba Valley, staying one or more nights in hotels at Urubamba or Ollantaytambo, for example, to allow more in-depth visits of the sites. The tours can sometimes seem rather rushed, especially with the cheaper agencies.

Dozens of companies offer inexpensive tours. The following seem to do a decent job most of the time: Kantu Tours (☎ 22-1381), Plaza de Armas, Luzma Tours (☎ 23-5468, fax 23-8793), Plaza de Armas, and EcoTours (☎ 23-1288), Heladeros 150 (by the Hotel Cuzco). Snow Tours (☎ 24-1313), Plaza de Armas, has received mixed reports over the years although comments have been favorable over the last year. Romulo Castillo (☎ 22-6858) speaks English and has been recommended.

Lima Tours (☎ 23-8857), Plaza de Armas, is the Cuzco office of this major Lima travel agency, and it caters to 1st class travelers and international tour groups. Milla Turismo (☎ 23-1710), Avenida Pardo 675, is geared to providing 1st class services to international tour groups.

Many agencies run adventure trips. An excellent general adventure agency is Explorandes (☎ 23-8380, fax 23-3784), in an alley off the 500 block of Avenida Sol, and in Lima (☎ 446-9889, fax 445-4686) at Bolognesi 159, Miraflores. It is the oldest established and among the most expensive of the adventure agencies, and it has a wide variety of services and equipment rental. Aventours (☎ 23-7307), Pardo 545, is run by Ricky Schiller, who provided me with excellent trekking and river-running services. Their Lima office (☎ 444-1067) is at La Paz 442, Miraflores.

The basic, one-day Urubamba River trip with lunch costs US$25 and is offered by many companies. A minimum of four paying passengers is normally required. The following are pretty good outfits. Luzma Tours (see above) is also known among kayakers because owner Luzmarina Anaya is very helpful in sorting out expedition problems. Loreto Tours (☎ 23-6331), Calle del Medio, seems to have almost a monopoly on cheap one-day river trips, and Kantu Tours (see above) also offers them. Eric Adventures (☎ 23-2244, fax 23-9772), Plateros 324, and Soqllaquasa (☎ 22-2224), Plateros 359, both offer one- and two-day trips on the Urubamba. The two-day trips are about US$60 and include food and camping.

Eric Arenas of Eric Adventures is a Peruvian kayaking champion who represented Peru in the 1992 Olympics. He also offers kayaking classes on the Apurimac, where he uses a hot spring to comfortably teach the eskimo roll! A two-day course is US$80. Another kayaking outfit is Río Sur, Procuradores 354, which does three-day courses on the Urubamba for US$100 as well as rafting trips.

Instinct (☎ 23-3451), Procuradores 50, and Mayuc (☎ 23-2666), on the Plaza de Armas, both do three-day rafting trips on the Río Apurimac for US$225 including transportation, food and camping. Both companies do other trips as well. For the Río Tambopata, Mayuc has infrequent departures costing about US$900 for nine days. Otherwise, you could book a Tambopata trip in advance with Amazonas Explorer (☎ /fax 23-6826). They are very professional, with top-quality equipment and guides, but currently are booking only international groups at (☎ /fax 41-1-361-4857) Seminarstrasse 76, 8057 Zurich, Switzerland. They are planning on opening a Cuzco office. Amazonas Explorer also does eight-day Apurimac trips. Another professional outfitter taking advance international bookings for Tambopata trips is Apumayo Expedition in Lima.

If mountaineering interests you, contact Peruvian Andean Treks (☎ 22-5701, fax 23-8911), Pardo 705, which is run by Tom Hendrickson. They have some of the best guides and equipment for climbing the local snowpeaks, as well as other adventure trips. Apu Expeditions (☎ 23-5408), Plaza de Armas, is another general all-round outfitter. Southern Cross Adventures (☎ 23-7649, fax 23-9447), Plaza de Armas, includes horse-riding among its activities.

Mountain bikes can be rented from Bicy Centro Atoq (☎ 23-6324), Saphi 674. Bikes are about US$7 to US$15 a day, depending on quality. The owner, Juan Salazar Chavez, also guides, does bike repairs, and can provide suggestions for bike tours. A new company, Eco Montaña (☎ /fax 25-2670), Procuradores 344, does one- and two-day guided biking trips for US$35 and US$80 (three people minimum) and also does longer trips by mountain bike to the jungle. Another new outfitter is All Adventure (☎ 24-0337), Triunfo 346, which does bike rental and river running.

Those who want to visit the jungle should contact Manu Nature Tours (☎ 22-4384, fax 23-4793), Avenida Sol 582, or Expediciones Manu (☎ 22-6671, 23-9974, fax 23-6706), Procuradores 50, for the best quality and environmentally sensitive (but not cheap) expeditions to Manu. Both these outfitters provide mountain biking options en route from Cuzco to the jungle. Cheaper trips from Pantiacolla Tours (☎ 23-8323, fax 23-3727), Plateros 360, have also been recommended. (See the Parque Nacional Manu section for more details.) If you're planning a trip to lodges in the Puerto Maldonado area, reservations for the Explorers Inn can be arranged at Peruvian Safaris (☎ 23-5342), Plateros 365, for the Cuzco Amazonico Lodge (☎ 23-2161, 22-3769) at Procuradores 48, for the Tambopata Jungle Lodge at Peruvian Andean Treks (above) and for the Tambo Lodge (☎ 23-6159) at Plateros 351. (Additional information is provided in the Puerto Maldonado section of the Amazon Basin chapter.)

There are many cheaper agencies on Procuradores, Plateros and around the Plaza de Armas. Check them out carefully – some offer good value but others are disappointing. For standard local tours, if you have a little extra time, you can visit most places using the cheap public transport system. Details of this option are given later in this chapter.

Books & Bookstores The best source of general information about Cuzco and the surrounding area, including maps of the Inca Trail, Machu Picchu and all the other sites, is the highly recommended book *Exploring Cuzco* by Peter Frost. It is available from bookstores in Cuzco and at the South American Explorers Club in Lima.

Also excellent are two books by John Hemming, *The Conquest of the Incas* and his large coffee-table book *Monuments of the Incas*, the latter illustrated with Edward Ranney's superb B&W photographs.

Three or four bookstores around the Plaza de Armas sell English-language guidebooks and books about Peru. One of the best is to the right of the church of La Compañía – it looks almost as if it's part of the church itself.

Laundry Cuzco has good laundry facilities. Places on Suecia, Procuradores, Plateros and Espaderos (just off the Plaza de Armas) advertise that they wash, dry

and fold your clothes in a day for just under US$2 per kg. During busy months, they can get overwhelmed, and their promise of 'in by 10 am, ready by 6 pm' can easily turn into 9 or 10 pm. However, if you are prepared to wait 24 hours, you'll find places up the hill along Suecia and Tecseccocha that will do it for about US$1 per kg.

Medical Services The best clinic is at the Hospital Regional (☎ 23-1131) on the Avenida de la Cultura. A recommended dentist is Dr Gilbert Armando Espejo H (☎ 22-8074), Centro Comercial Cuzco 7-III.

Emergency The Policia de Turismo has moved several times in the last few years. Recently, they were in the basement of the Torre de Pachacutec, southeast of downtown. They are open 24 hours a day. Some English is spoken and the police are trained to deal with problems pertaining to tourists. If you have something stolen, they'll help with the official police reports needed for insurance claims and will also tell you how to place a radio announcement offering a reward for the return of your property, particularly if it has little commercial value (such as your exposed camera film, journal or documents).

Recently, the tourism police busted several gringos for filing false reports of theft. Apparently, their 'stolen' property was in their hotel rooms and the police reports were to file a false insurance claim.

Visiting Prisoners You can visit the local prison on Thursday (for men) and Sunday (for women) between 9 am and noon. The prison, or *cárcel*, is en route to the airport and well known to taxi drivers. On entry, you have to leave your passport and state your purpose ('Christian goodwill work' is a good answer). The prisoners appreciate fruit, meat and cooking oil and sell various handicrafts at excellent prices.

Dangers & Annoyances More tourists are robbed in Cuzco than in any other Peruvian city. Avoid displays of wealth (expensive jewelry, wristwatches, wallets) and

CUZCO AREA

leave most of your money in a hotel safe (carry what you need in inside pockets and/or money belts). Avoid walking alone around town late at night – revelers returning late from bars and such have been mugged. Take special care going to and from the Machu Picchu railway station and the nearby market – these are prime areas for pickpockets and bag-slashers. Having said this, I have to point out that in scores of visits to Cuzco between 1982 and 1995, I have never been robbed on the street (though I had a camera taken from my hotel room once – I shouldn't have left it out in plain view).

Also, beware of altitude sickness if you're flying in from sea level. It's worth rereading the Altitude Sickness and Dangers & Annoyances sections of the Facts for the Visitor chapter.

Don't buy drugs. Dealers and police often work together, and Procuradores is only one of several areas in which you can make a drug deal and get busted, all within a couple of minutes.

Things to See

There are four things to remember when sightseeing: first, buy your Cuzco Visitor Ticket; second, carry a student card if you have one; third, don't get so excited by what you're seeing that you forget about your pockets and your camera – thieves congregate in the same places as sightseers; and fourth, opening hours are erratic and can change for any reason – from feast days to the caretaker wanting a beer with his friends.

Guided city tours are available from travel agencies. However, most of the sites listed below have local guides available, some of whom speak English. There is not normally a set fee, so you should come to some agreement. The minimum for a small group would be US$1 per person.

Plaza de Armas

In Inca times the plaza, called Huacaypata or Aucaypata was twice as large as it is today. It was the heart of Inca Cuzco and remains the heart of the modern city. Two flags often fly here – the red-and-white

Peruvian flag and the rainbow-colored flag of Tahuantinsuyo (representing the four quarters of the Inca Empire). Colonial arcades surround the plaza. On the northeastern side is the cathedral, fronted by a large flight of stairs and flanked by the churches of Jesus María and El Triunfo. On the southeastern side is the very ornate church of La Compañía. Some Inca walls remain, notably those of the palace of Pachacutec which were found in the Roma restaurant on the plaza's western corner. The quiet pedestrian alleyway of Loreto, both sides of which have Inca walls, is a pleasant means of access to the plaza.

Churches

Cuzco's numerous colonial churches are better preserved and much more ornate than those in other cities. Their maintenance directly correlates with the importance of the tourist industry in Cuzco. As there are literally scores of churches, only the most important are described in this section. They are usually open every day, but hours tend to vary. A good time to visit is in the early morning, when the churches are open for services. Officially, they are closed to tourists at this time, but if you go in quietly as one of the congregation, you can see the church as it should be seen – as a place of worship, not just a tourist site.

Religious festivals are a superb time to see the churches. One year, I visited the cathedral at Corpus Christi time. The church had been completely cleared of pews and in their place stood huge pedestals supporting larger-than-life statues of various saints in rich vestments. Each saint was being venerated by candlelight, and thousands of candles illuminated the ornate church interior. The place was thronged with people, including several bands of musicians who wandered around in the smoky atmosphere playing mournful Andean tunes in honor of the saints. As with many highland feast days, it was a fascinating combination of ancient and colorful pagan festivities, somber and prayerful Catholic ritual and modern Latin American mayhem.

Remember, though, that churches are places of worship and act accordingly, especially if you visit during a service. Photography, particularly flash photography, is normally not allowed – the intensity of repeated flashes seriously damages the pigment of the centuries-old art work inside.

The Cathedral Started in 1559 and taking almost a hundred years to build, the cathedral is Cuzco's main church and also one of the city's greatest repositories of colonial art. Many of the hundreds of canvases are from the Cuzco school of painting. This style combines the art of 16th- and 17th-century Europe with the imagination of Andean Indian artists who had only a few Spanish canvases as a guide to what was considered artistically acceptable.

The cathedral has been combined with two other churches. To the left, as you face it, is the church of Jesus María dating from 1733. The church of El Triunfo, to the right, is normally used as the entrance to the three-church complex during tourist opening hours. El Triunfo is the oldest church in Cuzco and dates from 1536. The cathedral proper is to your left after you enter El Triunfo.

Right in front of the entrance is a vault containing the remains of the famous Inca historian, Garcilaso de la Vega. Born in Cuzco in 1539, Garcilaso de la Vega left Peru in 1560 for Spain, where he died in 1616. His remains were returned to Cuzco several years ago by the king and queen of Spain.

As you enter the main part of the cathedral, turn right. In the far corner is the entrance to the **sacristy**, where you can sometimes see woodcarvers doing restoration work amid the smell of fresh cedar. The sacristy is covered with paintings of Cuzco's bishops, starting with Vicente de Valverde, the bloodthirsty friar who accompanied Pizarro during the conquest. Look for Manuel de Mollinedo, Bishop of Cuzco from 1673 to 1699 and one of the most influential supporters of the Cuzco school of art. The crucifixion at the back of the sacristy is attributed to the Flemish painter

Van Dyck, though some local guides claim it to be the work of the 17th-century Spaniard Alonso Cano. A similar painting hangs in the Museo de Arte Religioso.

In the corner of the cathedral, next to the sacristy, is a huge painting of the **Last Supper** by Marcos Zapata. This fine example of the Cuzco school depicts a supper consisting of the Inca delicacy *cuy*, or roast guinea pig!

The original wooden **altar** is at the very back of the cathedral, behind the present silver altar, which stands some 10 meters from the rear wall. Directly opposite the silver altar is the magnificently carved **choir**. It dates from the 17th century and is one of the finest in Peru.

On the far left outside wall of the main altar, you'll find a large painting of the great **earthquake** of 1650. The city of those days, as shown in the painting, is recognizable as Cuzco even today. The inhabitants are parading around the plaza with a crucifix, praying for an end to the earthquake. Miraculously, the earthquake stopped (don't they all?), and the city was saved. This crucifix, called **El Señor de los Temblores**, or 'The Lord of the Earthquakes,' can be seen in the alcove to the right of the door leading back into El Triunfo. The image has been blackened by the countless votive candles that have been lit beneath it, and the candles are now kept well away from the statue to prevent further smoke damage. The statue is paraded around on Easter Monday.

There are many splendid **side chapels**, some containing the elaborate silver trolleys used to cart the religious statues around during processions and others with intricate altars. The last side chapel to the left of the altar has a painting of Pope John Paul II during his visit to Sacsayhuaman in 1985.

The cathedral is open to tourists from 2 to 5.30 pm. Entrance is with the Cuzco Visitor Ticket through the side chapel of El Triunfo. The huge main doors are open for worship between 6 and 10 am – there is no admission charge during these hours, but tourism is officially prohibited. Discreet, respectful visits normally do not cause a problem.

CUZCO AREA

TONY WHEELER

La Compañía

La Compañía This church on the Plaza de Armas is often lit up at night and can be seen from the train as you come in from Machu Picchu after dark – a splendid sight. Its foundations are built from the palace of Huayna Capac, the last Inca to rule an undivided, unconquered empire.

The church was built by the Jesuits, hence its name: the Church of the Company of Jesus. Work commenced in 1571. The church was destroyed by the 1650 earthquake but reconstruction began almost immediately. The Jesuits planned to make this the most magnificent of Cuzco's churches. However, the Bishop of Cuzco complained that its splendor should not rival that of the cathedral, and finally, Pope Paul III was called upon to arbitrate. His decision was in favor of the cathedral, but by the time final word reached Cuzco, La Compañía was almost complete. It has an incredible baroque facade and is one of the most ornate churches in Cuzco.

The interior has the usual array of fine paintings and richly carved altars. Two large canvases near the main door show early marriages in Cuzco and are noteworthy for their wealth of period detail.

After the 1986 earthquake, La Compañía was temporarily closed. Although it has now been reopened, hours are erratic. Admission is free.

La Merced La Merced is considered to be Cuzco's third most important colonial church. It was destroyed in the 1650 earth-quake and rebuilt; the present structure, consisting of two sections, dates from 1654.

The church itself is open for worship from 7 to 9 am and 5 to 7.30 pm. To the left of the church, at the back of a small courtyard, is the entrance to the monastery and museum, which are open Monday to Saturday from 8 am to noon and 2 to 5 pm. Entry costs about US$1.50.

The Order of La Merced was founded in Barcelona in 1218 by San Pedro Nolasco. Paintings based on his life hang around the walls of the beautiful colonial cloister. The church on the far side of the cloister contains the tombs of two of the most famous conquistadors, Diego de Almagro and Gonzalo Pizarro. Also on the far side of the cloister is a small religious museum that houses vestments said to have belonged to the conquistador/friar Vicente de Valverde. The museum's most famous exhibit is a priceless, solid-gold monstrance, 1.3 meters high and covered with precious stones, including over 1500 diamonds and 1600 pearls.

San Francisco This church and monastery, dating from the 16th and 17th centuries, is more austere than many of Cuzco's other churches, but it does have a large collection of colonial religious paintings and a well-carved, cedar-wood choir. One of the paintings measures 9 by 12 meters, supposedly the largest painting in South America, and shows the family tree of St Francis of Assisi, founder of the order. His life is celebrated in the paintings hung around the colonial cloister.

Also of interest are the two crypts, which are not totally underground. Inside are plenty of human bones, some of which have been carefully arranged into phrases designed to remind visitors of the transitory nature of life.

The church is currently under restoration and was closed recently, but it may reopen by the time you read this.

Santa Clara This 16th-century church, part of a strict convent, is difficult to visit.

Seeing it became a minor challenge, and I finally found that you can usually get in for mass if you go around 6 or 7 am. It is worth making the effort because this is one of the more bizarre churches in Cuzco, indeed, in all Peru.

Mirrors cover almost the entire interior; I've heard that the early clergy used them to entice the local Indians into church for worship. The nuns provide the choir during mass, sitting at the very back of the church and separated from the priest and the rest of the congregation by an ominous-looking grille of heavy metal bars stretching from wall to wall and floor to ceiling.

San Blas This simple adobe church is comparatively small, but its exquisitely carved pulpit has been called the finest example of colonial wood carving in the Americas. Legend claims that its creator was an Indian who miraculously recovered from a deadly disease and subsequently dedicated his life to carving this pulpit for the church. Supposedly, his skull is nestled in the topmost part of the carving. In reality, no one is certain of the identity of either the skull or the woodcarver.

The church has been worked on recently, and the very ornate, baroque, gold-leafed principal altar is newly restored.

San Blas is open Monday to Saturday from 2 to 5.30 pm. Entry is with the Cuzco Visitor Ticket.

Santa Catalina This convent was closed for restoration in the early 1980s but has recently reopened. There is a colonial and religious art museum here, with many religious paintings of the Cuzco school, statues, an ornately friezed side chapel, and the convent's main altar behind steel bars. It's open Monday to Thursday and Saturday from 9 am to 6 pm. Friday hours are 9 am to 3 pm; closed Sunday. Entry is with the Cuzco Visitor Ticket.

Santa Teresa Santa Teresa is a closed convent and difficult to visit. Its church is said to be one of the most beautiful in Cuzco.

Santo Domingo The church of Santo Domingo is famous as the site of Coricancha, Cuzco's major Inca temple (see below). The church has twice been destroyed by earthquakes, first in 1650 and again in 1950. It was also damaged in the 1986 earthquake and briefly closed for repairs. Photographs in the entrance show the extent of the 1950 damage – compare the state of the colonial building with that of the Inca walls, which sustained minimal damage in these earthquakes. Also in the entrance is a doorway carved in the Arab style – a reminder of the centuries of Moorish domination in Spain. Remains of the Inca temple are inside the cloister. Colonial paintings around the outside of the courtyard depict the life of Santo Domingo (Saint Dominic). The paintings contain several representations of dogs holding torches in their jaws. These are God's guard dogs, or *dominicanus* in Latin, hence the name of this religious order.

It's open Monday to Saturday from 8 am to 5 pm. Admission to both the cloister and the Inca ruins is by the Cuzco Visitor Ticket.

Inca Ruins in Cuzco
Most Inca ruins are outside the city and are described in Around Cuzco, below. The main ruin within Cuzco is Coricancha. Other ruins have been converted into colonial or modern buildings but their walls remain visible.

Coricancha This Inca ruin forms the base of the colonial church of Santo Domingo. Today, all that remains of Coricancha, once the Inca empire's richest temple, is the stonework; the precious stones and metals were looted by the conquistadors.

In Inca times Coricancha, Quechua for 'Golden Courtyard,' was literally covered with gold. The temple walls were lined with some 700 solid gold sheets, each weighing about two kg. There were life-size gold and silver replicas of corn that were ceremonially 'planted' in agricultural rituals. Also reported were solid gold treasures such as altars, llamas and babies, as

CUZCO AREA

well as a replica of the sun, which was lost. Within months of the arrival of the first conquistadors, this incredible wealth had all been melted down.

Various religious rites took place in the temple. The mummified bodies of several previous Incas were kept here, brought out into the sunlight each day and offered food and drink, which was then ritually burnt. Coricancha was also an observatory from which priests monitored major celestial activities.

Most of this is left to the imagination of the modern visitor, but much of the stonework does remain and ranks with the finest Inca architecture in Peru. A curved, perfectly fitted wall six meters high can be seen from both inside and outside the site. This wall has withstood the violent earthquakes that destroyed most of Cuzco's colonial buildings.

Once inside the site, the visitor enters a courtyard. The octagonal font in the middle was originally covered with 55 kg of solid gold. Inca side chambers lie to either side of the courtyard. The largest, to the right, were said to be temples to the moon and stars and were, perhaps, appropriately covered with sheets of solid silver. However, the conquistadors looted the temple riches so fast and so thoroughly that records are hazy. The walls are perfectly tapered upward and, with their niches and doorways, are excellent examples of Inca trapezoidal architecture. The fitting of the individual blocks is so precise that, in some places, you can't tell where one block ends and the next begins as you glide your finger over them.

Opposite these chambers, on the other side of the courtyard, are smaller temples dedicated to thunder and the rainbow. Three holes have been carved through the walls of this section to the street outside. Their purpose is not known but various theories have been advanced. Perhaps they were drains, either for the sacrificial *chicha* drink, for blood or, more mundanely, for rainwater. Alternatively, they may have been speaking tubes connecting the inner temple with the outside. Another noteworthy feature of this side of the complex is the floor in front of the chambers. It dates from Inca times and is carefully cobbled with pebbles.

The buildings described cover only two sides of the square. There was a larger chamber on each of the other two sides but only small segments of their foundations remain.

After the conquest, Coricancha was given to Juan Pizarro. He was not able to enjoy it for long because he died in the battle at Sacsayhuaman in 1536. In his will, he bequeathed Coricancha to the Dominicans, and it has remained in their possession ever since. Today's site is a rather bizarre combination of Inca and colonial architecture, topped with a modern protective roof of glass and metal. Hours are as for Santo Domingo.

Other Inca Walls in Cuzco The other Inca buildings in Cuzco are not visitor sites in themselves but can still be admired, most of them from outside.

If you walk southeast away from the Plaza de Armas along the narrow alley of Loreto, there are Inca walls on both sides. The wall on the right-hand side belongs to Amarucancha, or the 'Courtyard of the Serpents.' Perhaps its name derives from the pair of snakes carved on the lintel of the doorway near the end of the enclosure. Amarucancha was the site of the palace of the 11th Inca, Huayna Capac. The church of La Compañía was built here after the conquest, and there is now a school behind the church. Behind the school is a popular tourist market. On the other side of Loreto is the oldest-surviving Inca wall in Cuzco. It's also one of the best. The wall belonged to the Acllahuasi, or the 'House of the Chosen Women.' After the conquest, the building became part of the closed convent of Santa Catalina and so went from housing the Virgins of the Sun to housing pious Catholic nuns.

Heading northeast away from the Plaza de Armas along Calle Triunfo, you soon come to the street of Hatunrumiyoc, named after the well-known 12-sided stone. The

TONY WHEELER

Inca wall: stones cut to fit perfectly

stone is on the right, about halfway along the second city block, and can usually be recognized by the small knot of Indians selling souvenirs next to it. This excellently fitted stone belongs to a wall of the palace of the sixth Inca, Inca Roca. It is technically brilliant but by no means an unusual example of polygonal masonry. In Machu Picchu, there are stones with more than 30 angles (though these are corner stones and are therefore counted in three dimensions) and a block with 44 angles in one plane has been found at Torontoy, a minor ruin roughly halfway between Machu Picchu and Ollantaytambo.

There is a great difference between the wall of Hatunrumiyoc and that of the Acllahuasi. The first is made of polygonal stone blocks in no regular pattern, while the second is made from carefully shaped rectangular blocks that are coursed, or layered, in the manner of modern-day bricks. Both styles are common in Inca architecture. In general, the polygonal masonry was thought to be stronger and

was therefore used for retaining walls in terraces. The coursed masonry, which was considered more aesthetically appealing, was used for the walls of Inca temples and palaces.

Museums & Colonial Buildings

Many museums are in colonial houses, the interiors of which are often as interesting as the exhibits.

Museo de Arqueología The museum building, at the corner of Tucumán and Ataud, a steep block northeast of the Plaza de Armas, rests on Inca foundations; it's also known as the admiral's house after the first owner, Admiral Francisco Aldrete Maldonado. It was badly damaged in the 1650 earthquake and rebuilt by Pedro Peralta de los Rios, the Count of Laguna, whose crest is above the porch. Further damage, which occurred during the 1950 earthquake, has now been fully repaired, restoring the building to its position among Cuzco's finest colonial houses.

The architecture has several interesting features, including a massive stairway guarded by sculptures of mythical creatures and a corner window column that looks like a statue of a bearded man but, from outside, appears to be a naked woman. The facade is plateresque, an elaborately ornamented 16th-century Spanish style suggestive of silver plate. The building's restored interior is filled with a fine collection of metal and gold work, jewelry, pottery, textiles, mummies, wooden *queros* (Inca vases) and more. The ceilings are ornate and the views from the windows are fine, but the collection is labeled only in Spanish and visitors complain that the labels are inadequate.

The museum is currently being expanded and may or may not be open when you're in Cuzco. Check locally.

Museo de Historia Regional This museum is in the Casa Garcilaso de la Vega, the house of the Inca historian buried in the cathedral. The chronologically arranged collection begins with arrowheads from pre-ceramic periods and continues with a few pots of the Chavín, Vicus, Mochica, Chimu, Chancay and Inca cultures. There is also a Nazca mummy, a few Inca weavings (some of which show a marked similarity to the older weavings available for sale in the Cuzco area today) and some small gold ornaments excavated from Coricancha between 1972 and 1979. Labels are in Spanish, and there weren't enough of them on my most recent visit. Some pieces from the archaeology museum may be exhibited here during expansion.

Also on display are a few dozen Cuzco school paintings as well as some more recent Mestizo art, mainly with religious themes. There are some changing local art shows. It's open Monday to Saturday from 9 am to 6 pm, and possibly on Sunday morning. Entrance is with the Cuzco Visitor Ticket.

Museo de Arte Religioso This building on Hatunrumiyoc was originally the palace of the Inca Roca and then used as the foundation for the residence of the Marquis of Buenavista. It later became the archbishop's palace and is sometimes referred to by that name. The church donated the mansion to house a religious art collection. Many of the paintings are notable for the accuracy of their period detail. There are some impressive stained-glass windows in one part of the museum. The colonial-style tile work of the interior is not original and was replaced in the 1940s.

It's open daily except Sunday (when it may be open in the afternoon) from 9 to 11.30 am and 3 to 5.30 pm. Entry is with the Cuzco Visitor Ticket.

Museo de Historia Natural This museum is run by the Universidad Nacional, and the entrance is to the right of La Compañía on the Plaza de Armas. It houses a collection of stuffed local animals and birds and a few other items. It's open weekdays from 9 am to noon and 3 to 6 pm; admission is US50¢.

Activities
Photography The best light for photography occurs in the early morning and late afternoon when the sun is low. The shadows in the middle of the day tend to come out very black in photographs.

Some locals dress in traditional finery and lead their llamas past the most photogenic spots. This is not a coincidence; they expect a tip for posing and see themselves as working models, not beggars. Some tourists object to paying for these photographs, in which case they shouldn't take them. On the other hand, if you make friends with your potential model, they will help you get shots that are worth paying for.

If you want natural-looking, unposed shots, please be sensitive and discreet. Some travelers seem more concerned with taking a good photograph than with their subject's feelings. Not everyone takes kindly to being constantly photographed doing such mundane things as selling vegetables, breast feeding their children, or loading their llama.

A wide selection of film is available in Cuzco, but it's expensive.

Trekking & Backpacking The best time to go trekking is during the May to September dry season. At other times, trails turn into muddy slogs and views are often clouded in. Many people still go off-season, of course, but be prepared for rain and mud.

The Inca Trail is a very popular adventure. You can hire porters, cooks and guides or just rent some equipment and carry it yourself. Tents, sleeping bags, backpacks, stoves – everything you might need for hiking – can be hired in Cuzco, usually from around US$2 per item per day. Check the equipment carefully before you rent it as some of it is pretty shoddy.

Cheap tours start as low as US$60 or US$70 per person, but the guides tend to speak little English or not be very informative or environmentally aware, and the food and equipment of minimal quality. Don't go on a trip that dumps its garbage on the trail. More expensive outfits provide better food, equipment and services and clean up after themselves, hauling the trash out rather than dumping it in the nearest ruin.

Other popular treks include Mollepata to Santa Teresa, which climbs over 4800-meter passes near the peak of Salcantay (6271 meters, the second-highest peak in the Cuzco area) and takes about five days, or the six-day circuit around the area's highest peak, Ausangate (6384 meters). There are many other options. The hugely popular Inca Trail is described below, but if you want to do other hikes I suggest you read Hilary Bradt's book *Backpacking & Trekking in Peru & Bolivia* (see Books in Facts for the Visitor).

River Rafting The most popular rafting trip is down the Urubamba. Trips typically last half a day, with about three hours of rafting plus transportation at either end. Costs are from about US$25. Full-day tours combining a raft trip with a lunch and a visit to the Pisac or Ollantaytambo ruins

are also offered for a little more. Two-day trips offer two half days of rafting on different sections of the river, with ruin visits and overnights in the Urubamba Valley all possible at extra cost. Many agencies in Cuzco offer these tours, particularly the standard half-day excursion.

The Urubamba is not very wild and offers a great introduction to whitewater rafting, spectacular scenery, and a chance to visit some of the best Inca ruins near Cuzco. Three sections are regularly run. The popular Huambutiyo to Pisac section is the easiest, with three or four hours of fun rafting and a chance to explore the Pisac ruins or market. This section can be run year round, although during the dry season it is far from wild.

The Ollantaytambo to Chilca run is also very popular, combining the ruins of Ollantaytambo with some exciting rapids, reaching Class III. This can be combined with the Inca Trail, if you want to trek the extra half day along the river from Chilca to the Inca Trail. The most exciting section is the short but action-packed Cañon Huaran, which can be run two or three times with a good crew. This is not a frequently offered trip, however. Farther downstream, the river becomes unraftable as it approaches Machu Picchu. Beyond Machu Picchu, from the village of Chaullay, it is possible to do a two-day run mixing exciting rapids with a look at the high jungle and staying overnight at Quillabamba. This is another seldom-offered option.

Other rivers that can be run are farther from Cuzco, but you can't find agencies closer than Cuzco. The Apurimac has three- to five-day options but can only be run from June to October. You definitely need to book with a top-quality outfit and check gear beforehand. The rapids are extremely exciting and the river goes through remote and wild scenery with deep gorges. Camping is on sandy beaches (where sand flies can be a nuisance) and sightings of deer, otters, condors and even pumas have been recorded. The end of the run enters the recently declared Zona Reservada Apurimac, a huge protected area of rainforest with no infrastructure or tourist services that I have ever heard of.

An even wilder expedition is the 10- to 12-day possibility on the Tambopata, starting in the Andes north of Lake Titicaca and ending at the Reserva Nacional Tambopata in the Amazon. It takes two days just to drive to the put-in point from Cuzco. The first days on the river are full of technically demanding rapids in wild Andean scenery, finishing with a couple of gentle floating days in the rainforest. Tapirs, capybara, caiman, giant otters and jaguars have all been seen by keen-eyed boaters.

Kayaking This is a new option, one that is just beginning in the Cuzco area. Ask around for an outfitter with a kayak.

Mountain Biking This is another new option, with only a few agencies offering bike rentals and guides, but it looks like this will be a growing industry over the next few years. Currently, the bikes available are no more than just adequate, so some people may prefer to bring their own (see Air in Getting There & Away for details of bicycle baggage restrictions). However, as more bikes start being imported, the selection will improve. The cheapest bikes can be hired for about US$8 a day, but they aren't really up to the rigors of unpaved roads on the wilder rides. Better bikes are available for US$15 to US$20 a day, but check these carefully as well. Make sure you get a helmet, puncture-repair kit, pump and tool kit.

There are several excellent one- or two-day trips around Cuzco, but they are difficult to describe accurately enough for you to follow them. It's worth hiring a local guide until you get to know the lay of the land. Ask around in Cuzco.

Longer trips are possible, but a guide and a support vehicle are recommended. From Ollantaytambo you can go by bike, bus or truck to the Abra de Malaga (4600 meters) and then downhill to the jungle in three or four days. If heading to Manu, you can break up the long bus journey by biking from Tres Cruces to La Unión, a

beautiful, breathtaking downhill. (The outfitters of Manu trips can arrange bicycle rental and guides.) The descent to the Apurimac River would make a great burn, as would the journey to the Tambopata, which boasts a descent of 3500 meters in five hours. Beat that if you can. (The descents to the Apurimac and Tambopata are reported by Paul Cripps – I believe him but don't know which roads. Ask in Cuzco.) A few bikers have done the over 500-km trip all the way to Puerto Maldonado, which gets hot and sweaty near the end but is a great challenge.

Bird-Watching Serious birders should definitely get Fjeldså and Krabbe's book (see Facts for the Visitor). One of the best birding trips is from Ollantaytambo to Quillabamba over the Abra de Malaga. This gives a fine cross section of habitats from 4600 down to 950 meters above sea level, but you need to hire a truck or jeep to do it. Barry Walker, owner of Expediciones Manu and the Cross Keys Pub in Cuzco, is the best resident ornithologist and can give serious birders plenty of enthusiastic advice and help setting up a birding expedition.

Mountaineering & Skiing Peruvian Andean Treks and Apu Expeditions (see Travel Agencies above) are your best source of information, guides and equipment rental to scale any of the high peaks in the Cuzco area. There are no skiing areas, but adventurous and expert mountain skiers have been known to carry their skis to a mountain summit and then ski back down.

Spanish Courses
The Excel Language Center (☎ 23-5298), Cruz Verde 336, charges about US$3.50 an hour for private lessons and has received several recommendations. They can arrange homestays with local families if you wish. A new school is Tumi's language school at Ahuacpinta 732, which offers Spanish lessons for about US$3 an hour and can also arrange homestays with local families.

Work

The Excel Language Center has hired English teachers in the past, but you'll need to commit yourself for several weeks. Tumi's also hires travelers wishing to stay in Cuzco for a few months and teach English in the evenings. Native English speakers are preferred. You may find other jobs if you ask around.

Special Events

The area celebrates many fiestas and holidays. Apart from the national holidays, the following dates mark crowded, lively occasions that are especially important in Cuzco:

Easter Monday
    The procession of the Lord of the Earthquakes dates from the earthquake of 1650 (see the statue in the cathedral).
May 2-3
    A hilltop Crucifix Vigil is held on all hillsides with crosses atop them.
Corpus Christi
    This movable feast usually occurs on a Thursday in early June (after Trinity Sunday) with fantastic religious processions and celebrations in the cathedral.
June 24
    Cuzco's most important festival is Inti Raymi, or the 'festival of the sun.' It attracts tourists from all over the world, and the entire city seems to celebrate in the streets. The festival culminates in a reenactment of the Inca winter solstice festival at Sacsayhuaman.
December 24
    This date marks the Santuranticuy, or 'Christmas Eve,' shopping festival.

Other festivals are important in particular villages and towns outside Cuzco, and these are mentioned in the appropriate sections.

Places to Stay

The most visited city in Peru, Cuzco has over a hundred hotels of all types, and prices tend to be higher than in less popular parts of the country. It gets rather crowded here during the dry season (June to August), which coincides with the North American and European summer holidays. At this time, accommodations can be tight, especially during the 10 days before Inti Raymi (the major annual summer solstice festival) on June 24, and around July 28 when the national Fiestas Patrias occur. The best hotels are often fully booked for Inti Raymi and accommodation prices usually rise substantially during these periods. Nevertheless, you can almost always manage to find somewhere to stay, though not necessarily at the price or comfort level you want.

During the rest of the year, many hotels are sometimes almost empty, and in this buyer's market, it is well worth bargaining for better rates. However, student groups from Lima and other major cities visit Cuzco during the low season, and sometimes they can make budget accommodations hard to find. Late October and November seem to be popular times for student groups, but at any time of the low season you may find a sudden influx of tourists pushes prices up and makes rooms temporarily hard to find. School holidays in January and February are also a busy time.

Many travelers want to spend time visiting nearby villages or hiking the Inca Trail, and most hotels in Cuzco will store excess luggage so that you don't have to lug it around with you. Always securely lock and clearly label all pieces of luggage. It's unlikely that anyone will razor blade your pack open inside a hotel, but light fingers may, occasionally, dip into unlocked luggage. Don't leave any valuables in long-term storage, lock and label your luggage and ask for a receipt.

I have stayed in about a dozen hotels in Cuzco, ranging from 1st-class to basic places charging about US$5 per night (as low as US$1.50 in the early '90s, but that is no more!). Whatever the price, I usually found the plumbing inadequate – even the best hotels occasionally have hot water problems, most of which are eventually resolved. You may also find that hot showers are available only at specified times of day or at haphazard intervals. The city cuts off water supply as a matter of course every afternoon, so those hotels without their own cisterns have no water during those times.

Places to Stay – bottom end

Things aren't great for shoestring travelers watching their budget carefully. The best cheap hotels are not in safe areas, and so what you save by staying there is offset by the need to take a taxi after dark or to walk in a large group. These areas are near the two railway stations and in the steep streets to the north and northwest of the Plaza de Armas. The hotels themselves are safe enough once you get inside, but people have been mugged or pickpocketed in the streets leading up to them. Nevertheless, it's not too bad if you can go with friends or take a cab. The cheapest hotels in safer areas are generally poor quality.

The reasonably clean and secure *Hostal Royal Qosco* (☎ 22-6221), Tecsecocha 2, is popular with budget travelers. Basic rooms are US$4 per person and there is hot water in the mornings. It has been raided by police for drug and passport violations. The *Espaderos Hotel* (☎ 23-8894), Espaderos 136, just off the west corner of the Plaza de Armas, has tepid water in the mornings but the bathrooms are dirty. Rooms are about US$5/7.50 for singles/doubles. Another option for budget travelers is the *Santo Domingo Convent*, Ahuacpinta 600, in the grounds of Colegio Martín de Porres. It's clean, safe and friendly, and has hot water, but there is a 10.30 pm curfew. Don't miss it if an atmosphere of nuns, daily prayers and posters of the pope appeals to you. Rates are about US$6 per person.

The basic but clean *Korichaska Chekol* (☎ 22-8974), Nueva Alta 458, is friendly and safe. Rooms are US$4 per person or US$5 with a private bath, and they have hot water at times. Other basic, cheap hotels where hot water is erratic or nonexistent are the *Hostal Matará* (☎ 22-4432), Matará 501, the *Hostal Royal* (☎ 23-3859), San Agustín 256, and the *Residencial Torres* (☎ 22-6697), Limacpampa Chico 485.

The *Hostal Cáceres* (☎ 22-8012), Plateros 368, has hot water at times and is reasonably clean and popular, though the security is lax. Rates are about US$5 per person and baths are shared. The basic *Hostal Chaski* (23-6093), Portal Confitería 257 on the Plaza de Armas, charges US$7/10 and has rooms with private bath for an extra US$2. Some hot water is available. The *Hostal Suecia I* (☎ 23-3282), Suecia 332, is popular with budget travelers, though thefts have been reported. There is hot water, and rooms are US$5 per person. Nearby, the *Hostal Rainbow Lodge*, Suecia 310, is a little cheaper and has been recommended as friendly, clean and a good value with hot water at times. The *Hostal Residencial Rojas* (☎ 22-8184), Tigre 129, is basic but OK for US$5/7.50 or US$10 for a double with bath. They have hot water in the early morning and early evening.

Hotels near the San Pedro railway station are cheap. Some are a good value, but the area is not a very safe one, so it is for budget travelers who are used to the travel realities of Peru – you know who you are! The *Hotel Imperio* (☎ 22-8981), Chaparro 121, across from the Mercado Central, is clean and friendly and has reliable hot water in the mornings and sometimes at other times. It has a hard-core support group of budget travelers who like the staff and the prices of US$3 per person for rooms with private bath or a little less without. It's a good value if you don't get mugged outside. On the other side of the Mercado Central is a slew of cheapish hotels in an unsafe area – the farther away you are from the market the better. Similar prices to the Imperio can be found at the *Hostals San Pedro* and *La Posada* and then, in increasing order of price (up to about US$15 a double with bath) are the *San Martín, Comercio, Belén, Trinitarias, Tambo Real, Milan* and *Hispano*. These hotels are OK and have hot water sometimes. The *Hostal Tambo Real* (☎ 22-1621), Belén 588, charges about US$10/15 for rooms with bath and hot showers in the morning; it's friendly and helpful and has been recommended. There are others in this area as well.

Another area to look for rock-bottom prices is around the Puno train station, also rather unsafe at night and the haunt of pickpockets during the day. There are a dozen or more hotels here that charge about US$3/5 for basic rooms. They may have hot water in the morning. Look along Tacna, Huayna Capac, Manco Capac, Manco Inca, Huáscar, Pachacutec, Tullumayo and Ahuacpinta and you'll find these cheap, basic places. A little farther away, the *Hostal Chavin* (☎ 22-8857), Cuichipunco 299, charges US$5/6 for singles/doubles.

The *Albergue Juvenil* (☎ 22-3320), on Huayruropata in the suburb of Huanchac, is clean and safe and charges about US$7.50 per person with breakfast in rooms with private bath, but it's a long way from the town center. Take a taxi. The *Albergue Municipal* (☎ 25-2506), Kiskapata 240, is up a steep hill with great city views from their balcony. Clean rooms have bunk beds for four to eight people, and there is hot water, a large common room, a small café, laundry facilities and safe left luggage. Rates are US$7 per person. The owners are helpful, but this area is not safe to walk around at night – take a cab. In the same area is the quite good *Hostal Huaynapata* (☎ 22-8034), Huaynapata 369, which charges US$16/22 for clean rooms with bath, or about half that price with shared bath. They are friendly, store luggage and have hot water in the mornings. Nearby, the *Hostal El Arqueólogo* (☎ 23-2569), Ladrillos 425, is clean, has hot water in mornings and evenings, kitchen privileges and a nice garden. It seems popular with French tourists. They charge about US$12/16 for rooms with private bath, less without. Also in this area is the *Hostal Corihuasi* (☎ /fax 23-2233), Suecia 561, which charges about US$18 for a double with bath and has a few cheaper rooms without bath. Some rooms have great views. They have a cafeteria and luggage storage, and their hot water is reliable.

The *Gran Hostal Machu Picchu* (☎ 23-1111), Quera 282, has OK rooms around two pleasant patios and has hot water most of the time. They charge US$7.50 per person and have clean bathrooms. The *Hostal Familiar* (☎ 23-9353), Saphi 661, charges US$12 for a double with bath but has few singles. Doubles with shared bath are about US$7.50. It has a pleasant courtyard and is clean, popular and often full, but I found it decidedly unfriendly. Farther up is the friendly, popular and often full *Hostal Cahuide* (☎ 22-2771), Saphi 845, where clean rooms with bath cost US$16/22 – OK, though nothing special. They have hot water in the mornings and afternoons.

The popular colonial-style *Hostal Suecia II* (☎ 23-9757), Tecsecocha 465, has friendly staff and is often full. There is hot water and a pleasant glassed-in courtyard for snacks and hanging out. Doubles with bath are about US$20, and there are very few singles, though some rooms sleep up to five. A few cheaper rooms lack bathrooms. Prices drop a lot in the low season. The *Hostal Incawasi* (☎ 23-8245), Portal de Panes 143 on the Plaza de Armas, has a great location and charges about US$12/18 for rooms with shared bath and occasional hot water, though a discount can be arranged in the low season. As with many of these hotels, the price is what the market will bear! The staff are friendly enough, but it's the location you're paying for here. Another possibility in this price range is the friendly *Hostal San Blas* (☎ 22-5781), Cuesta San Blas 526.

As we go to press, I have received a recommendation for *Hostal Tumi I*, Siete Cuartones 245, and *Hostal Tumi II* (☎ 22-8361), 312 Maruri, which opened recently. Both are friendly budget places with shared hot showers and charge about US$5 per person.

Places to Stay – middle

The wonderful, rambling old colonial house *Hostal Las Marqueses* (☎ 23-2512), Calle Garcilaso 252, is a lot of fun. They charge US$18/25 for eclectically furnished singles/doubles with bath around an attractive courtyard. There is hot water in early mornings and evenings. It's a good value that's often full in the high season; prices drop in the low season. The clean and friendly *Hostal Loreto* (☎ 22-6352), Loreto 115, just off the Plaza de Armas, has Inca walls in some rooms (which makes them rather dark, but how often do you get to sleep next to an Inca wall?). Rates are US$16/22 with bath, towels and hot water morning and evening. Rooms sleeping five go for US$36. This place is popular and often full, when they refer you to the owner's sister at *El Peregrino* (☎ 23-2072), a new recommendation on Medio, just off the Plaza de Armas. It's clean, secure and friendly and has hot water in the mornings. They charge US$20 for a double. The preceding places are rather disorganized with reservations.

The *Hostal El Solar* (☎ 23-2451), Plaza San Francisco 162, has hot water some of the time and is clean, comfortable and recommended. They charge US$16/22 and less in the low season. Another possibility in this price range is the *Hotel Virrey* (☎ 22-1771), Portal Comercio 165 right on the Plaza de Armas. It has two rooms with plaza views, but the service is reportedly poor. The *Hostal Inca World* (☎ 23-8469, 24-0559), Tecsecocha 474, has an erratic water supply and seems overpriced at US$16/22 in the high season, but they will charge a lot less when it's not busy. Also there is the *Hostal del Inca* (☎ 22-1110, fax 23-4281), Quera 251, which seems OK.

The following hotels charge about US$20/30, but even at this price they still only have hot water mornings and evenings. The *Hotel Carlos V* (☎ 22-3091), Tecsecocha 490, is pleasant enough, and they have a breakfast cafeteria, although a few of the rooms seem a litle musty. The *Hostal Colonial Palace* (☎ 23-2151), Quera 270, is pleasant and includes breakfast, though one reader reports that a recent armed robbery cleaned out the hotel safe and that it's not very secure. The *Hotel Conquistador* (☎ 23-3661, 22-4461, fax 23-6314), just off the Plaza de Armas, looks quite nice but unfortunately seems to be plagued with water problems. The *Hotel Garcilaso I* (☎ 23-3501), Calle Garcilaso

233, is in a nice old building, but a theft was reported recently by travelers who had left their luggage in storage there. There is a cheaper version a few doors away at the *Hotel Garcilaso III* (☎ 22-7951), Calle Garcilaso 285. The *Hotel del Angel* (☎ 23-1415, 23-2415), Afligidos 124, has been recently renovated. The *Tambo Hotel* (☎ 22-3221, 23-6788), Ayacucho 233, is clean and good and has a restaurant. The *Hotel Los Portales* (☎ /fax 22-2391), Matará 322, is clean and charges US$36 for a double, including continental breakfast. A nice touch is the large containers of purified water on each floor.

The *Hostal Wiracocha* (☎ 22-2351) is on the corner of the Plaza de Armas, but none of the rooms have plaza views. The restaurant is reasonable though, with excellent espresso coffee. Rooms are about US$30/40 for singles/doubles, but prices rise for Inti Raymi and fall in the off season. Also in this price range are the following. The *Hotel Cristina* (☎ /fax 22-7251), Avenida Sol 341, is a good, clean, friendly place, and rates include continental breakfast. The *San Agustín Plaza* (☎ 23-7331, 22-4231, 23-8121), Avenida Sol 594, is very helpful and friendly; its nice rooms have hot water all day. The *Hotel Espinar* (☎ 23-3091, fax 22-7061), Portal Espinar 142, is another reasonable choice, with friendly staff. Bargain in all these hotels during the low season.

Places to Stay – top end
Top-end hotels tend to be full during the high season (often with international tour groups), and advance reservations are recommended. At other times, walk-in discounts may be arranged if things are quiet. The following hotels charge about US$40 to US$50 for a single and about US$60 to US$70 for a double. You can expect 24-hour hot water at these prices, but this is Peru and occasional failures occur. They are usually resolved quickly. All these hotels have their own restaurant and bar and normally include breakfast in their rates.

Royal Inka I and *Royal Inka II* (☎ 23-1067, 23-3037, 22-2284, fax 23-4221) are

Monasterio Hotel

sister hotels almost next to one another at Plaza Regocijo 299 and Santa Teresa 335, respectively. Both are in interesting buildings dating from the early 1800s, with attractive public areas and rooms that vary somewhat in size and style. As with most hotels in Peru, street-side rooms can be noisy. The Royal Inka I, with about 35 rooms, is the smallest of Cuzco's top-end hotels. The larger Royal Inka II also has a sauna and is one of the few hotels in Peru that charges for left luggage (US$2 a bag). Most rooms are around an attractive central atrium, which also contains a restaurant and bar and tends to be noisy with early breakfasters and late revelers.

The *Hotel Cuzco* (☎ 22-4821, 22-1811, fax 22-2832), Heladeros 150, is the oldest of Cuzco's 1st-class hotels and has been operating for over half a century. There are many old-fashioned touches, and the ornately paneled bar is one of the most attractive in Cuzco. The hundred or so rooms are large and have a somewhat faded charm, but they are certainly adequate. This hotel's rates are among the cheapest of the top-end hotels. The *Hotel Internacional San Agustín* (☎ 23-3023, 22-7952, 22-1169, fax 22-1174), Maruri 390, is in an attractive old building with 80 rooms, and it has good facilities and service. The more modern *El Dorado Inn* (☎ 23-3112, 23-2573, 23-1232, fax 24-0993), Avenida Sol 395, has a glassed-in elevator and a good but pricey restaurant/bar with musicians and dancers in the evenings. The 54 rooms have heaters and individual hot water tanks that deliver enough water for one long or two very short showers. Roommates need to coordinate their showers accordingly. Rooms overlooking the elevator/restaurant area tend to be noisy with early morning departees.

The modern *Picoaga Hotel* (☎ 22-1269, 22-1291, 22-7691, fax 22-1246), Santa Teresa 344, has 70 good rooms but charges a few dollars more than the above hotels. The *Hotel Savoy* (☎ 22-4322, fax 22-4900), Avenida Sol 954, is one of two hotels in Cuzco supposedly in the five-star category. The 120 rooms are good but the restaurant

is overpriced, and the hotel's location, near the Puno railway station, is not a particularly safe one at night; you should take a taxi there. Rates are a high US$85/125. You're better off at Cuzco's best hotel, the *Hotel Libertador* (☎ 23-1961, fax 23-3152), San Agustín 400, which is in a huge old mansion with a fine courtyard. There are a few Inca foundations and parts of the building date back to the 16th century, when Francisco Pizarro was the occupant at one time. There are 113 rooms at US$125/140 and 18 suites for about US$50 more. All have central heating. The public rooms are opulently furnished with colonial sofas, iron chandeliers and antique paintings. The restaurants are overpriced, however.

Places to Eat

As you'd expect in a city with such a cosmopolitan range of visitors, Cuzco has a great variety of restaurants catering to every taste and budget. With literally hundreds of eateries from which to choose, I have limited this section mainly to places I have tried. They can be very popular, especially during the busy season, so make a reservation or be prepared to wait for a table, particularly at the better restaurants.

Breakfast & Snacks One of the best choices for breakfast and a popular meeting place throughout the day is the simple and reasonably priced *El Ayllu* café next to the cathedral. They open around 6 am, play classical music and offer a good selection of juices, coffee, tea, yogurt, cakes, sandwiches and other snacks. Next door, *La Yunta* offers a huge variety of juices, as well as cakes, coffee and inexpensive meals. Both of these are very popular and have plaza views.

Also popular, particularly for cheap breakfasts and lunches, is the *Café Haylliy* on the first block of Plateros. Other cafés that are good for breakfasts, snacks and meeting people are the *El Piccolo* on the Plaza de Armas and the *Café Varayoc* on Espaderos. The last is particularly popular and recommended. The *Hostal Wiracocha Café* on the Plaza de Armas has good coffee. A small bakery on Almagro, almost at the corner with San Andrés, has a stand-up counter and sells delicious hot meat or cheese empanadas (pies) for about US60¢.

Vegetarian If you're economizing, try the Hare Krishna *Govinda Vegetarian Restaurant* on Espaderos. The food is cheap and adequate, though the service is very slow. Their homemade bread lasts for several days if you want to take some on a trek.

The clean *Restaurant El Tordo*, Tordo 238, has good, cheap vegetarian food. Vegetables used for salads are washed in iodinized water.

Local Food A few inexpensive restaurants serve tasty, authentic Peruvian food. They often have outside patios and are usually open only for lunch or afternoon snacks. Monday seems to be the day off. People with very finicky stomachs might question the hygiene, but if you stick to cooked food, you're unlikely to get sick.

If you want something really Andean, try roast guinea pig, or cuy, an Inca delicacy. Often, this has to be ordered a day in advance. Other typical local dishes include anticucho de corazon (a shish kebab made from beef hearts), rocoto relleno (spicy bell peppers stuffed with ground beef and vegetables), adobo (a spicy pork stew), chicharrones (deep-fried chunks of pork ribs, called chancho, or of chicken, called gallina), lechón (suckling pig), choclo con queso (corn on the cob with cheese), tamales (boiled corn dumplings filled with cheese or meat and wrapped in a banana leaf), cancha (toasted corn) and various locros (hearty soups and stews). The meal is often washed down with chicha, which is either a fruit drink or a fermented, mildly alcoholic corn beer.

One of the best places and the closest to the central city area is the *Quinta Eulalia* (☎ 22-4951), which has a colorful courtyard. It's only open for lunch (as are most quintas) and there is no sign – go to Choquechaca 384. Farther afield, try the

How to Play Sapo
The local restaurants that serve Andean specialities are often called *picanterías*, literally 'spicy places,' or *quintas*, literally 'country houses,' but here referring to inns in the nearby suburbs. Often, they have a *sapo*. This is a popular picantería game, rather like darts in an English pub or pool in an American bar. The sapo, a metal toad, is mounted on a table and players toss a metal disk as close to it as possible. Top points are scored when the disk is thrown into the toad's mouth. Men will sometimes spend the whole afternoon drinking beer or chicha and competing at this old test of skill. ■

Quinta Zárate on Calle Tortera Paccha, on the eastern outskirts of town. It has a nice garden and good views, but it isn't easy to find so hire a taxi. *La Peña de Don Luis*, about 1½ km southwest of the center on Avenida Regional, is popular with Peruvians for lunch.

There are several very funky, local hole-in-the-wall places along Pampa del Castillo that serve chicharrones hot from the grill, which is often placed in the door of the restaurant. One of these is *Oh Que Rico* at number 445.

Peruvian Food These local restaurants are more likely to serve fish, chicken, or meat, perhaps with a small selection of the more traditional dishes and some international food.

Just off the plaza, along the first block of Calle Plateros, there are several good local restaurants, most of which have been recommended by one traveler or another, though I occasionally hear gripes from someone. These include the *Café Haylliy* (for good snacks), *El Tronquito* (good sopa criolla and cheap set meals), *Los Candiles* (good, cheap set meals), the *Pollería Haway* (for chicken), the *Kusikuy* (with the best selection of traditional dishes) and the Japanese-run *Pucará* (☎ 22-2027), which with dishes in the US$4 to US$10 range is the most expensive on this block. It has by far the best food, though portions aren't big. They are closed on Wednesday.

Around the corner on Calle Tigre are a couple of recommended budget restaurants, the *Victor Victoria* and *Miski Wasi*. Other recommended budget restaurants are *Chef Victor*, Ayacucho 217, and the chicken restaurant next to the Hostal del Inca on Quera.

On the Plaza de Armas, the *Inka Restaurant* and *Restaurant El Paititi* (☎ 22-6992) both have genuine Inca walls. El Paititi was part of the House of the Chosen Women and now offers good but pricey food in a white-tablecloth environment. They often have musicians at no extra charge. The cheaper Inka Restaurant was part of the Inca Pachacutec's palace, which became the house of Francisco Pizarro after the Spanish conquest. They may have a peña at night, for which there may be a small cover charge.

El Mesón de los Espaderos (☎ 23-5307), on the corner of the plaza (the entrance is just off the plaza on Espaderos 105, upstairs), is a place for dedicated carnivores. They served parilladas (mixed grills), steaks, cuy or chicken. Get there early or make a reservation to sit in the attractively carved balcony overlooking the Plaza de Armas.

Italian Food *Chez Maggy* (☎ 23-4861) and *Mia Pizza*, both on Procuradores, another *Chez Maggy* on Plateros and *Pizzería America*, also on Plateros, are currently the favored places for travelers looking to meet other people and eat good, reasonably priced pizza. Many have live music (a hat is passed for tips) in the evenings.

La Mamma Pizzería on Plaza Regocijo is quite good but not especially cheap. There are two other Italian/international restaurants next door to La Mamma – they look good, though I haven't tried them. The medium-priced *Trattoria Adriano* (☎ 23-3965) at the end of Avenida Sol is popular but has received mixed reviews. You decide, but I think it has tasty pasta dishes and often good dessert cake as well.

International These restaurants serve both international and Peruvian food. Some of the top hotels have decent restaurants where prices are high and often charged in dollars rather than intis. The food is somewhat bland and is popular with tourists who have particularly delicate stomachs or want to minimize health risks. Local musicians often play. The best hotel restaurant is at the *El Dorado Inn*.

The fanciest restaurant not attached to a hotel is *El Truco* (☎ 23-5295), Plaza Regocijo 262, which has a nightly dinner and show (from 8.30 to 10.30 pm) and is quite a good value. Make reservations in the high season because it's popular with tour groups. The food is good, as is the show. There is a cover charge, and a dinner for two with drinks could run as high as US$50, though you can get by with half that. A newer dinner-and-show restaurant with similar prices is the *José Antonio* (☎ 24-1364), Santa Teresa 356. This is a huge barn of a place.

On the northwest side of the Plaza de Armas, there are usually a couple of fairly upscale places that seem to change names every few years. The latest here are *La*

Gringo Alley

The alley leaving the Plaza de Armas on the northwest side – officially named Procuradores – has earned the nickname Gringo Alley because budget travelers have traditionally congregated there.

Gringo Alley has a good selection of cheap bars, pizzerias, restaurants and cafés, which are popular with backpackers and good places to meet people. Names and owners seem to change periodically, though the *Chez Maggy* pizzeria (see Italian food) has been there for years. It's a good street to explore if you're on a budget. *Los Cuates* is a Mexican restaurant on this street that has been recommended. ■

Estancia Imperial (☎ 22-4621) and *El Mesón Los Portales.*

My choice of the best restaurant in town is *La Retama* (☎ 22-5911), Pampa del Castillo 315, with delicious and innovative versions of some favorite Peruvian and international dishes. It's a cozy place that packs in a fair number of diners, particularly when they have live musicians and dancers performing in the evenings. Prices aren't cheap, but it's worth it.

Entertainment

Several restaurants have live entertainment with dinner every night. If you'd rather listen to music in a slightly looser bar environment, you'll find several places.

The current favorite seems to be the *Ukukus Bar*, Plateros 316, which has a variety of both live and recorded music and plenty of dancing and is a popular gathering spot for travelers. There's a US$1.50 cover charge after 9.30 pm, and a happy hour from 8 to 9.30 pm, so go early. It gets very crowded later on. The older *Kamikaze*, up the stairs at the northwestern corner of the Plaza Regocijo, has lively taped music and live performers (usually from 10.30 pm), but is currently less popular. They have an 8.30 to 9.30 pm happy hour and a variable cover charge.

The *Cross Keys Pub*, Portal Confituría 233, is easily identifiable from the Plaza de Armas by the huge metal keys hanging outside; it's an English pub run by a British ornithologist, Barry Walker. He knows the area well and is a good contact for the Manu area. There is a dart board and what may be the most challenging pool tables in town – every shot takes a bananalike trajectory. It's a great meeting place – you can have a conversation here without having to scream over the music – and though not as cheap as some other bars, it does have a happy hour from 6 to 7 and 9 to 9.30 pm. Note that these happy hours don't normally include beer. A recent recommendation is *Tumi's Video Bar*, Saphi 456-478, which shows recently released videos on a 52-inch screen in one room and has a friendly bar next to it. They have pool, darts and

food, and the place appears to be gaining popularity. They open for lunch and have an 8 to 9 pm happy hour.

Opened in 1995 and upscale, the *Kerara Jazz Bar* (☎ 23-5706) on Espaderos has about seven different barrooms with changing attractions, one showing videos of jazz and blues greats, another with a variety of live acts, yet another with snacks, one with a nice balcony view and so on. It's quite a place and worth checking out, though the cover charge may be rather higher than other places. Also in this building is the *Mama Africa Pub*, which has live music and is becoming something of a budget travelers' hangout.

Several places offer disco dancing. The fairly expensive *El Muki*, just off the plaza at Santa Catalina 114, is dark, with plenty of alcoves, and has a couples-only rule at the door (though they usually don't count when a mixed group goes in). This is the place where Peruvian teenagers with a little money go to make out. *Las Quenas*, in the Hotel Savoy basement, is also popular with Peruvians.

Several places have evening folklore dance shows. Usually there are some good dances in traditional costumes, but the music may be recorded and disappointing. Cover charges vary from US$3 to US$6 – shop around. The *Teatro Inti Raymi*, Saphi 605, and the *Qosqo Center of Native Dance* (☎ 22-7901), Avenida Sol 604, are two such places.

Things to Buy

The best place to see local artisans making and selling their handicrafts is around the Plaza San Blas and the streets leading to it from the Plaza de Armas. The San Blas area has a reputation as Cuzco's artisan quarter and is worth visiting not only to buy and to watch artisans at work but also to see the interior of some of the buildings. Prices and quality vary greatly, so shop around. The very best pieces may cost 10 times more than what, superficially, appear to be the same items in a store on the Plaza de Armas, but the difference in quality is significant. Bargaining is expected, except in a few of the more expensive stores where prices are fixed.

Going to the Mercado Central near the San Pedro (Machu Picchu) railway station to buy crafts is not a good idea – neither the prices nor the quality are any better than elsewhere and thieves abound. This market is a colorful affair, but if you must go don't bring much money or a camera because the thieves are extremely professional and persistent. If you want to look around, you should do so in a group and look out for one another. This is not the place for crafts.

If you like to shop in a market atmosphere, there's a crafts market on the corner of Quera and San Bernardo and another off Loreto. A nightly crafts market is also held under the arches around the Plaza de Armas and a block over on Espinar. You will often be approached on the street by people trying to sell you all kinds of crafts. This can become a little wearisome when you're not in a buying mood – the only thing to do is say 'No, gracias' as firmly as possible and show absolutely no interest; the slightest spark of curiosity will inevitably result in five minutes of pestering.

Some of the best places (though not the cheapest) include Taller Olave, to the left of Plaza San Blas, for exceptionally fine and expensive reproductions of colonial sculptures and precolonial ceramics; Santiago Rojas Alvarez at Suytuccato 751, for Paucartambo fiesta masks; Taller Mérida at Carmen Alto 133, for earthenware statues of Indians; the nationally known Mendivil family at the corner of Hatunrumiyoc and Tullumayo, for their hallmark religious figures with elongated necks and other items; and Josefina Olivera at Santa Clara 501, by the Machu Picchu train station, for old ponchos and weavings. There are many stores along Hatunrumiyoc and Cuesta San Blas and

around Plaza San Blas that sell almost any souvenir you can imagine. This is the best shopping area.

There are some warehouses with large selections of sweaters and crafts where you can shop with minimal pressure. A reader recommends La Perez (☎ 23-2186, 22-2137), Mateo Pumachahua 598, Tienda 1, Wanchaq. Serious shoppers can call them and they'll pick you up from your hotel and bring you back at no charge.

For grocery shopping (Inca Trail food and so on) good selections of food are found at Mercado El Chinito on Mesón de la Estrella between Quera and Ayacucho and at another market on the corner of Avenida Sol and Almagro. (These do not compare with the supermarkets found in Lima, however.)

Getting There & Away

Air Cuzco's airport claims international status because of the flights to La Paz, Bolivia. All departures and arrivals are in the morning because climatic conditions make landing and takeoff difficult in the afternoon. Airport departure tax is US$17.70 for international flights and US$4 for internal flights.

Flights to Bolivia cost about US$126. Both Lloyd Aereo Boliviano (LAB) and AeroPerú have flights to La Paz, but schedules change frequently. Flights are almost daily during the high season.

There are seven or more (mostly direct) flights a day to and from Lima with Faucett, AeroPerú, Americana, Aero Continente and Imperial Air. Be aware that many of these get canceled or lumped together with another flight during nonbusy periods. Your best bet is to get the earliest flight available as the late ones are the most likely to be delayed or canceled. Fares are about US$102, or less with Imperial. There are one to three flights a day to Arequipa (US$53), Juliaca (US$48), Puerto Maldonado (US$44) and Ayacucho (US$48) with one or more of the same airlines. These fares change frequently, and the Lima fare has varied from about US$60 to US$100 over the last few years. Transportes Aereos Andahuaylas (TAA) flies to Andahuaylas on Tuesday and Friday.

Same-day connections to Tacna via Arequipa and to most northern cities via Lima can be arranged, but allow several hours connecting time as flights from Cuzco are frequently late. Contrary to popular opinion, no direct flights operate between Cuzco and Iquitos; you have to fly to Lima and connect from there.

Airline offices are in central Cuzco along Avenida Sol or on the Plaza de Armas (see map). Airlines don't normally sell tickets at the crowded airport counters, although it is possible to buy a ticket at the airport on a space-available basis. The military airline, Grupo 8, sells tickets at the airport for its flights (usually on Thursday) to Lima and Puerto Maldonado. These flights don't always go, are usually full and normally cannot be booked in advance (though there's no harm in trying). Although fares are somewhat cheaper than those of the commercial airlines, Grupo 8 flights are difficult for tourists to get on. Go to the airport before 6 am on the day of the flight, packed and ready to go, get your name on the waiting list and hope. Grupo 8 also fly via Puerto Maldonado to Iberia or Iñapari for the Brazilian border.

Flights tend to be overbooked, especially during the busy season, so confirm your flight when you arrive in Cuzco, then reconfirm 72 hours in advance and again 24 hours before departure. If you buy your ticket from a reputable travel agent in Cuzco, they'll reconfirm for you. Having ensured that your flight has been properly and frequently reconfirmed, check in at least one hour before departure time. Check-in procedures at Cuzco airport are often chaotic and even people with confirmed seats and boarding passes have, occasionally, been denied boarding because of overbooking errors. (Don't get overly paranoid; this doesn't happen all the time.) During the rainy season, flights can be postponed for 24 hours because of bad weather. Baggage is often lost or delayed and routinely pilfered unless it is locked. Bring valuables and essentials (including medicines and hiking boots if you are doing the Inca Trail) with you on the plane and securely lock your checked luggage.

When flying from Cuzco to Lima, check in as early as possible to get a seat on the right-hand side of the plane for the best views of Salcantay's 6271-meter peak. Some pilots like to fly quite close to the mountain and the views are sometimes stupendous. (Sit on the left from Lima to Cuzco.) Occasionally, a different route is taken over Machu Picchu, but not often.

A taxi from the airport to the center of Cuzco costs about US$2 to US$3; the local bus costs about US25¢.

Helicopter Helicusco (☎ 23-1760, fax 23-1388), Portal Comercio 195, Plaza de Armas, began Cuzco-Aguas Calientes flights in 1995 after an environmental impact study enabled them to receive permission from the Peruvian authorities. The helicopter service of the 1970s was stopped because the vibration of the choppers was damaging the Machu Picchu ruins. The new service does not go to the ruins themselves but to Aguas Calientes, 8 km away. A 24-passenger Russian helicopter leaves Cuzco daily at 9.30 am and returns at 3.30 pm. The flight takes 25 minutes. The cost is about US$85 each way, or you can buy a package including Cuzco hotel transfer, bus from Aguas Calientes to Machu Picchu, entrance to the ruins, lunch and a guided tour for about US$220. Milla Turismo is the general agent for Helicusco.

Bus Cuzco has no central bus terminal, although there has been talk of building one near the airport. Buses to Pisac, Calca and Urubamba leave frequently with Transportes Pitusiray from Avenida Tullumayo from 5.30 am until dusk. Transportes Chican, on Intiqhawarina just off Tullumayo, has buses to Chincheros, some continuing to Urubamba and Ollantaytambo, at the same hours. These buses change their departure points every year or two, so check with the tourist office or other travellers before hiking out there with your gear. It takes over two hours to reach Urubamba, about an hour to Pisac. Buses are always crowded. The Pisac buses will also drop you off at the Inca site of Tambo Machay. You can walk back from there to Cuzco and visit the other nearby ruins en route. To get to Ollantaytambo from Pisac, change at Urubamba.

Buses to Oropesa, Urcos, Sicuani and Ocongate leave from the Coliseo Cerrado on Manco Capac, about five blocks east of Tacna. Buses for Urcos also leave from Avenida Haya de la Torre on the north side of Avenida de la Cultura between the University and Hospital Regional. Take these buses to visit the ruins of Tipón, Pikillacta, Rumicolca and Raqchi.

Trucks for Limatambo, Mollepata and on to Abancay and other destinations leave from Arcopata. Alternatively, take a long-distance bus to Abancay from one of several companies on the same street. There are also two or three companies on Granada, northwest of the Plaza San Francisco, with buses to Abancay (eight hours, US$6) and on to Andahuaylas (14 hours, US$9) leaving at 6 am, 10 am and 1 pm. To continue on to Ayacucho, you normally have to change at Andahuaylas, although there have been through buses in the past. Empresa Andahuaylas on Arcopata has buses to Ayacucho at 6 am, which stop to overnight in Andahuaylas and then continue a further 15 hours to Ayacucho (US$18). The road to these towns is absolutely atrocious and very cold at night, but it is no longer unsafe because of terrorism. The journey is often done in cramped minibuses, rather than full-size buses, and can be extremely uncomfortable.

There are no buses to the southeastern jungles except for those to Quillabamba. You have to fly, go by truck or go on an expedition. There are daily trucks to Puerto Maldonado during the dry season along a wildly spectacular but difficult road, and the trip from Cuzco takes two to three days. The trip takes a week or more in the wet, if the road is passable at all. Trucks leave from near the Plaza Tupac Amaru, two blocks east of Tacna along Avenida Garcilaso. You could also get a bus to Urcos or Ocongate and wait for a truck there. As I've never gone beyond Ocongate, except by air from Cuzco to Puerto Maldonado, I'd like to hear from anyone who has done this trip.

Getting to Manu is just as problematic. Transportes Sol Andino has buses to Paucartambo (six hours, US$3) at 10 am on Monday, Wednesday and Friday mornings leaving from the Coliseo Cerrado. They are very full, so you should get there by 7 am to get a seat or try and book one with the Andino office on Avenida Huáscar. Trucks also do the journey on the same days from the Coliseo Cerrado area – ask around. Continuing from Paucartambo to Manu there are only passing trucks or expedition buses. From Cuzco, trucks from the Coliseo Cerrado go to Pillcopata (11 hours), Atalaya (16 hours) and Shintuya (20 hours). See From Cuzco to the Jungle below for more details. Expediciones Manu is a source of information about these, or try Explorers Transportes (☎ 23-3498), Plateros 354-A; they rent buses, 4WDs and pickups (with or without drivers) for explorations to anywhere in the area.

There is a bus to Quillabamba (10 hours, US$6) every night with Empresa Carhuamayo at the Plaza Tupac Amaru. There is also an Ormeño office on Avenida Huáscar with buses to Lima and international buses to Chile.

Getting to other major cities is a lot easier. Cruz del Sur, on Pachacutec, provides bus services to the south of the country, with day buses to Sicuani and overnight buses to Juliaca and Puno (14 hours, US$10). Because the road is in such poor shape (see Puno), most people prefer the much more comfortable day train. Cruz del Sur also has a nightly service to Arequipa via Imata (16 hours, US$12); it's a rough journey on a little-traveled road. The service continues to Lima (40 hours, US$24). Expect delays in the rainy season. Several other companies on the same street also have buses to southern Peruvian towns. Try Civa, Expreso Cometa, Transportes Collasuyo and others for different prices. Ormeño also has buses to these destinations.

A cheaper and only slightly quicker route to Lima goes via Abancay, Puquio and Nazca. This used to be the most frequently traveled bus route between Cuzco and the capital. However, in the late '80s and early '90s, serious problems with the Sendero Luminoso guerrillas made the trip dangerous. Now that the guerrilla problem is under control, bandits have been attacking buses in the Puquio area, and this route is definitely not recommended; only a few minor companies use this route. If services on the Abancay route resume with major companies like Ormeño and Cruz del Sur, it will be an indication that travel there is becoming safer again.

All the journey times given are approximate and apply in good conditions. In the wettest months of the rainy season, especially January to April, long delays are possible.

Train Cuzco has two train stations. Estación Huancho (☎ 23-3592, 22-1992), near the end of Avenida Sol, serves Urcos, Sicuani, Juliaca, Puno and Arequipa. Estación San Pedro (☎ 22-1291, 23-8722 for reservations, 23-1207 for information), next to the Mercado Central, serves Machu Picchu and Quillabamba. It is therefore impossible to travel directly from Arequipa or Puno to Machu Picchu; you must change lines at Cuzco. To make matters worse, the two stations are not within easy walking distance of each other. However, there has been occasional talk about linking the Machu Picchu railway line with the line for Puno and Arequipa, though this is unlikely to happen in the near future.

The train for Puno leaves at 8 am on Monday, Wednesday, Friday and Saturday and takes about 10½ hours. It passes through Juliaca at about 5 pm, allowing you to connect with the nightly train from Juliaca to Arequipa, which leaves later.

First-class tickets for the Puno train are often sold out, so if possible, buy a ticket the day before. The ticket office is open weekdays from 9 to 11 am and 3 to 4 pm and on weekends from 9 to 10 am, though these hours change often. If you have problems getting a ticket, try booking through a travel agent. They may charge a fee; shop around for the best deal.

Fares have varied wildly for several years now, depending on currency fluctuations and railway regulations. See the Puno and Arequipa sections for details of classes and fares.

The Machu Picchu train departs several times a day and is the most frequently used train in Peru. This, combined with the station's location near the crowded Mercado Central, makes it a prime target for thieves. In recent years, Peruvian police have increased patrols around the station and on the trains, greatly reducing the risk of ripoffs, but because it's so crowded, you still have to be very vigilant.

Although popularly called the Machu Picchu train, it doesn't go there! The most important stops (for the traveler) are described below.

Ollantaytambo station can be reached by road. This enables travelers to visit the Sacred Valley ruins by bus and then continue from Ollantaytambo to Machu Picchu without returning to Cuzco. All trains stop here.

The halt at Km 88 is where hikers leave the train to begin the Inca Trail. Only the local train stops here.

The next important station is at Aguas Calientes, but it's misleadingly called Machu Picchu station. It is served by all trains except the tourist train (unless requested in advance) and is the place to go if you want to spend the night near the ruins without staying at the very expensive Machu Picchu Hotel. It is 8 km from the Machu Picchu ruins.

The closest train station to the Machu Picchu ruins themselves, Puente Ruinas, is 2 km beyond the Machu Picchu station at Aguas Calientes. All trains stop here, except the Quillabamba autovagon, which will also do so if you ask in advance. As the tourist train doesn't go beyond Puente Ruinas, you must travel on the local train or the Quillabamba autovagon if you plan to continue beyond this point.

Santa Teresa station is 18 km beyond Puente Ruinas. There is a tenuous road link with Cuzco (about 15 hours by truck) and a basic hotel. It is also the end of the Mollepata to Santa Teresa trek (see Bradt's *Backpacking & Trekking in Peru & Bolivia*).

The jungle-edge town of Quillabamba is the end of the line. There is a bus link from here back to Cuzco.

When leaving Cuzco, the train has to climb a steep hill. This is accomplished by a series of switchbacks and the train shunts backward and forward several times with grand views of Cuzco below. It takes about 30 minutes before you start leaving Cuzco proper. On the return to Cuzco, the same process occurs in reverse except that if it is dark, the view of Cuzco is enhanced by the beautifully floodlit church and cathedral on the Plaza de Armas.

There is a bewildering variety of trains. Some go only as far as Puente Ruinas while others continue to Quillabamba. Some are express and others are local, stopping everywhere. The electric autovagon is generally smaller, faster and more expensive than other trains. Some of these services are designated for tourists only and are better guarded and much more expensive, with reserved seating. Schedules change frequently and the following information can therefore be used only as a rough guide – before traveling, check with other travelers and at the station, the tourist information office, or a reliable local travel agent to determine current services. Often, an extra train runs during the height of the tourist season (June to August). Also, of course, the cheaper local trains are often late, though the tourist trains are on time surprisingly often.

The local train (tren local) is the cheapest and stops everywhere. As it is also the one with the worst reputation for robbery, you are better off traveling 1st class. The train leaves Cuzco daily at 6.20 am and daily except Sunday at 1.15 pm, and it takes about four hours to reach Machu Picchu and seven hours to Quillabamba. First-class fares are about US$4.50 to Machu Picchu and US$5.50 to Quillabamba. Second class is about 20% cheaper. There may be a more expensive Pullman or Special class available. The train makes very brief stops at some stations – be ready to jump of quickly, particularly at Km 88.

The autovagon to Quillabamba takes three hours to Aguas Calientes, 5½ hours to Quillabamba. In the past it left daily around 1.30 pm, but recently hasn't been running. Check locally. The fare is about US$14 to Quillabamba. Vendors are not allowed aboard and the autovagon doesn't stop at many stations, so bring some food.

The tourist train stops at Ollantaytambo and Puente Ruinas (for the Machu Picchu ruins) and does not continue to Quilla-bamba. Normally roundtrip tickets are sold. The idea is that you leave in the morning, spend two or three hours at the ruins and return in the afternoon – a tiring day with inadequate time at the ruins. Nevertheless, this is the way many, perhaps most, people visit Machu Picchu. It is possible to buy one-way tourist train tickets or to travel on separate days.

The tourist train leaves Cuzco about 6.30 am, and there may be another departure in the high season. In the past, passengers have been taken to Ollantaytambo by bus and continued from there by train. On the return trip, the same applied. More recently, passengers were taken by bus to the newly built Poroy station, about 6 km from Cuzco, and met the train there. Both of these avoid the long switchback section above Cuzco and speed up the overall journey. However, on my last trip in 1995, Poroy station had been closed and tourist trains were running all the way to or from Cuzco. Inquire locally about the current situation.

The trip to Puente Ruinas takes about three hours each way and costs about US$50 roundtrip, plus the fare for the 20-minute bus ride from the station to the ruins and admission to the site. Travel agents sell the trip for about US$90, including the bus from the Puente Ruinas station to the ruins, entrance to the ruins, and a guide.

The ticket office is open daily, suppos-edly all day, but in fact they close several times a day. Call them to ask when tickets are sold. Because it is in a dangerous area, you are advised not to carry valuables when going to buy a ticket and to go with friends or take a taxi.

Getting Around
Bus Local buses cost about US25¢. There is no easy bus link between the two rail-way stations.

Taxi A taxi ride is about US$1 in town, US$2.50 to just outside the airport or

US$3.50 to the airport terminal – drivers have to pay an extra fee to enter the airport.

You can hire a taxi for a whole day for about US$40 or US$50 to visit sites around Cuzco. Some drivers speak English.

AROUND CUZCO
The Nearby Ruins
'The Nearby Ruins' refers to the four ruins closest to Cuzco: Sacsayhuaman, Qenko, Puca Pucara and Tambo Machay. They are often visited in a day, even less if you're on a guided trip, and entry is with the Cuzco Visitor Ticket. The cheapest and most con-venient way to visit the ruins is to take a bus to Pisac and get off at Tambo Machay, the nearby ruin farthest from Cuzco and, at 3700 meters, the highest. From there, you can walk the 8 km back to Cuzco, visiting all four ruins along the way. Colorfully dressed locals often wait near the sites with their llama herds, hoping to be photographed. Tipping is expected (about US30¢ is usual), and photographers trying for a free shot will get an unfriendly recep-tion. Travelers wanting a more in-depth description of these and other ruins, as well as details of hikes in the area, are directed to Peter Frost's excellent book *Exploring Cuzco*. This is generally a safe, popular and rewarding walk, but it's advisable to go in a group and to return well before nightfall to avoid potential robbery.

Tambo Machay This small ruin, about 300 meters from the main road, consists of a beautifully wrought ceremonial stone bath and is therefore popularly called El Baño del Inca. Puca Pucara, the next ruin, can be seen from the small signaling tower opposite. There is usually a guard at Tambo Machay who will punch your Cuzco Visitor Ticket for this site and also for Puca Pucara.

Puca Pucara As you return from Tambo Machay, you'll see this small site on the other side of the main road. In some lights, the rock looks very red and the name literally means 'red fort.' It is the

TONY WHEELER

Sacsayhuaman

ROB RACHOWIECKI

Inca ceremonial center at Pisac ruins

ROB RACHOWIECKI

Church on the outskirts of Pisac

ROB RACHOWIECKI

Ollantaytambo village as seen from the ruins

ROB RACHOWIECKI

Ollantaytambo ruins

ROB RACHOWIECKI

TONY WHEELER

ROB RACHOWIECKI

ROB RACHOWIECKI

ROB RACHOWIECKI

ROB RACHOWIECKI

Machu Picchu

least interesting and least visited of the four ruins.

Qenko The name of this small but fascinating ruin is variously written qenqo, qenco, q'enqo or qenko and means 'zigzag.' Qenko consists of a large limestone rock completely covered with carvings, including the zigzagging channels that give the site its name. These are thought to have been used for the ritual sacrifice of chicha or, perhaps, blood. Tunnels are carved below the boulder, and there's a mysterious cave with altars carved into the rock. Qenko is about 4 km before Cuzco, on the left-hand side of the road as you descend from Tambo Machay.

Sacsayhuaman This huge ruin is the most impressive in the immediate Cuzco area. The name means 'satisfied falcon' but most local guides cannot resist telling visitors that the long Quechua name is most easily remembered by the mnemonic 'sexy woman.'

The most interesting way to reach the site is to climb the steep street of Resbalosa, turn right at the top, go past the Church of San Cristobal and continue until you come to a hairpin bend in the road. Here, you'll find the old Inca road between Cuzco and Sacsayhuaman. Follow it to the top; the ruins are to the left. The climb is short but steep and takes almost an hour from Cuzco, so make sure you're acclimatized before attempting it. (An acclimatized athlete wrote to me complaining that the walk took barely 20 minutes!) The old road is also a good descent route when returning from visits to the other nearby ruins. The site is open from dawn till dusk, and the guards are very active in demanding to see your Cuzco Visitor Ticket. Arriving at dawn will give you the site to yourself – tour groups begin arriving in midmorning. However, robberies have been reported early and late in the day so you should go with friends or a group.

Although Sacsayhuaman seems huge, what today's visitor sees is only about 20% of the original structure. Soon after the conquest, the Spaniards tore down many walls and used the blocks to build their own houses in Cuzco. They left the largest and most impressive of the original rocks, one of which weighs over 300 tons. Most of them form part of the main battlements.

The Incas envisioned Cuzco in the shape of a puma with Sacsayhuaman as the head. The site is essentially three different areas, the most obvious being the three-tiered zigzag walls of the main fortifications. The 22 zigzags form the teeth of the puma and are also a very effective defensive mechanism – an attacker must expose a flank when attacking any wall. Opposite is the hill called Rodadero with its retaining walls, curiously polished rocks and a finely carved series of stone benches known as the throne of the Inca. Between the zigzag ramparts and Rodadero Hill lies a large, flat parade ground that is used for the colorful tourist spectacle of Inti Raymi, held every June 24. The site is being actively excavated following the recent discovery of seven mummies behind the Rodadero Hill.

The magnificent zigzag walls remain the site's major attraction even though much of this fortification has been destroyed. Three towers once stood above these walls. Only the foundations remain, but the 22-meter diameter of the largest, Muyuc Marca, gives an indication of how big they must have been. Muyuc Marca, with its perfectly fitted stone conduits, was used as a huge water tank for the garrison. Other buildings within the ramparts provided food and shelter for an estimated 5000 warriors. Most of these structures were torn down by the Spaniards and by later inhabitants of Cuzco, and the resulting lack of evidence makes a precise description of Sacsayhuaman's function difficult. Most authorities agree, however, that the site had important religious as well as military significance.

The fort was the site of one of the most bitter battles of the Spanish conquest. About 2½ years after Pizarro's entry into Cuzco, the rebellious Manco Inca recaptured the lightly guarded Sacsayhuaman and used it as a base to lay siege to the conquistadors in Cuzco. Manco was very nearly successful in defeating the Spaniards and only a desperate last-ditch attack by 50 Spanish cavalry led by Juan Pizarro finally succeeded in retaking Sacsayhuaman and putting an end to the rebellion. Although Manco Inca survived and retreated to the fortress of Ollantaytambo, most of his forces were killed. The thousands of dead littering the site attracted swarms of carrion-eating Andean condors, hence the inclusion of eight condors in Cuzco's coat of arms.

The Urubamba Valley

The beautiful Vilcanota/Urubamba River valley is popularly called *El Valle Sagrado*, or the Sacred Valley of the Incas. It is about 15 km north of Cuzco as the condor flies. The climate is pleasant because of the elevation (600 meters lower than Cuzco) and there is much to do – visit Inca ruins, bargain in Indian markets, stroll through Andean villages or take an exciting river-running trip down the Urubamba. Rafting is one of the Sacred Valley's most pleasant activities, and this option is described under Activities in Cuzco.

The most important points of interest in the valley are the ruins at Pisac and Ollantaytambo, both of which require the Cuzco Visitor Ticket for admission. Other lesser sites can also be visited. Limited accommodations are available in the towns of Pisac, Calca, Yucay, Urubamba and Ollantaytambo. Various tour companies in Cuzco visit the Pisac and Ollantaytambo sites on half- and full-day guided bus tours of the Sacred Valley, but if you have a few days, taking local buses and staying in the valley itself is rewarding.

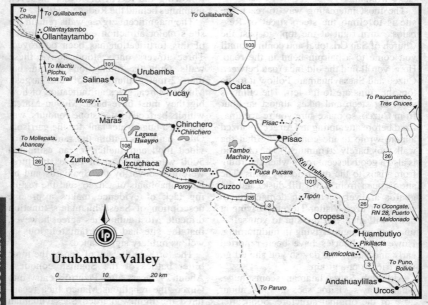

Urubamba Valley

PISAC

Pisac is 32 km from Cuzco by paved road and the most convenient starting point for a visit to the Sacred Valley. There are two Pisacs, one is the colonial and modern village lying beside the river and the other an Inca fortress on a mountain spur about 600 meters above. There is a telephone near the bridge into town if you need to make a call.

Colonial Pisac & Market

For most of the week, colonial Pisac is a quiet, Andean village and there's little to do except sit and relax in the plaza or visit the bakery for some bread fresh from the old-fashioned clay oven. The village comes alive on Sunday, however, when the famous weekly market takes place. This attracts traditionally dressed locals from miles around and garishly dressed tourists from all over the world. Despite being a big tourist attraction, this bustling, colorful market retains at least some of its traditional air (although some readers complain it is too touristy). Selling and bartering of produce goes on alongside stalls full of weavings and sweaters for the tourists. Many of the stallholders come from Cuzco, and even after hard bargaining, prices in Pisac are not any lower than those in Cuzco. The main square is thronged with people and becomes even more crowded after the mass (said in Quechua), when the congregation leaves the church in a colorful procession, led by the mayor holding his silver staff of office. Things start winding down about lunchtime, and by evening, the village returns to its normal somnolent state.

There is a smaller market on Thursday (few tourists but plenty of handicrafts) and one smaller still on Tuesday, and a few stallholders sell souvenirs every day during the high season, but it's pretty quiet compared to Sunday. Calle Bolognesi has several interesting-looking stores where you can see crafts being made.

Inca Pisac

The Inca ruins above the village are among my favorites, partly because the walk there is so spectacular and partly because the site is less visited than others on the tourist circuit, and so, except on Sunday, you don't see too many people. The ruins are reached either by a new, 10-km paved road up the Chongo Valley or by a shorter (about 5 km) but steep footpath from the plaza. There is little traffic along the road but it is sometimes possible to hire a pick-up truck in Pisac to drive you to the ruins. One reader reports that a pickup truck drives up from Pisac at 7 am to take locals up to work. Minibuses occasionally go up this road and drop you within a kilometer of the ruins, but they don't have a set schedule.

The footpath to the site leaves town from the left-hand side of the church. There are many crisscrossing trails but, as long as you generally head toward the terracing, you'll get to the ruins without much

Caracara

difficulty. Allow roughly two hours for the spectacular climb. This is a full-day trip if you take your time and don't rush things. Children and women will meet you at the top with bottled soft drinks that cost twice as much as in the store – but after climbing this far the kids deserve to make a few cents!

The ruins are on a hilltop with a gorge on either side. The western gorge (to the left of the hill as you climb up on the footpath) is the Kitamayo River gorge; to the right, or east, is the Chongo River valley where the road ascends. Pisac is particularly well known for its agricultural terracing, which sweeps around the south and east flanks of the mountain in vast, graceful curves, almost unbroken by steps – which would promote erosion, take up valuable cultivation space, require greater maintenance and make walking and working along the terraces more difficult. Instead, the different levels of terracing are joined by diagonal flights of stairs made of flagstones set into the terrace walls.

Above the terraces are some cliff-hanging footpaths, well defended by massive stone doorways, steep stairs and, at one point, a tunnel carved out of the rock. Walking along these paths is

exciting – the views are wonderful and a pair of caracara hawks often accompanies you. This highly defensible site guards not only the Urubamba Valley below but also a pass into the jungle to the northeast. Pisac's main religious center, near the top of the terraces, features extremely well-built rooms and temples. New excavations occur sporadically. At the back (north end) of the ruins you can see a series of ceremonial baths that were recently reconstructed. In the 1980s, this area was just a grassy hillside until the baths were excavated. As you look across the Kitamayo Gorge from the back of the ruins, you'll see hundreds of holes honeycombing the cliff wall. These are Inca tombs that, unfortunately, were robbed before being examined by archaeologists. The site is large and warrants several hours or a whole day of your time. People occasionally camp near the ruins, but there is no water or facilities. If you decide to spend the night, please don't break the law by lighting fires; use a stove for cooking or bring cold food. A recent fire ruined a large portion of the vegetation above the terraces. Fires also advertise your presence. People camping near the ruins have been robbed while sleeping, so keep a low profile.

Places to Stay & Eat

Pisac is a small village and accommodations are limited, especially before market day, so get there early or take a day trip from Cuzco. The *Parador Pisaq* on the square has two clean rooms with eight beds and charges US$5 per person. They may have food available. The *Residencial Beho* on the path to the ruins, charges a little less and has cold showers. Some families rent rooms in their houses; ask around. The *Hostal & Café Pisaq* charges US$6 a person for clean beds and has hot showers in the mornings. The *Royal Inka* is in an old farmhouse 1½ km from town. Once a good hotel, then a place used by couples from Cuzco for romantic getaways, then closed down, it now may reopen as a midpriced hotel. Ask in Cuzco. The *Samana Wasi* is considered the best of Pisac's several very basic cafés, though it is a little overpriced. The *Hostal Pisaq* café might be a better bet. There are a few basic eateries near the bridge. Stop by the bakery near the Plaza de Armas for hot-out-of-the-oven flat bread rolls typical of the area.

Getting There & Away
For a fare of about US60¢, you can catch one of the minibuses that leave frequently from the stop on Avenida Tullumayo in Cuzco, some continuing along the Urubamba Valley to Urubamba. This is the cheapest way to travel but also the most crowded. Be wary of pickpockets on the buses and around the bus stops. Many agencies in Cuzco operate more expensive tourist buses, especially on market day, or you can hire a cab for about US$20. When returning to Cuzco or continuing down the Urubamba Valley, wait for a bus by the bridge.

CALCA
About 18 km beyond Pisac, Calca is the most important town in the valley but is of little interest to the traveler. There are some small and unspectacular ruins in the vicinity and a couple of very basic hotels, such as the dirty *Hostal San Martín*, which has cold water and charges about US$3 per person, or the better *Hostal Pitusiray*, which charges about US$8/12. Few travelers stay in Calca.

YUCAY
The pretty little village of Yucay is approximately 18 km beyond Calca. It has the valley's fanciest hotel, the *Alhambra* (☎ 20-1107, 22-0204, 22-4076), which charges about US$60/80 for comfortable single/double rooms including breakfast, though discounts in the low season can be obtained if you just show up. The main building is a beautiful 300-year-old hacienda with 17 rather creaky and dark rooms – one of which is haunted. There are more modern rooms around attractive gardens in the back. There is hot water at any time, a decent restaurant and bar, helpful staff and

a small but high-quality gift shop. There is also an interesting little private museum.

URUBAMBA
Urubamba is about 4 km beyond Yucay, at the junction of the valley road with the Chinchero road. The town is pleasant, though not exceptional, and it's a convenient base from which to explore the Sacred Valley.

Pottery
Pablo Seminario (☎ 20-1002), Zavala 318, is a local potter. He has a workshop on the corner of Zavala and Mariscal Castilla, the main street leading from the gas station on the main valley road into the town center. Walk about eight blocks and you'll find El Retamal on the left. Pablo does attractive work with pre-Hispanic influence, as well as his own original work, which is different from anything else you'll see in Cuzco. He speaks English and is happy to explain his art to visitors. Pieces are for sale here.

Places to Stay & Eat
There are a couple of very basic cheap hotels in the town center. The best is the friendly *Hotel Urubamba*, on Bolognesi a couple of blocks from the central plaza and about 10 minutes from the main valley road, for US$6 for a double. Showers are cold. Another cheap and basic place is *Hostal Vera* on the main valley road. You'll find simple restaurants on the plaza and along the road leading from the gas station on the main valley road into the town center. About 100 meters up this road on the left is the inexpensive *Restaurant Hirano's*, which has been recommended as the best of the cheap places.

Along the main valley road are the following. The *Hotel Valle Sagrado de Los Incas* (☎ 20-1071, 20-1126, 20-1127), formerly the Centro Vacacional, has a very cold swimming pool, an adequate restaurant and comfortable, if impersonal, singles/doubles with clean hot showers for about US$18/25. The newly opened *Hotel Río Bravo* is affiliated with the top end Hotel El Dorado in Cuzco, which can provide information. They reportedly have a pool, disco, restaurant and pleasant rooms with private hot showers.

Best of the hotels is the *Hotel San Agustín Turquesa* (☎ 22-1025), where comfortable singles/doubles with heaters and hot water cost about US$35/50. (Discounts can be obtained during the low season.) New owners have converted the garden into an outdoor buffet-style restaurant, which is full with tour groups eating lunch on weekends and sometimes midweek during the high season. Opposite is the *Gran Casa Restaurant*, which also is popular with tour buses.

Also worth trying, especially for lunch, is the *Quinta Los Geranios* restaurant on the main valley road near the gas station. Here, you can get a good three-course lunch for about US$3. The best restaurant in town is the *El Maizal* (☎ 20-1054), which has the best buffet-style lunches as well as sit-down meals. They will prepare traditional Andean food (cuy, quinua, a variety of potatoes, beans, etc) if you ask for it in advance.

Getting There & Away
Buses leave Cuzco many times a day from the bus stop on Avenida Tullumayo.

In the mid to late 1980s, a railway construction project was busily under way, apparently extending the Machu Picchu railway line to Urubamba, but things seem to have ground to a halt. Who knows when the project might be finished.

Buses back to Cuzco or on to Ollantaytambo stop at the gas station on the main road.

SALINAS
About 6 km farther down the valley from Urubamba is the village of Tarabamba. Cross the Río Urubamba here by footbridge, turn right and follow a footpath along the south bank of the river to a small cemetery, where you turn left and climb roughly southward up a valley to the salt pans of Salinas. It's about a 3-km uphill hike.

Hundreds of salt pans have been used for salt extraction since Inca times. A hot spring at the top of the valley discharges a small stream of heavily salt-laden water, which is diverted into salt pans and evaporated to produce a salt that is used for cattle licks. The local salt-extracting cooperative charges about US$1 for entry to this little-visited and incredible site. However, there is rarely anyone there to collect the money if you enter from the path climbing up from the river.

A rough dirt road enters Salinas from above (giving spectacular views) but it is hard to find drivers who know the route. Milla Turismo in Cuzco can provide a vehicle and driver but it's not cheap. Also, you can hike in from Moray.

MORAY
The experimental agricultural terraces of Moray are fascinating. Different levels of terraces are carved into a huge bowl, part of which occurred naturally and part of which was further excavated by the Incas. The terraces supposedly have varied microclimates depending on how deep into the bowl they are, and so they were thought to have been used by the Incas to discover in which conditions their crops would grow most successfully. There are two large bowls and one small bowl each ringed by terraces. Some restoration work began in 1994 and a small on-site museum is planned.

This site is challenging to reach. First, catch a bus or get a ride up the steep road from Urubamba, across the river toward Chincheros. Ask the driver to drop you at the road to Maras. From here, take a track about 3 km to the village of Maras, then follow the trail a further 7 km to Moray. Ask locals for directions. The only facilities in Maras are very basic stores, so you should be self-sufficient.

It is possible to drive to Moray. The road is extremely rough and takes about 13 km from the paved Urubamba-Chinchero highway. You need high clearance and a driver who knows the route – not many do. Milla Turismo in Cuzco organizes tours there; again, not cheap.

From Moray you can continue on to Salinas, about 6 km away, and on down to Urubamba. This would be a long but satisfying day. There are usually workers in Moray who can point out the trail.

OLLANTAYTAMBO

This is the end of the road as far as the Sacred Valley is concerned. Like Pisac, Ollantaytambo is a major Inca site at which you use the Cuzco Visitor Ticket. (You can buy a single-entry ticket to Ollantaytambo at the ruins; this costs US$2, but it may go up soon.) The site, a massive fortress, is one of the few places where the Spanish lost a major battle during the conquest. Below the ruins is the village of Ollantaytambo, built on traditional Inca foundations and the best surviving example of Inca city planning. The village was divided into blocks called *canchas*, each cancha with just one entrance leading into a courtyard. Individual houses were entered from this courtyard, not directly from the street.

The huge, steep terraces guarding the Inca fortress are spectacular and bring gasps of admiration from visitors arriving in the square below. Ollantaytambo is the fortress to which Manco Inca retreated after his defeat at Sacsayhuaman. In 1536, Hernando Pizarro led a force of 70 cavalry here, supported by large numbers of native and Spanish foot soldiers, in an attempt to capture the Inca. The steep terracing was highly defensible and Pizarro's men found themselves continuously showered with arrows, spears, stones and boulders. They were unable to climb the terraces and were further hampered when the Inca, in a brilliant move, flooded the plain below the fortress through previously prepared channels. The Spaniards' horses had difficulty maneuvering in the water and Pizarro decided to beat a hasty retreat. This almost became a rout when the conquistadors were followed down the valley by thousands of the victorious Inca's soldiers.

Manco Inca's victory was short lived;

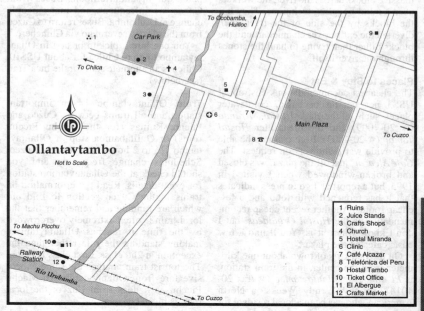

Ollantaytambo

Not to Scale

To Ocobamba, Huilloc
To Chilca
To Cuzco
To Machu Picchu
To Cuzco
Railway Station
Río Urubamba
Car Park
Main Plaza

1 Ruins
2 Juice Stands
3 Crafts Shops
4 Church
5 Hostal Miranda
6 Clinic
7 Café Alcazar
8 Telefónica del Peru
9 Hostal Tambo
10 Ticket Office
11 El Albergue
12 Crafts Market

CUZCO AREA

soon afterward, the Spanish forces in Cuzco were relieved by the return of a large Chilean expedition and Ollantaytambo was again attacked, this time with a cavalry force over four times the size of that used in the first attack. Manco Inca retreated to his jungle stronghold in Vilcabamba, and Ollantaytambo became part of the Spanish Empire.

It is probable that the Incas themselves saw Ollantaytambo as a temple rather than as a fortress, but the Spanish called it a fortress and it has usually been referred to as such ever since. The temple area is at the top of the terracing. Some extremely well-built walls were under construction at the time of the conquest and have never been completed. The stone used for these buildings was quarried from the mountainside 6 km away, high above the opposite bank of the Río Urubamba. Transporting the huge stone blocks from the quarry to the site was a stupendous feat and involved the effort of thousands of Indian workers. To move the massive blocks across the river, the workers used a mind-boggling technique. They left the blocks by the side of the river, then diverted the entire river channel around the blocks rather than trying to haul the stones through the river itself.

Places to Stay & Eat

The cheapest accommodations cost about US$3 per person in basic, cold-water places such as the dark *Hostal Miranda* (☎ 20-4009) and the pleasanter *Hostal Tambo* (☎ 20-4003). Both claim to be able to provide warm showers on request. The *Café Alcazar*, just off the plaza, was closed and broken-windowed when I visited in 1995, but a report as I go to press indicates that it has reopened with food and a few cheap rooms. Another recent cheap recommendation is the *Hostal Orquideas*, but I don't know where it is. You'll find a few basic cafés on the plaza.

On the outskirts of town about one kilometer from the center, in the train station, is *El Albergue Ollantaytambo* (☎ /fax 20-4014), run by Wendy Weeks, a North American who has been a local resident for over two decades. It is a very clean, pleasant, rustic hostal with hot showers, a lovely garden and a sauna. Rates are US$15 per person in singles, doubles and triples, with room for a maximum of 16 guests. Breakfast is available for about US$4, lunches at US$5 and dinners by advance request for about US$10. During the June to September season, El Albergue Ollantaytambo is often full, so don't rely on just showing up. Reservations are accepted.

Recently, the cheaper *Albergue Kapuly* has opened next door to the Albergue Ollantaytambo. I don't know if it's any good, but it is a different place. Readers' comments are welcomed.

Getting There & Away

You can get to Ollantaytambo from Cuzco by either bus or train, but you must use the train if you want to go on to Machu Picchu.

Bus Minibuses leave from Urubamba's gas station several times a day, but services peter out in midafternoon. Buses from Cuzco are infrequent, and many people change in Urubamba. Buses return to Cuzco from the plaza – several go via Chinchero.

You can hire a pickup or taxi in Ollantaytambo to go to Chilca for about US$10. Chilca is an alternate start for the Inca Trail (see below).

Train Ollantaytambo is an important station and all trains between Cuzco and Puente Ruinas (for the Machu Picchu ruins) or Quillabamba stop at Ollantaytambo 1½ to 2 hours after leaving Cuzco. Schedules change frequently and you should check at the Ollantaytambo station for exact details. Read the information on trains in the Cuzco section to find out which are running and remember that the local train is often extremely overcrowded by the time it reaches Ollantaytambo, making standing the rule rather than the exception in 2nd class. First class is better. The tourist train charges the same expensive fare from Ollantaytambo to Machu Picchu as it does from Cuzco; the local train is much cheaper.

CHINCHERO

Access to Chinchero requires a Cuzco Visitor Ticket. The site combines Inca ruins with an Andean Indian village, a colonial country church, wonderful mountain views and a colorful Sunday market.

The Inca ruins, consisting mainly of terracing, are not as spectacular as those at Pisac but are interesting nevertheless. If you walk away from the village through the terraces on the right-hand side of the valley, you'll find various rocks that have been carved into seats and staircases.

On the opposite side of the valley, a clear trail climbs upward before heading north and down to the Urubamba river valley about four hours away. At the river, the trail turns left (downstream) and continues to a bridge at Huayllabamba where you can cross the river. From here, the Sacred Valley road will take you to Calca (turn right, about 13 km) or Urubamba (turn left, about 9 km). You can flag down a bus until midafternoon.

The main village square features a massive Inca wall with 10 huge, trapezoidal niches. The colonial church just above the main square is built on Inca foundations. The church is in regular use but lack of funds has prevented restoration, and it's interesting to compare its interior to those of the highly restored churches of Cuzco.

The Sunday market is marginally less touristy than the Pisac market. There are two markets. One, in front of the old church, sells crafts and sweaters for tourists. Prices in the craft section are similar to those in Pisac or Cuzco, but it's good to see many of the local people still dressed in traditional garb. This is not done just for the tourists – if you come midweek when there is no market and few tourists, you'll still see the women dressed in traditional clothing.

The other market, held at the bottom of the village (you can't miss it), is the local produce market, which is important to inhabitants of surrounding villages.

Both markets are held to a smaller extent on other days, especially Thursday.

Places to Stay & Eat

There are no hotels at this time, though there has been one in the past. There are some basic places to eat.

Getting There & Away

Buses leave Cuzco from Avenida Tullumayo a few times each day, some continuing to Urubamba or even Ollantaytambo. Buses also go from the plazas in Urubamba and Ollantaytambo to Chinchero.

The Inca Trail & Machu Picchu

THE INCA TRAIL

The Inca Trail is the best known and most popular hike on the continent and is walked by thousands of people every year. Many of these adventurers are not prepared for the trip, though every guidebook to South America at least describes the trail and most provide a map. If walking to Machu Picchu is a lifelong ambition, go ahead and enjoy yourself – it certainly is an exceptional hike. The views of snowcapped mountains and high cloud forest can be lstupendous, weather permitting. Walking from one beautiful ruin to the next is a mystical and unforgettable experience. If you are an experienced backpacker looking for solitude or remote mountain villages, however, then I suggest hiking any one of the many other available trails.

Conservation

If you decide that the Inca Trail is not to be missed, please don't defecate in the ruins, don't leave garbage anywhere, don't damage the stonework by building fires against the walls (it blackens and, worse still, cracks the rocks), don't use a wood fire for cooking (the trail has been badly deforested over the past decade) and don't pick the orchids and other plants in this national park. I'm sure that 99% of readers would never consider doing any of these things but there always seems to be one

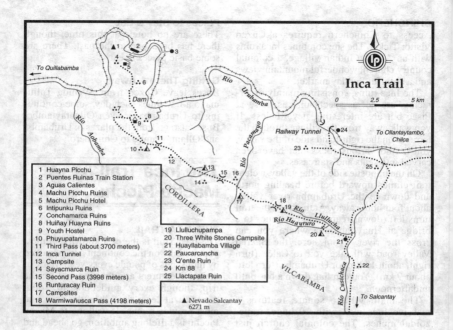

Inca Trail

0   2.5   5 km

To Quillabamba

Río Urubamba

Río Pacaymayo

Railway Tunnel

To Ollantaytambo,
Chilca

Dam

Río Aobamba

CORDILLERA

Río Llulucha

Río Huayruro

VILCABAMBA

Río Cusichaca

To Salcantay

1   Huayna Picchu
2   Puentes Ruinas Train Station
3   Aguas Calientes
4   Machu Picchu Ruins
5   Machu Picchu Hotel
6   Intipunku Ruins
7   Conchamarca Ruins
8   Huiñay Huayna Ruins
9   Youth Hostel
10 Phuyupatamarca Ruins
11 Third Pass (about 3700 meters)
12 Inca Tunnel
13 Campsite
14 Sayacmarca Ruin
15 Second Pass (3998 meters)
16 Runturacay Ruin
17 Campsites
18 Warmiwañusca Pass (4198 meters)

19 Llulluchupampa
20 Three White Stones Campsite
21 Huayllabamba Village
22 Paucarcancha
23 Q'ente Ruin
24 Km 88
25 Llactapata Ruin

▲ Nevado Salcantay
6271 m

person in a hundred who will thoughtlessly cause more damage than the other 99.

The South American Explorers Club organized an Inca Trail clean-up in 1980 and collected about 400 kg of unburnable garbage. Other clean-up campaigns since then have recorded similar figures. See Tours below for information about joining an Inca Trail clean-up trek. Please remove your empty cans and other rubbish and bury your feces away from the trail and water sources.

Preparation

You should take a stove (wood is scarce), a sleeping pad and warm bag, and a tent or other protection against the rain. All this equipment can be rented inexpensively in Cuzco, but check rental gear carefully as many rented tents leak badly. Also bring insect repellent, sunblock lotion, water purification tablets or iodine and basic first-aid supplies. I know of people who have hiked the Inca Trail with a sheet of plastic

and a bag of peanuts. Fine. They can go hungry and freeze if they want to but such behavior is irresponsible and foolish. The trek takes three full days (though a leisurely four is more fun), temperatures can drop below freezing at night, and it rains even in the May to September dry season. In the wettest months (January to April) trails can be a real mud slog. There is nowhere to buy food. The ruins are roofless and provide no shelter. Caves marked on some maps are usually wet, dirty overhangs. Although the total distance is only 33 km, there are three high passes to be crossed, one of which reaches a height of 4200 meters. The trail is often steep, so don't be lulled into a false sense of security by the relatively short distance. One reader called it 'the Inca Trial.' Hike prepared.

You can obtain detailed maps and information from the South American Explorers Club in Lima as well as from trekking agencies and the tourist office in Cuzco.

CUZCO AREA

Some maps do not include the new section of trail joining Phuyupatamarca with Huiñay Huayna or the newly excavated ruins of Conchamarca. Most maps do not have contours marked on them. The trail is fairly obvious for most of the way and it's difficult to get lost, especially if you carry a compass. The map in this book is perfectly adequate. There have been occasional reports of robberies on the trail, and you are advised not to travel alone and never leave gear unattended. The dry season from June to September is the most popular time and the most crowded. For the rest of the year the trail is fairly empty but also very wet – the mud can be 30 cm deep for long stretches.

Trail Fee
It costs about US$17 per person to hike the Inca Trail, which includes a one-day entrance to Machu Picchu (itself a US$10 expense). If taking a guided trek, check to see if this fee is included. This fee may increase in the future.

The Hike
It is interesting to note that various translations of Quechua names are possible and that those most frequently given are not necessarily the best or most accurate. Anthropologist Cristina Kessler-Noble has provided some interesting variations.

Most people begin the trail from the railway stop at Km 88 (see Getting There & Away). However, it is also possible to begin at the village of Chilca (accessible by train, by road from Ollantaytambo, or by river raft), from where a relatively flat five-hour hike along the south side of the Río Urubamba brings you to the Inca Trail at the Llactapata Ruins. It is also possible to begin at Mollepata, spend three or four days hiking past the magnificent glacier-clad Salcantay, and join the Inca Trail at Huayllabamba. Operators in Cuzco can arrange these options, or consult Bradt's *Backpacking & Trekking in Peru & Bolivia*. The description below is the standard hike from Km 88.

After crossing the Río Urubamba at Km 88 (2200 meters) and taking care of trail fees and registration formalities, you can either turn right (west) to see the little-visited site of Q'ente, or 'hummingbird,' one kilometer away, or turn left and begin the Inca Trail as it climbs gently through a eucalyptus grove for about one kilometer. You will see the minor ruin of Llactapata, or 'town on hillside,' to your right and soon cross the Río Cusichaca, or 'joyful bridge,' on a footbridge before heading south along the east bank of the river. Although there are camping possibilities just before Llactapata, most people elect to keep going to beyond the village of Huayllabamba, or 'grassy plain,' on the first day. It's about 6 km along the river to the village, climbing gently all the way and recrossing the river

Inca Trail Tours

Many adventure travel companies in the USA offer Inca Trail treks. This is the most expensive way to go but all the logistics and equipment are organized in advance. I have led treks for Wilderness Travel (☎ 800-247-6700, 510-548-0420, fax 510-548-0347), 801 Allston Way, Berkeley, CA 94710, USA, for many years and recommend them. There are several other good companies. If you'd like to go on an organized trek that includes an Inca Trail clean-up campaign, contact the Earth Preservation Fund, affiliated with Wildland Adventures (☎ 800-345-4453, 206-365-0686, fax 206-363-6615), 3516 NE 155th St, Seattle, WA 98155, USA. A 10-day trip to the Cuzco area, including four nights of trekking/clean up, costs about US$1300 plus air fare.

If you arrive without a previously organized trek, there are several options. You can hike with what you can carry on your back or you can hire porters, guides and cooks from an adventure travel agency in Cuzco. Some budget travelers hire just one porter to carry a pack, and this is inexpensive.

Guided tours are available from many outfitters in Cuzco from about US$60 and up per person. This includes the local train to the beginning of the trail at Km 88, a tent, food, a porter, a cook and entrance to the ruins. While this may seem like a good deal, consider the following. The lowest costs mean that the porters are not provided with camping equipment and food, and so have to fend for themselves. This leads to them cooking and warming themselves with scarce wood from the already badly damaged woodlands. The cheap guided tours generally have no idea of ecologically sensitive camping, and the result is garbage left everywhere. Some outfitters make no attempt to carry out garbage, bury shit or safeguard the delicate Andean woodlands. It has been over a decade since I first hiked the trail, and the degradation of the route and the ruins is clear. Do whatever you can to preserve this hike.

There are no easy solutions. You can rent gear in Cuzco (or use your own), avoid guided trips, and camp as cleanly as possible. You can even pack out garbage that you

after about 4 km. You can buy bottled drinks in houses near this bridge. Look over your shoulder for views of the snowcapped Veronica, 5750 meters above sea level.

Huayllabamba, at an elevation of about 2750 meters, is a village near the fork of the Llullucha (a Quechuan word for a type of herb) and Cusichaca Rivers. You cross Río Llullucha on a log bridge. It is possible to camp in the plaza in front of the school, but beware of thieves slitting your tent at night. Huayllabamba has a reputation for thievery. If you want to get away from the crowds, continue south (away from the Inca Trail) along the Cusichaca to the ruins of Paucarcancha about 3 km away. You can camp here, though if you do so, you'll need to carry water up from the river and watch your camp – Huayllabamba is not far away.

The Inca Trail itself climbs steeply up along the south bank of the Río Llullucha.

After a walk of about an hour, the river forks. Continue up the left fork for a few hundred meters, then cross the river on a log bridge. There are several flat campsites on both sides of the bridge. The area is known as 'three white stones,' but I've never worked out which boulders are referred to. This site could be your first camp, although there are bugs and local kids to bother you. If you have the energy, push on.

The trail turns right beyond the log bridge and sweeps back to the Llullucha. It is a long, very steep climb to the Warmiwañusca, or 'dead woman's,' Pass. At 4198 meters above sea level, this pass is the highest point of the trek, but there are campsites before it. Some people prefer to rest for the night at the Three White Stones campsite to further acclimatize before making the ascent. The trail passes through cloud forest for about 1½ hours before encounter. You can go on an expensive guided trip organized by companies used by international adventure travel companies. At least these folks make some effort to camp cleanly and provide adequate facilities for porters. They also contribute to Inca Trail clean-up campaigns and sometimes will advertise their own clean-up hikes, usually at the beginning or end of the dry season. Or you can use the cheap outfitters and insist on clean camping by setting an example and ensuring that there is enough fuel and tentage for the porters.

A recent letter reports that some travelers talked to an inexpensive agency and asked to go on a trek with a good guide and a small group. 'No problem!' Unfortunately, once they arrived at the trailhead, they found that several agencies had lumped their 'small groups' together, and there were now 23 tourists plus porters, cooks and a guide. The guide was strong, fit and acclimatized, and strode off down the trail leaving the tourists to find the way for themselves. He provided little information. Whatever an agency says, if you pay low prices you can't expect high-quality services – though you might get lucky. If you want a top-notch guide, good food and equipment and a small group, expect to pay as much as US$200 to US$300.

Another report suggests that you should make it clear if you don't want to carry anything. Some agencies ask that you carry 'a small day pack,' which ends up being your regular backpack, so clarify this. Find out how many people sleep in tents – two, three, or . . . ? Make your wishes clear and get them in writing and keep reconfirming them at every opportunity.

A third group reported paying US$70 per person for a trip that included new tents, simple but filling meals, all train/entrance fees and a good guide. So shop around and ask a lot of questions. I have received more negative than good reports about cheap Inca Trail treks.

It is normal to tip guides, cooks and porters. Don't forget the porters – they are woefully underpaid and work the hardest of all. Tip them as well as you are able. ■

emerging on the high, bare mountain. At some points the trail and stream bed become one, so be prepared for wet feet. Although the trail climbs steeply there are a couple of small, flat areas in the forest where you could camp. After emerging from the forest, you reach Llulluchupampa, a flat area above the forest where water is available and camping is good, though it is very cold at night. This is as far as you can reasonably expect to get on your first day from Km 88. It takes from four to nine hours, depending on your fitness, acclimatization and load.

From Llulluchupampa follow the left-hand side of the valley for the two to three hour climb to Warmiwañusca Pass. It takes longer than you'd expect because the altitude slows you down.

From Warmiwañusca, you can see the Río Pacamayo, or 'sunrise river' far below and the ruin of Runturacay halfway up the hill, above the river. The trail descends to the river where there are good campsites. There are guards from the Instituto Nacional de Cultura staying here. The downward climb is long, taking over an hour, and is a strain on the knees. People with knee problems may take longer. At an altitude of about 3600 meters, the trail crosses the river over a small footbridge – don't venture too far into the vegetation below.

Climb to the right toward Runturacay, or 'egg hut,' an oval-shaped ruin with superb views about an hour's walk above the river. You can also camp here, and a few minutes away from the ruins, to your left as you look out into the valley, there is a trickle of water. On one visit, I found that previous campers had left this ruin in an unsavory condition. Recently, it was better, perhaps because of the work of the nearby guards.

Above Runturacay, the trail climbs to a

CUZCO AREA

false summit before continuing past two small lakes to the top of the second pass at 3998 meters, about an hour above Runturacay. If it's clear, there are views of the snowcapped Cordillera Vilcabamba. The clear trail descends past another lake to the ruin of Sayacmarca, or 'dominant town,' which is visible from the trail one kilometer before you reach it. The site, a tightly constructed town on a small mountain spur, is the most impressive of those seen along the trail so far and offers superb views. A long, steep staircase to the left of the trail leads to the site. The trail itself continues downward and crosses the headwaters of the Río Aobamba, or 'wavy plain,' 3600 meters above sea level. There is enough room here for a small campsite, but the ground is boggy after rain.

As the trail goes through some beautiful cloud forest on the gentle climb to the third pass, you'll find a causeway across a swampy, dried-out lake and, farther on, a tunnel, both Inca constructions. The highest point of the pass, at almost 3700 meters, is not very obvious. There are great views of the Urubamba Valley from here. You soon reach the beautiful ruin of Phuyupatamarca, or 'town above the clouds,' about 3650 meters above sea level and approximately two or three hours beyond Sayacmarca.

Phuyupatamarca has been well restored and contains a beautiful series of ceremonial baths with water running through them (purify it before drinking). A ridge above the baths offers camping sites with spectacular views. There are sometimes camp guards here.

From Phuyupatamarca, the newly opened (1985) section of the Inca Trail is much shorter than the old route that traverses the mountain. The new section makes a dizzying dive into the cloud forest below, following an incredibly well engineered flight of many hundreds of Inca steps. This route is by far the more interesting of the two but is not marked on some older maps. It rejoins the old trail near the electric power pylons built down the hill to the dam on the Río Urubamba.

Follow the pylons down to a red-roofed, white hotel that provides youth hostel-type facilities for about US$5 per bed (there are 16), much less if you sleep on the floor. Hot showers (US$1.25), meals (US$3.50) and bottled drinks (US$1.25) are available and camping is possible nearby. The hostal is sometimes full in the high season but making a reservation is problematic. Ask in Cuzco travel agencies or the tourist office. A 500-meter trail behind the hotel leads to the beautiful Inca site of Huiñay Huayna, which cannot be seen from the hotel. This ruin is about a two- to three-hour descent from Phuyupatamarca.

Huiñay Huayna is normally translated as 'forever young' but a much more attractive translation was explained to me. As Huiñay is the Quechua infinitive for 'to plant the earth,' a more accurate translation may be 'to plant the earth, young,' perhaps a reference to the young, springtime earth of planting time. From planting comes growing; thus one has 'growing young,' as opposed to 'growing old,' and hence the popular catch-all translation 'forever young.' Peter Frost, meanwhile, writes that the name is Quechua for an orchid that blooms here. There are, no doubt, several other variations on the translation theme.

Whatever it means, this exquisite little place warrants the short side trip and an hour or two of exploration. Climb down to the lowest part of the town where it tapers off into a tiny and very exposed ledge overlooking the Río Urubamba far below. The very difficult climb down to the Urubamba is prohibited. The land is owned by the electric company and there are no trails.

About a kilometer above the hotel and Huiñay Huayna is Conchamarca, a recently discovered terraced ruin excavated in 1993. It can now be visited.

From Huiñay Huayna, the trail contours around through the cliff-hanging cloud forest and is very thin in places, so watch your step. It takes about two hours to reach Intipunku, or 'gate of the sun,' the penultimate site on the trail and the last point on the Inca Trail where you're allowed to camp. There's no water and there is room for only a couple of tents, so guided tours can't camp here. You'll get your first view of Machu Picchu from here.

The descent from Intipunku to Machu Picchu takes almost an hour. Backpacks are not allowed into the ruins, and immediately upon arrival, park guards ask you to check your pack at the lower entrance gate and have your trail permit stamped. It is rather a brusque return to rules and regulations when all you want to do is quietly explore the ruins. The pass is only valid for the day it is stamped, so try to arrive in the morning. Sometimes, you can persuade the guards to stamp it for the next day.

After you've explored the ruins, you can stay at the expensive hotel near the site, or camp by the river far below (see Machu Picchu), or take the 8-km road (buses are available) to the village of Aguas Calientes where there are cheap hotels and restaurants (see Aguas Calientes). You can also take the afternoon train and be in Cuzco, Ollantaytambo or Quillabamba by evening.

Getting There & Away
Most people take the train from Cuzco to Km 88. The tourist train and autovagon don't normally stop here (though, if you pay the full fare to Machu Picchu and make arrangements, you may be able to get off here from the tourist train or autovagon). Most hikers take the local train. It has a well-deserved reputation for thievery – watch your pack like a hawk and be particularly aware of thieves working in groups, some distracting your attention while others snatch your camera, slash your pack or pick your pockets, particularly in 2nd class. It's not too bad if you are in a group and watch one another's stuff.

One reader suggests going on to Aguas Calientes and then returning the next day on the first train. This gets you to Km 88 over an hour earlier than taking the first train from Cuzco. Make sure the conductor knows you are getting off at Km 88, because this is not a regular stop.

Either way, ask where to get off because,

although everyone knows the stop, it is very small and badly marked. At Km 88, you cross the river; there is now a footbridge as well as the curious ski lift-type contraption that used to be the only way across. At the river you have to either buy a US$17 trail permit (cash dollars or nuevos soles, have the right change) or present one obtained from the Ministerio de Cultura in Cuzco. It's easier to buy it at the trailhead (but check with the Cuzco tourist office for the latest of the ever-changing regulations and permit fees). You're ready to begin the walk.

Doing the hike in reverse (from Machu Picchu to Km 88) is officially not permitted. However, I have received a report that you can hike back as far as the hotel in Huiñay Huayna, overnight there, return, and pay for just one day at Machu Picchu plus a US$1.50 trail fee.

MACHU PICCHU
Machu Picchu is South America's best known and most spectacular archaeological site. During the busy, dry-season months of June to September, up to a thousand people a day come to visit the Lost City of the Incas, as it's popularly known. (This number dropped substantially during the early 1990s because of the general drop in tourist activity due to terrorism, but tourism is now returning.) Despite the huge tourist influx, the site manages to retain its air of grandeur and mystery and is considered a must for all visitors to Peru.

History
Machu Picchu is both the best and the least known of the Inca ruins. It is not mentioned in any of the chronicles of the Spanish conquistadors and archaeologists today can do no more than speculate on its function. Although Machu Picchu was known to a handful of Quechua peasants who farmed the area, the outside world was unaware of its existence until the American historian Hiram Bingham stumbled on it almost by accident on July 24, 1911. Bingham's search was for the lost city of Vilcabamba,

the last stronghold of the Incas, and at Machu Picchu he thought he had found it. We now know that the remote and inaccessible ruins at Espíritu Pampa, much deeper in the jungle, are the remains of Vilcabamba. Machu Picchu remains a mysterious site, never revealed to the conquering Spaniards and virtually forgotten until the early part of this century.

The site discovered in 1911 was very different from the one we see today. All the buildings were thickly overgrown with vegetation, and Bingham's team had to be content with roughly mapping the site. Bingham returned in 1912 and 1915 to carry out the difficult task of clearing the thick forest from the ruins, and he also discovered some of the ruins on the Inca Trail. Peruvian archaeologist Luis E Valcárcel undertook further studies and clearing in 1934, as did a Peruvian-American expedition under Paul Fejos in 1940-41. Despite these and more recent studies, knowledge of Machu Picchu remains sketchy. Over 50 burial sites were discovered containing over a hundred skeletal remains, about 80% female. An early theory that it was a city of chosen women who catered to the Incas' needs has lost support, and it is now thought that Machu Picchu was already an uninhabited, forgotten city at the time of the conquest. This would explain why it wasn't mentioned to the Spaniards. It is obvious from the exceptionally high quality of the stonework and the abundance of ornamental rather than practical sites that Machu Picchu must once have been an important ceremonial center.

There have been reports of new finds in the area. One, in the early 1980s, was of some burial sites on Huayna Picchu mountain. Another, in late 1986, involved the exciting discovery of a city about twice the size of Machu Picchu and 5 km north of it, according to a Peruvian government spokesperson. Local and US archaeologists have named the city Maranpampa (or Mandorpampa). Neither of the new sites is easily accessible to the general public at this time, though there are plans to eventually open Maranpampa to tourists.

Admission

The site is open daily. Hours vary from season to season but they are always open from 7.30 am to 5 pm. They may open as early as 6 am and close as late as 6 pm. Generally, I've found that if you arrive before the gate is open, you can find someone to open it by knocking at the office on the left a short distance before the gate.

Because the site is surrounded by high mountains, you can see sunrise and sunset over the ruins during visiting hours, though it's already broad daylight when the sun comes up over the surrounding mountains. The changes in color and light early and late in the day are very beautiful.

Machu Picchu is Peru's showpiece site and entrance fees are correspondingly high. Foreigners pay about US$10 for a single day's visit and there's no longer any student discount. The site is exceptionally difficult to enter other than through the gate and the guards (who wear hard hats) are very vigilant, so resign yourself to paying. If you want to visit the ruins for two days, the second day costs only US$5. Peruvian visitors pay only a small fraction of this price. For some years, it has been illegal for foreigners to be charged more than Peruvians for any services. Machu Picchu, however, appears to have been able to sidestep these regulations.

Many visitors buy a Machu Picchu combined-ticket book from one of the tourist agencies in Cuzco. This includes round-trip tickets for the tourist train, the bus to and from the ruins, admission to the ruins and lunch at the Machu Picchu Hotel. Make sure your ticket contains all these sections and shop around. The combined ticket costs about US$90, depending on the agency. Many agencies will also provide an English-speaking guide. This ticket doesn't enable you to cut corners by, for example, traveling on the cheaper local train or bringing a sandwich lunch, but if you want to go 1st class all the way, consider the combined-ticket book to save

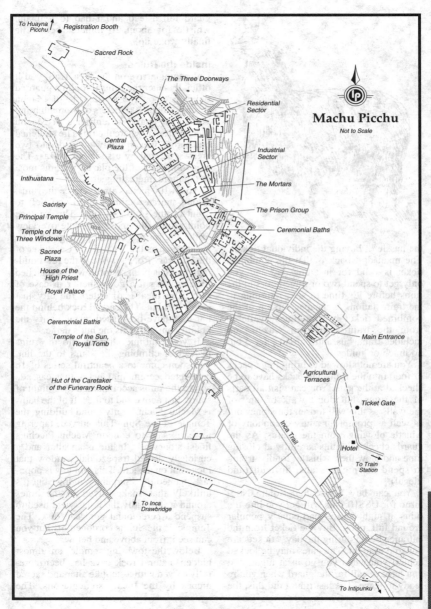

To Huayna Picchu

Registration Booth

Sacred Rock

The Three Doorways

Residential Sector

Machu Picchu

Not to Scale

Central Plaza

Industrial Sector

Intihuatana

The Mortars

Sacristy

The Prison Group

Principal Temple

Temple of the Three Windows

Ceremonial Baths

Sacred Plaza

House of the High Priest

Royal Palace

Ceremonial Baths

Temple of the Sun, Royal Tomb

Main Entrance

Hut of the Caretaker of the Funerary Rock

Agricultural Terraces

Ticket Gate

Inca Trail

Hotel

To Train Station

To Inca Drawbridge

To Intipunku

Alpaca

the hassle of buying the individual tickets. The main drawback is that the combined ticket is valid for just one day and you only get to spend two or three hours in the ruins before it's time to start returning to the train station. A cheaper version of the combined ticket is sometimes available from the train station in Cuzco and includes train, bus and entrance fees, but no lunch or guides.

You are not allowed to bring large packs or food into the ruins and packs have to be checked at the gate. You can visit all parts of the ruins, but don't walk on any of the walls as this will loosen the stonework as well as prompt an angry cacophony of whistle blowing from the guards. As the guards check the ruins carefully at closing time and blow their whistles loudly, trying to spend the night is also difficult (and illegal).

You can buy a so-called Boleto Nocturno for US$10; this will get you into the ruins at night and is particularly popular around full moon. Buy the ticket from the entrance booth during the day – tickets are not sold at night. The gates may be locked behind you when you go in at night, and you have to call for the guard when you're ready to leave. The last time I did this, the guard fell asleep and I had to yell and whistle for about 20 minutes before he finally woke up!

Inside the Ruins

Unless you arrive on the Inca Trail, you'll officially enter the ruins through a guarded ticket gate on the south side of Machu Picchu. About 100 meters of footpath bring you to the mazelike entrance of Machu Picchu proper, where the ruins lie stretched out before you, roughly divided into two areas separated by a series of plazas. The area to the left of the plazas contains most of the more interesting sites.

About 100 meters after you see the ruins, a long staircase climbs up to your left to a hut on the southeast spur. This vantage point affords the most complete overview of the site for that classic photograph. The hut, known as the 'Hut of the Caretaker of the Funerary Rock,' is one of the few buildings that has been restored with a thatched roof, making it a good shelter in case of rain. The Inca Trail enters the city just below this hut. The carved rock behind the hut may have been used to mummify the nobility and explains the hut's name.

If you continue straight into the ruins instead of climbing the stairs to the hut, you soon come to a beautiful series of 16 connected ceremonial baths that cascade across the ruins accompanied by a flight of stairs. Just above and to the left of the baths is Machu Picchu's only round building, the Temple of the Sun. This curved, tapering tower is said to contain Machu Picchu's finest stonework. Inside is an altar and a curiously drilled trapezoidal window that looks out on the site. This window is popularly named the 'Serpent Window' but it's unlikely that snakes lived in the holes around it. Probably the holes were used to suspend a ceremonial gold sun disk. The Temple of the Sun is cordoned off but you can see it from above and below.

Below the towering temple, an almost hidden, natural rock cave has been carefully carved with a steplike altar and sacred niches by the Inca's stonemasons. The mummies discovered at this site inspired its name – the Royal Tomb.

Climbing the stairs above the ceremonial baths, you reach a flat area of jumbled rocks, once used as a quarry. Turn right at the top of the stairs and walk across the quarry on a short path leading to the four-sided Sacred Plaza. The far side contains a small lookout platform with a curved wall and a beautiful view of the snowcapped Cordillera Vilcabamba in the far distance. Below, you can see the Río Urubamba and the modern buildings of a hydroelectric project. The remaining three sides of the Sacred Plaza are flanked by important buildings. The Temple of the Three Windows commands an impressive view of the plaza below through the huge, trapezoidal windows that give the building its name. With this temple behind you, the Principal Temple is to your right. Its name derives from the massive solidity and perfection of its construction. The damage to the rear right corner of the temple is the result of the ground settling below this corner rather than any inherent weakness in the masonry itself. Opposite the Principal Temple is the House of the High Priest, though archaeologists cannot say with certainty who, if anyone, lived in this building.

Behind and connected to the Principal Temple lies a famous small building called the Sacristy. It has many well-carved niches, perhaps used for the storage of ceremonial objects, as well as a carved stone bench. The Sacristy is especially known for the two rocks flanking its entrance; each is said to contain 32 angles, but I come up with a different number whenever I count them!

A staircase behind the Sacristy climbs a small hill to the major shrine in Machu Picchu, the Intihuatana. This Quechua word loosely translates as the 'hitching post of the sun' and refers to the carved rock pillar, often mistakenly called a sun dial, which stands at the top of the Intihuatana hill. This rock was not used in telling the time of day but, rather, the time of year. The Inca's astronomers were able to predict the solstices using the angles of the pillar. Thus the Inca, who was the son of the sun, was able to claim control over the return of the lengthening summer days. Exactly how the pillar was used for these astronomical purposes remains unclear, but its elegant simplicity is remarked upon by many modern observers. It is recorded that there were several of these Intihuatanas in various important Inca sites, but all with the known exception of this one were smashed by the Spaniards in an attempt to wipe out what they considered to be the blasphemy of sun worship.

At the back of the Intihuatana is another staircase. It descends to the Central Plaza, which separates the important sites of the Intihuatana, Sacred Plaza and Temple of the Sun from the more mundane areas opposite. At the lower end of this opposite area is the Prison Group, a labyrinthian complex of cells, niches and passageways both under and above ground. The centerpiece of the group is a carving of the head of a condor, the natural rocks behind it resembling the bird's outstretched wings. Behind the condor is a well-like hole and, at the bottom of this, the door to a tiny underground cell that can only be entered by bending double. This was being excavated in 1995.

Above the Prison Group is the largest section of the ruins, the Industrial & Residential Sectors. These buildings are less well constructed and had more mundane purposes than those across the plaza.

Walks near Machu Picchu

Several fairly short walks can be taken starting from and returning to the ruins, the most famous of which is the climb up the steep mountain of Huayna Picchu at the back of the ruins. Huayna Picchu is normally translated as 'young peak,' but it is interesting to note that picchu, with the correct glottal pronunciation, refers to the wad in the cheek of a coca-chewing, Quechua-speaking mountain dweller – the wad looks like a little peak in the cheek.

Huayna Picchu At first glance, it would appear that Huayna Picchu is a difficult climb, but there is a well-maintained trail; although the ascent is steep, it's not technically difficult. You begin by walking to the very end of the Central Plaza and turning right between two open-fronted buildings. Just beyond is a registration booth where you have to sign in; it's only open until about 1 pm. The one hour climb (less if you are athletic and fit) takes you through a short section of Inca tunnel. The view from the top is spectacular, but if you lack either time or energy, I think the view from the Hut of the Caretaker of the Funerary Rock is equally good.

Another walk begins with a climb part of the way up Huayna Picchu. About 10 minutes from the lowest point of the trail, a thin path plunges down to your left. It is possible to continue down the rear of Huayna Picchu along a recently cleared trail to the small Temple of the Moon. The trail is easy to follow, but involves steep up and down sections, a ladder, and an overhanging cave where you have to bend over to get by. The descent takes about an hour and the ascent back to the main Huayna Picchu trail rather longer. The spectacular trail drops and climbs steeply as it hugs the sides of Huayna Picchu before plunging into the cloud forest for a while. Suddenly, you reach a cleared area where the small, very well made ruins are found. Unfortunately, they are marred by graffiti.

From the Temple of the Moon, a newly cleared path leads up behind the ruin and steeply on up the back side of Huaynu Picchu. It was almost finished when I tried it in 1995 and should be open by the time you read this.

Inca Drawbridge On the other side of the ruins, a much less steep and very scenic walk from the Hut of the Caretaker of the Funerary Rock takes you past the top of the terraces and out along a narrow, cliff-clinging trail to the Inca drawbridge. The trail is marked; there is also a registration booth at which you're supposed to register before 3 pm, but its opening hours are

erratic. The 20-minute walk gives you a good look at the vegetation of the high cloud forest and a different view of Machu Picchu. The drawbridge itself is less interesting than the walk to reach it. You are not allowed to walk right up to the bridge and have to be content with viewing it from behind a barrier about a hundred meters away. Someone crossed both the barrier and the bridge some years ago and fell to their death.

Intipunku The Inca Trail ends just below the Hut of the Caretaker of the Funerary Rock after its final descent from the notch in the horizon called Intipunku, or the 'gate of the sun.' Looking at the hill behind you as you enter the ruins, you can see both the trail and Intipunku. This hill, called Machu Picchu, or 'old peak,' gives the site its name. It takes about an hour to reach Intipunku, and if you can spare about a full half day for the roundtrip, it's possible to continue as far as Huiñay Huayna (see the Inca Trail).

Machu Picchu The ascent of the hill of Machu Picchu is the most difficult and rarely done cleared hike near the ruins. Take the Inca Trail for a few minutes and look for a trail to your right passing through a gap in the walls of the terraces. It's not very obvious and there's no sign. If you find the trail, it will be very overgrown, but you can force your way through the thick vegetation to the top of the peak. Allow well over an hour for the climb and be prepared for disappointment unless the trail has recently been cleared.

Places to Stay & Eat
The *Hotel Machu Picchu Ruinas* (☎ 21-1038, 21-1052; in Lima 221-0822/4/5/6, fax 440-6197, the Lima phone is hard to get through to) is the only place to stay at Machu Picchu itself. Rooms without a view cost US$147/172, rooms with mountain views cost US$192. (None have views of the ruins.) The rates almost doubled after privatization in 1995 and are expensive for what you get. Despite the expense, it's

often full, so reserve as far ahead as possible in the high season. You can sometimes get a room on the day you arrive, especially during the low season, but don't rely on it. During the low season, you can often book a room here in Cuzco with a day or two's notice, and rates as low as half of the above have reportedly been obtained. Rooms are clean and good-sized, but bland. The best thing about this hotel is the never-ending supply of hot water in the showers in every room.

You can camp cheaply at the campsite by the river about 200 meters from the railway station, 6 km from the ruins by road. Floodlights discourage theft but you shouldn't leave anything unattended. Washrooms with cold showers are available. This still leaves the problem of looking after your gear while visiting the ruins. There are backpack-storage facilities at the ruins entrance (US50¢ a bag) but you have to lug your gear up the hill first. Staying at Aguas Calientes (see below) is a better budget option.

The only place to eat at the ruins is in the hotel. The hotel restaurant serves expensive breakfast and supper, and a cafeteria on the patio offers overpriced self-service lunches with three courses and a drink for about US$15. During the busy season, lunch queues can be very long. There is also a souvenir shop/snack bar where you can buy bottled drinks for about the same price as in the cafeteria. Bring a packed lunch and water bottle if you want to economize. It's illegal to bring food into the ruins themselves because many tourists litter the site. Don't leave any rubbish whatsoever.

Cheap snacks and drinks can be purchased at the train station in the afternoon.

Getting There & Away
Most visitors take the expensive autovagon or tourist train from Cuzco, arriving at the Puente Ruinas train station about 3½ hours later. (Puente Ruinas is the nearest train station to Machu Picchu. The station in Aguas Calientes is misleadingly named Machu Picchu, but don't get off there.)

Alternatively, you can get a bus to Ollantaytambo and catch the train there, perhaps after overnighting in Urubamba or Ollantaytambo. The local train is the slowest and cheapest option and is preferred by budget travelers. See Cuzco for train times and fares.

The train journey begins with a climb out of Cuzco. Because it is too steep for normal railroad curves, this is accomplished in four back-and-forth zigzags. The tracks then drop gently through mainly agricultural countryside to the important station of Ollantaytambo, where all trains stop. From here, you can see Mount Veronica (5750 meters) to your right and the Río Urubamba to your left. The train descends down the narrow gorge with superb views of the very difficult white water of the lower Urubamba.

At Puente Ruinas station, you are about 2000 meters above sea level and roughly 700 meters below the ruins of Machu Picchu. A fleet of buses waits to take you up to the ruins on a 6-km road (the Hiram Bingham Hwy, opened in 1948), which zigzags thrillingly up the mountainside. One-way bus tickets cost about US$3 and can be obtained at the train station ticket office, across the platform facing the left-hand side of the train as you come in. (People with combined tickets have the return bus ticket to the ruins included.) There are enough buses to handle the crowds coming off the train.

If you're staying in Aguas Calientes, there are buses from there as well (see below). Otherwise, you'll have to walk. (Many budget travelers prefer this to paying US$3 for a 20-minute bus ride.) Rather than climb 6 km by road, the shorter and much steeper footpath is a better hike. Cross the bridge behind the train station and turn right. The path, marked by arrows, crosses the road at several points on the ascent, but the drivers will not normally stop for passengers at intermediate points. It's a 1½ hour climb from the station but the descent takes only a knee-straining 40 minutes. (Note that Peruvians are charged less for the bus. If you descend on a bus other than the ones rushing for the train, you can often bargain a more reasonable rate.)

The tourist trains leave for the return trip in the afternoon. Departure times vary according to the season – there may be one train at 3.30 pm, or another may be added if there is demand. The buses start descending from the ruins about 1 pm, and during the high season, bus lines can get very long. Buying tickets for the tourist train can be a bit of a problem as the seats are often fully booked by passengers on day trips from Cuzco.

If you have time, the most economical way to travel is on the local train or the Quillabamba autovagon to Aguas Calientes. Spend the night there, a full day at Machu Picchu ruins and another night at Aguas Calientes, then return on the local train. This avoids the tourist train completely and maximizes your time at the ruins.

The ruins are most heavily visited between about 10.30 am and 2.30 pm. As many tours combine visits of Machu Picchu with the Sunday markets at either Pisac or Chinchero, Sunday is fairly quiet, but Friday, Saturday and Monday are busy. June to August are the busiest months. Try to plan your visit early or late in the day, especially during the dry season (the whole day is best), and you'll have several hours of peace and quiet. An early, wet, midweek morning in the rainy season will virtually guarantee you the ruins to yourself.

AGUAS CALIENTES

This tiny village is the closest to Machu Picchu and is therefore a frequent destination for travelers wanting to do more than just visit Machu Picchu on the standard one-day train trip from Cuzco. The scenery here is pretty, and it's a good place to meet other travelers and relax in the countryside.

Orientation

The village is 2 km before the Puente Ruinas train station, coming from Cuzco. The train station at Aguas Calientes is confusingly named Machu Picchu. A new road is now open that joins Aguas Calientes with Puente Ruinas and the ruins at Machu Picchu.

Information

There is a telephone office open from 7 am to 8 pm on the corner of the plaza. A medical center is next door. There is no bank, but small amounts of money can be changed in some of the hotels and restaurants.

Hot Springs

Trekkers completing the Inca Trail may want to soak away their aches and pains in the natural thermal springs from which the village of Aguas Calientes derives its name. To get there, follow the path past the youth hostel for about 10 minutes.

Unfortunately, a landslide in April 1995 destroyed the entire hot springs complex (pools, changing rooms, showers, etc). The latest report is that the hot springs still flow and you can soak in them, but the place is a mess. Before the landslide, hours were 6 am to 9 pm, admission was US$2.50, and bathing suits could be rented. Inquire locally about the current situation.

Places to Stay

The basic but clean *Hostal Los Caminantes* (☎ 21-1007), next to the railway line, charges US$6/9 for singles/doubles with shared bath or US$11 for a double with bath. Showers are cold. Some rooms sleep up to five people. Other cheap and basic cold-water places include *Hostal La Cabaña* with four rooms sharing one bathroom and *Hostal Ima Sumac*, both of which charge about US$5 per person or maybe more in the high season.

The *Hostal Qoñi* (☎ 21-1046), better known as *Gringo Bill's* because of its American owner, is a better choice and has been a budget travelers' favorite for many years. It attracts a laid-back crowd who enjoy the spacy wall murals and the friendly but slow service in the restaurant. There is 24-hour hot water. Rates are about US$6.50 per person in rooms sleeping several people, or US$20 for a double.

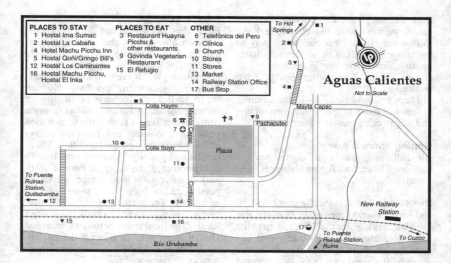

PLACES TO STAY	PLACES TO EAT	OTHER
1 Hostal Ima Sumac	3 Restaurant Huayna	6 Telefónica del Peru
2 Hostal La Cabaña	Picchu &	7 Clínica
4 Hotel Machu Picchu Inn	other restaurants	8 Church
5 Hostal Qoñi/Gringo Bill's	9 Govinda Vegetarian	10 Stores
12 Hostal Los Caminantes	Restaurant	11 Stores
16 Hostal Machu Picchu,	15 El Refugio	13 Market
Hostal El Inka		14 Railway Station Office
		17 Bus Stop

Some rooms have private bath. There is also the *Hostal Machu Picchu* (☎ 21-1034), near the train station, which is simple but clean and has a nice little patio with a river view. Rooms are US$10/15/20 for singles/doubles/triple with shared hot showers.

Formerly a government-run youth hostel, *Hotel Machu Picchu Inn* (☎ in Cuzco 21-1056, fax 21-1011; in Lima 221-0822/4/5/6, fax 440-6197) has clean and reasonably sized if rather spartan rooms. The bathrooms aren't as good. Bunkbeds in dorm rooms are about US$11 per person. Rooms with shared bath were last reported at US$15/25/36 and with private bath at US$24/31/50 – prices may go up, but have not been announced since privatization. There are about 200 beds so this place is almost never full. Breakfast is included and discounts are available for groups. Hot water is available in the mornings and evenings in the communal baths or all day in the private baths. Lunches and dinners are about US$6.

The new *Hostal El Inka* (☎ 21-1034), by the railway tracks, is very clean, helpful, friendly and often full. Rooms are US$22/35 with private bath and hot water.

The *Machu Picchu Pueblo Hotel* (☎ 22-0803; reservations in Lima 446-2775, fax 445-5598; in Cuzco 23-2161, 21-1038, fax 22-3769) is about a five-minute walk east of Aguas Calientes along the railway tracks, although a road extension is planned. The tourist train stops at the hotel's private station, from where a steep flight of stairs leads to the hotel. Large, comfortable bungalows are scattered around an attractive garden, and rooms are US$100/120. There is a good, though pricey, restaurant, which is several minutes walk from the farthest rooms – not much fun on a dark stormy night! There are about 28 rooms and reservations are usually required. Overbooking occurs so reconfirm reservations.

Places to Eat

Most of the restaurants are clustered along the railway tracks, and a few have been criticized for undercooked food or unhygienic conditions. The tap water is not safe to drink. Some reasonably good and clean places include the *Aiko, El Refugio, Samana Wasi* and *Chez Maggy*, the last of which is currently quite popular. Away from the tracks are the *Govinda Vegetarian Restaurant* near the church and the *Restaurant Huayna Picchu* on the way to the hotsprings. All of these are fairly inexpensive, and there are several others to choose from. The better hotels have restaurants, too.

There's not much to do in the evening except hang out in one of the restaurants and talk to other travelers over a beer.

Getting There & Away
Air Helicusco has a helicopter service between Cuzco and Aguas Calientes. See Cuzco for details.

Bus Buses to Machu Picchu cost US$3.50 and leave several times a day from the Río Urubamba bridge for the 8 km run up to the ruins. Departure times have changed frequently, but usually the first bus leaves about 6.30 am and then in the late morning and early afternoon. Buses return a couple of times in the afternoon. Ask locally for exact times.

If you miss a bus, you can walk 2 km to Puente Ruinas and catch one of the buses that meet trains there.

Train The Aguas Calientes train station is called Machu Picchu. The ticket office is on the north side of the railway tracks. A new station is under construction on the east side of town and may be operational by the time you read this. Usually, only the local train stops here, and some people prefer to walk 2 km to Puente Ruinas for a better selection of faster trains to Cuzco. The local train leaves Aguas Calientes for Cuzco daily at 7 am (except Sunday) and 4 pm. It takes about five hours to Cuzco. The trains to Quillabamba pass through daily at about 10.25 am (except Sunday) and 5.10 pm, take three hours and cost about US$2 in 1st class. Schedules are subject to change.

There is also a faster and more expensive local autovagon that doesn't always run and when it does is subject to changing timetables. Ask about departures at the railway station.

SANTA TERESA
From this village, about 20 km beyond Aguas Calientes on the way to Quillabamba, it is possible to find trucks to Cuzco. The rough journey takes about 15 hours during the dry season and is very difficult during the rainy months of November to April. Santa Teresa is a fruit growing center, particularly for *granadillas* (passion fruit). Santa Teresa is also the termination point for a four-day trek from the village of Mollepata through the Cordillera Vilcabamba and passing Salcantay (see Bradt's *Backpacking & Trekking in Peru & Bolivia*). A basic hotel here charges US$3 per person and a local lady serves decent meals; ask. There are hot springs at Colcamayo, less than an hour's walk away – ask locals. The local trains between Cuzco and Quillabamba stop in this off-the-beaten-track place, described by one correspondent as 'magical and fun.'

Southeast of Cuzco

The railway and the road to Puno and Lake Titicaca head southeast from Cuzco. En route are several sites of interest which can be visited from Cuzco in a day.

TIPÓN
This little-known Inca site consists of some excellent terracing at the head of a small valley and is noted for its fine irrigation system. To get there, take an Urcos bus from Cuzco and ask to be set down at the Tipón turn-off, 23 km beyond Cuzco and a few kilometers before Oropesa. A steep dirt road from the turn-off climbs the 4 km to the ruins.

PIKILLACTA & RUMICOLCA
Pikillacta is the only major pre-Inca ruin in the Cuzco area, and it can be reached on an Urcos minibus from Cuzco. Pikillacta means 'the place of the flea' and was built around 1100 AD by the Wari culture. Entry is with the Cuzco Visitor Ticket. The site is just past a lake on the left-hand side of the

road, about 32 km beyond Cuzco. It is a large city of crumbling, two-story buildings, all with entrances strategically located on the upper floor. A defensive wall surrounds the city. The stonework here is much cruder than that of the Incas. The floors were paved with slabs of white gypsum, and the walls were covered with gypsum as well. You can still see traces of this.

Over the past few years there has been some new excavation and research here, and some human burials were discovered. There are local guides available, particularly on weekdays.

Across the road from Pikillacta and about one kilometer away is the huge Inca gate of Rumicolca, built on Wari foundations. The cruder Wari stonework contrasts with the Inca blocks.

The area's swampy lakes are also interesting. You can see Indians making roof tiles from the mud that surrounds the lakes.

ANDAHUAYLILLAS

Andahuaylillas is about 40 km beyond Cuzco and 7 km before Urcos. (Don't confuse it with Andahuaylas, which is a long way west of Cuzco and described later in this chapter.) This pretty Andean village is famous for its beautifully decorated church, comparable to the best in Cuzco, and attractive colonial houses.

The Jesuit church dates from the 17th century. It houses many carvings and paintings, of which the best is considered to be a canvas of the Immaculate Conception by Esteban Murillo. There are reportedly many gold and silver treasures locked in the church, and the villagers are all involved in taking turns guarding it 24 hours a day. The church hours are erratic, but you can usually find a caretaker to open it for you (a tip is expected). You can reach Andahuaylillas on the Urcos minibus.

BEYOND URCOS

The road is paved as far as Urcos, 47 km southeast of Cuzco, where there is a basic hostal. From Urcos, one road heads north-

east to Puerto Maldonado in the jungle (see next section) while another continues southeast toward Lake Titicaca. About 60 km southeast of Urcos is the village of **Tinta**, which has another fine colonial church and a basic place to stay. About 25 km farther is **Sicuani**, a market town of about 40,000 people.

A few kilometers before Sicuani is the little village of San Pedro, and a short walk from here the ruins of **Raqchi** are visible both from the road and the railway; they look like a huge aqueduct. These are the remains of the Temple of Viracocha, which once supported the largest known Inca roof. Twenty-two circular columns made of stone blocks helped support the roof; most are now destroyed but their foundations are clearly seen. This was once one of the holiest shrines of the Inca Empire but was destroyed by the Spanish. The remains of many houses and storage buildings are also visible. An entry fee of about US$2.50 is charged and there are very few tourists here. In mid-June Raqchi is the site of a very colorful fiesta with much traditional dancing and other events.

Getting There & Away

These places can all be reached by bus from Cuzco; it takes less than three hours to reach Sicuani. Alternatively, the railway to Puno parallels this road and there are stops at the places mentioned. Accommodation in Sicuani is extremely basic, but if you leave Cuzco first thing in the morning you'll have plenty of time to visit Raqchi and return on a day trip.

Beyond Sicuani the road deteriorates and most travelers prefer the train on to Juliaca and Puno.

From Cuzco to the Jungle

There are three overland routes from Cuzco to the jungle. One is via the railway to Quillabamba (see below). The other two are poor dirt roads on which it's best to travel in the dry months (June to September); they can be very muddy and slow in the wet months, especially January to April. One road heads to Paucartambo, Tres Cruces and Shintuya for Parque Nacional Manu and the other goes through Ocongate and Quince Mil to Puerto Maldonado.

PAUCARTAMBO

The small village of Paucartambo lies on the eastern slopes of the Andes about 115 km from Cuzco along a very narrow, though well-maintained dirt road. There are fine views of the Andes and the high Amazon Basin beyond. Travel on the one-way dirt road is from Cuzco to Paucartambo on Monday, Wednesday, Friday and possibly Sunday, and return on Tuesday, Thursday and Saturday. Trucks for Paucartambo leave Cuzco early in the morning from near the Urcos bus stop. The journey takes about six hours.

Paucartambo is particularly famous for its very authentic and colorful celebration of the Fiesta de la Virgen del Carmen, held annually on and around July 16 with traditional street dancing, processions and wonderful costumes. Relatively few tourists have seen this fiesta simply because it's been difficult to reach and because, once you're there, you either have to camp, find a room in one of two extremely basic small hotels or hope a local will give you floor space. Tourist agencies in Cuzco, realizing the potential of this fiesta as a tourist attraction, have started running buses specifically for the fiesta. If you go this way, the agency can help arrange a floor or bed to sleep on.

Some Inca ruins are within walking distance of Paucartambo – ask for directions in the village.

TRES CRUCES

About 45 km beyond Paucartambo is the famous jungle view at Tres Cruces, about 15 km off the Paucartambo-Shintuya road. The sight of the mountains finally dropping away into the Amazon Basin is exceptionally beautiful and made all the more exciting by the sunrise phenomenon that occurs around the time of the winter solstice on June 21. For some reason, the sunrise here tends to be optically distorted, causing double images, halos and unusual colors, particularly during May, June and July (other months are cloudy). At this time of year, various adventure tour agencies advertise sunrise-watching trips to Tres Cruces. You can also take the thrice-weekly truck service to Paucartambo and ask around for a truck going on to Tres Cruces – Señor Cáceres in Paucartambo will reportedly arrange sunrise-watching trips. Alternately, ask at the police checkpoint. One of the policemen has a truck and can take you for US$45 – split the cost with friends. Make sure you leave in the middle of the night to catch the dawn, there's no point in going otherwise.

PARQUE NACIONAL MANU

Although this park belongs in the Amazon Basin section, I describe it here because the easiest access and tour services are from Cuzco.

This 1.8-million-hectare rainforest park is the biggest in Peru and one of the best places in South America to see a wide variety of wildlife. Many biologists believe that Manu has a greater biodiversity than any other park because it starts in the eastern slopes of the Andes and plunges down into the lowlands, thus covering a wide range of cloudforest and rainforest habitats. Several Indian groups continue to live here as they have for generations; some of these have had almost no contact with outsiders and do not appear to want contact anyway. Fortunately, these wishes are respected, and although the park is a huge one, less than 20% is open to visitation. The rest is the haunt of Indian tribes and wildlife, almost untouched by 'progress' as we know it. The most progressive aspect of the park is the fact that so much of it is so carefully protected – a rarity anywhere in the world.

The park was formed in 1973, and UNESCO declared the area a Biosphere Reserve in 1977 and a World Natural Heritage Site in 1987. One reason the park is so successful in preserving such a large tract of virgin jungle is that it is remote and relatively inaccessible and therefore has not been exploited by rubber tappers, loggers, oil companies or hunters, so wildlife is less wary and disturbed than in much of Peru's rainforest.

Visiting the national park on your own requires a great deal of time, self-sufficiency, money and an ability to travel in difficult conditions. It is now illegal to enter the park without a guide. It is easier and more worthwhile to go with an organized group. This can be arranged in Cuzco or with international tour operators. It is an expensive trip, but if you want to minimize expenses, you should arrange your trip in Cuzco and be very flexible with your travel plans. Travelers report returning from the park three or four days late! Don't plan on an international airline connection the day after a Manu trip.

The best time to go is during the dry season from June to October; the park may be inaccessible or closed during the rainy months. Recently the park was completely closed in January and open from February to April only to visitors staying at the one lodge (operated by Manu Nature Tours in Cuzco) within the park boundaries. According to national park records, there were 712 registered visitors in 1992, 848 in 1993, and over a thousand in 1994. There is talk of limiting the park to 500 visitors annually, and although this has not yet happened, you need to be aware of this. Permits are necessary to enter the park. Tour agencies will take care of all permits, transport, accommodation, food, guides and other arrangements. Most visits to the park are for a week, although four night stays at the lodge can be arranged.

The park is divided into the Reserve Zone and the Park Zone, but there is no real difference between the rainforest in the two areas. Visitors are only permitted to enter the Reserve Zone. (There is also a smaller Culture Zone containing a few villages, which can be entered by anyone.)

The first stage of the journey involves taking a truck from Cuzco via Paucartambo and Pilcopata to **Shintuya**. Trucks along the one-way road leave on Monday, Wednesday, Friday and possibly Sunday from the Coliseo Cerrado in Cuzco. In the dry season it takes about 20 hours to Shintuya. Breakdowns, flat tires, extreme overcrowding and delays are frequent, and during the rainy season (and even in the dry), vehicles slide off the road. It is safer, more comfortable and more reliable to take the costlier tourist buses (which are basically heavy-duty trucks modified with seats) offered by the Cuzco tour operators.

The trip is often broken at **Pilcopata**, which is the biggest village along the road and has places to sleep and TV in a couple of stores. (I stopped here for five minutes in 1994 and saw every goal of the World Cup Final – soccer, for the uninitiated – which was being transmitted live.) A bed costs about US$5 or floor/hammock space is US$2.50.

About 40 km before Shintuya is the village of **Atalaya** on the Río Alto Madre de Dios. About one kilometer away across the river is the *Amazonia Lodge* (☎ in Cuzco 23-1370, fax 22-2987) in an old hacienda in the foothills of the Andes. This is the best hotel on the whole road, and it offers clean, comfortable beds and communal cold showers for US$40 per person, with simple but satisfactory meals included. There is no electricity, but that is more than compensated for by the low numbers of mosquitoes. There are trails into the forest and the birding is excellent. Birders could profitably spend a few days here in relative comfort. The tour agencies in Cuzco can make reservations.

The village of **Salvación**, about 10 km closer to Shintuya, has a national park office and a couple of basic hotels. Ask around here for boats into the park – the park personnel may know of any trips planned for the near future, and if you're lucky, you might be able to join them.

Shintuya is the end of the road at this time and is the closest village to the park, but it has few places to stay. You may be able to camp at the mission station by talking to the priest. The Moscoso family lives 30 minutes down river from Shintuya and operate the *Pantiacolla Lodge* here, which can be booked through Pantiacolla Tours in Cuzco. The rate is about US$40 per person including food. The lodge is on the margin of the national park and good wildlife sightings have been reported from here.

Boats can travel from any of Pilcopata, Atalaya, Salvación and Shintuya toward Manu. People on tours often start river travel from Atalaya after a night in the Amazonia Lodge, or perhaps in a cheaper house. The few visitors who attempt to travel independently hire a boat in Shintuya, usually for at least several days. Expect to pay several hundred dollars for a week, plus US$100 to US$200 for gas. You might have to wait several days for a boat to become available unless you've made advance arrangements through the operators in Cuzco; they can rent you a boat and boatman even if you don't take a full tour.

The boat journey down the Río Alto Madre de Dios to its junction with the Río Manu takes almost a day, depending on how fast a boat you have. The airstrip at this river junction, known as **Boca Manu**, is often the starting point for commercial trips into the park, eliminating the time-consuming truck and boat approach. There are no regular air services, and a light plane must be chartered from Cuzco or, possibly, Puerto Maldonado. There is, however, talk of introducing a twice-a-week scheduled flight during the May to December season. Ask at the Cuzco agencies for the most recent information about this.

If you turn right (southeast) at Boca Manu on the Madre de Dios, you'll reach *Blanquillo Lodge* (also known as Parrot Lodge) about two hours away by boat. This lodge has simple accommodations and meals for US$40 per day and is a good place for birdwatching, since there is a salt lick nearby that attracts macaws and parrots. The area is within the private **Blanquillo Ecological Reserve**, which covers almost 10,000 hectares. There are trails and blinds, and local guides at the lodge will take you to the salt lick. The lodge is

expanding in 1995 and will eventually have 15 double rooms. Camping is reportedly possible here for US$15 a tent. Expediciones Manu can arrange for you to stay there. If you continue down the fairly busy Madre de Dios past gold-panning areas to Puerto Maldonado, you won't see much wildlife. This takes 14 hours to two days and may cost as little as US$10 if you can find a boat heading that way.

Although none of the lodges mentioned above are inside the national park, all offer a good chance of seeing wildlife, particularly birds.

The virgin jungle of the park lies up the Río Manu northwest of Boca Manu. At the Romero guard post, about an hour from Boca Manu, you pay a park entrance fee of US$15 per person. Near here are a few trails. (During a recent stop at this guard post, I saw a Muscovy duck, green ibis, rufescent tiger-heron and white-winged swallow all at the same time in a single binocular field!)

A further six hours upstream is Cocha Salvador, one of the largest and most beautiful lakes in the park, where there are camping and hiking possibilities. Other areas farther into the park also have trails and camping. If you're patient, wildlife can be seen in most areas. This is not wide-open habitat like the African plains. The thick vegetation will obscure many animals and a skilled guide is very useful in helping you to see them. During a one-week trip you can reasonably expect to see scores of different bird species, several species of monkey, and possibly a few other mammals. Jaguars, tapirs, giant anteaters, tamanduas (a kind of anteater), capybaras, peccaries and giant river otters are among the common large mammals of Manu, but they are elusive and you can consider a trip very succesful if you see two or three large mammals during a week's visit. Smaller mammals you might see include kinkajous, pacas, agoutis, squirrels, brocket deer, ocelots and armadillo. Other animals include river turtles and caiman, which are frequently seen, snakes, which are less often spotted, and a variety of other reptiles and amphibians. Colorful butterflies and less-pleasing other insects also abound.

There is only one place to stay within the park. This is the *Manu Lodge* operated by Manu Nature Tours. Rates are US$90 per person per day including food and guides. Rooms are screened and have comfortable beds; there are cold showers. The lodge is on Cocha Juarez, a 2-km-long oxbow lake, and is about one kilometer from the Río Manu. For an extra fee (about US$40) a climb up to a canopy platform can be arranged. There is a network of trails from the lodge around the lake and beyond.

If you don't stay at the lodge, the only other option is camping, usually on the sandy beaches of the Río Manu. During the high water of the January to April rainy season, these beaches are flooded and the park is closed to camping. During the rest of the year, campers should be prepared with plenty of insect repellant.

Tours
However you do it, an expedition to Manu will not be cheap, and unless you go on a guided tour, the park is not easy to reach. It is, however, the best place in Peru to see jungle habitat and wildlife. Allow at least one week for the trip.

Several travel agencies in Cuzco have banded together to form Ecotur Manu, a loosely-knit organization trying to promote low impact tours and conservation in the national park. Members include Manu Nature Tours, Expediciones Manu and Pantiacolla Tours (see under Cuzco travel agencies for addresses), and these three have consistently been recommended as the best operators. Cheaper outfitters exist, but I haven't had solid recommendations about them. As a minimum, check that they belong to Ecotur Manu.

Manu Nature Tours (which operates the Manu Lodge) is the most expensive outfitter. An eight-day/seven-night tour, with five nights at Manu Lodge, going in by road and out by air, will cost roughly US$200 per person per day, with a minimum of four people. This includes a bilingual naturalist guide and all meals. Cheaper tours can be arranged if you're prepared to spend time driving and boating out of the park instead of flying, if you want to camp rather than stay in the lodge, or if you would prefer a Spanish-speaking boatman to a bilingual naturalist guide. (The guide is recommended for a better appreciation of the rainforest.)

Expediciones Manu is highly recommended for camping trips. They have some fine guides, but if you are lucky enough to go with the owner, British ornithologist and long-time Cuzco resident Barry Walker, you will really be in excellent hands, particularly if birding is your main interest. All guides are experienced and knowledgeable about the flora, fauna and ecology of the rainforest.

Trips of five to nine days are offered, either going in and out by road or air. Costs depend on transportation used and number of people – a group of seven or eight people is usually the most economical without becoming excessively large. Individuals or small groups can arrange to join other people to make up numbers if they wish. Tours using land transportation are just under US$100 per person per day with a group of eight, but over US$200 per person per day with a group of two or three. Costs include bilingual guide (two guides for large groups), food and all camping gear. The overland section can include a mountain-biking descent if arranged in advance. The tents used are designed to sleep three or four people, but only one or two people sleep in them, allowing plenty of space. Thick mattress pads are used. Large screened dining tents with folding camp stools and table are provided. Cooks prepare three-course dinners and alcoholic beverages are available. A camp crew takes care of putting up tents, and the camping trips are as comfortable as conditions permit.

If you don't want to camp, Expediciones Manu can arrange six- to nine-day lodge-based trips staying in some of the lodges mentioned above. Costs are about the same as for camping trips. Barry Walker is very knowledgeable and enthusiastic about the area, and he will work with you to tailor trip to suit your needs if there is a group of you.

Pantiacolla Tours has been recommended for budget travelers. Their trips are usually based in their lodge and their guides speak limited English. Nevertheless, the owners were raised in the area and are very knowledgeable about it. Their costs are about US$500 per person for an eight-day trip.

Several other adventure tour companies in Cuzco arrange trips to Manu, sometimes acting as brokers for one of the agencies already mentioned in this section. I've heard of tours being offered for as little as US$50 per person per day and posters advertising Manu departures are often seen around Cuzco during the dry season. Shop around and don't automatically assume that the cheapest deal is the best one.

The South American Explorers Club in Lima can help members obtain up-to-date information.

THE ROAD TO PUERTO MALDONADO

This road is almost 500 km long and takes about 2½ days to travel in the dry season. Trucks leave daily from the Coliseo Cerrado or near the Plaza Tupac Amaru in Cuzco. Fares to Puerto Maldonado are about US$15; the cheapest places are in the back and the more expensive ones are in the cab with the driver. Most tourists travel on the daily flight from Cuzco to Puerto Maldonado, but the difficult, tiring trip by road is a good chance to see the beautiful scenery of the Andes' eastern slopes.

The road follows the southeastern route to Puno until it reaches Urcos, where the dirt road to Puerto Maldonado begins. To save time, you could bus to Urcos and wait there for a truck. About 125 km and seven or eight hours from Cuzco, you come to the highland town of **Ocongate**, which has a couple of basic hotels. From here, trucks go to the village of **Tinqui**, about an hour's drive beyond Ocongate. It is the starting point for a five- to seven-day hike encircling Ausangate, the highest mountain in southern Peru at 6384 meters. There

is a basic hotel and the locals rent mules (about US$7 per day plus US$6 for an *arriero*, or muleteer) to do the trek (see Bradt's *Backpacking & Trekking in Peru & Bolivia*).

Ausangate is the site of the traditional festival of Koyoriti (various spellings), which is held in early June. Thousands of local people converge on the mountain's icy slopes to celebrate the 'star of the snow' with a night trek to the top of a glacier. Tinqui is the gathering point for this. Outfitters in Cuzco have recently begun to arrange guided trips to this relatively little known (outside of Peru) festival.

After Tinqui, the road begins to drop steadily. The next town of any size is Quince Mil, 240 km from Cuzco and the halfway point. The area is a gold-mining center and the hotel here is often full. You are now less than a thousand meters above sea level, still in the Department of Cuzco.

The road drops a further 100 km into the jungle before reaching the flatlands, where it levels out for the last 140 km into Puerto Maldonado (see also the Amazon Basin chapter).

QUILLABAMBA

Quillabamba lies on the Urubamba River at the end of the railway line from Cuzco and Machu Picchu. At only 1050 meters above sea level, it is hot and humid and can properly be called a jungle town, the only one in Peru reached by train. Because it is so accessible and close to Cuzco, it is a worthwhile destination for travelers wanting a glimpse of the high jungle. The town has about 15,000 inhabitants and is quiet and pleasant, if not particularly interesting, and can be used as a base for trips deeper into the jungle.

The area is an important agricultural one, with cocoa, coffee, achiote (a dye), peppers, peanuts, tropical fruits and coca being grown for the Cuzco market. The coca farmers in this region have strong unions and work to prevent their crops becoming involved in narco-traffic. Coca, chewed rather than destined for the production of cocaine, plays an important part

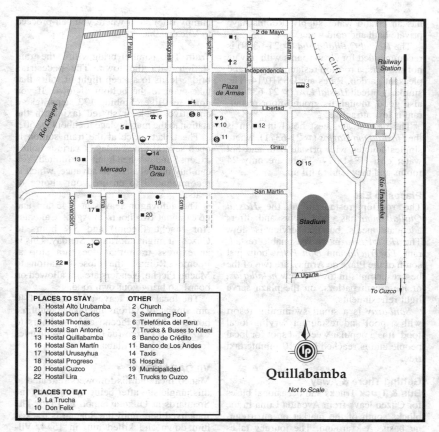

PLACES TO STAY
1 Hostal Alto Urubamba
4 Hostal Don Carlos
5 Hostal Thomas
12 Hostal San Antonio
13 Hostal Quillabamba
16 Hostal San Martín
17 Hostal Urusayhua
18 Hostal Progreso
20 Hostal Cuzco
22 Hostal Lira

PLACES TO EAT
9 La Trucha
10 Don Felix

OTHER
2 Church
3 Swimming Pool
6 Telefónica del Peru
7 Trucks & Buses to Kiteni
8 Banco de Crédito
11 Banco de Los Andes
14 Taxis
15 Hospital
19 Municipalidad
21 Trucks to Cuzco

Quillabamba

Not to Scale

of the socioeconomic structure of the high-land inhabitants. Because the plant can be harvested every three or four months, it is an economically attractive alternative to annual plants.

There is no tourism office. There is a Banco de Crédito for changing money. The area code is 084.

Places to Stay

There are about a dozen hotels from which to choose, none very expensive and some quite good. The cheapest seems to be the *Hostal Borraneche*, on Espinar three blocks north of the Plaza de Armas.

They charge about US$2.50/4 for basic rooms with shared bath. Other cheap and basic places are the *Hostal Progreso* (no singles), *Hostal San Antonio* (dormitory accommodation), *Hostal San Martín* (dirty), *Hostal Thomas* and *Hostal Uru-sayhua*, all with cold-water communal bathrooms only.

Clean, cheap and recommended, the *Hostal Alto Urubamba* (☎ 21-6131) charges US$4/6 for singles/doubles with shared bath, US$5/7.50 with private bath. There are 50 rooms with shared bath and only 18 with private. The similarly priced and pleasant *Hostal Cuzco* is also clean but has an erratic water supply. Rooms have private bath and cold water.

The *Hostal Quillabamba* (☎ 21-6369) is recommended for clean rooms with private hot showers, a rooftop restaurant, pool and pleasant garden. Rates are US$10/14. The similarly priced *Hostal Lira* (☎ 21-6324) is also good, though its ground-floor restaurant is less attractive.

The newest and best hotel in town is the *Hostal Don Carlos* (☎ 21-6371), where singles/doubles with private bath and hot water cost US$14/17. There are only 24 rooms and they tend to fill up.

Places to Eat
The rooftop restaurant at the *Hostal Quillabamba* has good views and offers adequate meals, but the service is slow. The *Hostal Lira* has a reasonable restaurant. *La Trucha* and *Don Felix*, both just south of the Plaza de Armas, are two of the best restaurants in town. A few *heladerías*, or ice-cream parlors, on the plaza serve light refreshments.

Sanbaray is a small swimming resort with a pool and restaurant serving local food. It is a popular weekend spot for local people and is reached by a 10-minute taxi ride.

Getting There & Away
Bus & Truck Trucks and occasional buses for Cuzco leave from Avenida Lima in the blocks south of the market on an irregular basis. Ask around. The journey takes roughly 11 hours and costs about US$6. This rough route, high over the spectacular pass of Abra de Malaga, is a favorite road for ornithologists, who see many different species of birds as the ecological zones change from subtropical to subglacial. The Abra de Malaga area is also one of Peru's most important tea-producing regions.

Pickup trucks (there is also one bus) leave every morning from the market area for the village of Kiteni, farther into the jungle. The trip is variously reported as 6 to 12 hours.

A correspondent suggests asking around the plaza for trucks to Huancacalle (a long, bumpy ride) from where you can proceed to Vilcabamba.

Train Two parallel bridges link the train station with the town. The pedestrian bridge leads to a steep flight of stairs that takes you to the bottom of town. If you don't feel like climbing 172 steps, take a colectivo truck or shared taxi from the station to the marketplace for about US50¢.

The ticket office at the train station is open several times a day at various hours, except Sunday when hours are limited. You can buy tickets a day in advance, which is recommended to ensure your choice of seats.

The autovagon leaves at 3.45 am and takes about two hours to Aguas Calientes (for Machu Picchu) and 5¼ hours to Cuzco. It might not run on Sunday. This is an express train that does not stop at Puentes Ruinas, the closest station to Machu Picchu. Vendors are not allowed on board, so bring your own food.

The local trains leave at 4 am and 1.40 pm, stop at all stations and take about three hours to Machu Picchu and 7½ hours to Cuzco. See Cuzco for fares and schedules from Cuzco to Quillabamba.

VILCABAMBA
Manco Inca and his followers retreated to this jungle site after being defeated by the Spaniards at Ollantaytambo in 1536. The Inca lived here until the Spaniards tracked him down and killed him in 1544. Vilcabamba (also called Espíritu Pampa) slowly fell into disrepair and was forgotten for centuries until it was rediscovered by the American explorer, Gene Savoy, during expeditions in the mid-1960s. The area, about 70 km due west of Quillabamba, was off-limits because of terrorism and other problems in the 1980s, but is now again open to visitation. Although the ruins are of great importance, they have not been properly excavated and are still overgrown.

To get there, you have to walk for several days. The starting point is the village of **Huancacalle**. One way to get there is to take a morning train south from Quilla-bamba to Chaullay Puente, about 19 km from Quillabamba. There is nowhere to stay here but trucks pass through here to Huancacalle, usually a few times a day. It is reportedly possible to find trucks direct from Quillabamba as well, so ask around. In Huancacalle, there are basic places to stay in people's houses. The ruins of **Vitcos** are about an hour's walk away and other ruins are nearby. Also in Huanca-calle, you can hire mules, arrieros and guides to Vilcabamba. This hike takes several days, and small villages and ruins are passed along the way. It is rough going, with many steep ascents and descents before reaching Vilcabamba at about a thousand meters above sea level. (More details are found in Frost's *Exploring Cuzco* and Bradt's *Backpacking & Trekking in Peru & Bolivia*.)

While the Huancacalle route is the most direct one, adventurous travelers can find several other routes.

KITENI & BEYOND
Kiteni is the end of the road as far as this section of the jungle is concerned. This small jungle town has one cheap, basic hotel.

It is possible to continue by river, but as food and accommodations are often nonex-istent, you're advised to be self-sufficient. The first major landmark is the Pongo de Manique, a steep-walled canyon on the Río Urubamba. There is a basic hotel in the area. The canyon is dangerous, and in the rainy season (from December to April), the river runs high and boat owners are reluc-tant to go through it (though some report-edly will). Boats as far as the pongo can occasionally be found, on inquiry, in Kiteni – it takes a day.

During the dry season, a few boats con-tinue through the pongo – the river after the canyon is relatively calm, though there are still some rapids. There are few settlements until you reach the oil town of Sepahua, two to four days beyond the pongo. There is basic food and accommodation here, and the oil workers are often interested in a new face.

From Sepahua, there are flights to Satipo with light aircraft and some flights to Lima for the oil workers. These are not cheap.

Sometimes, it is possible to continue down the Urubamba to the village of Atalaya two or three days away. A member of the South American Explorers Club says that the trip to Atalaya is difficult on public transport because there are few boats between the pongo and Sepahua. Instead, you could build (or have someone else build) a balsa raft after passing the Pongo de Manique (which is too dangerous to raft). En route are the communities of San Iratio (the last place before the pongo), Timpia (where you can have a raft built), Choquorian, Camisea, Liringeti, Miaria, Sepahua, Boteo Pose, Sepal, Puerto Inca and Atalaya. Basic food and accommoda-tions can be obtained from friendly locals in these villages. In return, they often prefer useful gifts to money – flashlights and batteries, fish hooks and lines or basic medicines are good. In Atalaya, there are simple hotels and an airstrip with light air-craft connections to Satipo (see Amazon Basin chapter). Boats can be found to con-tinue down the river, now the Ucayali, as far as Pucallpa (about one week). The route from Kiteni onward is obviously little trav-eled and adventurous, especially beyond the Pongo de Manique, but it is possible for experienced and self-sufficient travelers.

West of Cuzco

Until the mid-1980s, most buses between Cuzco and Lima went via Limatambo, Abancay, Chalhuanca, Puquio, Pampas Galeras and Nazca, a route frequently taken by budget travelers who didn't want to fly and who wanted to see some of the spec-tacular scenery as the road drops from the Andes to the desert coast. Unfortunately, guerrilla activity made the route dangerous in the late 1980s and now banditry and hold-ups are a continuing problem, particu-larly around Puquio. Most buses to Lima now go via Arequipa instead. When the major companies (such as Ormeño and Cruz del Sur) start using the Abancay-Puquio route again, it will be a good indication that the region is returning to normal. Meanwhile, the trip through Piquio is not recommended.

Going west through Limatambo, Abancay, Andahuaylas and on to Ayacucho (in the Central Highlands chapter) is a tough ride on a rough road, but is otherwise not particularly dangerous and is being used by independent travelers again.

LIMATAMBO

The infrequently visited little village of Limatambo is 80 km west of Cuzco by road. Most people do no more than pass through Limatambo on the bus, which is a shame because it's worth a visit.

The village is named after the small, well-made Inca ruin of Rimactambo, or 'speaker's inn.' The site, better known as Tarahuasi after the hacienda in whose grounds it is located, is about 2 km from Limatambo on the road toward Cuzco and easy to find. It is better constructed than many other *tambos* because it was probably used as a ceremonial center as well as a resting place for the Inca *chasquis* or 'runners' who carried messages from one part of the empire to another. For those interested in ruins, the exceptional polygonal retaining wall with its 12 man-sized niches is, in itself, worth the trip.

There is a basic and inexpensive hostal in Limatambo, as well as a swimming pool that is popular with the locals. The village is in pretty, mountainous countryside at the upper end of the valley of a headwater tributary of the Río Apurimac and is a retreat for Cuzco citizens wanting a weekend away from the city.

You can get to Limatambo from Cuzco on the bus to Abancay or on the truck to Mollepata. If you leave early in the morning, you can visit the ruins here and return to Cuzco on an afternoon bus, making a good day trip.

MOLLEPATA

The old village of Mollepata is a few kilo-

meters off the main Cuzco to Abancay road and a couple of hours beyond Limatambo. It is the starting point for a trek to Santa Teresa, beyond Machu Picchu, and a longer alternate start to the Inca Trail. Directions for both hikes are given in Bradt's *Backpacking & Trekking in Peru & Bolivia*. You can also hire an arriero in Santa Teresa for the trek – they know the trails. Allow about four days to Huayllabamba on the Inca Trail and five days to Santa Teresa. Mules are not allowed on the Inca Trail, so after Huayllabamba, you'll have to carry your own gear or hire porters (you can do this at Huayllabamba).

Getting to Mollepata is straightforward if not particularly comfortable. Trucks leave Cuzco from the end of Calle Arcopata early every morning, usually about 7 am. The dusty but scenic drive takes five hours. Alternatively, take a bus heading to Abancay. Sit on the right if the weather is clear for views of the Salcantay snow caps. Although you can buy basic supplies in Mollepata, it's best to bring everything from Cuzco. There is no hotel; you can camp if you ask around but don't leave belongings unattended. If you plan to carry your own gear and dispense with mule drivers and guides, there's no need to stay.

ABANCAY

This sleepy rural town is the capital of the Andean Department of Apurimac, one of the least-explored departments in the Peruvian Andes. It is a seven-hour drive west of Cuzco (in the dry season) and 2377 meters above sea level. The population is about 95,000, although it doesn't look that big! Despite its status as a departmental capital and the main town between Cuzco and the coast or Cuzco and Ayacucho, Abancay has no scheduled air service and the place has a forlorn, forgotten air. Travelers use it as a resting place on the long, tiring bus journey between Cuzco and Ayacucho.

The Banco de Crédito changes money. The area code is 084.

Things to See

Abancay is not totally devoid of interest. Its

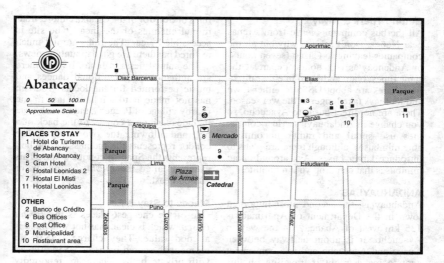

Abancay

0   50   100 m
Approximate Scale

PLACES TO STAY
1 Hotel de Turismo
   de Abancay
3 Hostal Abancay
5 Gran Hotel
6 Hostal Leonidas 2
7 Hostal El Misti
11 Hostal Leonidas

OTHER
2 Banco de Crédito
4 Bus Offices
8 Post Office
9 Municipalidad
10 Restaurant area

particularly colorful carnival, held in the week before Lent, is a chance to see Andean festival celebrations uncluttered by the trappings of international tourism and includes a nationally acclaimed folk-dancing competition. Hotels tend to fill early, so get there a few days before the carnival gets underway, or make reservations if you can. Another festival is held on November 3, Abancay Day.

Those with an interest in Inca ruins may want to visit the Hacienda of Saihuite, 45 km from Abancay on the main road toward Cuzco, near the turnoff to Huanipaca and Cachora. Here, you'll find several large, carved boulders, the Stones of Saihuite. These intricately decorated stones are similar to the more commonly visited carved rock at Qenko, near Cuzco, but are considered more elaborate.

During the dry season (late May to September), walkers and climbers may want to take advantage of the best weather to head for the sometimes snowcapped peak of Ampay (5228 meters), about 10 km north-northwest of the town. For the rest of the year the weather tends to be wet, especially during the first four months of the year.

The mountain is center of the 3635 hectare **Santuario Nacional Ampay**.

Places to Stay & Eat

Most hotels are poor. The cheapest is the pretty grim *Hostal El Misti*, which charges just over US$2 per person. Slightly cleaner and with bigger rooms, but otherwise still very basic and with cold water, is the *Gran Hotel*, which charges US$3.50/5.50 in rooms with private bath or a little less with shared bath. The *Hostal Leonidas* (☎ 32-1199) is better and has clean rooms with private cold showers for US$5.50/8 or with shared showers for a dollar less. The *Leonidas 2* is similar but a little less attractive. The best hotel in town is the *Hotel de Turismo de Abancay* (☎ /fax 32-1017; in Cuzco 22-3339), at Avenida Diaz Barcenas 500 in a pleasant, old-fashioned country mansion. Singles/doubles with shared bath cost US$19/31 with bath; some rooms without bath are cheaper. The restaurant offers meals for about US$3.

The best place to eat may be the restaurant in the Hotel de Turismo de Abancay. Otherwise, you'll find plenty of cheap cafés near the bus stations.

CUZCO AREA

Getting There & Away

All the bus companies leave from Arenas near Nuñez. Don't ask me why but all the companies leaving to Cuzco (seven hours) or Andahuaylas (six hours) depart at the same times: 6 am and 1 pm in either direction. Fares are about US$5 to either town and journeys take longer in the wet season. There are no direct buses to Ayacucho, so you change in Andahuaylas. Most companies use small and rather uncomfortable minibuses, although there are plans to introduce larger buses. Ask around about minibuses that can drop you in Sahuite.

ANDAHUAYLAS

Andahuaylas, the second most important town in the Department of Apurimac, is 135 km west of Abancay on the way to Ayacucho. It is about halfway between Cuzco and Ayacucho and is a convenient spot to rest a night if traveling on this very rough but scenic route. When taking buses from Cuzco, don't confuse it with Andahuaylillas, which is in the opposite direction.

There are some 26,000 inhabitants, most of whom seem to speak Quechua as their first language and Spanish as the second. This is a very rural part of Peru and one of the poorest. Only parts of the town center have electricity. The elevation here is 2980 meters.

Information

There is no tourism office. The Banco de Crédito changes dollars, but traveler's checks may be a problem. I couldn't find a telephone office except at the airport. The area code is 084. Tourists were supposed to register with police until recently – this requirement has been waived since 1994.

Things to See & Do

The colonial **cathedral** on the Plaza de Armas is much more sober than its counterparts in most Peruvian cities.

Andahuaylas' main attraction, the beautiful **Laguna de Pacucha**, is 17 km from town and accessible by bus or car. Fishing and rowboat rental are available. A one-hour hike from the lake brings you to the ruins of **Sondor** of the Chanka culture, traditional enemies of the Incas. The site is accessible by car. The ruins are not much restored but there are good mountain views.

The annual fiesta is June 21 when there are authentic and traditional dances and music performed for the locals. Tourism has not made it to Andahuaylas. In the nearby village of Pacucha, the annual fiesta includes lashing a condor to the back of a bull and allowing the two to fight. The condor represents the Indians and the bull represents the Spanish conquistadors. This event is called the *Fiesta de Yahuar*, or 'Blood Feast.'

Places to Stay & Eat

One of the cheapest places is the *Hostal Cusco*, which is clean, has hot water and is a good value. They charge US$3/5 in rooms with shared baths or US$4.50/6.50 with private baths. There are reportedly a couple of cheaper cold-water places. The *Hostal Los Libertadores Wari* (☎ 72-1434) is also a good value. It is clean and safe and has hot water, but it closes its doors at 11 pm. Rates are US$4.50/7 with shared baths and US$6/8 with private baths. Similar rates are charged at the equally good *Hostal Las Americas*. The best hotel, although in a poor neighborhood, is the modern *Hotel Turístico Andahuaylas* (☎ 72-1224; in Cuzco 22-3339), Avenida Lazarro Carillo. Rates are about US$18/25 including breakfast.

The simple *Aji Seco* serves good, inexpensive, highland Peruvian food. There are several other equally good restaurants along this street, Ramon Castilla. None are particularly outstanding. A popular place for a drink is the *Garabato Pub* on the Plaza de Armas, although some visitors are put off by the dozens of animal skins (mainly Andean mammals) hanging on the walls.

Getting There & Away

Air The regional airport is about a 20-minute drive south of town and is reached by colectivo taxis at US$1 per person. It was closed for some years because of terrorism but is now operational again. After the

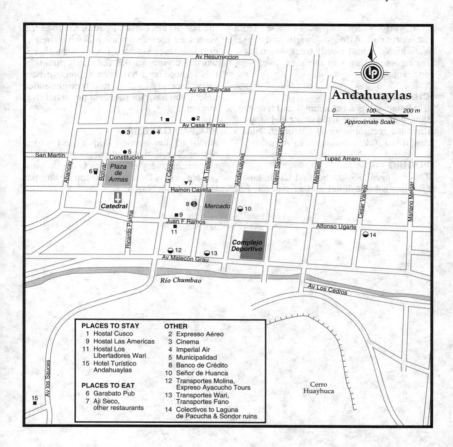

Andahuaylas

0   100   200 m
Approximate Scale

PLACES TO STAY
1 Hostal Cusco
9 Hostal Las Americas
11 Hostal Los
   Libertadores Wari
15 Hotel Turístico
   Andahuaylas

PLACES TO EAT
6 Garabato Pub
7 Aji Seco,
   other restaurants

OTHER
2 Expresso Aéreo
3 Cinema
4 Imperial Air
5 Municipalidad
8 Banco de Crédito
10 Señor de Huanca
12 Transportes Molina,
   Expreso Ayacucho Tours
13 Transportes Wari,
   Transportes Fano
14 Colectivos to Laguna
   de Pacucha & Sondor ruins

Cerro
Huayhuca

airport reopened in 1994, several airlines tried to get a piece of the market. At time of writing, however, the following were operating, and this will, no doubt, change. Imperial Air flies daily to and from Lima (US$57); Expresso Aéreo flies to Lima three times a week, and Transportes Aereos Andahuaylas (TAA) (☎ 72-1891) flies to Lima daily and to Cuzco twice a week (currently Tuesday and Friday mornings).

Bus Señor de Huanca has uncomfortable minibuses to Abancay (six hours, US$5) at 6 am and 1 pm. The 6 am departure continues to Cuzco (14 hours, US$9). Transportes Wari has large buses to Cuzco and Ayacucho but its schedule is erratic. Transportes Molina and Transportes Faro both have a 1 pm large bus to Ayacucho (17 hours in the dry season, US$9). Both companies continue to Lima (30 hours, US$18). Expreso Ayacucho Tours has minibuses to Ayacucho, occasionally continuing to Huancayo and Chanchamayo. The road to Ayacucho goes over very high puna and may be snow-covered and is very cold at night. Bring adequate clothing or a sleeping bag.

Minibuses to Laguna de Pacucha, Sondor

and various local places leave from the corner of Alfonso Ugarte and Cesar Vallejo. Vehicles (mainly trucks) also leave for remote villages in the area, over very poor roads.

CHALHUANCA
Chalhuanca has a basic hotel and a restaurant, which is often used as a meal stop on the (not recommended) Cuzco to Nazca run. It is 120 km southwest of Abancay.

PUQUIO
This village, 189 km beyond Chalhuanca, also has a basic hotel and restaurant. For the last 50 km before Puquio, the road traverses an incredibly wild-looking area of desolate, lake-studded countryside that is worth staying awake for. Unfortunately, this remote area has been subject to banditry recently and is not recommended unless you have more recent positive information.

PAMPAS GALERAS
About 65 km beyond Puquio and 90 km before Nazca, the road passes through the vicuña sanctuary of Pampas Galeras. Most people visit Reserva Nacional Pampas Galeras from Nazca.

The Central Highlands

The central Peruvian Andes is one of the least visited and most neglected areas of Peru. The harsh mountain terrain has made ground communications especially difficult and the region also suffers from a lack of air services. Huancayo, for example, is both the capital of the Department of Junín and Peru's fifth largest city, yet it lacks a commercial airport. Two of the area's other departmental capitals, Huancavelica and Cerro de Pasco, also lack a commercial airport. The departmental capital of Ayacucho, founded in 1540, received its first permanent public telephone link with the outside world in 1964, at a time when there were still only a few dozen vehicles servicing the city. These remote cities of the central Andes are surrounded by a rural population involved in subsistence agriculture and among the poorest in Peru.

It was in this environment of isolation and poverty that the terrorist organization, Sendero Luminoso, or 'Shining Path,' emerged in the 1960s and grew in the '70s. The violent activities of the Sendero escalated dramatically in the 1980s and headlines all over the world proclaimed Peru's internal unrest. Following reports of atrocities and mass murders in the central Peruvian highlands, committed not only by the terrorists but also by government troops during incompetent attempts to subdue the insurgents, tourism declined from the high levels of the late '70s. During 1983 and '84, the Departments of Ayacucho, Huancavelica and Apurímac were all but abandoned by tourists and Peruvian authorities strongly discouraged travelers from visiting them.

By 1985, however, things had quieted down considerably and tourists once again returned to these areas, albeit very slowly. I spent several weeks traveling here at the time and found little external evidence of the Sendero. Unfortunately, this situation did not last and, in the late 1980s, much of

the area was again under Sendero control. Finally, in 1992, Abimael Guzmán, former professor of philosophy at the university in Ayacucho and the founder/leader of the Sendero, was captured and sentenced to life imprisonment. Soon afterwards, several of his top lieutenants were also captured and the Sendero lost the control it once had over most of central Peru. Places covered in this chapter are again safe to visit.

This region has several delightful, friendly colonial towns which are among the least spoiled in the entire Andean chain. The travel itself is exciting too, not only because of the magnificent mountain views but also because it involves a certain amount of effort. The region still has more communications problems than most other areas of Peru and traversing the bad roads is a minor challenge, but the rewards of getting off the beaten 'gringo trail' make the hard travel worthwhile. If you want to travel to a lesser-known part of Peru, read on.

LA OROYA

The highland industrial town of La Oroya, population 35,000, proudly calls itself 'the metallurgical capital of Peru.' Unless you're interested in metallurgy, which, in La Oroya, translates into the huge, state-run, CENTROMIN smelter and refinery with its attendant slag heaps, you'll not want to linger in this cold, unattractive place. However, because La Oroya is a major junction, most travelers to central Peru's interior at least pass through the town.

From La Oroya, roads lead in all directions: east to Tarma (and down into the central jungle), south to Huancayo, Huancavelica and Ayacucho (and on to Cuzco), north to Cerro de Pasco and Huánuco (and then down into the northern jungle), and west to Lima. All these central highland towns are described in this chapter.

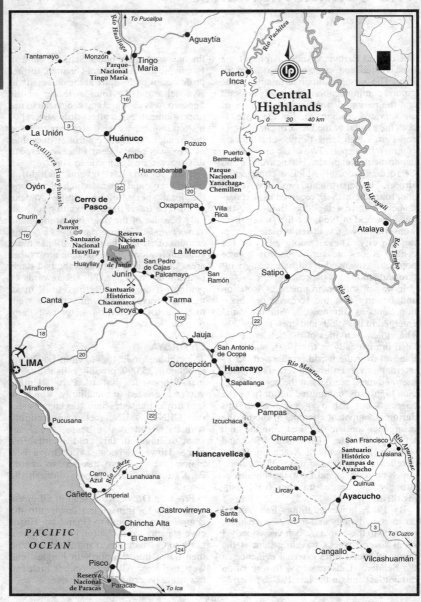

Central Highlands

0   20   40 km

Riding the Rails

La Oroya is over 3700 meters above sea level; the railway line from Huancayo through La Oroya to Lima (187 km from La Oroya) passes through the station of La Galera. At 4781 meters above sea level, La Galera is the world's highest station on a standard-gauge track. On the trip from Lima, oxygen is available in 1st class, and if you're not yet acclimatized, you may be glad to know it's there – even sitting quietly in your seat is a breathless experience. During the second half of the trip, the scenery is stark and bare, awesome rather than pretty, and the snow line often comes to below 5000 meters. You'll sometimes see llama and alpaca but, unfortunately, La Oroya's several mining operations tarnish the landscape's natural splendor.

As you can imagine, the huge vertical change in such a relatively short length of track makes this stretch of railway line one of the most exciting in the world for train enthusiasts (not to mention ordinary travelers). The *South American Handbook* claims that, along its whole length, the railway traverses 66 tunnels, 59 bridges and 22 zigzags. I lost count but the figures seem about right. (This route has been closed to passenger trains but there are plans to reopen it in 1996; see Huancayo and Lima for details.) ∎

Information

For obvious reasons, La Oroya is a place to travel through, not to. It is possible to reach several other central highland towns from Lima in a day and, rtherefore, few travelers stop here. If you should be stranded, the *Hostal San Martín*, 2 or 3 km out of the town center towards Lima, is better than the places in the center such as the *Hostal El Viajero* and the very basic *Hostal Lima*. Buses leave from near the train station.

East of La Oroya

TARMA

This small town on the eastern slopes of the Andes, 60 km east of La Oroya, is known locally as 'the pearl of the Andes.' It is a pleasant town, 3050 meters above sea level and with about 80,000 inhabitants.

Tarma has a long history. The overgrown Inca and pre-Inca ruins to be found in the hills and mountains surrounding the town are not well known and there's plenty of scope for adventurers to discover ruins on the nearby peaks. The town seen today was founded by the Spanish soon after the conquest (the exact date is uncertain – I've read 1534, 1538 and 1545). Nothing remains of the early colonial era but there are a number of attractive 19th- and early-20th-century houses with white walls and red-tiled roofs.

Information

In the absence of a tourist office, information is available from Servicios Turisticos Maeedick (☎ 32-2530), 2 de Mayo 547, who are very helpful and have leaflets (in Spanish) describing local villages and attractions. One of the staff, José Luís Orihuela, is a local writer who is very knowledgeable about the area and will give you information or work as a guide to see the ruins in the area.

The Banco de Crédito (see map) changes money. The post office and telephone company are shown on the map. The area code is 064.

Things to See & Do

Tarma is high in the mountains and the clear nights of June, July and August provide some good opportunities for star-gazing. There is a small **astronomical observatory** run by the owner of the Hostal Central (see Places to Stay – bottom end). The owner is usually away in Lima, so serious astronomers should call the hotel and ask when he might be there and if it is possible to use the telescope.

CENTRAL HIGHLANDS

PLACES TO STAY
3 Hostal Internacional
4 Hostal Anchoraico
6 Hostal Central
7 Hotel El Dorado
9 Hostal Ritz
10 Hostal Cordova
17 Hotel Tuchu
19 Los Portales
25 Hostal Tarma
26 Hotel Galaxia
27 Hotel Vargas

PLACES TO EAT
23 Restaurant Don Lucho
26 Restaurant Chavín
28 Restaurant El Rosal

OTHER
1 Pick-up Trucks to San Pedro de Cajas
2 Empresa de Transportes San Juan
5 Buses to Acobamba, Palcamayo
8 Baños Del Sol (Public Hot Showers)
11 Transportes Chanchamayo
12 Transportes DASA
13 Señor de Muruhuay, Los Canarios
14 Post Office
15 Comité 20 (Colectivos to Chanchamayo)
16 Servicios Turisticos Maeedick
18 Police
20 Gas Station
21 Empresa Hidalgo
22 Expreso Tarma
24 Banco de Crédito
29 Telefónica del Peru

Tarma

0   100   200 m

The **cathedral** is modern (built in 1965) and is of interest because it contains the remains of Peruvian president, Manuel A Odría. He was born in Tarma and organized construction of the cathedral during his presidency. The clock in the tower dates from 1862.

Several nearby excursions are described at the end of the Tarma section. These include visits to the religious shrine of Señor de Muruhuay in Acobamba (9 km from Tarma), the cave of Guagapo (33 km), and the weaving village of San Pedro de Cajas (50 km).

Special Events
The big annual attraction is undoubtedly Easter. Many processions are held during Semana Santa (Holy Week), including several by candlelight after dark. They culminate on the morning of Easter Sunday with a marvelous procession to the cathedral along a beautiful route entirely carpeted with flower petals. This attracts

many Peruvian visitors and the hotels are usually full.

The annual fiesta of El Señor de Los Milagros, or 'the Lord of the Miracles,' takes place in late October; 18, 28 and 29 are the main feast days. (No, I don't know why there's a 10-day gap.) This is another good opportunity to see processions marching over beautiful flower-petal carpets.

Other fiestas include Tarma Week near the end of July and San Sebastián on January 20.

Places to Stay – bottom end
The following cheap and basic, cold-water hotels are found near the Mercado Modelo. At US$3.50/5 for singles/doubles, the OK *Hostal Ritz* on the market is one of the cheapest places, though the outside rooms are noisy. The nearby *Hostal Anchoraico* is similarly priced but dirty and poor, and the dingy-looking *Hostal Tarma* is a little better. The *Hostal Cordova* has a sign for *agua caliente* – hot water – but doesn't

have any; it charges US$3.50/5.50. If you're staying in a cold-water cheapie, you can use the hot public showers at *Baños del Sol*, half a block from the market.

The following have hot water occasionally, particularly in the morning, though they may claim to have it all day: The old but adequate *Hostal Central* (☎ 32-2466) has the observatory mentioned above. Rooms are US$4/5, or US$5.50/7.50 with private bath. Among the better cheap hotels is the *Hotel Tuchu* which charges US$5/7.50 with private bath and is good value. The *Hotel Vargas* has spacious rooms and some hard beds if you're fed up with soft and sagging mattresses. Rooms with private bath and hot water in the morning cost US$5 per person, or less with shared bath. The *Hotel El Dorado* (☎ 32-2598) can be noisy, but is otherwise quite good; rooms with private bath and hot water go for US$6.50/8.50, a little less with cold, shared showers.

The clean *Hotel Galaxia* on the Plaza de Armas has only 16 rooms, so it's often full. Rooms are US$9.50/13 with private bath. The newer *Hostal Internacional* (☎ 32-2830) is also quite good and charges US$10/14 with private bath, or US$7.50/12 with shared showers.

Places to Stay – middle
The town's best accommodations are the *Los Portales* (☎ 32-1411, fax 32-1410). Set in pleasant gardens at the west end of town, the hotel charges US$40/55 including continental breakfast. However, the hotel is usually half empty and if you just show up you'll get much better rates.

Places to Eat
Plenty of cheap restaurants line Avenida Lima (which becomes Avenida Castilla in the west end of town). The *Restaurant Chavín* on the Plaza de Armas is good and the *Restaurant Don Lucho* is acceptable and cheap. The best in town is the *Restaurant El Rosal*.

Getting There & Away
There are two areas of town from which transport leaves frequently: near the Mercado Modelo and at the western end of Avenida Castilla. On market days (Thursday and Sunday) service is disrupted around the Mercado Modelo area and companies near here leave from other streets – ask around.

If continuing to Chanchamayo (US$2) in the central Amazon Basin (see that chapter), the most frequent service is with Empresa de Transportes San Juan with buses every hour or two during the day. Some buses continue to Villa Rica or Oxapampa. Transportes Chanchamayo has about three buses a day. The colectivo taxis of Comité 20 are the most convenient way to get to Chanchamayo. They leave from the market when they're full and charge US$3.25 per passenger for the precipitous descent to La Merced at about 600 meters. It's worth doing the trip just for the views.

San Juan also has buses almost every hour to Huancayo (US$2.25). Los Canarios has five buses a day. During the rainy season the route is usually through La Oroya, but in the dry season they may take a more direct secondary road through Lomo Largo. This scenic route goes over high puna where you might glimpse vicuñas.

Vicuñas

If heading to La Oroya and on to Lima (about US$4), there are three or four buses a day with each of Los Canarios, Transportes DASA, Transportes Chanchamayo and Hidalgo. Note that most buses coming or going almost anywhere will stop by the gas station on Castilla. If you want to act like an experienced Peruvian traveler, you can wait here and hop on the next bus heading to your destination. I hope they have a seat for you!

Getting Around

Several companies provide service to the nearby towns. Señor de Muruhuay has frequent buses to Acobamba (US30¢) and the religious sanctuary there. A bus stop next to Transportes San Juan has minibuses going to Acobamba and Palcamayo. A couple of blocks away on Huancavelica, pick-up trucks leave for San Pedro de Cajas, usually leaving around noon. Several small companies have buses by the coliseum that go to local villages.

ACOBAMBA

The village of Acobamba, 10 km from Tarma, is famous for the religious sanctuary of El Señor de Muruhuay, visible on a small hill about 1½ km away.

The sanctuary is built around an image of Christ crucified, etched onto the rock. Historians claim that it was carved with a sword by a royalist officer who was one of the few survivors after losing the Battle of Junín (a major battle of independence fought on August 6, 1824). Despite this, legends relating to the image's miraculous appearance persist. The first building erected around the image was a roughly thatched hut. It was replaced in 1835 by a small chapel. The present sanctuary (the third) was inaugurated on April 30, 1972. It is a very modern building with an electronically controlled bell tower (the bells came from Germany) and is decorated with huge weavings from San Pedro de Cajas.

The colorful feast of El Señor de Muruhuay, held throughout May, has been celebrated annually since 1835. Apart from the religious services and processions, there are ample opportunities to sample local produce and to see people dressed in traditional clothes. Stalls sell *chicha* (corn beer) and *cuy* (roast guinea pig) but be wary unless your stomach is used to local food. There are dances, fireworks, very few gringos and no hotels – most visitors stay in nearby Tarma.

PALCAMAYO

This attractive village is 28 km from Tarma

The Gruta's Bottomless Depths

About 1500 meters into the Gruta de Guagapo is an underwater section, first reached in 1972 by an expedition from Imperial College, London. The underwater section was named 'The Siphon' and a French expedition got through it in 1976. Peruvian teams led by Carlos Morales Bermúdez reached 2000 and 2400 meters into the cave during two 1988 expeditions. In 1994, Carlos Morales Bermúdez and local Ramiro Castro Barga, accompanied by US and German cavers, reached 2745 meters into the cave. No one knows how much further it goes.

To get to the cave, ask in Palcamayo. You'll be shown a dirt road winding off into the hills – it's a pleasant 4-km walk. The cave is accessed through a large opening in the side of the mountain to the right of the road; Señor Castro's house is on the left. Bottled drinks are available and prospective expeditions can camp.

The Palcamayo area is also known for the many little-explored Inca and pre-Inca ruins in the surrounding hills. Although they are not very interesting to the casual tourist, an adventurer equipped with camping gear could spend days wandering the hilltops looking for ruins. José Luís Orihuela (see Tarma Information) knows many of these places. He has also entered the cave as far as The Siphon and has information about that. ■

and serviced by several colectivos a day. From Palcamayo, you can visit the Gruta de Guagapo, a huge limestone cave in the hills about 4 km away. The gruta has been the subject of various expeditions from all over the world. It is one of Peru's largest and best known caves and is officially protected as a National Speleological Area. Several other lesser-known caves in the area would also be of interest to speleologists (those who study caves).

A descent into the Gruta de Guagapo requires caving equipment and experience. It contains waterfalls, squeezes and underwater sections (scuba equipment required), and although it is possible to enter the cave for a short distance, you soon need technical gear. A local guide, Señor Modesto Castro, has explored the cave on numerous occasions and can provide you with ropes, lanterns and so on to enter the first sections. He lives in one of the two houses below the mouth of the cave and has a collection of photographs and newspaper clippings describing the exploration of the cave. He doesn't do much caving himself any more, but his son, Ramiro, can be of assistance.

SAN PEDRO DE CAJAS
The village of San Pedro de Cajas, high in the Andes at an altitude of 4040 meters, is known throughout Peru for the excellence of its unique tapestries, which are often exported. Made of stuffed rolls of wool (difficult to visualize until you actually see some), the tapestries can be bought from the weavers for less than you'd pay in Lima. However, as the village is not oriented to tourists, facilities are very limited and you'll need some elementary Spanish.

A bed at the basic hotel run by the Oscanoa family will cost under US$3.50. Not surprisingly, there are no hot showers, but the people are friendly. You can eat at the basic restaurant or arrange simple meals at the hotel. Some weavings are available here; ask around if you want to see more. The village has no money changing facilities, so change as much money as you'll need before you get there.

Getting There & Away
Catching a bus from Tarma to Palcamayo is easy enough, but buses continuing on to San Pedro are infrequent. You can walk along the 16-km dirt road from Palcamayo, past the Gruta de Guagapo, to San Pedro. Pick-up trucks from Tarma pass by in the early to mid afternoon and there are occasional minibuses and other vehicles, so you probably will get a ride along the way. The road climbs most of the way to San Pedro, which is about 800 meters higher than Palcamayo.

Instead of returning to Tarma the way you came, you might walk beyond San Pedro for about 7 km or so and come to the main La Oroya to Cerro de Pasco highway. Flag down a bus here.

South of La Oroya

JAUJA
The main road to Huancayo heads southeast from La Oroya along the central Andes, passing several towns of importance along the way. The first of these is the historic town of Jauja which lies on a junction about 80 km southeast of La Oroya, 60 km south of Tarma and 40 km north of Huancayo.

Before the time of the Incas, this area was the home of an important Huanca Indian community and Huanca ruins can be seen on the skyline of the hill about 3 km southeast of Jauja. With many other little-known ruins, the area is ideal for adventurous walking. Jauja was Pizarro's first capital in Peru, though this honor was short lived. Some finely carved wooden altars in the main church are all that remains of the early colonial days.

About 4 km from Jauja is **Laguna de Paca**, a small, pleasant resort offering a hotel, a few rowing boats and fishing. A boat ride around the lake will cost about US$8 which can be split between several people. There are ducks and gulls to look at and you can stop at the 'Isla del Amor' – a tiny artificial island not much bigger than the boat you're on!

There is a colorful weekly market on Wednesday mornings.

Places to Stay & Eat
Many visitors to Jauja stay in Huancayo and travel to Jauja on one of the frequent buses linking the two towns. If you do choose to stay in Jauja, try the basic *Hotel Ganso de Oro* in front of the train station. Rooms cost about US$3/5 and hot water is sometimes available. This hotel tends to fill up by early afternoon. The *Hotel Santa Rosa*, on the corner of the main plaza by the church, is similar but has no hot water. The best accommodations are offered by the *Hotel de Turistas de Paca*, next to the lake of that name, where rooms cost about US$25/35, including continental breakfast.

Jauja has several cheap, basic restaurants near the Plaza de Armas. The *Hotel Ganso de Oro* has one of the best restaurants in town and the *Hotel de Turistas* is also good. Trout and, during the rainy season, frog are local specialties.

Getting There & Away
The train from Lima to Huancayo used to stop at Jauja and may do so again if the route reopens. (See the Lima and Huancayo sections for further train information.)

Minibuses leave for Jauja from the corner of Amazonas and Calixto in Huancayo as soon as they are full – about twice an hour. The fare is under US$1 and the trip takes under an hour.

CONCEPCIÓN
South of Jauja, the road branches to follow both the west and east sides of the Río Mantara valley to Huancayo. Traveling along the east side, you come to Concepción, a small village about halfway between Jauja and Huancayo. Although the village itself is of no more than passing interest, the nearby convent of Santa Rosa de Ocopa is well worth a visit.

Set in a pleasant garden, this beautiful building was built by the Franciscans in the early 1700s as a training center for their

missionaries heading down into the jungle regions, especially those working to convert the Ashashinka tribe. During the years of missionary work, the friars built up an impressive collection which is on display in the convent museum. Exhibits include stuffed jungle wildlife, Indian artifacts, photographs of early missionary work, old maps, a fantastic library of some 20,000 volumes (many are centuries old), a large collection of colonial religious art, mainly of the Cuzqueño school, and many other objects of interest.

The convent is open daily, except Tuesday, from 9 am to noon and 3 to 6 pm and entry is US$1.50 (less for students). Frequent colectivos leave from Concepción for Ocopa, about 5 km away. The bus stop is a few blocks from the Plaza de Armas – ask someone where it is.

Places to Stay & Eat
The best of the few basic hotels is the pleasant *Hotel Royal* on the main plaza. It charges about US$5 per person and has hot water in the morning. The *Hotel El Paisanito*, about a half block from the plaza, is cheaper and even more basic.

There are a couple of simple restaurants in the 'center' that tend to close soon after dark. On the main road are some 'restaurantes turisticos' which stay open a bit later and look nicer.

Getting There & Away
Buses leave frequently from the corner of Calixto and Mantaro in Huancayo and charge about US30¢.

HUANCAYO
Huancayo is a modern city with a population of about 360,000. It lies on the flat Río Mantaro valley, which is one of the most fertile in the central Andes and supports a large rural population. At an altitude of 3260 meters and about 300 km from Lima, Huancayo is the capital of the central Andean Department of Junín. As the major commercial center for the area, it is of great importance as a market town for people living in the many nearby villages.

However, despite its size and departmental capital status, Huancayo is still relatively undeveloped.

The town itself is not particularly interesting but its weekly Sunday market, where both crafts and produce from the Río Mantaro valley are sold, is famous among locals and travelers. In addition, Huancayo is a good base from which to visit the many interesting villages of the Río Mantaro valley.

Information
Tourist Office The tourist office is on the corner of Calle Real at Breña. Hours are 8 am to 1.30 pm and 4 to 6 pm, Monday to Friday. The office is a great source of information about sightseeing in the Río Mantaro valley, things to do and how to get around on public transport. The enthusiastic young woman with whom I spoke bemoaned the fact that Huancayo always seems to be forgotten in the tourist scheme of things and then provided me with a huge list of places in the Río Mantaro valley that I should see. To visit everything would take a couple of weeks, so I'll try to outline the best places in this section. Definitely visit this tourist bureau if you want to spend some time in the area and especially if you speak Spanish. Also in the tourist office is a big display of crafts from all over the Río Mantaro valley.

La Cabaña restaurant and the Incas del Peru tour agency, Giráldez 652, are recommended sources of help and information on just about anything in the area. They have maps of Huancayo and the surroundings.

Money There are several casas de cambio on Calle Real, between the civic center and the Plaza de Armas, and these are usually the best places to change cash. You may find traveler's checks difficult to change in casas de cambio, but the Banco de Crédito will often change them, albeit at a loss. Velitours, Calle Real 552, changes traveler's checks at a 5% commission. Reportedly, a new Banco Wiese opened in late 1995 in the center of town and charges 1.5% commission on traveler's checks and

1% on MasterCard advances – of course, this may be an 'opening special.' The situation varies from year to year (and from month to month), so you may find that changing travelers' checks is no problem.

Post & Telecommunications The telephone company will send faxes to Europe for about US$5 to US$6 per page. New telephone booths have been installed all over central Huancayo. The area code for Huancayo (and the surrounding towns) is 064. Incas del Peru (see below) will also hold and send faxes for you.

Dangers & Annoyances Huancayo has a reputation for theft; the bus and train stations and the Sunday market are said to be crawling with thieves. I've had no problems (admittedly, I'm used to this kind of situation) but stay alert.

Beware of the altitude if arriving straight from Lima.

Things to See
The **Museo Salesiano** (see map) can be entered from the Salesian school. There are stuffed animals (in better condition than in most Peruvian museums), especially from the Amazon, as well as some pottery. Hours are 9 am to noon and 3 to 6 pm; admission is about US$1.

Head northeast on Avenida Giráldez for a good view of the city. About 2 km from the town center is **Cerro de la Libertad** where, apart from the city view, there are snack bars and a playground. About 2 km farther (there is a sign and an obvious path), you come to the eroded geological formations known as Torre Torre.

In the city itself, the cathedral and the church of La Inmaculada are both modern and not particularly noteworthy. **La Merced**, on the first block of Calle Real, is the most interesting church; although there isn't much to see, this is where the Peruvian Constitution was approved in 1839.

Organized Tours & Treks
Incas del Peru (☎ 22-3303, fax 22-2395), Giráldez 652 (same building as La Cabaña),

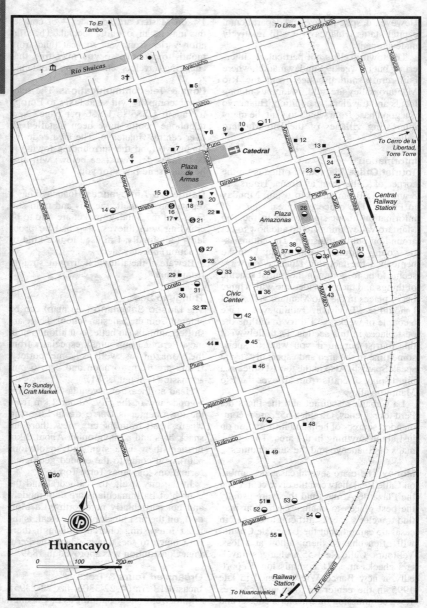

Huancayo

PLACES TO STAY	PLACES TO EAT	27	Casa de Cambio

PLACES TO STAY
4 Hostal Los Angeles
5 Hotel Plaza
7 Hostal Tivoli
12 Residencial Baldeón
13 Residencial Huancayo
18 Hotel Kiya
19 Hotel Santa Felicita
22 Hotel Roger
24 Hostal Pussy
25 Hostal Universal
29 Hotel Centro
30 Hostal Roma
34 Hotel Prince
36 Turismo Hotel
37 Hostal Will Roy
44 Hotel Torre Torre
46 Hotel El Dorado
48 Hotel Palace
49 Hotel Presidente
51 Hostal Villa Rica
55 Percy's Hotel

PLACES TO EAT
6 Restaurant El Inca
8 El Parque
9 Chifa Central
17 El Pino
19 Pinky's Restaurant
20 Restaurant Olímpico
24 Lalo's Restaurant

OTHER
1 Museo Salesiano
2 Sauna Blub
3 Iglesia La Merced
10 Duchas Tina
11 ETUCSA & Cruz del Sur Buses
14 Transportes Costa Sierra
15 Tourist Office
16 Banco de Crédito
17 Banco de la Nación
21 Casa de Cambio
23 Empresa de Transportes San Juan
26 Buses to Chupaca & Pilcomayo

27 Casa de Cambio
28 Cine Pacifico
31 Comité 12 Colectivos to Lima
32 Telefónica del Peru
33 Comité 22 Colectivos to Lima
35 Buses to San Jerónimo & Concepción
38 Expreso Huaytapalana
39 Buses to San Jerónimo, Concepción & Jauja
40 Buses to La Oroya
41 Buses to Hualhuas, Cajas & Huamancaca
42 Central Post Office
43 Iglesia La Inmaculada
45 Municipalidad
47 Mariscal Cáceres
50 Taj Mahal
52 Empresa Molina
53 Empresa Hidalgo, Antezana, many small bus companies
54 Empresa Ayacucho

offers tours arranged by Luis 'Lucho' Hurtado, a local man who speaks English and knows the surrounding area well. He can guide you on adventurous treks down the eastern slopes of the Andes and into the high jungle on foot, horseback or public transport. It isn't luxurious but it's a good chance to experience something of the 'real' rural Peru. Lucho's father has a ranch in the middle of nowhere at which you can stay and meet all kinds of local people. I have heard several recommendations of his trips. If you are unable to get a group together, you may be able to join up with another group. The trips last anywhere from three to eight days and cost about US$30 per person per day, including simple food. Accommodations are rustic and trips may involve some camping.

Guided day hikes can be arranged for about US$20 per person including lunch. Longer trips beyond the Huancayo area can also be arranged.

The best standard travel agent that has bus tours in the Río Mantara valley is Huancayo Tours (☎ 23-3351), Calle Real 543.

Bicycle Rental
Incas del Peru (above) rents mountain bikes for US$20 per day including a guide, or less if you want to strike out on your own. Multi-day rentals can be arranged at a discount.

Language Courses
Incas del Peru also arranges Spanish lessons which include meals and accommodations with a local family (if you wish) for about US$150 a week. Lessons can be modified or extended to fit your interests and you can learn to cook local dishes, play the panpipes, or weaving and other local crafts.

Special Events
There are hundreds of fiestas or ferias in Huancayo and surrounding villages – some locals say that there's a party every day somewhere in the Río Mantaro valley. Ask at a tourist information center. One of the biggest events in Huancayo is Semana Santa, with big religious processions attracting people from all over Peru. Hotel

rooms fill up and raise their prices during the festival.

Places to Stay – bottom end

Many cheap hotels are to be found in the area between the Plaza de Armas and the train station to Lima. There are also a couple of cheap hotels in front of the train station to Huancavelica, but the central ones are better.

The clean *La Casa de la Abuela*, Giráldez 1081, charges US$5 per person and includes continental breakfast with good coffee. They have hot showers and a games room, and are recommended. Reservations can be made at Incas del Peru. At the same price is the popular *Residencial Baldeón*, Amazonas 543, in a friendly family house, with hot water and kitchen privileges; breakfast is included. The *Residencial Huancayo* (☎ 23-3541), Giráldez 356, charges US$6/7 and has hot water in the communal showers all day. It is basic but popular with budget travelers. A recent report says they now have rooms with private bath as well.

Other cheap hotels include the *Hostal Universal*, Pichis 100, the *Hostal Roma*, Loreto 447, and the *Hostal Tivoli*, Puno 488, which are very basic, cold-water hotels offering the cheapest rooms in town at about US$4/6. The *Hotel Centro*, Loreto 452, has similarly priced rooms as well as rooms with private bath (cold showers) for a couple of dollars more. Other cold-water hotels that don't charge much more include the *Hotel Prince*, Calixto 578, and the

clean *Hostal Villa Rica*, Calle Real 1291, both of which have rooms with or without private bath.

Note that if you stay in a cold-water hotel, hot showers (US$1) and a sauna (US$2) are available at *Duchas Tina*, behind the cathedral. There's also the delightfully named *Sauna Blub* (☎ 22-1692), Pasaje Veranal 187, just off Ayacucho.

The basic *Hostal Will Roy*, Calixto 452, has erratic hot showers and charges US$6/8 in rooms with shared bath. The *Hotel Torre Torre*, Calle Real 873, is basic but clean and has hot water. Rates are US$5.50/7.50, or US$2 more with private bath. The similarly priced *Hostal Los Angeles*, Calle Real 245, has hot water in the mornings. *Percy's Hotel*, Calle Real 1339, is clean and has hot water in the morning. Rates are US$7.50/10 with private bath.

Places to Stay – middle

Hostal Pussy (☎ 23-1565), on the 300 block of Giráldez, has been recommended as clean and safe, with a friendly, English-speaking landlady. Rates are US$9/12.50, or a little less with shared bathrooms. Similar rates are charged at the following, all of which have clean rooms with private baths: The *Hotel Roger* (☎ 23-3488), Ancash 460, is centrally located. The *Hotel Palace* (☎ 23-8501), Ancash 1127, has hot water during early mornings and early evenings. The friendly *Hotel Plaza*, Ancash 171, has 24-hour hot water and TVs in some of the rooms. For a couple of dollars more, the *Hotel El Dorado* (☎ 22-3947), Piura 428, is another fine choice.

The *Hotel Santa Felicita* and the *Hotel Kiya* (☎ 23-1431) are both on the Plaza de Armas. The Kiya charges US$20/25 for clean rooms with telephone, bath, hot water, soap and towel. The Santa Felicita has similar facilities and prices.

The centrally located *Turismo Hotel* (☎ 23-1072), Ancash 729, is a pleasant-looking old building with some wooden balconies. Rooms with bath and telephone cost about US$35/45, including

---

Papa à la Huancaína

Visitors to Huancayo should try the local specialty, *papa à la huancaina*, which consists of a boiled potato topped with a tasty white sauce of cheese, milk, hot pepper and butter. The whole concoction is served with an olive and eaten as a cold potato salad. Despite the hot pepper, it's not too spicy – in fact, I find that it has a distinctly peanut-like flavor. ■

continental breakfast. There are some cheaper rooms with shared bath. The hotel also offers a pleasant restaurant and bar, and is probably the best in Huancayo at the moment, though the more modern *Hotel Presidente* (☎ 23-1275), Calle Real 1138, is a few dollars cheaper and also recommended.

Places to Eat

Restaurants recommended by budget travelers for cheap set meals include *El Pino*, Calle Real 539, and *Pinky's*, Giráldez 147. The *Chifa Central* on the north corner of the plaza is the best value for Chinese food and the *El Parque* on Ancash near the plaza is a good chicken place.

There are several notable restaurants on or near the Plaza de Armas. The best is the *Restaurant Olímpico* which has good set menus for about US$2 and Peruvian à la carte plates from about US$5, efficient service and a huge open kitchen allowing you to watch your food being prepared. Other similarly priced places near the plaza are the *Restaurant El Inca*, Puno 530, and *Lalo's Restaurant*, Giráldez 363. The restaurant in the Turismo Hotel is also worth trying.

La Cabaña (☎ 22-3303), Giráldez 652, has good pizzas, sandwiches, anticuchos and is probably the only place in Peru that serves New Zealand-style lamb, courtesy of Kiwi co-owner Beverly Stuart. There is a book exchange, live music from Thursday to Saturday nights and travel information. It's a popular hangout for travelers and locals.

Away from the town center you'll find several restaurants serving typical food in a slightly rural atmosphere. Northwest of town, Calle Real becomes Avenida Mariscal Castilla in the El Tambo district. Here, you'll find *La Estancia* (☎ 22-3279), M Castilla 2815, which does a great lunchtime *pachamanca* – a dish containing cuy, pork, lamb, potatoes, beans and tamales, among other possible ingredients, wrapped in leaves and cooked in an underground earth oven (basically, a hole in the ground!). Go early and watch them disinter

it. A filling lunch is about US$8. Another place to try is *Recreo Huancahuasi* (☎ 23-5330), 2222 M Castilla, which has a pachamanca for Sunday lunch. Nearby is *Los Maderos* (☎ 22-3034), M Castilla 1860, which is open in the evening for pizza and barbecues.

Entertainment

Huancayo offers little in the way of nightlife. A lot of travelers end up at the *La Cabaña Restaurant* which has the liveliest action at night and quite good music, both folklórico and various forms of rock most Thursdays through Sundays. The *Taj Mahal*, Huancavelica 1052, is a popular club with video karaoke and dancing. You can also dance at a new disco, *Coconut*, at Huancavelica 430, near Puno. The people at La Cabaña know other places where you can dance or party.

Calientes

Calientes, or 'hot ones,' are drinks sold on cold Andean nights. All through the night, you will find people selling these drinks from little stoves on wheels on street corners. Here's a recipe to warm the cockles of your heart.

- half a cup of black tea leaves
- 1 stick of cinnamon
- 1 teaspoon aniseed

a generous pinch of each of the following:

- lemon grass
- lemon balm
- chamomile
- fennel
- fig leaves

Put all the above ingredients into a kettle and boil for 10 minutes. In a cup put the juice of one lime, two teaspoons of sugar or honey, one measure of pisco or rum, then fill the cup with the hot tea mixture. Drink it while it's hot! ■

recipe courtesy of Beverly Stuart

Things to Buy

There are two main markets in Huancayo: the Mercado Mayorista (daily produce market) and the Feria Dominical (Sunday craft market). The very colorful produce market spills out along the railway tracks from the covered Mercado Mayorista off Ica east of the railway tracks. In the meat section, you can buy various Andean delicacies such as fresh and dried frogs, guinea pigs, rabbits and chickens. Although it's a daily market, the most important day is Sunday, coinciding with the weekly craft market.

The Sunday craft market occupies five or six blocks along Calle Huancavelica to the northwest of Ica. A variety of weavings, sweaters and other textile goods, embroidered items, ceramics and wood carvings is sold here, as well as the carved gourds in which the area specializes. These are made in the nearby villages of Cochas Grande and Cochas Chico. The non-craft items range from cassette tapes to frilly underwear. You must bargain hard here to get the best prices; gourds are reputedly the best buy. This is definitely a place to keep an eye on your valuables.

Kamaq Maki (☎ 23-3183), Santa Isabel 1865 (in the Miraflores suburb – take a cab), is Quechua for 'Creative Hand.' This craft cooperative has a fine selection of high-quality sweaters and also a few items from the departments of Junín and Huancavelica. Kamaq Maki involves local craftspeople who preserve traditional techniques and designs in their work. Hours are 9 am to 2 pm, Monday to Saturday, but call ahead to check. Their store has moved several times over the last few years.

Buyers of handicrafts would do well to familiarize themselves with local crafts by visiting the display at the tourist information office. The folks at Incas del Peru sell some good-quality stuff and can take you to meet the craftspeople.

Getting There & Away

Bus With no airport and a limited train system, Huancayo depends heavily on bus services and there are many companies to choose from. Shop around if you're on a tight budget, as fares vary substantially, as do levels of comfort.

Mariscal Cáceres (☎ 23-1232), Huánuco 350, has nine buses to Lima every day. Most cost about US$7 but their US$9 presidential service is recommended for being uncrowded and not stopping. Others recommended for Lima are ETUCSA (☎ 23-2638), Puno 220, and Cruz del Sur (☎ 23-4251), Puno 250, both of which have comfortable non-stop buses with toilet aboard and may serve you a snack en route. Companies with cheaper and less frequent service to Lima include Empresa Molina, Angaraes 334, Transportes Costa Sierra, Antezana, Hidalgo and several other companies – they are marked on the map. Some companies have buses for as cheap a US$4.50 to Lima, which takes from six to eight hours. If you're in a hurry, consider taking one of the colectivo taxis. Comité 12 (☎ 23-3281), Loreto 421, and Comité 22 (☎ 23-5841), Loreto 345, have several cars to Lima every day which take five to six hours and charge about US$13 per passenger.

Buses to Huancavelica take about seven hours and charge about US$3 or US$4. Empresa Molina and Empresa Hidalgo both have buses there, though the first leaves in the middle of the night for a morning arrival. Buses to Ayacucho take 12 to 14 hours if the going is good and charge about US$8. Empresa Molina and Empresa Ayacucho are the best for this route, and Hidalgo and Antezana also go to Ayacucho every day. This rough road is receiving maintenance and is being improved, but still expect delays in the rainy season.

Empresa de Transportes San Juan, Quito 136, has minibuses almost every hour to Tarma (US$2.50) which can drop you at Concepción or Jauja. Some continue to La Merced/San Ramón and even to Oxapampa.

Empresa Ayacucho goes to many small destinations, mainly within a few hours of Huancayo. Once a week they actually go to Ayacucho, continuing on through Andahuaylas and Abancay to Cuzco (US$20, a couple of days on atrocious roads). Travelers to Cuzco would do best to take the journey in stages, stopping at Huancavelica, Ayacucho, Andahuaylas and Abancay. This is one of those situations where the more time you have, the better. Money isn't going to buy you much. It's wild mountainous country with few services but great scenery.

The route to Satipo, in the jungle, is open again. I haven't been there but there are buses available with Empresa de Transportes San Juan. You can also find buses north to Cerro de Pasco, Huánuco and Tingo María.

Local buses to most of the nearby villages leave from the street intersections shown on the Huancayo map. The companies rarely have offices or fixed schedules. You just show up and wait until a bus is ready to leave. Ask other people waiting with you for more details. The tourist office is a good source of local bus information.

Train Huancayo's two train stations are in different parts of town and are not linked by train (though the tracks do connect). The central station serves Lima but the passenger train was discontinued in the 1980s, although recent investment (see Lima) may reopen the route. The most spectacular part of this route is described earlier under La Oroya. The journey used to take about 10 hours.

The Huancavelica train station is at the southeastern end of town. Train is the best mode of transport to Huancavelica because the road is not very good. There are two trains: the faster *expreso* and the slower *extra*.

The expreso takes 4½ hours, costs US$2.50 and leaves at 6.30 am daily, except Sunday when it leaves at 2 pm. Try to buy your ticket before you travel, as this service is very popular and the train is often full. Tickets are sold from 3 to 6 pm on the previous day and at 6 am on the day of travel. They start selling numbered tickets for 1st-class carriages but, when these run out, they have been reported to sell unnumbered tickets in 2nd class where you have to fight for a seat.

The extra takes about 6½ hours, leaves at 12.30 pm daily, except Sunday, and costs US$2 in 1st class, a few cents less in 2nd class. Tickets are sold from 9 am. All these times are definitely subject to change.

When these trains reach Huancavelica, they turn around and come back again.

RÍO MANTARO VALLEY

Two main road systems link Huancayo with the villages of the Río Mantaro valley and are known simply as the left and right of the river. With Huancayo lying in the southern part of the valley, left translates into west and right into east. It is best to confine your sightseeing on any given day to one side or the other because there are few bridges.

Perhaps the most interesting excursion is on the east side of the valley where you can visit the twin villages of Cochas Grande and Cochas Chico, about 11 km from Huancayo. These villages are the major production centers for the incised gourds which have made the area famous. Oddly enough, the gourds are grown mainly on the coast and imported into the highlands from the Chiclayo and Ica areas. Once they reach the highlands they are dried and scorched, then decorated using

---

Market Days Around Huancayo

Each little village and town in the Río Mantaro valley has it's own *feria* or market day. If you enjoy these, you'll find one on every day of the week.

Monday
    San Agustín de Cajas, Huayucachi
Tuesday
    Hualhuas, Pucara
Wednesday
    San Jeronimo, Jauja
Thursday
    El Tambo, Sapallanga
Friday
    Cochas
Saturday
    Matahuasi, Chupaca, Marco
Sunday
    Huancayo, Jauja, Mito, Comas ■

woodworking tools. The gourds are available at the Huancayo Sunday craft market but, if you speak Spanish and can hit it off with the locals, you can see them being made and buy them at Cochas.

Other villages of interest for their handicrafts include San Agustín de Cajas, Hualhuas and San Jerónimo de Tunán. Cajas is known for the manufacture of broad-brimmed wool hats, though this industry seems to be dying. Hualhuas is a center for the manufacture of wool products – ponchos, weavings, sweaters and other items. San Jerónimo is known for its filigree silver work and also has a 17th-century church with fine wooden altars. While the villages can easily be visited from Huancayo, most buying and selling is done in Huancayo and the villages have few facilities for shopping or anything else. The key here is the ability to speak Spanish and make friends with the locals. Going on a tour, guided hike or bike ride (as described above) helps getting into this as well.

HUANCAVELICA

Huancavelica, 147 km south of Huancayo, is the capital of the department of the same name. High and remote; most of the department lies above 3500 meters and has a cold climate, though it can get T-shirt-hot during the sunny days of the dry season (May to October). The rest of the year tends to be wet, and during the rainiest months (between February and April) the roads are sometimes in such bad shape that Huancavelica can be virtually cut off from the rest of Peru.

This historic city is nearly 3700 meters above sea level and has a population of well over 30,000. (Many of these have arrived recently, escaping from the deadly problems of terrorism in the late '80s and early '90s.) Before the arrival of Europeans, Huancavelica was a strategic Inca center, and shortly after the conquest, the Spanish discovered its mineral wealth. By 1564, the Spaniards were sending Indian slaves to Huancavelica to work in the mercury and silver mines. The present town was founded in 1571 under the name of Villa Rica de Oropesa and retains a very pleasant colonial atmosphere and many interesting churches. It's a small but attractive town visited by few tourists, partly because it's not on the main Central Highland road between Huancayo and Ayacucho. This means that visitors usually must travel from Huancayo and then backtrack.

Information
Tourist Office There is no official tourist office, though one may open soon. Meanwhile, you can try the Ministerio de Turismo, Nicolás de Piérola 180, or the Instituto Nacional de Cultura (INC), on Plaza San Juan de Dios.

Money Changing traveler's checks may be difficult; try the Banco de Crédito but don't rely on it. Changing cash dollars is no problem.

Post & Telecommunications The post office on the Plaza de Armas is worth a look because of the tumbledown old colonial building in which it is housed. The area code is 064.

Police Over the last few years, foreign tourists were required to register with the PIP police, although this rule may be relaxed by this time. Ask. In both 1992 and 1993, the register showed only two foreign visitors, but about 30 registered in 1994, showing the return of tourism. The registration procedure is quick if your passport is in order.

Churches
There are seven churches of note: Santa Ana, now in a bad state of disrepair, was founded in the 16th century and was followed in the 17th century first by the cathedral, then by Santo Domingo, San Francisco, San Cristóbal, La Ascensión and finally San Sebastián. San Francisco is famous for its 11 intricately worked altars. The cathedral has been restored and contains what has been called the best colonial altar in Peru. It is certainly a magnificent

Huancavelica

0   100   200 m

PLACES TO STAY
14 Hotel Tahuantinsuyo
22 Hotel Presidente
   de Huancavelica
23 Hostal Mercurio
24 Mi Hotel
25 Hotel Savoy
26 Hostal Santo Domingo
27 Hostal Virrey

PLACES TO EAT
5 Restaurant Joy
12 Restaurant
   Gansa de Oro
15 Restaurant
   La Estrellita
   & others
21 Las Magnolias
28 Césars

OTHER
1 Plaza & Church of
   La Ascensión
2 San Cristóbal
   Hot Springs
3 Plaza & Church of
   San Cristóbal
4 Ministerio de Turismo
6 Post Office
7 Municipalidad
8 Telefónica del Peru

9 Santo Domingo Church
10 San Sebastían Church
11 Banco de Crédito
13 Instituto Nacional
   de Cultura
16 Empresa Hidalgo
17 Expreso Huancavelica
18 PIP
19 Santa Ana Church
20 San Francisco Church
29 Transportes Oropesa

church. Santo Domingo has also recently been restored and San Sebastían is currently under restoration.

Huancavelican churches are noted for their silver-plated altars, unlike the rest of Peru's colonial churches which are usually gold-plated.

Visitors find that many of the churches are often closed to tourism. You can go as a member of the congregation when they are open for services, usually early in the morning on weekdays, with longer morning hours on Sundays. Those with a particular interest in colonial churches can

contact Señor Gilmar Torres Velasquez, Manuel Segura 243, beside the cathedral. He is the director of the church restoration projects and has the keys to the churches, though he doesn't speak English.

Hot Springs
The San Cristóbal hot springs (marked on the Huancavelica map) are fed into a large, slightly murky swimming pool in which you can relax for about US25¢. For US35¢ you can have a (private) hot shower. There is a bar and café and it's reasonably pleasant. You can rent a towel, soap and a

bathing suit if you've forgotten yours (though their selection of bathing wear is limited and unlovely). The springs are open from 7 am to 4 pm daily (ticket sales stop at 3 pm).

Market
Market day in Huancavelica is Sunday and, although there are smaller daily markets, Sunday is the best day to see the locals in traditional dress (see the next town, Lircay, for a description). The main market area is near the river and there is a smaller market off the main street, M Muñoz.

Mercury Mine Hike
An interesting hike of about three hours' duration leads to the old mercury mines. Leave town from near the train station, heading south; it's a bit difficult to find the right path at first, but after a few hundred meters it becomes obvious. It is a steep ascent going to over 4000 meters above sea level, so take time to become acclimatized. The hike brings you to the village of Santa Barbara, with its now-deserted colonial church. Nearby are the abandoned modern mining installations, which were finally closed in 1976. Between the village and the mining installations you can find the old entrance to the original 16th-century mine, carved into the rock and with a coat of arms beside it. If you have a good flashlight it's possible to enter it a little ways, but do so at your own risk.

Apart from the deserted church and mine, the walk is of interest because of the many llama and alpaca herds in the mountain landscape. Huancavelica has many other little-known areas that have been closed to tourism for years but will soon be ready for the adventurous traveler.

Special Events
Colorful traditional fiestas occur on major Peruvian holidays, with Carnaval, Semana Santa, Todos Santos and Christmas being particularly important. Other local fiestas are held on January 6 and 12.

Places to Stay
Most hotels are very cheap and have only cold water, but with the natural hot baths in town, this is not a great hardship. The cheapest place is the *Hostal Santo Domingo*, Barranca 366, which charges US$2.50/3.50 and is better than the very basic, not very clean *Hotel Savoy* and *Hostal Virrey*, which charge US$3/4.

Better cheap places include *Mi Hotel*, Carabaya 481, which is clean, friendly, has hot water in the morning in shared showers, and charges about US$3 per person. Also quite good is the nearby *Hotel Tahuantinsuyo*, Carabaya 399, which has some well-lit rooms with table and chair for US$3.50/5 and others with private bath and hot water in the mornings at US$4/5.50.

A better hot water supply is found in the *Hostal Mercurio*, Torre Tagle 455. This place is clean, but the rows of rooms painted institutional green make it look somewhat grim. Rates are US$4.50/6.50, or US$6/8 with private bath.

The best in town is the *Hotel Presidente de Huancavelica* (☎ 95-3070, fax 95-2760) in a nice old building on the Plaza de Armas. It's about US$21/28 with bath, or US$15/21 with shared bath. Prices include a continental breakfast, and hot water is available.

Places to Eat
There are no particularly good restaurants in Huancavelica. The restaurant at the *Hotel Presidente de Huancavelica* is the most expensive and no more than mediocre. Elsewhere in town you can eat decent set menus for about US$1.50 or less. There are some cheap restaurants along M Muñoz. *La Estrellita*, S Barranca 255, serves excellent trout. This is fished from the large nearby Andean lake of Chochococha which, at 4600 meters above sea level, must be one of the highest commercial fish sources in the world. There are several other OK places on the same block, including *El Misti*, *La Amistad* and others.

Another street worth trying is V Toledo. Here you'll find the *Ganso de Oro*, V Toledo 283, and the recommended

Restaurant Joy, V Toledo 230. Others which have been recommended are *Césars*, M Muñoz 390, and *Las Magnolias*, just off the Plaza de Armas.

Getting There & Away

Despite being the capital of its department, Huancavelica has no commercial airport, so to reach it you must travel overland. The train from Huancayo is more comfortable than the buses, but the road goes higher than the train and has better views. Take the bus one way and the train the other.

Bus Almost all major buses depart from Avenida M Muñoz. The bus trip to Huancayo takes six hours and costs about US$3.50. Empresa Hidalgo, Transportes Oropesa and Expreso Huancavelica all have three buses a day, usually leaving around 6 am, noon and 5 pm. Some buses continue to Lima (14 hours); if you wish to continue, check whether you are on a through bus. Companies will sell you Lima tickets for a bus going to Huancayo without telling you that you have to change buses in Huancayo. Occasional buses and trucks take the spectacular high route southwest to Pisco and then to Lima. This goes through the villages of Santa Inés and Castrovirreyna, reaches an altitude of about 4800 meters, and passes many Andean lakes and herds of alpaca, llama and vicuña. The route can take 20 hours or more and you should be prepared for freezing temperatures. Buses might not get through in the December to April rainy months.

There are no direct services to Ayacucho. The easiest way to get there is to go back to Huancayo. It is possible to take a bus to the village of Santa Inés or the bigger town of Castrovirreyna, from where you can catch one of the buses going from Lima to Ayacucho via Pisco (see Ayacucho for a route description). However, I don't know what kind of accommodations you'll find in Santa Inés (probably none) or Castrovirreyna. This is an option for experienced, self-sufficient, off-the-beaten-track travelers with a working knowledge of Spanish.

Train The trains that arrive from Huancayo turn around in Huancavelica and go straight back again. See the Huancayo section for more information. The Extra leaves Huancavelica at 6.30 am and the Expreso leaves at 12.30 pm, except on Sundays when the Expreso leaves at 7 am. You should by tickets in advance. Ticket sales are 6 to 6.30 am, 9 am to 12.30 pm and 3 to 6 pm.

LIRCAY

The small, colonial town of Lircay is almost 80 km southeast of Huancavelica. Its main claim to fame is as the center for the department's traditional clothing, which can be seen at Huancavelica's Sunday market. The predominant color is black, but the men wear rainbow-colored pompoms on their hats and at their waists (supposedly love tokens from women) and the women wear multicolored shawls over their otherwise somber clothing. The town has a couple of basic hotels.

IZCUCHACA

Izcuchaca, the main village between Huancayo and Huancavelica, has a basic hotel, a pottery center, hot springs and archaeological ruins, which are accessible only on foot. There is also a historic bridge which, legend has it, was built by the Incas and defended bitterly by Huascar against the advance of Atahualpa's troops during the civil war which was raging in the Inca Empire when the Spaniards arrived.

AYACUCHO

Founded by the Spanish in 1539, Ayacucho is a small city lying 2731 meters above sea level. It has a population of 100,000 and is the capital of its department. Despite its remoteness and small size, Ayacucho is arguably Peru's most fascinating Andean town after Cuzco and is well worth a visit.

Five hundred years before the Inca Empire, the Wari (also written Huari) Empire dominated the Peruvian highlands. The Wari's ruined capital, 22 km northeast of Ayacucho, is easily reached along the paved road which now links it with Ayacucho.

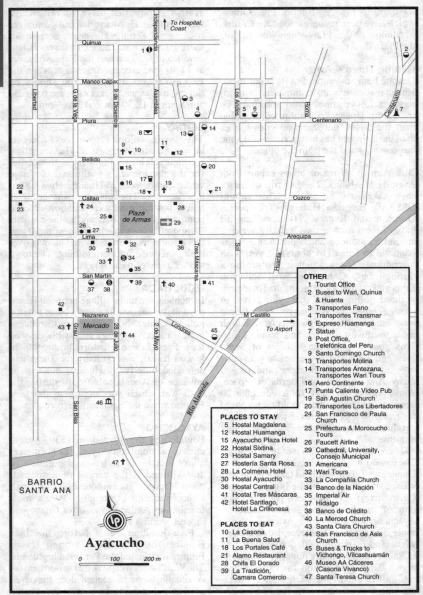

Ayacucho

0   100   200 m

OTHER
1   Tourist Office
2   Buses to Wari, Quinua & Huanta
3   Transportes Fano
4   Transportes Transmar
6   Expreso Huamanga
7   Statue
8   Post Office, Telefónica del Peru
9   Santo Domingo Church
13 Transportes Molina
14 Transportes Antezana, Transportes Wari Tours
16 Aero Continente
17 Punta Caliente Video Pub
19 San Agustín Church
20 Transportes Los Libertadores
24 San Francisco de Paula Church
25 Prefectura & Morocucho Tours
26 Faucett Airline
29 Cathedral, University, Consejo Municipal
31 Americana
32 Wari Tours
33 La Compañía Church
34 Banco de la Nación
35 Imperial Air
37 Hidalgo
38 Banco de Crédito
40 La Merced Church
43 Santa Clara Church
44 San Francisco de Asis Church
45 Buses & Trucks to Vichongo, Vilcashuamán
46 Museo AA Cáceres (Casona Vivanco)
47 Santa Teresa Church

PLACES TO STAY
5   Hostal Magdalena
12 Hostal Huamanga
15 Ayacucho Plaza Hotel
22 Hostal Sixtina
23 Hostal Samary
27 Hostería Santa Rosa
28 La Colmena Hotel
30 Hostal Ayacucho
36 Hostal Central
41 Hostal Tres Máscaras
42 Hotel Santiago, Hotel La Crillonesa

PLACES TO EAT
10 La Casona
11 La Buena Salud
18 Los Portales Café
21 Alamo Restaurant
28 Chifa El Dorado
39 La Tradición, Camara Comercio

Ayacucho played a major part in the battles for independence and a huge nearby monument marks the site of the important Battle of Ayacucho, fought in 1824.

As mentioned at the beginning of this chapter, the central Andes is one of Peru's least visited areas. Ayacucho is no exception to this. Its first road link with the Peruvian coast was not finished until 1924 and, as late as 1960, there were only two buses and a few dozen vehicles in the city. Departmental statistics show that in 1981, there were still only 44 km of paved roads in the department, only 7% of the population had running water in their houses and only 14% had electricity. Thus, Ayacucho has retained its colonial atmosphere more than most Peruvian cities and many of its old colonial buildings have been preserved.

Information
Tourist Office The Dirección General de Indústria y Turismo, Asamblea 481, is a good, friendly and helpful source of information, maps and leaflets. Local travel agencies (see below) are also helpful.

Money The Banco de Crédito will change traveler's checks at low commissions. Cash dollars are readily exchanged.

Post & Telecommunications These offices are marked on the map. The area code for Ayacucho is 064.

Travel Agencies Morocucho Tours and Wari Tours, both on the Plaza de Armas, organize local excursions and have information. They cater mainly to Peruvian tourists and their guides speak Spanish.

Medical Services The hospital is on Independencia on the north side of town.

Churches
The 17th-century cathedral on the Plaza de Armas has a religious art museum which has been closed for years but may reopen. The cathedral and a dozen other colonial churches from the 16th, 17th and 18th centuries are well worth a visit for their incredibly ornate facades and interiors. The most important of Ayacucho's churches are marked on the map. Opening hours are

Sendero Luminoso
It was in the remote environment of Ayacucho that the Sendero Luminoso (Shining Path) guerrilla movement was born, beginning in 1962 as the Huamanga Command of the Frente de Liberación Nacional (FLN). In 1965, the Huamanga Command broke with the national FLN organization and, in the late 1960s, flirted with communism. In the 1970s, when the Sendero was a little-known local organization headquartered at Ayacucho's University of Huamanga, nonviolent political discussion and dissent within the confines of the campus were its main activities.

The violence with which the world press has frequently identified the Sendero began in the early 1980s and peaked in 1982. The strong military measures taken in 1983, in an attempt to control the organization, were frequently criticized because of the killing of civilians. The spread of the Sendero was halted for a few years in the mid-'80s but, by the end of the decade, strong Sendero presence was felt not only in Ayacucho but through much of the central Peruvian Andes. The Sendero's objectives appeared to be the overthrow of Peru's present democratic system, the destruction of all bourgeois elements in the country and the return of land to the peasant farmers. The violence employed in the pursuit of these aims contributed to the fact that the Sendero had relatively little popular support in Peru.

In the early 1990s, Ayacucho was considered a dangerous destination but the situation stabilized in 1993 after the Sendero leaders were captured and imprisoned for life. Since that time, increasing numbers of Peruvian and foreign visitors have visited the area and it is a safe destination again. ■

erratic but the tourist office can help with scheduling a visit.

Colonial Houses

Most of the old mansions are now mainly political offices and can be visited. The offices of the Department of Ayacucho (the *prefectura*) on the Plaza de Armas is a good example. The mansion was constructed between 1740 and 1755 and sold to the state in 1937. On the ground floor is a pretty courtyard where a visitor can see the cell of the local heroine of independence, María Parado de Bellido. Go upstairs to see some excellent tile work.

Also worth a look is the Salon de Actas in the Consejo Municipal, next to the cathedral, with its excellent view of the plaza. On the north side of the plaza are several more fine colonial houses; the tourist office can suggest which ones to visit.

Museo Andres Avelino Cáceres

This collection is housed in the Casona Vivanco, 28 de Julio 512, a mansion dating from the 16th century. Cáceres was a local man who commanded Peruvian troops during the War of the Pacific (1879-1883) against Chile. Accordingly, the museum houses maps and military paraphernalia from that period, as well as some colonial art. Admission is free but opening hours are erratic (supposedly 9 am to 6 pm).

Museo Arqueológico Hipolito Unanue

The museum is in the Centro Cultural Simón Bolívar, a little over a kilometer from the town center on your right – you can't miss it. Wari ceramics make up most of the small exhibit.

They are supposedly open from 8.30 am to 5 pm, Monday to Saturday, but there are few visitors and the caretakers often take extended lunch breaks or whatever. The best time is usually in the morning. Entry is US$1.50. To get there, walk north from the Plaza de Armas along Asamblea, which soon turns into Independencia, or take one of the minibuses along the route.

Special Events

Ayacucho's Holy Week celebration, held the week before Easter, has long been considered Peru's finest religious festival and it attracts visitors from all over the country, though relatively few foreigners. Rooms in the better hotels are booked well in advance and even the cheapest places fill completely. The tourist office has lists of local families who provide accommodations for the overflow. In 1994, there reportedly were more visitors during Santa Semana than at any other time in the previous 12 years.

Each year, the tourist bureau prints a free brochure describing the Holy Week events with street maps showing the main processions. Visitors are advised to get this detailed information. The celebrations begin on the Friday before Palm Sunday and continue for 10 days until Easter Sunday. Each day is marked with solemn yet colorful processions and religious rites which reach a fever pitch of Catholic faith and tradition. The Friday before Palm Sunday is marked by a procession in honor of La Virgen de los Dolores, or 'Our Lady of Sorrows,' during which it is customary to inflict 'sorrows' on bystanders by firing pebbles out of slingshots. Gringos have been recent targets, so be warned.

In addition to the religious services, Ayacucho's Holy Week celebrations include numerous secular activities – art shows, folk-dancing competitions and demonstrations, local music concerts, street events, sporting events (especially equestrian ones), agricultural fairs and the preparation of typical meals.

The tourist office is a good source of information about the large number of minor fiestas – there seems to be one almost every week – held throughout the department.

Places to Stay

The recent revival of tourism has left Ayacucho a little short on hotel rooms. They tend to fill up, so try to avoid arriving very late in the day. New hotels will probably be available by the time you read this.

Places to Stay – bottom end

One of the cheapest is the very basic *Hostal Ayacucho* (☎ 91-2759), Lima 165, at US$3.50/5. It isn't very clean and lacks hot water. Other basic cold-water cheapies include the *Hostal Sixtina* (☎ 91-2018), Callao 336, at US$5/7, and the *Hostal Central* (☎ 91-2144), Arequipa 180, at US$5/9.

The *Hotel Santiago* (☎ 91-2132), Nazarena 177, is basic and noisy because of the nearby market, but does have some hot water in the mornings. Rates are US$4/6.50 or US$10 for a double with bath. Next door is the slightly better (but still noisy) *Hotel Crillonesa* (☎ 91-2350), Nazarena 165, also with hot water in the morning. Rooms are US$4.50/8.

The *Hostal Magdalena* (☎ 91-2910), Centenario 277, is clean and has hot water in the morning, but rooms vary in size. Rates are US$5/9 or about US$15 for a double with bath. The *Hostal Huamanga* (☎ 91-3527), Bellido 535, has hot water in the morning, but is not as good for US$5.50 per person or US$7.50 with private bath. The *Hostal Samary* (☎ 91-2442), Callao 329, is simple but clean, has great rooftop views and hot water in the early morning and evening. Rates are UD$7.50/9.50, or US$9/11 with private bath.

Places to Stay – middle

The recommended *La Colmena Hotel* (☎ 91-2146), Cuzco 140, has an attractive courtyard and is clean, safe and a good value, which means it's often full by lunchtime. Rates are US$8/12 or US$12/15 with private bath and hot water in the morning and evening. Also good value is the friendly new *Hostal Tres Máscaras* (☎ 91-3520, 91-2921), Tres Máscaras 194, which has a pleasant garden, hot water and rooms for US$8 per person, or US$11 per person with private bath. The quiet *Hostería Santa Rosa* (☎ /fax 91-2083), Lima 166, has a nice patio with a restaurant, but is a little pricey for US$10/16 or US$15/21 with private bath.

The *Ayacucho Plaza Hotel* (☎ 91-2202/3/4, fax 91-2314), 9 de Diciembre 184, is the best in town. It is comfortable but unexciting, and rooms with bath and hot water cost US$50/66, with continental breakfast. Rooms with shared bath are about half price. The restaurant is just OK.

Places to Eat

The *Alamo Restaurant* starts serving breakfast at 7 am, offering pancakes and yogurt as well as the usual eggs and sandwiches. It is open all day and serves good, cheap food. They don't serve beer, but this restaurant is recommended to budget travelers. Marginally more expensive, but still reasonable (there are no fancy or expensive restaurants in Ayacucho), *La Casona* is popular and recommended by several travelers. *La Tradición* is also worth trying, as is the nearby restaurant *Camara Comercio* for cheap set menus. *Los Portales Café*, on the Plaza de Armas, is a good place with a sawdust-on-the-floor ambiance. For desserts, try the *San Agustín Café* next to the church of the same name. The *Chifa El Dorado*, next to La Colmena Hotel has also been recommended. The simple, signless, *La Buena Salud* vegetarian restaurant is at Asamblea 204.

Entertainment

Punto Caliente Video Pub, Asamblea 131, is a good place to have a drink at night. There are no specific places for peñas, but this is a university town with a good number of students, and tourism is again returning, so you can expect to find some kind of música folklórica action. Ask around.

Things to Buy

Ayacucho is famous as a crafts center, and though it slumped in production during the Sendero years, it's picking up again. The tourist office can recommend local artisans who will welcome you to their workshops (particularly if you buy something!). Noted crafts include carpets, rugs and tapestries woven in the Barrio Santa Ana (see map), *retablos* (colorful wooden boxes ranging from the size of a matchbox to a meter or more in height, containing intricate papier-mâché models – Peruvian rural scenes or the nativity are particularly popular), carved churches made of alabaster and ceramic altars.

Getting There & Away

Ayacucho is most easily reached by air and there are several flights available. If you travel by road, be prepared for long delays during the rainy season (the worst months are February to April), especially if you're coming from the direction of Cuzco, though other routes are only marginally better. All routes are spectacular.

From Ayacucho to Lima you can go via Pisco on the coast or via Huancayo. The Pisco route has long been considered the better and faster option, but improvements on the Ayacucho-Huancayo road now make it a toss-up. Ask locally. Bus companies claim 18 hours to Lima but it's often closer to 22 or 24 hours, even more during the wet months.

Coming up from the coast near Pisco, the road heads up to Castrovirreyna, a small mountain town 12 to 14 hours from Lima. Castrovirreyna has several basic restaurants, and buses usually stop here for meals. The road climbs to Castrovirreyna in an incredible series of hairpin bends, hugging the mountainside and often wide enough for only one vehicle, which makes the journey a little more exciting.

Beyond Castrovirreyna, the road reaches an altitude of about 4800 meters as it passes several blue, green and turquoise Andean lakes. The road flirts with the snow line for over an hour with dramatic views of high-Andean scenery and snowcaps. This section is often done at night, so travel on a full moon to see anything and dress warmly. Finally, the road begins its descent towards Ayacucho and the countryside becomes greener as forests of the dwarf polyepsis trees appear. Those who suffer from *soroche* (altitude sickness) in the high

passes are relieved by the arrival in Ayacucho, a mere 2731 meters above sea level.

Air In 1994, all five of the major domestic airlines flew from Lima to Ayacucho, but in late 1995, it was only Aero Continente, Americana, Faucett and Imperial Air. The last named has just two flights a week, while Aero Continente has two flights a day, and Americana and Faucett each have daily flights. One of Aero Continente's daily flights continues to and from Cuzco. This situation will probably change again soon. Fares to Lima are US$47 and to Cuzco US$42. Airport departure tax is US$4. Airline offices are shown on the map.

The airport is a walkable 3 km from the town center. Alternatively, catch a taxi for about US$1.50 or one of the irregular buses from the Plaza de Armas.

Bus For Lima, Transportes Molina, Los Libertadores, Transmar and Fano all have departures leaving mid-afternoon. The fare is US$10 to US$12. Hidalgo, Transportes Antezana and Transportes Molina have night buses to Huancayo; Molina also has one Huancayo departure at 6.30 am. The fare is US$7 to US$8. There are two routes; the one through Acobamba is currently a couple of hours faster than the one through Churcampa. The trip takes 12 to 14 hours in the dry season.

Transportes Wari Tours claims to have a daily departure to Cuzco (25 to 30 hours, US$18) at 7 am, but I wouldn't rely on this. It's a rough trip and the journey can be broken at Andahuaylas (about 15 hours, US$9). Transportes Molina and Transportes Fano have dawn departures to Andahuaylas. Note that these companies change their routes and services rather frequently. There are other possibilities if you ask around.

The cheapest way to get to Cuzco is to wait at the Grifo (gas station) Chakchi for a truck and ride in the back with the locals. This is slow and uncomfortable but the views are great and you will experience the Andes from a very different perspective.

A rough road drops about 200 km

northeast of Ayacucho to San Francisco and Luisiana, in the jungle on the Río Apurimac. This is a good take-out point for rafters after an adventurous descent of the river (see Cuzco). This road is traveled mainly by trucks, though occasional buses may do it. Ask around. There are basic hotels in San Francisco and a better one at Luisiana. This route was off-limits to all travelers because of Sendero problems for several years – if you decide to go there, you'll be a curiosity. Like any highlands-to-jungle road, it's rough, tough and spectacular.

Getting Around
Pick-up trucks and occasional buses will take you to many local villages, including Quinua, and to the Wari ruins, departing from beyond the statue at the east end of Avenida Centenario.

There are four local city buses, one of which goes from the Plaza de Armas to the airport. Trucks and buses to Cangallo and Vischongo leave from the Puente Nuevo area which is the bridge on Londres over the Río Alameda. Departures are normally in the morning. Some vehicles may continue on to Vilcashuamán if there is enough demand. It takes five or six hours to get to

Vischongo. Buses don't leave every day but trucks usually do. Note that the area southeast of Puente Nuevo is a bad one, so don't wander around there.

AROUND AYACUCHO
There are several places of interest that travelers to Ayacucho often visit. The area most frequented is the village and battlefield of Quinua, which is often combined with a visit to the Wari ruins. The Inca ruins of Vilcashuamán can also be visited, with other sites of interest nearby.

Wari Ruins & Quinua
Pick-up trucks leave for Quinua from the end of Avenida Centenario in Ayacucho about once an hour. The fare for the one-hour ride is US50¢. The attractive 37-km road climbs about 550 meters to Quinua, 3300 meters above sea level. After about 20 km, you will pass the extensive Wari ruins sprawling for several kilometers along the roadside. The small site museum is usually closed, but there are more Wari artifacts to be seen in the Ayacucho museum. The five main sectors of the ruins are marked by road signs; the upper sites are in rather bizarre forests of *Opuntia* cacti. If you

visit, don't leave the site too late to look for onward or return transport – pick-ups can get hopelessly full in the afternoon.

The ruins have not been much restored, and there is not much for the untrained eye to see. Interested travelers should find a guide from Morocucho or Wari Tours in Ayacucho. These agencies can arrange a tour at any time, but if you are on a budget, wait for the weekend when there is usually an inexpensive Peruvian group tour going (you need to speak Spanish).

Wari is built on a hill and, as the road from Ayacucho climbs through it, there are reasonable views from the pick-up truck. The road climbs beyond Wari until it reaches the pretty village of Quinua; pick-up trucks usually stop at the plaza. Steps from the left-hand side of the plaza, as you arrive from Ayacucho, lead up to the village church. The church is on an old-fashioned cobblestone plaza and a small museum nearby displays various relics from the major independence battle which was fought in this area. The museum is open from 8 am to 5 pm daily, except Mondays, and costs about US$1.35 to visit. It is not of much interest, however, unless you are particularly fascinated by the battle fought here. Beside the museum you can see the room where the Spanish Royalist troops signed their surrender, leading to the end of colonialism in Peru.

To reach the battlefield, turn left behind the church and head out of the village along Jirón Sucre which, after a walk of about 10 minutes, rejoins the main road. As you walk, notice the red-tiled roofs elaborately decorated with ceramic model churches. Quinua is famous as a handicraft center and these model churches are especially typical of the area. Local stores sell this craft.

The **white obelisk**, which is intermittently visible for several kilometers as you approach Quinua, now lies a few minutes' walk in front of you. The impressive monument is 40 meters high and features carvings commemorating the Battle of Ayacucho, fought here on December 9, 1824. The walk up from Quinua and the views are pleasant. The whole area is protected as the 300-hectare **Santuario Histórico Pampas de Ayacucho**.

There are no accommodations in Quinua (at this time) and only very basic food supplies. There is a small market on Sunday.

Vilcashuamán & Vischongo

Vilcashuamán, or 'sacred falcon,' was considered the geographical center of the Inca Empire. It was here that the Inca road between Cuzco and the coast crossed the road running the length of the Andes. Little remains of the city's earlier magnificence; Vilcashuamán has fallen prey to looters and many of its blocks have been used to build more modern buildings. The once-magnificent Temple of the Sun now has a parish church on top of it. The only structure still in a reasonable state of repair is a five-tiered pyramid, called an *usnu*, topped by a huge double throne carved from stone and used by the Inca.

To get there, take a vehicle from Ayacucho to Vischongo (about 110 km, five to six hours). There is a basic hotel in Vischongo. From here, it's about 45 minutes by car or almost two hours uphill on foot to Vilcashuamán. Reportedly, there is now a restaurant and basic hotel in Vilcashuamán, too. From Vischongo, you can also walk to an Intihuatana ruin, where there are reportedly thermal baths (about an hour) or you can also walk to a *Puya raimondii* forest (see The Huaraz Area for a description of this plant) which is less than an hour away by foot.

Morochuco and Wari Tours can provide a guided service.

North of La Oroya

So far, this chapter has described travel east or south from the central Andean crossroads town of La Oroya. If you decide to go north instead, you will pass through the highland towns of Junín, Cerro de Pasco, Huánuco and Tingo María, ending up in the important jungle town of Pucallpa.

JUNÍN

The village of Junín is at 4125 meters above sea level, about 55 km due north of La Oroya. I have never heard or read of a hotel here but there must be some kind of basic accommodations available. An important independence battle was fought at the nearby Pampa of Junín, just south of the village. This is now protected as the 2500-hectare **Santuario Histórico Chacamarca** and there is a monument.

About 10 km beyond the village is the interesting Lago de Junín. This lake is about 30 km long and 14 km wide and is Peru's largest lake after Titicaca. At more than 4000 meters above sea level, it is the highest lake of its size in the Americas. Lago de Junín is known for its bird life, some authorities claiming that one million birds live on the lake or its shores at any one time. It is a little-visited area and an excellent destination for anyone interested in seeing a good variety of the water and shore birds of the high Andes. The lake and its immediate surroundings are part of the 53,000-hectare **Reserva Nacional Junín**.

The wide, high plain in this area is bleak, windswept and very cold, so be prepared with warm, windproof clothing. There are several small unattractive villages along the road and buses stop quite often. Between these settlements, herds of llama, alpaca and sheep are seen.

CERRO DE PASCO

Cerro de Pasco is 4333 meters above sea level and has a population of about 30,000. I can't think of any town of this size that is higher anywhere in the world. It is the capital of its department and rather a miserable place. The altitude makes the town bitterly cold at night and its main reason for existence is mining. Cerro de Pasco is about 40 km north of Lago de Junín and, although it has the closest hotels to the lake, accommodations are poor. The area code is 064.

Southwest of Cerro de Pasco

A poor and not frequently used road goes southwest of Cerro de Pasco to Lima. West of Lago de Junín, the road goes near the village of Huayllay, near to which is the 6815-hectare **Santuario Nacional Huayllay**, known for its strange geological formations. Several hours further southwest is the small town of **Canta**, which has a basic hotel and restaurant and is a few kilometers away from the pre-Columbian ruins of Cantamarca, which can be visited on foot.

Places to Stay

In the town center, the *Hotel El Viajero* (☎ 72-2172) and the *Hotel Santa Rosa* (☎ 72-2120), both by the Plaza de Armas, are the best of a basic few. Both claim to have warm water in the morning and both charge about US$4/6 for rooms with shared baths. There are also the poor and very basic *Hostal Internacional* and *Hostal Comercio* on the street between the plaza and the bus terminal area.

A better hotel is the *Villa Minera* (☎ 72-1113) in the suburbs. It's a 10-minute, US$1 cab ride. They have rooms with private baths and hot water for US$7/11.

Getting There & Away

The bus terminal area is three blocks from the Plaza de Armas. There are buses to Huánuco (US$2.50, three hours), Huancayo (six hours), and Lima, most going through La Oroya and a few through Canta.

The railway to La Oroya has been used only for freight for several years.

HUÁNUCO

Huánuco is 105 km north of Cerro de Pasco and almost 2500 meters lower, providing welcome relief for soroche sufferers. The elevation is only 1894 meters above sea level. Huánuco is on the upper reaches of the Río Huallaga, the major tributary of the Río Marañon before it becomes the Amazon. Huánuco is also the capital of its department and the site of one of Peru's oldest Andean archaeological sites, the Temple of Kotosh (also known as the Temple of the Crossed Hands). The town has an interesting museum and a pleasant Plaza de Armas. Although Huánuco dates

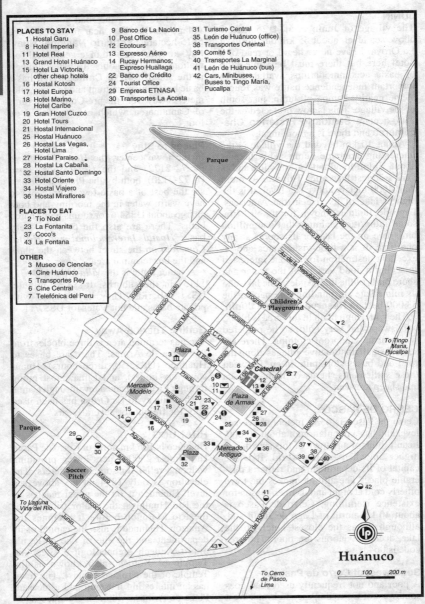

PLACES TO STAY
1 Hostal Garu
8 Hotel Imperial
11 Hotel Real
13 Grand Hotel Huánaco
15 Hotel La Victoria,
   other cheap hotels
16 Hostal Kotosh
17 Hotel Europa
18 Hotel Marino,
   Hotel Caribe
19 Gran Hotel Cuzco
20 Hotel Tours
21 Hostal Internacional
25 Hostal Huánuco
26 Hostal Las Vegas,
   Hotel Lima
27 Hostal Paraiso
28 Hostal La Cabaña
32 Hostal Santo Domingo
33 Hotel Oriente
34 Hostal Viajero
36 Hostal Miraflores

PLACES TO EAT
2 Tío Noel
23 La Fontanita
37 Coco's
43 La Fontana

OTHER
3 Museo de Ciencias
4 Cine Huánuco
5 Transportes Rey
6 Cine Central
7 Telefónica del Peru

9 Banco de La Nación
10 Post Office
12 Ecotours
13 Expresso Aéreo
14 Rucay Hermanos;
   Expreso Huallaga
22 Banco de Crédito
24 Tourist Office
29 Empresa ETNASA
30 Transportes La Acosta

31 Turismo Central
35 León de Huánuco (office)
38 Transportes Oriental
39 Comité 5
40 Transportes La Marginal
41 León de Huánuco (bus)
42 Cars, Minibuses,
   Buses to Tingo María,
   Pucallpa

Huánuco

0   100   200 m

from 1541, not much is left of its colonial buildings.

About 25 km before reaching Huánuco from Cerro de Pasco, the road goes through the village of **Ambo**, noted for its *aguardiente* distilleries. This locally popular liquor is made from the sugar cane which can be seen growing in the area. Sometimes the bus stops and passengers can buy a couple of liters.

Information
Tourist Office This is on the Plaza de Armas at General Prado 714. Hours are 8 am to 1.30 pm and 4 to 6 pm, Monday to Friday. Ecotur (☎ 51-2410 ext 16), 28 de Julio 1033, also has tourist information and local sightseeing tours.

Money As usual, the Banco de Crédito is your best bet.

Post & Telecommunications These offices are shown on the map. The area code is 064.

Museo de Ciencias
This museum at General Prado 495 is small but well organized and the exhibits are labeled. They are mainly stuffed animals from Peru, but there are also a few ceramic and archaeological pieces. The museum director, Señor Nestor Armas Wenzel, is dedicated and enthusiastic, and delights in showing visitors around. He particularly likes to talk to foreign visitors and has flags and 'welcome' signs in many languages decorating the entrance lobby. Admission is about US50¢. Hours are 9 am to noon and 3 to 6 pm weekdays and 10 am to 1 pm on Sunday.

The Temple of Kotosh
This archaeological site is also known as the Temple of the Crossed Hands because of the life-size molding, made of mud, of a pair of crossed forearms that was discovered in the ruins by an archaeological team in the early 1960s. The crossed hands can now be seen in the Museo de la Nación in Lima. The molding is dated to between 4000 and 5000 years old and no others are known to exist.

Little is known about Kotosh, one of the most ancient of Andean cultures. The temple site is overgrown and difficult to reach, though it lies only 5 km from Huánuco, and unless you are very interested in Kotosh, there is little to see. Most people are better off seeing the Crossed Hands in the Lima museum. If you really want to visit the ruins, head south on Abtao for about 1½ km from the town center until you come to a lake, Laguna Viña del Río, on your right. Here turn right (west) and proceed out of town on the road to La Unión. You may need to wade across a stream – ask locals. I haven't actually been to the ruin, but the tourist information office can give you more precise information.

Places to Stay
Huánuco is the most pleasant town between Lima and Pucallpa, so its hotels, though not very good, tend to fill quickly. You can usually find a bed, but the choice can be very limited by late afternoon, so start looking as early as possible.

Places to Stay – bottom end
The cheapest place in town is the *Hostal La Cabaña* for US$3/5, but it usually lacks water and is dirty. Slightly nicer rooms at about the same price can be found near the noisy market in the *Hotel La Victoria* and three other cheap hotels near by. All have shared cold showers.

The best cheap hotel seems to be the *Hotel Imperial*, Huánuco 581, which charges US$5/7, or US$7/10 with private bath. It's reasonably clean and quiet, but has only cold water. Across the street are the similarly priced Hotels *Marino* and *Caribe*.

Other pretty basic hotels in this price range are mainly near the market and have little to recommend them other than their cheapness. They include the *Hotel Oriente*, *Hostal Viajero*, *Hostal Internacional* and the *Hotel Europa* which does have a lot of rooms, so you'll probably get a bed there later in the day.

The *Hostal Santo Domingo* charges US$6/8 with shared bath and US$7/10 with private bath, has cold water, but seems OK. For the same rate with bath and, if you're lucky, hot water, try the *Hotel Paraiso* (☎ 51-1953) on the Plaza de Armas. Also on the plaza is the *Hotel Lima* (☎ 51-3020), which charges US$7/10 for rooms with private bath, may have hot water, and has an inexpensive café. Almost next door is the *Hostal Las Vegas* (☎ 51-2315) which has hot water sometimes and charges about US$8/12 for rather musty rooms with bath. It has a café as well. The *Hotel Kotosh* is US$7/10 with bath and cold water and the similar *Hotel Tours* is US$8/11.

Places to Stay – middle
The pleasant and secure *Hostal Huánuco* (☎ 51-2050), Huánuco 777, has a good hot-water supply and is often full. They charge US$11/14 in rooms with private bath. The *Hostal Garu* (☎ 51-3096, fax 51-3097), P Puelles 459, is decent and well-run, offering clean rooms with private hot showers for US$17/25. The *Gran Hotel Cuzco* (☎ 51-3263, 51-2244), Huánuco 616, is old but isn't bad and has clean, bare but good-sized rooms with private hot showers for US$17/27. It has a cafeteria and is popular with Peruvian businessmen.

The *Hotel Real* (☎ 51-2973), on the Plaza de Armas, is a fairly comfortable modern hotel charging US$20/28. The old-fashioned *Grand Hotel Huánuco* (☎ 51-2410, fax 51-4222) on the Plaza de Armas looks pleasant and has rooms with private bath and TV for US$28/38. It has a restaurant.

Places to Eat
Every hotel on the Plaza de Armas has a restaurant. There are several chifas or chicken places on or within a block of the plaza. The *La Fontanita* Italian restaurant on the corner of the plaza has been recommended. *La Fontana*, on the Malecón, has Italian food and steaks and seafood in the US$3 to US$7 range. It has a dance club upstairs and is locally popular on weekends. For typical local lunches only, try *Tío Noel*, which has a nice garden, or *Cocos*. Also good for local lunches are several restaurants near the Laguna Viña del Río, including the *Mukichu, Huanuceño* and *Viña del Río*. They are about 1½ km south of the Plaza de Armas along Abtao – cab drivers know them.

Entertainment
A couple of *cinemas* are shown on the map and there's *La Fontana* for dancing at weekends.

Getting There & Away
Air In 1990, only AeroPerú had a few flights a week from Lima. In 1994, daily service was provided only by Expresso Aéreo. By late 1995, there were daily flights with both Expresso Aéreo and Aero Continente, and three flights a week with AeroCóndor. Obviously, schedules and carriers change frequently. The fare is about US$65. Airport tax is US$4.

Aero Continente continues on to Tingo María and Expresso Aéreo continues on a milk run to Tingo María, Tocache, Juanjui, Saposoa, Tarapoto and Trujillo, with connecting flights to other northern cities. The airport is 8 km from town.

Bus For Lima, the best service is with León de Huánuco, which has 8 am and 8 pm departures (US$9, nine hours). Note that there is an office for tickets near the Plaza de Armas, but the bus leaves from the Malecón. Other companies operating buses to Lima are Transportes Rey, with departures at about the same time, and the not-so-good ETNASA, with only night buses.

ETNASA also has night buses to Pucallpa (US$11.50, 15 hours). Both day and night buses to Pucallpa are provided by Transportes Oriental. Empresa La Marginal has several slow buses a day to Tingo María. If you walk to the general transport stop beyond the Río Huallaga bridge (10 minutes from the town center), you'll find shared taxis or cheaper minibuses all heading to Tingo María. You can also flag down passing buses to Tingo María and

Pucallpa. Comité 5 colectivos also go to Tingo María.

Transportes Oriental has both day and night buses to Huancayo (US$6, eight hours). Rucay Hermanos and Expreso Huallaga have several buses a day to Cerro de Pasco and Huancayo. Turismo Central also goes to Huancayo daily.

To visit the remote towns of La Unión, Tantamayo and other villages, head for Jirón San Martín, a couple of blocks south of the market. Here you'll find a daily morning Transportes Acosta bus to La Unión (seven hours, US$6). For Tantamayo (10 hours to cover 150 km!), ETNASA has an 8 am bus (US$7). This is also the place to look for transport to other remote villages in the area.

LA UNIÓN

This town is roughly halfway between Huánuco and Huaraz. It is feasible to travel this way to the Cordillera Blanca. La Unión has a couple of basic hotels and transport is available from here on to Chiquián, near the Cordillera Huayhuash. From Chiquián (where there are basic hotels), you can continue on to Huaraz and the Cordillera Blanca. This is a little-traveled and, by all accounts, spectacular route.

About two to three hours' walk from La Unión are the Inca ruins of Huánuco Viejo.

TANTAMAYO

The small, remote village of Tantamayo is in the mountains north of Huánuco. The hotel can provide information for visiting the several ruins which are within a few hours' walk. Guides can be hired.

TINGO MARÍA

The 129 km road north from Huánuco climbs over a 3000-meter pass before dropping steadily to Tingo María, which lies in the lush, tropical slopes of the eastern Andes at an altitude of 649 meters. The town is on the edge of the Amazon Basin and is hot and humid most of the year. Tingo María could thus be described as a jungle town, yet it is surrounded by steep Andean foothills. Whether Tingo María

should be included in the Central Highlands or the Amazon Basin chapter is typical of the somewhat arbitrary decisions a guidebook writer must make.

Tingo María is a thriving market town. Among its main products are coca (for cocaine) and to a lesser extent, marijuana, so the town is rather unsavory and not particularly friendly to tourists. It also has a bad reputation for theft. It is definitely not a good place to buy drugs. I saw few foreign visitors here; most people go on to the jungle at Pucallpa.

Nevertheless, the town center is not any more dangerous than any other city. The dangerous area is the Río Huallaga valley north of Tingo María, which is best avoided. Remember that growing coca is not necessarily illegal and coca leaves are legally sold for chewing or making maté in most highland towns. It is the mashing of coca into *pasta básica* for use in cocaine production that is illegal. Local authorities are encouraging the production of other tropical crops, notably cocoa. Bus travel on the Huánuco-Tingo María-Pucallpa route is safe, particularly during the day.

Information

There is no tourist office. Cash dollars can be changed on the west side of the market or in the Banco de Crédito, which may change traveler's checks but don't rely on it. The area code for Tingo María is 064. The hospital is at the south end of Ucayali.

Universidad Nacional Agraria de la Selva (UNAS)

The university runs a **Jardín Botánico** (botanical garden) which, though rather run-down and overgrown, has labels on some of the plants allowing you to learn something about them. The garden is often locked but the gate keeper who lives in the shack behind the gate will open it up for you if you whistle and yell. The posted hours are 8 am to 2 pm, Monday to Friday, and 8 to 11 am on Saturday. The garden is at the south end of Alameda Peru.

The university itself, which is about 3 km south of town, has a small **Museo**

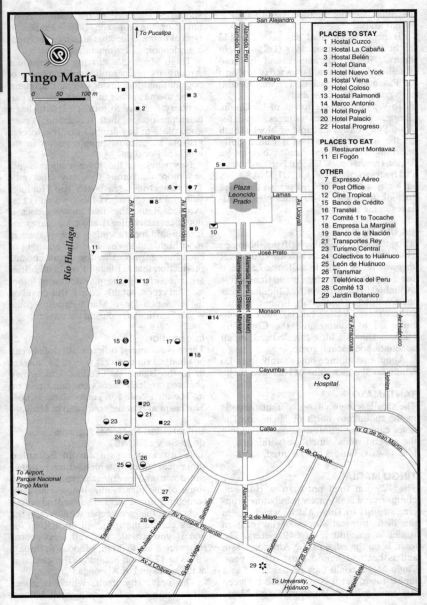

Tingo María

0   50   100 m

Río Huallaga

To Pucallpa

San Alejandro

Chiclayo

Pucallpa

Plaza Leoncido Prado

Lamas

José Prato

Monson

Cayumba

Hospital

Callao

9 de Octubre

To Airport,
Parque Nacional
Tingo María

To University,
Huánuco

Alameda Peru

Alameda Peru (Street Market)

Av A Raimondi

Av M Benavides

Av Ucayali

Av Amazonas

Av Huánuco

Uchiza

Av G de San Martín

Av J Chávez

Av Juan Ericsson

Av Enrique Pimentel

Surquillo

G de la Vega

Ramsaca

2 de Mayo

Sucre

Av Jiro RG

Miguel Gral

PLACES TO STAY
1   Hostal Cuzco
2   Hostal La Cabaña
3   Hostal Belén
4   Hotel Diana
5   Hotel Nuevo York
8   Hostal Viena
9   Hotel Coloso
13 Hostal Raimondi
14 Marco Antonio
18 Hotel Royal
20 Hotel Palacio
22 Hostal Progreso

PLACES TO EAT
6   Restaurant Montavaz
11 El Fogón

OTHER
7   Expresso Aéreo
10 Post Office
12 Cine Tropical
15 Banco de Crédito
16 Transtel
17 Comité 1 to Tocache
19 Empresa La Marginal
19 Banco de la Nación
21 Transportes Rey
23 Turismo Central
24 Colectivos to Huánuco
25 León de Huánuco
26 Transmar
27 Telefónica del Peru
28 Comité 13
29 Jardín Botanico

Zoológico with a collection of living and mounted animals from around the region.

Parque Nacional Tingo María

This 18,000-hectare park lies on the south side of town around the mouth of the Río Monzón, a tributary of the Río Huallaga. Within the park is the **Bella Dormiente** (Sleeping Beauty), a hill overlooking the town from the south which, from some angles, looks like a reclining woman.

Also in the park is **La Cueva de las Lechuzas** (the Cave of the Owls) which, despite its name, is known for the colony of oilbirds that lives inside. In addition, there are stalactites and stalagmites, and bats, parrots and other birds are seen around the cave entrance. But the oilbirds are the main attraction.

Comité 13 colectivos run every 30 minutes or so out to La Cueva de las Lechuzas for about US$1.25 (continuing beyond to the village of Monzón). The caves are about 6 km away and you'll be charged a US$2.50 national park fee. There are no facilities, however, apart from an urchin manning a few planks nailed together into a toll booth – there are no guides, no lights and little information. Locals say the best time to visit is in the morning when sunlight shines into the mouth of the cave; bring a flashlight anyway.

Places to Stay

Although there seem to be a lot of hotels, they are generally of a low standard. Hotels are often full so you should look for a room as soon as you arrive. I ended up staying in one of the 'better' hotels (the Nuevo York) because it was the first of the half dozen I tried that had a room available. The management told me that the room wasn't ready and I would have to

---

Oilbirds

There is only one species of *guacharo*, or oilbird, and it is so unusual that it is placed in its own family, the Steatornithidae, related to the nightjars. Oilbirds are nocturnal, and spend most of the day roosting in caves in colonies that may number in the thousands. La Cueva de las Lechuzas is one such cave. At dusk, huge numbers of oilbirds leave the cave in search of fruit, particularly that of palm trees, making oilbirds the world's only fruit-eating nocturnal birds.

Palm fruits are known for having a high fat content that gives the oilbirds a very fatty or oily flesh. In 1799, when oilbirds were first described in Venezuela by the German explorer/scientist, Alexander von Humboldt, the local people already knew about them. Oilbirds were captured in their roosting colonies and boiled down into a valuable oil used for cooking and lighting. This practice is now discouraged although it still occurs occasionally.

Oilbirds feed on the wing and their feet are poorly developed. For shelter, they require caves with ledges upon which to build their cone-shaped nests, which are constructed of regurgitated fruit and are enlarged regularly. Two to four eggs are laid and incubation is a relatively long 32 to 35 days. After hatching, the young are fed regurgitated fruit for up to four months, and during this time a nestling can reach a weight of over 1½ times that of an adult. These fat chicks were the most highly prized as a source of oil. Once the chicks leave the nest, they lose their accumulated baby fat. Adults weigh about 400g and reach a length of about 45 cm.

Oilbirds are adapted to their dark environment by having well-developed eyes and an exceptional sense of smell (which may help them detect the palm fruits, which have a distinctive fragrance). To avoid crashing into the cave walls (and into other birds), oilbirds emit audible, frequently repeated clicks which they use for echolocation, much as bats do. In addition they have a loud screaming call that they use for communication. The combination of screams and clicks made by thousands of birds within the confines of a cave can be deafening. ■

wait half an hour for the maid to finish cleaning it. I asked for the key so that I could go up and drop off my pack. When I reached my room, I found all the doors and windows open and a very harassed-looking maid attempting to clean the badly scuffed linoleum-tiled floor of what appeared to be bird dung. Upon inquiry, I learned that the previous occupants were a couple of machos in town for a cockfighting competition who were traveling with their prize cocks. The birds had evidently shared the bedroom. My opinion of cockfighting and its aficionados, never very high, took a turn for the worse. Perhaps I should be thankful that the men weren't bullfighters.

Places to Stay – bottom end
Almost all the hotels in Tingo María have cold showers (occasionally no showers!). One of the cheapest in town is the *Hostal Cuzco* (☎ 56-2095), Raimondi 671. It is an adequate hotel, popular with Peruvians, and is therefore often full. Rates are US$3.50/5.50. The *Hostal La Cabaña* is reasonably clean and charges US$5/8. The *Hostal Diana* has poor rooms with private bath at US$6/9. The similarly priced *Hostal Belén* has nicer rooms with shared showers. Other basic cheapies include the *Hostal Raimondi* (☎ 56-2095), Raimondi 344, which seems secure, the *Hotel Royal*, which has some rooms with private bath, and the *Hostal Progreso*.

The *Hostal Viena* (☎ 56-2194), Lamas 254, is clean and a reasonable value. Rooms are US$6/9, or US$8/11 with private bath. The *Hotel Coloso* (☎ 56-2027), Benavides 440, is also US$8/11 with private bath, is clean, but has occasional water failures (which is probably true of all of these places). The *Hotel Palacio* (☎ 56-2319), Raimondi 158, looks well run and clean, though the rooms are a bit spartan. Rates are US$7.50/10.50, or US$9/13 with private bath. Another hotel in this price range is the *Marco Antonio*.

The best of the bottom-end hotels at this time is the *Hotel Nuevo York* (☎ 56-2406), Alameda Peru 553, which charges US$12/17 for rooms with private bath and tepid water.

Places to Stay – middle
The best hotel at this time is the *Madera Verde Hotel* (☎ 56-2047, fax 56-1608), just over 1 km south of town. Any taxi can get there. Full price is about US$38/50, or US$75 for a four-person bungalow, but walk-in rates can be substantially less and continental breakfast is included. Good-sized rooms have private bath and hot water, TV and mini-fridge. The hotel is set in pleasant gardens with a pool, playground and simple but adequate restaurant and bar.

Places to Eat
El Fogón is a pleasant shady place with river views. Pizzas, meat and fish meals are in the US$3 to US$6 range – this is the best place I could find. The *Restaurant Montavaz* is a little cheaper and sells local dishes, and there are several other inexpensive restaurants along Raimondi.

Getting There & Away
Air As with the air service to Huánuco, carriers and schedules change frequently. Currently, there are daily flights from Lima with Aero Continente, stopping at Huánuco. Expresso Aéreo has both direct flights and flights stopping at Huánuco and continuing to Tocache, Juanjui, Saposoa, Tarapoto and Trujillo, with connections to other northern towns. AeroCóndor has direct flights several times a week.

The fare to/from Lima is about US$60. Airport tax is US$4. The airport is about 1½ km from town and a cab should cost about US$2. Cab drivers meeting passengers at the airport will try and charge you US$5, then drive you on a circuitous route around the edge of town before arriving in the center. This is not a pleasant sightseeing tour – it's just a rip-off. (OK. I admit it. It happened to me.) The airport is on the west side of the Río Huallaga (the town is on the east) and there is one bridge linking the two. The bridge is south of the airport and you can walk if you like.

If you go to the airport and ask around,

you can find light aircraft flying to other nearby towns. Cancellations are frequent in the rainy season (January to April), or if there are not enough passengers. In 1995, I flew to Tingo María from Lima with AeroCóndor on an airplane with about 20 seats. It had about eight or nine passengers, but still flew, so flights don't have to be full to go. The in-flight service was provided by a small, pleasant man who had to crouch to get up the aisle. A soft drink and pastry were a pleasant surprise on what I thought would be a no-frills flight. The views of the Cordillera Huayhuash and, beyond, of the Cordillera Blanca, were excellent. Sit on the left if flying from Lima to Tingo María.

Bus As with anywhere in Peru, the bus situation changes frequently, but it seems that Tingo María is prone to more than the average changes. Whatever . . . you'll get

to where you want to go if you ask around. Transtel seems like a good bet for early-morning buses to Pucallpa (about 12 hours, US$9). They also have buses north to Tocache in the Río Huallaga valley (see Across the Northern Highlands for Tocache). Outside, there are minibuses leaving later in the day. Empresa La Marginal also goes to Pucallpa, and there are others. The journey from Tingo María to Pucallpa is described in the Pucallpa section of the Amazon Basin chapter.

Empresa, Transmar and Transportes Rey have night buses to Lima (US$12, 12 hours). León de Huánuco has day buses. Turismo Central has a night bus to Huancayo (US$8, 12 hours). Colectivo taxis and minibuses leave for Huánuco from Raimondi at Callao. Empresa Marginal has slow buses to Huánuco. Comité 1 has colectivo taxis to Tocache in the Río Huallaga valley.

The North Coast

The scenery of the Peruvian coast north of Lima is similar to that of the south coast; both areas are part of the great South American coastal desert. On the coastal drive north from Lima you pass huge, rolling sand dunes, dizzying cliffs, oases of farmland, busy fishing villages, relaxing beach resorts and fascinating archaeological sites dating back thousands of years, as well as some of Peru's largest and most historic cities.

Few travelers are able to fully appreciate this area of Peru. Most are so wrapped up in visiting the world-famous Inca ruins and Lake Titicaca to the south that the northern part of the country is largely ignored. Those who do travel north tend to head either straight to the Ecuadorian border, 24 hours away, or along the coast for four hours then inland to the Callejón de Huaylas and the beautiful mountains of the Cordillera Blanca. Slowly traveling the north coast, however, allows greater involvement with the local people and often gets you away from the gringo 'scene.' In addition, the many archaeological ruins here are uncrowded and interesting.

ANCÓN

The first town north of Lima is Ancón, a seaside resort about 40 km from the capital. The beaches are poor and crowded with Limeños on day trips during the January to March season.

En route from Lima to Ancón on the Panamericana, you'll see many pueblos jovenes, or 'young towns.' These shanty towns often have no running water, electricity or other facilities. They are built by peasants migrating to Lima from the highlands in search of jobs and a higher standard of living.

CHANCAY

Beyond Ancón are the spectacular Pacasmayo sand dunes. There are two roads –

one snakes along a narrow ledge at the bottom of the dunes and the other goes over the top. Both offer superb views of the dunes, which stretch on for some 20 km to the small village of Chancay. The Chancay subculture existed in this area from about 1100 AD to 1400 AD. The black-on-white ceramic style for which this coastal culture is noted is best seen at the excellent Amano Museum in Lima. Chancay itself is a small fishing village of some 10,000 inhabitants and has little to see, apart from a mock castle, 'El Castillo,' visible on the west side of the highway. There is a restaurant at the castillo and a resort hotel is planned, although the beaches are not particularly good. There are a few hotels and restaurants.

At the north end of Chancay, a road goes inland to the village of Huaral, 10 km away, and on up the Río Chancay valley where there are a number of little-known ruins.

THE CHURÍN RD

About 20 km north of Chancay, a turn-off to the right leads to the small mountain towns of Sayán, Churín and Oyón. This road follows the Río Huaura valley and a bus from Lima travels this road daily. Buses leave from opposite Lima's Ormeño terminal; ask for Empresa Espadín.

Between Sayán and Churín, the road climbs through strange rock formations and tropical scrub vegetation. Churín, 190 km from Lima, is a minor resort known for its good hot springs. There are a couple of cheap hotels on Avenida Larco Herrera, the main street, the best of which is the *Hostal Internacional Churín*. Several inexpensive restaurants serve local food such as trout and cuy (guinea pig).

Beyond Churín, the road continues through the village of Oyón and on to the southern parts of the Cordillera Raura, a remote, snowcapped mountain range.

RESERVA NACIONAL LACHAY

About 2 km north of the turn-off for the Churín road, just before Km 106, a dirt road heads 3 km east of the Panamericana to Loma de Lachay within a 5070-hectare reserve. This is a hill that seems to gain most of its moisture from the coastal mists, creating a unique micro environment of dwarf forest with small animals and birds. There are camping and picnicking areas.

HUACHO & HUAURA

The small town of Huacho (population 40,000) is almost 150 km north of Lima at the mouth of the Río Huaura. Buses from Huacho go up the valley reaching Sayán (see The Churín Rd above). Across the river is the village of Huaura, where San Martín proclaimed Peru's independence. Anyone can show you the building, where there is a very small museum with a Spanish-speaking guide. Entrance to the museum and the balcony from where San Martín spoke is almost US$1, or you can see the balcony from outside for free. There are two or three basic hotels in Huacho, of which *Hotel Pacífico* seems OK. The *Hostal La Villa* is better but more expensive.

BARRANCA

About 190 km north of Lima you reach Barranca. Though small, Barranca is the biggest town in the area and has the best facilities. Most buses along the coast stop here on their way to Supe, Pativilca, Paramonga and the turn-off for Huaraz and the Cordillera Blanca, all of which lie within a few kilometers of Barranca. Everything happens on the main street, which is also the Panamericana, but there's little to see here.

At the small fishing port of **Supe**, a few kilometers south of Barranca, there are a couple of basic hotels. The archaeological site of Aspero is nearby. Although Aspero is one of the oldest sites in Peru, it has little to offer the untrained eye and few locals know anything about it.

The village of **Pativilca** is a few kilometers north of Barranca. It has one very

NORTH COAST

basic hotel and a few simple restaurants, but most people stay at Barranca. Simón Bolívar once lived here and his house is now a small museum. Just north of Pativilca, the road to Huaraz and the Cordillera Blanca branches off to the right. This spectacular road climbs through cactus-laden cliff faces and is worth traveling in daylight. Many people see no more of the north coast than the Panamericana between Lima and the mountain turn-off at Pativilca.

Just 3 or 4 km beyond the Huaraz turn-off is the archaeological site of **Paramonga**. This huge adobe temple is attributed to the Chimu civilization, which was the ruling power on the north coast before being conquered by the Incas in the mid-1400s. The massive temple, surrounded by seven defensive walls, is clearly visible on the right-hand side of the Panamericana and is worth a visit. Entry is about US$2.50 and the small on-site museum is open from 8 am to 5 pm. Local buses traveling between Barranca and the port of Paramonga will drop you off 3 km from the entrance, or take a taxi from Barranca for a few dollars.

Places to Stay & Eat
You'll find several hotels along the main street. The best of these is the *Hotel Chavín* (☎ (034) 35-2358, 35-2253, fax 35-2480) which charges about US$14/23 for clean singles/doubles with bath. Nearby, just off

the main street, is the *Hostal Residencial Continental* (☎ (034) 35-2458), A Ugarte 190, which is clean, secure and charges US$6/10 with bath. The *Hostal Jefferson*, Lima 946, is clean and friendly at US$8 for a double with bath. There are half a dozen cheaper places, of which the *Pacífico* is quite good. There are plenty of cheap restaurants, the best of which is the *Chifa Lung Fung* on the main street (but beware of the overcharging of gringos for 'servicio especial' – check your bill).

Entertainment
There are a couple of cinemas or you could check out the *Disco Pub 'No Nerds'* (I'm not making this up) on the main street near the Hotel Chavín.

HUARMEY
North of Paramonga, the Panamericana enters a particularly deserted stretch and soon crosses the line dividing the departments of Lima and Ancash. The *Hotel de Turistas* (☎ (044) 32-0292) at Huarmey, 290 km north of Lima, is the best hotel on the 420 km stretch of road between Lima and Chimbote. A double room with bath costs about US$25. There is also a cheap basic hotel.

There's nothing to do in Huarmey except spend the night in the hotel, though if you have your own transport, you'll find some excellent deserted beaches nearby.

CASMA & SECHÍN

The small town of Casma is 370 km north of Lima. The archaeological site of Sechín is about 5 km away and easily reached from Casma. Casma was once an important colonial port that was sacked by various pirates during the 1600s, but its importance has declined greatly and the town was largely destroyed by the earthquake of May 31, 1970. There's not much to do in either the port (11 km from the town) or the town itself, and most people only come here to visit the Sechín ruins or to travel to Huaraz via the Punta Callán road, a route offering excellent panoramic views of the Cordillera Blanca.

Information

There is no tourist office. Changing traveler's checks is difficult. The area code is 044. The Telefónica del Peru office is on the 300 block of Huarmey.

Sechín

This site is one of the oldest in Peru (about 1600 BC) and among the more important and well-preserved of the coastal ruins. First excavated in 1937 by the renowned Peruvian archaeologist, JC Tello, it has suffered some damage from grave robbers and natural disasters. The site is 5 km

southeast of Casma and easily reached on foot or by taxi; there are good road signs. To get there, head south of Casma on the Panamericana for 3 km, then turn left and follow the paved road to Huaraz for a further 2 km to the site. If you're descending from Huaraz, you can visit the ruins en route to Casma if you don't have too much gear.

The site at Sechín, part of which is thought to have been buried by a landslide, is still being excavated and only some of the area is open to visitors. This consists of three outside walls of the main temple that are completely covered with bas-relief carvings of warriors and of captives being eviscerated. The gruesomely realistic carvings are up to four meters high. Which warlike peoples were involved in building this temple remains a mystery and is one of the site's main points of interest. Inside the main temple are earlier mud structures still being excavated; you can't go in but there is a model in the small but modern on-site museum.

There are several other early sites in the Sechín area, most of them still unexcavated because of a lack of funds. From the museum you can see Sechín Alto in the distance – a large, flat-topped hill. The fortress of Chanquillo, consisting of several

The ruins at Sechín have a mysterious origin.

towers surrounded by concentric walls, can be visited but is best appreciated from the air. Aerial photographs are on display at the museum. If you wish to explore more than just Sechín, the museum attendant can give directions and there is a detailed area map in the museum.

The Sechín ruins and museum are open daily from 9 am to 5 pm and cost US$1.80 to visit. There is a small shady garden and picnic area – bring your own food. The entry ticket also allows you to visit the Mochica ruins of **Pañamarca**, 10 km inland from the Panamericana on the road to Nepeña (the turn-off is about halfway between Casma and Chimbote). The ruins are badly weathered but some murals can be seen if you ask the guard (they are normally covered up for protection).

Places to Stay

Casma has several hotels. The cheapest is the basic, unattractive *Hostal Central* on the Plaza de Armas which charges US$4 per person. A better budget choice is the clean and friendly *Hostal Gregori* (☎ 71-1073, 71-1173), L Ormeño 579, which charges US$5/7.50 for singles/doubles and shared cold showers. The *Hostal Indoamericano* (☎ 71-1235), just off the plaza on the first block of Huarmey, is also clean and good, though a little pricey. Rooms are US$6/11 or US$8/14 with private cold bath. The new and pleasant *Hostal Ernestos* (☎ 71-1475) charges US$10/15 in clean rooms with private cold bath.

The best place to stay is the pleasant *Hotel El Farol* (☎ /fax 71-1064, in Lima 424-0517). It's set in a garden and has a simple cafeteria and bar and helpful, friendly staff. There's a useful map in the lobby if you plan to explore some of the ruins in the area. The hotel is just off the main road, between the bus stop area and the Plaza de Armas and a couple of blocks from each – there's a sign on the main road. Singles with communal shower are US$7.50 and singles/doubles with private hot shower are US$12.50/17.50, including breakfast. The hotel reportedly has cold-water bungalows at a local beach,

Balneario Tortuga, which cost US$10/20 or US$30 for a family of five.

Places to Eat

There are no particularly good restaurants in Casma. One of the best is the inexpensive *Chifa Tio Sam* next to the Hostal Indoamericana, near the plaza. There are several other inexpensive and satisfactory places along the same street, including the *Venecia*. Just off the plaza, *Café Dulcería Lucy* is a friendly place and good for breakfast. The restaurant in the Hotel El Farol does a decent ceviche.

My wife and I stayed at El Farol several years ago and wanted to have breakfast. We were the only customers in the hotel's cafeteria but were told that breakfast would be no problem. We asked what they had (you soon learn to ask *¿Qué hay?* before choosing in small restaurants). The assistant strode purposefully to the refrigerator and swung the door open and we all peered hopefully inside. We couldn't help but laugh at the half full bottle of Pepsi and the small, sadly wrinkled papaya. The assistant, slightly crestfallen, soon recovered and offered to go out and buy some eggs and bread. We returned 30 minutes later to a good breakfast, complete with papaya juice.

Getting There & Away

Many companies run buses north and south along the Panamericana but, because Casma is so small, most don't have offices there. If you're heading for Trujillo or Lima, you can flag down a bus as it comes through and hope for a seat. Transportes Vista Alegre has an office on L Ormeño and sell a limited number of seats on their buses traveling between Trujillo and Lima. Empresa Turismo Chimbote, with an office on the main street, has five buses a day to Lima but only two or three seats are available from the Casma office – the rest are sold in Chimbote. There are a couple of other bus offices. Trips to Lima average six hours; buses to Trujillo take about three hours.

There are also frequent colectivos to

Chimbote, 50 km to the north, where there are better facilities. These take 1¼ hours and charge US$1. Expreso California, near the plaza, goes to Chimbote.

Several small companies run buses to Huaraz along a dirt road over the Cordillera Negra. The route begins with good views of the desert foothills of the western Andes and climbs up a fertile river valley, finally emerging over the Punta Callán Pass. The pass is 30 km from Huaraz and, from its altitude of 4225 meters, you will have one of the best panoramic views of the Cordillera Blanca. It's worth doing the journey during the day with Empresa Moreno (seven hours, US$6). There are other companies going to Huaraz but most go overnight.

Most of the bus offices and stops are within a few blocks of one another, clustered together on the main road at the junction where the Panamericana arrives in Casma from Lima. You won't have any trouble finding the buses – it's a small town and there are plenty of signs.

Getting Around
Colectivos leave from outside of the Telefónica office heading for Buena Vista. They can drop you outside the Sechín ruins for US50¢. A mototaxi charges about US$1 to the ruins.

CHIMBOTE
This is the first major town along the north coast; it is 420 km north of Lima. Chimbote is Peru's largest fishing port and millions of tons of fish were landed here in the 1960s. Since then, the industry has declined because of overfishing. Despite this and despite the 1970 earthquake (which destroyed much of the city), the population has continued to grow dramatically and is now close to 300,000 – about the same as Cuzco's. The comparison stops there, however. The town's several large

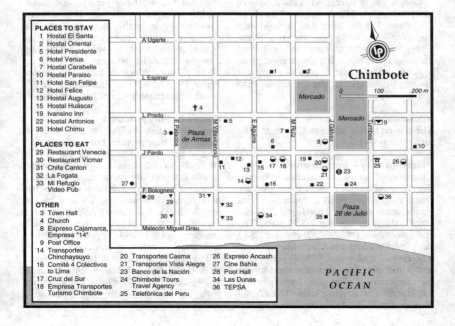

PLACES TO STAY
1 Hostal El Santa
2 Hostal Oriental
5 Hotel Presidente
6 Hotel Venus
7 Hostal Carabelle
10 Hostal Paraiso
11 Hotel San Felipe
12 Hotel Felice
13 Hostal Augusto
15 Hostal Huáscar
19 Ivansino Inn
22 Hostal Antonios
35 Hotel Chimu

PLACES TO EAT
29 Restaurant Venecia
30 Restaurant Vicmar
31 Chifa Canton
32 La Fogata
33 Mi Refugio
    Video Pub

OTHER
3 Town Hall
4 Church
8 Expreso Cajamarca,
    Empresa "14"
9 Post Office
14 Transportes
    Chinchaysuyo
16 Comité 4 Colectivos
    to Lima
17 Cruz del Sur
18 Empresa Transportes
    Turismo Chimbote
20 Transportes Casma
21 Transportes Vista Alegre
23 Banco de la Nación
24 Chimbote Tours
    Travel Agency
25 Telefónica del Peru
26 Expreso Ancash
27 Cine Bahía
28 Pool Hall
34 Las Dunas
36 TEPSA

Chimbote

A Ugarte
L Espinar
L Prado
J Pardo
F Bolognesi
Malecón Miguel Grau

Plaza de Armas
Mercado
Plaza 28 de Julio

PACIFIC OCEAN

Río Santa Valley
The Río Santa flows into the ocean at Santa, about 20 km north of Chimbote. The river valley is a little-explored area and poorly serviced by public transport – only a few buses go up this road en route to Huaraz. Aerial reconnaissance has revealed dozens of pre-Inca sites (read Gene Savoy's *Antisuyo*), including a Great Wall about 50 km long.

Adventurous travelers could explore the valley on foot – you don't need too much gear because it doesn't rain or get cold. A blanket and sleeping pad will suffice. Climbing the hills on either side of the valley will bring you to ruins that are very rarely visited. A possible place to start from is Tanguche. It is the first place inland from Santa and is marked on most maps. Parts of the Great Wall can be seen nearby and many more ruins lie further inland in the hills edging the Río Santa valley.

Carry your own food and plenty of water bottles – the Río Santa runs year round but you should purify the water before drinking it. This trip is only for self-sufficient travelers experienced in traveling rough and with an interest in exploring the desert.

On the north side of the Río Santa valley is the **Reserva Nacional de Calipuy**, covering 68,000 hectares at elevations ranging from under 1000 meters to almost 4000 meters above sea level. This is reputedly the haunt of pumas, condors and spectacled bears, but I don't know of any access or facilities. ■

fish meal factories give the town a pervasive and distinctive odor. There are also some steel mills. The beaches are dirty but good for watching bird life.

Unless you're interested in the fishing or steel industries, there's not much to do in Chimbote, but the town can be used as a base for excursions into the Río Santa valley, where there are some little-explored archaeological ruins. It's also a good place to stay overnight if you're heading for Huaraz by the spectacular Cañon del Pato route.

Information
There is no tourist office in Chimbote. The area code is 044.

Places to Stay – bottom end
Chimbote offers a good selection of hotels. For those on a tight budget, there are very basic cold-water hotels, generally with erratic water supplies. The *Hostal Huáscar* (☎ 32-1925) is OK for US$3.50/5. The *Hostal Oriental* (☎ 32-3272) charges US$3 per person but looks and feels like a prison! The *Hostal Unión* is US$3.50 per person and is just bearable. It is near the Moreno bus terminal if you are leaving early for Huaraz (or arriving late). The *Hostal Paraiso* (☎ 32-3718) is convenient for the

Expreso Ancash terminal and clean enough for US$4 per person or US$14 for a double with private cold shower. The *Hostal El Santa* (☎ 32-1161) has OK rooms with bath at about US$4.50 per person, and some slightly cheaper rooms with shared bath. Rooms vary in quality here so look at a couple of them. The reasonably clean *Hostal Augusto* (☎ 32-4431) is OK and charges US$6/10 with shared bath or US$8.50/14 with private bath. The *Hostal Felice* (☎ 32-5901) is similar. The *Hotel Venus* is comparably-priced but not as good.

Places to Stay – middle
The *Hotel San Felipe* (☎ 32-3401) is clean and has private hot showers for US$12.50/17.50. The *Hostal Carabelle* (☎ 32-2571) is similar, though its hot water supply is reportedly sporadic. *Hostal Antonios* (☎ 33-3026, 32-5783) has clean rooms with private hot showers, TV and phone for US$23/33. They have a café. The *Hotel Presidente* (☎ 32-2411), is also quite nice and charges US$30/44 for good rooms, but their attached café is overpriced.

The best place in town is the *Hotel Chimu* (☎ 32-5451, 32-1741, fax 33-5987; in Lima ☎ 241-2202, fax 241-6149). Good rooms with TV and hot bath cost US$50/67, including continental breakfast. Larger suites cost US$90. They have a decent restaurant and a bar. The new *Ivansino Inn* (☎ 33-1395) is giving the Hotel Chimu some competition and has cable TV and mini-bars in its rooms. Rates are US$38/50.

Places to Eat
There are no fancy restaurants in central Chimbote. *La Fogata* is a new and attractive restaurant for parrilladas (grills) at reasonable prices. The *Chifa Canton* is very clean and has fast service and moderate prices. *Restaurant Vicmar* has good set lunch menus and *Restaurant Venecia* has been recommended for seafood. There are many cheap chicken restaurants along L Prado. *Mi Refugio Video Pub* serves various meat and fish dishes after which you can dance to disco music. The restaurant at the Hotel Presidente is poor but the one in the Hotel Chimu is perhaps the best in town, serving set lunches for about US$6.

Getting There & Away
Air There are daily flights from Lima with AeroCóndor, some continuing to Cajamarca. AeroCóndor is at J Gálvez 667. Expresso Aéreo has flights from Lima on most days, some continuing to Cajamarca and Chachapoyas. There have, in the past, been services to other north coast cities, but these have not been offered recently. The fare to Lima is about US$58.

Bus & Colectivo The most frequent service to Lima (US$7, six hours) is with Empresa Transportes Turismo Chimbote; there are buses every one or two hours. They also have a night bus to Huaraz. Cruz del Sur has a daily bus to Lima. Comité 4 colectivos to Lima are a couple of hours faster than buses but they charge a ridiculous US$28.

Going north along the coast to Trujillo, Chiclayo and Piura, as well as south to Lima, are Cruz del Sur and Expreso Ancash (both good), Las Dunas (more expensive but comfortable), TEPSA (kamikaze drivers) and Transportes Vista Alegre (to Lima and Trujillo only). Transportes

Chinchaysuyo has buses going north to Cajamarca as well as Chiclayo and inland to Moyobamba and Tarapoto. They have an overnight bus to Huaraz. Expreso Cajamarca has an overnight bus to Cajamarca (eight hours, US$8).

Transportes Moreno and Empresa 14 operate services to Huaraz. Most buses go via Casma, but some travel via the Río Santa valley through Huallanca and the wild Cañon del Pato to Caraz and Huaraz. This route is the most spectacular approach to Huaraz from the coast. Empresa Moreno does this route daily, leaving at 8 am, taking almost 10 hours and charging US$6.50. The Moreno terminal is in a poor area off the map, at J Gálvez 1178, and has a bad reputation for pickpockets (take a taxi after dark).

TRUJILLO
The coastal city of Trujillo, with 750,000 inhabitants, is Peru's third largest city, though locals claim it vies with Arequipa for the status of Peru's second largest city. It is the capital of the strangely H-shaped Department of La Libertad and its only important city. Trujillo is about 560 km (nine hours) north of Lima and warrants a visit of several days. Founded in 1536 by Pizarro, it is an attractive colonial city and retains much of its colonial flavor.

Nearby is the ancient Chimu capital of Chan Chan, which was conquered by the Incas (local guides say that the Chimu surrendered to the Incas, rather than being conquered), and several other Chimu sites. Also in the area are the immense Moche Pyramids of the Sun and Moon (Las Huacas del Sol y de la Luna), which date back about 1500 years. If so much ancient culture wears you out, you can relax at one of the pleasant beaches around Trujillo.

Information
Tourist Offices The tourist office (☎ 24-6941), Pizarro 402 on the Plaza de Armas, is run by the tourist police who can be distinguished by their smart white uniforms. They are very friendly and helpful and can provide a map of the city and information.

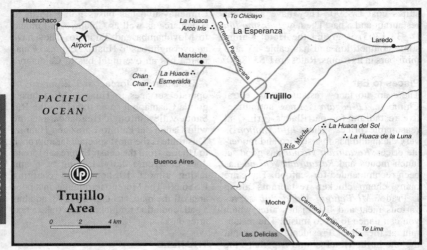

Some speak English and will also act as guides, although they have not had any professional guide training. The office is open daily from 8 am to 7.30 pm.

The government-run tourist office has closed, but has been replaced by a private office, Caretur, which has changed addresses several times. Recently they were at Independencia 620.

Visas Migraciones are at Almagro 225 on the corner of San Martín. Visas and tourist cards can be renewed here for 30 days for the usual US$20 fee, plus stamped paperwork (an extra US$1) from the Banco de la Nación next door. It can be a long process. It's best to go when they open at 9 am, get the official form, then go to the window marked *Pago de Impuestos – Extranjeros* in the Banco de la Nación. There shouldn't be much of a line here; other windows have long lines. You may be asked for proof of funds or onward tickets.

Money Changing money in Trujillo is a distinct pleasure because some of the banks are housed in colonial buildings. One of my favorites is the Casa de la Emancipación housing the Banco Continental – they give good rates for cash but charge a commission on traveler's checks. You can also change traveler's checks at the more modern Banco de Crédito or with one of the other banks – shop around for the best rate. Bank lines are long so go when they open around 9.30 am. Casas de cambio near Gamarra and Bolívar give good rates for cash. There are street changers as well – take the usual precautions. You'll find them on the Plaza de Armas or along Gamarra, near Pizarro and Bolívar. Watch for pickpockets, particularly along Gamarra south of Bolívar.

Money can be withdrawn on Visa cards at Interbanc and Banco de Crédito, on Amex at Banco de Crédito, and Mastercard at Banco Wiese (in another fine colonial building). Check commissions carefully – some have been reported as high as 8%.

Post & Telecommunications The main offices are shown on the map. The area code for Trujillo is 044.

Travel Agencies Chacón Tours (☎ 25-5722, ☎ /fax 25-5212), España 106, has been recommended for good flight arrangements. Guía Tours (☎ 24-5170, ☎ /fax 24-6353), Independencia 519, organizes daily tours that last three hours and go to several of the local archaeological sites for about US$15 per person. Some agencies have been criticized for supplying guides who speak English but don't know much about the area.

Guides It's best to go with a certified official guide who knows the area well and will take you to wherever you want to go, as well as suggesting places you may not have thought of.

Official guides charge about US$6 to US$8 an hour but will take several people for the same price as one, so get a group together if your budget is tight. A guide who has been highly recommended by travelers (and by me) is Clara Luz Bravo D (☎ 24-3347, radio ☎ 26-0003, fax 24-8644), Huayna Capac 542, Urbanización Santa María, Trujillo. Along with her partner, Englishman Michael White, she leads tours to all the local sites of interest, speaks some English and German, and is extremely helpful to tourists who want information beyond the normal tours (such as shopping, staying with local families and entertainment). Clara has been guiding for 25 years, is very enthusiastic and really knows Trujillo and other parts of Peru. Michael is also recommended and he has a car.

Pedro Puerta is also recommended by travelers. He speaks English and is enthusiastic and knowledgeable about all the ruins in the area. His office is at Km 560 on the Panamericana, just past the Templo Arco Iris, and he can be contacted through the Hotel Americano and other hotels.

Medical Services The best place for general medical services is the Hospital Americano-Peruano (☎ 23-1261), Mansiche 702, behind the Cassinelli Museum. They have English-speaking receptionists and doctors, and charge according to means. If you don't have medical insurance, let them know.

Dangers & Annoyances In my last edition, I wrote that single women tend to receive a lot of attention from males in Trujillo bars – to exasperating, even harassing levels. This continues to be the case. Locals tell me that Trujillo is one of the more conservative towns in Peru and women are not expected to be out alone in the evenings. As one woman reports, 'This is the only place in Ecuador and Peru where I was hit on by numerous men, some of whom were very persistent and all of whom were a nuisance.'

Plaza de Armas
Trujillo's very spacious and attractive main square has an impressive central statue of the heroes of Peruvian independence. The plaza is fronted by the cathedral that was begun in 1647, destroyed in 1759 and rebuilt soon afterwards. The cathedral has a famous basilica and is often open in the evenings around 6 pm.

There are several elegant colonial mansions around the plaza. One is now the Hotel Libertador Trujillo. Another, the Casa Urquiaga, now belongs to the Banco Central de la Reserva del Peru. It has a small ceramics museum and can be visited during banking hours for free. On the same block is the Casa Calonge.

On Sundays at 10 am there is a flag-raising ceremony on the Plaza de Armas complete with a parade. On occasional Sundays, there are also *caballos de paso* or 'pacing horses' and *marinera* dances.

Colonial Buildings
The colonial mansions and churches are most attractive and worth visiting. Unfortunately, they don't seem to have very regular opening hours and the listed times may change without notice. Some are closed for days on end. Mornings are often the best times to enter. Several are mentioned under Plaza de Armas (above) or Art Galleries (below). Hiring a local guide is recommended if you are seriously interested in visiting as many of them as possible.

The single feature which makes Trujillo's colonial center especially distinctive is the beautiful wrought-iron grillwork fronting almost every colonial building in the city. This, combined with the buildings' pastel shades, results in a distinct Trujillano ambiance not found in Peru's other colonial cities.

Palacio Iturregui This early 19th-century mansion is unmistakable and impossible to ignore – it's painted an overpowering shade of blue. Built in neoclassical style, it has beautiful window gratings outside and slender columns and gold moldings on the ceilings inside. Its main claim to fame is that General Iturregui lived here when he proclaimed Trujillo's independence from Spain in 1820. (Trujillo was the first city in Peru to declare its independence.) The building is now used by the swanky Club Central, Pizarro 688, which will allow you to visit the mansion between 11 am and noon on weekdays.

Other Buildings Also of interest, although not often visited and difficult to find information about, are the Casa Aranda, Bolívar 621, and the Casa de Mayorazgo de Facala, Pizarro 314.

Churches
Apart from the cathedral, the colonial churches of El Carmen, Santo Domingo, San Francisco, La Compañía, San Agustín, Santa Clara and La Merced are worth a look, though getting inside is largely a matter of luck. (They often are open for early morning mass as well as evening mass at 6 pm, but visitors at those times should respect the worshippers and not wander around too much.) The churches are close to one another and it's easy to stroll from one to the next. San Agustín, with its finely gilded high altar, dates from 1558 and is usually open. La Merced has a dome with noteworthy carvings under a balcony.

Art Galleries
Several of the colonial buildings contain art galleries with changing shows. Admission is normally free or a nominal few

cents. Hours are variable, so check locally. The Santo Domingo Art Gallery and the Casa de los Léones (also known as the Ganoza Chopitea Residence) are usually open on most days of the week for some hours in the morning and the afternoon. Good modern Peruvian art is sometimes shown, as are some rather arcane pieces that you may never have a chance to see elsewhere, thus offering relief from the interminable religious and colonial art that is the stock of most museums.

The cathedral has a museum of religious and colonial art, as does the Carmelite Museum in the Monastery of El Carmen. The latter reputedly has Trujillo's best collection of colonial art.

The Casona Orbegoso, Orbegoso 553, named after a former president of Peru, is a beautiful 18th century mansion with a collection of art and furnishings of that period.

Museo Cassinelli
The Museo Cassinelli is a private archaeological collection on the western outskirts of Trujillo – in the basement of a gas station.

When I visited this museum, I found the gas station without difficulty and spotted several pots and other pieces through the windows. I went inside and asked to see the collection and was told to wait a few minutes. I looked at the haphazardly displayed pots in the garage office and wondered if this was it. After all, what could I expect in an oily garage? After a few minutes, however, I was led through a locked door, down a narrow flight of stairs and through a second locked door – this one heavily armored. On entering the basement, I was astonished to see hundreds of ceramics carefully displayed on shelves that filled the room. The curator showed me dozens of his favorite pieces, letting me hold and examine several as he explained where they came from and what they represented.

Among the most interesting were the whistling pots, which produced clear notes when they were blown. I was especially intrigued by a pair of pots representing a male and a female bird – they appeared to be tinamous. Superficially, they were very similar, but when they were blown, each produced a completely different note. These notes corresponded to the distinctive calls of the male and female birds.

All in all, this was among the best museum experiences I have had in Peru and I give this place a whole-hearted recommendation. It's open from 8.30 to 11.30 am and 3.30 to 5.30 pm from Monday to Saturday and admission is about US$1.50.

Museo de Arqueología
This university-run museum at Pizarro 349 has variable opening hours depending on the season and academic year. It's usually open at least on weekday mornings. There's an interesting collection of art and pottery and a reproduction of the murals found in the Moche Pyramid of the Moon. Entry costs about US$1.50.

Museo de Zoología
This museum at San Martín 368 is also run by the university but the Peruvian stuffed animals in the collection are in poor condition.

Beaches
The beach at the Trujillo suburb of Buenos Aires is easily reached by local buses but theft has frequently been reported here. There are several seafood restaurants on the waterfront that are safe enough to eat in. Walking along the beach away from the restaurant area is dangerous and the 4 km walk from Buenos Aires to Chan Chan is especially notorious for muggings. Visit Chan Chan by road instead.

There is a much better and safer beach in the village of Huanchaco, 11 km to the north (see the Huanchaco section).

Caballos de Paso
Breeding, training and watching the caballos de paso (pacing horses) is a favorite Peruvian activity. The idea is to breed and train horses that pace more elegantly than others. Trujillo and Lima are both centers of this upper-class pastime. Trujilleños will tell you that the activity originated in the Department of La Libertad.

Special Events
Trujillo's major festival is called El Festival Internacional de la Primavera, or 'International Spring Festival,' held annually for well over 40 years. Its attractions include international beauty contests, parades, national dancing competitions (including, of course, the marinera), caballos de paso displays, sports and various other cultural activities. It all happens in the last week in September and better hotels are fully booked well in advance.

The last week in January is also busy with the national Fiesta de la Marinera contest. The marinera is a typical coastal Peruvian dance involving much romantic waving of handkerchiefs. Students of folk dance should not miss this one. Again, hotels are booked up.

Places to Stay – bottom end
Many cheap hotels, especially in the poor area east of Gamarra and Bolívar, are used for short stays by young local couples, but aren't dangerous or horribly sleazy. The cheapest is the very basic and poor-looking *Hostal Peru* at about US$3/5. Opposite is the slightly better *Hotel Paris* (☎ 24-2701). The basic *Hostal Lima* (☎ 24-4751), Ayacucho 718, is quite popular with gringos. It looks like a jail but is secure and friendly at US$7.50 for a double. The *Hostal Central* (☎ 24-6236), next door, is similarly priced and OK. None of these hotels have private showers or hot water and their standards of cleanliness are not very high.

The *Hostal Acapulco* (☎ 24-3524), Gamarra 681, is US$5/6 with private cold bath and reportedly has warm showers for US$2 more. They are friendly and have been recommended as good value among the basic hotels. The *Hostal Colón* (☎ 23-4545) charges US$5/7.50, or US$10 for a double with warm shower. The cold-water *Hotel Oscar* (☎ 24-2523) looks OK for

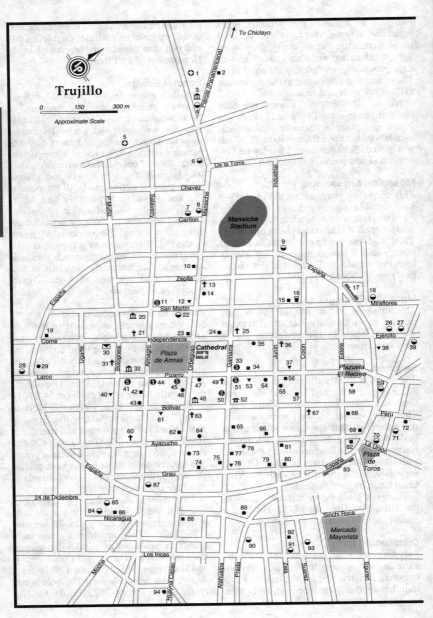

Trujillo

0   150   300 m

Approximate Scale

To Chiclayo

Pizarra (Panamericana)

De la Torre

Chavez

P Muñiz

Salaverry

Carrion

Mansiche

Mansiche Stadium

España

Zepita

España

San Martin

Independencia

España

Corne

Ugarte

Bolognesi

Almagro

Orbegoso

Plaza de Armas

Cathedral

Gamarra

Junin

Colón

Estete

Larco

Pizarro

Bolivar

Ayacucho

Grau

Miraflores

Ejército

Plazuela El Recreo

Peru

La Union

Plaza de Toros

24 de Diciembre

Nicaragua

Moche

Los Incas

Huayna Capac

Grau

Atahualpa

Pizarro

Zela

Suarez

Junin

Sinchi Roca

Mercado Mayorista

Plaza de Toros

PLACES TO STAY

2 Hotel Primavera
10 Hotel Oscar
15 Hotel San Martín
19 Hostal Rosell
23 Libertador Trujillos
34 Cassino Real Hotel
42 Hotel Los
   Conquistadores
56 Hotel Americano
57 Hostal Colón
62 Residencial Los
   Escudos
65 Hotel Continental,
   Hostal Acapulco
66 Hostal Vogi
68 Hostal Recreo
69 Hotel Paris
74 Hotel Sudamericano
75 Hotel Opt Gar
77 Hotel Turismo
79 Hostal Rosalia
80 Hostal Palacios
81 Hostals Central, Lima
82 Hostal Peru
86 Hostal Roma
88 Hotel Chan Chan
92 Hotel La Querencia

PLACES TO EAT

12 ABC Chicken
   Restaurant
37 Marco's Café,
   Café Romano
38 Restaurant Big Ben
40 Parrillada Tori Gallo
53 El Maizal; Restaurant
   Vegeteriano El Sol
58 Las Tradiciones,
   othet bar/restaurants
61 La Mochica Ramos
76 Restaurant Oasis,
   Restaurant 24 Horas
77 Chifa Oriental,
   Chifa Ak Chan

OTHER

1 Hospital Americano-
   Peruano
3 Museo Cassinelli
4 Buses to Chan Chan,
   Huanchaco, Arco Iris
5 Hospital Regional
6 Transportes
   ETHMOPESA
7 Vulcano
8 El Dorado, ITTSA,
   Transportes Guadalupe
9 Buses to Chan Chan,
   Huanchaco, Arco Iris
11 Banco de la Nación,
   Migraciones Office
13 Santa Ana Church
14 Cine Primavera
16 Peña Catana
17 Old City Wall
18 EMTRAFESA
20 Museo de Zoológica
21 La Compañía Church
22 Trujillo Express Buses
23 Guía Tours
24 Santo Domingo
   Art Gallery
25 San Francisco Church
26 Ormeño
27 Cruz del Sur
28 Local Buses to
   Buenos Aires Beach
29 Chacón Tours
30 Post Office
31 San Pedro Church
32 Museo de Arqueología
33 Interbanc
35 Casa de los Léones
   (Casa Ganoza Chopitea)
36 Santa Clara Convent
39 Olano
41 Banco Wiese
43 AeroPerú
44 Tourist Office,
   Tourist Police
45 Casa de Urquiaga
46 Cine Ideal
47 Faucett Airline
48 Casona Orbegoso,
   Museo Republicano
49 La Merced Church
50 Banco de Crédito
51 Casa de la Emancipación,
   Banco Continental
52 Telefónica del Peru
54 Palacio Iturregui
55 Americana Airline
59 Las Dunas
60 Ruined Church of Belén
63 San Agustín Church
64 Mercado Central
67 El Carmen Church,
   Art Museum
70 Empresa Antisuyo
71 Expreso Sudamericano
   (Buses North)
72 Cine Trujillo
73 Cine Star
78 Teatro Ayacucho
83 Old City Wall
84 Empresa El Aguila
85 Expreso Sudamericano
   (Buses South)
87 TEPSA Bus Station
89 Cine Chimú
90 Chinchaysuyo Buses
91 Buses to Chan Chan,
   Huanchaco, Arco Iris
93 Local buses to
   Las Huacas del Sol
   y de La Luna
94 Clara Luz Bravo D

US$5/7.50. The similar *Hotel España* is near the Antisuyo Bus Terminal, and the *Hostal JR*, a block away, has rooms with bath for US$6/8.

The perennially popular *Hotel Americano* (☎ 24-1361), Pizarro 792, is in a rambling and dilapidated old mansion with lots of character. The rooms are basic but fairly clean for US$8/11 with bath or a bit less without. I've found the showers to be cold, but readers have reported hot ones. The *Hostal Roma*, on Nicaragua, is clean and secure (US$9 for a double with cold bath). The *Hotel La Querencia* is clean but noisy at US$6/9 with bath and warm water.

The following hotels have rooms with private bath and hot shower. The clean *Hostal Rosell* (☎ 25-3583, 25-6282), España 250 (look for the small hostel sign), charges US$9/14 and gives discounts to youth hostel members. The *Hotel Chan Chan* (☎ 24-2964), on Huayana Capac and Sinchi Roca, is basic but OK at US$8/12. The *Hotel Primavera* (☎ 24-4146), Piérola 872, is out of the center but is clean, modern and good value at US$10/15. The clean and friendly *Hotel Sudamericano* (☎ 24-3751), Grau 515, is OK for US$9/14, but check the water – some showers are cold.

Home Stays Budget travelers can also stay with local families who charge about US$5 to US$9 per person. Local guide Clara Luz Bravo D (☎ 24-3347) is a good source of addresses and can help set you up (see Guides, above).

Places to Stay – middle

The line between the best bottom end and the cheapest middle hotels is blurred. The *Hotel San Martín* (☎ 23-4011), 745 San Martín, has over 100 rooms and therefore is rarely full. It is characterless but fair value, at US$13/20. The clean *Hostel Recreo* (☎ 24-6991), Estete 647, has rooms with telephone, TV and (usually) hot water at US$12/18. Other reasonable choices with doubles in the high teens are the *Hotel Rosalia* (☎ 25-6411), Grau 611; *Hostal Palacios* (☎ 25-8194), Grau 709; and the *Residencial Los Escudos* (☎ 25-5691),

Orbegoso 676. All have hot water some of the time and Los Escudos has a nice garden.

The *Hotel Turismo* (☎ 24-3411, 24-4181, fax 25-4151), Gamarra 747, has clean, good-sized, but slightly stuffy rooms with telephone, bath, TV and hot water in the mornings and evenings. Rates are about US$13/20. The clean *Hostal Vogi* (☎ 24-3574, 23-1069), Ayacucho 663, is about the same price and has similar features, though rooms are smaller. The *Hotel Continental* (☎ 24-1607), Gamarra 663, has clean, carpeted singles/doubles with telephone, music, bath and hot water (some of the time) for US$14/21. Their attached restaurant isn't bad. The clean, friendly and well-run *Hotel Opt Gar* (☎ 24-2192), Grau 595, has a good restaurant and singles/doubles with quite reliable hot water at US$17/26. This is the best hotel in this class.

Places to Stay – top end

The quite new *Los Conquistadores Hotel* (☎ 24-4505, fax 23-5917), Almagro 586, has comfortable carpeted rooms with TV, telephone, mini bar and room service. Rates area US$25/38 including breakfast. For a couple of dollars more, there's the new *Casino Real Hotel* (☎ 25-7034, fax 25-7416), Pizarro 651, which has similar rooms and includes breakfast and airport pickup in its prices.

These compete with the Grand Dame of the city's hotels, the *Hotel Libertador* (☎ 23-2741, 23-1741, fax 23-5641; in Lima 442-1995, 442-1996) in a beautiful old building right on the Plaza de Armas. There is a pool, sauna, good restaurant, pleasant bar, 24-hour coffeeshop and comfortable rooms for about US$96. They have a few suites at US$160. Try to avoid streetside rooms unless you want to watch the goings-on, as they are apt to be noisy.

Places to Eat

There are plenty of restaurants near the market, and for the impecunious, the food stalls in the market itself are among the cheapest places to eat in Trujillo. Restaurant prices are also very reasonable. A block from the market are several Chinese restaurants: the *Chifa Oriental* and *Chifa Ak Chan* are recommended. The nearby *Restaurant 24 Horas* is inexpensive and always open. The *Restaurant Oasis* next door is good for fritadas and other local food. Across the street, the restaurant in the *Hotel Opt Gar* serves some of the best international food in town.

Simple but recommended restaurants on the 700 block of Pizarro include the *Café Romano* with strong espresso coffee and *Marco's Café* for good homemade cakes and pies as well as ice cream. Both cafés offer a variety of good food. If you're economizing, ask for the set lunch or dinner at under US$2. On the 600 block of Pizarro, the *Restaurant Vegetariano El Sol* offers inexpensive vegetarian meals. Another good choice for a cheap set lunch in pleasant surroundings is *El Maizal* on the same block. They often have coastal music and dance shows on Friday and Saturday evenings and sometimes on weekend afternoons. *Las Tradiciones* and other places around the Plazuela El Recreo have inexpensive menus and a variety of meat, chicken and fish dishes.

If you like fried chicken, the *ABC* chicken restaurant has large portions. *Restaurant Big Ben* is recommended for good ceviches and local seafood at medium prices. *La Mochica Ramos* is recommended for a variety of mid-priced steaks and local dishes but is closed on Monday and Tuesday. *Parrillada Tori Gallo* (☎ 25-7284, 25-3901) has a variety of mid-priced grills as well as some Mexican dishes and music at weekends. *La Taberna*, on Husares de Junín off Larco about a kilometer southwest of town, serves chicken dishes and is a locally popular place for folkloric music on weekends.

Entertainment

Trujillo's several cinemas often offer the best choices for an evening out. Some of the restaurants above have music on weekends. The shows at the *El Maizal* feature criolla music and salsa. The national dance champions of the marinera, tondero and huayno dances sometimes give demonstrations. The *Peña Catana* at Colón and Miraflores has live music on weekends. There are other peñas away from the center. The local newspaper *La Industria* is the best source for local entertainment, cultural exhibitions, etc.

Getting There & Away

Trujillo is Peru's major north-coast city and is serviced by scores of buses making the 24-hour run along the Panamericana between Lima and the Ecuadorian border (and intermediate coastal points). There are also daily flights to and from Lima and other cities.

Air The airport is 10 km northwest of town. Faucett, AeroPerú and Americana have offices in central Trujillo and soon Aero Continente will too. They all fly to Lima (US$69) on most days. Faucett has daily flights to Chiclayo. Aero Continente has two flights a week to Tarapoto (US$71) and Rioja. AeroPerú has flights most days to Piura and twice a week to Iquitos (US$92). Americana has a daily flight to Piura (US$40). Expresso Aéreo flies from Lima daily, stopping at about five towns. Transportes Aéreos Andahuaylas (TAA) flies from Lima and on to Chachapoyas on Thursdays. Schedules and destinations vary often. The usual US$4 domestic departure tax is levied at the airport.

Bus & Colectivo Many major companies operate up and down the coast along the Panamericana Norte. A few go inland. Prices and schedules vary widely from company to company and from month to month. Some companies have luxury buses with video, bathroom and reclining seats that cost twice as much as regular buses, so you should shop around for the service/ price combination that you want. The details given below are only intended as a rough guide. Bear in mind that buses to Lima tend to leave at night, so if you want to travel by day, book in advance. Most buses leave Trujillo full and advance booking is recommended for any departure.

If you're heading north, the first major stop is Chiclayo. This journey costs about US$3 and takes three to four hours. The locals stand on Avenida Mansiche outside the stadium and catch the next bus heading north. All northbound buses with empty seats will stop here. If you'd rather not bother about watching your luggage while you wait on the side of the road, the most frequent Chiclayo service is with EMTRAFESA (☎ 24-3981), on Miraflores near España, with Chiclayo buses leaving every half-hour during the day. Vulcano also has frequent Chiclayo buses.

Several bus companies provide services to Piura (US$5 to US$9, seven to nine hours) and/or Tumbes (about 15 hours). EMTRAFESA goes to Piura quite cheaply, Vulcano and El Dorado have good buses to Piura and Tumbes and Expresso Sudamericano has cheaper, slower buses there. ETHMOPESA, Cruz del Sur (good buses), ITTSA and TEPSA (older buses driven fast!) are among other possibilities.

The trip to Lima takes 8 to 10 hours and prices fluctuate wildly. In 1995, fares were US$7 to US$15 depending on the class of service. The best services to Lima are said to be Ormeño (Continental) and Trujillo Express. Las Dunas, España 1445, has overnight luxury buses to Lima. EMTRAFESA, Cruz del Sur, Chinchaysuyo and Expresso Sudamericano are others going to Lima.

There are various bus services inland. Chinchaysuyo and Cruz del Sur have buses to Huaraz (10 hours) but most departures are at night. If you want to travel by day and can't find a day bus leaving Trujillo, take a bus to Huaraz from Chimbote instead. The route up into the highlands is spectacular and daytime travel is recommended for the scenery. Empresa El Aguila is good for Chimbote.

Connections from Chiclayo to Cajamarca are better than those from Trujillo, so if you plan to visit both Chiclayo and Cajamarca, it makes sense to visit Chiclayo first. Vulcano, El Dorado, Expresso Sudamericano and Empresa Díaz buses run from Trujillo to Cajamarca (eight hours).

The Empresa Díaz terminal is on the Panamericana, about a kilometer northeast of the town center. If you can't find a direct bus, you can take any bus to Chiclayo and get off at the Cajamarca turn-off (about 15 km past Pacasmayo) and then wait for a Cajamarca-bound bus. It's a hot place to wait but there are a couple of basic cafés for cold drinks. If you leave Trujillo fairly early in the morning, you should be able to connect with a bus from Chiclayo.

If you want to head east from Trujillo to Otuzco, Santiago de Chuco, Huamachuco and Cajabamba (this is the much rougher and longer old route to Cajamarca), there is service with Empresa Antisuyo. Several small buses leave in the morning on the interesting side trip to Otuzco (2½ hours) but may not go further. For buses beyond to Santiago de Chuco and Huamachuco, try Empresa Sanchez López on Avenida Vallejo, away from the center.

For the long northern route into the jungle via Chiclayo, Bagua Grande and Moyobamba to Tarapoto, Transportes Guadalupe is a reasonable choice, though there are others. For the spur off that road down to Chachapoyas, Olanó is the most popular choice. A description of that route, quite along and rough one but with some spectacular scenery, is given in the Chachapoyas section of Across the Northern Highlands.

Getting Around
To/From the Airport The airport, about 10 km northwest of Trujillo, can be reached cheaply on the bus to Huanchaco, though you'll have to walk the last kilometer or so. Ask the driver where the airport turn-off is. A taxi to or from the city center will cost about US$5.

To/From Archaeological Sites White-yellow-and-orange 'B' colectivos pass the corner of España and Industrial (and other places – see map) for Huaca Esmeralda, Chan Chan and Huanchaco every few minutes. Red-blue-and-white minibuses or green-and-white buses for Esperanza go northeast along Mansiche and can drop you at La Huaca Arco Iris. Minibuses leave every half hour from Calle Suarez for the Huacas del Sol y de la Luna. Fares are roughly US25¢ on these routes. Note that these buses are worked by professional thieves looking for cameras and money – the tourist police may be able to warn you of particularly bad places. At any rate, keep cameras hidden and watch your bags carefully.

A taxi or tour group isn't a bad idea, even for budget travelers. The ruins certainly will be more interesting and meaningful with a good guide – some recommended ones are listed above. They can arrange a taxi or their own vehicle. Alternatively, a taxi to most of these sites will cost US$3 to US$4, then you can hire an on-site guide in most cases.

If you want to go to Huaca Prieta (see below), it's about 30 km north of Trujillo on the south side of the Chicama Valley, by the coast. Colectivos go from Avenida España to Cartavio; from there, it's a walk of about 7 km.

Taxis A taxi ride within Avenida España shouldn't be more than US$1. For sightseeing, taxis charge about US$6 to US$8 per hour, depending on how far you expect them to go.

ARCHAEOLOGICAL SITES AROUND TRUJILLO
The Moche and Chimu cultures left the greatest marks on the Trujillo area, but are by no means the only ones. In a March 1973 *National Geographic* article, Drs ME Moseley & CJ Mackey claimed knowledge of over 2000 sites in the Río Moche valley. Many of these sites are small and well-nigh forgotten, but others include the largest pre-Columbian city in the Americas (Chan Chan) as well as pyramids that required in excess of an incredible 100 million adobe bricks to construct.

Five major archaeological sites can be easily reached from Trujillo by local bus or taxi. Two of these sites are Moche, dating from about 500 AD. The other three, from the Chimu culture, date from about 1200 AD to 1300 AD. The recently excavated Moche ruin called El Brujo (60 km from Trujillo) can also be visited, but not as conveniently.

Dangers & Annoyances
I have heard several reports of single travelers – especially women – being mugged, robbed or raped while visiting the more remote archaeological sites. You are advised to stay on the main footpaths at all times, not to visit the ruins late in the day and to go with friends or hire a guide to accompany you.

Archaeology & History
Huaca Prieta One of the earliest groups in Peru to be studied are the Huaca Prieta people, who lived at the site of that name around 3500 BC to 2300 BC. These hunters and gatherers also began to develop simple agriculture. They grew cotton and varieties of bean and pepper – but corn, now a staple, was unheard of. Finds of simple fishing nets and hooks indicate that the Huaca Prieta people primarily ate seafood. They lived in single-room shacks half buried in the ground and most of what is known about them has been deduced from their middens, or garbage piles. Hence we know that they were a preceramic people, didn't use jewelry and had developed netting and weaving. At their most artistic, they decorated dried gourds with simply carved patterns; similarly decorated gourds are produced today as a Peruvian handicraft. Hot stones may have been dropped into these gourds to cook food.

Huaca Prieta has been one of the most intensively studied early Peruvian sites but, for the nonarchaeologist, it's more interesting to read about than to visit. After all, it's simply a prehistoric pile of garbage.

After the decline of the Huaca Prieta a developmental era began. It is called the Guañape, after a tiny fishing village near the mouth of the Río Virú where burial sites of this era were excavated. Weaving improved, agriculture developed with the advent of corn and, particularly importantly,

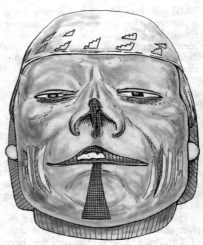

Pot rendering official with severed nose and lip, Florescent Epoch, Mochicha IV

the making of ceramics began and simple funerary offerings were made. Burial sites in the Chicama and Virú valleys have given archaeologists an insight into this development, but no specific site is particularly important to the traveler.

Chavín About 850 BC, a major new cultural influence, that of the Chavín, began to leave its mark on the area. This was a cultist period, named after Chavín de Huácar, on the eastern slopes of the Cordillera Blanca, where a feline-worshipping cult had one of its main centers. The Chavín influence swept over the northern mountains and the northern and central coasts of Peru. At its most simple, the Chavín influence consisted of a highly stylized art form based especially on jaguar motifs. Formerly called the Chavín Horizon (many archaeologists now prefer the term Early Horizon) this may have been the first major culture in Peru as well as one of the most artistically developed. The various areas and groups it encompassed were typified by the rapid development of ceramic ware and a common art form. In the Trujillo area, the Chavín influence was represented by the Cupisnique culture. Examples of Cupisnique pottery can be seen in the museums of Lima and Trujillo, though there are no especially noteworthy ruins for the visitor to see.

Archaeologists identify several other geographically smaller and less important cultures of the Trujillo area which coincided with the later Cupisnique period. These include the Salinar, Vicus and Gallinazo.

Moche With the decline of the Cupisnique period came the beginnings of the fascinating Moche period, a culture that has left impressive archaeological sites and some of the most outstanding pottery to be seen in Peru's museums.

The Moche culture is named after the river that flows into the ocean just south of Trujillo. The word Mochica has been used interchangeably with Moche and refers to a dialect spoken in the Trujillo area at the time of the conquest, though not necessarily spoken by the Moche people. Moche is now the preferred usage.

The Moche culture evolved from the Cupisnique at about the time of Christ. The Moche didn't conquer the Cupisnique; rather, there was a slow transition characterized by a number of developments. Ceramics, textiles and metalwork improved greatly, architectural skills allowed the construction of huge pyramids and other structures and there was enough leisure time for art and a highly organized religion.

Mochica running fox god

As with the Nazca culture, which developed on the south coast at about the same time, the Moche period is especially known for its ceramics, considered the most artistically sensitive and technically developed of any found in Peru. The thousands of Moche pots preserved in museums are so realistically decorated with figures and scenes that they give us a very descriptive look at life during the Moche period. As there was no written language, most of what we know about the Moche comes from this wealth of pottery. Pots were modeled into lifelike representations of people, crops, domestic or wild animals, marine life and houses. Other pots were painted with scenes of both ceremonial and everyday life. From these pots, archaeologists know that Moche society was very class conscious. The most important people, especially the priests and warriors, were members of the urban classes and lived closest to the large ceremonial pyramids and other temples. They were surrounded by a middle class of artisans and then, in descending order, farmers and fishermen, servants, slaves and beggars.

Moche ceramics usually depicted priests and warriors being carried in litters wearing particularly fine jewelry or clothing. Further evidence is given of the authority of priests and warriors in pots showing scenes of punishment, including the mutilation and death of those who dared to disobey. Other facets of Moche life illustrated on the pots include surgical procedures such as amputation and setting of broken limbs. Sex is realistically shown; one room in the Museo Rafael Larco Herrera in Lima is entirely devoted to (mainly Moche) erotic pots depicting most sexual practices, some rather imaginative. The Museo Cassinelli in Trujillo also has a fine collection. Clothing, musical instruments, tools and jewelry are all frequent subjects for ceramics.

The ceramics also show us that the Moche had well-developed weaving techniques but, because of rare rainstorms that occurred every few decades, most of their textiles have been destroyed. Metalwork,

Huaqueros

The word 'huaquero' is heard frequently on the North Coast of Peru. The word literally means 'robber of huacas.' Huacas are temples, shrines and burial sites of special significance. They are often characterized by their richness. Temples were decorated with sheets of precious metals and royalty was buried with a treasure trove.

Ever since the Spanish conquest, huaqueros have worked the ancient graves of Peru. They make their living by finding and opening these graves, then removing the valuables and selling them to anybody prepared to pay for an archaeological artifact. To a certain extent, one can sympathize with a poor campesino grubbing around in the desert, hoping to strike it rich; but the huaquero is one of the archaeologist's greatest enemies. So thorough has the huaqueros' ransacking been that an unplundered grave is almost never found by archaeologists – someone else has always been there first.

Today, visitors to Trujillo and the surrounding sites are sometimes offered a 'genuine' archaeological artifact. These are not always genuine – but if they are, it is illegal to export them from Peru. ∎

on the other hand, has survived. They used gold, silver and copper mainly for ornaments but some heavy copper implements have also been found.

Two Moche sites survive, side by side, a few kilometers south of Trujillo. They are known as the Huacas del Sol y de la Luna, or the 'Temples of the Sun and the Moon,' and are easily visited. The Temple of the Sun is the largest pre-Columbian structure in South America and is described in more detail later in this section.

The Moche period declined around 700 AD and the next few centuries are somewhat confusing. The Wari culture, based in the Ayacucho area of the central Peruvian Andes, began to expand and its influence was felt as far north as the Chicama Valley.

Chimu The next important period in the Trujillo area, the Chimu, lasted from about 1000 AD to 1470 AD. The Chimu built a huge capital at Chan Chan, just north of Trujillo. The Chimu was a highly organized society – it must have been to have built and supported a city such as Chan Chan. Its artwork was less exciting than that of the Moche, tending more to functional mass production than artistic achievement. Gone, for the most part, is the technique of painting pots. Instead, they were fired by a simpler method than that used by the Moche, producing the typical blackware

Chimu god

seen in many Chimu pottery collections. Despite its poorer quality, this pottery still shows us life in the Chimu kingdom. And while the quality of the ceramics declined, metallurgy developed and various alloys, including bronze, were worked. The Chimu were also exceptionally fine goldsmiths.

It is as an urban society that the Chimu are best remembered. Their huge capital contained approximately 10,000 dwellings of varying quality and importance. Buildings were decorated with friezes, the designs molded into the mud walls, and the more important areas were layered with precious metals. There were storage bins for food and other products from throughout the empire, which stretched along the coast from Chancay to the Gulf of Guayaquil (in southern Ecuador). There were huge walk-in wells, canals, workshops and temples. The royal dead were buried in mounds with a wealth of funerary offerings.

The Chimu were conquered by the Incas in about 1460 but the city was not looted until the arrival of the Spanish. Heavy rainfall has severely damaged the mud moldings, though a few survive and others have been restored.

Chan Chan

Most visitors to the North Coast want to see Chan Chan, the huge ruined capital of the Chimu Empire. Built by the Chimu around 1300 AD and covering about 28 sq km, it is the largest pre-Columbian city in the Americas and the largest mud city in the world. At the height of the Chimu Empire, it housed an estimated 50,000 inhabitants and contained a vast wealth of gold, silver and ceramics. After Chan Chan's conquest by the Incas, the wealth remained more or less undisturbed. The Incas were interested in expanding their imperial control, not in amassing treasure. As soon as the Spaniards arrived, however, the looting began and within a few decades there was little left of the treasures of Chan Chan. The remainder have been pillaged through the centuries by huaqueros, though remnants can be seen in museums. Chan

Chan must have been a dazzling sight at one time. Today, only the mud walls and a few molded decorations remain and the visitor is amazed by the huge expanse of the site as much as anything else.

The damage at Chan Chan has not been caused only by the huaqueros. Devastating floods and heavy rainfall have severely eroded the mud walls of the city. Several decades can go by with almost no rain but occasionally the climatic phenomenon of El Niño can cause rainstorms and floods in the coastal desert.

The Chimu capital consisted of nine major subcities, each built by a succeeding ruler – hence the nine areas are often referred to as the Royal Compounds. You can spend hours wandering around these ruins. Each contains a royal burial mound where the ruler was buried with an appropriately vast quantity of funerary offerings, including dozens of sacrificed young women and chambers full of ceramics, weavings and jewelry. The Tschudi compound, named after a Swiss naturalist who visited Peru in the 1800s and published *Peruvian Antiquities* in Vienna in 1851, is partially restored and open to visitors. (Most of the other compounds have also been named after archaeologists and explorers.)

Chan Chan is about 5 km west of Trujillo. See Getting Around (above) for how to get here. Tschudi lies to the left of the main road; it's a walk of almost 2 km along a dusty dirt road. As you walk, you'll see the crumbling ruins of the other compounds all around you. Stick to the footpath and do not be tempted to stroll off into the ruins on either side. Not only are these ruins in a very poor state of repair, but they are also the haunt of muggers who hope some unsuspecting, camera-toting tourist will enter alone. Stay on the path and go with a friend or guide if possible.

At the Tschudi complex you'll find an entrance booth, a snack and souvenir stand and a third booth where guides are available. There is usually a pair of tourist police on duty. Entry is from 9 am to 4 pm daily (except New Years, May 1 and Christmas) and costs US$2.50. The ticket, which can also be bought at either the Huaca Esmeralda or Huaca Arco Iris ruins, is valid for all three sites but must be used within two days. You can hire a local guide for about US$5 an hour to make sure you don't miss anything and to be shown the original, not the restored, friezes and decorations. The complex is well marked by arrows, so you can see everything without a guide if you prefer.

Tschudi Complex Entry is through a thick defensive wall. Inside, you turn right and almost immediately enter the huge and largely restored Ceremonial Courtyard. All four interior walls are decorated with geometric designs, most of which are new. Just to the right of the massive doorway, as you enter, you'll see a few designs at ground level. I'm told those closest to the door, representing three or four nutria (large aquatic rodents, also called coypu), are unrestored. They're slightly rougher looking than the modern work. The design is repeated all the way around the Ceremonial Plaza and is topped by a series of lines representing waves. A ramp at the far side of the plaza accesses the second level (stairways are not a frequent feature of the major Chimu structures). Note also the great restored height of the walls in this plaza. Though all the Chan Chan walls have crumbled with time, the highest of Tschudi's walls once stood over 10 meters high.

Follow the arrows out of the Ceremonial Courtyard through a door to the right and make a sharp left-hand turn to walk along the outside wall of the plaza. This is one of the most highly decorated and best restored of Tschudi's walls. The adobe friezes show waves of fish rippling along the entire length of the wall above a line of seabirds. See if you can tell where the original moldings end and the restored ones begin. As with the nutria designs, the rougher-looking fish are the originals. Despite their time-worn appearance, they retain a fluidity and character somehow lacking in the modern version. Nevertheless, the modern work has been done with care and succeeds in restoring the entirety of the wall.

At the end of this wall, the arrowed path goes through a labyrinthine section known as the Sanctuaries. The function of these sanctuaries is not clear but their importance is evident in both the quantity and quality of the decorations. Though less restored than the waves-and-fish wall, they are the most interesting section of friezes in Tschudi. Their square- and diamond-shaped geometric designs represent, quite simply, fishing nets. Being so close to the ocean, the Chimu based much of their diet on seafood and the importance of the sea reached venerable proportions. As we have seen, fish, waves, seabirds and sea mammals are represented throughout the city and here, in the Sanctuaries, you find all of them interspersed with the fishing nets. The moon was also very important and there are several series of full-moon symbols in the Sanctuaries. For the Chimu, the moon and the sea were of religious importance (unlike the Incas, who worshipped the sun and venerated the earth).

From the Sanctuaries, arrows lead the visitor into a second ceremonial plaza smaller in size than the main Ceremonial Plaza but similar in shape. It also has a ramp to the second level. From behind this plaza, you can see a huge rectangular depression resembling a drained swimming pool. In fact, it was once a walk-in well which supplied the daily water needs of the Tschudi royal compound. The water level was reached by a series of ramps from the surface and each compound had its own cistern. The Tschudi cistern is the largest in Chan Chan and measures 130 by 45 meters.

To the left of the cistern is an area of several dozen small cells that have been called the military sector. Perhaps soldiers lived here, or the cells may have been used for storage. These constructions are not very well preserved. A straight path leads you from the military sector almost back to the main entrance, passing a series of storage bins. The final area visited is the Assembly Room. This large rectangular room has 24 seats set into niches in the walls and its acoustic properties are such that speakers sitting in any one of the niches can be clearly heard all over the room. Try it.

You are now back by the main entrance, free to wander around again to inspect more thoroughly those areas of particular interest to you.

Chan Chan has eight compounds similar to Tschudi. Unfortunately, as they are in much worse states of repair and there are no guards, visiting the others is neither as worthwhile nor as easy. It is possible to be robbed in these remote and dusty old ruins and it's recommended that those seriously interested in seeing less developed areas of Chan Chan do so in a group and with a knowledgeable professional guide. The path behind Tschudi leading down to and along the beach is particularly notorious for robberies and muggings. If you stay on the dirt road joining the main road with Tschudi, you shouldn't have any problems.

La Huaca Esmeralda

This temple was built by the Chimu at about the same time as Chan Chan. The site is open daily from 9 am to 4 pm and entry costs US$2.50. The ticket is valid for Chan Chan and the Huaca Arco Iris on the same or the next day. Huaca Esmeralda lies at Mansiche, which is halfway between Trujillo and Chan Chan, so you can take the same bus as to Chan Chan or walk from either direction. If you're returning from Chan Chan to Trujillo, the huaca is to the right of the main road, about four blocks behind the Mansiche Church. Thieves reportedly prey on unwary tourists wandering around so go with friends or a guide and keep your eyes open.

The site was buried by sand and was accidentally discovered by a local landowner in 1923. He attempted to uncover the ruins but the El Niño of 1925 began the process of erosion which was exacerbated by the floods and rains of 1983. Little restoration work has been done on the adobe friezes but it is still possible to make out the characteristic designs of fish, seabirds, waves and fishing nets. The temple consists of two stepped platforms and an on-site guide will take you around for a tip.

ROB RACHOWIECKI
Carved wall, La Huaca Arco Iris

La Huaca Arco Iris

This is the third Chimu site that can be visited with the same ticket as Chan Chan and Huaca Esmeralda. Huaca Arco Iris, or the 'Rainbow Temple,' is also known locally as the Huaca del Dragón. It is just to the left of the Panamericana in the suburb of La Esperanza, about 4 km northwest of Trujillo. (See Getting Around for bus information.)

La Huaca Arco Iris is one of the best preserved of the Chimu temples simply because it was covered by sand until the 1960s. Its location was known to a handful of archaeologists and huaqueros but excavation did not begin until 1963. Unfortunately, the 1983 El Niño caused damage to the friezes.

The excavation of the temple took about five years and the upper parts were rebuilt. It used to be painted but now only faint traces of yellow paint can be seen. The temple consists of a defensive wall over two meters thick enclosing an area of about 3000 sq meters. Through the single entrance in this rectangular wall is one large structure, the temple itself. This building covers about 800 sq meters in two levels with a combined height of about 7½ meters. The walls are slightly pyramidal and covered with repeated rainbow

ROB RACHOWIECKI

Author nose to nose with warrior, Sechín ruins

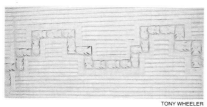

TONY WHEELER

Chan Chan, near Trujillo

TONY WHEELER

La Huaca Arco Iris, near Trujillo

TONY WHEELER

Chan Chan

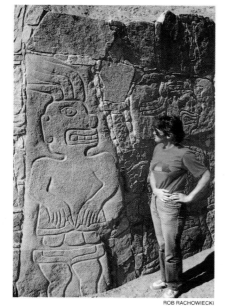

ROB RACHOWIECKI

Carving of warrior, Sechín ruins

TONY WHEELER

Cathedral, Trujillo

Caballitos – boats made of totora reeds – are still used today by fishermen on Peru's north coast.

Caballitos ashore at Huanchaco

Caballito, north coast

Trujillo's colonial architecture

designs, most of which have been restored. Some of the decorations are said to show Recuay, Tiahuanaco and Wari influence. Ramps lead the visitor to the very top of the temple. From here, you can look down into a series of large storage bins. These almost surround the structure and have openings only at the top. There are also good views from the top level of the temple.

There is a tiny on-site museum and local guides, some speaking a little English, are available to show you around the ruin and museum. A tip is expected. You can buy inexpensive, well-made reproductions of Chimu ceramics from the souvenir stand near the entrance.

Las Huacas del Sol y de la Luna

The Temples of the Sun and the Moon were not built by the Chimu. They are about 700 years older than Chan Chan and are attributed to the Moche period. They are on the south bank of the Río Moche, about 10 km southeast of Trujillo by rough road. (See Getting Around above for bus information.)

The site is officially open from 8 am to 1 pm – closing before afternoon wind storms start whipping up the dust. Entrance is about US$1. Because the site is out of the way, single travelers, especially women, are advised to go with a friend or hire a guide.

The two huacas, both roughly pyramidal in shape, are usually visited together. The Huaca del Sol is the largest single pre-Columbian structure in Peru. Estimates of its size vary, depending on the points of reference used, but recent measurements give a maximum length of 342 meters, breadth of 159 meters and height of 45 meters. The structure was built with an estimated 140 million adobe bricks, many of them marked with symbols. These are not evidence of writing or hieroglyphics; they are merely the hallmarks of the workers who made them. Over 100 symbols have been identified and one theory holds that groups or communities of workers were taxed a certain number of adobe bricks and

marked their contributions with distinctive hallmarks to keep track of how many bricks they had provided.

At one time, the pyramid consisted of several different levels connected by steep flights of stairs, huge ramps and walls sloping at 77° to the horizon. A millennium and a half have wrought their inevitable damage and today the pyramid looks like a giant pile of crude bricks partially covered with sand. Despite this, the brickwork remains very impressive from some angles. It appears that there are few graves or rooms within the structure and that it must have been used primarily as a huge ceremonial site. Certainly, its size alone makes the pyramid an awesome structure and the views from the top are excellent.

The smaller Huaca de la Luna is about 500 meters away across the open desert. Dozens of pottery shards lie around this open area. Although less impressive in size than the Huaca del Sol, the Huaca de la Luna has yielded many more artifacts. Unlike the almost solid Pyramid of the Sun, the Pyramid of the Moon is riddled with rooms which contained ceramics, precious metals and some of the beautiful polychrome friezes for which the Moche were famous. These are currently under restoration by archaeologists and students from the Universidad Nacional de Trujillo (UNT) and you may be allowed to seem some of them. Reproductions of some of the murals are displayed in the Museo de Arqueología in Trujillo.

La Huaca El Brujo

This newly excavated Moche ruin is 60 km from Trujillo on the coast and is rather hard to find without a guide. The main section of El Brujo is a 90-foot-high truncated pyramid with some of the best friezes in the area, including stylized designs of fish, priests, and human sacrifices. There are also many burial sites here, reportedly from the Lambayeque culture, which followed the Moche. Many other ruins are in the area, mainly of archaeological rather than touristic interest.

The most direct way of reaching the site is to drive north for 40 km on the Panamericana to the village of Chocope, then go west for 20 km via an unpaved road to the coastal village of Magdalena de Cao, near the ruins. Chocope is easy enough to reach but transport from there may be problematical. It may be easier, if relying on public transport, to take buses north on the Panamericana to the village of Chicama and then west to Cartavio. From there, you might find a bus going to the coast. If not, it is a shorter taxi ride to the ruins from Cartavio than from Chocope. I recommend going with a guide – Clara Luz Bravo D and Michael White have both been there many times (see Guides under Trujillo Information).

SUGAR ESTATES

Sugar cane is an important crop all along the northern Peruvian coast. A reader suggests that several sugar estates in the Trujillo area can be visited by those interested in sugar manufacturing. It is best to go in the morning when guided tours can be arranged. The Casa Grande and Hacienda Cartavio estates in the Chicama Valley, some 40 km north of Trujillo, can be reached by bus. Departure points change regularly, so ask in Trujillo if you are interested.

HUANCHACO

The fishing village of Huanchaco, a 15 km bus ride northwest of Trujillo, is the best beach resort in the Trujillo area. It's not very good for swimming, though, and you won't find expensive high-rise buildings. Huanchaco is still very low key and retains its fishing-village ambience.

Of particular interest are the totora reed boats. These look superficially like those found on Lake Titicaca in the southern highlands, but differ from the highland boats in that they are not hollow. Because the fishermen ride on them rather than in them, these high-ended, cigar-shaped boats are called *caballitos*, or 'little horses.' The caballitos are similar to the boats depicted

on Moche ceramics 1500 years ago. The inhabitants of Huanchaco are among the few remaining people on the coast who still remember how to construct and use these precarious-looking craft and you can always see some stacked up at the north end of the beach. When the surf is good, the fishermen paddle the boats beyond the breakers to fish and then surf back to the beach with their catch. It's well worth seeing.

Apart from walking on the beach and waiting for the caballitos to go into action, there's not much to do in Huanchaco and that's one of its attractions. It's a quiet, laid-back, relaxing sort of place. You can swim in the ocean but it's a little too cold for most of the year local newspapers have reported fecal contamination in summer. When the El Niño current warms the water from January to March, Huanchaco gets a little busier. You can climb the tower of the massive church at the north end of the village for a good view of the surrounding area. And you can enjoy a seafood meal on the coast.

Dangers & Annoyances

Although the beach of Huanchaco is no more dangerous than anywhere else, people have been mugged when walking a long way from the village. You'll be OK if you stay in Huanchaco and use the bus to get to Trujillo.

Special Events

Huanchaco is host to the Festival del Mar, held every other year (that's even years) during the first week in May. This festival reenacts the legendary arrival of Takaynamo, founder of Chan Chan. There are various events such as surfing and dancing competitions, cultural conferences, food and music.

Places to Stay

Huanchaco is a small town and most people know where the hotels are or where people rent rooms. Heidi, a Swiss lady at Los Pinos 451, charges about US$3.50 per person. Señora Lola, Manco Capac 136, has cheap rooms. Ask about others.

The clean *Hostal Huanchaco* (☎ 23-0813), Larco 287, is US$6 per person (communal cold showers) or US$8 (private hot bath). There is a small pool and pleasant courtyard. The rundown *Hostal Caballito de Totora* (☎ 22-3389) is US$10/16 with bath. The similarly priced *Hostal Esteros* (☎ 23-0810) is a little better. Best is the popular, friendly and secure *Hostal Bracamonte* (☎ 23-0808), Los Olivos 503, with a pool and nice gardens. Rooms with private hot showers are US$12/18. Bargain for reduced rates in the off season.

Places to Eat

Huanchaco has several seafood restaurants, especially near the totora reed boats stacked at the north end of the beach. None are luxurious but several are adequate – take your pick. Some places occasionally offer entertainment of sorts and they usually advertise this in the hotels a few days in advance.

The *Restaurant Lucha del Mar* is in a large, white, two-story building on the waterfront. This locally popular restaurant serves large and tasty seafood dishes for about US$4 to US$5. Next door, *La Estrella Marina* has also been recommended as a good typical restaurant. Both have balconies with ocean views. The more elegant *Club Colonial* restaurant on the plaza is very good but a little pricier.

Getting There & Away

Buses leave from Industrial at España in Trujillo at frequent intervals during daylight hours. The fare is about US30¢. The bus can drop you off near the hotel of your choice – ask the driver or you'll end up driving away from the hotels, through to the north end of the village. To return, just wait on the beachfront road for the bus as it returns from the north end, picking up passengers along the way. This service stops soon after sunset.

OTUZCO

The small town of Otuzco is at 2627 meters above sea level, two or three hours drive inland from Trujillo. There is a large modern church built next to a smaller, older one that is usually closed. Outside, stairs lead to the shrine of La Virgen de la Puerta, the site of a major pilgrimage every December 15, when all the (few) hotels are full and people sleep in the Plaza de Armas. Otherwise, this is a little-visited but typical town of the western Andean slopes. The drive up through coastal sugar-cane fields and other subtropical crops irrigated by the Río Moche and into the highland agricultural regions irrigated by the Río Otuzco is an interesting cross-section that only a few off-the-beaten-track travelers experience. It's a rough but scenic drive on unpaved roads.

Places to Stay & Eat

There are about half a dozen basic places to stay. The best is the *Hostal Los Portales*, Santa Rosa 680, which charges US$5 and is not especially good and has cold private showers. There are several cheaper places with shared showers.

A few inexpensive restaurants serve cheap Peruvian food. *Lima 2* on the Plaza de Armas is one suggestion, but none seem outstanding.

Getting There & Away

Empresa Antisuyo has buses from Trujillo. Otuzco is a few kilometers off the Trujillo-Santiago de Chuco road and it is difficult to find buses on to Santiago de Chuco. You may need to return a few kilometers to the main road. It is reportedly possible to take an early bus from Trujillo, spend a few hours in Otuzco, and return in the afternoon.

PUERTO CHICAMA

This small port is famous for its surf and has the longest left-handed wave in the world. Not being a surfer, I have no idea what that means but I guess it's pretty important. Surfers tell me that you can get a kilometer-long ride if there's a big swell;

otherwise, the waves aren't too good for surfing. There is no gear available here – you have to bring it all. The water is cold and a wet suit is recommended.

Places to Stay
Puerto Chicama is a surfer's hangout and there are few other visitors. There are a couple of basic hotels and restaurants but no electricity at night. The *El Hombre* faces the ocean and charges US$6 a double, has good simple meals, but lacks running water. Another hotel has a shower. I've also heard that you can camp.

Getting There & Away
To get to Puerto Chicama, wait for a bus near the Mansiche Stadium in Trujillo. There are a few direct buses but it may be easier to take a bus about 40 km north along the Panamericana to Paiján and change there for a local bus to Puerto Chicama, another 16 km away.

I once met an Australian surfer who was traveling from beach to beach along the Pacific coast. He had his board with him and seemed to have no problems transporting it on the buses.

PACASMAYO & PACATNAMÚ
The small port of Pacasmayo is 105 km north of Trujillo on the Panamericana. The private Rodriguez Razzetto collection has museum-quality textiles, pottery and jewelry of the Jequetepeque culture. Visits can be arranged by appointment.

The turn-off to Cajamarca is 15 km beyond Pacasmayo. A few kilometers further along the Panamericana, just before the village of Guadalupe, a track leads towards the ocean. The little-visited ruins of Pacatnamú lie several kilometers along this track. This large site has been inhabited by various cultures: The Gallinazo, Moche and Chimu have all left their mark.

Places to Stay
There are a few cheap, basic but clean hotels in Pacasmayo. These include the *Ferrocarril*, which has cold water and is supposedly the best – but ask locally. A

reader suggests the *Hostal Peru* on the plaza with dark but adequate rooms for about US$15 a double with bath. Others suggest the *Panamericano* and the *Hostal Pakatnamú* (☎ 52-2368, 52-3352), on the boardwalk.

CHICLAYO
The next major coastal city north of Trujillo is Chiclayo, just over 200 km away on the Panamericana. Founded in the 16th century, Chiclayo remained no more than an outlying district of the older town of Lambayeque through the 19th century. Today, however, Lambayeque is small and almost forgotten while Chiclayo has become one of Peru's fastest growing modern cities. Although the city itself has little to see of historical interest, it is a vibrant and thriving city with good opportunities to meet Peruvians. It is an important commercial center and the capital of the coastal desert department of Lambayeque. With a population of over 400,000, it is the fourth largest city in Peru.

In 1987, there was dramatic news of the discovery of a royal Moche tomb at Sipán, about 30 km southeast of Chiclayo. This find proved to be extraordinary – it has been called the most important archaeological discovery in Peru in the last 50 years – and Peruvian archaeologists have recovered hundreds of dazzling and priceless artifacts from the site. Excavation continues at the site and a tourist infrastructure is developing. Sipán is best visited from Chiclayo. The spectacular finds are displayed in the Bruning Museum in Lambayeque, 11 km north of Chiclayo. Other sites worth visiting from Chiclayo are the archaeological ruins at Túcume as well as a number of coastal villages, described after the Chiclayo section.

Information
The tourist information office has closed (but may reopen).

Money The Banco de Crédito and the Banco Nor Peru, on the 600 block of Balta by the Plaza de Armas, change traveler's

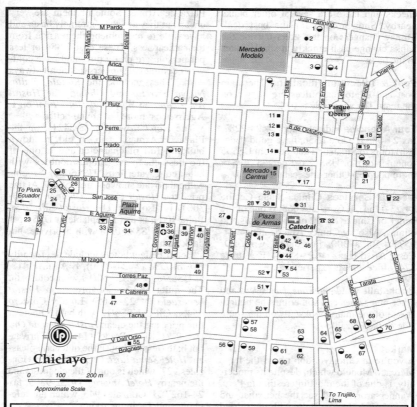

NORTH COAST

Chiclayo

0   100   200 m

Approximate Scale

To Piura,
Ecuador

To Trujillo,
Lima

PLACES TO STAY
9 Hotels Santa Rosa, America
11 Hostal Chimu
12 Hostal Cruz de Chalpón
13 Hostal Americano
14 Hostal Adriático
15 Hostals Balta,
   Nueva Estrella
16 Hostal Venezuela
18 Hostal Señor de los Milagros
19 Hostal Tumi de Oro
23 Gran Hotel Chiclayo
24 Hotel El Sol
29 Hostal Ronald
30 Hotel Royal
35 Hotel Real
38 Inca Hotel
39 Hotel Lido
40 Hotel Europa
47 Hotel Aristi
49 Hostal Sol Radiante
55 Sipán Hotel
62 Garza Hotel

PLACES TO EAT
17 La Nueva Barcarola
28 Kafé D'Kaly
45 Las Americas,
   Elio's Snack Bar
46 Restaurant Maritimo
50 Italian Restaurants
51 Chifa Pollería San Pablo
52 Restaurant Imperial
53 Restaurant Romana
54 Restaurant Le Paris
55 Oasis

OTHER
1 Mini Buses to Sipán
2 Sports Stadium
3 Buses to Monsefú
4 Buses to Puerto Etén
5 Buses to Túcume
6 Buses to Motupe
7 Buses to Monsefu,
   Nearby Towns
8 Empresa D Olano

10 Buses to Pimentel
20 Buses to Chongoyape
21 Peña Hermanos Balcázar
22 Peña El Brujo
25 Empresa Chiclayo
26 Transportes San Pablo
27 Aero Continente
31 Cine Colonial
32 Telefónica del Peru
33 Post Office
34 Hospital Las Mercedes
36 Clínica Santa Cecilia
39 Americana Airline
41 AeroPerú Airline
42 Cine Tropical
43 Banco de Crédito,
   other banks
44 Faucett (Airline)
48 Cine Oro
56 TEPSA Buses
57 Atahualpa Buses
58 Expreso Sudamericano
59 Vulcano, El Aguila

60 EMTRAFESA Buses
61 Cruz de Chalpon
63 CIVA, LTTSA,
   Cruz del Sur,
   Roggero
64 Peru Express
65 Transportes Piura
66 Expreso Continental
67 Empresa D Olano
68 Chiclayo Express
69 Transportes
   El Cumbe
70 Empresa Diaz

checks and there are several other banks nearby. Shop around for the best deal. Money changers on the street outside the banks change cash quickly at similar rates to the bank.

Post & Telecommunications The main post and telefónica offices are shown on the map. The area code is 074.

Tour Agencies Indiana Tours (☎ 24-2287, fax 24-0833), Colón 556, have good (English) tours to Sipán or Túcume from US$35 (one person), or US$17 per person (five or more people.) Other sites can be toured.

Medical Services Clínica Santa Cecilia (☎ 23-7154), L Gonzales 668, is one of the better of Chiclayo's 10 or so hospitals and clinics. Also try Clínica Americana (☎ 24-0571), Balta 300. For dental work, Dr César Aristi Ugaz (☎ 23-8405), E Aguirre 374, office 205, is experienced.

Bookstalls Outdated *Time, Newsweek* and other magazines can sometimes be bought at one of the many bookstalls on the south side of the Plaza de Armas.

Market

If you're in Chiclayo, don't miss the huge Mercado Modelo which, despite its modernity, is one of the most interesting in Peru. Wander around and see the herbalist and *brujo* (witch doctor) stalls with their dried plants, bones, bits of animals and other healing charms. Other things to look for include heavy woven saddlebags called *alforjas*, an item typical of the area that can be worn over the shoulder with one bag on your front and the other on your back. Woven straw items such as hats, baskets, mats and ornaments are also popular. And, of course, there is the usual cacophonous animal section and a food market. As always in a crowded market, watch your belongings.

Places to Stay – bottom end

Many of the cheaper hotels are along the main street of Avenida Balta, north of the Plaza de Armas. Some of them are very cheap but they are also extremely basic and have little to recommend them aside from their cheapness. These cost US$4 or less per person, are pretty dirty and have cold-water communal showers that don't always work. They include the *Ronald, Balta, Nueva Estrella* and *Chimu*. The *Hostal Americano* on Balta and *Hotel Real* on E Aguirre cost more but are no better.

The *Hotel Royal* (☎ 23-3421), on the Plaza de Armas, is in an old, rundown building full of character and is one of the best cheapies. Singles/doubles with bath (cold water) cost US$6/8 and rooms without private showers are US$5/7. At this price the *Hostal Cruz de Chalpón* (☎ 23-3004) is also OK. The *Hostal Adriático*, Balta 1009, is just acceptable at US$4 per person or US$8.50/10 with a private, but dank bath.

Better budget hotels include the friendly *Hostal Lido* (☎ 24-4050), E Aguirre 412, at US$5/8, or US$7.50/10 with cold bath. The quiet and reasonably clean *Hostal Venezuela* (☎ 23-2665), Lora y Cordero 954, is OK at US$8/12 with bath. Others at this price are the clean *Hostal Tumi de Oro* (☎ 22-7108), L Prado 1145, with private hot bath (less without); the quiet and pleasant *Hotel Santa Rosa* (☎ 22-4411), L Gonzales 927, which is one of the cleanest; and the nearby *Hotel America* (☎ 22-9305, fax 24-1627), L Gonzales 943, which has telephone and TV in the rooms.

The *Hostal Señor de los Milagros* looks OK for US$9/13. The *Hostal Sol Radiante* (☎ 23-7858), Izaga 392, is a quiet, family-run place at US$10/14 with hot bath. The *Hotel Europa* (☎ 23-7919), E Aguirre 466, looks nice and charges US$14/17/21 for one to three people with private hot bath or less with communal showers.

Places to Stay – middle

The clean and comfortable *Hotel El Sol* (☎ 23-2120, tel/fax 23-1070), E Aguirre 119, charges US$18/24 for singles/doubles with bath and hot water. Rooms have TV and phone but vary in quality and size so look around. There is a small pool and parking area. The similarly-priced *Hotel Aristi* (☎ 23-1074, 23-3873, fax 22-8673), F Cabrera at M Grau, has a restaurant attached and adequate rooms with private hot showers, TV and telephone. There are a few more expensive 'suites.' Although this is quite a good hotel by local standards, one reader reports that his bed collapsed in the middle of the night. The management were apologetic and friendly, fixed the problem, but did not offer a refund! The *Inca Hotel* (☎ 23-5931, 23-7803, fax 22-7651), L Gonzales 622, has similar features and charges about US$26/38 but is open to bargaining if things are slow. (A reader reports he paid about US$20 for a double.)

Places to Stay – top end
The *Sipán Hotel* (☎ 24-2563, 24-2564, fax 24-2408), V Dall'Orso 150, is a small, comfortable hotel with a very good restaurant. Rooms are US$40/45. The *Gran Hotel Chiclayo* (☎ 23-4911, fax 22-4031; in Lima ☎ 444-0352, Fax 444-1671), F Villareal 115, has comfortable if slightly worn rooms, some with balcony, a pool and a decent restaurant. It suffers somewhat from street noise, which is the case in almost all of Chiclayo's hotels. Rates are about US$40/55. Deluxe doubles cost US$75 and double suites are US$90. The *Garza Hotel* (☎ 22-8172, 23-8968, fax 22-8171), Bolognesi 756, is a good, new hotel with efficient service, a pool, a tourist agency, a decent restaurant and comfortable if bare singles/doubles for US$75/105, which seems overpriced. You can probably get the rooms cheaper on a walk-in basis if they aren't busy.

Places to Eat
There are plenty of cheap restaurants on Avenida Balta. Although not the cheapest, *Restaurant Romana* (☎ 22-8856), Balta 512, is a good, locally popular place open from 7 am to 2 am and serving a wide variety of food. The *Restaurant Imperial*, across the street, is cheaper and still quite good. A block south, *Chifa Pollería San Pablo* is OK for inexpensive chicken and Chinese dishes, and the next block south

has a couple of decent Italian restaurants. There are plenty of others to choose from on this street.

La Nueva Barcarola, Vicente de la Vega 961, is also recommended for cheap but tasty meals. The clean *Kafé D'Kaly* (☎ 23-5623), on the plaza, has sandwiches, snacks and good inexpensive set lunches. On the southwest corner of the plaza, the clean and modern *Las Americas* and *Elio's Snack Bar* have also been recommended for snacks and light meals. Less than a block away *Restaurant Maritimo* serves good seafood.

A more expensive restaurant in the city center is *Le Paris* (☎ 23-5485), M Izaga 716, which has a decent international menu. Another good, but pricey, restaurant is *Oasis* beneath the Sipán Hotel. They serve grilled steak and chicken, international food and a selection of dishes with a middle-Eastern influence. Perhaps the best in Chiclayo is *Restaurant Típico La Fiesta* (☎ 22-8441), Avenida Salaverry 1820 in the Residencial 3 de Octubre suburb. Salaverry is the western extension of E Aguirre and the restaurant is about 2 km west of the Gran Hotel Chiclayo. It's expensive by Peruvian standards, but the food is a delicious variety of local meats and seafoods.

Entertainment
Chiclayo has several movie theaters, including two on the Plaza de Armas, and some have English language films. For live music, there's *Peña Hermanos Balcázar* (☎ 22-7972), Lora y Cordero 1150, and *Peña El Brujo* (☎ 23-1224), Vicente de la Vega 1238, both with food and a peña late on Friday and Saturday nights. Also try *Recreo Parrillada La Tranquera* (☎ 23-4441), F Cabrera 1291 (just east off the map).

Getting There & Away
Air The airport is 2 km southeast of town (US$1 taxi). AeroPerú (☎ 24-2865, 23-7151, 23-6475), E Aguirre 712; Faucett (☎ 23-7312, 22-7932, 22-1728), M Izaga 711; Americana (☎ 23-8707, 22-9283), A

Ugarte 687; and Aero Continente, west side of the Plaza de Armas, have offices in central Chiclayo. Between them there are four or five flights a day to Lima (US$83). There are cheaper flights once or twice a day to Piura (with Aero Continente or AeroPerú), to Tumbes (with Americana or Faucett) and to Trujillo (with Faucett). There are two flights a week to Iquitos (with AeroPerú), and Rioja and Tarapoto (both with Aero Continente). These services, of course, are likely to change. As always, there's a US$4 airport departure tax.

Charter and sightseeing flights in small aircraft are available from Aero Servicio Andino (☎ 23-3161, 24-4772, fax 24-1575; at the airport 24-2298). The company is run by a friendly Swiss-Peruvian couple. They have well-maintained aircraft and are knowledgeable about the area.

Bus There is a large cluster of bus companies near the south end of town, at the corner of Saenz Peña and Bolognesi. This is often the best place to start looking for a long-distance bus, especially to Lima or other major north coast cities. Buses for local destinations usually leave from other parts of town.

A good number of the bus companies in the Saenz Peña/Bolognesi corner area have one or more buses a day to Lima, a journey taking 11 to 13 hours and costing US$7 to US$20. Cruz del Sur (☎ 24-2164), Bolognesi 751, has a variety of regular and luxury services. CIVA (☎ 24-2488), Bolognesi 757, has mainly regular services. There are several other companies in this area with reliable service to Lima. These buses can drop you at intermediate towns such as Trujillo. Frequent service to Trujillo is provided by EMTRAFESA (☎ 23-4291), Balta 110, Vulcano (☎ 23-2951) and El Aguila (☎ 23-3497), both at Bolognesi 638.

Empresa Chiclayo (☎ 23-3632, 23-7984), L Ortiz and Vicente de la Vega, has the most frequent service to Piura with about a dozen buses throughout the day. The three-hour trip costs US$3.50. Transportes Piura has early morning buses to

Piura. Cruz del Sur and Continental also go north.

Travelers heading inland to Cajamarca (US$5.50 to US$7.50, seven hours) can find transport with Empresa Diaz at noon but the buses are old. El Cumbe (☎ 23-1454), Quiñones 425 and Mariscal Nieto, has newer buses that also leave during the day. Vulcano and Expreso Sudamericano (☎ 23-8566), Colón 272, have night buses to Cajamarca. Others to try for Cajamarca include CIVA, Cruz del Sur, Atahualpa and Empresa D Olano. CIVA and Olano also have buses for Chachapoyas (12 to 18 hours, US$8 to US$10). This is a rough journey because parts of the road are poor (see Bus under Chachapoyas for a description of the journey). Olano and Cruz de Chalpon have buses on to Moyobamba and Tarapoto, usually leaving in the middle of the day and arriving the following afternoon, if you are lucky. It's a tough trip.

Getting Around
For destinations near Chiclayo, white Transportes San Pablo minibuses to Lambayeque leave from the west end of San José every few minutes. They'll drop you right in front of the Bruning Museum for about US25¢. There are other services to Lambayeque if you ask around.

To get to Chiclayo's three coastal towns of Pimentel, Santa Rosa and Puerto Etén, look for colectivos on 7 de Enero at Amazonas, east of the Mercado Modelo, or at the corner of Gonzalez and L Prado. Several other local destinations are served by minibuses and colectivos leaving from the market area. To Sipán, look on 7 de Enero by J Fanning; for Túcume at P Ruiz and L Gonzales; others are marked on the map or ask around. Departure points change fairly often.

CHICLAYO'S COASTAL AREA
Three coastal villages can be conveniently visited from Chiclayo. These are, from north to south, Pimentel, Santa Rosa and Puerto Etén. All three can be reached quickly from Chiclayo by public transport,

though the service to Puerto de Etén is relatively infrequent. It's better that you go to Pimentel or Santa Rosa first and change there to local transport for Puerto Etén.

Pimentel is 14 km from Chiclayo and the closest of the three villages. The good sandy beach here gets very crowded on summer weekends (January to March) but is quiet during the off season. A few kilometers south of Pimentel is **Santa Rosa**, a busy fishing village where a few caballitos (totora reed boats, described in the Huanchaco section) may still be seen. There is also a modern fishing fleet. You can walk from Pimentel to Santa Rosa in less than an hour or take a local bus. There is an inexpensive hotel in Santa Rosa and both villages have good seafood restaurants, though many are closed in the low season.

Colectivos operate from Santa Rosa to the small port of **Puerto Etén**. Here, you can see a 19th century train engine in the (disused) train station. There are plans to open a railway museum, but this doesn't look likely to happen in the near future. From Puerto Etén, you can return to Chiclayo via the village of **Monsefú**, 15 km

away from Chiclayo. Monsefú is known for its handicrafts. Several stores sell basketwork, embroidery and woodwork and a craft festival called Fexticum is held in the last week of July. The village has a few simple restaurants.

Colectivos to Pimentel leave from the corner of L Gonzalez and L Prado in Chiclayo, continuing on from Pimentel along the so-called *circuito de playas* (beach circuit) through Santa Rosa, Etén and Monsefú before returning to Chiclayo the same day. Most beach-goers stay in Chiclayo because accommodations are very limited. However, simple rooms and apartments can be rented if you want to stay awhile – ask around.

LAMBAYEQUE

Lambayeque, 11 km north of Chiclayo, used to be the main town in the area. Today, it has a population of only 20,000 and has been completely overshadowed by Chiclayo. Some colonial architecture can be seen but the town's Bruning Museum is its best feature.

Bruning Museum

Named after a local collector and businessman, the Bruning Museum (☎ 28-2110, 28-3440) was opened on its present site in the 1960s. The modern building houses a good collection of archaeological artifacts from the Chimu, Moche, Chavín and Vicus cultures and a new exhibit features finds from the newly discovered site of Sipán. Labels are in Spanish, but even if you don't read Spanish the museum is worth a visit. The director of the museum is Dr Walter Alva, who was responsible for the discovery, protection and archaeological investigation of Sipán. Museum hours are 8 am to 6.30 pm Monday to Friday, and 9 am to 6 pm on weekends and holidays. Entry is US$1.50 and a guide (some speak English) is US$2.50. There is a small giftshop selling well-made and attractive replicas of the jewelry found at Sipán. Buses from Chiclayo drop you a block from the museum.

NORTH COAST

ARCHAEOLOGICAL SITES

Several sites are easily accessible from Chiclayo and are well worth a visit, especially Sipán and Túcume. Chiclayo provides the best (almost only) accommodations in the area.

Sipán

This site, also known as 'La Huaca Rayada,' was discovered in 1987 by huaqueros (grave robbers) from the nearby village of Sipán. When local archaeologist Dr Walter Alva became aware of a huge

influx of beautiful objects on the black market early in 1987, he realized that a wonderful burial site was being ransacked in the Chiclayo area. Careful questioning led Alva to the Sipán pyramids which, to the untrained eye, look like earthen hills with holes excavated in them.

By the time Alva and his colleagues found the site, at least one major tomb had been pillaged by looters. Fast protective action by local archaeologists and police stopped the plundering. Scientists were then fortunate to discover several other, even better, tombs that the grave robbers had missed, including an exceptional royal Moche burial which became known as 'The Lord of Sipán.' One huaquero was shot and killed by police in the early, tense days of the struggle over the graves. The Sipán locals were obviously unhappy that this treasure trove had been made inaccessible to them and were not friendly to outside archaeologists. To solve this problem, the locals were invited to train to become excavators, researchers and guards at the site, which now provides steady employment to many of the local villagers.

The story, an exciting one of buried treasure, huaqueros, police, archaeologists and at least one killing, is detailed in articles by Alva in the October 1988 and June 1990 issues of *National Geographic* magazine, and in the May 1994 issue of *Natural History* magazine. Also read the book *Royal Tombs of Sipán* by Walter Alva and Christopher B Donnan, University of California, 1993.

Archaeologists continue to work at the site and photography is not allowed where the excavations are under way. (The National Geographic Society, which is one of the major sponsors of the excavations, gets first dibs on photography.) Several areas not currently under excavation can be photographed. The site is fascinating to those interested in seeing archaeology in action. Some of the tombs have been restored with replicas to show what they looked like just before being closed up over 1500 years ago. (The actual artifacts

---

Maybe You *Can* Take It with You

The tomb of the Lord of Sipán is the most interesting of the Moche burial sites – indeed, it is considered by some archaeologists to be the most important intact tomb found in Peru. The Lord was a divine Mochica leader who was buried in all his finery. His death spelled the doom of several of his subjects, who were buried alive with him. These included a warrior guard whose feet had been amputated (to ensure that he did not run off, perhaps?), three young women, two assistants, a servant, a child, a dog and two llamas. The Lord also took with him a treasure trove of gold, silver, copper and semi-precious stones, and hundreds of ceramic pots containing food and drink for the journey beyond. ■

ROB RACHOWIECKI

themselves went on a world tour and returned to the Lambayeque's Bruning Museum where they are now on display.)

Information Sipán is open daily from 8 am to 6 pm and admission to the site is US$1. Opposite the entrance is a small on-site museum which is worth a visit. Nearby are simple snack bars and gift shops. Climb the hill behind the museum for a good view of the entire site and surrounding area.

Getting There & Away Public buses to Sipán (US50¢) leave from Avenida 7 de Enero, near the market, several times a day at erratic hours. It is best to go in the morning if traveling by public transport, as buses peter out in the afternoon. (There are no hotels at Sipán).

Daily guided tours are available (according to demand) from Indiana Tours (see under Chiclayo). Guided tours take about three hours.

Túcume
This vast and little known site can be seen from a spectacular cliff-top *mirador* (viewpoint) about 30 km north of Lambayeque on the Panamericana. It's worth the climb to see over 200 hectares of crumbing walls, plazas and no less than 28 pyramids. Túcume is currently being investigated by a team led by Thor Heyerdahl (of *Kon Tiki* fame). There is a small but attractive and interesting on-site museum. Little excavation has been done and no spectacular tombs have been found (and perhaps never will be) but it is the sheer size of the site which makes it a memorable visit. More details are found in *Pyramids of Túcume – The Quest for Peru's Forgotten City* by Thor Heyerdahl, Daniel H Sandweiss & Alfredo Narváez, Thames & Hudson, 1995.

Information The site and museum are open from 8.30 am to 4.30 pm on weekdays and to 6 pm on weekends. Admission is US$1. There is a small snack bar.

Getting There & Away Although buses go to Túcume (US50¢) from Chiclayo (from the corner of P Ruiz and L Gonzales), I recommend that you go to Lambayeque first thing in the morning, visit the Bruning Museum, then continue on to Túcume. Ask anyone at the museum where buses to Túcume leave from; it's just a short walk to the bus stop. At Túcume, you have to walk almost a kilometer from where the bus drops you off.

Indiana Tours in Chiclayo has tours, but several readers have reported that some of the guides at the Bruning Museum will accompany visitors to Túcume in return for bus fare and a reasonable tip. They do a good guiding job.

La Huaca Chotuna
This 40-meter-high adobe pyramid can be climbed via a series of zig zag slopes and affords good views of the coast and ocean. The site is also called El Templo de Chot and, legend has it, was built by Naymlap, the founder of the Lambayeque culture.

Chotuna is a few kilometers inland from the coastal fishing village of San José. You can get buses to San José and walk from there. Taxi drivers from Chiclayo can take you there, but the road is poor. Make sure that the taxi driver knows where the ruin is – many of them don't.

The Chongoyape Area
Chongoyape is an old village about 65 km east of Chiclayo in the foothills of the Andes. A good road links Chiclayo with Chongoyape; buses leave from near the corner of L Prado and Sáenz Peña in Chiclayo and take about 1½ hours. About halfway to Chongoyape, a few kilometers beyond Tumán, a minor road on your left leads to the ruins of **Batan Grande** 31 km away. This is a major archaeological site where about 50 pyramids have been identified and several burials have been excavated. With the urging of Dr Walter Alva, among others, the site has recently become a National Reserve but there is no tourist infrastructure. As there is almost no public

transport, you will have to find a taxi or tour to take you. There are also poor roads to Batan Grande from the villages of Chongoyape and Ferreñafe.

Chongoyape has a cheap and basic hotel. The Chavín Petroglyphs of Cerro Mulato are 3 km away and there are a few other minor archaeological sites. The irrigation complex of Tinajones forms a large reservoir just before Chongoyape.

A rough but scenic road climbs east from Chongoyape into the Andes until it reaches Chota at 2400 meters, a 170 km journey that takes about eight hours. Two or three buses a day from Chiclayo go through Chongoyape and continue on to Chota, where there are basic hotels. From Chota, a daily bus makes the rough journey via Bambamarca and Hualgayoc to Cajamarca.

ZAÑA

Also called Saña, this is a ghost town about 50 km southeast of Chiclayo. Founded in 1563, this city held a wealth of colonial architecture, with a number of rich churches and monasteries. During the 17th century, it survived attacks by pirates and slave uprisings, only to be destroyed by the great flood of 1720. Today, great walls and arches poke eerily out of the desert sands. I don't know of public buses going there, but you can certainly visit by taxi or on a tour.

THE SECHURA DESERT

The coastal desert between Chiclayo and Piura is the widest in Peru. South of Chiclayo, the Andes almost reach the coast, leaving only a narrow strip of flat coastal desert. North of Chiclayo, this strip becomes over 150 km wide in places. This is the Sechura Desert.

Two main roads run between Chiclayo and Piura. The shorter, less interesting one is the Panamericana Nueva (new Panamericana) which goes via Mórrope, while the longer Panamericana Vieja (old Panamericana) goes via Motupe. These two roads divide at Lambayeque. In addition, there is a minor unpaved coastal road from

Chiclayo via San José and Bayovar to Piura. This last road has very little traffic but gives access to a few remote fishing settlements and some excellent surfing beaches. Surfers here must be completely self-sufficient as there are no facilities.

The 1983 El Niño flooded and devastated the Sechura Desert. Before the floods, the bus ride between Chiclayo and Tumbes took as little as eight hours, but for several months in 1983 the roads were washed away and impassable in places. One year after the floods, the journey was still taking twice as long as before, but the roads were improving. For some years, the longer old Panamericana was in better condition and therefore used more by buses. Despite intense rains in the early 1990s (which did more damage between Piura and the Ecuadorian border than they did between Chiclayo and Piura), both roads have been repaired and direct Chiclayo-Piura buses prefer the shorter new route. This may change if another El Niño event occurs. If you want to visit some of the towns between Chiclayo and Piura, find out which route your bus is traveling.

Panamericana Nueva

On the shorter, new Panamericana, **Morropé**, about 20 km north of Lambayeque, is the only settlement of any size and can be visited from Chiclayo. It is an old colonial town, founded in 1537. The church of San Pedro is the most notable building and has been declared a National Historic Monument. June 29, the feast of San Pedro, is an important holiday with religious processions. Another religious feast day is November 10, in honor of the Cruz de Pañala. Apart from these feast days, which attract hundreds of pilgrims and tourists from Chiclayo and Piura, Morropé is famed for its ceramics and other local crafts.

Beyond Morropé, the new Panamericana is a long straight run through the desert, with no settlements beyond a couple of simple restaurant/service station stops. The scenery is flat and bare. It is almost

200 km between Lambayeque and Piura. This is the shortest driving route, but I have read reports of strong headwinds from the north and possible muggings making this a poor choice for those touring the country by bike. The older, inland route is suggested.

Panamericana Vieja
The old Panamericana between Chiclayo and Piura passes the archaeological site of Túcume (see above). Also nearby is the little-visited site of El Purgatorio where there are pyramids from the Chimu period.

Motupe, almost 80 km north of Chiclayo, is the site of a major religious celebration every August 5. Thousands of pilgrims come from Chiclayo and all over Peru to honor the miraculous *Cruz de Chalpón*, a wooden crucifix kept in a hillside shrine above the town. Accommodations are extremely basic and many pilgrims camp out. The pre-Inca irrigation canals of Apurlec are 12 km away from Motupe and can be visited by taxi.

PIURA
Piura, with a population of over 300,000, is the fifth largest city in Peru and the capital of its department. Intense irrigation of the desert has made Piura a major agricultural center with rice and cotton being the main crops. Corn and plantains (bananas) are also cultivated. The department's petroleum industry, based around the coastal oil fields near Talara, is as valuable as its agriculture.

Piura's economic development has been precarious, buffeted by extreme droughts and devastating floods. The department was among the hardest hit by the disastrous El Niño floods of 1983, which destroyed almost 90% of the rice, cotton and plantain crops as well as causing serious damage to roads, bridges, buildings and oil wells in the area. Piura was declared a disaster area – crops were destroyed, land was flooded, and people had no food, homes or jobs. The area has now more or less recovered, though signs of flood damage can still be seen. El Niño

of 1992 washed out roads and bridges north of Piura, and going by bus to Tumbes involved a relay of buses, with passengers frequently wading rivers to meet a successive bus. Bridges on the Panamericana north of Piura have now been repaired, but you are advised to check locally about the latest climactic upheaval.

Piura is referred to as the oldest colonial town in Peru. Its original site on the north banks of the Río Chira was called San Miguel de Piura and was founded by Pizarro in 1532, before he headed inland and began the conquest of the Incas. The settlement moved three times before construction at its present location began in 1588. Piura's cathedral dates from that year and the city center still has a number of colonial buildings, though many were destroyed in the earthquake of 1912. Today, the center of the city is the large, shady and pleasant Plaza de Armas.

The center of the Vicus culture, which existed around the time of Christ, was roughly 30 km east of Piura. Although no buildings remain, tombs have yielded a great number of ceramics that can be seen in the museums of Piura and Lima.

Information
There is no official tourist information office. The best place to change cash and traveler's checks is the Banco de Crédito, just off the Plaza de Armas. The area code is 074.

Museums
The small **Museo de la Cultura**, Huánuco at Sullana, has archaeology and art exhibits. Hours are 9 am to 1 pm and 4 to 8 pm Tuesday to Saturday; entry is free.

On Tacna near Ayacucho is **Casa Grau**, the house where Admiral Miguel Grau was born on July 27, 1834. The house was almost completely destroyed by the 1912 earthquake; it was later restored by the Peruvian navy and is now a naval museum. Admiral Grau was a hero of the War of the Pacific against Chile (1879-80) and captain of the British-built warship *Huascár*, a model of which can be seen in the museum. Hours change often and admission is free.

NORTH COAST

Piura

0   100   200 m

PLACES TO STAY
1 Hotel Esmeralda
7 Hostal Terraza,
  Hotel Dallas
8 Hotel Tambo
9 Hotel Peru
10 Hostal Oriental
11 Hostal El Sol
14 Hostal El Almirante
15 Hostal Cristina
16 Hostal Ica
17 Hotel Hispano
20 Hostal Tangara
25 Hostal Lalo
26 Hostal California
28 Hotel Eden
32 Los Portales
35 Hostal San Jorge
36 Residencial Piura
37 Hostal Continental
40 Hostal Amauta
42 Hotel Plaza Suite
52 Residencial Bolognesi

PLACES TO EAT
6 Chifa Tay Loy
19 Restaurant Las
   Tres Estrellas
27 Pizzería La Cabaña,
   Snack Bar Romano
30 Heladería Chalan
34 El Puente Viejo
35 Ferny's
38 Las Tradiciónes
39 La Posada Vasca
44 Las Redes Bar,
   Italian Restaurant
47 El Arrero
48 Heladería Venecia

OTHER
2 Telefónica del Peru
3 EPPO (Buses to
  Tumbes & Chiclayo)
4 Comité 2 Colectivos
  to Sullana
5 Museo de la Cultura
12 El Carmen

13 Local Ceramics Shop
18 Transportes Piura
   (Bus Tickets)
21 Americana Airline
22 San Francisco Church
23 Grau Monument
24 Cine Variedades
29 Telefónica del Peru
31 Banco de Crédito, AeroPerú,
   Aero Continente
33 Faucett Airline
43 Casa Grau (Naval Museum)
45 Banco de la Nación
45 Municipalidad
46 Post Office
49 Colectivos to Catacaos
50 Bolognesi Monument
51 TEPSA
53 San Sebastian Church
54 ITTSA
55 Chinchaysuyo
56 Cruz del Sur
57 Expreso Sudamericano

Churches

The cathedral on the Plaza de Armas is the oldest church in Piura. Although parts of the cathedral date from 1588, the main altar was built in 1960. The side altar of the Virgin of Fatima, built in the early 17th century, was once the main altar and is the oldest. The famed local artist Ignacio Merino painted the canvas of St Martin of Porres in the mid-19th century.

Other churches worth seeing are the Church of San Francisco, where Piura's independence was declared on January 4, 1821, and the colonial churches of El Carmen and San Sebastian.

Jirón Lima

This street, a block southeast of the Plaza de Armas, has preserved its colonial character as much as any in Piura.

The Goulden Home

A traveler writes that Anita Goulden moved here from England in 1958 and has worked in Piura with orphans, the poor and handicapped people since then. Her home is at Jirón Procer Merino 128 in the Urbanización Club Grau district. The postal address is Apdo 77, Urb Club Grau. Those interested in contributing time or money may like to visit. For more information see the *South American Explorer* No 43, Spring 1996.

Catacaos

The village of Catacaos, 12 km southwest of Piura, is famous for its craft market and for its local restaurants, which are particularly recommended for lunch. You can get there by colectivo from the Plaza Pizarro in Piura.

The craft market sells a good variety of products, including gold and silver filigree ornaments, wood carvings, leather work and Panama hats.

There are a number of little picanterías (local restaurants) serving chicha and dishes typical of the area. Most picanterías are only open two or three days a week, but as there are so many of them you won't have any difficulty finding several open on the day you visit. They open for lunch rather than dinner and live music is sometimes played. Typical *norteño* (northern) dishes include seco de chabelo (a thick plantain-and-beef stew), seco de cabrito (goat stew), tamales verdes (green corn dumplings), caldo de siete carnes (a thick meat soup with seven types of meat), copus (made from dried goats' heads cured in vinegar and then stewed for several hours with vegetables such as turnips, sweet potatoes and plantains), carne aliñada (dried and fried ham slices, served with fried plantains) and many other dishes, including the familiar seafood ceviches of the Peruvian coast.

Catacaos is also famous for its elaborate Holy Week processions and celebrations.

Places to Stay – bottom end

Water shortages are reported and few hotels have hot water. The cheapest and most basic are the *Hotel Eden*, on Arequipa near Huancavelica; the *Hotel Hispano* (☎ 32-5901), Ica 650, which *claims* to have hot water; and *Hostal Ica* (☎ 32-6411), Ica 760. None are very clean and are suggested only for those on a tight budget.

The friendly *Hostal California* (☎ 32-8789), Junín 835, is cleaner, has occasional warm water, and charges US$4.50 per person. Opposite, the *Hostal Lalo* (☎ 32-5798), Junín 838, looks basic but is reasonably decent. The friendly *Hostal Continental* (☎ 33-4531), Junín 924, has clean doubles for US$9. The *Hostal Oriental* (☎ 32-8891), Callao 446, is very clean at US$5/8 for singles/doubles or US$6/11 with private cold bath. The *Hostal Amauta* (☎ 32-2976), Apurimac 580, is also reasonably clean and charges US$7.50/9 or US$15 for a double with bath. The *Hostal Terraza* (☎ 32-5043), Loreto 530, charges US$6/10 with bath, a little less with communal bath. It's dark and worn, and the rooms are small but clean though. Next door is the unsigned *Hotel Dallas*, at US$8/13 with bath. The *Hotel Tambo* (☎ 32-5379), Callao 546, is good, clean and friendly but noisy at US$8/12 with bath and warm water. The

Hotel Atenas (☎ 32-3212), R Castilla 161, is a cheap and basic hotel a couple of blocks beyond the Huancavelica bridge. It is convenient for the regional bus stations for Huancabamba and other nearby towns.

If hot showers are important, try the good and recommended *Hostal San Jorge* (☎ 32-7514, fax 32-2928), Loreto 960, with almost spotless carpeted rooms at US$12/16. This place is often full. The similarly-priced *Residencial Bolognesi* (☎ 32-4072), Bolognesi 427, is a huge, ugly-looking building offering over a 100 acceptable rooms with cold showers. There is a restaurant. Others to try at this price include the clean and quiet *Residencial Piura* (☎ 32-5680), Loreto 910, which has hot water, and *Hostal El Almirante* (☎ 32-9137), Ica 860.

Places to Stay – middle

The *Hostal El Sol* (☎ 32-4461, fax 32-6307), Sanchez Cerro 455, has decent rooms with hot water, TV and phone at about US$16/20. In an attractive old-fashioned building, the similarly-priced *Hostal Cristina* (☎ 32-2031, 33-4729), Loreto 649, has a bar and restaurant and rooms with TV, telephone and private cold showers. Also at this price, the *Hotel Plaza Suite* (☎ /fax 32-8769), Apurimac 420, has a restaurant and room service. Rooms have private baths with tepid showers, telephone, TV and (they claim) air-conditioning.

The modern-looking *Hotel Esmeralda* (☎ 33-1205, 33-1782, fax 32-7109), Loreto 235, has quite good carpeted rooms with TV, telephone and hot showers for US$23/30. The similarly-priced *Hostal Tangara* (☎ 32-6450, 32-6479, 32-8322), Arequipa 691, also has decent rooms with TV and phone but lacks hot water. The clean *Hotel Peru* (☎ 33-3421, 33-3919, fax 33-1530), Arequipa 476, charges a few dollars more but also lacks hot water.

The 'best' place in town is *Los Portales* (☎ 32-1161, 32-3072, fax 32-5920; in Lima 421-7270, 441-7755, fax 442-9196), in an attractive building at Libertad 875 on the Plaza de Armas. They have a swimming pool, restaurant and rather ordinary rooms with hot water for a very pricey US$63/82.

Places to Eat

Restaurants in Piura seem generally a bit pricey. Some cheap ones are on the 700 block of Junín near Avenida Grau.

The corner of Ayacucho and Cuzco has several popular and good restaurants. The *Snack Bar Romano* (☎ 32-3399), Ayacucho 580, is a local favorite and has been recommended several times by readers. Meals start at about US$2 and are good value. They are open all day. Next door, *Pizzería La Cabaña* is good but more expensive. Opposite, *Las Tradiciones* (☎ 32-2683), Ayacucho 579, has an art gallery and is somewhat pricier than the Romano but has good food and is also recommended. Round the corner, *La Posada Vasca* seems like a good place to try.

Another popular restaurant area is at Libertad and Apurimac. Here, the *Heladería Venecia* offers ice cream and sweet snacks, *Las Redes* offers good but pricey Italian food in a cozy restaurant within a small shopping mall, and *El Arrero* (☎ 32-9041), Libertad 951, is good for seafood. Also recommended for seafood is *El Puente Viejo* (☎ 32-1030), Huancavelica 167 (just before the Huancavelica bridge).

Others to try are *Ferny's*, at the Hostal San Jorge, which is clean and good. There are a couple of snack bars on the Plaza de Armas including the popular *Heladería Chalan* with a good selection of juices, cakes, ice creams, sandwiches and other snacks. The best place for Chinese food is the elegant-looking *Chifa Tay Loy*. *Restaurant Las Tres Estrellas* (☎ 32-8472) has also been recommended.

Getting There & Away

Air The airport is on the southwest bank of the Río Piura, about 2 km from the city's center. AeroPerú, Faucett, Americana and Aero Continente have offices in the center (see map). They all have daily flights to Lima (US$98). There are one or two flights a day to Trujillo with Americana or Aero-Perú. Aero Continente has daily flights to

Chiclayo, and AeroPerú goes there a couple times a week. Faucett has daily flights to Talara. Destinations and schedules change often so check with the airlines or a travel agent.

Local pilot Felix Perez used to work for the companies doing Nazca lines overflights. He now works in Piura and flies light aircraft to destinations like Huancabamba or other remote northern Peruvian towns. His office (☎ 32-4979), Corpac 212, is close to the airport.

Bus December to April is the rainy season and, as described above, every decade or so roads north and south of Piura may be closed by floods or washed-out bridges as the result of an El Niño event. Make local inquiry about current conditions.

Buses, cars and trucks for various local destinations leave from the fifth block of Avenida Sullana Norte. Empresa Chiclayo and Transportes El Dorado have buses for Tumbes (roughly US$5, six hours), Chiclayo (three hours) and Trujillo leaving from Sanchez Cerro a couple of blocks northwest of Sullana. Also here, EPPO has buses to Sullana. Expreso Sudamericano, Chinchaysuyo, Cruz del Sur and ITTSA are at the river end of Bolognesi, and TEPSA is at Bolognesi and Loreto, by the monument. These companies are best for Lima (US$10 to US$22, 14 to 18 hours). Chinchaysuyo goes to Huaraz. CIVA, across the river on Huancavelica, has buses to Huancabamba (US$12, 8 to 10 hours) and other small towns in the Andes east of Piura. There are other small bus companies here for local destinations. These include Chulucanas, with buses leaving several times a day. For Cajamarca and across the northern Andes, it's best to go to Chiclayo and change.

The standard route to Ecuador is via Tumbes, but the route via La Tina is a longer, more difficult, but also more scenic alternative. Take an early morning bus to Sullana (US50¢, one hour) and continue from Sullana to La Tina by truck (the bus driver will show you where). Sullana has poor, basic hotels; Piura is a better place to stay.

There is reportedly direct bus service from Piura to La Tina – ask around at the market.

CHULUCANAS
This village is about 55 km east of Piura, just before the Sechura Desert starts rising into the Andean slopes. It is locally known for its distinctive ceramics – rounded, glazed, earthen-colored pots representing people. These pots are now becoming famed outside of Peru and can be bought in Chulucanas and Piura (see the ceramic shop marked on the Piura map), as well as in Lima and even abroad.

The village is reached by taking the Panamericana Vieja due east for 50 km, then north on a side road for about 5 km more. There are direct buses from Piura (ask around the market area or east of the Huancavelica bridge). There are a couple of basic hotels (*Hostal Junín* is OK according to one traveler) and some restaurants.

SECHURA
The fishing village of Sechura is on the estuary of the Río Piura, about 54 km by road southwest of Piura. It is famous for its 17th-century cathedral and for its nearby beaches, which are crowded with folks from Piura on summer weekends. The most interesting beach is at San Pedro, 11 km along a dirt road that branches off the Piura to Sechura road to your right about 10 km before Sechura. The excellent beach and lagoon are the haunt of many seabirds, including flamingos.

The beaches have few facilities (San Pedro, above, has none). Sechura has a few simple restaurants and a basic hotel, which is usually full. Camping is possible but carry plenty of drinking water with you. The best way to visit is on day trips.

PAITA
Piura's main port is the historic town of Paita (population about 50,000), 50 km due west by paved road. Paita's secluded location on a natural bay surrounded by cliffs did not protect it from the seafaring conquistadors; Pizarro landed here in 1527 on his second voyage to Peru.

Since then, Paita has had an interesting history. It became a Spanish colonial port and was frequently sacked by pirates and buccaneers.

According to local historians:

In 1579, Paita was the victim of the savage aggression of the English filibuster, Francis Drake. Apparently, he heard that the Spanish galleon *Sacafuego* was in the area, laden with treasure destined for the Spanish crown. With shooting and violence, he attacked the port, reducing its temple, monastery and houses to ashes, and fleeing with his booty.

And to think that I was taught that Sir Francis was a hero! Drake was not the only one making life miserable for the Spaniards. Numerous privateers arrived during the centuries that followed, with another notable episode occurring in the 18th century when the Protestant buccaneer George Anson tried to decapitate the wooden statue of Our Lady of Mercy. The statue, complete with slashed neck, can still be seen in the church of La Merced. The feast La Virgen de la Merced is held annually on September 24.

Paita is also famous as the home of Manuela Sáenz, the influential mistress of Simón Bolívar. She was Ecuadorian, and arrived here upon Bolívar's death in 1850. Forgoing the fame and fortune left her by her lover, she worked as a seamstress until her death over 20 years later. Her house still stands (people live there) and a plaque commemorates its history. Across the street is La Figura, a wooden figurehead from a pirate ship.

The port has good beaches to the north and south that are popular with holiday-makers from Piura during the summer season. A few kilometers to the north is the good beach of Colán. The church there is reputedly the oldest colonial church in Peru. The beach of Yasila, some 12 km to the south, is also popular.

Despite Piata's historic interest and beaches, the town has only a few cheap and basic hotels, none of which are particularly good. They'll do if you're not too fussy, but most visitors stay in Piura.

SULLANA

Sullana is a modern city 38 km north of Piura. It is an important agricultural center and has a surprisingly large population of about 150,000. Despite its size and importance, most travelers find Sullana of little interest and prefer to visit and stay in nearby Piura. There is nothing much to see in Sullana except the hustle and bustle of a Peruvian market town. Watch your belongings – several thefts have been reported.

The main reason to stop here is to take a bus on to La Tina on the Ecuadorian border. Where the bus from Piura drops you off take a taxi (under US$1) or walk to El Mercadillo. At El Mercadillo, pickup trucks, cars and minibuses leave for La Tina (about US$3 to US$5, four hours) as long as there are passengers. Most departures are in the morning.

Places to Stay

Sullana has about 10 cheap hotels and plenty of restaurants. One of the best hotels is the friendly and reasonably priced *Hostal San Miguel* (☎ 502-541), Avenida Farfán 204, near the Plaza Grau. They have cheap rooms with shared bath and more expensive rooms with private bath, but none are over US$20. There are several bus offices nearby. The *Hostal La Siesta* (☎ 50-2264), 404 Avenida La Panamericana (on the outskirts), is the most expensive and the best of a poor lot. *Hotel Aypata* (☎ 50-2013), J de Lama 112, is cheaper but adequate. The *Residencial Wilson* (☎ 50-2050), Tarapaca 378, is one of the cheapest.

HUANCABAMBA

The eastern side of the department of Piura is mountainous, has few roads and is infrequently visited by travelers. Huancabamba, 210 km east of Piura by rough road, is one of the most important and interesting of the department's highland towns.

The western slopes of the Andes in the Department of Piura are an important fruit and coffee-growing area. As you travel east from Piura, first on the asphalted Panamericana Vieja and then, after 64 km, along the dirt road to Huancabamba, you pass citrus groves, sugarcane fields and coffee plantations. You can break the journey at Canchaque, two-thirds of the way from Piura to Huancabamba, where there are a couple of simple hotels. Beyond Canchaque, the road climbs steeply over a 3000-meter pass before dropping to Huancabamba at 1957 meters. This last 70 km stretch is very rough and there may be long delays in the wet season (December to March).

Huancabamba is an attractive country town in a lovely setting – at the head of the long, very narrow Río Huancabamba valley and surrounded by mountains. The Río Huancabamba is the most westerly major tributary of the Amazon. Although only 160 km from the Pacific Ocean, the waters of the Huancabamba empty into the Atlantic, some 3500 km away as the macaw flies. The banks of the Huancabamba are unstable and constantly eroding. The town itself is subject to frequent subsidence and slippage and so has earned itself the nickname *la ciudad que camina*, or 'the town that walks.'

Huancabamba has a long history. In Inca times, it was a minor settlement along the Inca Andean Hwy between Ecuador and the important town of Cajamarca. Although the Inca town is lost, you can still see remnants of Inca paving along the Río Huancabamba.

But Huancabamba is not just geographically, geologically and historically interesting; it is also one of Peru's major centers of *brujería*, loosely translated as witchcraft or sorcery. Traditional brujería methods are used both to influence a client's future and to heal and cure. The use of local herbs or potions is combined with ritual ablutions in certain lakes said to possess curative powers. People from all walks of life and from all over Peru (and other Latin American countries) visit the *brujos* (shamans) and *curanderos* (medicine men or healers), paying sizable sums in their attempts to find cures for ailments which have not responded to more modern treatments or to remedy problems such as unrequited love, bad luck or infertility.

Although a few curanderos can be found in Huancabamba, those with the best reputation can be found in the highlands north of the town in a lake region known as the Huaringas, almost 4000 meters above sea level. The main lake in the region is Shumbe, about 35 km north of Huancabamba, though the nearby Laguna Negra is the one most frequently used by the curanderos. Trucks go as far as Sapalache, about 20 km north of Huancabamba, and you can hire mules from there. There is also a bus that reportedly leaves Huancabamba for the Shumbe before dawn. Many local people (but few gringos) visit the area, so finding information and guides is not difficult. However, the tradition is taken very seriously and gawkers or skeptics will get a hostile reception. This is not a trip for the faint of heart.

Places to Stay & Eat
There are few places to stay and those available are very basic – bring a sleeping bag. The best of Huancabamba's cheap and basic hotels is the clean, centrally located *Hotel El Dorado* at Medina 118. It has a decent restaurant and helpful owner. Other hotels include the *Minerva* at Medina 208 and the *Andino* at Grau 310.

Getting There & Away
The daily CIVA bus from Piura takes 8 to 10 hours if the going is good, but in the wet season, the trip can easily take twice as long. The CIVA office in Huancabamba is on the Plaza de Armas.

AYABACA
Ayabaca (altitude 2715 meters) is a small highland town in the northeastern part of the Department of Piura, close to the Ecuadorian border. It is in an isolated and very rarely visited region but of interest to the adventurous traveler.

There is an Inca ruin at Ayapata, several hours away on foot. The site contains walls, flights of stairs, ceremonial baths and a central plaza, but is overgrown. Other Inca sites can be found in the region, many unexplored, as well as a variety of pre-Inca ruins. There are also mysterious caves, lakes and mountains, some of which are said to be bewitched. Those with time could mount an expedition to find unexplored ruins; mules and guides are indispensable.

Visit the area in the dry season (late May to early September) when the trails are easily passable; the wet months, especially December to April, are best avoided. You should not attempt to travel through this remote region alone as it's easy to become lost. Señor Celso Acuña Calle has been recommended as a knowledgeable guide.

The very colorful religious festival of El Señor Cautivo, held from October 12 to 15, is rarely seen by tourists.

Places to Stay & Eat
There are a few small, basic hotels. The *Hotel Señor de Cautivo*, Cáceres 109, is perhaps the best. Others are the *San Martín* at Cáceres 192 and the *Alex* at Bolívar 112. They are not well marked.

Ayabaca has a few simple restaurants and shops. If you're planning an expedition, bring what you need with you, as supplies in Ayabaca are limited and basic.

Getting There & Away
There is no regular bus service from Piura at this time. One way to get to Ayabaca is on a morning bus to La Tina. Get off at the Ayabaca turn-off at Santa Ana de Quiroz, about three hours from Piura and 83 km from Ayabaca. From here, there is a dirt road to Ayabaca; if you arrive in Santa Ana in the morning you can usually find a truck to Ayabaca. Ask around the bus offices in Piura to see whether a better service is now available.

LA TINA
The small border post of La Tina is too small to qualify as a town. There are no hotels but if you cross the border to the Ecuadorian town of Macará, you'll find adequate facilities. La Tina is reached by daily buses, colectivos and trucks leaving Sullana early in the morning. (There may be a direct bus from Piura.) The road is paved as far as Las Lomas and is rough and slow thereafter. There are several passport checks and the journey takes four to six hours from Sullana.

This international route continues from Macará to the Ecuadorian mountain town of Loja and is much less frequently traveled but more scenic than the desert route via Tumbes and Huaquillas.

Crossing the Border
The border is open from 8 am to 6 pm daily with irregular lunch hours. Formalities are fairly relaxed as long as your documents are in order, though attempts by officials to obtain bribes have been reported. There are no banks. If you ask around, you'll find money changers at the border or in the Macará market. They'll change cash but traveler's checks are hard to negotiate.

Travelers entering Ecuador are rarely asked to show onward tickets or money. Normally, only a valid passport is required. You are given a tourist card at the border that you must surrender when leaving the country. It is about 3 km from the border to the town of Macará and there are pick-up trucks and taxis doing the journey. Macará has several hotels, the best of which is the *Parador Turistico* on the outskirts of town. There are cheaper hotels in the town center. Also in the town center is Transportes Loja, which has three buses a day to Loja (US$4.50, six hours), and daily buses to Guayaquil (15 hours) and Quito (22 hours). The last departure for Loja is at 3 pm, so you could make it from Sullana to Loja in one long day. See Lonely Planet's *Ecuador & the Galápagos Islands* for further information.

Travelers entering Peru, especially those who require a visa, are occasionally asked for a ticket out of the country. If you don't need a visa, you probably won't be asked. If you are asked, and you don't have an airline ticket, you can usually satisfy the exit-ticket requirement by buying a roundtrip bus ticket to Sullana or Piura. The unused portion is nonrefundable. Most nationalities, however, require only a tourist card, obtainable from the border authorities, and a valid passport. Australians, New Zealanders, Spaniards and some other nationals do require visas. There is a Peruvian consul in Macará. If you arrive at Macará in the afternoon, it is best to stay the night there. The last bus from La Tina to Sullana leaves at 2 pm. (Expect several passport checks.) There is a basic hotel in El Suyo, 15 km away, then no hotels until Sullana.

TALARA

Talara lies on the coast, in the center of Peru's major coastal oil-producing region. On the 120 km desert drive along the Panamericana from Piura, you'll see plenty of *lufkins*, the automatic pumps used in oil extraction. Although there are some good beaches near Talara, the town has little to interest the tourist, particularly since floods severely damaged the town, including its hotels, in 1983. Though the town's few hotels are often full of oil workers, authorities are promoting the beaches in an attempt to attract tourists. One of the better beaches is at Las Peñitas, 3 km to the north.

Forty years ago, Talara was a small fishing village. Today, it has a population of 45,000 and is the site of Peru's largest oil refinery, producing between 60,000 and 100,000 barrels of petroleum a day. Talara is a desert town, so everything, including water, must be imported.

Negritos, 11 km south of Talara by road, is on Punta Pariñas, the most westerly point on the South American continent. The tar pits of La Brea, where Pizarro dug tar to caulk his ships, can be seen on the Pariñas Peninsula.

On the north side of Talara are the Pariñas Woods. According to a local tourist information booklet, the woods 'are perhaps the city's major tourist attraction, where one can encounter magnificent examples of wild rabbits and squirrels, etc, as well as a diversity of little birds that belong to the fauna of the place.' Don't miss them.

Information
The area code for Talara is 074.

Places to Stay
Talara's five or six hotels are often full and not very cheap. I haven't stayed in any of them. A decent mid-priced possibility is the *Hostal Grau* (☎ 38-2841), Grau 77. A cheaper choice is the *Hospedaje Talara* (☎ 38-2186), Ejercito 217. The most luxurious is the *Club Hotel Nautilus* (☎ in Lima 424-3162), a resort hotel outside of town. Rates here are US$62/95 for singles/doubles. There are plenty of restaurants, cafeterias and bars.

Getting There & Away
Air Faucett (☎ 38-1694, 38-1183) has daily flights to Piura and Lima (US$115). They also have flights from Tumbes to Talara (but not from Talara to Tumbes) twice a week. Other airlines have flown here in the past and schedules change often.

Bus Plenty of buses go to Talara from Piura or Tumbes.

TALARA TO TUMBES
From Talara, the Panamericana heads northeast for 200 km to the Ecuadorian border. The road runs parallel to the ocean with frequent views of the coast. A number of beaches, resorts and small villages are passed on the drive from Talara to Tumbes on the Panamericana. Buses between the two towns (except for direct express services) can drop you wherever you want.

The water is fairly warm at around 18°C/70°F all year, though few Peruvians (except for the fishermen) venture into the sea outside the hottest months of January, February and March. Women are advised not to visit the beaches alone.

Cabo Blanco
About 40 km north of Talara is Cabo Blanco, famous for sport fishing. Ernest Hemingway fished here in the early 1950s. The largest fish ever landed on a rod, a 710-kg black marlin, was taken here in 1953 by

Alfred Glassell, Jr. The angling is still good, though it has declined somewhat and the scenery has not been improved by the oil pumps and related buildings. The fishing club can usually provide accommodations or you can camp nearby. There is also the newly opened *Cabo Blanco Hotel*.

Máncora

The small fishing village of Máncora, about 30 km further north, has the next well-known beach. This beach has recently become popular with Brazilian surfers. It's been described as 'quite a scene' and the surf is particularly good from November to March. It's also good for swimming and fishing.

Places to Stay & Eat The *Hostal Bamboe* on the main street is cheap and there are several other adequate basic hotels. The *Hostal Punta Ballenas* charges about US$15 for a clean room and has a good restaurant. *Las Pocitas* (☎ in Lima 472-2065) is a beach resort with a few small but attractive bungalows for about US$55 per person including meals. Another pleasant resort is *Las Arenas* at about US$60 per person with meals. There are several inexpensive restaurants serving fresh seafood.

Punta Sal

This beach is about 28 km north of Máncora and 70 km south of Tumbes, making it a popular spot for Tumbeños. The best place to stay is the *Punta Sal Beach Resort* (in Lima ☎ 442-5992, fax 442-5961) where it's about US$60 per day with meals. They have a nice pool and beach and water activities. A couple of kilometers away is the *Puerto Azul Beach Resort* (☎ in Lima 444-4131, 444-4306), which is also comfortable.

Cancas

About 8 km north of Punta Sal is the fishing village of Cancas with hundreds of fishing boats and thousands of seabirds wheeling overhead, including pelicans and the large distinctive black frigate birds with scissors-like tail feathers. There are

seafood restaurants here but I didn't see any hotels.

Zorritos

About 35 km south of Tumbes, Zorritos is the biggest fishing village along this section of coast and has beaches frequented by the people of Tumbes. The village is interesting for fishing activities and for coastal bird life. You can see frigate birds, pelicans, egrets and many migratory birds.

On the outskirts of town, about 4 km north of the town center, is the *Hotel de Turistas* (☎ 23-6222). They charge about US$18/25 for singles/doubles with bath and has a restaurant. There are other more basic restaurants in the town. *Hostel Casa Grillo* is a youth hostel/restaurant a couple of kilometers south of Zorritos at Km 1236.5 on the Panamericana. They have information about nearby national parks. Rates are US$6 or US$7 per person and camping is US$3 per person. Camping is popular along the beaches (but there are no facilities).

Colectivos to Zorritos (about one hour, US$1) leave from the market in Tumbes, as do cheaper, slower buses.

Caleta La Cruz

This popular beach is about 10 km north of Zorritos. There are sandy beaches all the way along the coast from Zorritos and you'll see many surf fishermen catching shrimp larvae in red nylon hand nets. The larvae are transferred to commercial shrimp farms for rearing. Caleta La Cruz also has a picturesque fishing fleet. The road passes banana plantations soon after it leaves the coast on the way to Tumbes. Caleta La Cruz has a couple of basic seafood restaurants.

TUMBES

Tumbes was an Ecuadorian town until Peru's victory in the 1940-41 border war but is now about 30 km away from the border. A garrison town with a strong military presence and a population of about 50,000, it is also the capital of its department. (Tumbes is Peru's smallest department.) Be careful taking photographs in the Tumbes area – it is illegal to photograph anything remotely concerning the military.

History
Most travelers pass through Tumbes without realizing that the city has a long history. Ceramics found in the area are up to 1500 years old.

At the time of the conquest, Tumbes was an Inca town on the coastal highway. It was first sighted by Pizarro in 1528 during his second voyage of exploration (the first voyage never reached Peru). Pizarro invited an Inca noble to dine aboard his ship and sent two of his men ashore to inspect the Inca city. They reported the presence of an obviously well-organized and fabulously rich civilization. Pizarro returned a few years later and began his conquest of Peru.

Present-day Tumbes is about 5 km northeast of the Inca city marked on maps as San Pedro de los Incas. The Panamericana passes through the site but there is little to see.

Information
There is no official tourist office. The main street is Avenida Tumbes, which is still sometimes called by its old name of Teniente Vásquez. The Ecuadorian Consul is shown on the map, but has moved several times in recent years. Hours are weekdays from 8.30 am to 1 pm.

Money The Banco de Crédito changes traveler's checks, though rates are better further south. Money changers in Tumbes hang out on the Plaza de Armas and give fairly good rates for cash if you bargain. Money changers will sometimes hope to mislead you into accepting a low rate, thinking you may have just arrived from Ecuador and won't know any better. The same is true of money changers at the border. Ask around before changing large sums of money. It is best to change excess nuevos soles to dollars in Peru and then dollars to sucres in Ecuador (or vice versa) to get the best rates.

Beware of 'fixed' calculators and other rip-offs. If you don't bargain, especially on the Ecuadorian side of the border, they'll cheerfully give you an exchange rate anywhere from 5% to 50% lower than it really is. Try to find out what the dollar is worth in both Ecuador and Peru from travelers going the other way. Also, beware of being short-changed and make sure you understand the rate (some changers will quote an exchange such as 2.30 nuevos soles and give you only 2.13, hoping you didn't clearly understand their quote).

Telecommunications As in all Peruvian towns, long-distance and international phone calls can be made from the Telefónica del Peru office. It is normally open from 8 am to 10 pm daily. The area code for Tumbes is 074.

Things to See & Do
The small, dusty town **library** on the Plaza de Armas displays a few ceramics discovered by workers on the site of the Hotel de Turistas Costa del Sol. These pottery vessels have been tentatively dated at about 1500 years old. Calle Grau, east of the Plaza de Armas, has several **old houses** dating to the early 19th century. The Plaza itself has several outdoor restaurants and is a nice place to hang out. The **pedestrian streets** north of the Plaza (especially Bolívar) have several large modern monuments and are favorite hangouts for young and old alike. They are lined with chicken restaurants, ice cream shops and hamburger stands and are full of vibrant Peruvian life. During the day, you can walk along the **Malecón** for views of the Río Tumbes.

Beaches
The beaches of Caleta La Cruz and Zorritos, southwest of Tumbes, have been described above.

Another side trip is to **Puerto Pizarro**, about 30 minutes north of Tumbes. Colectivos leave from near the bus stations and charge US80¢. Here, the character of the ocean front changes from the coastal desert, which stretches over 2000 km north from central Chile to northern Peru. At Puerto Pizarro begin the mangrove swamps which dominate much of the Ecuadorian and Colombian coastlines. This change of environment also signals a different variety of birdlife.

Although the water is a bit muddier, it is still pleasant enough for swimming and is less crowded with fishermen than the beach at Zorritos. If you don't want to stay at the cheap, basic *Hotel Venecia*, try the pleasant *Motel Pizarro* on the waterfront (about US$15 for a double with cold bath). Its restaurant has good meals, though the service is desperately slow. If you have the time, money and inclination, the motel can arrange fishing boat and water-skiing trips (skis can be rented).

Many people choose to stay in Tumbes and just visit Puerto Pizarro on a day trip.

La Reserva de Biosfera de Noroeste
The Northwestern Biosphere Reserve consists of four protected areas (detailed below) covering a total of 2344 sq km in the Departments of Tumbes and northern Piura, abutting the Ecuadorian border. Although the four areas are protected by the government, lack of funding means that there is relatively little infrastructure such as ranger stations or tourist facilities. Much of what is available is funded by private organizations such as the Fundación Peruana para la Conservación de la Naturaleza (FPCN, also called ProNaturaleza) with assistance from international bodies such as the World Wide Fund for Nature and the International Union for the Conservation of Nature.

Information about all four areas is available from the Tumbes FPCN office (☎ 52-3412), Avenida Tarapacá 4-16, in the Urbanización Fonavi suburb (a short taxi ride from the center). They can help set up a visit if you have spare time and money. Insect repellent is strongly advised.

Parque Nacional Cerros de Amotape
The desert-dry tropical forest ecosystem of Cerros de Amotape has been protected by the creation of the 913 sq km national

park in 1974. The flora and fauna is interesting; crocodiles, jaguars, condors and anteaters have been reported, though you are unlikely to see much in the way of wildlife without a guide. More common sightings are parrots, deer, squirrels and peccaries. Large-scale logging, illegal hunting and overgrazing are some of the threats facing this habitat, of which there is very little left anywhere.

Guides are available from the village of Rica Playa just within the park. Two have been recommended: Manuel Porras Sanchez and Roberto Correo. The FPCN suggests the Mellizos Hidalgo family as a good source of local information. There is a national park control post at Rica Playa.

During the dry season, a morning bus leaves for Rica Playa from the Tumbes market (about 2½ hours), though the road may be impassable during the wet months (January to April). Trucks also make the trip – one is Señor Esteban Hidalgo's truck *Flecha de Oro*. Señor Hidalgo can be contacted at San Ramon 101 in Tumbes.

Rica Playa is a small, friendly village. Although there are no hotels, you can camp and local families will sell you meals. It's a good idea to bring some of your own food.

Another way to visit the park is to go to the village of Casitas near Caña Veral, where there's a ranger station. The park chief comes into Tumbes every week and can help you get out there. Buses go to Casitas once a day from the market in Tumbes.

Bosque Nacional de Tumbes
This 751 sq km national forest adjoins Cerros de Amotape to the northeast. This forest is similar to the tropical dry-forest of Cerros de Amotape, but because it lies more on the easterly side of the hills, it is wetter and has a slightly different flora and fauna, including monkeys and nutria. Visiting during the wet months of January to May is very difficult. During the dry months, visits can be arranged but there is no public transport and you'll have to hire a truck or jeep. Again, the FPCN people can help.

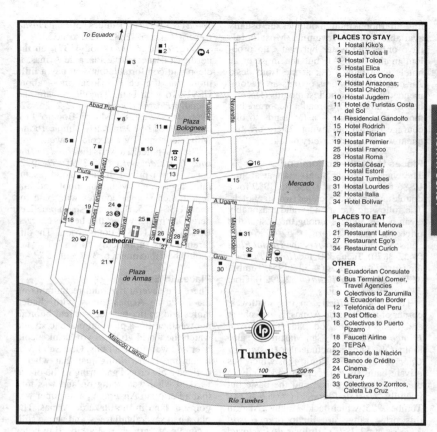

NORTH COAST

PLACES TO STAY
1   Hostal Kiko's
2   Hostal Toloa II
3   Hostal Toloa
5   Hostal Elica
6   Hostal Los Once
7   Hostal Amazonas;
    Hostal Chicho
10 Hostal Jugdem
11 Hotel de Turistas Costa
    del Sol
14 Residencial Gandolfo
15 Hotel Rodrich
17 Hostal Florian
19 Hostal Premier
25 Hostal Franco
28 Hostal Roma
29 Hostal César,
    Hostal Estoril
30 Hostal Tumbes
31 Hostal Lourdes
32 Hostal Italia
34 Hotel Bolívar

PLACES TO EAT
8   Restaurant Menova
21 Restaurant Latino
27 Restaurant Ego's
34 Restaurant Curich

OTHER
4   Ecuadorian Consulate
6   Bus Terminal Corner,
    Travel Agencies
9   Colectivos to Zarumilla
    & Ecuadorian Border
12 Telefónica del Peru
13 Post Office
16 Colectivos to Puerto
    Pizarro
18 Faucett Airline
20 TEPSA
22 Banco de la Nación
23 Banco de Crédito
24 Cinema
26 Library
33 Colectivos to Zorritos,
    Caleta La Cruz

Coto de Caza El Angolo This 650 sq km extension has recently been added to the southwest border of Cerros de Amotape and is the most remote and difficult to visit section of the tropical dry forest.

Santuario Nacional Los Manglares de Tumbes This national sanctuary is on the coast and not linked to the other three dry-forest areas. Only about 30 sq km in size, it plays an essential role in conserving Peru's only region of mangroves and was established in 1988.

Los Manglares de Tumbes can be visited by going to Puerto Pizarro and taking a dirt road northeast for a few kilometers along the coast to the tiny community of El Bendito. There, ask for Agustín Correa Benites who has a canoe and can show you the mangroves.

Places to Stay
The large amount of border traffic means that the hotels tend to be crowded, and during the major annual holidays and occasional trade fairs, they are often full by early afternoon. During the rest of the year, it can be difficult to find single rooms by

mid-afternoon, though doubles are usually available into the evening. Most hotels have only cold water but that's no problem in the heat. All but the most basic hotels have fans – ask at the front desk. Air-conditioned rooms or fans are recommended during the hottest months (December to March). One reader reported bad mosquitoes in June – a fan tends to discourage them from flying. There are frequent water and electricity outages.

Places to Stay – bottom end

The cheapest basic hotels start at around US$6 for a single and US$8 or US$9 for a double and are locally called two-star hotels. The following are friendly and reasonably clean hotels and are among the best at this price: the *Hostal Estoril* (☎ 52-4906), 361 Huáscar, with hot showers; the *Hostal Elica* (☎ 52-3870), Tacna 319; the *Hostal Tumbes*; the *Hostal Amazonas* (☎ 52-3495), Tumbes 317; and the *Hostal Italia* (☎ 52-2925), Grau 733, with private baths.

The *Hotel Bolívar*, on the southwest corner of the Plaza de Armas, is also cheap and basic but not too bad. The *Hostal Franco* (☎ 52-5295), San Martín 107, also looks OK. Others include the *Hostal Los Once* (☎ 52-3717), Piura 475, which has private baths, is fairly clean and handy to the buses, but is noisy; and the basic but friendly *Hostal Premier* (☎ 52-3077), Tumbes 225, which lacks singles. Also in this price range are the poorer *Hostal Kiko's* (☎ 52-3777), Bolívar 462; *Hostal Toloa II* (☎ 52-4135), Bolívar 458; and *Hostal Chicho* – all of which have private baths. Poorer still are the *Residencial Gandolfo* (☎ 52-2868), Bolognesi 420; *Hotel Rodrich* (☎ 52-3237), Piura 1000; *Hostal Jugdem* (☎ 52-3530), Bolívar 344, and a few other places around the market.

Places to Stay – middle

Locally known as three-star hotels, they start at about 50% more than the two-star bottom end places. The *Hostal Florian* (☎ 52-2464), Piura 414, charges US$10/14 with private hot bath and is recommended. Also decent at this price are the *Hostal*

Toloa (☎ 52-3771), Tumbes 430, and *Hostal César* (☎ /fax 52-2883), Huáscar 353.

The *Hostal Roma* (☎ 52-4137), on the northeast corner of the Plaza de Armas, is clean and comfortable but you pay a little more for the central location – about US$12/16 with bath. The clean, safe and friendly *Hostal Lourdes* (☎ 52-2126, 52-2966, fax 52-2758), Mayor Bodero 118, charges US$14/19 in fairly simple rooms with telephone, TV and cold shower.

The best hotel in town is the *Hotel de Turistas Costa del Sol* (☎ 52-3991, 52-3992) but it is over-priced. It has a good restaurant, a garden, swimming pool and air-conditioned singles/doubles with bath for about US$45/55. Beware of sharp practices here. One reader writes that he was charged US$85 for his US$55 double room. The difference was supposedly 'taxes.' The tax should be a maximum of 31% not 55%!

Places to Eat

There are several bars and restaurants on the Plaza de Armas, many with shaded tables and chairs outside – a real boon in hot weather. It's a pleasant place to sit and watch the world go by as you drink a cold beer and wait for your bus. One Sunday at lunchtime I was doing just that when I noticed a big crowd gathering in the plaza. I asked what was going on and was told that a Peruvian Air Force paratrooper was going to land in the Plaza de Armas. The plaza had several tall trees, and worse still, a couple of very sharp-looking flag poles in the center. The thought of jumping onto one by accident was so unpleasant that I had to order another beer. An hour later the paratrooper made a dramatic appearance, his descent marked with smoke canisters. Despite the hazards of flag poles, trees and spectators, he made a perfect landing right in front of the restaurant where I was sitting.

The best (and priciest) restaurants on the plaza seem to be on the west side. The *Restaurant Latino* (☎ 52-3198) is popular and my have live music shows at weekends. Meals average US$5 to US$8. The nearby *Restaurant Curich* is similarly priced. Both serve a variety of tasty dishes, including excellent local seafood. Travelers arriving from Ecuador should try the ceviche – this marinated seafood dish is much spicier than the Ecuadorian version and goes down very well with a cold beer. If you're economizing but want to enjoy plaza views, *Restaurant Ego's* on the north side of the plaza has decent meals for under US$5. North of the plaza, the pedestrian street of Bolívar has inexpensive chicken restaurants and ice cream parlors and is a popular hangout.

If you're in a hurry to catch a bus or are on a budget, the *Restaurant Menova* is within a block of most bus terminals and sells good, cheap food. Most meals are about US$2.

It's unlikely that you will be in Tumbes very long but if you are, there are plenty of other inexpensive places to choose from in the bus terminal area.

Getting There & Away
Air Faucett (☎ 52-2655) has daily afternoon flights to Lima (US$128) via Talara on Friday and Saturday and via Chiclayo (US$53) on other days. Americana has a daily late morning flight to Lima via Chiclayo. If coming from Ecuador, look into discounted multi-city Americana tickets available outside Peru. Flights are often full so reconfirm.

Carriers, schedules and routes change frequently, but you can rely on flights to Lima. Promotional deals are available at times – as this book went to press, Faucett was offering the Lima flight for US$65 in the low season.

Bus Most long-distance bus company offices are on Avenida Tumbes, especially around the intersection with Avenida Piura. You can usually find a bus to Lima within 24 hours of your arrival in Tumbes but they're sometimes booked up a few days in advance. In that case, take a bus south to any major city and try again from there. Carry your passport with you – there are several passport control stops south of Tumbes.

Buses to Lima take 22 to 24 hours; fares vary from US$16 to US$30. Some companies offer limited-stop 'luxury service,' with air-conditioning, bathrooms and video. There are several buses a day; most stop at Piura (six hours), Chiclayo (12 hours), Trujillo (15 hours) and other intermediate cities. If you arrive in Tumbes in early morning, there's a reasonable chance you'll get out the same day if you are in a hurry; otherwise, be prepared to overnight. Most major companies have at least two departures a day. Shop around for the one that suits you. Expreso Sudamericano buses are usually the slowest and cheapest. Olano and Ormeño (represented by Expreso Continental) are pretty reliable. TEPSA is fast but has older buses.

Getting Around
To/From the Airport The airport is north of town, about US$2 by taxi. For about the same price, the airlines will pick you up from your hotel if you reconfirm with them the day before your flight. If you have confirmed flights and are coming from Ecuador, it's faster and cheaper to go direct from the border to the airport and avoid Tumbes altogether.

Local Transport If you're heading for Puerto Pizarro, use the colectivos that leave from the east end of Avenida Piura, near the market area. Colectivos to the beaches of Zorritos and Caleta La Cruz also depart from near the market. The market area is the place to find colectivo taxis, buses and trucks to most local destinations.

To/From the Border Colectivos for the border leave from the corner of avenidas Bolívar and Piura and cost about US$1 for the 26 km journey. Ask around for the exact price as not all the drivers are honest. (One tried to charge me US$2 for the trip, though he wasn't successful.) If you're in a group, hire a car to take you to the border. A taxi to the border charges about US$4.

TO/FROM ECUADOR

Some years ago, Peru built a new immigration office in the middle of the desert about 2 km from the border at Aguas Verdes. This operated for a couple of years and was then temporarily closed. It has now reopened again, but be aware of the possibly changing situation.

Before leaving Peru, travelers must surrender their Peruvian tourist cards and obtain an exit stamp from the immigration office. Assuming your documents are in order, exit formalities are usually fairly quick. Although an exit ticket out of Peru is officially required, gringo travelers are rarely asked for one unless they look thoroughly disreputable. Latin American travelers are often asked for an exit ticket, so be prepared for this eventuality if you're a non-Peruvian Latin American (or are traveling with one). A bus office in Aguas Verdes sells (nonrefundable) tickets out of Peru. The immigration official can tell you where it is. The immigration office is open daily from 8 am to noon and 2 to 6 pm. From the immigration office, mototaxis take you to the border town of Aguas Verdes for US50¢.

Aguas Verdes is basically a long street full of stalls selling consumer products. It has a bank and a few simple restaurants but no hotels.

The long market street of Aguas Verdes continues into the Ecuadorian border town of Huaquillas via an international bridge across the Río Zarumilla. You will probably have to show your documents again as you cross the bridge. Huaquillas, on the Ecuadorian side, has similar stalls of clothes, calculators and cooking pots.

The Ecuadorian immigration office is on the left-hand side of the street, about 200 meters beyond the international bridge, and is identified by the yellow, blue and red striped Ecuadorian flag. The office is open from 8 am to noon and 2 to 5 pm daily and all Ecuadorian exit and entrance formalities are carried out here.

Ecuadorian entrance formalities are usually straightforward. Few tourists need a visa but everyone needs a T3 tourist card, available free at the immigration office. You must surrender your T3 when you leave Ecuador, so don't lose it. Exit tickets out of Ecuador and sufficient funds (US$20 per day) are legally required but very rarely asked for. Stays of up to 90 days are allowed but often only 30 days are given. Extensions can be easily and freely obtained in Guayaquil or Quito. Note that you are allowed only 90 days per year in Ecuador. If you've already been in the country for 90 days and try to return, you will be refused entry. (Recently, for some reason, UK passport holders were able to stay longer than 90 days. Check this if you are a Brit and want to stay longer.) If you have an international flight from Ecuador, you can usually get a 72-hour transit visa to get you to the airport and out of the country.

There are some basic hotels on the main street of Huaquillas but most people make the two-hour bus trip to the city of Machala, where there are much better facilities. See Lonely Planet's *Ecuador & the Galápagos Islands* for further information.

Plenty of people will offer their services as porters and guides. Most are very insistent and usually overcharge, so unless you really need help, they're more of a hassle than they're worth. Even if you do need help, bargain hard. Many readers have written that not only porters but border guards, taxi drivers and money changers all try to rip you off. There are no entry fees into either country so be polite but insistent with border guards, bargain hard with drivers, and find out exchange rates ahead of time before changing money.

Travelers leaving Ecuador for Peru must surrender their Ecuadorian T3 card at the immigration office in Huaquillas and obtain an Ecuadorian exit stamp in their passports. Cross the international bridge (guards usually inspect but don't stamp your passport) and continue for a short distance to the mototaxi rank to take you to Peruvian immigration.

North Americans and most European nationals don't need a visa to visit Peru.

Australians, New Zealanders, South Africans and Spaniards do. Visas are not available at the border and you have to go back to the Peruvian Consul in Machala to get one. Other nationalities usually just need a tourist card, available at the Peruvian immigration office near the border. Remember to look after your tourist card – you will need to surrender it when you leave Peru.

The Huaraz Area

Huaraz is the most important climbing, trekking and backpacking center in Peru, perhaps even in all of South America. The city of Huaraz has been demolished several times by massive earthquakes and is therefore not particularly attractive. The surrounding mountains, however, are exceptionally beautiful and many travelers come to Peru specifically to visit the Huaraz area.

The mountains offer a wide range of attractions, most evident of which are the many permanently glaciated peaks jutting up to 6000 meters and above. There are glacial lakes and hot springs. There are Inca and pre-Inca ruins, particularly the fascinating 3000-year-old Chavín de Huántar ruins, the most important site in the Americas at that time. There are friendly, interesting people living in remote villages, accessible only by mule or on foot. And there are fascinating flora and fauna, including the 10-meter-high *Puya raimondii*, the tallest flower spike and largest bromeliad in the world, and the magnificent Andean condor, one of the largest flying birds on earth.

The Andes around Huaraz

Huaraz is 3091 meters above sea level and lies in the Río Santa valley, flanked to the west by the Cordillera Negra and to the east by the Cordillera Blanca. The valley between these two mountain ranges is popularly referred to as 'El Callejón de Huaylas,' after the district of Huaylas at the northern end. A paved road runs the valley's length, linking the main towns and providing spectacular views of the mountains. The Callejón de Huaylas is roughly 300 km north of Lima, about eight hours by bus.

The Cordillera Negra, though an attractive range in its own right, is snowless and completely eclipsed by the magnificent snowcapped mountains of the Cordillera

Blanca. The lower range is sometimes visited by road from the coast en route to the Cordillera Blanca.

The Cordillera Blanca is about 20 km wide and 180 km long. In this fairly small area, there are more than 50 peaks of 5700 meters or higher. In contrast, North America has only three peaks in excess of 5700 meters (Orizaba in Mexico, Logan in Canada and Denali in Alaska) and Europe has none. Only in Asia can mountain ranges higher than the Andes be found. Huascarán, 6768 meters, is Peru's highest mountain and the highest peak in the tropics anywhere in the world. However, this string of statistics does not do the Cordillera Blanca justice. Its shining glaciers, sparkling streams, awesome vertical walls and lovely lakes must be seen to be appreciated.

South of the Cordillera Blanca is the smaller, more remote, but no less spectacular Cordillera Huayhuash. It contains Peru's second highest peak, the 6634-meter-high Yerupajá, and is a more rugged and less frequently visited range. The main difference between the two ranges, for the hiker at least, is that you walk *through* the Cordillera Blanca surrounded by magnificent peaks and you walk *around* the smaller Huayhuash, one of the most spectacular mountain circuits in the world. Both ranges are highly recommended for climbers and hikers.

For a few years in the early '90s, the Cordillera Huayhuash area was considered dangerous because of terrorist activity. This is no longer a significant problem at this writing.

PARQUE NACIONAL HUASCARÁN

Protecting the beauty of the Cordillera Blanca was first suggested by the well-known Peruvian mountaineer César Morales Arnao in the early 1960s. The idea did not become reality until 1975 when Parque

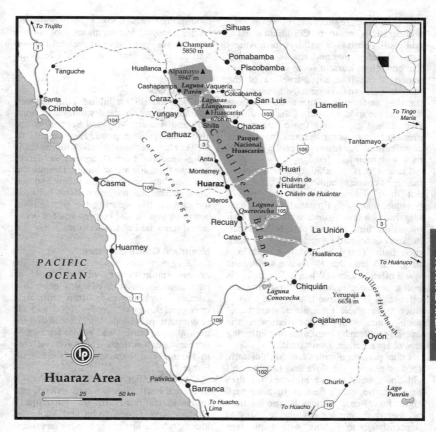

Huaraz Area

Nacional Huascarán was established. The 3400-sq-km park encompasses not only the highest peak in Peru, but also the entire area of the Cordillera Blanca above 4000 meters, except Champará in the extreme northern part of the range.

The objectives of the park are the protection and conservation of the Cordillera Blanca's flora, fauna, archaeological sites and scenic beauty, the promotion of scientific investigation of its natural resources, the publicizing of the park's natural and historic attractions on regional, national and international levels, the stimulation and

control of tourism in the park and the raising of living standards for the people living within its boundaries.

Visitors to the park should register at the park office (see the Huaraz section) and pay a small park fee. This is about US$1 per person per day, but may change in the future. You can also register and pay your fee at one of the control stations on the main trails entering the park, but these stations are not often staffed. The money from the fees is used to help maintain trails, pay park rangers (there are a few) and offset the effects of so many visitors in the area.

Some oppose regulation; however, the number of visitors to the Cordillera Blanca, while still relatively small by North American or European standards, is increasing fast enough to warrant some sort of governance if the inherent attraction of the mountains is not to be damaged. It seems to me that as foreign visitors are the ones who get the most joy out of the Cordillera Blanca, and are among those causing the greatest change within the area, they should contribute to the financing of the national park with their user fees.

Present park regulations are largely a matter of courtesy and common sense. 'Do not litter' is the most obvious one – obvious, that is, to almost all of us. There are always a few visitors who leave a trail of yellow film cartons, pink toilet paper, broken bottles and jagged tin cans to mark their path. This is thoughtless, rude and illegal. It's true that locals are among the worst offenders, but 'When in Rome . . . ' is not a sensible reason for imitating the offense. It is also true that people tend to litter more where litter already exists, so each candy wrapper contributes to the overall problem by beginning or continuing this chain reaction. Don't do it.

Other park regulations are: don't disturb, feed or remove the flora and fauna, don't cut down trees or live branches for fires or other use, don't destroy or alter park signs, no off-road vehicle use, no hunting, no fishing during the off season (May to September), no fishing with explosives or nets and no taking of fish less than 25 cm in length.

Visiting the Mountains

Basically, there are two ways to visit the mountains. One is to stay in the towns of the Callejón de Huaylas and take day trips by bus or taxi. A casual glance at the map reveals that the summit of Peru's highest peak is a mere 14 km from the main valley road and spectacular views can certainly be obtained from public transport or day tours. For many people, that is enough. The more adventurous will want to take their backpacks and hike, trek, camp or climb in the

mountains. This book gives details of public transport and mentions some of the major hikes, but does not pretend to be a trail guide (see Trail Guidebooks & Maps below).

When to Go

The best months for hiking, climbing and mountain views are the dry months of June, July and August. May and September are also usually quite good. For the rest of the year, the wet season makes hiking difficult, especially from December to March, because the trails are so boggy. Despite the wet weather, you may be lucky and see some spectacular mountain views between the clouds. Even during the dry season, however, you should be prepared for occasional rains, hail or snow storms.

Mountain Guide Services

Guiding services range from a single *arriero* (mule driver) with a couple of pack animals for your camping gear, to a complete trekking expedition with arrieros, mules, cooks, guides, food and all equipment provided. You can also hire high-altitude porters and guides for mountaineering expeditions. These are available in Huaraz and, to a much lesser extent, Caraz.

If your Spanish is up to it and you're not in a great hurry, you can hire arrieros and mules in trailhead villages, particularly Cashapampa, Colcabamba and Vaquería, among others. The going rate for an arriero is about US$7 a day, for a mule is US$2 to US$4 a day (cheaper mules are likely to be old and decrepit), and this does not include the cost of the arriero's meals (which you provide). You also have to pay for the days the arriero and mules are walking back, unloaded, to the point of origin. It's difficult to hire a pack animal for yourself; the arrieros will not send out burros without experienced drivers. Horses and mules for riding purposes are also available. Bear in mind that it is easier to make arrangements in Huaraz than anywhere else in the area, and that in some towns and villages arrieros are difficult to find.

North face of Nevado Santa Cruz, Cordillera Blanca

ROB RACHOWIECKI

ROB RACHOWIECKI

Laguna Cullicocha, below Nevado Santa Cruz

ROB RACHOWIECKI

Entertaining local children, Jancapampa

ROB RACHOWIECKI

Sunset on Alpamayo, Cordillera Blanca

ROB RACHOWIECKI

Jancapampa and Nevado Taulliraju, Cordillera Blanca

The floating town of Belén, Iquitos

A variety of transport, Iquitos

Giant Amazonian lily pads near Explorama Inn

Jungle trail near the Río Tambopata

Watching the river flow

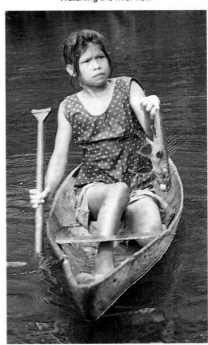

Girl selling fish on the Amazon

As you enter a valley, you often find a locked gate. The locals will unlock it for you and charge you to go through 'their' valley. The fees have been variously reported as US$2 an animal or US$5 to US$15 per group. Ask the arrieros about these fees. Backpackers without animals can often just climb over the gate.

Trail Guidebooks & Maps

Backpacking & Trekking in Peru & Bolivia (6th ed, 1995, Bradt Publications, UK, and Globe Pequot Press, USA) by Hilary Bradt is recommended. Several Cordillera Blanca hikes and the Cordillera Huayhuash circuit are included in this book, which also has plenty of background information, including a useful natural history section.

The Peruvian Andes (1988, Glenat, France; Cordee, UK; Cloudcap Press, USA) by Phillipe Beaud is a trilingual book in Spanish, English and French and describes hiking and climbing in the Cordilleras Blanca and Huayhuash.

Jim Bartle's *Trails of the Cordilleras Blanca & Huayhuash of Peru*, 1981, is now out of print, but a new edition is planned in Spanish. Meanwhile, the South American Explorers Club has a reference copy that details 18 different hikes in the Cordillera Blanca and the complete circuit of the Cordillera Huayhuash, provides a wealth of background information and has plenty of detailed maps and photographs.

Felipe Díaz's *Cordilleras Blanca & Huayhuash* is a useful map showing the major trails as well as having town plans. It is updated every few years and available in Huaraz and the South American Explorers Club. More detailed IGN topographical maps are hard to find in Huaraz; get them in Lima. With 24 hours notice, ElectroPeru (see Huaraz) can provide detailed dye line maps of the mountains.

HUARAZ

The Río Santa valley, in which Huaraz lies, has long been a major Andean thoroughfare and the Incas' main Andean road passed through here. However, little remains of the valley's archaeological heritage due to a series of devastating natural disasters that have repeatedly destroyed the towns of the Callejón de Huaylas.

The major cause of these natural disasters has been the build-up of water levels in high mountain lakes, causing them to breach and water to cascade down to the valley below. These high lakes are often held back by a relatively thin wall of glacial debris that can burst when the lake levels rise. This can occur suddenly, as when an avalanche falls from high above the lake, or more slowly with rain and snow melt. Earthquakes can also cause the lakes to breach. When this happens, a huge wall of water, often mixed with snow, ice, mud, rocks and other matter, flows down from the lakes, wiping out everything in its path. Such a mixture of avalanche, waterfall and landslide is referred to as an *aluvión*.

Records of aluviones date back almost 300 years and three recent ones have caused particularly devastating loss of life. The first of these occurred in 1941 when an avalanche in the Cojup valley, west of Huaraz, caused the Laguna Palcacocha to break its banks and flow down onto Huaraz, killing about 5000 of its inhabitants and flattening the center of the city. Then, in 1962, a huge avalanche from Huascarán roared down its western slopes and destroyed the town of Ranrahirca, killing about 4000 people. The worst disaster occurred on May 31, 1970, when a massive earthquake, measuring 7.7 on the Richter scale, devastated much of central Peru, killing an estimated 70,000 people. About half of the 30,000 inhabitants of Huaraz died and only 10% of the city was left standing. The town of Yungay was completely buried by an aluvión caused by the quake and almost its entire population of 18,000 was buried with the city. Evidence of the disaster can still be seen throughout the valley.

Since these disasters, a government agency has been formed to control the lake levels by building dams and tunnels, thus minimizing the chance of similar catastrophes. The agency concerned is the Hidrandina (formerly INGEMMET).

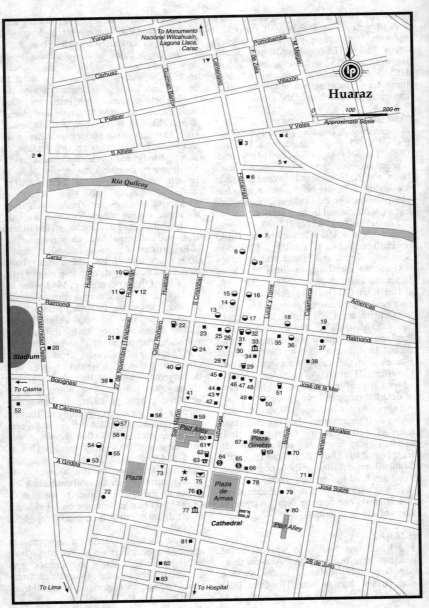

PLACES TO STAY
4   Hostal Colombo
6   Hostal Yanett
19 Hostal Los Portales
20 Hostal Alpamayo
21 Hotel Casablanca
23 Hotel Barcelona
25 Hostal Cataluña
34 Alojamiento Tany
35 Hostal Raimondi
38 Hostal Monte Rosa
39 Hotel Los Andes
42 Hostal Huaraz
47 Hostal Oscar
52 Edward's Inn,
    Señora López
53 Casa de Jaime
55 Pensión Maguina
56 Pensión Galaxia
58 Alojamiento Quintana
59 Hostal Estoico
60 Hostal El Pacífico
66 Hotel Landauro
67 Hostal Montañero
68 Casa de Guías
70 Hostal Copa
71 Hotel Santa Victoria
81 Hostal Continental
82 Hostal Tumi I
83 Hostal Tumi II

PLACES TO EAT
1   Pío Pío
5   Recreo La Unión

12 Huaraz Querido
27 Creperíe Patrick,
    Chifa Min Hua
28 Monte Rosa
30 Restaurant Familiar
41 Las Puyas
43 Chez Pepe
48 Restaurant Samuels
61 Montrek
66 Café Pizzería Piccolo
68 Casa de Guías
73 Miski Huasi
80 Rinconcito Huaracino
81 Café Central

OTHER
2   ElectroPeru
3   Pacccha'k Pub
7   Lavandería Fitzcarrald
8   Empresa 14
9   Empresa Huandoy
    (Buses to Monterrey,
    Carhuaz, Yungay
    & Caraz)
10 Virgen del Carmen
11 El Rápido
13 Empresa Norpacifico
14 Expreso Sudamericano
15 Turismo Chimbote
16 Paradise Tours
17 Taxis 1 & 2 (Local &
    to Caraz)
18 Expreso Ancash
22 Gas Station

24 Transportes Huascarán
    & TROME (Buses)
26 Transportes Rodriguez
27 Imantata Bar
29 El Pub
31 Campo Base
32 Movil Tours
33 Museo de Miniaturas
36 Transportes Moreno
37 Duchas Raimondi
40 Civa Cial
44 Pyramid Adventures,
    Milla Tours
45 Chavín Tours
46 Pablo Tours
49 Mountain Bike Adventures
50 Cruz del Sur
51 El Tambo Bar
54 Transportes Rodríguez
57 Chavín Express
61 Montrek
62 La Cueva del Oso Peña
63 Telefónica del Peru
64 Banco de Crédito
65 Interbanc
69 Taberna Amadeus
72 Ames River Runners
74 Police Station
75 Post Office
76 Tourist Office
77 Museo Regional
    de Ancash
78 Cine Radio
79 Lavandería Liz

HUARAZ AREA

Most of Huaraz has been rebuilt and it is now a modern, not especially attractive city of about 80,000 and the capital of the Department of Ancash. Its renown as the center for visiting the Cordillera Blanca has led to the development of a thriving tourist industry, with a multitude of hotels and other facilities.

Information
Tourist Offices The tourist office on the Plaza de Armas is supposedly open from 9 am to 1 pm and 4.30 to 6 pm on weekdays, but actual hours are somewhat erratic. They have general information about the area.

The Parque Nacional Huascarán office is in the Ministerio de Agricultura building at the east end of Avenida Raimondi.

Working hours are 7 am to 2.15 pm Monday to Friday, but avoid arriving just before they close. Staff can help you with information about visiting the national park.

Trekkers and climbers will find that the Casa de Guias (see Travel Agencies & Guides, below) is the best source of information for these activities.

During the May-to-September season, Huaraz is a mecca for climbers and hikers from all over the world. These visitors are a great source of up-to-date information. You'll find them hanging out in the popular bars and restaurants between climbs.

Money There are several banks on the north side of the Plaza de Armas and on the 600 block of Luzuriaga. The Banco de

Crédito (☎ 72-1182), Luzuriaga 669, will give advances on a Visa card and change most kinds of traveler's checks. Hours are 9.15 am to 1.15 pm and 4.30 to 6.30 pm, Monday to Friday, and possibly Saturday morning as well. Interbanc (☎ 72-1502), José Sucre 913, will also give an advance on a Visa card and will change American Express checks. Money changers on the street outside the banks also give good rates for cash US dollars with less hassle than the banks (which can have long lines), but check your money carefully before handing over your dollars. Many of the better hotels and tourist agencies will accept cash US dollars at reasonable rates.

Post & Telecommunications Both are found on the northwest corner of the Plaza de Armas. The area code for Huaraz (and the surrounding area) is 044.

Travel Agencies & Guides There are several tour agencies in Huaraz that will provide vehicles for local tours – you'll find a few along Avenida Luzuriaga. Pablo Tours (☎ 72-1145), Luzuriaga 501, has received several recommendations for its local bus tours. Other possibilities on the same block are Milla Tours (☎ 72-1742), No 528, and Chavín Tours (☎ 72-1578), No 508, but these are by no means the only ones. Prices are fixed and include transport (usually in minibuses) and a guide (who may or may not speak English). You should bring a packed lunch, warm clothes, drinking water and sun protection. Any admission fees are extra. There are tours almost daily during the high season, but at other times, departures depend on whether there are enough passengers. Often, agencies will pool their passengers.

The four most popular trips around Huaraz each take a full day and cost in the US$7 to US$12 range, depending on the tour and number of passengers. One tour visits the ruins at Chavín de Huántar, another passes through Yungay to the beautiful Lagunas Llanganuco, where there are superb views of Huascarán and other mountains, a third takes you through Caraz

to Laguna Parón, spectacularly surrounded by glaciated peaks, and a fourth goes through Catac to see the giant *Puya raimondii* plant and continues to Nevado Pastoruri where there are ice caves and mineral springs. These destinations are described in greater detail in the appropriate sections later in the chapter.

Mountaineers and trekkers should check out the Casa de Guías (☎ 72-1811), on the Plaza Ginebra one block northeast of the Plaza de Armas. They have a list of registered guides and are a good source of hiking and climbing information. The going rate for guides is about US$15 for a trekking guide and from US$40 for a climbing guide, per day, plus food and transportation to and from the trek or climb. These rates have been established for five years now, and may go up in the future. Make sure your guide is a member of the Asociación de Guías de Montaña del Peru, particularly if you are hiring a mountain guide. You are putting your life in their hands.

One of the best outfitters, though certainly not the cheapest, is Pyramid Adventures (☎ 72-1864, fax 72-2525), Luzuriaga 530, Casilla 25, Huaraz, Ancash, Peru, run by the five Morales brothers (Marcelino, Pablo, Eleazar, Eudes and Néstor). They are knowledgeable, hardworking, honest and friendly, and provide every level of service at fair prices. The brothers are accomplished mountaineers and have been involved in new ascents and mountain-rescue activities. They specialize in providing full service to trekking and climbing groups, but can also put you in contact with a couple of arrieros if that's all you want. Eudes Morales speaks English.

Some cheaper guide services are available if you shop around, but try to get references from other travelers or the Casa de Guías before contracting with them. The cheapest option is to hire arrieros directly, though this involves speaking Spanish and perhaps some bargaining. Again, get references first. The national park office (see Tourist Offices, above) has a list of arrieros.

Maps Detailed dye line maps of the Cordillera Blanca (US$12) and Huayhuash (US$7) can be obtained with 24 hours advance notice from ElectroPeru (☎ 72-1661), Confraternidad Oeste 195. Their hours are 8 am to noon and 2 to 5 pm, Monday to Friday.

Equipment Rental The better guide services will be able to supply everything from tents to ice axes. There are also rental agencies in Huaraz that will rent equipment without your having to hire guides. You'll find plenty of rental agencies along Luzuriaga, so if the first one you try doesn't have what you want, don't give up. Recommended rental places are at the Casa de Guías and at Montrek, Luzuriaga 646. Prices are fairly similar, but the quality of the equipment varies a good deal – check around before you rent.

If you bring your own equipment, remember that *kerex* (kerosene, paraffin) can be purchased from gas stations, and *bencina* (white gas, stove alcohol) is found in hardware stores and pharmacies. Camping Gaz canisters are usually available in rental places. Firewood is in short supply and what there is should not be burned indiscriminately; carry a stove. As it often freezes at night, you'll need to bring a warm sleeping bag – a lightweight tropical one won't do. It can rain even in the dry season, so rain gear and a waterproof tent are needed. Sun protection is also essential. Wear a brimmed hat and sunglasses, and bring strong sunblock with you as it is difficult to find in Huaraz. The same applies to effective insect repellent.

Food is no problem. Expensive, lightweight, freeze-dried food is occasionally left over from mountaineering expeditions and can be bought at the trekking and rental agencies. You can easily make do with oatmeal, dried soups, fast-cooking noodles and the usual canned goods, all of which are readily available in Huaraz.

Laundry The Casa de Guías has laundry service and there are a couple of other lavanderías shown on the map. Rates are around US$1.50 to US$2 per kilogram.

Medical Services The Hospital Regional is on the 13th block of Luzuriaga, at the south end of town. It is suitable for emergencies, though if you get really sick, you'd be better off going to Lima.

Emergency The police, just off the Plaza de Armas, have a Policia de Turismo branch. Some of those officers speak English and can help you to report a robbery. For climbing accidents, the Casa de Guías can arrange a rescue, but suggest that all trekkers and climbers carry rescue insurance. A helicopter rescue will cost several thousand dollars as a minimum. A guided evacuation by land will cost several hundred dollars a day.

Dangers & Annoyances Acclimatization is important. Huaraz's altitude of 3091 meters will make you feel a little breathless and may give you a headache during your first few days, so take it easy and don't over-exert yourself. The surrounding mountains are high enough to ensure that you will definitely get altitude sickness if you venture into them without spending at least a couple of days acclimatizing in Huaraz. See the introductory Health section in the Facts for the Visitor chapter for more information.

Things to See

The **Museo Regional de Ancash** (☎ 72-1551), on the Plaza de Armas, is small but quite interesting. There are a few mummies, some trepanned skulls and a garden of stone monoliths from the Recuay culture (400 BC to 600 AD) and the Wari culture (800 to 1200 AD). Hours are 9 am to 6 pm from Tuesday to Saturday and 9 am to 2 pm on Sunday and Monday. Admission is US$1.50 which can also be used at Wilcahuaín (see below). There is also a **Museo de Miniaturas**, Lúcar y Torre 460, which has about 100 dolls dressed in traditional costumes, a scale model of Chavín de Huántar and some pre-Inca carved stones from the area.

You can make an unusual and interesting excursion to the **Piscigranja de Truchas** (trout hatchery) on the eastern outskirts of town. The best way to get there is to walk east on Raimondi to Confraternidad Este (just past the national park offices), then turn left and cross the Río Quilcay on a small bridge. The hatchery is a little beyond. Hours are 9 am to 5 pm daily and admission is US50¢. Also east of town is **Jirón José Olaya**, on the right hand side of Raimondi a block beyond Confraternidad. This is the only street that remained intact through the earthquakes and gives a look at old Huaraz.

For a view of the city as well as mountains behind it, you can climb up to the **Mirador de Retaquenua** lookout point, about a 45 minute walk southeast of the city. Ask locally for directions.

Monumento Nacional Wilcahuaín

This small Wari ruin about 8 km north of Huaraz is in quite a good state of preservation. It can be reached on foot or you can hire a taxi for a few dollars. To get there, head north out of town on Avenida Centenario. A few hundred meters past the Gran Hotel Huascarán and just before a Mobil gas station, a dirt road to your right climbs 6 or 7 km (passing through the small communities of Jinua and Paria) to the ruin. (The road continues on for another 20 km to **Laguna Llaca**, where there are excellent mountain views. There is no regular transport.) Another way to get to the ruin is along a more attractive footpath which is harder to find without local help. You could climb up by road and return along the footpath, asking locals the way back to Huaraz.

The site dates to about 1100 AD and is an imitation of the temple at Chavín done in the Tiahuanaco style. The name means 'Grandson's House' in Quechua. The three-story temple has a base of about 11 by 16 meters and each story has seven rooms, some of which have been filled with rubble. Kids in the area will take you inside the ruin with a flashlight and show you around for a tip.

The site can be visited daily for a US$1.50 fee, which also includes the Museo Regional in Huaraz.

Instead of returning to Huaraz, you could walk down to the hot springs at Monterrey (see North of Huaraz below) along a footpath which takes about 30 minutes. Locals will show you the way or hire a kid to walk down with you. From Monterrey, take a bus back to Huaraz.

Activities

Hiking & Climbing Clearly, this is Peru's premier area for hiking and climbing and there are plenty of outfitters with whom to arrange trips (see above). Of course, many experienced backpackers go camping, hiking and climbing in the mountains without any local help and you can too. Just remember that carrying a backpack full of gear over a 4800-meter pass requires a lot more effort than hiking at low altitudes. People hike year round, but the dry season of mid-May to mid-September is the most popular and recommended. Climbers pretty much stick to the dry season for serious mountaineering.

Mountain Biking This is a newcomer to the Huaraz outdoor activities scene. Mountain Bike Adventures (☎ 72-1203, 72-4259), Lúcar y Torre 538, is run by Julio Olaza, a life-long resident of Huaraz who speaks English and has spent time mountain biking in the USA. He understands what is required to run a successful mountain biking operation – though bikers should remember that this is Huaraz, not Moab!

The company offers bike rentals if you want to do it yourself or guided tours ranging from an easy five-hour cruise to a 10-day trip. Rates start at US$15 a day. You can fax them at 72-4888 Attn: Julio Olaza.

Skiing There are no ski lifts in the Cordillera Blanca, but there is skiing, especially during the Semana de Andinismo (see Special Events). Skiers carry their skis to the tops of icy runs and then ski down.

Nevado Pastoruri is probably the most popular area, though people have skied in a few other places. This is mountain skiing for diehards only.

River-Running The Río Santo can be run year round, though it's pretty low during the dry, high season, and options are limited. It's better in the wettest months of December to April.

Outfitters who do river trips include Montrek, Luzuriaga 646, which has been recommended, and Ames River Runners (☎ 72-3375), 27 de Noviembre 773, which I know nothing about.

Special Events
Holy Week is very busy with many Peruvian tourists. Shrove Tuesday (the Tuesday before Easter) is a day of intense water fights – stay inside your hotel if you don't want to get soaked. Ash Wednesday is much more interesting and colorful, with funeral processions for Ño Carnavalon converging on the Plaza de Armas. Here, a 'will' is read, giving opportunity for many jabs at local politicians, police and other dignitaries, before the procession continues to the river where the coffin is thrown in. Participants dress in colorful costumes with papier-mâché heads, some of which are recognizable celebrities.

Semana de Andinismo is held annually in late May or, more often, sometime in June. This attracts climbers and skiers from several countries, and various competitions and exhibitions are held. Many Peruvians like to spend Fiestas Patrias, July 28, in the Huaraz area.

Places to Stay
Hotel prices can double (even triple!) during the periods mentioned above, and bargains can be found or made in the rest of the October to April low season. Some of the cheaper hotels have only cold water, but you can get a hot shower at *Duchas Raimondi*, Raimondi 904. The hot showers are open to the public from 8 am to 6 pm daily and cost about US$1.

Prices given below are average dry/high season rates.

Places to Stay – bottom end
Especially during the high season, family members meet buses from Lima and offer inexpensive accommodations in their houses. One of the cheapest places is *Casa de Jaime*, A Gridilla 267, which is basic but friendly, and has cooking and laundry facilities and a hot shower. They charge about US$2.50 per person. Another recommended private house is *Pensión NG*, Pasaje Valenzuela 837, run by Norma Gamarra. The street is parallel to 28 de Julio and a few blocks south along Gamarra. She charges about US$5 per person including breakfast and dinner and has a hot shower. Another budget possibility is *Señora López* behind Edward's Inn.

Edward's Inn (☎ 72-2692), Bolognesi 121, is friendly, helpful and has plenty of local information available. It is clean, with hot water, laundry facilities and a café, and is popular with international backpackers. Edward speaks English and rents camping gear. Rates are US$5 per person in dorm rooms or about US$13 for a double. Some rooms have private baths. Showers are heated with solar panels, so take your shower in the afternoon. The *Casa de Guías* (☎ 72-1811), Plaza de Ginebra, charges US$6 per person in dorm rooms with kitchen and laundry facilities, hot water and a popular restaurant. This is a climbers' meeting place with bulletin boards and information. They also run the mid-priced Hostal Montañero.

Small, family-run places with shared showers and occasional hot water include the basic but clean, friendly and popular *Alojamiento Quintana*, Cruz Romero 593, charging US$5 per person, and *Pensión Galaxia* (☎ 72-2230), Romero 638, charging US$8 for a double. Other places charging about US$4 or US$5 per person include the dingy-looking but OK *Pensión Maguina* (☎ 72-2320), Tarapaca 643, and the *Hotel Barcelona*, Raimondi 612, which has great mountain views from the balconies, but no hot water and some rooms with rather smelly private bathrooms. They also have very basic dorm space for under US$3 a person on the top floor. The *Hotel Landauro* (☎ 72-1212), Sucre 109 on the Plaza de Armas, has mainly cold water and some more expensive rooms with private bath. The friendly and helpful *Hotel Los Andes* (☎ 72-1346), Tarapaca 316, charges US$5 per person. The similarly priced *Hostal Alpamayo* by the stadium has had several robberies reported. The *Hostal Estoico* (☎ 72-2371), San Martín 635, and the *Alojamiento Tany* (☎ 72-2534), Lúcar y Torre 468-A, are both basic but clean and friendly, and charge about US$4 per person.

The *Hostal Cataluña* (☎ 72-1117), Raimondi 822, has excellent balcony views, but may close in the off season. Clean rooms with private showers are about US$7/11 and there is hot water from 7 to 9 am and 7 to 9 pm. This was formerly Pepe's Place and it is still run by him. The *Hostal Oscar* (☎ 72-1314), José de la Mar 624, charges about US$6/10 and has hot water. The *Hostal Huaraz* (☎ 72-1314), Luzuriaga 529, is clean but shabby, and has hot water problems. They charge US$8/13. The *Hostal Raimondi* (☎ 72-1082) (☎ 72-1082), Raimondi 820, has a pleasant courtyard, but is rather cold and charges US$10 for a double. Also in this price range are the *Hostal Copa*, Bolívar 615, which has been popular in the past, but has had some recent reports of theft; and the *Hostal Monte Rosa*, Bolívar 419, which is frequently full.

Places to Stay – middle

The clean, pleasant and safe *Hostal Yanett* (☎ 72-1466), Centenario 106, has a small garden and is recommended. Rooms with bath cost US$8 per person and there is hot water morning and evening. The *Hostal Continental* (☎ 72-1557), 28 de Julio 586, is about US$7 per person and is clean with private bathrooms and hot water. The *Hostal El Pacífico* (☎ 72-1683), Luzuriaga 630, charges US$10 per person in rooms with private bath and hot water in the mornings. It is popular with Peruvian

tourist groups. Some of the interior rooms are windowless and dark.

The *Hostal Tumi I* (☎ 72-1784), San Martín 1121, is clean, comfortable and quiet and many of its rooms have great mountain views. There is a good and inexpensive hotel restaurant. Rooms with bath and hot water are officially US$13/24, but discounts are often offered. Almost next door is the slightly cheaper and also good *Hostal Tumi II* (☎ 72-1784 ext 51), San Martín 1089. Closer to the center is the *Hostal Los Portales* (☎ 72-1402), Raimondi 903. It is bare and modern looking and has clean rooms with bath and hot water for US$15 per person. They also have a decent restaurant.

The *Hostal Colombo* (☎ /fax 72-1422), Francisco de Zela 210, has comfortable bungalows set in a large and pleasant garden full of plants and bird cages. Rates are about US$15 a person. The *Hotel Santa Victoria* (☎ 72-2422), Gamarra 690, has simple but spacious rooms with private bath and phone for about the same price. There is a restaurant. The new, clean and comfortable *Hotel Casablanca* (☎ 72-2602), Tarapaca 138, charges about US$25 for a double room; there are no singles.

The *Hostal Montañero* (☎ 72-1811) shares its telephone with the Casa de Guías on Parque Ginebra. It's a clean, European-style boarding house with large, comfortable rooms with private bath and hot water for about US$25 to US$30 per person.

Places to Stay – top end

The best two hotels are both about a 15-minute walk from the center. The modern *Gran Hotel Huascarán* (☎ 72-1640, 72-1709, fax 72-2821), 10th block of Centenario, has clean, spacious rooms with bath for about US$45/60, including breakfast. There is a restaurant, but it is no more than adequate.

The best is the Swiss-run *Hostal Andino* (☎ 72-1662, fax 72-2830), Pedro Cochachín 357, with the best restaurant in Huaraz. It is very popular with international trekking and climbing groups and reservations are a good idea during the high season. Rooms with bath and oodles of hot water cost about US$50/60. Rooms with a balcony and a great view of the mountains are about US$75 for a double. Rates are lower in the off season when reservations are not needed.

Places to Eat
Budget travelers have plenty of inexpensive options. The *Restaurant Familiar*, Luzuriaga 431, is one of the better cheap restaurants with a wide choice. Slightly away from the center, the simple, inexpensive *Pío Pío*, Centenario 329, has been recommended by travelers. For a cheap and typical local lunch, try the *Recreo La Unión*. It's not fancy, but it is quite authentic. *Restaurant Samuels*, on La Mar, is inexpensive, serves big helpings and is popular with both locals and gringos. *Las Puyas*, Morales 535, has very large, inexpensive meals and is popular with budget travelers. *Miski Huasi*, Sucre 476, is cheap, good and friendly. They'll prepare vegetarian dishes with a few hours' notice.

For breakfasts, *Café Central*, Luzuriaga 808, is good and cheap. *Casa de Guías* is not as cheap, but good and extremely popular with visitors. They offer granola, yogurt and fruit as well as the more usual fare. *Rinconcito Huaracino*, in a little square just off Bolívar behind the cathedral, serves good typical Peruvian food and ceviche, and there are another couple of good restaurants there. *Huaraz Querido*, Huacarán 180, is a good, cheap and popular place for ceviche.

The influx of European and North American climbers and hikers has led to the appearance of several good pizzerias and international restaurants, which are good, but pricier than the Peruvian places. Many of them add a 31% tax and tip to the menu price, so check if you're on a budget. The best pizzerias are *Chez Pepe*, Luzuriaga 568, which is probably the most expensive, but also has a good selection of meat and fish dishes; *Montrek*, Luzuriaga 646, which has a climbing wall on the premises; and the slightly cheaper but also good *Monte Rosa*, Luzuriaga 496, which happens to be

the Swiss Army knife distributor in town as well. The *Café Pizzería Piccolo*, Sucre 109, below the Hotel Landauro, is one of the cheapest.

The *Creperie Patrick*, Luzuriaga 422, is recommended for crepes, ice creams and continental dinners. They sometimes put tables out on the sidewalk if the weather is good. Next door is the decent *Chifa Min Hua* for Chinese food. The best and priciest restaurant in town is the Swiss kitchen in the *Hostal Andino*. The food is delicious, but they open at meal times only, primarily for guests of the hotel, though casual diners will also be served if there's room, particularly if you make a reservation.

Entertainment
There are several bars, discos and peñas. *El Pub*, La Mar 661, is currently the most popular hangout for climbers and trekkers and a good place to meet people. It has taped rock music, friendly management and a dartboard. *El Tambo Bar*, a couple of blocks away, is popular with gringos and Peruvians and has good live and recorded music and crowded dancing, though it doesn't get underway until about 10 pm. Backpackers on a budget could save a night's lodging by dancing here until 4 am and then taking the first bus out of town.

The *Imantata Bar*, near Creperie Patrick at Luzuriaga 424, is a peculiarly low-roofed drinking and dancing establishment, which also gets underway at about 10 pm – it used to be the best place to go for dancing to live music, but has been eclipsed by El Tambo. *La Cueva del Oso Peña*, Luzuriaga 674, also has dancing and a variety of music. *Campo Base*, Luzuriaga 407, is the most recently opened bar with music and dancing – let's see how long it lasts. The promisingly named *Pacccha'k Pub* looks good, but is very quiet most nights. The *Taberna Amadeus* seems to cater to a local teen crowd. Bear in mind that there is much less entertainment outside the tourist season.

Cine Radio by the Plaza de Armas sometimes screens English-language movies.

HUARAZ AREA

Things to Buy

An outdoor crafts market is held along Luzuriaga every evening during the tourist season. Inexpensive thick woolen sweaters, scarves, hats, socks, gloves, ponchos and blankets are available for travelers needing warm clothes for the mountains. Tooled leather goods are also popular souvenirs. There is a sprinkling of other souvenirs for those who aren't planning on spending time in Cuzco or Lima, where the selection is better.

Attractive T-shirts with appropriately mountainous designs are made by Andean Expressions (☎ 72-2951). They are sold in several outlets in town or you can get them from the home-factory where they are made at J Arguedas 1246, near the Iglesia Soledad on the east side of town. Cab drivers can find it.

Getting There & Away

Air The Huaraz area airport is at Anta, about 23 km north of town. Scheduled air services from Lima and Chimbote are reported occasionally, though I have not found any scheduled flights available on my recent visits to Huaraz. You could check with Expresso Aéreo and AeroCóndor in Lima – they seem the most likely to offer occasional flights in the high season. The only aircraft normally seen here are the topiary ones decorating the perimeter of the terminal area. You can charter a flight here.

Bus Buses heading north along the length of the Callejón de Huaylas stop near the corner of Fitzcarrald and Raimondi when coming from Lima. Local transport goes as far as Caraz. Empresa Huandoy (☎ 72-2502), Fitzcarrald 216, has buses to Caraz every half hour. The 67 km journey takes about 1½ hours and costs US$1.25. There are frequent departures throughout the day, but not after nightfall, so plan to travel early. These buses will drop you in any of the towns between Huaraz and Caraz. This company also has a few buses a week across the Cordillera Blanca. One route goes via Carhuaz and the spectacular Quebrada Ulta, through a tunnel at the top

of the valley and down to the village of Chacas (with basic accommodations) on Tuesday, Thursday and Saturday mornings. Another goes via Chavín de Huántar to the village of Llamellin on Tuesday and Saturday. Outside the Empresa Huandoy terminal, faster minibuses also go north to Caraz, taking less than an hour.

A plethora of companies have departures for Lima (US$5 to US$9, about eight hours), so shop around. Some of these begin in Caraz and stop in Huaraz to pick up passengers, but if you have a numbered ticket there should be no problem in getting a seat. Cruz del Sur (☎ 72-2491), Lúcar y Torre 585, has nightly Imperial non-stop service with a coffee and sandwich along the way – this is the most comfortable and expensive. Other companies include Civa Cial (☎ 72-1947), San Martín 408, with nice day and night buses; Movil Tours (☎ 72-2555), the 700 block of Raimondi, also with good newish buses; Paradise Tours (☎ 72-2207, 72-1834), Fitzcarrald 317; Transportes Rodriguez (☎ 72-1353), has two offices at Raimondi 616 and Tarapaca 622, with one day bus and two night buses; Expreso Ancash (the subsidiary of Ormeño, ☎ 72-1102), Raimondi 825, with a morning, afternoon and night bus; Empresa 14 (☎ 72-1282), Fitzcarrald 216, with one departure in the morning and one at night; Expreso Sudamericano (☎ 72-1576), Fitzcarrald 360, with one of the cheapest night buses; and TROME (☎ 72-1542), San Martín 485, with a daily bus – the cheapest. Empresa NorPacifico has among the poorest buses and service.

There are three main bus routes to Chimbote (US$7 or US$8, eight hours) on the north coast. One follows the Callejón de Huaylas and passes through the narrow, spectacular Cañón del Pato before descending to the coast at Chimbote. This is a scenic route, but, unfortunately, most buses travel it by night. A route more frequently followed by day crosses the 4225-meter-high Punta Callán, 30 km west of Huaraz, and provides spectacular views of the Cordillera Blanca. This road comes out at Casma and continues north along the coastal Panamericana to Chimbote. Some buses take the road to Pativilca (the same route as Lima-bound buses) and then head north on the highway. Transportes Moreno (☎ 72-1344), the 900 block of Raimondi, has day buses on both the Cañón del Pato and Casma routes and a night bus on the Casma route. Transportes Rodriguez, Comite 14, and Turismo Chimbote (☎ 72-1984), Fitzcarrald 286, all have buses to Chimbote, mainly through Casma. Turismo Chimbote has buses to Lima and Trujillo as well. Some of the other companies going to Chimbote may continue to Trujillo, about three hours north of Chimbote.

Chavín Express, Cáceres 338, has buses for Chavín de Huántar (five hours, US$3.50), continuing on to Huari (seven hours), daily at 12.20 pm. Transportes Huascarán, at the TROME office at San Martín 485, also has buses to Chavín and Huari. A company called Lanzón de Chavín is also reported to do this route, but I don't know where it is. Write and tell me if you find it.

For Chiquián (and the Cordillera Huay-huash) El Rápido (☎ 72-2610), Huascarán 129 and, on the same block, Virgen del Carmen, have buses leaving daily around 2 pm taking three to four hours and charging US$2. If you want to go earlier, take any Lima-bound bus and get off at Conococha, a high, cold lake with a little huddle of buildings nearby, and wait for any transport to Chiquián, a further 32 km by dirt road.

Transportes Huallanca has two vehicles a week to La Unión, about seven hours from Huaraz to the east. From there, it is possible to find daily trucks to Huánuco. Transportes Huallanca doesn't have a terminal, but its vehicles leave from San Martín near Morales at about 1 pm on Sunday and Thursday.

Trucks leave for villages in the Cordillera Blanca area. Ask around about them.

Getting Around
A taxi ride around Huaraz costs about US$1.25. A taxi to Caraz is about US$25. Other rides can be arranged. A central taxi rank is at the corner of Fitzcarrald and Raimondi.

North of Huaraz

The Callejón de Huaylas road north of Huaraz follows the Río Santa valley, and is paved for the 67 km to Caraz. This road passes within 14 km of Peru's highest peak and links the departmental capital with the other main towns in the area. Buses for all towns mentioned in the following sections leave from or near Empresa Huandoy in Huaraz.

MONTERREY
Just five km north of Huaraz is the small village of Monterrey, famous for its natural *baños termales* (hot springs). The bus terminates right in front of the springs, so you won't have any difficulty in finding them. The hot springs are divided into two sections; the lower pools are cheaper (US$1), in worse condition and more crowded than the upper pools (US$1.50), which are within the grounds of the Hotel Baños Termales Monterrey. The pools are open from 8 am to 6 pm, and tickets for either level are sold at the lower entrance.

Places to Stay & Eat
There are no budget hotels. The *Hotel Baños Termales Monterrey* (☎ 72-1717) is a pleasant building set in gardens right next to the hot springs. There is a good, simple restaurant with outdoor dining (overlooking the pool) and reasonably priced meals. Rooms with bath are about US$30/40. You needn't stay at the hotel to use the pool or the restaurant. The similarly priced *El Patio* (☎ 72-4965) nearby is also good, with bungalows in a pleasant garden. Outside of the hotels, the *El Cortijo* seems to be the best restaurant.

Getting There & Away
Monterrey is reached by local buses from Huaraz, which pass the Plaza de Armas and continue north along Avenidas Luzuriaga, Fitzcarrald and Centenario. Try to catch a bus early in the route, as they soon fill up. The fare for the 15-minute ride is US25¢.

HUARAZ AREA

MONTERREY TO CARHUAZ

About 16 km north of Huaraz, the road goes through the little village of **Taricá**, famous as a local pottery center. There is a basic hotel here. About 23 km north of Huaraz, the road passes the rarely used **Anta** airport (look for the topiary airplanes around the terminal). A few kilometers beyond is the small village of **Marcará**. From here, minibuses leave regularly for the hot springs of **Chancos**, 3 km to the east, and occasionally continue a further 4 km to the ruins at **Vicos**. Beyond Vicos, the Quebrada Honda trail (for hikers only) continues across the Cordillera Blanca. The rather rustic and dilapidated Chancos hot springs are popular with locals at weekends, when they tend to be crowded. There are private cubicles and steam baths for US$1 per person.

CARHUAZ

The small town of Carhuaz is 31 km north of Huaraz. It is not a particularly interesting place, but trekkers heading into the Cordillera Blanca via the beautiful Quebrada Ulta may want to stay there. Vehicles from Carhuaz to Shilla and Llipta (in the Quebrada Ulta) are frequent on Sunday, which is market day, but there's usually only one truck in the morning on other days.

Carhuaz's annual La Virgen de La Merced fiesta is celebrated on and around September 24 with processions, fireworks, dancing, bullfights and plenty of drinking. This is the most interesting time to visit Carhuaz.

Places to Stay & Eat

The *Hotel La Merced*, Ucayali 600, half a block from the Plaza de Armas, has hot water and appears to be the best in the town center. They charge US$6 per person. The *Hostal Carhuaz*, a block from the Plaza on Progreso, has a pleasant courtyard, but is otherwise a basic hotel, though they have hot showers. They charge US$5 per person. At the northwest exit of town is the *Hostal Delicias* which claims to have hot water. The basic *Hotel Victoria*, Comercio 105, is another option.

About 1½ km east of town is the friendly and recommended *La Casa de Pocha*, a farm growing organic vegetables and using solar panels to heat the shower. They have a sauna. Rates are US$20 a day including meals and use of sauna. Natural hot springs at La Merced are a short hike away and horse riding can be arranged.

There are a few cheap and basic restaurants. The *Las Mercedes*, Progreso 153, and *Los Pinos*, Amazonas 634, look OK.

CARHUAZ TO YUNGAY

Six or 8 km north of Carhuaz, the road goes through the little village of **Tingua** where the *Rancho Chico* restaurant prepares typical pachamancas, particularly for weekend lunches. A few kilometers beyond is the village of **Mancos**, from where there are excellent views of Huascarán. A road east goes through Musho to the base camp for climbing Huascarán.

YUNGAY

Not far from Mancos is the newly rebuilt village of Ranrahirca (devastated in the 1962 earthquake), followed by the rubble-strewn area of old Yungay, site of the single worst natural disaster in the Andes. It was near here that the earthquake of May 31, 1970, loosened some 15 million cubic meters of granite and ice from the west wall of Huascarán Norte. The resulting alluvion picked up a speed of about 300 km/h as it dropped over 3 vertical km on its way to Yungay, 14 km away. The town and almost all of its 18,000 inhabitants were buried. The earthquake also killed about 50,000 people in other parts of central Peru.

Today, the site is known as **Campo Santo** and is marked by a huge white statue of Christ on a knoll overlooking old Yungay. The path of the alluvion can plainly be seen from the road. It costs US50¢ to enter the site, walking through flower-filled gardens and past occasional gravestones and monuments commemorating the thousands of people who lie buried beneath your feet. At the old Plaza de Armas of Yungay, you can see just the very top of the cathedral tower and a few palm trees which are all that remain of the devastated village.

New Yungay has been rebuilt just beyond the alluvion path, about 59 km north of Huaraz. A stark, hastily built town, it offers no attraction in itself, but it is from here that you begin one of the most beautiful and popular excursions in the Cordillera Blanca, the drive to the Lagunas Llanganuco.

Places to Stay & Eat

Although there are several cheap places to stay in Yungay, there's little point in spending more than a night here en route to the mountains. One of the best hotels is the very friendly *Hostal Gledel*, a block from the plaza, at about US$5/7.50 with hot water and meals available.

Other similarly priced hotels include the *Yuly*, with no hot water, and the *Yungay*, with hot water, both on the plaza, The cheaper *Confort* on the road south of town is a basic cold-water place. Hotels may close in the off season and private homes often offer accommodations during the high season.

There are several cheap and simple places to eat in the market next to the plaza. The best restaurant is the *Restaurant Turístico Alpamayo*, three blocks from the plaza, serving cheap, typical local food.

Getting There & Away

Frequent minibuses run from the Plaza de Armas to Caraz (US50¢, 15 minutes) and buses en route from Caraz will pick up passengers to Huaraz (US80¢, about an hour) from the southwest side of the plaza.

Buses from Caraz to Lima and buses from Huaraz to Chimbote pick up passengers at the Plaza de Armas.

LAGUNAS LLANGANUCO

A dirt road goes up the Llanganuco valley to the two lovely lakes of the same name, about 28 km east of Yungay. There are great views of the giant mountains of Huascarán (6768 meters), Chopicalqui (6354 meters), Chacraraju (6112 meters), Huandoy (6395 meters) and others, particularly if you drive a few kilometers beyond

the lakes. The road continues over the pass beyond the lakes and down to Yanama on the other side of the Cordillera Blanca; there is often an early morning truck from Yungay going to Yanama and beyond.

It is also from Yungay that the walker begins the Llanganuco-to-Santa Cruz loop, the most popular and spectacular trek of the Cordillera Blanca. This takes an average of five fairly leisurely days (though it can be done in four days) and is a good hike for everybody, especially beginners, because the trail is relatively well defined. See the Bradt book for a hike description or use the adequate maps available in Huaraz.

The Llanganuco road is also the access route to the Pisco base camp, where the ascent of Nevado Pisco (5800 meters) begins. This is considered one of the most straightforward high-snow ascents in the range, though it is not to be taken lightly and requires snow and ice-climbing equipment and experience.

To get to the Lagunas Llanganuco, you can go on a tour from Huaraz or take buses or taxis from Yungay. During June, July and August (the height of the dry season) minibuses carrying 10 or more passengers leave from the Yungay Plaza de Armas. The roundtrip costs about US$5 and allows about two hours in the lake area. A national park admission fee of around US$1 is also charged. During the rest of the year, minibuses do the trip if there is enough demand, which there often is in April and May and from September to December. Taxis are also available. Go in the early morning for clear views; it's often cloudy in the afternoon.

CARAZ

The pleasant little town of Caraz lies 67 km north of Huaraz and is the end of the road as far as regular and frequent transport is concerned. Caraz is one of the few places in the area which, while suffering some damage, has managed to avoid total destruction by earthquake or alluvion. The town has an attractive Plaza de Armas and several hotels and restaurants, and you can take pleasant walks in the surrounding hills. The population is about 14,000 and the elevation is 2270 meters.

Caraz is both the end point of the popular Llanganuco-to-Santa Cruz trek and the point of departure for rugged treks into the remote northern parts of the Cordillera Blanca. The town makes a particularly good base for treks to the north side of Alpamayo (5947 meters), for views of what one magazine called the most beautiful mountain in the world. Excursions can be made by road to the beautiful Laguna Parón and to the Cañón del Pato.

The bright blue Laguna Parón is 32 km east of Caraz and surrounded by spectacular snowcapped peaks, of which Pyramide (5885 meters) at the end of the lake looks particularly magnificent. The road to the lake goes through a canyon with 1000-meter-high granite walls. Although this excursion takes you further from Huaraz than a visit to the Lagunas Llanganuco and is therefore neither as popular nor as crowded, it is just as attractive as the Llanganuco tour.

The spectacular Cañón del Pato is at the far north of the Callejón de Huaylas and its narrowest point. Buses en route to Chimbote take this road every day or you can take a pick-up truck or taxi from Caraz. There is a cheap, clean hotel in Huallanca at the north end of the Cañón (not to be confused with Huallanca at the southeast end of the Cordillera Blanca).

Although much smaller than Huaraz, Caraz is beginning to develop some infrastructure for tourism.

Information

Tourist information is available in the Oficina de Promoción Turística, on the 2nd floor of the Municipalidad on the Plaza de Armas, or at Pequeña Pony.

Alberto Cafferata, who speaks English, French and Spanish, runs Pequeña Pony (☎ 72-0221, fax 72-0255), Daniel Villar 416, and is a good source for local information. He rents and sells camping and climbing equipment and arranges transportation, guides, arrieros, mules, local tours and horseback riding.

There are banks and stores where you can change cash US dollars though traveler's checks are not as easy to change. Post and telephone offices are shown on the map.

Things to See & Do

There is a small **Museo Arqueológico** near the Municipalidad. About a 30-minute walk on a dirt road north of town are the pre-Inca ruins of **Tumshukayko**.

Places to Stay

Apart from the Independence holidays at the end of July, hotel prices remain quite stable throughout the year, probably because Caraz has not yet been overrun by visitors. Small, family-run lodgings include the basic, clean and friendly *Señor Caballero*, Daniel Villar 485, which has hot showers and is owned by the same folks that run the tour agency above.

The cheapest place is probably the friendly *Hostal Morovi* on Luzuriaga which charges US$3/4 with bath. The *Albergue Los Pinos* in Parque San Martín – ask someone how to get there – charges about US$4/5 and has hot water and breakfast available. Also cheap, but noisy and basic, is the *Alojamiento Ramírez* above the Moreno bus terminal. The *Hostal La Casona* (☎ 72-2335), on Raimondi, is one of the best cheap hotels. It's clean, has hot water and charges about US$4/7 or US$7/10 with private bath. The *Hostal Suizo Peruano* (☎ 72-2166), San Martín 1133, charges about a dollar more but is no better. Next door, the *Hostal Chavín* (☎ 72-2171) is friendly and charges US$8/12 in clean rooms with hot showers. The *Hostal El Cafetal* is another option on San Martín.

On the outskirts is the German-run *Hostal Chamanna*, Nueva Victoria 185, about a 20-minute walk from the center on the road to Cashapampa (ask locals for directions). They have pleasant cabins set in a pretty garden for about US$15 per double. There are shared hot showers, but private showers are planned. They serve good German food in their garden restaurant.

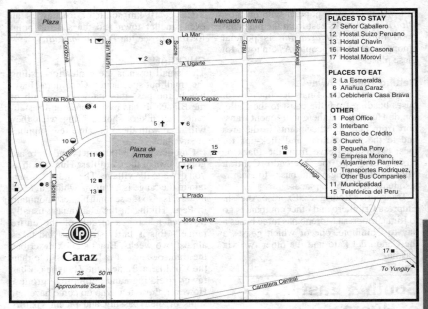

Plaza

Mercado Central

PLACES TO STAY
7 Señor Caballero
12 Hostal Suizo Peruano
13 Hostal Chavín
16 Hostal La Casona
17 Hostal Morovi

PLACES TO EAT
2 La Esmeralda
6 Añañua Caraz
14 Cebichería Casa Brava

OTHER
1 Post Office
3 Interbanc
4 Banco de Crédito
5 Church
8 Pequeña Pony
9 Empresa Moreno,
    Alojamiento Ramírez
10 Transportes Rodríquez,
     Other Bus Companies
11 Municipalidad
15 Telefónica del Peru

La Mar
Sucre
Grau
Bolognesi
Cordova
San Martin
A Ugarte
Santa Rosa
Manco Capac
D Villar
Plaza de
Armas
Raimondi
Lizurriaga
M Cáceres
L Prado
José Galvez

Caraz

0   25   50 m
Approximate Scale

To Yungay
Carretera Central

HUARAZ AREA

Places to Eat

There are several simple restaurants on or
near the Plaza de Armas. *Cebichería Casa
Brava* is OK and has nice plaza views from
the balcony. *Añañua Caraz* is clean and
friendly and has a cheap menu. *Los Portales* next to the Municipalidad is clean and
has drinks, snacks and ice cream – it is
often the last place to close at night. *La
Esmeralda*, A Ugarte 404, is the best place
in the center for lomo saltado. There are
several other pretty basic restaurants.

My favorite restaurant in Caraz is *La
Punta*, a short walk from the town center
(at the end of Daniel Villar) and particularly good for lunch. They serve cheap,
typical highland dishes (including guinea
pig) and there is a garden to eat in. If you
don't feel like guinea pig, try a hearty bowl
of soup. There are two La Punta's on either
side of the street. *La Punta Grande* (☎ 72-
2321) has the plant-filled garden with
a sapo game and I like it better – if I

remember correctly it's the one on the
right as you are walking out of Caraz. If it's
not that one it's the one on the left.

Also good for typical lunches is the
pleasant *Restaurant La Capullana*, about
1½ km west of town on the road to Cañón
del Pato. It offers outdoor dining around a
small lake and prices are very reasonable.
Service is spotty however – on some days
you have to yell for the waiter who has to
go find a cook. Holidays and weekends are
the best times here.

I've received recommendations for
Recreo Palmira on the south side of town
just off the main road; they are said to have
great trout, pachamanca and other local
dishes. Like other typical restaurants on the
outskirts, it's best for lunch.

Entertainment

The following bars (with music) are recommended by Alberto Cafferata – I haven't
been to any of them. The *Gato Negro*, north

of town, is the most popular with gringos; *Olturis*, two blocks east from the plaza has good music; *Alpamayo Inn* is popular among local young people. Ask in town for these places.

Getting There & Away
Caraz is often the final destination for buses heading from the coast to the Callejón de Huaylas and there is frequent transport from here to other points in the area and to the coast. Taxis and pick-ups for local excursions leave from the Plaza de Armas or from the Mercado Central. Minibuses to Yungay and buses to Huaraz also leave from these places.

Transportes Rodriguez, Expreso Ancash, Empresa Cribillero and other companies go to Lima. Empresa Moreno has three buses a day to Chimbote, one of which goes via the Cañón del Pato and the other two via Casma.

South & East of Huaraz

The road south of Huaraz is the one most travelers to and from Lima use to enter the Callejón de Huaylas, but, apart from this, the road is little traveled by tourists. Local buses and trucks heading south of Huaraz leave from the *frigorífico* bus stop on Avenida Tarapaca, near the Hostal Los Andes. Scheduled services are described under Huaraz.

The first place of interest south of Huaraz is the Puente Bedoya (bridge) about 18 km away. From here, a dirt road leads 2 km east from the highway to the village of Olleros, the starting point for the easy three-day trek across the Cordillera Blanca to Chavín.

Recuay is 25 km from Huaraz and the only town of any size south of Huaraz. It has a basic hotel and a small museum, but is otherwise of little interest to most travelers.

Catac, 10 km south of Recuay, is an even smaller town and the starting point for trips to see the *Puya raimondii*.

CHIQUIÁN
This small town is the center for visiting the small but spectacular Cordillera Huayhuash, the next mountain range south of the Blanca. It has basic hotels and restaurants, but hikers should bring what they will need with them because few supplies are available.

Chiquián is at 3400 meters and there are good views of the Cordillera Huayhuash as you drive to the village. The highest mountain in the range is Yerupajá which, at 6634 meters, is also the second-highest mountain in Peru. Hiking in the Huayhuash usually involves making a circuit of the entire range – this is fairly strenuous and takes almost two weeks. Bradt's book describes the trail. Because it is less accessible than the Cordillera Blanca, the Huayhuash has fewer trekking and climbing groups. However, those few who do come have left signs of their passing and recent visitors have complained of trash-strewn campsites. Please . . . .

In May 1989, Sendero activity put the Huayhuash off-limits to trekkers, but by 1993 people were hiking through here again with no problems. One attempted robbery was reported during the '94 season and no problems were reported in the '95 season.

Burros and arrieros can be hired here.

Places to Stay & Eat
The best hotel in Chiquián is the *Hostal San Miguel* at Comercio 233, about seven blocks from the Plaza. It is basic but clean and charges about US$4 per person per night. They have no sign. If the San Miguel is full, there are a couple of other even more basic places, and people have slept in the church when all else failed.

The town has a couple of simple restaurants. The best seems to be *El Rincón de Yerupajá*, Tarapaca 351, off the 500 block of Comercio.

Puya Raimondii

The giant *Puya raimondii* is a strange plant that is frequently confused with others. It belongs to the bromeliads, or the pineapple family, of which it is the largest member. Many people think it's an agave, or century plant, to which it has a certain resemblance, but is not closely related; the century plants belong to the amaryllis family. One guidebook claims that the *Puya raimondii* is a cactus, but there is no comparison – they belong to different classes and are about as closely related as a bird and a mammal.

The *Puya raimondii* is a huge, spiky rosette of long, tough, waxy leaves. This rosette can be two meters or more in diameter and takes about 100 years to grow to full size. It then flowers by producing a huge spike, often 10 meters in height, which is covered by approximately 20,000 flowers – a magnificent sight. This spiky inflorescence is the largest in the world and remains in flower for about three months, during which time it is pollinated by hummingbirds. After flowering once, the plant dies.

Obviously, with flowering occurring only once at the end of a century, most of the plants you'll see won't be flowering. When they do flower, they tend to do so in groups and this occurs about every three or four years; it is not known why this happens, nor is it clear when the best time for flowering is. Some guides claim the end of the wet season (May) is best. Most say the beginning of the wet season (October and November) is the time to go. You should make local inquiries if you hope to see the *Puya raimondii* in flower, though even when not flowering, it is a fascinating sight. The spiky rosette offers protection to a variety of birds and you may find several nests within the leaves of one plant.

The giant bromeliad is also considered to be one of the most ancient plant species in the world and has been called a living fossil. It is rare and found only in a few isolated areas of the Peruvian and Bolivian Andes. The sites in the Cordillera Blanca are among the best known and receive protection as part of the Parque Nacional Huascarán.

There is a small *Puya raimondii* site on the southern slopes of the upper Quebrada Queshque, about 20 km southeast of Catac. You can hike on a trail from Catac, as described in Bartle's book. Another site is on a little-traveled road about 50 km west of Huaraz (not so far if you hike, but this site is hard to find).

Most people visit the site at the intersection of the Quebrada Raria with the Río Pachacoto, which can be reached by road. Drive 10 km south of Catac on the main road and turn left at the Río Pachacoto (there is a national park sign which reads Sector Carpa). Follow the dirt road for about 18 km to the Quebrada Raria where the puyas are to be seen. These areas are also the best place in the Cordillera Blanca to watch for the beautiful vicuña, an infrequently seen wild relative of the alpaca and llama. Camping is possible in both areas.

Tour companies in Huaraz make trips to this last site. If traveling by public transport, take any early-morning, Lima-bound bus to the Sector Carpa turnoff and wait for a truck going along the Río Pachacoto road (there are usually several a day). Start heading back by early afternoon if you don't want to spend the night. These trucks act as buses for the locals and you are expected to pay a bus fare.

The road continues as far as La Unión, where you can find basic hotels and transport on to Huánuco. ■

Getting There & Away

If you are interested in Chiquián and the Cordillera Huayhuash, you'll find direct buses from Lima. However, Chiquián is not a particularly exciting town in which to acclimatize and so you could spend a few days in Huaraz first.

TUBSA and Transfysa have bus service to Lima (US$7.50, 10 hours) every other day. Their offices are on the 9th and 10th blocks of Comercio, by the Plaza de Armas. Transfysa seems to have the best buses. Turismo Cavassa, Bolognesi 421, just off the plaza, has a night bus to Lima. Transportes Virgen del Carmen, on the 8th block of 2 de Mayo, and Transportes Huandoy, Comercio 850, both just off the plaza, have buses to Huaraz. Trucks occasionally go north from Chiquián, past the small Cordillera Huallanca to the village of Huallanca. Here there is a basic hotel and transport continues on to La Unión and Huánuco.

CAJATAMBO

This is the only other village on the Cordillera Huayhuash trek which is accessible by road. At least one old, slow bus runs from Cajatambo to Lima every morning at 6 am; there may be others. There are three or four basic hotels in Cajatambo. All have very cold water and charge around US$3 or US$4 a person. The best is probably the *Hotel Miranda*.

CHAVÍN DE HUÁNTAR

This small village is of little interest in itself, but the ruins of Chavín on the southern edge of the village are well worth a visit.

The Chavín Culture

The Chavín culture is named after its type site at Chavín de Huántar and is the oldest major culture in Peru. It existed from about 1300 to 400 BC, predating the Incas by about 2000 years. The major period of influence was from about 800 to 400 BC, and the Chavín's culture certainly was influential. Its people didn't conquer by warfare – they simply influenced the artistic and cultural development of all of northern Peru. Archaeologists formerly referred to this cultural expansion as the Chavín Horizon, though Early Horizon is now the preferred usage. Signs of Chavín influence are evident in ruins ranging from the present-day Ecuadorian border to as far south as Ica and Ayacucho. None of these sites are as well preserved or as frequently visited as Chavín de Huántar.

The principal Chavín deity was feline (a jaguar or puma), and lesser condor, snake and human deities also existed. Highly stylized representations of these deities are carved in Chavín sites. The experienced eye can see similarities in the precise yet fluid lines of these carvings, while the non-expert can tell that any culture capable of such fine work 3000 years ago must indeed have been well advanced.

The artistic work of Chavín is much more stylized and cultist than the naturalistic art of the later Moche and Nazca cultures. Because of this, archaeologists lack an accurate picture of life in Chavín times. However, excavations of middens (garbage dumps) indicate that corn became a staple food and agriculture improved with the introduction of squash, avocados, yucca and other crops. Better agriculture meant less reliance on hunting, fishing and gathering, and more importantly, allowed leisure time. Thus, art and religion could develop, and so the Chavín horizon, linking art and religion in its feline-worship cults, was able to influence a large part of Peru.

For detailed information, read the excellent *Chavín and the Origins of Peruvian Civilization* by Richard Burger, Thames and Hudson, 1992.

Visiting the Ruins

At first glance, the site at Chavín de Huántar is not particularly prepossessing. There are two reasons for this: most of the site's more interesting parts were built underground and the area was covered by a huge landslide in 1945. To visit the site properly and to get the most from your visit, you should enter the underground chambers. Although these are electrically lit, the lighting system sometimes doesn't work and you are advised to bring your own flashlight. It is also worth hiring a guide to show you around.

The site contains a huge central square, slightly sunken below ground level, with an intricate and well-engineered system of channels for drainage. From the square, a broad staircase leads up to the single entrance of the largest and most important building in Chavín de Huántar, the Castillo. With an area of about 75 sq meters and height of up to 13 meters, the Castillo was built on three different levels, each of dry stone masonry. At one time the walls were embellished with tenons – keystones consisting of large projecting blocks carved to resemble a stylized human head. Only one of these remains in its original place; the others have been moved inside the Castillo in the underground chambers or to museums.

The underground tunnels are an exceptional feat of 3000-year-old engineering; they are so well ventilated that the air is not musty, yet the main entrance is the only external window or doorway. In the heart of the underground complex is an exquisitely carved rock known as the Lanzón de Chavín. It is a thrilling and distinctly mysterious experience to come upon this four-meter-high, dagger-like rock stuck into the ground at the intersection of four narrow passageways, deep within the Castillo.

Travelers interested in the Chavín culture are advised to visit the Museo de la Nación in Lima. Two carved rocks, the Raimondi Stela and the Tello Obelisk, smaller but similar to the Lanzón de Chavín, and several of the large, carved keystones which once decorated the Castillo may be examined at the museum.

The site is open daily from 8 am to 4 pm. Entry is about US$2, with an extra fee for photography. If the gate is closed, look around for a guard to open it. Spanish-speaking local guides are available to show you around for a small fee or you can come on one of the frequent guided tours from Huaraz.

Places to Stay & Eat

Hotels in the village of Chavín de Huántar are found on or near the Plaza de Armas and are very cheap and basic. The best of a not-particularly-good lot is the *Hostal Inca*, which may manage hot water occasionally. They charge about US$4/6. Other choices are the *Montecarlo* and *Gantu*.

There are some basic restaurants in town with a reputation for closing soon after sunset, so eat early. *Las Chositas*, on the main road between the town center and ruins; and *Mi Ranchito*, Enero Norte 427, are probably the best. There are other cheap ones along Enero Norte and Sur.

Camping is reportedly possible at the hot springs about 3 km south of town; try to go in a group and watch your belongings.

Getting There & Away

Tour buses make day trips from Huaraz to Chavín for about US$9 per passenger, not including the ruin entry fee. See the Huaraz section for daily public buses from Huaraz (US$3.50, five hours).

Transportes Cóndor de Chavín runs buses to and from Lima (US$9, 11 hours). Buses leave Lima on Tuesday and Saturday at 6 am, continuing on to Huari, Piscobamba and Pomabamba. Their Lima office (☎ 428-8122) is at Montevideo 1039. Other trucks and buses leave Chavín to the north most days.

The drive across the Cordillera Blanca from Catac is a scenic one. The road passes the Laguna Querococha at 3980 meters; from here, there are good views of the peaks of Pucaraju (5322 meters) and Yanamarey (5237 meters). The road deteriorates somewhat as it continues climbing to the Cahuish tunnel at 4178 meters above sea level. The tunnel cuts through the Cahuish Pass, which is over 300 meters higher, before the road descends to Chavín at about 3145 meters.

Hikers can walk to Chavín from Olleros in about three days (see Bartle's book or Bradt's book).

NORTH OF CHAVÍN

The road north of Chavín goes through the villages Huari (40 km, two hours), San

Luis (100 km, five hours), Piscobamba (160 km, eight hours), Pomabamba and Sihuas. The further north you go, the more difficult transport becomes and it may stop altogether during the wet season. Basic accommodations are available in all of these towns, which may be the end of various cross-cordillera hikes. From

Sihuas, it is possible to continue on to Huallanca (at the end of Cañón del Pato) via Tres Cruces and thus return to the Callejón de Huaylas. This roundtrip is scenic, remote and rarely made by travelers. It shouldn't be too difficult to find transport during the dry season if you really want to get off the beaten track.

Across the Northern Highlands

The traveler heading farther north into the highlands from the Cordillera Blanca is unable to do so conveniently without returning to the coast. You must then travel north along the coast before returning inland and into the mountains again. The first major city north of Huaraz is Cajamarca, reached by three roads from the coast. The dirt roads from Trujillo and Chiclayo are both rough and difficult but the

road that leaves the Panamericana between these two cities is paved all the way to Cajamarca. All three routes are described in this chapter.

From Cajamarca, a very poor road continues northeast across the Andes to Chachapoyas, capital of the Department of Amazonas. A better road to Chachapoyas via Bagua leaves the Panamericana north of Chiclayo. Beyond Chachapoyas, this

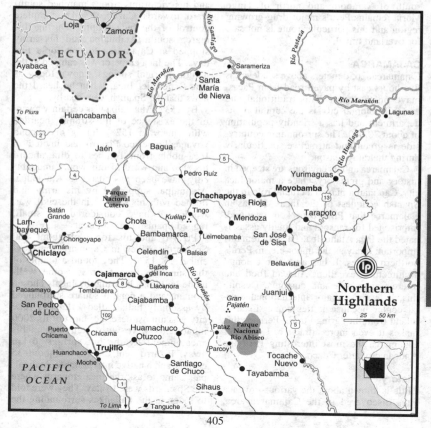

road continues down the eastern slopes of the Andes to the jungles of the Department of San Martín. Although travel in this region was inadvisable in the early '90s because the Sendero Luminoso and drug cartels had formed a strange alliance, this is no longer the case since the imprisonment of Sendero leaders. One can safely travel beyond Chachapoyas by road through the towns of Moyobamba and Tarapoto as far as the jungle port of Yurimaguas, where the road stops and overland travelers must continue by river (as described in the last chapter of this book). However, the Río Huallaga valley south of Tarapoto and north of Tingo María remains Peru's major drug-growing region and this particular route is not safe for overland travel.

CAJAMARCA

Cajamarca, 2650 meters above sea level, is five hours east by paved road from Pacasmayo on the coast. This traditional and tranquil colonial city is the capital of its department and has a friendly population of about 70,000. The surrounding countryside is green and attractive, particularly during the rainy season.

Cajamarca and its environs are steeped in history and prehistory. Once a major Inca city, Cajamarca played a crucial role in the Spanish conquest of the Incas. It was in Cajamarca that Pizarro tricked, captured, imprisoned for ransom and finally assassinated the Inca Atahualpa. The city remains important today as the major city in Peru's northern Andes. It has attractive colonial architecture, excellent Andean food and interesting people and customs. Despite this, it is not a major international tourist center because it lies some distance inland from the 'gringo trail.' Perhaps this makes it even more attractive. I consider Cajamarca the most interesting Peruvian Andean city after Cuzco.

History

Little is known about the various pre-Inca sites discovered in the Cajamarca area,

though they are generally attributed to the Chavín-influenced Cajamarca culture.

About 1460, the Incas conquered the Cajamarca people and Cajamarca became a major Inca city on the Inca Andean highway linking Cuzco with Quito.

After the death of the Inca Huayna Capac in 1525, the Inca Empire, by then stretching from southern Colombia to central Chile, was divided between the half-brothers Atahualpa and Huáscar. Atahualpa ruled the north and Huáscar ruled the south. Civil war soon broke out and Atahualpa, who had the support of the army, gained the upper hand. In 1532 he and his victorious troops marched southward towards Cuzco to take complete control of the Inca Empire. During this march south, Atahualpa and his army stopped at Cajamarca to rest for a few days. The Inca emperor was camped at the natural thermal springs, known today as Los Baños del Inca, when he heard the news that the Spanish were nearby.

By 1532, Atahualpa was certainly aware of the existence of the strange, bearded white men. In 1528, during his second voyage, Francisco Pizarro had invited an Inca noble from Tumbes to dine aboard his ship and word of this would undoubtedly have been passed on to Atahualpa. Atahualpa, supported by his army and flushed with his victory in the civil war, would not have considered the small, ragged Spanish force a threat.

Pizarro and his force of about 160 Spaniards arrived in Cajamarca on November 15, 1532. They found a temple of the sun, the Inca fortress, some well-made buildings housing the Inca's chosen women, and a central square surrounded by assembly halls called *kallankas*. The city was almost deserted; most of its 2000 inhabitants were with Atahualpa at his encampment by the hot springs, 6 km away. Pizarro sent a force of about 35 cavalry and a native interpreter to Atahualpa's camp to ask the Inca emperor where the Spaniards were to stay. They were told to lodge in the kallankas surrounding the plaza and that the Inca would join them the next day.

The small force of Spaniards spent an anxious night, fully aware that they were severely outnumbered by the Inca troops, estimated at 40,000 to 80,000. The Spaniards plotted throughout the night, deciding to try and entice Atahualpa into the plaza and, at a prearranged signal, capture the Inca should the opportunity present itself. If this did not occur, they were to maintain a 'friendly' relationship and hope for another chance to capture Atahualpa. The next morning Pizarro stationed his troops in the kallankas, which were perfect for his plan. The kallankas surrounded three sides of the plaza and each had about 20 doorways so that a large number of the Spaniards could emerge and attack at the same time.

Atahualpa kept the Spanish waiting all day, much to their consternation. He didn't break camp until the afternoon and reached Cajamarca early in the evening, accompanied by his vast army. Upon arriving at the outskirts of the city, the Inca emperor ordered the majority of his troops to stay outside while he entered the plaza with a retinue of nobles and about 6000 men armed with slings and hand axes. He was met by the Spanish friar, Vicente de Valverde. The friar, Bible in hand, attempted to explain his position as a man of God and presented the Inca with the Bible. Atahualpa angrily threw the book to the ground and Valverde saw this action as an insult to Christianity. This provided the excuse he needed to absolve the Spaniards in advance for an attack upon the Inca. He rushed back to the kallankas and prevailed upon Pizarro to order the firing of his cannon into the group of Indians. This was the prearranged signal to attack.

The cannon were fired and the Spanish cavalry attacked with much trumpeting and yelling. The Indians, who had never seen cannon or horses before, were terrified and bewildered by the fearsome onslaught. Their small hand axes and slings were no match for the well-armored Spaniards who were swinging razor-sharp swords from the

Francisco Pizarro

advantageous height of horseback. The Indians tried to flee but the entrance to the plaza was too narrow to allow escape. By sheer weight of numbers, they knocked down a section of wall two meters thick and swarmed out of the plaza in total disarray. Pizarro's horsemen charged after them, hacking down as many Indians as they could. Meanwhile, Pizarro himself led a small contingent that succeeded in capturing Atahualpa. As the sun set over Cajamarca on the evening of November 16, the course of Latin American history was changed forever. With an estimated 7000 Indians dead and Atahualpa captured, the small band of Spaniards had succeeded beyond their wildest hopes. Now they literally were conquistadors.

Almost immediately after his capture, Atahualpa became aware of one of the weaknesses of the Spaniards – their lust for gold. Accordingly, he offered to fill a large room once with gold and twice with silver in return for his freedom. Astounded by their good fortune, the conquistadors quickly agreed to the offer and led Atahualpa to believe that they would not only release him after the ransom was paid, but would also return him to his northern lands around Quito.

Papers confirming the conquest of
Peru – showing Pizarro, the priest
Valverde and Atahualpa.

This was a wily move on the part of Pizarro. By promising Atahualpa's return to Quito, he effectively controlled the northern part of the Inca Empire. And by holding Atahualpa captive, Pizarro also maintained control of the southern half of the empire whose inhabitants, having just been beaten by Atahualpa in a civil war, considered Pizarro a liberator rather than an invader. Playing one Inca faction against the other in this way was Pizarro's strongest weapon. If the Inca Empire had been united when the Spanish arrived, the story of the conquest would have been entirely different.

The gold and silver slowly began to arrive at Cajamarca. Pizarro sent some of his men to Cuzco to ensure the collection of the ransom. Meanwhile, Atahualpa was held as a royal prisoner, with the servants and comfort to which he was accustomed.

The Spanish were in no great hurry to collect the ransom; they were also waiting for reinforcements. On April 14, 1533, Diego de Almagro arrived from the coast with 150 soldiers, almost doubling the Spanish force at Cajamarca. Atahualpa began to suspect that the Spaniards were lying to him and that he wouldn't be released and allowed to return to Quito on payment of the ransom.

Finally, in mid-June of 1533, the ransom was complete and Pizarro ordered the melting down and distribution of the treasure. Careful records were kept of these procedures and it is known that about 6000 kg of gold and 12,000 kg of silver were melted down into gold and silver bullion. At today's prices, this is worth roughly US$76 million but the artistic value of the ornaments and implements that were melted down is impossible to estimate or recover. The gold and silver was distributed among the conquistadors in strictly controlled quotas.

Atahualpa, still a prisoner, now knew he was not going to be released. He sent desperate messages to his followers in Quito to come to Cajamarca and rescue him. The Spaniards heard of the rescue attempt and became panic-stricken. Although Pizarro was not anxious to kill the Inca emperor, intending instead to further his own aims by continuing to hold Atahualpa hostage and using him as a puppet ruler, the other leading Spaniards insisted on the Inca's death. Despite the lack of a formal trial, Atahualpa was sentenced to death for attempting to arrange his own rescue. On July 26, 1533, Atahualpa was led out to the center of the Cajamarca plaza to be burnt at the stake. At the last hour, Atahualpa accepted baptism and his sentence was changed to a quicker death by strangulation.

Immediately after Atahualpa's death, the Spaniards crowned Tupac Huallpa, a younger brother of Huáscar, as the new Inca emperor. With this puppet ruler, the Spaniards were free to march into Cuzco as liberators. During the march, the new Inca died of an unknown illness and the Spanish arrived in Cuzco on November 15 without an Inca ruler.

NORTHERN HIGHLANDS

Today, little remains of Inca Cajamarca. Most of the great stone buildings were torn down to be used in the construction of Spanish homes and churches. The great plaza where Atahualpa was captured and later killed was in roughly the same location as today's Plaza de Armas, though in Atahualpa's time it was a much larger plaza. The ransom chamber, which Atahualpa purportedly filled once with gold and twice with silver, is the only building still standing.

For a much more detailed description of the momentous events that took place in Cajamarca in 1532 and 1533, see John Hemming's excellent *The Conquest of the Incas*.

Information
Tourist Office A tourist office at the Complejo de Belén is open weekdays from 7.30 am to 1.30 pm and 3.30 to 5.30 pm.

Money The Banco de Crédito, on Lima near Tarapaca, and Interbanc, on the Plaza de Armas, change traveler's checks. Cash dollars can be changed more quickly with money changers on the street near the Plaza de Armas, with the usual precautions.

Post & Telecommunications The post office at the corner of Lima and Gálvez is open from 8 am to 8 pm daily, except Sunday when it's open from 8 am to noon. You can make long-distance telephone calls every day from 8 am to 10 pm at Telefónica del Peru on the Plaza de Armas. The area code for Cajamarca and the surrounding area is 044.

Tour Agencies These provide tourist information and inexpensive guided tours of the city and surroundings. They claim to have English-speaking guides but, in reality, few guides speak passable English. Cumbe Mayo Tours (☎ 92-2938), Puga 635, and Cajamarca Tours (☎ 92-2813), 2 de Mayo 323, are the ones most recommended by readers but there are others.

Tuesday is a bad day to tour the town as the museums are usually closed.

Laundry There's a lavandería (☎ 92-3454) at Puga 545.

Medical Services The Hospital Regional is at Urteaga and Urrelo.

Dangers & Annoyances In Cajamarca, there aren't many dangers or annoyances to speak of. On the whole, it's a nice city, but there are thieves so take the usual precautions. Liquid fights during carnival (see Special Events) can be annoying.

El Cuarto del Rescate
The Ransom Chamber is the only Inca building still standing in Cajamarca. Although called the Ransom Chamber, the room shown to visitors is where Atahualpa was imprisoned and not where the ransom was stored. The small room has three trapezoidal doorways and a few trapezoidal niches in the inner walls – a typical sign of Inca construction. Although well constructed, it does not compare with the Inca buildings to be seen in the Cuzco area.

In the entrance, there are a couple of

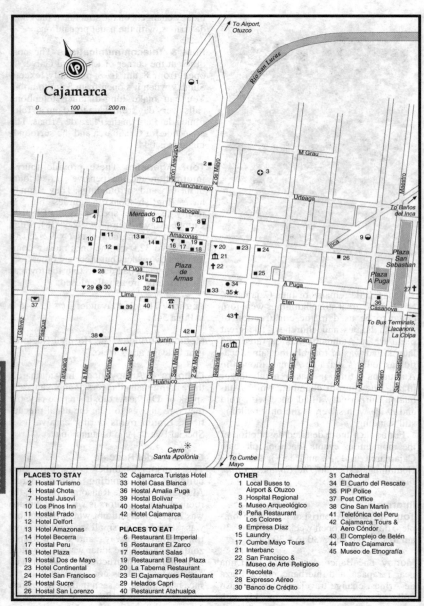

Cajamarca

0   100   200 m

PLACES TO STAY
2 Hostal Turismo
4 Hostal Chota
7 Hostal Jusovi
10 Los Pinos Inn
11 Hostal Prado
12 Hotel Delfort
13 Hotel Amazonas
14 Hotel Becerra
17 Hostal Peru
18 Hotel Plaza
19 Hostal Dos de Mayo
23 Hotel Continental
24 Hotel San Francisco
25 Hostal Sucre
26 Hostal San Lorenzo

32 Cajamarca Turistas Hotel
33 Hotel Casa Blanca
36 Hostal Amalia Puga
39 Hostal Bolívar
40 Hostal Atahualpa
42 Hotel Cajamarca

PLACES TO EAT
6 Restaurant El Imperial
16 Restaurant El Zarco
17 Restaurant Salas
19 Restaurant El Real Plaza
20 La Taberna Restaurant
23 El Cajamarques Restaurant
29 Helados Capri
40 Restaurant Atahualpa

OTHER
1 Local Buses to
   Airport & Otuzco
3 Hospital Regional
5 Museo Arqueológico
7 Peña Restaurant
   Los Colores
9 Empresa Díaz
15 Laundry
17 Cumbe Mayo Tours
21 Interbanc
22 San Francisco &
   Museo de Arte Religioso
27 Recoleta
28 Expresso Aéreo
30 Banco de Crédito

31 Cathedral
34 El Cuarto del Rescate
35 PIP Police
37 Post Office
38 Cine San Martín
41 Telefónica del Peru
42 Cajamarca Tours &
   Aero Cóndor
43 El Complejo de Belén
44 Teatro Cajamarca
45 Museo de Etnografía

modern paintings depicting Atahualpa's capture and imprisonment. The site is open from 9 am to noon and 3 to 5 pm daily except Tuesday. Entrance is US$1.50; the ticket can be used to visit the church and hospital of the Complejo de Belén and the Museo de Etnografía.

El Complejo de Belén

Construction of the church and hospital of Belén began in the latter part of the 17th century. The hospital was run by nuns. Inside, 31 tiny, cell-like bedrooms line the walls of the T-shaped building. In what used to be the women's hospital there is a small archaeology museum. Local guides point out that the building's facade has strange carvings of women with four breasts. The kitchen and dispensary of the hospital now houses an art museum.

The church next door has a fine cupola and a well-carved and painted pulpit. There are several interesting wood carvings, including an extremely tired-looking Christ sitting cross-legged on his throne, propping up his chin with a double-jointed wrist and looking as though he could do with a pisco sour after a hard day's miracle working. The outside walls of the church are lavishly decorated.

Opening hours and admission are the same as at El Cuarto del Rescate.

Museo de Etnografía

This small, attractively housed museum is just a few meters from the Complejo del Belén and has the same opening hours and admission fee. Here, you can examine local costumes and clothing, domestic and agricultural implements, musical instruments and craft work in wood, bone, leather and stone, as well as other examples of Cajamarcan culture.

Plaza de Armas

The plaza is pleasant and has a well-kept topiary garden. The fine central fountain dates to 1692 and commemorates the bicentennial of Columbus's landing in the Americas. The town's inhabitants congregate in the plaza every evening. Strolling and discussing the day's events are traditionally popular activities, more so in this area of northern Peru than anywhere else in the country.

Two churches face onto the Plaza de Armas: the cathedral and the church of San Francisco. Both are often illuminated in the evening, especially on weekends. The cathedral is a squat building that was begun in the late 1600s and has only recently been finished. Like most of Cajamarca's churches, the cathedral has no belfry. This is because the Spanish crown levied a tax on finished churches and so the belfries were not built, leaving the church unfinished and thereby avoiding taxes. San Francisco's belfries were finished this century – too late for the Spanish crown to collect its tax!

San Francisco

The church of San Francisco and its small Museo de Arte Religioso are open from 2 to 5 pm on weekdays. Admission is about US50¢. The intricately sculpted Capilla de La Dolorosa (to the right of the church) is considered one of the finest chapels in the city.

Museo Arqueológico

This small but well-stocked museum (not related to the even smaller one in the Belén Complex) is well worth a visit. Its remarkably varied collection of ceramics includes a few examples of Cajamarca pots and an unusual collection of ceramic ceremonial spears also from the same culture. The Cajamarca culture, which existed in the area before the Inca Empire, is little studied and not very well known. The museum also has b&w photographs of various historic and prehistoric sites in the Cajamarca area; its director is knowledgeable and willing to talk about the exhibits.

The museum is run by the Universidad de Cajamarca. Hours are 8 am to 1.30 pm daily except Tuesday but you may have to knock on the door to get in. Admission is US50¢.

Feast Days in Cajamarca

Like most Peruvian Andean towns, Cajamarca is famous for its carnaval – this one is a particularly wet affair and its water fights are worse (or better, depending on your point of view) than usual. Local teenagers don't necessarily limit themselves to soaking one another with water – paint, oil and urine have all been reported! The action begins on the Saturday preceding Lent and continues through Shrove Tuesday. The Corpus Christi processions are also very colorful.

Both of these are Catholic feast days and the dates vary each year, depending on the dates for Easter. Carnaval is the last few days before Lent (which, in turn, is 40 days before Palm Sunday, which is the Sunday before Easter). Corpus Christi is the Thursday after Trinity Sunday, which is the Sunday after Whitsunday, which is the seventh Sunday after Easter. Confused fiesta-goers would do well to buy a Catholic calendar for the year they plan on being in Peru. ■

Cerro Santa Apolonia

This hill overlooks the city from the southwest and is a prominent Cajamarca landmark. It is easily reached by climbing the stairs at the end of Jirón 2 de Mayo. The pre-Hispanic carved rocks at the summit are mainly Inca but are thought to originally date back to the Chavín period. One of the rocks, known as the Seat of the Inca, has a shape that suggests a throne. The Inca is said to have reviewed his troops from here. There are pretty gardens around the carved rocks and a fountain in the shape of a campesino. The water comes out of an appropriate part of the statue's anatomy! Admission to the hilltop is US50¢.

Special Events

Carnaval and Corpus Christi are popular feast days in Cajamarca – see the sidebar for more information about those. Independence day celebrations at the end of July may include a bullfight. Cajamarca's Tourist Festival is around the second week in August. The various cultural events include art shows, folk music and dancing competitions, beauty pageants and processions. Hotel and other prices go up during all these events and are usually slightly higher in the dry (May to September) season.

Places to Stay – bottom end

Many of the cheapest hotels have only cold water, but you can get a hot bath at Baños del Inca (see below). Cheap hotels that advertise hot water usually have it only a few hours a day – ask when.

If you're on a really tight budget, some of the cheapest places include the very basic *Hostal Chota* (☎ 92-2610), La Mar 637, which charges about US$3 or US$4 per person and has communal cold showers. Similar is the *Hostal Bolívar* (☎ 92-2969), Apurímac 670, and the *Hostal Amalia Puga* (☎ 92-2117), Puga 1118. The *Hostal Sucre* (☎ 92-2596), Puga 811, has rooms with private cold showers in the mornings for US$5 per person but is otherwise very basic. The *Hotel San Francisco* (☎ 92-3070), Belén 790, also charges about US$5 per person in rooms with private cold shower and is reasonably clean. The similar *Hotel Becerra* (☎ 92-3490), Arequipa 195, charges US$7/12. The similarly priced *Hostal Peru*, Puga 605, has private cold showers and is OK.

One of the best cheap hotels is the *Hostal Prado* (☎ 92-3288), La Mar 582, which is clean and has hot water. Rates are US$5/9 for singles/doubles or US$10/15 with private bath. The *Hotel Plaza* (☎ 92-2058), Puga 669, is in an old and colorful building on the Plaza de Armas. They have some hot water and a few rooms with balconies and plaza views. A double with private bath and plaza view is US$14; cheaper rooms (without views and with dirty communal showers) are available. The *Hostal Dos de Mayo* (☎ 92-2527), 2 de Mayo 585, has hot communal showers in the evening and charges US$6/10 in rooms with sink and toilet, but not a shower. The *Hotel Delfort* (☎ 92-3375), Apurímac 851, looks OK and has rooms with private hot showers for US$8/13. The bare-looking *Hostal Turismo* (☎ 92-3101), 2 de Mayo 817, has clean, carpeted rooms with comfortable beds and private hot showers US$9/15.

The clean *Hostal Jusovi* (☎ 92-2920), Amazonas 637, has cold water in the rooms and occasional hot water in communal showers. They charge US$10/18. Also in this price range is the *Hostal Atahualpa* (☎ 92-2157), on Lima near Atahualpa, which looks good and reasonably clean and has private warm showers. A few rooms with shared showers are cheaper. The *Hotel Amazonas* (☎ 92-2620, 92-3496), Amazonas 528, has singles with private cold showers for US$8 and doubles with private hot showers for US$20.

Places to Stay – middle
A memorable choice is the *Hotel Casa Blanca* (☎ 92-2141, fax 92-2013), 2 de Mayo 446, a thick-walled, creaky-floored, interesting old building on the Plaza de Armas. It has an excellent 24-hour hot-water supply and charges about US$20/30 for singles/doubles with bath. All rooms are very spacious and some have up to five beds. These work out more cheaply if you are traveling with a group. Bargain in the low season. The hotel café isn't bad.

The clean, pleasant *Hotel Cajamarca* (☎ 92-2532, fax 92-2813), 2 de Mayo 311, is in a colonial house and is recommended for reasonable comfort. It has a decent restaurant and charges US$21/31 for singles/doubles with bath and hot water. This hotel often has promotional discounts of up to 40%. Another reasonable choice in this price range is the *Hostal San Lorenzo* (☎ 92-2909), Amazonas 1070, with clean rooms and hot showers.

The *Hotel Continental* (☎ 92-2758, 92-3063, fax 93-3024), Amazonas 760, is over a modern shopping mall, which makes some rooms noisy but means that shops, a café and a bar are conveniently close. Good, clean singles/doubles with bath and hot water are US$25/32 and the hotel

has been recommended. The rooms at the back are a bit dark. The small *Los Pinos Inn* (☎ 92-5992), La Mar 521, charges US$25/33 for clean, pleasant rooms with hot showers and breakfast included.

The *Cajamarca Turistas Hotel* (☎ 92-2470, fax 92-2472; in Lima ☎ 442-3090, fax 442-4180), Lima 773 on the Plaza de Armas, is the most comfortable hotel in town. Rates are US$36/48 and may include breakfast. The quality of the rooms varies somewhat. There are a couple of suites for about US$65.

If you want quiet country comfort, go to the Baños del Inca, 6 km away. Here, the excellent *Hostal Laguna Seca* (☎ 92-3556, 92-0203 ext 205, fax 92-3149, in Lima 446-3270, 422-3008, fax 441-8560) will charge you US$30/40 for pleasant rooms with bath. They also have four-bed bungalows for US$55. The hotel has a warm swimming pool and the hot water in all rooms is fed by the natural thermal springs nearby. Horseback riding can be arranged. There is a pleasant garden and an adequate restaurant.

Places to Eat
My favorite restaurant in Cajamarca is the *Salas*, a big barn of a place on the Plaza de Armas. It's popular with the locals and serves various local dishes such as cuy, delicious corn tamales and sesos (cow brains), which I must admit I've never tried. Prices are very reasonable. Similar to the Salas but a little cheaper, the recommended *El Zarco* on Arequipa at Amazonas serves Chinese food as well as local Peruvian dishes and sells almost every beer produced in Peru. *El Real Plaza*, at 2 de Mayo 569, has a pleasant courtyard and serves local dishes and good cheap breakfasts. The *Atahualpa*, next to the Hostal Atahualpa, and *El Imperial*, on the 600 block of Amazonas, have good, cheap fixed menus and other meals. *La Casita del Cuy*, opposite the Hostal Jusovi on Amazonas, is clean, inexpensive and popular with locals.

La Taberna, on the corner of the plaza, is more modern and serves good 'international' food at prices that are only a little

NORTHERN HIGHLANDS

higher than the other places. The restaurant in the *Hotel Cajamarca* has a nice ambiance and decent food and often has musicians in the evenings. Although it's pricier than most restaurants in Cajamarca, it really isn't expensive. Also good is *El Cajamarques* (☎ 92-3092), next to the Hotel Continental. For a good, though not very cheap, early breakfast, the Cajamarca Turistas Hotel is worth checking out. Try *Helados Capri* for good ice cream.

For a typical local lunch, try *La Namorina*, about 1½ km from the town center on the road to the Baños del Inca. Cuy is the main attraction at this inexpensive and authentic highland restaurant. It is a fly-blown, hole-in-the-wall place but the cuy is good and the restaurant is close to most of the bus stations. Nearby, *Sabor Cajabambino*, on La Paz next to the bus stations, is another OK place for a meal while waiting for a bus.

Entertainment

Cajamarca has a couple of cinemas and there may be a reasonably good English-language film screening at one of them.

A few restaurants have live music; these include *El Cajamarques* restaurant or in the *Hotel Cajamarca* restaurant. *Peña/Restaurant Los Colores*, 2 de Mayo 643, looks like a fun, locally-popular place. For dancing, try *Discoteca Chalan* in the Cajamarca Turistas Hotel or the *Discoteca La Caverna*, Cinco Esquinas 648. There are other places – ask around.

Things to Buy

The market on Calle Amazonas is lively and interesting. Local products to look for include alforjas (heavy wool or cotton saddle bags), which can be worn over the shoulder or used on horseback. Woven baskets and leather work are also local crafts; the latter can be bought cheaply (if you bargain) from prisoners in the jail, which is just past the arch on Jirón Lima. They are open from 8 to 11.30 am and 2 to 4.30 pm. The local eucalyptus honey sold at the market is worth trying.

Getting There & Away

Air Flight schedules to Cajamarca are subject to frequent changes, cancellations and delays. AeroCóndor and Expresso Aéreo are the airlines with the most regular service, usually with daily morning flights from Lima, some stopping in Chimbote. Occasionally, there are afternoon flights.

Some Expresso Aéreo flights continue to Chachapoyas (currently Thursday and Sunday mornings, but subject to change). Flights to Trujillo, Chiclayo and other destinations have been sporadically scheduled. One of the other airlines may have direct flights to and from Lima; in 1994 it was Imperial Air, in 1995 it was Aero Continente. Who knows which airline will be flying there in 1996.

The AeroCóndor office (☎ 92-2813) is at 2 de Mayo 323; the Expresso Aéreo office (☎ 92-3480, 92-5113) is at Puga 442. The fare to Lima is about US$104, to Chachapoyas about US$50. Local buses for Otuzco pass the airport (US30¢) or take a taxi.

Bus Cajamarca is at an ancient crossroads dating back many centuries before the Incas. Today, daily buses leave Cajamarca on roads heading for all four points of the compass.

Most bus terminals are on or close to the third block of a street called Atahualpa (not to be confused with the Atahualpa on the map, in the town center), about 1½ km southeast of the town center on the road to the Baños del Inca. No address is given for these companies. A few companies are on Independencia, off the first block of the same Atahualpa. You can buy tickets at the bus terminals, or from agents in the center. Cumbe Mayo Tours, Puga 635, sells tickets for Sudamericano buses. Cajamarca Tours, 2 de Mayo 323, sells tickets for Empresa Atahualpa.

The most important road is the west-bound one, which is paved all the way to the Panamericana near Pacasmayo on the coast. From here, you can head north to Chiclayo or south to Trujillo and Lima. Services to Trujillo (US$6 to US$8, eight to nine hours), Chiclayo (US$5.50 to

US$7.50, seven hours) and Lima (US$10 to US$15, 15 to 17 hours) are provided by many companies. Most buses to Lima travel overnight, though a few leave as early as 1 pm, arriving before dawn. CIVA (☎ 92-1460), Independencia 386, has the most expensive and comfortable night bus. Empresa Atahualpa (☎ 92-3075) also has good buses. Cheaper Lima services are provided by TEPSA (☎ 92-3306), Sudamericano (☎ 92-3270), Cruz del Sur, Nor Peru (☎ 92-4550) and Palacios (☎ 92-2600). For Trujillo, most companies leave in the afternoon and arrive late at night. The earliest bus is often with Vulcano (☎ 92-1090) or Empresa Díaz (☎ 92-5630), Ayacucho 753, near the center. The Lima-bound companies also stop in Trujillo. For Chiclayo, El Cumbe (☎ 92-3088), Independencia 236, has three or four buses a day and is the best bet for daytime travel. Jarcer Express, (☎ 92-3337), on Independencia, has a fast small bus at noon. Sudamericano and Vulcano also have buses to Chiclayo.

The southbound road is the old route to Trujillo via Cajabamba and Huamachuco. The trip to Trujillo takes two or three times longer on this rough dirt road than it does along the newer paved road via Pacasmayo, although the old route is only 60 km longer. The scenery is supposedly prettier on the longer route but most buses are less comfortable and less frequent beyond Cajabamba. Transportes Atahualpa has a noon bus to Cajabamba (US$5, about seven hours) but the buses are already half full with passengers from Lima and Trujillo when they reach Cajamarca and the best seats are taken. Others serving Cajabamba include Nor Peru and Palacios. For Huamachuco and on to Trujillo, you have to get another bus at Cajabamba.

The rough northbound road passes through wild and attractive countryside via the towns of Hualgayoc (US$5) and Bambamarca (US$5.50) to Chota (US$6, nine hours). **Hualgayoc** is a mining village in a beautiful setting. **Bambamarca** has a colorful Sunday morning market. There are basic hotels in Bambamarca and more hotels in **Chota**. Buses run from Chota to Chiclayo along a very rough road. Daily Empresa Diáz buses to Chota leave Cajamarca at 7 am and with Nor Peru at 11 am.

The eastbound road heads to Celendín, then across the Andes, past Chachapoyas and down into the Amazon lowlands. The road between Celendín and Chachapoyas is very bad and transport is unreliable; if you're going to Chachapoyas, you are advised to travel from Chiclayo via Bagua, unless you have plenty of time and patience. Daily buses to Celendín (US$5, five hours) leave Cajamarca in the morning with Empresa Atahualpa and around midday with Empresa Atahualpa, Palacios and Empresa Díaz.

Getting Around
It is easy to find transport to the Baños del Inca. Colectivo taxis leave frequently from in front of the church of San Francisco. The fare is US50¢. Cheaper Comité 3M buses travel along Jirón Lima and through the Plaza de Armas to the Baños.

Buses for the Ventanillas de Otuzco leave frequently from the end of Jirón Arequipa, about 500 meters from the Plaza de Armas and two blocks past the bridge. The fare is US50¢. The buses go past the airport (US30¢) and on to Otuzco, leaving you within 500 meters of the archaeological site.

Bus routes and departure points change occasionally, so ask at the tourist office for the latest details. Other local places are not served by public bus, though it is worth checking with the tourist office to see if this has changed. Walk, hitchhike, take a taxi or join a tour.

AROUND CAJAMARCA
There are several places of interest around Cajamarca. Some can be reached on public transport while others must be visited on foot, by taxi or with a guided tour. The tour agencies may pool their clients to form a tour group for any trip, although more expensive individual outings can be arranged.

Baños del Inca
These natural hot springs are 6 km from

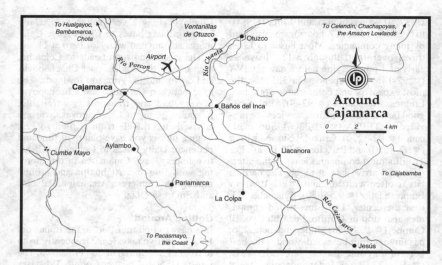

Cajamarca. The water is channeled into many private cubicles, some large enough for up to six people at a time. These are available for US$1 an hour. There is a cheaper public pool.

Atahualpa was camped by these hot springs when Pizarro arrived in the area, but there is nothing to see today except for the springs themselves.

Aylambo
Just a few kilometers south of Cajamarca via Avenida Independencia is the village of Aylambo. Here there is the *Escuela Taller de Alfarería* (a pottery trade school) where students learn to combine traditional elements with modern ceramic techniques. The school can be visited and pottery is for sale.

Cumbe Mayo
According to the locals, the name of this site is derived from the Quechua term *kumpi mayo*, or 'well-made water channel.' The site, about 23 km from Cajamarca by road, has some extraordinarily well-engineered pre-Inca channels running for several kilometers across the bleak mountain tops. Nearby are some

caves containing petroglyphs. The countryside is high, windswept and slightly eerie. Locals tell superstitious stories about the area's eroded rock formations, which look like groups of shrouded mountain climbers.

The site can be reached on foot via a signposted road from the Cerro Santa Apolonia. The walk takes about four hours if you take the obvious short cuts and ask every passer-by for directions. Guided bus tours are offered in Cajamarca for about US$8 or US$9 per person and last four to five hours. They have been recommended.

Ventanillas de Otuzco
This pre-Inca necropolis consists of hundreds of funerary niches built into the hillside, hence the name *ventanillas*, or 'windows.' The site is in beautiful countryside about 8 km northeast of Cajamarca, and it is possible to walk here from either Cajamarca or the Baños del Inca. There are also local buses. Further away are the larger Ventanillas de Combayo, but these are rarely visited because the road is in bad shape. Guided bus tours cost about US$7 per person.

Llacanora & Hacienda La Colpa
The picturesque little village of Llacanora is 13 km from Cajamarca. Some of the inhabitants still play the traditional three-meter-long bamboo trumpets, called *claríns*. A few kilometers away is the Hacienda La Colpa, which is usually visited on a tour combined with Llacanora (about US$6 per person). The hacienda is a working cattle ranch, and in the afternoons the cattle are herded into their stalls one by one, the ranch-hands calling each animal by name. This is a locally famous tourist attraction.

The Road from the Coast
The highway from the coast to Cajamarca is paved all the way, passing through **Tembladera** 46 km from the Panamericana junction. Interestingly enough, Tembladera is named not after the tremors of earthquakes but after the trembling and shivering of malaria victims. The disease was once common in this rice-growing area. Nearby is a new dam and reservoir visible on the right side.

A further 41 km brings you to the mining village of **Chilete** and a basic hotel. A partially paved road southwest of Chilete comes out at Chicama on the coast and offers a shorter but much rougher route between Trujillo and Cajamarca.

On a side road 24 km north of Chilete is the village of **San Pablo**. It has a basic hotel and two or three buses a day to Chilete. An hour's walk from San Pablo is the Chavín site of **Kuntur Wasi** with its stone monoliths. Tours can be arranged to Kuntur Wasi in Cajamarca. You can also walk to San Pablo from Cajamarca via Cumbe Mayo; the walk takes three or four days and is described in Hilary Bradt's book.

The drive from the coast goes from desert coastal scenery to green mountains in a matter of a few hours and becomes more attractive the closer one gets to Cajamarca.

CAJABAMBA
The old route from Cajamarca to Trujillo takes 15 to 22 hours along 360 km of dirt road via Cajabamba and Huamachuco. Although this route passes through more interesting scenery and towns than the new road, bus travel is very rough and some buses travel only at night.

Cajabamba is a very quiet, pleasant small town with a 19th-century atmosphere. You'll see more mules than cars in the streets and the whitewashed houses and red-tiled roofs give the place a colonial air. There is a cinema on the pretty Plaza de Armas. The feast of La Virgen del Rosario is celebrated around the second week of October with bullfights, processions, dances and general bucolic carousing. Hotels tend to be full at this time.

Places to Stay & Eat
All hotels suffer from periodic water shortages and dim light. The best place to stay is the *Hostal Flores* on the Plaza de Armas, next to the Banco de Crédito – there is a very small sign on the door. They charge US$3 or US$4 per person. Ask for a room with a balcony onto the plaza.

The cheaper *Hotel Ramal*, Grau 624, and *Hostal Bolívar*, Ugarte 603, are both within a block of the plaza. On the street behind the Flores, at José Sabogal 692, is a cheap basic hotel without a sign (knock on the door).

There are a few passable restaurants on or near the plaza.

Getting There & Away
Travel to and from Cajabamba is by road only. Empresa Díaz, at Balta 132 on the outskirts of town, has a daily 5 am bus to Cajamarca (US$5, five hours). Transportes Atahualpa, one block from the Plaza de Armas at Alfonso Ugarte 601, has better maintained buses leaving at 5.30 am daily for Cajamarca and continuing on to Trujillo and Lima.

On the corner of Lloza and Caceres, by the main market, is Empresa Antisuyo and, nearby, Empresa Quiroz. They have daily buses to Huamachuco (US$2.50, three hours). There are also trucks leaving from the market in the morning.

HUAMACHUCO

The small town of Huamachuco is about 50 km beyond Cajabamba and 190 km from Trujillo. It has a few places to stay and an impressive Plaza de Armas.

The ruins of the pre-Inca hilltop fort of **Marcahuamachuco** lie within reach of Huamachuco itself, two to three hours away on foot.

During the dry season, you can find transport east to **Pataz**, a mining town in the Marañón valley. From Pataz, expeditions can be mounted to the little-explored ruins of various jungle cities, including the recently discovered **Gran Pajatén**. This is an undertaking for explorers and archaeologists only. The ruins are north of the recently formed Parque Nacional Río Abiseo, which has no infrastructure for travelers at this time and is very hard to get to.

West of Huamachuco, the road heads to the coast at Trujillo, passing the mining village of Shorey after 60 km. Here, a branch road to the south traverses about 40 km to the village of **Santiago de Chuco**, birthplace of César Vallejos (1892-1938) who is considered to be Peru's greatest poet. His house is now a museum.

Places to Stay & Eat

There are three or four cheap hotels in Huamachuco, the best of which is the *Hostal San Francisco*, Sánchez Carrión 380. It boasts hot water – the others don't. Rates are about US$4 per person. The *Hostal Fernando*, Bolívar 361, is a clean and basic hotel. There are others.

Most restaurants are either along Sánchez Carrión or on the Plaza de Armas.

CELENDÍN

This pleasant village is 118 km away from Cajamarca and at approximately the same altitude. However, the bus journey takes about five hours because the road is so rough and hilly. There's not much to do in Celendín and most travelers just pass through en route to Chachapoyas. There is one cinema that, when I was there in October, was unseasonably showing a film about the resurrection. Market day is Sunday. The annual fiesta, held from July 29 to August 3, coincides with the Fiestas Patrias and features bullfighting with matadors from Mexico and Spain. La Virgen del Carmen is celebrated on July 16.

Places to Stay & Eat

There are three basic hotels on the 300 block of 2 de Mayo, the cheapest of which is the *Maxmar*. It's just acceptable and some rooms even have private, if smelly, bathrooms with cold showers. A little more expensive and slightly better are the *Hotel José Gálvez* and the *Amazonas* at about US$4 per person with cold water. Best of all is the clean *Hostal Celendín* on the Plaza de Armas. It charges US$14 for a double with a toilet and sink. Hot water is available in the communal shower for a few hours a day. There are a couple of other basic hotels.

The best restaurant (though nothing to get excited about) is *Jalisco* on the Plaza de Armas.

Getting There & Away

Although both roads into Celendín are terrible, the road from Cajamarca is better than the one from Chachapoyas. Transport from Celendín to Chachapoyas consists of pick-up trucks because most buses are unable to negotiate the very demanding but beautiful road, which may be impassable during the wet season. During dry months, there may be a weekly bus, usually on Sunday. Road improvements are planned and bus connections may improve – ask in Cajamarca.

The road to Chachapoyas climbs from Celendín at 2625 meters over a 3085 meter pass before dropping steeply to the Río Marañón at **Balsas**, 62 km away from and 1600 meters lower than Celendín. From Balsas (where there is a basic pensión), the road climbs again through spectacular rain and cloud forest to emerge at the 3678-meter high point of the drive, the aptly named Abra de Barro Negro, or 'Black Mud Pass,' which gives you an idea of the road conditions during the rainy season. From the pass, the road drops to **Leimebamba** at the head of the Río Utcubamba valley and follows the river as it descends past Tingo (near the Kuélap ruins) and on to Chachapoyas. According to Peruvian road maps, the distance from Celendín to Chachapoyas is 228 km, though some travelers think it to be well under 200 km. Leimebamba has a couple of basic hotels and is surrounded by poorly known and almost unexplored ruins to tempt the truly adventurous. Chachapoyas, Tingo and Kuélap are described below.

Pick-up trucks charge around US$15 for the entire trip, depending on road conditions. They don't leave every day, so you can be stuck in Celendín for several days waiting for the next departure, particularly in the wet season. The trip can take from 12 to 24 hours, more if there's a landslide or less if projected road improvements come to fruition. The route from the coast at Chiclayo to Chachapoyas via Bagua is much more frequently traveled, though not as spectacular as the Celendín route.

Both Empresa Díaz, on the Plaza de Armas, and Transportes Atahualpa, at 2 de Mayo 630 (one block from the plaza), have daily 6.30 am departures to Cajamarca (US$5, five hours). The latter company connects with and sells tickets for their afternoon bus from Cajamarca to Trujillo and Lima.

CHACHAPOYAS

This quiet, pleasant little town of 20,000 inhabitants stands on the eastern slopes of the Andes. According to IGN maps, the altitude is 1834 meters but locals assure me it's about 2340 meters and some guide books claim 2400 meters. Anyone with an altimeter out there?

The Chachapoyan culture was conquered but not completely subdued by the Incas a few decades before the Spaniards arrived. When the Europeans showed up, local chief Curaca Huáman supposedly aided them towards their conquest. Local historians claim that San Juan de la Frontera de las Chachapoyas was the third town founded by the Spaniards in Peru (after Piura and Lima) and, at one time, was the seventh largest town of Peru.

Chachapoyas is the capital of the Department of Amazonas and, despite its name, is a mainly Andean department. It used to include the lowland regions east to the Brazilian border but, after the 1942 war with Ecuador, parts of it became the new Department of Loreto while Chachapoyas remained capital of Amazonas. The department's contact with the Amazon is chiefly through the Río Marañón, which is one of Peru's two major tributaries of the Amazon and the one which reaches furthest west into the Andes. The Marañón bisects the department and forms most of its western border with the Department of Cajamarca.

The Department of Amazonas has long been difficult to reach, and even today it remains one of the least visited areas of Peru. Along with the neighboring Department of San Martín, it contains vast tracts of the little-explored cloud forest of the Andes' eastern slopes. Within these highland forests are some of Peru's most fascinating and least known archaeological ruins. Although the ravages of weather and time and the more recent attentions of grave robbers and treasure seekers have caused damage to many of the ruins, some have survived remarkably well and can be visited by the adventurous traveler. The best known and one of the most accessible is the magnificent ruin of Kuélap, described later in this chapter. Chachapoyas provides an excellent base for visiting ruins and has been called 'the archaeological capital of Peru.'

Information

Chachapoyas is a military zone and foreign travelers have, in the past, been required to register with the PIP (see the Chachapoyas map). They simply check that your passport and tourist card are valid – it only takes a minute. In late 1994, this requirement was lifted but could become reinstated at any time.

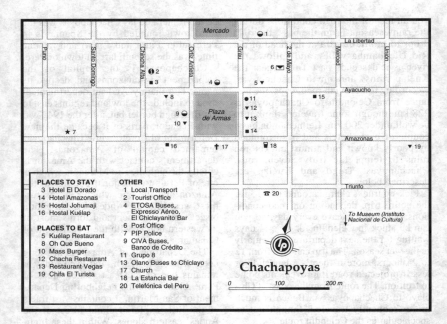

PLACES TO STAY
3 Hotel El Dorado
14 Hotel Amazonas
15 Hostal Johumaji
16 Hostal Kuélap

PLACES TO EAT
5 Kuélap Restaurant
8 Oh Que Bueno
10 Mass Burger
12 Chacha Restaurant
13 Restaurant Vegas
19 Chifa El Turista

OTHER
1 Local Transport
2 Tourist Office
4 ETOSA Buses,
  Expresso Aéreo,
  El Chiclayanito Bar
6 Post Office
7 PIP Police
9 CIVA Buses,
  Banco de Crédito
11 Grupo 8
13 Olano Buses to Chiclayo
17 Church
18 La Estancia Bar
20 Telefónica del Peru

Chachapoyas

0   100   200 m

Tourist Office A tourist office is open sometimes and moves frequently – see the map for the most recent location.

Money The Banco de Crédito will change US$ cash and traveler's checks. Several stores will change cash dollars.

Post & Telecommunications These offices are marked on the map. The area code for Chachapoyas is 074. A new telephone system was recently installed and Chachapoyas' old three-digit telephone numbers have all been prefixed with 757.

Guides & Tours Martin Antonio Olivo Chumbe (☎ 75-7212), Piura 909, can be contacted at the Reina de la Selva radio station above Expresso Aéreo. He is a recommended local guide and can take you to many local ruins, including an expedition to see the enigmatic sarcophagi (coffins in the shape of human beings) left high on a cliff wall in the jungle. Trips can last from a day to over a week if you want. He speaks Spanish and doesn't have any gear, so you need to be self sufficient with equipment.

Books A useful book about the region is *Antisuyo: The Search for the Lost Cities of the Amazon* by Gene Savoy. The British edition is entitled *Vilcabamba: The Lost City of the Incas*. This is an account of explorations in the region during the 1960s. Most professional archaeologists pooh-pooh Savoy's rather unscientific style but it makes entertaining and informative reading.

Things to See & Do
There is a small museum at the Instituto Nacional de Cultura, Merced 800. Booklets (in Spanish) about local archaeological sites may be available here as well as information about visiting archaeological sites.

Chachapoyas is a quiet, friendly town. The traditional evening pastime of strolling around the Plaza de Armas is a favorite way of relaxing and socializing.

A visit to the ruins of Kuélap is definitely the most rewarding and representative of the available trips to ruins in the area. Travelers or archaeologists who want to visit one of the scores of other sites in the Chachapoyas area should seek further information in Chachapoyas. Most trips will require at least sleeping bags and sometimes tents and food as well. One good center for exploration is Levanto, a small village about three hours walk away.

Most basic supplies can be obtained in Chachapoyas. Items such as specialized foods, camera gear and film, suntan lotion and so on are best brought with you.

Places to Stay
Chachapoyas had a new water system installed in 1994 that, one hopes, will solve the chronic water shortage problems of earlier years. The following hotels charge about US$6 per person in rooms with private bath and hot water. The *Hostal Johumaji* (☎ 75-7138), Ayacucho 711, has small, carpeted rooms with good light and is one of the best. Also good is the *Hotel El Dorado* (☎ 75-7147), Ayacucho 1062, which is clean, safe and friendly and has some rooms with up to four beds, at cheaper rates per person. A few rooms have only cold water. Also recommended is the *Hostal Kuélap* (75-7136), Amazonas 1057, which has a variety of rooms at different prices depending on whether you want a private or communal bath and hot or cold water. A cheaper option is the *Hotel Amazonas* on the main square. Some of its rooms have a view over the plaza and not all have a private bath. A new hotel is under construction on the same block as the Johumaji and may be open by the time you get there. There are a couple of cheaper and more basic pensions if you ask around.

Places to Eat
The most locally popular restaurant is the *Chacha* on the plaza – people go there to socialize as well as eat. On the other side of the plaza is *Mass Burger*, with decent

A Lively Way to Fly
Grupo 8, the military airline, has two flights a month flying Lima-Saposoa-Rodriguez de Mendoza-Chachapoyas-Chiclayo and back to Lima. These flights cost 50% less than the commercial flights and are mainly designed to aid Peruvians living in remote towns. Foreigners can get on sometimes if there is space available (not very often) and it is always easier to get on one of these flights in a town other than Lima. Flights are usually delayed but can be quite an incredible experience.

A friend tells me that Grupo 8 uses old Russian Antonovs to serve Chachapoyas. Passengers sit on benches along the fuselage walls and mountains of cargo, chickens, etc, are piled in between. On one flight, a passenger's two guinea pigs escaped. He ran up and down the plane trying to capture the animals and an air force crew member appeared demanding to know what was going on. After hearing the explanation, he replied reassuringly, 'You'd better catch them fast, because they might chew through the cables and the controls won't respond.' ■

baked goods and fruit salads, as well as the obvious burgers. Nearby, the restaurants *Vegas*, *Kuélap*, *Oh Que Bueno* and *Chifa El Turista* serve OK cheap Peruvian food. There are several other choices.

Entertainment
The evening promenade around the plaza is the main entertainment. *La Estancia* and *El Chiclayanito* are OK bars for a drink, though frequented mainly by men. At the north end of Santo Domingo is the *El Salonazo Disco*, a pretty basic dancing place.

Getting There & Away
Air An airport was built in the early '80s and flights started in 1985. Although various companies have flown here, only two are operating regular flights at this time – but this is subject to change. Expresso Aéreo has flights on Sunday and

NORTHERN HIGHLANDS

Thursday flying from Lima through Chimbote and Cajamarca to Chachapoyas. The fare from Lima is about US$104 (about the same as flying Lima to Cajamarca – weird, isn't it?) Transportes Aereos Andahuaylas (TAA) flies to Lima via Trujillo on Thursday.

Bus There are two routes from the coast. The one through Cajamarca and Celendín is more difficult but also more spectacular – it is described in the Celendín section earlier in this chapter. The more frequently traveled route from Chiclayo via Bagua normally takes 12 to 15 hours (or up to 30 hours in the wet season when landslides are possible if it has rained heavily). This route is described below.

The route follows the Panamericana north for 100 km to Olmos. From here, a paved road heads east into the Andes and climbs over the Porculla Pass which, at 2145 meters, is the lowest pass across the Peruvian Andes. The road then drops to the Río Marañón valley. About 190 km from the Panamericana turn-off, you reach **Jaén** where there are a couple of basic hotels and restaurants. The town is a few kilometers off the main road and not all buses go there. From Jaén, a rough northbound road heads to San Ignacio near the Ecuadorian border, about 100 km away. Because of the 1942 border war and continued hostilities as recently as 1995, it is not possible to enter Ecuador at this point.

After Jaén the road is unpaved, although there are plans to pave it. About 50 km beyond the Jaén turn-off on a side road is the village of **Bagua**. It is in the Marañón Valley, is Peru's most westerly jungle town, and offers basic accommodations. Because it is in a low enclosed valley (elevation about 500 meters), many Peruvians claim that Bagua is the hottest town in the country. From Bagua, a long and difficult trip can be made by road and river to Iquitos (see Saramenriza in the Amazon Basin chapter). The bus usually goes through **Bagua Grande** on the main road about 20 km away from Bagua. Buses and pick-up trucks make the

journey between Bagua Grande and Moyobamba. The road follows the Río Utcubamba valley upwards for about 70 km to the crossroads town of Pedro Ruíz, which is not marked on most maps. From here, a southbound road branches down to Chachapoyas, 54 km away. This is a poor road at this time, though has been better in the past.

In Chachapoyas, Olano, CIVA and ETOSA bus companies have daily (except Sunday) departures for Chiclayo via Bagua (US$8 to US$10).

Small minibuses and pick-up trucks leave from near the market (see map) for various destinations. About three minibuses leave early in the day to Tingo (US$2, two hours) and may continue on to Leimebamba. Later in the day this route is served by pick-up trucks. (This is also the service for Kuélap). Almost every day in the dry season, pick-up trucks depart for Leimebamba and travel on to Celendín – ask around. It can take anywhere from 12 to 24 hours to Celendín.

To continue further down the eastern slopes of the Andes into the Amazon Basin, you must first take a bus to the crossroads at Pedro Ruíz (US$2, two hours). The buses to Chiclayo will drop you off at Pedro Ruíz if they aren't full of passengers traveling further. There are also a few minibuses that make the journey. No direct buses run from Chachapoyas to Moyobamba at this time, so you have to wait in Pedro Ruíz to continue eastwards.

Other local destinations are serviced by pick-up trucks that leave from the Plaza de Armas or market areas. It's a matter of asking around.

AROUND CHACHAPOYAS
Tingo
From the village of Tingo, you can visit the important ruin of Kuélap. Tingo was badly damaged by floods in 1993, and many buildings, including a couple of cheap hotels, were destroyed. Ask locally to determine what accommodations may be available (I'm told that cheap hotels have reopened).

The *Hacienda Chillo*, about 5 km south of Tingo, has been recommended as a good place to stay, to get information about local ruins and to arrange mule hire. The owner's name is Oscar Arce – most locals know him. Clean accommodations are about US$10 per person, pricey home-cooked meals are available, but the plumbing is problematical. Hot water (indeed, any water) may or may not be available. A German anthropologist, Pieter Lerche, lives nearby and is a good source for archaeological/anthropological information about the area.

Kuélap

This immense ruined city in the mountains southeast of Chachapoyas is, for most travelers, the main reason to spend time in the region. Kuélap is the best preserved and most accessible of the major ruins in the area – note that by 'most accessible' I do not mean 'easily accessible.' Reaching the ruins takes several hours of very steep hiking from the village of Tingo, so it is remote enough to discourage casual tourists. A rarely used dirt road almost reaches the ruins, but you still have to walk for about a kilometer to get to the entrance. It's easier to arrange transportation in Chachapoyas than in Tingo. The site averages about one or two small groups of visitors per day. Hiking up into the mountains to finally emerge at Kuélap, which is not easy to see until you are almost in front of the ruins, is an exhilarating experience. The majority of the (still few) visitors hike up from Tingo.

In common with the other sites in the area, Kuélap is referred to as a pre-Inca city, though little is known about the people who built it. The Chachapoyas area was the center of a highland people, known variously as the Chachapoyans or the Sachupoyans, who were incorporated into the Inca Empire by the Inca Huayna Capac in the late 1400s. They left massive walled cities and fortresses on many of the area's mountain tops. The stonework of these sites is somewhat rougher looking than Inca stonework but is embellished with patterns and designs missing from the Inca work.

Kuélap is about 3100 meters above sea level on a ridge high above the left bank of the River Utcubamba. It is an oval-shaped city about 600 meters long and entirely surrounded by a massive defensive wall six to eight meters high. Three entrances pierce this wall. The principal entrance, and the one used today to gain access to the site, leads into an impressive, funnel-shaped, high-walled passageway. This is a highly defensible entrance; it would have been well-nigh impossible for attackers to scale these high walls without being repulsed by projectiles from the defenders perched high on the walls. Once inside the site, the visitor will find about 300 or 400 buildings, most of which are round. One, named *El Tintero* (the inkpot), is a mysterious underground chamber where, it is locally said, pumas were kept and human sacrifices were thrown in. Another is a lookout tower. The views are excellent.

Information The guardians at Kuélap are very friendly and helpful. At least one of them is almost always on hand to show visitors around and answer questions. When I was there, I was helped by Don José Gabriel Portocarrero Chávez. He gave me a guided tour of the ruins and his wife cooked me a meal. He is a good source of information on this and other ruins in the area.

The small hotel on the site is run by the guardians. It has a few very cheap beds but, if there are more of you, sleeping on the floor is no problem (bring sleeping bags). If you have a tent, camping is also possible. You should carry or purify water, though soft drinks are usually for sale. Basic food is available – but bringing your own is still a good idea. A small tip or present for the guardians is appreciated – flashlight batteries, a magazine or newspaper, chocolate or canned (or other) food are good gifts.

Entry to the site is US$4.

Getting There & Away Several vehicles a day travel from Chachapoyas to Tingo, where locals can point out the path to you.

You can hire mules to take you or your gear up to the ruins, but most people walk.

The trail climbs from the south end of Tingo at 1900 meters to the ruins about 1200 meters above. There are some signposts on the way and the trail is not very difficult to follow; the main problem is the steepness of the climb. It takes about five hours to climb to Kuélap, so it's best to spend the night there. If you leave Chachapoyas in the morning, you can reach the ruins by midafternoon. Remember to bring water because there is little available at Kuélap and none on the trail. During the rainy season (October to April), especially the latter half, the trail can become very muddy and travel difficult.

PEDRO RUÍZ TO RIOJA

Pedro Ruíz is the small village at the junction of the road to Chachapoyas from the Bagua to Moyobamba road. For some reason that I haven't figured out, Pedro Ruíz is not marked on most maps. If traveling from Chachapoyas, you usually have to wait here for vehicles to Rioja and Moyobamba. If arriving in the afternoon, you may need to spend the night at Pedro Ruíz before continuing the rough journey eastward. There are a couple of cheap and basic hotels. One, the *Hotel Amazonas*, next to the police station, is clean but has only cold showers. Rates here are US$4/6. The town's electricity gets cut off in the middle of the night, so pack in the evening if planning a pre-dawn departure.

Very crowded and uncomfortable pick-up trucks travel from Pedro Ruíz to Rioja every hour or two throughout the morning and early afternoon. These vehicles come from Bagua and are often full to overflowing when they arrive (I counted 33 people in the back of the Datsun pick-up I rode on). They claim that the journey takes six hours but it often takes more like nine hours, longer in the wet season when landslides can close the road.

More comfortable buses with two companies, Jesus Luz del Mundo and Olano, leave Pedro Ruíz at 4 and 5 am and take about 10 to 12 hours to Moyobamba

(US$7.50) and 14 to 16 hours to Tarapoto. Large trucks also do the journey but are much slower. If you're lucky, you might get onto one of the daily buses plying this route from the coast, but these are often full. Ask the locals what time the buses are expected to come through.

The journey east from Pedro Ruíz is spectacular – the road climbs over two major passes and drops into fantastic high jungle vegetation in between. It's definitely worth traveling this section in daylight, though the very rough road and uncomfortable, overcrowded conditions sometimes make appreciating the beauty of the landscape a bit difficult.

About two hours (depending on your form of transport) east of Pedro Ruíz is Laguna Pomacocha. Just before the lake is the village of **Florida**, where there is a basic cheap hotel used by truck drivers. Just beyond the lake is the village of **Balzapata**. Pick-up trucks and minibuses provide service between Pedro Ruíz and Balzapata (US$2.50) several times a day during daylight hours. Balzapata is on a ridge overlooking the lake, has a few cheap hotels and restaurants and is a nicer place to spend the night than Pedro Ruíz. You can catch the Moyobamba-bound buses that left Pedro Ruíz at 4 and 5 am as they come through Balzapata two hours later.

A brand-new town built in the 1970s, **Nueva Cajamarca** is inhabited by colonists from the highlands. It has a couple of basic cheap hotels. Tired travelers can stop here – the hotels are reportedly safer than in Rioja. From Nueva Cajamarca, pick-up trucks and minibuses leave frequently along the improved road to Rioja. The fare for the 45-minute trip is about US$1.50.

RIOJA

Rioja is the first town of importance on the road heading inland across the Andes from the Panamericana. It is a small but busy town. The nearby airport serves both Rioja and nearby Moyobamba, the capital of the Department of San Martín. Both towns were severely damaged by earthquake on May 29, 1990, and again in a smaller quake in 1991, but they have been partly rebuilt since then.

Places to Stay

There are two or three basic hotels along Avenida Grau. The *Hostal San Martín*, Grau 540, about a block from the Plaza de Armas, is just acceptable at about US$4 per person. The best is the *Hostal Residencial Vanessa* at Faustino Maldonado 505. I'd go on to Moyobamba for a better selection.

Getting There & Away

Air Aero Continente has flights to and from Lima via Tarapoto on Monday, Tuesday, Thursday and Saturday. Faucett has similar flights on Monday and Friday. Imperial Air flies on Sunday via Juanjui and Tarapoto. These schedules are definitely subject to change. Other destinations are occasionally served. The fare from Lima is US$90. Taxis to the airport leave from the Plaza de Armas.

Bus Pick-up trucks leave for Pedro Ruíz and Bagua from the corner of the Plaza de Armas. Both pick-up trucks and plenty of minibuses leave from the plaza for Moyobamba (US$1, 30 minutes) and on to Tarapoto.

MOYOBAMBA

A good road links Rioja, at 1400 meters, with the small town of Moyobamba, at 860 meters. Moyobamba is the capital of the Department of San Martín and was one of the first towns to be founded in the Peruvian eastern lowlands, soon after the conquest. Moyobamba used to be a pleasant town, but the 1990 and 1991 earthquakes did serious damage. There are still many collapsed buildings visible.

Information

There is no tourist office but you can try asking at the Instituto Naciónal de Cultura (INC) for information. They also have a very small exhibit of local stuffed animals, including many frogs in little costumes, if you're interested.

Money can be changed at the Banco de Crédito, but traveler's checks may be a problem.

The area code for Moyobamba is 094.

Things to See & Do

The local **hot springs** or *baños termales* are about an hour's walk south of town on the Jepelacio road – ask anyone for directions. A mototaxi will cost about US$1 or

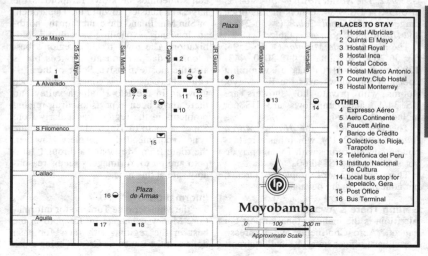

PLACES TO STAY
1 Hostal Albricias
2 Quinta El Mayo
3 Hostal Royal
8 Hostal Inca
10 Hostal Cobos
11 Hostal Marco Antonio
17 Country Club Hostal
18 Hostal Monterrey

OTHER
4 Expresso Aéreo
5 Aero Continente
6 Faucett Airline
7 Banco de Crédito
9 Colectivos to Rioja, Tarapoto
12 Telefónica del Peru
13 Instituto Nacional de Cultura
14 Local bus stop for Jepelacio, Gera
15 Post Office
16 Bus Terminal

Moyobamba

0   100   200 m
Approximate Scale

take a Jepelacio bus. There are both hot and cold swimming pools and the place is overcrowded at weekends. Admission is US30¢ and they are open till 10 pm.

The **Cataratas del Gera** are quite impressive waterfalls near the Gera hydro-electric project. They can be visited with a free permit available from the offices of Proyecto Especial Huallaga Central y Bajo Mayo, on the main road into town. Take a bus to Jepelacio (US$1.50) and then it's a one to two hour walk, though you may be able to find a ride. Ask anyone in Jepelacio. Go in the morning so as not to get stranded on the way back.

Places to Stay & Eat

Several new hotels have opened since the quake and a few old ones have survived. The cheapest is the *Quinta El Mayo*, which charges US$3/5 and has shared showers. The basic *Hostal Monterrey* (☎ 56-2145) charges US$5/6 for rooms with private cold showers. Better rooms are available at the *Country Club Hostal*, which charges US$7/12 and has private baths and a garden. One of the nicest cheap hotels is the clean *Hostal Albricias* (☎ 56-2142), which also has a garden and charges US$9/12. The *Hostal Royal* (☎ 56-2564) is also OK at US$9/14. Others in this price range are the *Hostal Cobos* (☎ 56-2153) and *Hostal Inca*, both acceptable.

The *Hotel Puerto Mirador* (☎ 56-2594, fax 56-2050; in Lima ☎ 442-3090, 442-1298, fax 442-4180) has a swimming pool and fine views over the Río Mayo. Rooms with private hot showers are US$34/47 and bungalows are US$66, including breakfast.

The best hotel is the *Hostal Marco Antonio* (☎ 56-2319), which has a restaurant and decent rooms with TV and private hot showers for US$40/60.

There are plenty of simple restaurants, but none of them are outstanding.

Getting There & Away

Air Rioja is the main regional airport but Faucett, Aero Continente and Expresso Aéreo have offices here. A smaller airport in Moyobamba started operating with a few scheduled flights in 1995. The most recent information is that Expresso Aéreo has three flights a week from Tarapoto and Imperial Air has one flight a week from Lima via Juanjui and Tarapoto. This is definitely subject to change.

Bus & Colectivo Colectivos (shared cars and vans) to Rioja (US$1.50, 45 minutes) and Tarapoto (US$7, 3½ hours) leave about every 30 minutes from the taxi rank on Canga. Colectivos to Nuevo Cajamarca (U$2.50, 1½ hours) also leave frequently. Local buses to Jepelacio and Gera leave from the stop on Varcadillo.

The bus terminal on the Plaza de Armas has daily departures for Chiclayo (US$14) at 1 pm. Buses to Tarapoto are US$4 and take about five hours. Buses from Tarapoto to Chicalyo stop here as well – ask about hours.

TARAPOTO

From Moyobamba, the road drops still further down the Río Mayo valley to Tarapoto, 356 meters above sea level, on the very edge of the eastern Andean foothills. It is a 116 km journey but the road was damaged in the earthquake and the going can sometimes be slow. Tarapoto is the largest and busiest town in the Department of San Martín and the center for the northern lowlands' expanding agricultural colonization. The town has the region's best accommodations and air services but is also the most expensive. Some of the agricultural expansion has come from the coca growing in the Río Huallaga valley and there have been reports of drug-related problems in the region, particularly from Saposoa south to Tingo María. That route is not recommended to travelers. However, the route from Moyobamba through Tarapoto and on to Yurimaguas seems reasonably safe at this time.

Information

Try the Ministerio de Turismo for information. Money exchange in Tarapoto is the best in the region, with rates for cash dollars at the Banco de Crédito being close

Tarapoto

0   125   250 m

To Yurimaguas

To Moyobamba

PLACES TO STAY		PLACES TO EAT	OTHER	
2 Hostal Misti	27 Hostal El Dorado	1 El Camarón	4 Minibuses to Juanjui	25 Guadalupe Buses
3 Hotel Tarapoto	28 Hostal Meléndez	5 Restaurant Real	6 Post Office	26 Ministerio de Turismo
7 Hotel Acosta	30 Hostal Lily	9 La Terraza Café	12 Local Museum	29 Cruz de Chalpón
8 Hostal Las Palmeras	31 Hostal Viluz	11 El Farolito	13 Telefónica del Peru	Buses
10 Hostal Central		16 La Mesón Restaurant	14 Aero Continente,	32 La Perla Buses
17 Hostal San Antonio			Expresso Aéreo	
18 Hotel Edinson			15 Faucett Airline	
20 Hostal San Martín			18 Imperial Air	
21 Hostal Miami			19 Banco de Crédito	
22 Hostal Juan Alfonso			23 Trucks to Yurimaguas,	
24 Hostal Pasquelandia			Juanjui, Laguna Sauce	

to Lima rates, except when a flood of drug-related dollars hits, in which case rates may drop 2% or so. Traveler's checks can be exchanged. Street changers hang out in front of the bank. The area code for Tarapoto is 094.

Things to See & Do

There is not much to do in Tarapoto itself apart from hanging out in the Plaza de Armas or visiting the small local museum just off the plaza, but there are a few local excursions.

A few small travel agencies have opened on or near the Plaza de Armas and can provide information and buses to most of the following places. Nearby **Lamas** is worth a day trip. This interesting Indian village is well off the normal tourist circuit and has an early morning market, a small museum and a reasonable restaurant, but no hotels. The **Laguna de Sauce** is a popular local destination reached by crossing the Río Huallaga on a raft. There is good swimming here and expensive bungalows are available (see Places to Stay).

Cheaper, and easier to reach by public transport, is **Laguna Venecia** and the nearby **Cataratas de Ahuashiyacu**, about 45 minutes away on the road to Yurimaguas. A small restaurant is nearby and a 10 minute walk takes you to a locally favored swimming spot.

Motorcycles can be hired at or near the Plaza de Armas at about US$3 per hour (bargain for multi-hour discounts).

A recent attraction is running the **Río Mayo**, 30 km from Tarapoto. Trips are fairly short and easy and inexpensive. One outfitter with modern rafting equipment is Los Chancas Expeditions (☎ 52-2616, fax 52-5279), Jirón Rioja 357. A 90 minute run on Class III rapids costs from US$15 and can be done year round. Multi-day adventures are offered from July through September. They are planning to make inflatable kayaks available for the 1996 season.

Places to Stay – bottom end
None of the hotels in town have hot water at this time. Some of the cheaper hotels have water available at only certain times of the day, so ask about this if you're desperate for a shower. Many hotels have mosquito netting in the windows, but no glass, which makes them extra noisy from street traffic.

The *Hostal Juan Alfonso* (☎ 52-2179) charges US$3.50/5.50 for basic singles/doubles with communal cold showers and US$5/7.50 for rooms with private showers and is one of the better cheap hotels. The staff is friendly. Other basic places at about this price include the *Hostal Meléndez* and *Hostal Las Palmeras*, both with communal showers only, and the *Hostal Pasquelandia* (☎ 52-2290), which has rooms with or without private bath and has fans in every room. The *Hostal Misti* (☎ 52-2439) has a shower and fan in every room. The *Hostal Central* (☎ 52-2234) is clean and reasonable and all rooms have private bath and fan, although the disco next door can be very loud. The *Hostal El Dorado* is not much better but charges about US$6/10 for rooms with private shower. The clean *Hostal Viluz* is similarly priced.

The recommended *Hostal San Antonio* has clean rooms with private shower, fan and cable TV (with some US channels) for US$10/12.50. The *Hotel Tarapoto* (☎ 52-2150) charges US$10/15 and is also quite good, but doesn't offer TV. Other clean and OK places in this price range are the *Hostal Miami* (☎ 52-238) and the *Hostal San Martín*, which will give you a discount if you stay for a few days.

Places to Stay – middle
A recommended hotel near the town center is the *Hotel Acosta* (☎ 52-3145; in Lima 444-4454, fax 446-5505), which has comfortable rooms with cable TV for US$24/32, including breakfast. The good *Hotel Edinson* (☎ 52-2723, 52-2293, fax 52-4153, in Lima 436-9214) is similarly priced and has cable TV and air-con, but the rooms aren't quite as nice.

The *Hotel Río Shilcayo* (☎ 52-2225, fax 52-4236; in Lima ☎ 447-9359) is almost 2 km out of town at Pasaje Las Flores 224, just off Jirón Pablo Cruz. It is quiet and cool and has a swimming pool that is free for hotel residents and open to others for a small fee. Rates are about US$40/50, including breakfast. The best downtown place is the *Hostal Lily* (☎ 52-3154, 52-3341, fax 52-2394), Pimental 405, with a swimming pool, air-con, cable TV and rooms for US$40/58 including breakfast – but still no hot water.

A new resort hotel, *Puerto Palmeras* (☎ 52-3978, in Lima 472-1257), opened in 1995. It's 3 km south of town on the road to Juanjui. It claims to be the most luxurious in the department and charges about US$80. The same company operates the similarly priced *Puerto Patos Sauce Lodge* (same phone) at the Laguna de Sauce.

Places to Eat
El Mesón and *La Terraza*, both on the Plaza de Armas, have decent set lunches and are among the cheaper places in this pricey town. Nearby, the *El Farolito* opens in the afternoon and has sandwiches, burgers and pizzas and is a place to hang out. If you are

economizing, head to the market area for the cheapest restaurants. The best restaurants are *El Camarón* and *Restaurant Real*, both preparing the local giant river shrimp in various ways.

Entertainment
El Papillón and *Las Rocas* are locally popular night clubs in the Morales district. A mototaxi can take you there at night for under US$2.

Getting There & Away
Air The busy Tarapoto airport is one of the most important airports in northern Peru. There are no buses going to town, 2 or 3 km away; a mototaxi will cost about US$1.50. The major airlines have offices in central Tarapoto or at the airport. In addition, smaller airlines have offices at the airport and offer frequent light-aircraft flights to several jungle destinations.

Aero Continente and Faucett both have daily nonstop flights from Lima (US$89, about one hour). Imperial Air has five flights a week from Lima, stopping in either Juanjui or Pucallpa. Expresso Aéreo has a daily flight from Lima, stopping in about five jungle towns en route and taking about 3½ hours. Aero Continente has several flights a week to Rioja, Yurimaguas (US$28), Iquitos (US$62), Trujillo (US$67) and Chiclayo (US$67). Faucett flies to Iquitos, Rioja and Yurimagus two or three times a week. Imperial Air has three weekly flights to Pucallpa (US$54) and one or two flights a week to Juanjui, Rioja and Moyobamba. Expresso Aéreo's milk runs provide connections to Huánuco, Tingo María (US$55), Juanjui, Tocache, Saposoa, Bellavista, Moyobamba, Pucallpa, Chiclayo and Trujillo.

AeroTaxi Iberico has an office at the airport and flies light aircraft to Yurimaguas (US$40), Juanjui, Tocache and other jungle towns. These are good alternatives to the difficult journeys by road, but remember that there isn't much room for baggage and you may have to pay for an extra seat if you're lugging a huge backpack around. AeroTaxi Iberico doesn't take

reservations – just go to the airport in the morning. Flights leave as soon as the plane is full. Most have five passenger seats, so it doesn't take long for them to fill up. Departures start around 9 am and continue all day – it's a great way to see some of the jungle from the air. When I flew from Tarapoto to Tocache, the pilot pointed out what he claimed were clandestine airstrips used by drug runners. In this respect, the area is becoming increasingly dangerous – make local inquiries.

You can charter a flight to other jungle destinations – you have to pay for all five passenger seats but that's no problem if you can get a group together.

If you have to spend a few hours at the airport, an inexpensive snack bar sells sandwiches and ice-cold beer.

Bus Tarapoto is an important junction. From here, roads head west to Moyobamba, north to Yurimaguas and the Amazon Basin, and south to Juanjui and Tingo María, in descending order of road quality.

The southbound journey via Bellavista to Juanjui (145 km) and on to Tocache and Tingo María (485 km) is not recommended because of drug-running problems and because the road is in very bad shape – several bridges have not yet been repaired since the Sendero blew them up in the early 1990s. The trip to Juanjui takes about eight hours in colectivo taxis, minibuses and trucks, which often travel in convoys for greater safety. The journey to Tingo María takes about two or three days and should be broken at Juanjui or Tocache (described below) if you take it at all. Definitely don't travel at night. I would fly if you want to see these places. Tingo María is described in the Central Highlands chapter.

Heading west from Tarapoto to Moyobamba takes about three to four hours in Comité 1 colectivo taxis. They leave from the eighth block of Ramon Castilla and charge US$7 per person. Cheaper and slower minibuses and pick-up trucks also make the trip but leave less frequently. A block away is the taxi and pick-up truck stand for Lamas (US$2.50, one hour).

A Tough Drive

I had a memorable trip from Tarapoto to Yurimaguas. I was waiting at the usual departure point when a man offered me a ride to Yurimaguas. I couldn't see any trucks or jeeps, but he told me he was ready to go right away and pointed to a Volkswagen standing a few meters away. I looked at it in disbelief – how was a little VW going to negotiate a road that buses didn't dare attempt? Nevertheless, the thought of riding in comfort soon overcame my worries and I climbed in.

The road was absolutely terrible. The driver couldn't get out of first gear and, when he tried using second, the car would invariably stall. While we moved along at walking pace, the driver told me the story of his trip. The car was new – he had bought it in Lima and was driving it to Yurimaguas, a distance of well over 2000 km. He was planning to ship it from Yurimaguas to Iquitos, where it would be sold as new at the Iquitos VW dealership. I was amazed by the story and asked why he didn't just air freight it from Lima to Iquitos. I was told that driving it over 2000 km of bad road plus several days on the river was cheaper.

At last, we managed to get over the final pass and were on the flat 60 km stretch to Yurimaguas. The driver became very confident and even managed to get into third gear. While we splashed through the few puddles in the road, the driver happily began telling me that the worst part was over and we were as good as there. Unfortunately, one of the puddles turned out to be extremely deep and, just as the driver was blithely telling me how close we were to Yurimaguas, the vehicle sank almost up to its windows and the engine stopped. Despondently, the driver opened the door to see how bad the situation was and a 30-cm wall of water gushed into the car. So much for delivering a new car to the Iquitos dealership!

We tried pushing it out, but to no avail – the car was well and truly stuck. After about two hours, a large truck came along (giving you an idea of the frequency of traffic on this road) and pulled the car out. Another two hours were spent drying the starter and engine. Finally, we managed to get the car started and sputtered into Yurimaguas. Here, the driver dried out and cleaned up the car as best he could before arranging river transport to Iquitos. I guess the moral of that story is 'Don't buy a new car in Iquitos.' ∎

There is talk of moving these departure points even further out of town.

Guadalupe, Cruz de Chalpón, La Perla and Paredes Estrella have big old buses to the coast on most days. It takes about 36 hours to Chiclayo (US$20) and 48 hours to Lima (US$32). You have to be a real masochist to want to put yourself through a ride like this – break it up.

Pick-up trucks and other vehicles for Yurimaguas leave from the end of Jirón Ursua and take four to six hours in the dry season, possibly a lot more in the wet. The fare is about US$7 in the back (mind the sunburn), or US$9 in the cabin. Though vehicles leave several times a day, I'd leave early in the morning to enjoy the scenery and avoid the hottest hours. The 130 km road climbs over the final foothills of the Andes, and emerges on the Amazonian plains before continuing on to Yurimaguas. It is one of the most beautiful drives in the area. For more information about Yurimaguas and river travel into the jungle, see the Amazon Basin chapter.

BELLAVISTA, JUANJUI & TOCACHE

These are the main towns in the Río Huallaga valley between Tarapoto and Tingo María. The area is one of the most expensive in Peru and a story circulates that everything is priced in dollars. This is where much of Peru's clandestine coca and marijuana crops are produced so the area is not recommended at this time. The worst section of road is reportedly between Juanjui and Tocache and the most dangerous part is from Tocache to Tingo María.

Southwest of Juanjui is the Río Abiseo, a tributary of the Huallaga. This river is within the Parque Nacional Río Abiseo, a very remote area of a quarter of a million hectares more accessible from Huamachuco (see earlier in this chapter).

East of the Río Huallaga is the Reserva Forestal Biabo-Cordillera Azul, an officially protected area of over a million hectares. It has no infrastructure that I know of.

Places to Stay

The best hotel in Bellavista is the *Hostal Cardenas*, San Martín 599, and the best in Juanjui is the *Hostal Capricornio*, Peña Meza 1185. There are others. Tocache has four basic hotels: the *Bolívar, Sucre, San Martín* and *Comercio*. The showers don't always work but the hotels still are often full. Try to get into town early or you'll end up sleeping on the floor in one of the hotel lobbies.

Getting There & Away

All three towns have an airport and flying is the recommended way to reach them (see Tarapoto for flight details). Also see Tarapoto for a description of the road, which is not recommended.

The Amazon Basin

About half of Peru is in the Amazon Basin, yet it merits only one chapter in this book. Why is this? The answer is inaccessibility. Few roads penetrate the rainforest of the Amazon Basin and, therefore, few towns of any size have been built. Those that exist started as river ports and were connected with towns further downstream, usually in Brazil or perhaps Bolivia. Only a few decades ago, the traveler from Peru's major jungle port of Iquitos had to travel thousands of kilometers down the Río Amazonas to the Atlantic and then go either south around Cape Horn or north through the Panama Canal to reach Lima – a journey taking several months. With the advent of roads and airports, these jungle areas have slowly become a more important part of Peru. Nevertheless, they still contain only about 5% of the nation's population.

Five main jungle areas are accessible to the traveler. Starting in the southeast, near the Bolivian border, the first of these is Puerto Maldonado, which lies at the junction of the Tambopata and Madre de Dios rivers. Puerto Maldonado is most easily reached by air (there are daily flights from Cuzco) or by an atrociously bad dirt road (an uncomfortable two- or three-day journey by truck). West of Puerto Maldonado is Parque Nacional Manu, which is more easily accessible from Cuzco.

In central Peru, almost due east of Lima, is the area known as Chanchamayo. It consists of the two small towns of San Ramón and La Merced, both easily accessible by road from Lima, and several nearby villages.

A new jungle road has almost been completed from La Merced north to the important port of Pucallpa, the capital of the Department of Ucayali and the third region described in this section. Most travelers to Pucallpa, however, take better roads from Lima via Huánuco and Tingo María, or fly.

Further north is the small port of Yurimaguas, reached from the North Coast by road (the difficult journey is described in Across the Northern Highlands) or by air from Lima.

Finally, travelers can reach Peru's major jungle port, Iquitos, by river boat from Pucallpa and Yurimaguas or by air from Lima and other cities. It is impossible to reach Iquitos by road.

PUERTO MALDONADO

Founded at the turn of the century, Puerto Maldonado has been important as a rubber boom town, a logging center, and more recently as a center for gold and oil prospectors. It is also important for jungle crops such as Brazil nuts and coffee. Because of the logging industry, the jungle around Puerto Maldonado has been almost totally cleared. There is also some ranching.

The various commercial enterprises centered on Puerto Maldonado have made it the most important port and capital of the Department of Madre de Dios. It is an unlovely, fast-growing town with a busy frontier feel and a population of about 17,000. It is interesting to experience this boom-town atmosphere, but otherwise there isn't much to see. Puerto Maldonado can be used as a starting point for trips into the jungle. The best of these are at the nearby jungle lodges. It is also possible to continue into the Brazilian or Bolivian jungle or to Parque Nacional Manu, but these trips are not straightforward.

Information
Immigration If you're attempting to leave Peru via Iñapari (for Brazil) or Puerto Heath (for Bolivia), check first with immigration officials in Puerto Maldonado or Cuzco – recently, exit stamps were not obtainable at the borders. In Puerto Maldonado, the migraciones office is found in the riverside complex opposite the Hotel

432

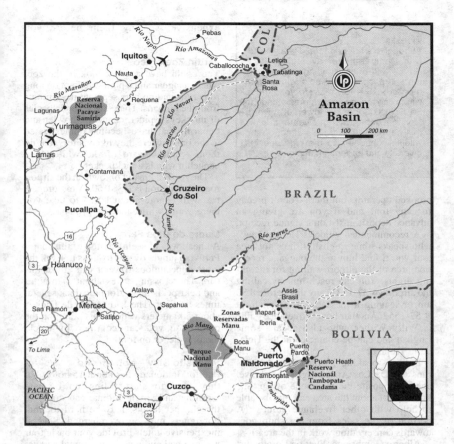

Moderno. Foreign visitors can extend their visas or tourist cards here for the standard US$20 fee. They like to give you just 30 days but will give you 90 if you are politely insistent. If you're flying from Cuzco to Iñapari, check with migraciones in Cuzco.

There is no Bolivian or Brazilian consul at this time (though there has been a Bolivian consul in the past).

Money The Banco de Crédito on the Plaza de Armas will change US cash dollars or traveler's checks. You can also try the Banco de la Nación on the same block, or a casa de cambio on the corner of Puno and G Prada. Brazilian cruzeiros and Bolivian pesos are hard to negotiate.

Post & Telecommunications The offices are shown on the map. The area code for Puerto Maldonado is 084 (the same as for Cuzco).

Tour Guides Many visitors arrive with a prearranged tour, staying at one of the jungle lodges described below. If you're not one of these visitors, you can arrange a tour when you arrive. Beware that there are

Friajes

Although it's hot and humid year round, with temperatures averaging 81°F (27°C) and often climbing above 90°F, there are occasional cold winds from the Andes. Known as *friajes*, these winds can make temperatures plunge to 50°F (9°C) or even lower. It's worth having a light jacket or sweater in case this happens. The friaje's effect on the wildlife contibutes to the high species diversity and endemism of the region. ■

crooked operators out there – don't prepay for any tour and if you are giving an advance deposit, insist on a signed receipt.

A recommended guide is Hernan Llave who speaks some English. If he's not on a tour you'll find him in the baggage reception area of the airport waiting for incoming flights. You can reach him by calling the airport (☎ 57-1531) any day before 8.30 am or leaving a message, in Spanish, at ☎ 57-1552. Another honest freelance guide is Willy Wither, who also speaks some English and can be contacted at the Heladería Tropico.

English-speaking María Luisa Angeles runs the De Los Angeles gift shop/travel agency opposite the telephone office. She knows a lot about the area and may be able to help with other freelance guides. (A portion of the sales from her shop goes towards conservation work in the area.)

Alberto Gombringer lives on Loreto, just off the Plaza de Armas towards the river. He is well known locally and has a two-story hacienda near a lake, several hours down the Madre de Dios, from where he organizes excursions.

The *motorista* (boatman) Victor Yarikawa, and guides Alberto Amachi, Arturo Balarezo, Benigno Diaz, Arturo Revilla and Victorio Suárez are other possibilities.

Other There's not much to do apart from shoot pool in one of the many pool halls (mainly frequented by men). Personal items such as film, soap and batteries are expensive, so buy them before you arrive.

Jardín Zoológico
You could have a quick look in the zoo, where a jaguar and a puma are kept on long rope runs and no bars separate the animals from the humans. There are several species of monkeys (spider, capuchin, howler and tamarin) that have become domesticated to the point where they like visitors to hold them – but beware of the white-faced capuchin who is a pickpocket.

The zoo is 2 km out of town on the airport road. Admission is US$1.50. A motorcycle taxi will charge about US$4 to take you there, wait a while, and bring you back.

Madre de Dios Ferry
A cheap way of seeing a little of this major Peruvian jungle river is to cross it. Even the most impecunious traveler can afford this trip. The crossing takes about 5 minutes and peki-pekis leave from the dock several times an hour. The Río Madre de Dios is about 500 meters wide at this point; on the other side you can continue by truck, motorcycle, or on foot.

Places to Stay – bottom end
Puerto Maldonado has about 15 hotels but they tend to start filling up by late morning and single rooms, especially in the cheaper hotels, may be hard to find. Foreigners may be overcharged. Several inexpensive hotels provide your basic four walls, a bed and a cold communal shower for about US$2.50 or US$3 per person. One of the best of these is the *Hostal Moderno*, which is friendly and clean but run down and has very thin walls and can be noisy. It has a café attached, as does the *Hostal Español*. The *Hotel Oriental*, a typical, basic Amazonian hotel with a tin roof and rough wooden walls painted an unappealing green, is described by one visitor as hostile and with a bad atmosphere. The *Hostal Chávez* is the cheapest in town at US$2 per person and it looks it. Other cheapies to try are the *Hotel Tambo de Oro, Hotel Central* and *Hotel Cross*,

which aren't too bad and have some rooms with private bath for about US$5/8. Also at this price is the *Hotel El Astro*, which is OK but has small rooms.

The recommended *Hotel Wilson* (☎ 57-1296), G Prada 355, has long had a reputation for being the best value hotel in the town center. It has clean rooms with communal showers for US$3.50 per person, singles/doubles with private cold shower and fan for US$6/10, and a basic cafeteria and pool room on the premises. Some rooms actually have a bit of a view. If you make an advance reservation, you'll be charged twice as much. The *Hotel Rey Port* is similarly priced and is just adequate. The *Hostal Royal Inn* has large clean rooms with private bath for US$6/10. Others in this price range are the *Hostal Gamboa* and *Hotel del Solar*.

Places to Stay – middle

The *Hostal Cabaña Quinta* (☎ 57-1863, 57-1864), Cuzco 535, is the best in the town center and has a decent restaurant and friendly staff. Rooms with fans are US$6/10 and with fans and private cold shower are US$10/16.

About a kilometer southwest of the town center on Jirón Velarde and pleasantly located above the banks of the Río Tambopata, is the *Cadena Hotelera Turística Puerto Maldonado* (☎ 57-1029, fax 57-1323; in Lima ☎ 224-0263, fax 224-8581). They charge US$35/30 for clean singles/doubles with cold shower, fan and air-conditioning. There is an adequate restaurant that opens on demand.

Outside Puerto Maldonado are some jungle lodges, described later in this section.

Places to Eat

There are no fancy restaurants in Puerto Maldonado and most are fairly basic. *Huasoroco* has a nice atmosphere and serves typical Peruvian food. *El Mirador* has a cool, screened-in dining area that overlooks the Río Madre de Dios and they have a peña on Friday nights. *La Cusqueñita* is clean and has a good variety

of dishes. *El Tenedor* and *Chifa Wa-Seng* are also satisfactory cheap places and there are many others that offer a set meal for as low as US$1.

Heladería Tropico has a friendly and helpful staff. They serve juices and ice creams made from local fruits as well salads and hamburgers. It's the only place in town that prepares well-balanced vegetarian food. They also donate a portion of their profits to local conservation work.

A little way from the town center (10 minutes' walk), by the pioneer cemetery (itself a tourist attraction) on Piura near Cuzco, is the local restaurant *El Califa*; taxi drivers know it. This place is only open for lunch and usually serves regional dishes. Get there early for the best selection of food.

In the Mercado Modelo look for homemade hot chocolate and other jungle staples such as fariña, a muesli-like yucca concoction eaten fried or mixed in lemonade. Also in the market, look out for children selling hot, fresh *pan de arroz* in the early morning (7 to 8 am). This bread is made from rice flour, yucca and butter and takes three days to prepare.

Regional specialities include *juanes* (fish or chicken steamed in a banana leaf with rice or yucca), *chocana* (a broth of fish chunks flavored with the native cilantro herb) and *parrillada de la selva* (a barbecue of marinated meat in a Brazil-nut sauce). The banana-like plantain (*plátano*) is served boiled or fried as a side dish to many meals.

Getting There & Away

Most people fly from Cuzco; this is cheap and convenient. The road or river-trips are only for adventurous travelers who are prepared to put up with both discomfort and delay.

Air The airport is about 7 km out of town. Colectivos leave from the airport after plane arrivals and charge about US$1. Motorcycle taxis cost about US$3.50 or US$4.

PLACES TO STAY
4   Hostal Moderno
6   Hotel Oriental
13 Hostal Cabaña Quinta
14 Hostal Chávez
16 Hotel Rey Port
17 Hostal Español
19 Hostal Royal Inn
22 Hotel Tambo de Oro
24 Hotel del Solar
28 Hotel Wilson
30 Hotel Central,
    Hotel El Astro
33 Hostal Gamboa
34 Hotel Cross

PLACES TO EAT
3   El Mirador
8   El Califa
10 Heladería Tropico
15 El Tenedor
18 Chifa Wa-Seng
21 Huasoroco
32 La Cusqueñita

OTHER
1   River Boat Hire
2   Migraciones
5   AeroPerú Airline
7   Imperial Air
9   Banco de la Nación
11 Banco de Crédito
12 Explorer's Inn Office
20 Americana Airline
23 AeroSul
25 Telefónica del Peru
26 De Los Angeles Agency
27 Casa de Cambio
29 Motorcycle Hire
31 Post Office
35 Trucks to Cuzco,
    buses to Laberinto

Puerto Maldonado

0   100   200 m

There are daily scheduled flights every morning to and from Lima via Cuzco with either AeroPerú, Americana or Imperial Air but these may be cancelled because of rain (the wet season is December to April, but cancellations are possible at other times), so allow some flexibility in your schedule. Flights to Lima cost about US$108, to Cuzco about US$44, and there is the usual US$4 departure tax for nonresidents. Imperial Air offers discounted fares but doesn't fly every day. The airline offices are shown on the map.

Grupo 8 has one flight a week to Iberia on Thursday and occasionally flies to Iñapari. (It is a 7 km walk from the Iñapari airstrip to the village.) Flights are subject to delay, cancellation or overbooking. Grupo 8 can be contacted at the Cuzco and Puerto Maldonado airports. If you want to fly, get to the airport early on the day of the flight and be persistent.

AeroSul has an office in Puerto Maldonado (see map) and you can charter light aircraft to anywhere as long as you pay for five seats and the return trip. This service has been offered by a number of companies in the past – AeroSul is the latest of them.

If you can't find them in town, go to the airport in the morning and ask about charter companies.

Truck Ha! You noticed – the heading doesn't read 'Bus.' During the dry season, trucks to Cuzco leave from the Mercado Modelo on E Rivero. Although it's only about 500 km, the road is so rough the trip takes three days or more, depending on weather conditions. A Peruvian road engineer I met in Chiclayo told me that this was undoubtedly Peru's worst road between two major towns. The journey costs roughly US$15, though you can pay a few dollars more and talk the driver into letting you ride in the cab if you don't want to stand up in the back. (See the Road to Puerto Maldonado section in the Cuzco chapter.)

River Boat You can hire boats at the Río Madre de Dios ferry dock for local excursions or to take you downriver to the Bolivian border. It is difficult to find boats up the Madre de Dios (against the current) to Manu, and though it is possible to fly to Boca Manu on chartered light aircraft, this is more frequently done from Cuzco. Cuzco is a better place than Puerto Maldonado from which to reach Manu, so the national park is described near the end of the Cuzco chapter.

Occasionally, people reach Puerto Maldonado by boat from Manu (with the current) or from the Bolivian border (against the current), but transport is infrequent and irregular. Be prepared for long waits of several days or even weeks.

Getting Around
Three-wheeled motorcycle taxis (locally called *MotoKars)* can take two or three passengers (and light luggage) to the airport for about US$4. Short rides around town are about US$1.

There are also *TaxiMotos*. These are Honda 90s (small motorcycles) that will take one passenger around town for about US25¢, but don't expect a motorcycle helmet!

Motorcycle Rental You can rent motorcy-

cles if you want to see some of the surrounding countryside; go in pairs in case of breakdowns. The motorcycle rental place marked on the Puerto Maldonado map charges about US$4 per hour and has mainly small 100cc bikes. Bargain for all-day discounts. (The motorcycle rental place has moved several times over the last few years.)

AROUND PUERTO MALDONADO
Laberinto
There is a bus service from Puerto Maldonado to the nearby gold-rush town of Laberinto (US$2.50, 1½ hours). Buses leave several times during the morning from the corner of Ica and E Rivero, supposedly at fixed times but usually not until they are full. Faster colectivo pick-ups also leave from here. This is the only local bus journey you can take to see the countryside around Puerto Maldonado. You can leave in the morning and return in the afternoon, but don't miss the last bus as the one hotel in Laberinto is a real dive and usually full of drunk miners.

Laberinto itself is just a shanty town. However, you can take trips up and down the Río Madre de Dios to various nearby communities, some of which are involved in gold panning. The miners come into Laberinto to sell their gold at the Banco de Minero. You may see buyers blow torching the gold to melt and purify it. If the bank runs out of money, the miners may barter their gold in exchange for gas, food and other supplies.

Down the Río Madre de Dios
A pleasant jungle lake, **Lago Sandoval**, is about two hours away down the Madre de Dios. Half the trip is done by boat and the other half on foot (about a 5 km hike). Bring your own food and water. For about US$25 to US$30 (you have to bargain but several people can travel for this price), a boat will drop you at the beginning of the trail and pick you up later. The boatman will also guide you to the lake if you wish. If you're lucky, you might see caiman, turtles, exotic birds and perhaps other wildlife. A cheap lodge recently opened at

the lake – ask around in Puerto Maldonado about it. This is the cheapest option for budget travelers wishing to get a taste of the rainforest.

About 20 minutes before Lago Sandoval there is a cacao plantation, Fondo Concepción, that can be visited. In the nearby jungle there is an abandoned steamship, which local guides will tell you is the boat of the rubber baron, Fitzcarraldo. (The story is told in Werner Herzog's movie *Fitzcarraldo*.) In fact, this boat has nothing to do with Fitzcarraldo, but it makes too good a story for guides to resist.

Various overnight trips can be undertaken. One is to **Lago Valencia**, just off the Madre de Dios about 60 km away, near the Bolivian border. At least two days are needed, though three or four days are suggested. This lake reportedly offers the region's best fishing as well as good bird watching and nature observation (bring binoculars). There are trails into the jungle around the lake.

South of the Río Madre de Dios and along the Río Heath (the latter forming the border between Peru and Bolivia), a 102,000-hectare reserve has been established – the **Santuario Nacional Pampas del Heath**, known locally as Las Pampas. This is another good place for nature study.

Apart from fishing and nature trips, visits to beaches, Indian communities, salt licks and gold-panning areas can be made in the Lago Valencia/Las Pampas area. Most excursions involve camping or staying in simple thatched shelters, so bring a sleeping bag and hammock if you have them. Be prepared for muddy trails – two pairs of shoes are recommended, a dry pair for camp use and a pair that can get thoroughly wet and covered with mud. Insect repellent, sun protection and a means of purifying water are essential.

For trips to Lago Valencia or Las Pampas, it may be necessary to register with the *capitanía* (harbor master) in Puerto Maldonado; ask your motorista. There are control points near the Bolivian border, so carry your passport. It is normal to negotiate trip costs beforehand and to

bargain hard. Roughly US$30 to US$40 per day seems to be the going rate. It is cheapest to go as a group because most boats will accommodate eight or more people with ease.

Down the Río Tambopata

Southwest of Las Pampas is Reserva Nacional Tambopata-Candama, established in 1990. At almost 1.5 million hectares, this reserve is one of the largest protected areas in the country and there are proposals to upgrade it to national park status. Visiting the reserve is quite straightforward if you book a guided stay at one of the lodges within the reserve (see below). If you aren't staying in one of the lodges, it would be feasible to hire a boatman in Puerto Maldonado and go into the reserve, but there are no developed facilities for visitors. One of the highlights of the reserve is the *Colpa de Guacamayos* (macaw and parrot salt lick), one of the largest natural salt licks in the country. It attracts hundreds of birds and is a spectacular sight – see the January 1994 *National Geographic* for more information.

See Tour Guides, above, for suggestions about reaching these places.

Places to Stay – jungle lodges

The area's jungle lodges can only be reached by boat. Reservations should be made in Cuzco or Lima as it can be difficult to contact the offices in Puerto Maldonado. However, the closer to the lodge you are the cheaper the cost, so if you are flexible and have time on your hands, you'll bargain a cheaper rate here than in Cuzco or Lima or (most expensive of all) from your home country. Advance reservations simply give you the peace of mind that there will be room for you. These lodges do deal with international tour groups and can be full at any time, but also are fairly empty quite often.

Although two day/one night packages are available, I recommend a minimum stay of three days/two nights because the first and last day are geared to plane connections from Cuzco. This means that the last day usually involves departing the lodge after a pre-dawn breakfast to catch the late-morning flight to Cuzco, and you only get one day and one evening (but two nights) in the jungle. All prices should include transfers to and from Puerto Maldonado airport by vehicle to the river and by boat to the lodge, as well as meals, accommodations and some local guided tours. The guides come and go and the quality and depth of their knowledge is highly variable. Airfare to Puerto Maldonado is extra. If it's the low season (December to April) or you are traveling as a group (usually five or more) or planning a long stay, discounts can normally be arranged. All the lodges will happily arrange longer stays.

Accommodations are rustic but comfortable enough. Lodges normally lack electricity, except for perhaps a generator to run a refrigerator in the kitchen. Lighting is by kerosene lantern and you should definitely pack a flashlight. Showers are cold, which is normally very refreshing at the end of a sweaty day, and beds usually have mosquito netting. Visitors will see a large variety of tropical plants, insects and birds, but remember that mammals are elusive and hard to see in the rainforest. Don't go with high expectations of seeing jaguars and tapirs – most likely you won't. Monkeys are the most frequently sighted mammals.

The closest lodge to Puerto Maldonado is the *Albergue Tambo Lodge*, 10 km downstream on the Río Madre de Dios. It is the cheapest of the jungle lodges; three days/two nights cost about US$100 per person (double occupancy) and extra days are US$35. Being so close to Puerto Maldonado means that you won't see virgin jungle around the lodge; nevertheless, nearby walks and tours to Lake Sandoval or to gold-panning areas give the visitor a good look at jungle life. Reservations can be made in Cuzco (☎ 23-6159), Plateros 351.

Further down the Madre de Dios, about 15 km away from Puerto Maldonado, the more comfortable *Cuzco Amazonico Lodge* also offers local tours and perhaps a better look at the jungle. Rooms here are all with private bathroom and porch with hammock. They charge US$143 per person (double occupancy) for three days/two nights but will offer low season discounts if you arrive at their Cuzco office and space is available (usually no problem). There are 18 km of trails in a private reserve around the lodge. Reservations for the Cuzco Amazonico Lodge can be made in Lima (☎ 446-2775, fax 445-5598), at Andalucia 174, and in Cuzco (☎ 23-2161, 23-3769), at Procuradores 48.

The *Explorer's Inn* is 58 km from Puerto Maldonado on the Río Tambopata. It takes three to four hours of river travel to reach the lodge, located in the protected 5500-hectare Zona Preservada Tambopata (itself surrounded by the much larger Reserva Nacional Tambopata-Candamo). Over 540 species of birds have been recorded in this preserved zone, which is a world record for bird species sighted in one area. There are similar records for other kinds of wildlife, including over 1100 butterflies. Despite these records (which are scientifically documented), the average tourist won't see much more here than anywhere else during the standard two night visit. The 38 km of trails around the lodge can be explored by yourself or with naturalist guides. These are usually British or American university students who may or may not know much about the area, depending on how long they have stayed here. Some of them are enthusiastic guides though others find guiding to be an imposition on their studies. I have received several reports about a series of inept managers here, but most of the guides try hard and the area is more pristine than the previous lodges. Rates here are about US$160 for three days/two nights. Tours to the salt lick cost extra. Reservations can be made at Peruvian Safaris (☎ 23-5342), Plateros 365, Cuzco, or (☎ 33-9213, 33-7963), Garcilaso de la Vega 1334, Lima. They have an office in Puerto Maldonado (see map).

About 45 minutes further up the Río Tambopata is the newer *Tambopata Jungle Lodge*, with individual bungalows set

AMAZON BASIN

Ants

Of the hundreds of ant species in the Amazonian rainforests, two kinds are frequently observed: leaf-cutter ants and army ants.

Colonies of leaf-cutter ants numbering hundreds of thousands live in huge nests dug deep into the ground. Foraging ants search the vegetation for particular types of leaves, cut out small sections and, holding the leaf segments above their heads like a small umbrella, bring them back to the nest. The ants can be quite experimental, bringing back a variety of leaves and even pieces of discarded nylon clothing or plastic wrappers that they may discover on forays into the forest.

Workers within the nest sort out those kinds of leaves that will mulch down into a type of compost; unsuitable material is ejected from the nest after a few days. The composted leaves form a mulch on which a fungus grows. Ants tend these fungal gardens with care, for they provide the main diet for both the adult ants and for the young that are being raised inside the nest.

When a particularly good source of leaves has been located, ants lay down a trail of chemical markers, or pheromones, linking the nest with the leaf source, often 100 yards or more away into the forest. People frequently come across one of these trails in the jungle, with hundreds of ants scurrying along them carrying leaf sections back to the nest, or returning empty-handed for another load.

Other species – for example, army ants – may want to prey upon this ready and constant supply of foragers. To combat this, the leaf-cutter ants are morphologically separated by size and jaw structure into different castes. Some specialize in tending the fungal gardens, others have jaws designed for cutting the leaf segments, and yet others are soldiers, armed with huge mandibles, who accompany the foragers and protect them from attackers. Close observation of the foragers will sometimes reveal yet another caste, a tiny ant that is so small that it rides along on the leaf segments without disturbing the foragers. The function of these riders is still unclear, but biologists suggest that they may act as protection against parasitizing wasps that try to lay their eggs on the foragers when they are occupied with carrying leaves.

A colony of leaf-cutter ants can last for a decade or more. New colonies are founded by the emergence of a number of potential queens, who mate and then fly off to found another nest. They carry some of the fungus used for food with them. This is essential to 'seed' the new nest. The rest of the new queen's life is spent in laying tens of thousands of eggs, destined to become gardeners, foragers, soldiers, riders, or perhaps even new queens. ■

in secondary jungle. Although there are several farms in the area, the lodge is within the Reserva Nacional Tambopata-Candama and a short boat ride will get you out into primary forest. Tours to nearby lakes and to the salt lick are offered and naturalist guides are available. Rates here are about US$140 for three days/two nights. Reservations can be made in Cuzco at Peruvian Andean Treks (☎ 22-5701, fax 23-8911), Pardo 705.

Close to the salt lick, just a few hours further up the Río Tambopata, is the recently established *Colpa Lodge*, also called the Tambopata Research Center. Ornithologists stay here and there is an on-going research program. It is the most basic of the lodges with shared sleeping and showering facilities but, because of the distances involved, rates are higher than the other places. If you're interested in seeing more macaws than you ever thought possible, it's worth the expense. Travel time varies depending on water levels (and the size of your boat motor) – it might be an all day river trip to get there from Puerto Maldonado. Reservations can be made with Manu Nature Tours (☎ 22-4384, fax 23-4793), Avenida Sol 582, Cuzco; Rainforest Expeditions (☎ 438-9325), Galeon 120, Lima 41; or International Expeditions (☎ 1-800-633-4734), One Environs

Park, Helena, AL 35080, USA. International Expeditions will arrange a complete package including air from the USA.

GOING TO BOLIVIA

You can hire a boat at the Madre de Dios dock to go to the Bolivian border at Puerto Pardo. The trip takes half a day and costs about US$80 – the boat will carry several people. With time and luck, you may be able to find a cargo boat that's going there anyway and will take passengers more cheaply.

It is possible to continue down the river on the Bolivian side, known as Puerto Heath, but this can take several days (even weeks) to arrange and is not cheap. It's best to travel in a group to share costs and avoid the drier months when the water is too low. Basic food and accommodations (bring a hammock or sleeping pad) can be found.

Travelers should have their passports checked at the migraciónes office in Puerto Maldonado before leaving. I have received a report that the Bolivian border officials are unfriendly and demand bribes. From Puerto Heath, you can continue down the Madre de Dios as far as Riberalto (at the confluence of the Río Madre de Dios and Río Beni, far into northern Bolivia), where road and air connections can be made.

This trip is rarely done by foreigners. In 1992, a traveler reported that a sugar boat from Puerto Maldonado to Riberalta charged US$30 for passengers. I have no more recent reports.

GOING TO BRAZIL

A track to Iñapari, on the Brazilian border, is open but the end of it is in bad shape. Because it is a dirt road, heavy trucks traveling in the wettest months churn up the road leaving almost impassable ruts when the mud dries. Wet season travel is now, reportedly, not allowed; if that's true the road should be passable in the drier months.

You can reach the Iñapari road by taking the ferry across the Madre de Dios. Pick-up

trucks leave every day from the other side of the river and reach Iñapari the same day, charging about US$10. Along the road there are a few small settlements of people involved in the Brazil nut industry and some cattle ranching and logging. These settlements have only a few hundred inhabitants, a couple of stores, a place to eat and possibly a basic place to stay. After some 170 km you reach Iberia, where there are a couple of basic hotels. This is the largest town on the road, with about 4000 inhabitants and weekly air service from Cuzco with Grupo 8.

The village of Iñapari is another 70 km beyond Iberia. Iñapari is occasionally served by Grupo 8 flights (the airport is 7 km from town) but most people arrive by pick-up truck. There is a basic hotel.

From Iñapari, it is possible to cross the Río Acre to Assis in Brazil, but I've heard that the river must be waded. At Assis, you'll find a better hotel and a dry season road to Brasiléia and Río Branco, which is served by pick-up trucks. Travel along the Río Acre is possible. There is Brazilian immigration in Assis but no Peruvian immigration in Iñapari; instead, travelers arriving from Brazil should see the police: They will provide you with a permit to travel to Puerto Maldonado, where you can stop by the migraciones office for an official entry stamp. A Peruvian migraciones may open in Iñapari in the future, but until then travelers leaving Peru should get their exit stamps in Puerto Maldonado. (More information on Brazilian visa and entry requirements is provided in the Iquitos section. If you need a visa for Brazil, get one in Lima or in your home country.)

Charter flights can be arranged in Puerto Maldonado to Iberia, Iñapari or Río Branco in Brazil. Money changing facilities are poor. Small US$ bills are often negotiable.

CHANCHAMAYO

The jungle region east of Lima most accessible from the capital is known as Chanchamayo and comprises the neighboring towns of **La Merced** and **San Ramón**. These towns are entry points for further excursions into the jungle. San Ramón is about 300 km east of Lima and La Merced a further 11 km. Chanchamayo and the surrounding jungle regions are popularly called La Selva Central, or Central Jungle. The area is noted for coffee and fruit production.

All buses to the region terminate in La Merced, the center for ground transport in the region and the more important of the two towns. It has a population of over 10,000 and is a major coffee-marketing center. La Merced has a greater choice of hotels and restaurants, though the region's best hotel is in the smaller and quieter San Ramón. Although less important, San Ramón boasts the regional airport nearby. The two towns are linked by frequent colectivos and locals consider them to be one unit (as do I in this section).

La Merced is the center for vehicles heading north to Oxapampa and Pozuzo, northeast to Puerto Bermúdez and southeast to Satipo.

Information
Money Both towns have a Banco de Crédito that might change traveler's checks at a poor rate, though I wouldn't count on it. Cash dollars are changed on the streets near the banks at rates below those in major cities.

Post & Telecommunications There is a post office in La Merced and telephone offices in both towns – see maps. The area code is 064.

Medical Services A small hospital in La Merced is marked on the map, but I'd go to Lima if I was sick.

Things to See & Do
There is a colorful daily market in La Merced, and a weekend market at San Luis de Shuaro, 22 km beyond La Merced, is also interesting – local Indians visit it. You'll find a basic hotel here. Campa Indians occasionally come into La Merced to sell handicrafts.

Avenida 2 de Mayo is good for views of La Merced; the stairs at the north end afford a good view of the town, and from the balcony at the south end there is a wonderful view of the river – excellent for photography.

An interesting botanical garden is on the grounds of El Refugio Hotel in San Ramón.

Places to Stay
Some hotels claim that they are busier from April to September, so rates may be a little higher.

La Merced This is the most convenient place to stay if you are continuing by road rather than by air. Most hotels lack hot water. The town has several cheap, very basic hotels that are not particularly clean and may have an erratic water supply, though you can always bathe in the river as the locals do. The most basic places are the *Hostal Roca*, Ayacucho 256, with rooms at US$3.50/5 for singles/doubles, the *Hostal Básico Chuncho* (☎ 53-1161), Lima 128, for US$3 per person, and the *Hostal Iquitos*, Callao 210, which is even cheaper.

Slightly better cheapies include the following. The *Hostal Santa Rosa* (☎ 53-1012), 2 de Mayo 447, charges US$3.50/5. They have one double with private bath for US$6. Less than a block away is the *Hostal Lima*, which is clean and charges US$5/7. The *Hostal Romero* (☎ 53-1106), Palca 419, is a decent cheapie at US$4/5. They have a few slightly more expensive rooms with private bath.

If you want something a little better than basic, try the clean and friendly *Hostal Villa Dorada* (☎ 53-1221), Pirola 265, with rooms for US$4.50/7.50 or US$7/10 with private bath. The *Hostal Residencial San Felípe* (☎ 53-1046), 2 de Mayo 426, is friendly and charges US$4.50/7. Also good is the *Hotel Cosmos* (☎ 53-1053), Pirola at Pasuni, which has reasonably clean rooms with private bath at US$7/9. The *Hotel Cristina* (☎ 53-1276), Tarma 582, is

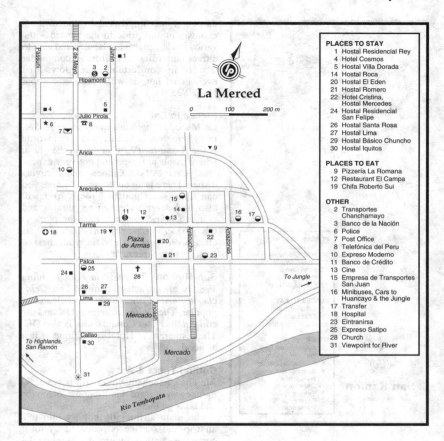

La Merced

PLACES TO STAY
1 Hostal Residencial Rey
4 Hotel Cosmos
5 Hostal Villa Dorada
14 Hostal Roca
20 Hostal El Eden
21 Hostal Romero
22 Hotel Cristina,
   Hostal Mercedes
24 Hostal Residencial
   San Felípe
26 Hostal Santa Rosa
27 Hostal Lima
29 Hostal Básico Chuncho
30 Hostal Iquitos

PLACES TO EAT
9 Pizzería La Romana
12 Restaurant El Campa
19 Chifa Roberto Sui

OTHER
2 Transportes
   Chanchamayo
3 Banco de la Nación
6 Police
7 Post Office
8 Telefónica del Peru
10 Expreso Moderno
11 Banco de Crédito
13 Cine
15 Empresa de Transportes
   San Juan
16 Minibuses, Cars to
   Huancayo & the Jungle
17 Transfer
18 Hospital
23 Eintranirsa
25 Expreso Satipo
28 Church
31 Viewpoint for River

US$8/11.50 for rooms with private bath. The *Hostal Mercedes* (☎ 53-1304), next door at Tarma 576, has hot water and charges US$13/17.

The *Hostal Residencial Rey* (☎ 53-1185), Junín 103, provides towels, soap and toilet paper and sometimes has hot water. There are telephones in the rooms and a cafeteria on the top floor serves good breakfasts. Climb onto the roof for a good view of the town. Rooms are US$16/20. The *Hostal El Eden* (☎ 53-1183), Ancash

347 on the plaza, has OK rooms with TV, fans, private bath, hot water, towels, etc, for US$18/25.

San Ramón Most of San Ramón's hotels are clustered within a block of the intersection of Avenida Paucartambo and the main street, Avenida Progreso. The cheapest are the basic *Hostal Comtur* (☎ 33-1084), Progreso 366, at US$4/6; and the nearby *Hotel Colón* (☎ 33-1120), at US$4.50/7. The *Hostal Venus* (☎ 33-1004), Paucartambo

AMAZON BASIN

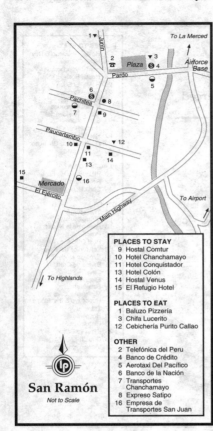

PLACES TO STAY
9 Hostal Comtur
10 Hotel Chanchamayo
11 Hotel Conquistador
13 Hotel Colón
14 Hostal Venus
15 El Refugio Hotel

PLACES TO EAT
1 Baluzo Pizzería
3 Chifa Lucerito
12 Cebichería Purito Callao

OTHER
2 Telefónica del Peru
4 Banco de Crédito
5 Aerotaxi Del Pacífico
6 Banco de la Nación
7 Transportes
   Chanchamayo
8 Expreso Satipo
16 Empresa de
   Transportes San Juan

San Ramón
Not to Scale

garden. I was impressed by the owner's enthusiasm and pride in the garden – the various exotic plants are labeled and tend to attract butterflies and birds. Accommodation is in comfortable bungalows that even boast hot showers; rates are about US$20/25.

Places to Eat

La Merced There are many more restaurants here than in San Ramón. My favorite is the *Restaurant El Campa*, on the plaza, where meals are good and not very expensive. It serves both Chinese and Peruvian dishes. There is an outdoor area where you can dine under thatched roofs. You will also find several chicken restaurants and chifas; *Chifa Roberto Sui* on the plaza is OK. *Pizzería La Romana*, Arica 309, is closed on Sunday, and is your best – perhaps only – pizza choice.

San Ramón The *Pizzería Baluzo*, Junín 198, is an attractive choice. The *Cebichería Purito Callao* looks nice, clean and popular. The *Chifa Lucerito* is OK and the chifa in the Hotel Conquistador is also OK. The restaurant in Hotel El Refugio is just as good.

Getting There & Away

Air The Chanchamayo airstrip is about 30 minutes walk from San Ramón. Colectivos and taxis go there.

The main airlines do not fly into this airstrip and service is provided by local companies with light aircraft. Aerotaxi del Pacífico (☎ 33-1438), Pardo 296, has daily flights to Ciudad Constitución (US$58) and Puerto Bermúdez (US$40) in five-passenger planes. A minimum of three passengers is required. Taapsa has flights to Pozuzo. SASA and other companies at the airport are other possibilities for flights to local jungle villages. Your best bet is just turning up at the airport early (before 9 am) and waiting for a flight. Planes carry between five and nine passengers and leave as soon as they are full. The most frequent other destinations are Atalaya, Satipo and Puerto Inca. If you are traveling in a group,

247, is US$5/7.50 or US$7.50/10 with a private bath. The *Hotel Chanchamayo*, Progreso 291, is quite good at US$4.50/7.50 or US$11/13 with private bath. The *Hotel Conquistador* (☎ /fax 33-1157), at Progreso and Paucartambo, is a good hotel that charges US$14/20 but raises rates in the 'high season.' They have a good chifa restaurant.

My favorite hotel in the Chanchamayo region is *El Refugio* (☎ 33-1082), Ejército 490, which is about a 10 minutes' walk from the town center. The hotel grounds are also a small but well-laid-out botanical you can charter your own plane to almost anywhere in the region (you can charter a plane by yourself, too, but you have to pay for the empty seats).

There is a simple airport cafeteria serving snacks and cold drinks, including beer.

Bus There are direct buses from Lima to Chanchamayo, though some travelers find it convenient to break the journey at Tarma. The 70 km stretch from Tarma to San Ramón (at 850 meters above sea level) drops 2200 meters so it is worth trying to travel on this section in daylight hours for the views.

Most buses leave from La Merced and pick up passengers in San Ramón, so there is a better seat selection in La Merced. Companies that make the eight- to 10-hour journey to Lima are Transportes Chanchamayo, Expreso Moderno and Expreso Satipo. Fares vary from US$6 to US$8.

Empresa de Transportes San Juan and Transfer charge about US$4.50 for the six hour journey to Huancayo (with stops at Tarma and Jauja, etc). Colectivo cars to Huancayo from Avenida Tarma at Amazonas are faster and charge a bit more. San Juan also has buses to Oxapampa and Villarica. Transfer runs two buses a week on the long and grueling route to Andahuaylas (US$23, 36 hours), though I haven't the faintest idea why anybody would want to go direct from La Merced to Andahuaylas. They also have buses to Satipo (US$4.50) and intermediate jungle towns. Eintranirsa has minibuses every half hour to Villarica (two hours).

If you are looking for transport into the jungle, go to the east end of Avenida Tarma where you'll find all kinds of trucks, cars, minibuses and jeeps. Minibuses will take you to Satipo (US$4.50, six hours), Oxapampa (US$3.50, four hours) and Puerto Bermúdez (US$6.50, seven hours), as well as to intermediate towns such as San Luis de Shuaro en route to Oxapampa. Colectivo taxis are more expensive. Schedules are haphazard – go down there as early as you can and ask around. Sometimes you can buy tickets the night before, but as things

are generally disorganized you may have to rely on luck and persuasiveness.

Getting Around
Minibuses cruise around La Merced picking up passengers to San Ramón (US35¢). In San Ramón, buses head northeast on Progreso and then along Pardo en route to La Merced.

SATIPO
This small jungle town lies about 130 km by road southeast of La Merced. Satipo is the center of a small fruit-producing region but its main claim to fame at this time is as the southernmost town of any size on the Carretera Marginal de la Selva (the Marginal Jungle Hwy).

This huge road project was devised by the Peruvian architect and president for two terms, Señor Fernando Belaúnde Terry. Belaúnde's dream was to open up the Amazon Basin, not by a road cutting across it but by a road encircling the entire western boundary of the Amazon Basin. The scheme called for a road beginning in Asunción, the capital of Paraguay, and going through the jungle lowlands of Bolivia, Peru, Ecuador and Colombia before terminating at the Caribbean near Caracas, the capital of Venezuela. Only relatively small sections of this highway have been built and it is unlikely that the project will be completed. The section from Satipo to La Merced is fairly well established but further north there are breaks in the highway.

Satipo is also linked by road to the highlands of Huancayo and a roundtrip is possible by public transport. Although the scenery is spectacular, the trip is rarely made.

Places to Stay
For such an isolated little town, Satipo has a surprising number of hotels. The best is the *Hotel Majestic*, at Plaza Principal 408, where a double room with bath costs US$18. The fairly basic *Hostal Palermo*, Manuel Prado 228, charges US$8 for a double with bath. There are several other cheap and basic hotels.

Getting There & Away

Air There is an airport where light aircraft can be chartered. Flights to Pucallpa and other jungle towns leave irregularly when there are enough passengers.

Bus Minibuses leave many times a day for La Merced. Empresa de Transportes Selva has a daily 6 am departure to Huancayo (US$7, 12 hours) via La Merced. On Monday and Friday mornings there is transport to Huancayo along the spectacular but difficult direct road through Comas.

OXAPAMPA & POZUZO

About 75 km north of La Merced is the ranching and coffee center of Oxapampa. It used to be important for logging but most of the trees have now been cut down. Look around at your fellow passengers on the bus north from La Merced – you'll see some blonde heads and blue eyes. This is because several hundred German settlers arrived in the area in the mid-1800s. Their descendants live in Oxapampa or in Pozuzo (about four to six hours north of Oxapampa by daily minibus) and have preserved many Germanic customs: buildings have a Tyrolean look to them, Austrian-German food is prepared and an old-fashioned form of German is still spoken by some families. Although the area has been settled for over 100 years, it is still remote and rarely visited. The people are friendly and interested in talking with tourists. La Fiesta de Santa Rosa de Lima, August 30, is the major holiday here.

East of the Oxapampa-Pozuzo road is the **Parque Nacional Yanachaga-Chemillén**, which covers 122,000 hectares, is largely inaccessible and has no tourist services. It is reputedly famous for its orchids, but such a large area situated in hilly Andean foothills falling into jungle has many different habitats and will doubtlessly have a huge variety of flora and fauna. You could try asking in Oxapampa about access.

Oxapampa has half a dozen simple hotels. Pozuzo has two or three, of which the *El Tirol* is quite good.

PUERTO BERMÚDEZ

Puerto Bermúdez is a sleepy port on the Río Pichis, about nine hours northeast of La Merced by bus. Looking at the huddle of dugout canoes tied up to the mud bank of the small river flowing past the town, it is difficult to imagine that one could embark here on a river journey that would eventually lead down the Amazon to the Atlantic. Until recently, this was the only way to continue past Puerto Bermúdez, but in the mid-1980s the new Carretera Marginal de la Selva was opened as far as Pucallpa. I thought it would be interesting to travel this new section of road and see how Peru is opening up its frontier.

The area southeast of Puerto Bermúdez is the home of the Ashaninka Indians. This is the largest Amazon Indian group in Peru. In the late 1980s and early '90s, attempts were made to indoctrinate them by the Sendero Luminoso guerrillas. When the guerrillas were unable to get the Indians' total support, they retaliated by massacring dozens of Indians and torturing many others in an attempt to intimidate them. Thankfully, the Sendero problem has been reduced since the capture of the guerrilla leaders. People interested in learning more about the Ashaninka can contact the *Jefe* (leader) of the official local native organization, ANAP, based in Puerto Bermúdez. Permission to visit villages with a local guide can be obtained.

Places to Stay & Eat

There are basic hotels right by the river, including the *Hostal Tania* and the *Hotel Prusia*, both providing a bed, four walls and a river view. Both charge about US$2.50 per person and you get what you pay for. At least the river view is pretty, especially at dawn and dusk. The newer *Hostal Shelagh* is similarly priced and clean. If these places are full, there are a couple of other even more basic hotels a few streets away from the river. The town has one main street, where you'll find places to eat.

Getting There & Away

It's easy enough to get here by bus from La Merced or plane from San Ramón. Continuing north, the road deteriorates and erratic transport to Ciudad Constitución is often by truck. Boats also are available to go north to Ciudad Constitución and Puerto Inca, but have no particular schedule. Ask around.

There have been problems reported with drug-running and nighttime assaults. Travel during the day for safety.

CIUDAD CONSTITUCIÓN

This is a recently conceived major town that is to be built in the middle of the jungle along a particularly unpopulated stretch of the Río Palcazu and near the new highway. Schools, a hospital, a cathedral, political offices and many blocks of streets with shops and housing have all been mapped out and an area of the jungle has been cleared. That's about as far as the project had gone when President Belaúnde's second term of office came to a close. Since then, with new presidents and different political priorities, Ciudad Constitución has remained a forgotten and fly-blown huddle of huts.

Although the road has been built, only heavy trucks and road-building equipment were able to get through when I did the trip. (I have heard that pick-up trucks are doing it now.) At Puerto Bermúdez, I found someone heading down the Río Pichis to Constitución who gave me a ride in his peki-peki. The journey took seven hours and was much more pleasant than grinding over the newly churned mud of the highway. The fare is about US$8. If you're lucky, you might be able to find a boat with an outboard motor that will do the trip in about four hours. It's a walk of a few kilometers from the point where the boat drops you off to the huts that comprise the 'town.' Pick-up trucks are reportedly available.

The only place to stay is a hut with mud floors and no locks on room doors. There is a small store where cold drinks and a simple meal are available.

THE NEW ROAD TO PUCALLPA

North of Constitución, the road improves and there are several vehicles a day going via Zungaro to Pucallpa (US$8, six hours). You'll pass occasional small communities and the closer you get to Pucallpa, the more open the country becomes, a sign of the logging followed by ranching that is typical of the opening up of the Peruvian rainforest. Public buses and trucks run during the day, which is the safest time to travel and affords the better views.

About 1½ hours beyond Ciudad Constitución, where a small river is crossed by raft, is the village of Zungaro. Here you'll find a basic hotel and restaurant. From Zungaro, there are both road and river communications with Puerto Inca on the Río Pachitea, about 10 km away. During the wet season the road is often closed, and during the dry season the river between Zungaro and Puerto Inca is too low, so ask around for the best way to go. At Puerto Inca, ask for Don José, an old Czech gentleman who has lived in the area for many years and who is a great source of local information. He is something of a local identity and owns a simple hotel pleasantly situated on the river.

Beyond Zungaro, the scenery is all forest for about an hour, but this soon gives way to ranch land and small homesteads. Alternatively, you can travel to Pucallpa by boat from Puerto Inca.

PUCALLPA

With a population of about 200,000, Pucallpa is Peru's fastest growing jungle town and the biggest to be linked directly with Lima by road. Until 1980, it played second fiddle to Iquitos, capital of the huge Department of Loreto, but since then the new Department of Ucayali has been formed and Pucallpa is now experiencing political and economic growth as its capital.

Despite a few pleasant modern buildings, such as the Hotel del Oriente, Pucallpa is not a particularly attractive city. Many of its buildings have been hastily constructed in concrete with tin roofs. Its roads are slowly

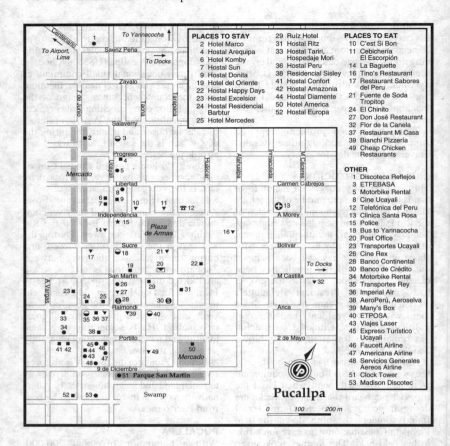

PLACES TO STAY
2 Hotel Marco
4 Hostal Arequipa
6 Hotel Komby
7 Hostal Sun
9 Hostal Donita
19 Hotel del Oriente
22 Hostal Happy Days
23 Hostal Excelsior
24 Hostal Residencial Barbtur
25 Hotel Mercedes
29 Ruíz Hotel
31 Hostal Ritz
33 Hostal Tariri, Hospedaje Mori
36 Hostal Peru
38 Residencial Sisley
41 Hostal Confort
42 Hostal Amazonia
44 Hostal Diamente
50 Hotel America
52 Hostal Europa

PLACES TO EAT
10 C'est Si Bon
11 Cebichería El Escorpión
14 La Baguette
16 Tino's Restaurant
17 Restaurant Sabores del Peru
21 Fuente de Soda Tropitop
24 El Chinito
27 Don José Restaurant
32 Flor de la Canela
37 Restaurant Mi Casa
39 Bianchi Pizzería
49 Cheap Chicken Restaurants

OTHER
1 Discoteca Reflejos
3 ETFEBASA
5 Motorbike Rental
8 Cine Ucayali
12 Telefónica del Peru
13 Clinica Santa Rosa
15 Police
18 Bus to Yarinacocha
20 Post Office
23 Transportes Ucayali
26 Cine Rex
28 Banco Continental
30 Banco de Crédito
34 Motorbike Rental
35 Transportes Rey
36 Imperial Air
38 AeroPerú, Aeroselva
39 Many's Box
40 ETPOSA
43 Viajes Laser
45 Expreso Turístico Ucayali
46 Faucett Airline
47 Americana Airline
48 Servicios Generales Aereos Airline
51 Clock Tower
53 Madison Discotec

Pucallpa

0   100   200 m

being paved but many of those away from the center are still red mud quagmires in the wet season and choking red dust in the dry. The huge flocks of vultures circling lazily over the markets, plazas and dock areas are one of Pucallpa's most startling sights. The roofs of the buildings around the food market are often crowded with scores of the huge black birds silently waiting for scraps to be thrown out. The town is dirty and noisy and few travelers enjoy it. Though locals take pride in the town's progress and growth, the visitor, having felt the pulse of the city and

watched the languid flapping of the vultures, isn't left with much to do. The Plaza de Armas isn't up to much (though it is improving). The intersection of Raimondi and Ucayali is considered to be the town center. There are a couple of cinemas that occasionally show English-language films.

The best thing to do is take the short bus trip to nearby Yarinacocha, a lovely oxbow lake where you can go canoeing, observe wildlife, visit Indian communities and purchase their handicrafts. Yarinacocha is the tourist area of Pucallpa, yet it is far from touristy – simple hotel, restaurant and boat services are provided in a casual, easy-going atmosphere. It's worth spending a couple of days here. (There is a full description after the Pucallpa section.)

When you are ready to move on, go down to the Pucallpa docks to find a river boat heading to Iquitos; while you're looking, you can experience first hand the rough-and-tumble atmosphere of a busy, hard-working river port.

One hint: Just as you've become used to remembering that 'll' is always pronounced 'y' in Spanish, you come to one of the very few exceptions to this rule; Pucallpa is pronounced 'pukalpa.'

Information

I couldn't find a tourist information office, though there has been one here in the past.

Cash dollars and traveler's checks can be changed at the Banco de Crédito. Other banks, some stores, the better hotels, travel agents and airlines normally change money for their clients. There are street changers outside the Hotel Mercedes.

The area code for Pucallpa is 064.

Tourism is returning slowly to the area after the problems of the early '90s. Viajes Laser (☎ 57-1120, fax 57-3776), 7 de Junio 1043, is one of the better travel agencies in Pucallpa, but for jungle guides go to Yarinacocha.

The Clínica Santa Rosa on A Morey is quite good for stool, urine or blood tests if you get sick.

Places to Stay

Hotels are often full by early afternoon, so start looking as soon as you arrive. Many travelers prefer to stay at Yarinacocha, though it has fewer hotels.

Places to Stay – bottom end

One of the cheapest hotels in town is the *Hostal Europa*, which is dirty and run down, though probably the best of the three dives on the same block. I wouldn't recommend any of them for single female travelers. Rates are under US$4 per person and rooms vary in quality, so look at several if you are determined to economize. Other similarly priced cheapies that aren't much better are the *Hostal Excelsior* and *Hospedaje Mori*.

The *Hostal Sun* (☎ 57-4260), Ucayali 380, is a better budget bet and charges US$5/7.50 for fairly clean singles/doubles or US$7.50/11 with private cold showers. Another decent cheap choice is the *Hostal Confort* (☎ 57-5815) with rooms with private bath at US$7/9. Almost next door is the similarly priced *Hostal Amazonia* (☎ 57-1080), Portillo 729, which looks OK. One of the best of the cheap hotels is the small, friendly, reasonably clean and popular *Hostal Residencial Barbtur* (☎ 57-2532), Raimondi 670. Rates are US$6/9 for singles/doubles or US$9/14 for rooms with private cold showers and fan. Almost as good is the nearby and similarly priced *Hostal Peru* (☎ 57-5128), Raimondi 639, which has more rooms and is less likely to be full.

Other cheap and basic places to try include the *Hostal Diamante*, charging US$6/10 for rooms with private cold showers and fan; and the similar *Residencial Sisley* (☎ 57-5137), Portillo 658, which charges US$8/10. The *Hostal Marco* (☎ 57-1048), 7 de Junio 307, is basic but clean enough and has rooms with windows at the front that are noisy and rooms without windows in the back that are quiet. Rates are US$9/12 with bath. The *Hostal Tariri* (☎ 57-5147), Raimondi 733, looks pretty basic and beat from the outside but the beds are clean, the place is secure and has plenty of water. Rates are US$10/15 with bath and fan. The *Hostal Donita* (☎ 57-1480), Ucayali 369, is adequate at US$6 per person or US$9 per person with private bath.

Places to Stay – middle

All the following have rooms with private baths and fans. The *Hotel Komby* (☎ 57-1184), Ucayali 360, seems like a good deal at US$15/22 for clean rooms and there is a swimming pool. One of the best midrange hotels is the clean *Hotel Arequipa* (☎ 57-1348, 57-3171, 57-3112), Progreso 573. They charge US$15/22 for rooms with fans or US$28/35 for rooms with air-conditioning. The *Hostal Happy Days* (☎ 57-2067, fax 57-1940), Huáscar 440, has small but clean rooms on a quiet street for US$16/22. The similarly-priced *Hostal Ritz* (☎ 57-5112) is OK and has TVs in the rooms.

The *Hotel America* (☎ /fax 57-1378), Portillo 357, has small, simple rooms with TV, phone and air-conditioning for US$28/35. The similarly priced *Hotel Inambu* (☎ 57-5234, 57-1601), Centenario 271, also has air-conditioned rooms and a decent restaurant. The central *Hotel Mercedes* (☎ 57-1191, 57-5120), Raimondi 600, was Pucallpa's first good hotel and has a certain dated charm and character. It has a pool, restaurant, and bar and charges US$30/40.

Places to Stay – top end

The modern, central *Hotel del Oriente* (☎ 57-5154, fax 57-5510), San Martín 552, has a swimming pool, bar, good restaurant and rooms with telephones and TVs. Rooms are overpriced at US$53/70, including continental breakfast. Suites start at US$106. The *Ruíz Hotel* (☎ 57-1280, fax 57-1028), San Martín 475, charges US$37/50 including breakfast. Rooms are spartan but bigger than average and have TV, telephone, warm showers, mini-bar and air-conditioning.

Places to Eat

The town abounds with cheap or mid-range restaurants, though few are especially noteworthy. Because of the heat, I prefer shaded pavement tables rather than eating indoors – most of the restaurants below have them. The heat in the middle of the day means that restaurants tend to open early (by 7 am) for breakfast.

As Pucallpa is usually hot, places to drink are as important as places to eat. For a variety of cold, freshly squeezed fruit juices, *Don José's* is good. As well as juices, they serve reasonably priced meals.

For cheap local breakfasts, the pavement cafés on Portillo near 7 de Junio are OK. For about US$1 you might order local breakfasts like *cecina* (smoked pork) or *tacu tacu* (rice and beans with bananas). *La Baguette*, at Ucayali 490, is squeaky clean and sells bread, snacks and good-looking cakes and pastries. For ceviches and other meals in the US$3 to US$6 range, a good place is *Cebichería El Escorpión* on the northwest side of the plaza. It is clean and has sidewalk tables for viewing the plaza. Ice cream and snack places are nearby, including *C'est Si Bon* and *Fuente Soda Tropitop*.

Near the Raimondi-Ucayali intersection there are several popular places with outdoor tables. These include *El Chinito* with set lunches for US$1.50, *Restaurant Mi Casa* and the *Bianchi Pizzería & Bar*, the latter a popular hangout for young people. After pizza, they move on to *Many's Box*, an outdoor bar with a loud juke box.

Restaurant Sabores Peru is a local place that has pizza, chicken, a small meat and fish selection and ice cream. Prices range from US$2 for a quarter chicken, to US$4 for a meat or fish dinner, to US$10 for a pizza for four. A couple of decent, cheap and popular chicken restaurants are on Tacna by the Parque San Martín. A quarter chicken with an order of fries is about US$2.25. *La Flor de La Canela*, away from the center on M Castilla, is good for local food. *Tino's* has recently been recommended as the best local restaurant. The better hotels have decent, if not particularly cheap, restaurants.

The local beer, San Juan, has the distinction of being the only beer brewed in the Amazon – whether that is the entire Amazon or just the Peruvian Amazon is open to discussion. At any rate, because it is brewed locally, it is cheaper than the coastal beers and, for a light bottled beer, it is good and refreshing.

If you want to splash out a little, go to *El Establo* steak house; it's out of town on the road to the airport (take a taxi) and serves the best steaks in town.

Entertainment

Local young folk tend to hang just out at one of the central pavement places; *Many's Box* is currently popular. A couple

of cinemas shown on the map occasionally
have decent movies. The *Madison Discoteca* is open from 9 pm onwards nightly
except Monday, though not much happens
before 10 pm. They may have a live band
on weekends. Another dancing place is the
Discoteca Reflejos, which is hot and
crowded on weekends but dead mid-week.

Things to Buy
The local Shipibo Indians wander the
streets with souvenirs. More of their work
is seen near Yarinacocha, described below.

Getting There & Away
Air Pucallpa's airport is small but busy.
Most airlines have offices in the city center
and at the airport, about 5 km northwest of
town. Aero Continente, AeroPerú, Ameri-
cana and Faucett all have daily direct
flights to and from Lima (US$75). Imperial
Air has three flights a week from Lima and
Transportes Aéreos Andahuaylas has a
Wednesday flight from Lima via Atalaya.
This service is subject to change.

Aero Continente and Americana have
daily flights to Iquitos (US$53) while
AeroPerú and Faucett have flights two
or three times a week. Services to other
towns are provided but schedules change
frequently. Imperial Air flies to Tarapoto
(US$53) three times a week. Expresso
Aéreo has flights via Tarapoto and Moyobamba to Chiclayo three times a week.
Most passengers use one of the small local
airlines to fly to other jungle towns.

AeroSelva (☎ /fax 57-1138, 57-2637),
Portillo 644, has flights in small planes to
Ciudad Constitución, San Francisco, Tarapoto, Juanjui, Atalaya, Sepahua, Contamaná, Bellavista, Tingo María, Tocache,
Uchiza and other small towns. Servicios
Generales Aéreos has fewer flights to many
of the same places. It is often best to just go
to the airport and ask around if you plan on
flying to a jungle town. Often, a small plane
will go as soon as it has filled its seats.

Float planes sometimes fly from Yarinacocha to towns down the Río Ucayali. Ask
at the TASA office in the Hotel Arequipa or
ask around in Yarinacocha.

Bus A direct bus from Lima takes about 24
hours but you can break the journey in
several places; Huánuco and Tingo María
are the best of these. A journey from coastal
Lima takes you up the steep western slopes
of the Andes to a breathless 4843 meters
above sea level, continues along the Andes
at an average of over 4000 meters for
several hours, then begins the dizzying
descent down the cloud-forested slopes of
the eastern Andes to Pucallpa at a mere 154
meters. This incredible change of scenery
and altitude gives the traveler an exceptional look at Peru in cross section and is
one of the continent's most exciting and
demanding 24-hour intercity bus journeys.

The journey as far as Tingo María is
mainly paved and described in the Central Highlands chapter. From Tingo, the
unpaved road climbs over a final pass in
the eastern Andes before descending to
Pucallpa in the Amazon Basin proper.
There is an interesting story connected with
building the road over this pass. Until the
1930s, the road reached only as far as
Huánuco and engineers were carrying out
surveys to assess the easiest route for the
road on to Pucallpa. They were unable to
find an obvious pass over the last range
of the Andes and were preparing for an
expensive road-building project. One of the
engineers had been studying historical documents and maps of the region, some of
which had been made as long ago as the
1700s by Franciscan missionaries exploring the area. One document, recounting a
1757 expedition by Padre Abad, led to the
rediscovery of an extremely narrow, steep-
walled gorge through the final mountain
barrier. The road was built through this
pass, saving much time and money, and
reached Pucallpa in 1941. The pass is now
named El Boquerón del Padre Abad.

Driving through the pass is spectacular
and should be done in daylight. Exotic vegetation clings to waterfall-covered vertical
walls and there are several natural pools
where it is possible to swim. The bird life is
prolific and the careful observer may see
troops of monkeys scurrying along the cliff
ledges.

Unfortunately, public transport only takes you through the pass; it's not a destination. Ideally, you could take a Tingo-Pucallpa bus and get off at the pass, walk through it (it's about a 4 km walk along the road) and flag down a later bus. Otherwise, you'll have to be content with tantalizing glimpses through the bus windows. If you can't find a bus on to Pucallpa, you could stop at the village of Aguaytía (see below). Between Aguaytía and Pucallpa there are several police checkpoints; these take up a lot of time but are not a problem if your papers are in order. There are fewer of them now than there used to be in 1993 and early 1994. Whereas before guerrilla problems necessitated increased police checkpoints, the problems now are with drug-running. Don't travel at night. I have not heard of any problems on this road recently for people taking daytime buses.

Although the bus trip between Pucallpa and Lima is supposed to take 24 hours, it can take two days or more during the rainy months (especially January to April) if the road has been closed by mud slides. During the rest of the year, buses are known to sometimes do the trip in 20 hours. There are several companies shown on the map and most of them leave at 6 or 7 am and charge about US$12 to US$15. Along 7 de Junio there are small bus companies that have faster, but less comfortable, minibuses to Aguaytía and Tingo María. Also ask around here for minibuses and trucks heading south to Zungaro, Ciudad Constitución and Puerto Bermúdez. Once in a while a large bus will go somewhere other than the standard Lima route. On a recent visit, one company was offering a weekly departure to Huancayo and Ayacucho (US$27).

Some maps show roads continuing east of Pucallpa to Cruzeiro do Sul in Brazil. This is wishful thinking in the extreme because there is not even a jeep track part of the way there. Absolutely nothing. Japanese lumber importers are making an effort to get this road built so they can import Amazonian timber from Brazil more cheaply. Environmentalists are concerned that this will contribute drastically to the felling of the Amazon rainforest, which is already out of control.

River Boat Pucallpa's port, called La Hoyada, is about 2½ km northeast of the town center along unpaved roads. During the drier months (June to October) boats cannot reach the port and leave from El Mangual, 3 km away along a very dusty road. Minibuses from the center charge about US50¢ for the ride. Locals tell me that during the wettest months (February to April) boats have been known to reach the Plaza San Martín in Pucallpa, but I don't know if I was getting my leg pulled about that one!

Anyway, wherever the port is, you can get river boats along the Río Ucayali from Pucallpa to Iquitos (three to five days, US$25). It's easier to get a passage when the river is high. In the dry season the river is too low for many of the boats and passages are slower.

Finding a boat to the ports of Contamaná and Requena is not difficult. Expreso Turístico Ucayali, Portillo 671, has speed boats taking about five hours to get to **Contamaná** (about five hours, US$22) and back, against the current (six to seven hours, US$27). They leave daily about noon in each direction. However, accommodations are very basic in Contamaná, where there are reportedly two dirty, noisy hotels charging about US$2.50 per person. Contamaná has a frontier-town atmosphere and continuing from there north to Iquitos is not any easier than from Pucallpa. Although Contamaná, like most river towns, is settled mainly by mestizo colonists, the village of Roroboya, a little over half way between Pucallpa and Contamaná, is a Shipibo Indian community.

The town of **Requena** has a better *Hotel Municipal* at US$5 per person. It is clean but one traveler reports that nearby church bells ring every 15 minutes, all night long! There is another more basic and cheaper hotel. From Requena, boats to Iquitos leave on most days, taking about 12 hours. Locals in the small villages along the river are often helpful and friendly.

Because air fares are not much more expensive than river boat fares, there are fewer passenger boats than there used to be and travel conditions are rough. Food is provided but it is very basic and travelers often get sick – bring some of your own food. Hammocks and mosquito repellent are essential but not provided. The market in Pucallpa sells hammocks but the mosquito repellent is of poor quality. The Capitanía should be able to provide you with a list of boats and their destinations, though their information is rarely reliable until after the boat has gone! Passengers from Pucallpa to Iquitos may need to have their passport inspected by both the PIP and the Capitanía before beginning the trip. If you are heading on to Brazil, it is more convenient to fly as far as Iquitos and then begin your river journey from there.

Jungle 'guides' approaching you on the Pucallpa waterfront are usually unreliable and sometimes dishonest. There isn't much to do in the way of jungle trips from the dock anyway. If you want to make an excursion into the jungle, you should look for a reliable service in Yarinacocha. For a river boat passage, ask on any likely looking boat but don't hand over any money until you and your luggage are actually aboard the boat of your choice. Then pay the captain and no one else.

Don't wander around the docks with your luggage looking for a boat; arrange a trip, then return with your luggage. Boats are sometimes delayed for some days before the cargo is loaded but captains will often let you sling your hammock and stay aboard at no extra cost while you wait for departure. Be aware of the danger of theft in the La Hoyada dock area and the fact that drug-running boats leave from here, too. However, police vigilance has decreased the number of drug-running boats considerably in recent years.

Getting Around

Mototaxis will take you to the airport for about US$1 and to Yarinacocha for about US$2 but you'll probably have to bargain. Car taxis are twice as expensive.

Buses to Yarinacocha (US30¢) leave from the corner of Ucayali and Sucre. Colectivo taxis charging US50¢ leave from the same corner.

Motorcycles can be rented for about US$3 per hour or US$22 for 12 hours (6 am to 6 pm). Try at Portillo 730 and Ucayali 235.

YARINACOCHA

Yarinacocha lies about 10 km northeast of Pucallpa. This attractive oxbow lake, once part of the Río Ucayali, is now entirely landlocked, though a small canal links the two bodies of water during the rainy season. The road from Pucallpa goes to the small port of Puerto Callao, which is the main population center on the lake. Here, there are a few places to stay, several bars and restaurants and boats for trips around the lake. You can visit Shipibo Indian villages and buy handicrafts or watch for wildlife in and around the lake. My wife and I have seen freshwater dolphins in the lake, a sloth and a meter-long green iguana in the trees, and plenty of exotic birds, ranging from the curiously long-toed wattled jacana, which walks on lily pads and other floating vegetation, to the metallic green flash of the Amazon kingfisher.

Tours & Guides

Whether your interest lies in bird-watching, photography, visiting Indian villages, fishing or just relaxing on a boat ride around the lake, you'll find plenty of peki-peki boat owners ready to oblige. Take your time in choosing; there's no point in going with the first offer unless you are sure you like your boatman. Ask around and be aware that some boatmen are dishonest and may be involved in drug trafficking. Guides are also available for walking trips into the surrounding forest, including some overnight trips. If you are interested in fishing, the dry season is said to be the best.

A recommended guide is Gilber Reategui Sangama who owns the boat *La Normita* on Yarinacocha. He has expedition supplies (sleeping pads, mosquito nets, purified drinking water) and is both knowledgeable and environmentally aware about the wildlife and people. As with all the local guides, he speaks little English. He is safe and reliable, and will cook most of your meals for you. He charges about US$30 per person per day, with a minimum of two people, and he runs tours of three to five days. If he is not available he recommends his uncle, Nemecio Sangama, who owns the boat *El Rayito*. Mauricio (nicknamed 'Boa') is a good guide but has no equipment. Others who have been recommended include Marly Alemán Arévalo with the *Julito*, and the boatmen Roy Riaño and Jorge Morales.

A good afternoon trip is up the northeast arm of the lake (to your right as you look at the lake from Puerto Callao). Ask the boatman to float slowly along and look for bird life at the water's edge or sloths *(perezoso)* in the trees. Sunset is a good time to be on the lake. A day trip up the northwestern arm is a good way to visit San Francisco and perhaps another Shipibo village.

There is also a botanical garden reached by a 45 minute boat ride followed by a 30 minute walk. For short trips, boatmen charge about US$7 an hour for the boat. It is always worth bargaining over the price but the best way to do it is to set a price for the boat and then ask the boatman if you can bring a couple of friends. As long as there are only two or three of you, they don't normally complain and you can split the cost.

The Mission

There is a large, modern American missionary base on the outskirts of Puerto Callao that is affiliated to the SIL (Summer Institute of Linguistics). The missionaries have made contact with various Amazonian tribes and work to translate the Indian languages into English and Spanish. By making a workable alphabet for these previously unwritten languages, the missionaries hope to translate the New Testament into the area's many different Indian languages.

Shipibo Indians & Their Handicrafts

The Shipibo Indians live along the Ucayali and its tributaries in small villages of simple, thatched platform houses. They are a matriarchal society. San Francisco, at the northwest end of the lake, is one village that is often visited.

The Shipibo women make fine ceramics and textiles decorated with highly distinctive, geometric designs. Some of the women come into Pucallpa to sell their pottery and material. It is also possible to buy direct from their villages, but the selection is not very good and the villagers distrustful of outsiders, particularly because of problems with guerrillas and drug-runners in recent years.

The Shipibo also run a very fine cooperative craft store that collects work from about 40 villages. The store, called Maroti Shobo, is on the main plaza of Puerto Callao. There are many ceramics to choose from and because each piece is hand made, it can be considered unique. Lengths of decorated cloth and other handicrafts are also available but it is the ceramics that make the place really worthwhile. The pieces range from small pots and animal figurines to huge urns. The friendly staff (Spanish essential) will arrange international shipping if you buy a large piece. Prices are fixed (no bargaining) but I found them very fair. I bought my favorite South American handicraft here and every time I look at my sensitively molded, two-headed, ceremonial drinking pot, I am reminded of Peru. ∎

There are opponents to the mission who feel the Indians will lose their tribal and cultural idenities by becoming Christianized.

Places to Stay

There are two small hotels in Puerto Callao near the waterfront; anyone can point them out to you. The *Hotel El Pescador* is the cheapest place to stay. Its main attraction is its waterfront location; otherwise it's a pretty basic hotel with an erratic water supply. Rooms are about US$4/6.

A short dirt road to the left along the waterfront leads to the *Hostal El Delfin* (☎/fax 57-1129). Rooms here are better and only a little more expensive than those at El Pescador. Old wooden cabins with a basic private bath are US$5/7.50. Newer rooms are large and clean with fans, TV and private bath for US$8/11. El Delfin is full more often than El Pescador. By asking around, you can sometimes find a room in a private home.

There used to be several jungle lodges around the lake but terrorist problems closed most of them. Things are looking up again, however. The Swiss-run *La Cabaña* is a 15 minute peki-peki ride across the lake from Puerto Callao. The owner also runs the *Mercedes* in Pucallpa, so you can make inquiries there. The lodge is good, quiet, has a restaurant and charges about US$35 per person including meals. Guided tours are available and have been recommended. La Cabaña is the only lodge that has made it through the problem years intact. A little further away is the German-run *La Perla*, which is more expensive but I haven't heard any recommendations for it.

Places to Eat

Several inexpensive restaurants and lively bars line the Puerto Callao waterfront.

AGUAYTÍA

A little over half way from Pucallpa to Tingo María is the small and fairly pleasant jungle town of Aguaytía, a possible base for visiting the nearby Boquerón del Padre Abad, on the main Pucallpa-Tingo María route (see Buses under Pucallpa). Aguaytía is on a river of the same name, which is spanned by an impressive suspension bridge.

Places to Stay & Eat

There are a few cheap and basic hotels. The most pleasant seems to be an unnamed place above a store opposite the main bus offices. It's clean and friendly and charges about US$5/7.50 in rooms with shared bath. The similarly priced *Hostal Rimay* has rooms with private bath but they don't work very well and the place smells of sewage (maybe they'll solve their plumbing problems). The *Hostal Oriente* is cheaper but very basic. Others to try are the *Hostal Nelly* and *Hostal San Antonio*.

Most of the restaurants are along Calle Sargento Suarez and charge US$1 for a simple set lunch.

Getting There & Away

Bus The main road, just above the town, has a police control point. Minibuses to Tingo María (US$4, four hours) leave from here every hour or so during daylight. Nearby are bus offices with daily departures for Pucallpa and Lima.

Boat Dugout canoes with outboards leave in the mornings for various small settlements on the Río Aguaytía.

YURIMAGUAS

Locals call Yurimaguas 'the pearl of the Huallaga.' It is the major port on the Río Huallaga and boats to Iquitos can be found here. Reaching Yurimaguas can involve a long road trip (see Across the Northern Highlands) or a simple flight from Lima. With a population of about 25,000, Yurimaguas is a quiet, pleasant little town, quite different from the bustling boom-town atmosphere of Pucallpa. There are signs of the rubber-boom days, such as the expensive imported tiles that decorate the walls of the buildings at the end of Avenida Arica, but generally it is a sleepy port where you may have to wait a couple of days for a river boat to Iquitos. Bring a couple of good books.

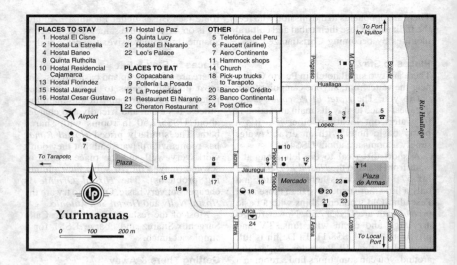

PLACES TO STAY
1 Hostal El Cisne
2 Hostal La Estrella
4 Hostal Baneo
8 Quinta Ruthcita
10 Hostal Residencial Cajamarca
13 Hostal Florindez
15 Hostal Jauregui
16 Hostal Cesar Gustavo
17 Hostal de Paz
19 Quinta Lucy
21 Hostal El Naranjo
22 Leo's Palace

PLACES TO EAT
3 Copacabana
9 Pollería La Posada
12 La Prosperidad
21 Restaurant El Naranjo
22 Cheraton Restaurant

OTHER
5 Telefónica del Peru
6 Faucett (airline)
7 Aero Continente
11 Hammock shops
14 Church
18 Pick-up trucks to Tarapoto
20 Banco de Crédito
23 Banco Continental
24 Post Office

Yurimaguas

Guerrilla activity has not been a problem since 1993. The town is a major US Drug Enforcement Agency (DEA) base and agents maintain quite a high profile in the area. Their mission seems mainly to be the prevention of the exportation of *pasta básica* (partially processed coca leaves for use in cocaine production) to Colombia. They have a huge radar to detect the small aircraft that are used to haul the pasta básica.

A small but growing number of visitors pass through en route to Iquitos.

Information
Tourist Office There is no tourist office but the Consejo Regional on the Plaza de Armas can give tourist information.

Money Banco de Crédito or Banco Continental give rates close to what they are in Lima and will change traveler's checks.

Post & Telecommunications The offices are shown on the map. The area code for Yurimaguas is 094.

Places to Stay
None of the hotels have hot water at this time, though most have private bathrooms. Shoestring travelers can try the following very basic hotels. The *Quinta Ruthcita* has shared baths and charges US$2.50 per person. The *Quinta Lucy* has private baths and charges US$3/5. The *Hostal Jauregui* has dark and dingy rooms with bath but no fan for US$3.50/5. The *Hostal Baneo* has shared baths and charges US$4/6 as does the *Hostal El Cisne* with private baths and the *Hostal La Estrella* with private baths but no fans. The best of the basic places is the clean and quiet *Hostal Cesar Gustavo*, which has rooms with private bath and fan for US$5/7.

The *Hostal Florindez* has air-conditioning and private baths in its otherwise basic rooms for US$7/9.50. The new *Hostal de Paz* (☎ 35-2123) is good value with clean rooms with bath, fan and TV for US$8.50/11. Also good is the new and quiet *Hostal Residencial Cajamarca*, which charges US$11/14 in rooms with bath, fan and TV. They serve breakfast (at an extra cost). The *Hostal El Naranjo* (☎ 35-2650, 35-0554) is brand new, clean, quiet and recommended. Rooms with bath, fan and TV are US$13.50/16. *Leo's Palace* (☎ 35-2213, 35-2544) is the oldest of the better hotels. It has a few simple but spacious clean rooms with bath, fan and a balcony overlooking the Plaza de Armas, though not all the rooms are this good (they may be smaller or lack balconies). Rates are about US$12/16. They have cable TV available but charge an extra US$2 for it.

Places to Eat
The *El Naranjo Restaurant* in the Hostal El Naranjo and *Cheraton* in Leo's Palace are among the best, though neither of them is anything special. Also OK is the *Copacabana* for general food, the *Pollería La Posada* for chicken and *La Prosperidad* for tropical juices and sandwiches.

Things to Buy
Stores selling hammocks for river journeys are on the north side of the market.

Getting There & Away
Air Faucett and Aero Continente fly here at this time, though carriers, schedules and routes change frequently. Recently, Aero Continente flew to and from Lima via Tarapoto on Wednesday, Friday and Sunday and to Iquitos on the same days. Faucett flew to Lima via Tarapoto on Wednesday and Sunday. Don't ask me why they don't schedule flights on different days! Fares are US$90 to Lima, US$24 to Tarapoto, and US$62 to Iquitos. Aero Taxi Iberico has an office by the airport and flies light aircraft to various nearby towns – ask at the airport.

Bus The only route out of Yurimaguas is the rough road to Tarapoto, which has improved considerably. Pick-up trucks leave from J Riera several times a day from 4 am to 6 pm, though I would leave in the morning to enjoy the great scenery and to avoid the slight chance of being assaulted on the road at night (reports of nighttime hold ups are now diminishing). It takes

from four to six hours, depending on the weather, and costs US$9 in the cabin or US$6.50 in the back (mind the sunburn!). The trip may take longer in the wet season.

River Boat Cargo boats from Yurimaguas follow the Huallaga to the Río Marañón and on to Iquitos. The trip usually takes about three days (captains insist they can do it in 36 hours, but there are numerous stops for loading and unloading cargo). There are several departures a week. Passages should cost less than US$20, or a little more in a cabin. Boat information is available from the Agencia Fluviales, by the river. As with other river trips, bring a hammock, mosquito repellent, purified water or tablets and a supply of food, unless you're prepared to eat the very basic and monotonous food available on board. Because Yurimaguas has fewer air and road services than Pucallpa, the river link is more important and the cargo boats are used to taking passengers. The journey can be broken at Lagunas (see below), just before the Huallaga meets the Marañón.

Getting Around
Mototaxis charge about US60¢ to the port, or walk 13 blocks north.

LAGUNAS
This village is the best point from which to begin a trip to the Reserva Nacional Pacaya-Samiria, described below. Lagunas is small and remote so you should bring most supplies with you. There are no money-changing facilities and food is limited and expensive.

Guides
Guides are available here to visit Pacaya-Samiria and they charge less than guides in Iquitos. They speak only Spanish. Some guides will hunt and fish but this is to be discouraged because you are, after all, visiting a reserve! If you tell the guides not to hunt, they'll abide by your request. Fishing for the pot is OK. The going rate is about US$8 to US$10 per passenger per day for

guide and boat; food is extra. Very small groups may have to pay more per person.

Very good guides are Job and Luís Gongora (nephew and uncle), who can be contacted at the Hostal La Sombra. They are reliable and knowledgeable and will cook and paddle for hours in the park. Paddling is better than motor boat if you want to approach animals quietly. They recently charged US$150 plus food for a six day trip for two tourists.

Other guides who have been recommended are Edinson Saldaña Gutiérrez and Juan Huaycama, both well known locally. Ask anyone.

Places to Stay & Eat

The hotels are very basic but you don't have much choice! The *Hostal La Sombra* (also known as Hostal Piñedo) has hot, stuffy little rooms at US$2 per person. The owners are friendly and the place is safe. Shared showers and food are available. The smaller *Hotel Montalbán* is another OK possibility. You can stay in a hostal above the Farmacía, but they don't have showers (buckets of water are provided). *Doña Dina* in a blue-fronted building just off the plaza serves good cheap meals.

Getting There & Away

Boats from Yurimaguas take about 12 hours and leave most days.

RESERVA NACIONAL PACAYA-SAMIRIA

At 20,800 sq km, this reserve is the largest of all of Peru's protected areas. In common with many reserves in South America, Pacaya-Samiria both provides local people with food and a home and protects ecologically important habitats. In this case, an estimated 30,000 people live on and around the reserve, and juggling the needs of the human inhabitants with the protection of wildlife is the key to managing the area. During 1994 and 1995, 25 rangers were hired and trained, paid for by contributions from the US government and private organizations in partnership with the Fundación Peruana para la Conservación de la Naturaleza (FPCN). Currently, a project is underway in teaching inhabitants how to best harvest the reserve's natural renewable resources in order to benefit the local people and to maintain thriving populations of plants and animals.

The reserve is the home of aquatic animals such as the Amazonian manatee, pink and grey river dolphins, two species of caiman, the giant South American river turtle and many others. Monkeys and birds are quite abundant and there are also many of the less commonly seen species of wildlife.

The best way to visit the reserve is to go by dugout canoe with a guide from Lagunas and spend several days camping and exploring. The area close to Lagunas has suffered from depletion by hunting, so you need several days to get deep into the least disturbed areas. The new ranger stations will charge a nominal fee to enter the reserve (US$5 recently) and you can then stay as long as you want.

The best time to go is during the drier season, when you are more likely to see animals along the river banks. Although the rains ease off in late May, it takes a month or so for the waters to drop and so July and August are the best months. September to November aren't too bad and December and January often have fairly low water. The heaviest rains begin in January and the months of February to May are the worst times to go and see wildlife here. February to June tend to be the hottest months.

Travelers should bring plenty of insect repellant, plastic bags to cover luggage, and be prepared to camp out.

SARAMERIZA

Sarameriza is a tiny port on the upper Marañón and the most westerly point from which to start a river journey down the Amazon, though this trip is very rarely done. I have heard from one source that permits (which are expensive and difficult to obtain) are asked for on this route. I've also heard that you can get through if your passport is in order. This is a developing region and roads may improve compared to my description below.

To get to Sarameriza (or Puerto Delfus, a few kilometers away), you must first get to Bagua, on the Chiclayo to Chachapoyas route in the northern Andes. Beyond Bagua, the going gets rough. Trucks travel daily via Aramongo to Nazareth (or the neighboring village of Chiriaco), about 80 km to the northeast, and continue to Imazita (where there is a basic hotel), about 30 km further on. Your documents will be checked at a police checkpoint about halfway between Chiriaco and Imazita. Bear in mind that, as you are close to the disputed Ecuadorian border here, police may be sensitive to anyone wearing a 'Galápagos' T-shirt or even to the presence of an Ecuadorian stamp in a passport.

From the checkpoint, a road branches off to Sarameriza, about 150 km to the northeast. This road is in very bad shape and you have to hitch a ride (expect to pay) on any vehicle that comes along. Vehicles do the trip about two or three times a week and may take days, depending on the state of the road. Be self-sufficient with food and sleeping gear. It is best to sleep in Nazareth or Chiriaco while waiting for a ride to Sarameriza.

Alternatively, you can get a boat from Imazita along the Marañón to Santa María de Nieve (about eight hours, departures every few days). The river is relatively narrow and the scenery is good. The village is at the confluence of the Marañón and Nieve rivers and has a basic hotel. From Santa María, the boat trip to Sarameriza takes a further 12 hours, though the trip can be broken at the army base of Pingo; there are no hotels in Pingo but you can stay with local families.

This area is the home of Aguaruna Indians and there is much pressure on them from Peruvian settlers. Mestizo settlers in the villages of Imazita and Santa María de Nieve routinely travel between the two places, but they consider it dangerous to stop en route at any of the Aguaruna settlements. Adventurers have tried to float down this section of the Marañón on rafts. In 1989, three French citizens and a Peruvian were shot to death while floating down-river. In 1995, two Americans were shot and one was killed on the same stretch (see the US magazine *Outside*, November 1995, for a full report).

Cargo boats leave Sarameriza for Iquitos every 10 or 15 days, so be prepared to wait. The river journey takes about five days. Obviously, this is a trip for the self-sufficient traveler with a spirit of adventure, plenty of common sense and a lot of spare time. Good luck!

IQUITOS

With a population approaching 400,000, Iquitos is Peru's largest jungle city and the capital of the huge Department of Loreto, largest of Peru's 24 departments. Iquitos is linked with the outside world by air and the Río Amazonas – I can't think of a larger city anywhere in the world that can't be reached by road. There are cars to get you around, but motorcycles seem to be the preferred mode of transport (as in many jungle towns) and this makes Iquitos a very noisy city!

Iquitos has a varied and interesting history. It was founded in the 1750s as a Jesuit mission, fending off attacks from Indian tribes who didn't want to be missionized. The tiny settlement survived and grew very slowly until, by the 1870s, it had some 1500 inhabitants. Then came the great rubber boom and the population increased about 16-fold by the 1880s. For the next 30 years, Iquitos was at once the scene of ostentatious wealth and abject poverty. The rubber barons became fabulously rich and the rubber tappers, mainly local Indians and poor mestizos, suffered virtual enslavement and sometimes death from disease or harsh treatment. Signs of the opulence of those days can still be seen in some of the mansions and tiled walls of Iquitos.

The bottom fell out of the rubber boom as suddenly as it had begun. A British entrepreneur smuggled some rubber-tree seeds out of Brazil and plantations were seeded in the Malay Peninsula. It was much cheaper and easier to collect the rubber from the orderly rows of rubber

PLACES TO STAY
- 3 Hostal José In
- 4 Hostal Baltasar
- 5 Hostal Bon Bini
- 6 Hotel Ambassador
- 12 Hostel La Pascana
- 14 Roland's Amazon River Lodge
- 16 Hotel El Dorado
- 18 Hotel Safari
- 21 Hostal Florentina
- 23 Hostal Amazonas
- 28 Grand Hotel Iquitos
- 30 Hostal Jhuliana
- 32 Hostal Karina
- 33 Hostal Acosta I
- 47 Hostal Libertad
- 48 Hostal Perú
- 49 Hostal Maynas
- 51 Hostal Loreto
- 58 Hotel Europa
- 59 Hostal Fortes
- 60 Hostal Isabel
- 61 Hostal Tacna
- 63 Hotel Acosta II
- 65 Hostal Caravel
- 66 Hostal Lima
- 68 Hostal Dos Mundos
- 72 Hostal Monterico
- 73 Hostal María Antonia
- 75 Hostal San Antonio
- 80 Hostals Anita, Lozano
- 82 Hostal Internacional
- 85 Hostal Alfert
- 86 Hostal Iquitos
- 88 Hostal Económico

PLACES TO EAT
- 15 La Barca
- 19 El Mesón
- 22 La Terracita
- 24 Ari's Burger
- 29 La Maloka
- 31 Olla de Oro
- 42 Don Giovanni
- 43 El Tuquito
- 44 Casa de Jaime
- 69 Chifa Wai Ming
- 71 Several Chifas
- 79 Pollería El Pollo Suave
- 81 La Pascana

OTHER
- 1 Museo Regional
- 2 Extasis Discoteca
- 7 Anaconda Lara Lodge (office)
- 8 Rapido Expresso Boat Office
- 9 Francesco Pub
- 10 Motorcycle Rental
- 11 El Amauta Café Bar
- 13 Dreams Discotheque
- 17 Municipalidad
- 20 Marandú Bar
- 25 Tourist Office
- 26 Craft shops, galleries
- 27 Iron House
- 34 Church
- 35 Colombian Consulate
- 36 Banco de Crédito
- 37 Telefónica del Peru
- 38 Servicios Aéreos Amazónicos
- 39 Banco Wiese
- 40 AeroPerú, Three Roses Travel
- 41 Americana (airline)
- 45 Brazilian Consulate
- 46 Adventure Tours Amazonia
- 50 Aero Continente
- 52 Banco Continental
- 53 TANS Airline
- 54 Bambolea Discoteca
- 55 Migraciones
- 56 Police
- 57 Post Office
- 62 Moisés Torres Viena
- 64 Interbanc
- 67 Motorcycle Rental
- 70 Cine Bolognesi
- 74 Faucett Airline, Paucar Tours
- 76 Motorcycle Rental
- 77 Dirección Regional de Turismo
- 78 Local Buses to Laguna Quistacocha & Airport
- 83 Colectivos to Laguna Moronacocha
- 84 Cine Iquitos
- 87 Boats for Hire to Belén Area

Iquitos

0   100   200 m

Río Amazonas

BELÉN

Mercado

To Airport

AMAZON BASIN

trees in the plantations than from the wild trees scattered in the Amazon Basin and, by WWI, Peru's rubber industry was at an end.

Iquitos suffered a period of severe economic decline during the ensuing decades, supporting itself as best it could by a combination of logging, agriculture (Brazil nuts, tobacco, bananas and barbasco – a poisonous vine used by the Indians to hunt fish and now exported for use in insecticides) and the export of wild animals to zoos. Then, in the 1960s, a second boom revitalized the area. This time, the resource was oil and its discovery made Iquitos a prosperous modern town. In recent years, tourism has also played an important part in the economy of the area.

Although most travelers use Iquitos as a base for excursions into the jungle or as a place to wait for river boats along the Amazon, there are several interesting places to see in and around the city itself.

Information

Tourist Offices The tourist office is in an unsigned office at Napo 176. They are open from 7.30 am to 1.30 pm on weekdays and can give you maps of the area as well as up-to-date information. You can also try the Dirección Regional de Turismo on the 6th block of R Hurtado on the waterfront.

Various commercial jungle guides and jungle lodges give tourist information. This is obviously biased towards selling their services, which is fine if you are looking for guides, tours or jungle lodges.

Consulates & Documents The Brazilian consul (☎ 23-2081) is at Sargento Lores 363 and the Colombian consul (☎ 23-1461) is at Putumayo 247 on the south side of the Plaza de Armas.

There are different entry requirements for travelers of different nationalities when crossing into Brazil or Colombia; regulations change often, so it is worth checking with the Brazilian or Colombian embassy at home or in Lima or Iquitos before you go.

The most recent Brazilian regulations require consular visas for citizens of the USA, France, Canada, Australia and New Zealand, while most other citizens of Europe and Latin America need only their passport to obtain a tourist card (valid for 90 days) at the border. Visa fees vary according to your country of origin (France US$50, Canada US$40, many others US$20, Australia free). A yellow fever vaccination certificate is required and you may need to show a ticket out of the country, though showing sufficient funds to buy a ticket should satisfy that requirement. A recent report indicates that the Iquitos consul does not ask to see an onward ticket but does ask to see the vaccination certificate and takes 24 hours to issue the visa. A passport photo is needed.

Colombia recently lifted regulations requiring visas from many countries, but it's always worth checking before being turned back at the border.

Immigration Migraciones (☎ 23-1021, 23-1072) is in the Prefectura building at Malecón Tarapaca 368. You can extend your tourist card or visa there. If you are arriving from Brazil or Colombia, you will get your entry stamp at the border.

Money There are several banks shown on the map where you can change traveler's checks or get advances on a credit card. They have competitive rates. For changing cash US$ quickly, you'll find street changers on Lores between Próspero and Arica. They are generally OK, though a few might have 'fixed' calculators. Use your own. Western Union money transfers can be arranged at Western Union (☎ 23-5182), Napo 359. Changing Brazilian or Colombian currency is best done at the border.

Post & Telecommunications The post office (☎ 23-4091), Arica 403, is open from 8 am to 6 pm, Monday to Saturday. Telefónica del Peru (☎ 23-5555), Arica 251, is open from 8 am to 8 pm, Monday to Saturday. You can send and receive faxes here at ☎ 23-1111. The area code for Iquitos is 094.

Travel Agencies For booking airline tickets, Paucar Tours next to the Faucett office has been recommended as reliable and will provide a free ride to the airport if you buy a ticket from them. Three Roses Agency, Próspero 246, has also been recommended. There are many other travel agents.

Jungle lodge operators have offices in Iquitos. Their addresses are given along with the description of the lodges in Around Iquitos, below.

Medical Services There are about five hospitals but you'll probably get better care at a private clinic such as the Centro Medico at Huallaga 353, open during business hours, or Clínica Ana Stahl (☎ 23-5231, 23-5801), on Avenida La Marina (parallel to the Amazon, north of downtown), which has 24-hour emergency service. English speaking private doctors include Dr Victor Antonioli (☎ 23-2684), Fitzcarrald 156, the gynecologist Dr Joel Rivera, Dos de Mayo 326, and the dentist Dr Rafael Urrunaga (☎ 23-5016), Fitcarrald 201. Farmacia Melendez (☎ 23-2411), Prospero 1035, has a pharmacist who speaks English.

Emergency The police are on the first block of Morona.

The Iron House
Every guidebook tells of the 'majestic' Iron House designed by Eiffel (of Eiffel Tower fame). It was imported, piece by piece, into Iquitos during the opulent days of the rubber boom to beautify the city. Unfortunately, no one knows exactly which building it is – during my research, I have read of three different buildings that are supposedly the famous Iron House. Even the people at the tourist office were vague when I asked them. To me, the most likely building seems to be the one on the northeast corner of Putumayo and Raimondi, on the Plaza de Armas. It looks like a bunch of scrap-metal sheets bolted together and is certainly nothing to get excited about. (There is now a small cake/snack shop inside.) I can't help wondering whether the famous Iron House is a myth perpetrated by generations of guides.

Azulejos
Some impressive remnants of those boom days remain, however. The best are the *azulejos*, hand-made tiles imported from Portugal to decorate the mansions of the rubber barons. Many buildings along Raimondi and the Malecón (literally, dike or seawall) are lavishly decorated with azulejos. Some of the best are various government buildings along or near the Malecón.

Belén
A walk down Raimondi (which turns into Próspero) and back along the Malecón is interesting, not only to see some of the tile-faced buildings but also to visit the Belén market area at the southeast end of town. Belén itself is a floating shanty town with a certain charm to it (the locals call it an Amazonian Venice but others would call it a slum). It consists of scores of huts built on rafts, which rise and fall with the river. During the dry months, these rafts sit on the river mud and are dirty and unhealthy but, for most of the year, they float on the river – a colorful and exotic sight. Several thousand people live here and canoes float from hut to hut selling and trading jungle produce. If you speak a few words of Spanish, you can find someone to paddle you around for a fee. Ask at the end of 9 de Diciembre. Although it is a very poor area, it seems reasonably safe, at least in daylight hours.

The city market, within the city blocks in front of Belén, is the usual raucous, crowded affair common to most Peruvian towns. All kinds of strange and exotic products are sold here among the mundane bags of rice, sugar, flour and cheap plastic and metal household goods. Look for the bark of the Chuchuhuasi tree that is soaked in rum for weeks and used as a tonic drink (served in many of the local bars). All kinds of other medicinal and culinary offerings are on sale: piles of dried frogs and fish, armadillo shells, piranha teeth and a great variety of tropical fruits. Pasaje Paquito is the block where they sell medicinal plants. It makes for exciting shopping or sightseeing but remember to watch your wallet.

Nicole Maxwell's *The Sorcerer's Apprentice* has been recommended for good background on medicinal plants in the Iquitos area.

Museo Regional
The museum is open daily except Sunday and has erratic opening hours. Admission is about US$1 and isn't really worth it unless you want to see stuffed rainforest animals that, as one might expect in the heat and humidity, are not in a very good state of repair.

Laguna Moronacocha
This lake forms the western boundary of the town. To get there, take the colectivo that departs from 2 de Mayo and leaves the city center along Ejército. The ride takes about 15 minutes. There really isn't much to see but there are a couple of very basic bars with views of the lake. It's a good place to relax with a cold beer and watch the sun set.

Laguna Quistacocha
This lake lies roughly 15 km south of Iquitos and makes a pleasant day trip. Minibuses leave several times an hour from Plaza 28 de Julio and charge US$1.20. There is a small zoo of local fauna displayed in sadly under-sized cages and a fish hatchery where you can see two-meter-long paiche fish swimming around. This huge river fish is one of the tastiest I've eaten but its popularity has apparently caused a severe decline in its numbers (see the sidebar, Fruit-Eating Fish). An attempt to rectify the situation is being made with the breeding program at the fish hatchery. There is a pedestrian walk around the lake (in which people swim though it looks rather unsavory) and paddle boats are for

Fruit-Eating Fish

Fruits are born on plants growing on land while fish spend their lives in the water. This simple and self-evident statement leads to the assumption that fish don't eat fruit and it was not until recently that exactly the opposite became generally known.

In fact, dozens of Amazonian fish species rely on fruit as the mainstay of their diet. Every year the river bursts its banks and floods up to 100,000 sq km of riverside forest. Thus fish can swim into the forest and eat floating or sunken fruit – there are even vegetarian piranhas. Some fish have developed extremely strong jaws that work like nut-crackers to enable them to eat the hardest seeds. One of the largest Amazonian fish, the *paiche* (also called the *pirarucu*, which can grow to well over two meters in length and weigh in at almost 90 kilos, is a fruit-eater.

During the rainy months, frugivorous fish glut themselves and fatten up for the lean times ahead. As the flood waters recede during the drier months, the fish lose their main source of food and simply stop eating until the next flood gets them back into the fruit. Fish biologist Michael Goulding reports that of 167 frugivorous fish caught during a dry season fishing trip, none had had a recent meal.

Fish like the delicious paiche play an extraordinarily important part in the economy of the Amazon. Even the poorest families can fish for food and this is the main source of protein for Amazon dwellers. From 1970 to 1975, the fish catch in the Amazon basin declined by 25% – a serious threat. Studies showed that logging along the river banks caused a loss of habitat for frugivorous fish. Apart from losing their main source of food, these fish also lost their breeding grounds. Many species of carnivorous fish that rely upon the frugivores for food were adversely affected. Goulding estimates that as much as 75% of the fish sold in the major Amazon fish market of Manaus, Brazil, rely ultimately on the flooded forest. These are among the most compelling reasons against logging and clearing the riverside forest. ∎

hire. It's fairly crowded with locals at the weekend but not midweek. Admission is US$1.50.

Places to Stay

There are plenty of hotels to choose from but the nicest and cheapest tend to fill up early, so for the best choice look as soon as you arrive. Many of the budget places are near the Belén area and some have an erratic water supply. Even some of the mid-range hotels suffer from a water shortage and it is important to look at your room and check the water supply before paying. Almost all the hotels, even if they have water problems, provide private bathrooms, though this can be a hindrance if you can't flush the toilet. Mosquitoes are rarely a serious problem and mosquito netting is not provided, though there should always be a fan. If there isn't one in your room, ask the management for one.

Places to Stay – bottom end

All these hotels have private baths and fans unless I write otherwise. The hotels in this paragraph are amongst the best in their price ranges. The clean and friendly *Hostal Alfert* (☎ 23-4105), G Saenz 001, is popular with travelers on a tight budget. Rooms are US$7 for one or two people and the hotel is quiet, with a view of the Amazon. They have water problems, though the management will keep up a steady stream of buckets of water. The *Hostal Tacna* (☎ 23-2839), Tacna 516, is basic and noisy, but clean and one of the cheapest at US$4.50/6.50 for singles/doubles. Also one of the cheapest is the *Hostal Monterico* (☎ /fax 23-5395), Arica 633, which is basic but OK for US$7/8. Also decent is the *Hotel Fortes* (☎ 23-5221), Próspero 665, which charges US$7/9. The simple *Hotel La Pascana* (☎ 23-1418), Pevas 133, has a small garden and is good, safe, friendly, popular with travelers and often full. Call ahead if possible. Rooms are US$10/13. The quiet and clean *Hostal Lima* (☎ 23-5152), Próspero 549, has fair rooms (their business card describes them as 'soberly decorated') for US$9/12.

Those on a budget can also try the very basic and noisy *Hostal San Antonio* (☎ 23-5221), Prospero 655, which is the cheapest in town at US$4.50/5.50 and lacks fans. The similarly priced but even more basic *Hostal Anita*, Hurtado 742, is friendly but has water problems. Next door, the slightly better *Hostal Lozano* (☎ 23-2486), Hurtado 772, charges US$6/9. The *Hostal Iquitos* (☎ 23-9015), R. Hurtado 955, is just OK for US$7/10. The *Hostal Perú* (☎ 23-4961), Próspero 318, and the *Hostal Loreto*, Próspero 311, are basic and noisy and have erratic water but are reasonably clean for US$7/9. Others in this price range are the basic but friendly *Hostal Karina* (☎ 23-5367), Putumayo 467, and the *Maynas Hotel* (☎ 23-5861), Próspero 388, which isn't very clean, and the *Hostal Económico*, Moore 1164, which is clean and away from the center.

The *Hostal Libertad* (☎ 23-5763), Arica 361, has air-conditioning, a restaurant and TVs in some rooms, which are otherwise fairly simple. It's worth the US$10/15 for the air-conditioning. Others at about this price or a little less are the *Hostal Bon Bini* (☎ 23-8422), Pevas 386, which is clean and quiet, the *Hostal Baltasar* (☎ 23-2240), Condamine 265, which is clean and acceptable, the *Hostal José In*, which is overpriced, the *Hostal Isabel* (☎ 23-4901), Brasil 164, which has varied rooms ranging from poor to quite good, and *Roland's Amazon River Lodge*, which is dirty, dark and a poor choice.

The *Hostal Florentina* (☎ 23-3591), Huallaga 212, has clean, pleasant rooms with fan for US$12/16. The *Hostal Dos Mundos* (☎ 23-2635), Tacna 631, has clean rooms with telephones for US$17/23, but often offers discounts.

Places to Stay – middle

All of the hotels in this section have rooms with air-conditioning and private bath, though most lack hot water (which isn't a major problem in the heat of Iquitos). A few may have some cheaper rooms with a fan. The *Hostal María Antonia* (☎ 23-4761, fax 23-4264), Próspero 616, is adequate for US$26/32 in rooms with TV and phone. There is a cafetería. The *Hotel Internacional* (☎ 23-9598, ☎ /fax 23-4684), Próspero 835, has decent rooms with TV and fridge for US$24/35. There is a restaurant. The similarly priced *Hotel Safari* (☎ 23-5593), Napo 118, has adequate rooms with TV and phone.

The *Hostal Caravel* (☎ 23-2176), Próspero 568, has a nice atmosphere and claims to have hot showers. Rooms with a TV and phone are US$26/36, but long-stay discounts are offered. The friendly *Hostal Europa* (☎ 23-1123, 23-4744, fax 23-5483), Brasil 222, has rooms with hot water (which rarely works), telephone, fridge and cable TV for US$32/46. They have a cafetería. The *Grand Hotel Iquitos* (☎ 23-1322, 23-6222; in Lima ☎ 241-2202, fax 241-6149), on the Malecón Tarapaca, is the Grand Dame of Iquitos' hotels. Its rooms are a bit shabby, though clean enough and the view over the Amazon compensates for the deteriorated decor. Rooms are US$35/45, including a continental breakfast; cheaper rooms with fans are available.

Also around US$35/45 are the modern *Hostal Amazonas* (☎ 23-2015, ☎ /fax 24-2431), Arica 108, and the *Hostal Ambassador* (☎ 23-3110, 23-8684), Pevas 260. Both have good rooms with hot water, fridge, TV and telephone, and the Amazonas has a prime location on the Plaza de Armas.

Places to Stay – top end

The *Hostal Jhuliana* (☎ /fax 23-3154), Putumayo 52, boasts a swimming pool, cafetería and bar and carpeted rooms with hot water, fridge, cable TV and phone for US$48/58. The *Hotel Acosta 2* (☎ 23-1282,

23-1286), Ricardo Palma 252, also has a restaurant, bar, swimming pool and good rooms with the above amenities for about US\$60/70. The *Hotel Acosta 1* (☎ 23-5974), Huallaga at Araujo, lacks the pool and is a bit cheaper, but still good. The *Hotel El Dorado* (☎ 23-7326, 23-1742), Napo 362, has all the facilities described above and is a good hotel. Rooms here are about US\$65/80. Note that these top end hotels are generally quite small, with only a few dozen rooms, and are often full, so reservations aren't a bad idea.

Places to Eat

Those wishing to economize can eat at small restaurants and stalls in the market area, but this is not recommended if your stomach is unaccustomed to Peruvian food. There are several inexpensive chifas near the Plaza 28 de Julio, the best of which is *Wai Ming*, which is a little more expensive than the others but is worth it. More cheap restaurants are found on Tacna and Huallaga in the blocks north of Plaza 28 de Julio. A good cheap chicken place is *Pollería El Pollo Suave* on Plaza 28 de Julio. Also on this plaza is *Heladería D'Onofrio* with good ice cream. *La Barca*, Fitzcarrald 137 just off the Plaza de Armas, is clean, has OK food and is quite cheap. Nearby, on the corner of the plaza, *La Terracita* is another OK cheap choice.

Slightly pricier but good eateries include the following. *La Pascana* (☎ 23-9021), R Hurtado 735, on the waterfront, is a simple place with good ceviches and fine Amazon river views. *La Olla de Oro* (☎ 23-4350), Araujo 579, has a good selection of local and Peruvian food at reasonable prices. *Ari's Burger* (☎ 23-1470), on the corner of the Plaza de Armas, is a brightly lit and clean joint known locally as 'gringolandia.' They are open almost always, will change US\$, are generally helpful and popular with foreign travelers. *El Tuquito* (☎ 23-6770), Putumayo 157 just off the Plaza de Armas, has good seafood.

Don Giovanni on the corner of the Plaza de Armas has medium-priced Italian food. *El Mesón* (☎ 23-1197), Napo 116, is a little pricey and serves local specialities. *La Casa de Jaime* (☎ 23-9456) on the Malecón has good local food, steaks, fish, and is friendly and recommended – I liked the food here the best. *La Maloka* (☎ 23-3126), a floating restaurant on the Amazon, has quite good local and Peruvian food in a romantic setting. It's not cheap but not terribly expensive and how often do you get to dine overlooking the Amazon!

Entertainment

There are a couple of cinemas, of which the *Cine Bolognesi* on the Plaza 28 de Julio shows the better films. *Alianza Francés* (☎ 23-2088), on the first block of Napo, has occasional French movie screenings, often on Wednesday evenings, and dance performances.

There are several places to meet for a cold beer or other drink and hear music, both recorded and live. These are especially found in the blocks between the Plaza de Armas and the waterfront. The *Marandú Bar* and *Francesco Pub* on the Malecón have both been recommended. *El Amauta Café Bar* (☎ 23-3109), Nauta 250, has live Peruvian music on most nights. There are other places nearby. *La Pergola*, Napo 735, is a nice bar in a tropical garden and has live music some nights.

For dancing, the most locally popular place is the *Agricobank* on Condamine a couple of blocks north of the map. It's a huge outdoors place where hundreds of locals gather for drinking, dancing and socializing. The trendy and more expensive dance clubs include the *Bamboleo Discoteca* on the Malecón and the *Latin Limits* on the road to the airport. A couple of others are shown on the map but I haven't checked them out.

Things to Buy

There are several shops on the first block of Napo selling jungle crafts, some of high quality and price. Shipibo Indians also hang out on the street here, on the Plaza de Armas and on the Malecón, selling their wares. A good place for crafts is Mercado de Artesanía San Juan on the road to the

AMAZON BASIN

airport – bus and taxi drivers know it. Although items made from animal bones and skins are available, I discourage their purchase. Most visitors come to the jungle to see some of the wildlife, not to help destroy it by purchasing animal products. It is illegal to import many of them into North America and Europe.

Film and camera batteries are sold at Kodak Photo, Raimondi 142 just off the Plaza de Armas.

Getting There & Away
Plane or river boat are your only choices – all roads into the jungle stop within 20 km or so.

Air Iquitos has a small international airport with flights to Miami and Colombia, as well as local flights. There have been flights to Brazil in the past, but none at this writing.

AeroPerú, Faucett, Aero Continente and Americana have offices in town. In the past, Imperial Air and Expresso Aéreo also served Iquitos but don't at this writing. There are about six flights a day from and to Lima (US$95), mostly leaving in the afternoon and evening, although Faucett has one early morning flight from Lima, returning from Iquitos in mid-morning. Some of these flights are direct and some stop in Pucallpa, Chiclayo, Trujillo, or Tarapoto.

There are two or three flights a day to Pucallpa (US$53) from where you can continue anywhere you want by bus. Tarapoto (US$62) is served daily except Monday by Aero Continente or Faucett. AeroPerú has flights on Friday and Sunday to Trujillo (US$75) and on Monday and Wednesday to Chiclayo (US$75). Aero Continente flies to Yurimaguas (US$61) on Wednesday, Friday and Sunday. All this information is subject to change but it gives you an idea of frequency.

Faucett flies Lima-Iquitos-Miami and vice versa every Saturday. Remember that airline tickets bought in Peru are subject to 18% tax so try to plan ahead if you want to fly internationally. Faucett advertises an Iquitos-Cuzco flight early on Sunday mornings. This flight is supposedly direct but when I flew it, they stopped in Lima. The fare of US$123 is a lot cheaper than buying Iquito-Lima and Lima-Cuzco tickets. This flight is useful for passengers arriving from Miami who want to take a one-week tour of the jungle and then continue to Cuzco.

Grupo 8 used to operate cheap military flights to Lima but no longer do. TANS (☎ 23-4632), Lores 127, has flights to remote jungle towns like Caballococha (US$46) near the Colombian border on Saturdays. (Caballacocha has one basic and one better hotel on the plaza and you can get boats from there to Leticia every day.) Twice a month TANS flies to the Río Ucayali villages of El Estrecho, Angamos, Requena, Orellana, Punta Hermosa, Contamaná and possibly on to Pucallpa. Fares are US$23 to US$46. Servicios Aéreos Amazónicos (☎ 23-5776), Arica 273, flies to **Caballacocha** (US$52) and Leticia, Colombia (US$69) on Tuesday, Thursday and Saturday. Flights are often full and subject to cancellation or postponement. Schedules, destinations and fares change frequently so check locally.

Charter companies at the airport have five passenger planes for hire to almost anywhere in the Amazon. Rates are around US$300 an hour.

Airport departure tax is US$17.70 for international flights and US$4 for domestic flights. Other international flights may be available in the future.

Boat Iquitos is Peru's largest and best organized river port and is quite capable of accepting ocean-going vessels as it did in the rubber-boom days. Most boats today, however, ply only Peruvian waters and voyagers must change boats at the border. Read the River Boat section in the Getting Around chapter for more detailed descriptions of these journeys.

Boats used to leave from the north end of the Malecón but because of changes in the river they can only reach that point occasionally when the water is high. Now boats leave from Puerto Masusa, on Avenida La

Marina about 2 or 3 km north of the center.

Boats have a chalkboard system to tell you which boats are leaving when, for where, and whether they are accepting passengers.

Upriver passages to Pucallpa (six to eight days) or Yurimaguas (four to six days) cost about US$20 to US$30 per person. Boats leave about once a week to Pucallpa, more often to Yurimaguas, less often if the river is low, but there are more frequent departures for the closer intermediate ports. Agencia Javier, Loreto 141, has information about upriver boats, although it's usually better to go down to the dock and look around.

Downriver boats to the Peruvian border with Brazil and Colombia leave about twice a week and take two to three days. Fares are US$15 to US$20 per person but gringos have to bargain hard.

If you are on a tight budget, you can often sleep aboard the boat while waiting for departure. Boats often leave many hours or a few days late!

If you're in a hurry, Expreso Loreto (☎ 23-8652), Loreto 171, has fast motor launches to the border at 6 am on Tuesday, Thursday and Sunday. The fare is US$50 for the 12-hour trip, including lunch.

Amazon Camp (see Around Iquitos, below) has weekly cruises on comfortable ships that go from Iquitos to Leticia leaving on Sunday. Most passengers are foreigners on a one-week roundtrip tour but one-way passages are sold on a space available basis.

Getting Around
Taxis & Buses A distinctive local taxi is the *motocarro* – a two-passenger motorcycle rickshaw. These strange-looking contraptions cost a little less than a taxi and are fun to ride.

Taxis tend to be more expensive than in other Peruvian cities and a taxi ride to the airport costs about US$5 or US$6, less in a motocarro.

Buses and trucks for several nearby destinations, including the airport, leave from the Plaza 28 de Julio.

Motorcycle You can find someone to rent you a motorcycle if you are persistent enough – there are three places shown on the map. Make sure you get a *Tarjeta de Propieded de la Motocicleta* (registration) and a *Documento Libre de Multas* (which will help if you are stopped by a bribe-hungry policeman).

EXPLORING THE JUNGLE
Basically, excursions into the jungle can be divided into three types: visits to jungle lodges (which is what most visitors do), a cruise on a river boat outfitted for tourism (an increasingly popular option) and more demanding camping and walking trips.

Jungle Lodges
There are quite a wide range of options at varying prices. Most can be booked from abroad or in Lima, but if you show up in Iquitos without a reservation, you can certainly book a lodge or tour and it'll cost you less. Bargaining is not out of the question if you are on a tight budget, even though operators show you fixed price lists. If the lodge has space and you have the cash, they'll nearly always give you a discount, sometimes a substantial one. If planning on booking after you arrive, avoid the major Peruvian holidays when many places are full with Peruvian holidaymakers. June to September (the driest months and the summer holiday for North American and European visitors) are also quite busy, though bargains can be found if you're flexible with time. It's worth shopping around.

The lodges are some distance from Iquitos, so river transport is included in the price. Most of the area within 50 km of the city is not virgin jungle and the chance of seeing big game is remote. Any Indians will be acculturated and performing for tourism. Nevertheless, much can be seen of the jungle way of life, and birds, insects and small mammals can be observed. The more remote lodges have more wildlife.

A typical two-day trip involves a river journey of two or three hours to a jungle lodge with reasonable comforts and meals, a 'typical jungle lunch,' a guided visit to an

Indian village to buy crafts and perhaps see dances (though tourists often outnumber Indians), an evening meal at the lodge, maybe an after-dark canoe trip to look for caimans by searchlight and a walk in the jungle the following day to see jungle vegetation and, if you are lucky, monkeys or other wildlife. A trip like this will set you back about US$50 to over US$100, depending on the operator, the distance traveled and the comfort of the lodge. On longer trips you'll get further away from Iquitos and see more, and the cost per night drops.

Places to Stay All prices quoted here are approximate, bargaining is acceptable, and meals, guided tours and transport from Iquitos should be included.

The best established and recommended agency is Explorama (☎ 23-5471, fax 23-4968), Avenida La Marina 340, which owns and operates three lodges and is an involved supporter of the Amazon Center for Environmental Education and Research (ACEER) laboratory. You could arrange a trip to visit one or more lodges combined with the ACEER Lab, each of which is very different.

The *Explorama Inn* is 40 km northeast of Iquitos on the Amazon and is their most modern lodge. Rustic thatched cottages all have screened windows, fans, lighting, private bath with heated water and private porch. Good food and short guided walks and boat rides are available for a taste of the jungle; there is some primary forest nearby. One highlight is the *Victoria regia* or giant Amazonian water lily with floating leaves almost two meters across, large enough for a child to lie down on without sinking! This lodge is a good option for people who really don't want to rough it at all. Rates are US$135 per person, double occupancy, for a two-day/one-night package and extra nights are US$70.

The *Explorama Lodge* is 80 km away on the Amazon near its junction with the Río Napo. Built in 1964, this was one of the first lodges constructed in the Iquitos area and is much more rustic than the others.

ROB RACHOWIECKI

Yagua dancers and musicians perform on the Amazon.

Lighting is by kerosene lanterns and bathrooms with cold water are shared. The lodge can accommodate up to 100 people and guides accompany visitors on several trails that go further into the forest than do those at the Inn. Rates here are US$250 for three days/two nights and extra nights are US$75.

The *Explornapo Camp* is 160 km from Iquitos on the Río Napo and is the most rustic and most fun. Guests sleep on comfortable mattresses spread out on a communal open-sided sleeping platform. Each mattress is covered with a mosquito net and that is the extent of your privacy, so don't plan a passionate honeymoon here! Good showers and latrines are available. The highlights are guided trail hikes in remote primary forest, birdwatching and a visit to the canopy walkway at the nearby ACEER Lab. Overnight hikes into the rainforest, staying in simple shelters, can be

ACEER's Canopy Walkway

Until a couple of decades ago, biologists working in the rainforest made their observations and collected specimens from the forest floor and along the rivers, unaware that many plant and animal species spent their entire lives in the canopy. When scientists began to venture into the tree tops, they discovered so many new species that the canopy has become known as the new frontier of tropical biology. It is very difficult to visit the canopy unless you are a researcher, but it is possible for interested and adventurous travelers to climb to the top of the rainforest on the ACEER walkway.

By making the canopy more accessible, it is hoped to draw attention to the value of the tropical rainforest habitat. It has been estimated that two-thirds of rainforest species live in the canopy – literally millions of species, most unknown to science. One way to slow the destruction of the rainforest is to make it a valuable cash resource as it stands. With access to the canopy, the rainforest will attract more tourist dollars and encourage countries with rainforests to preserve more of them.

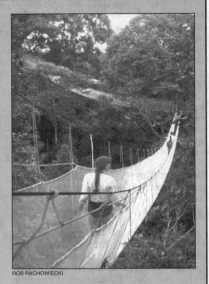
ROB RACHOWIECKI

Ornithologists Paul Donahue and Teresa Wood are co-project managers for the walkway. Paul first became involved in canopy research over a decade ago by constructing platforms in treetops high above the ground. These platforms were simply a metal girder reached by climbing up a rope! Things have come a long way since those days. I was fortunate enough to spend a day both on one of Paul's early platforms (now collapsed) in the 1980s and on the canopy walkway recently and recommend the experience most highly for birdwatchers and those interested in the rainforest. The canopy is accessible by stairs and so any able-bodied visitor won't have too much trouble in climbing to it. A couple of warnings, however. It can get hot up there so bring sun protection and a water bottle. Also, go with realistic expectations. Binoculars will enable you to see scores of tropical bird species but you are not likely to spot many mammals in the canopy. ∎

arranged from here. Because of the distance involved, on five-day/four-night packages you spend the first and last night at the Explorama Lodge. Costs are US$1025 for one person, but much less if you go in a group (eg, US$600 per person for a group of five). Overnight hikes are US$120, extra nights at the Camp are US$90.

The *ACEER Lab* is unique in the Amazon and many people come to Peru solely to visit it. If I were asked to choose only one place in the Amazon in which to spend a few days, this would be my first choice. ACEER is a non-profit foundation created in 1991 by International Expeditions with Conservación de la Naturaleza Amazónica del Peru AC (CONAPAC), and supported by various individuals and private companies, including Explorama. The main goal is to preserve rainforest habitats through sustainable natural resource development including ecologically responsible tourism and through local and global education.

The ACEER is located on the Amazon Biosphere Reserve (a non-government organization) that currently covers over a thousand sq km but is planned to expand to 4000 sq km. For more information, contact ACEER Foundation, 10 Environs Park, Helena, AL 35080, USA.

The highlight at the ACEER Lab is an awe-inspiring hanging walkway that stretches almost half a kilometer through the rainforest canopy, reaching a height of 35 meters above the ground. It is about 10 minutes' walk from the ACEER Lab. See the sidebar for more details.

You can either visit the ACEER Lab from the Explornapo camp (half hour walk) or you can stay at the Lab. This should be booked ahead because accommodations are often used by researchers, workshop groups, or international tours. Accommodations are similar to those at the Explorama Lodge, described above. Rates are US$145 a night if added to the Explornapo five-day/four-night trip, or you can exchange nights at the Explornapo Camp for nights at the ACEER Lab by adding US$55 a night. All visitors contribute US$25 per night (included in the cost) towards the ACEER foundation.

International Expeditions (☎ 1-800-633-4734, 205-428-1700, fax 205-428-1714), One Environs Park, Helena, AL 35080, USA, arranges regular guided expeditions from the USA to the ACEER Lab, including all flights and other arrangements. They also present a recommended annual International Rainforest Workshop, usually held at the ACEER Lab in late March.

Admittedly, visiting the ACEER walkway is not for everyone. It's not cheap, involves a lot of travel, is quite rustic and may terrify you if you are afraid of heights. There are many other good lodges in the Iquitos area that are easier and cheaper to reach and will give you a rewarding look at the rainforest. One of the better established ones is the *Amazonas Sinchicuy Lodge* (☎ 23-3110), Pevas 246, in Lima at Paseos Amazónicos (☎ 446-3838, fax 446-7946). The lodge is on a small tributary of the Amazon, only 25 km northeast of Iquitos,

and offers fairly standard but well-run tours ranging from US$80 for a one day trip to US$210 for a three-day/two-night trip – these are advertised costs for a single passenger but substantial reductions for groups and walk-up discounts can be easily arranged. They also do longer trips visiting other parts of the jungle. Rooms are screened and showers are shared.

Ecological Jungle Trips (☎ 23-7154), Soledad 1321, has very rustic cabins at various points from 75 to 180 km beyond Iquitos. I don't know much about these, but they sound like they may be worth checking out, particularly for travelers on a budget. Rates are about US$40 a night. A recent recommendation is for the small *Amazon River House* about 60 km south of Iquitos. It is near both a village and primary forest and has room for about a dozen people in basic accommodations. Bathing is in a pool near the lodge though showers are planned. The owner (Andres) is a local guide whose main interests lie in rainforest preservation and wildlife. Contact Andres A Peña Guerra, Calle Piura 162, Distrito Punchana (two blocks west of Avenida La Marina and about 2 km north of downtown), or write to Apartado 181, Iquitos, Peru, or the public fax at Telefónica del Peru (☎ 23-1111), marked 'Atención: Andres A Peña Guerra.' This sounds like a good, locally run and reasonably priced operation but I haven't stayed there.

One of the newest is the *Yacumama Lodge*, run by Eco Expeditions (☎ 305-279-8494, 1-800-854-0023, fax 305-279-8093), 10629 N Kendall Drive, Miami, FL 33176 USA. They probably have an Iquitos office by now, but I don't where it is – ask around. The lodge is almost 200 km south of Iquitos on the Río Yarapa, a small tributary of the Río Ucayali. There are about 20 cabins, all carefully screened. A cheaper dormitory-style building is planned for students and budget travelers. The lodge has been built with some thought as to minimum impact on the rainforest. Although bathrooms are shared (separate facilities for men and women) in an effort to consolidate waste in environmentally acceptable septic tanks, hot showers are available through solar panels. Treated water is provided for brushing teeth. Meals and jungle excursions have been recommended. A one-week package from Miami, including air fare, five nights at the lodge with a night at Iquitos at either end, all meals and guided excursions, is about US$1600 from Eco Expeditions.

Amazon Camp is run by Amazon Tours & Cruises (see Cruises, below) and is near the mouth of the Río Momón, an Amazon tributary just north of Iquitos. It is used for first/last nights in Iquitos for passengers on one of the many river cruises offered by this company and can also be used by individual travelers who want to experience a jungle lodge close to Iquitos. Note that you can't get there from Iquitos by car; a river taxi is required and will be provided at the beginning and end of your stay. The lodge has about two dozen rooms with private toilets and lit by kerosene lanterns. Cold showers are in a separate building. Rates are about US$125/190 for singles/doubles for one night including river taxi, meals and short excursions with a discount for passengers taking a cruise or tour. Extra nights are US$85/120. This company also operates several small, remote and very rustic expedition camps and can provide a variety of cruise/lodge options.

Anaconda Lara Lodge (☎ 23-9147), Pevas 210, is on the Río Momón about 40 km from Iquitos. It is used both for day trips to get a taste of the jungle and for overnights. A day trip may include a fast boat to the lodge (one hour), a two hour hike to a village, lunch and drinks, and a stop on the return at a Boras Indian village with a dance for the tourists and craft sales. This costs about US$40, less if you bargain or there's a big group going. An overnight stay is about US$70 including meals and a nighttime river excursion.

There are other places but several closed down during the slump in tourism in the early 1990s. No doubt a number will reopen or new ones emerge now that tourism is recovering.

Cruises

Amazon Tours & Cruises (☎ 23-3931, 23-1611, fax 23-1265), Requena 336, has been operating comfortable cruises for over two decades using a number of boats. You can also reach them in the US: (☎ 305-227-2266, 1-800-423-2791, fax 305-227-1880), 8700 W Flagler St, Suite 190, Miami, FL 33174, USA.

The 44-passenger *M/V Río Amazonas* is their largest ship (length 146 feet) and has 21 air-conditioned cabins with private showers and two or three beds. The 37-passenger *M/V Arca* has 16 small air-conditioned cabins with upper and lower bunks and private showers. The 20-passenger *M/V Delfin* has 10 double cabins with fans and four shower/toilets. All these are typical three- or four-decked Amazon river boats with a lot of romantic charm, and they are comfortable but not luxurious. All have dining areas and bars and plenty of deck space for watching the river go by. Each is accompanied by a full crew including an experienced bilingual local naturalist guide. Small launches are carried for side trips. Smaller boats carying 16 passengers (one has air-conditioning) or six passengers are also available for tours or charter.

The *M/V Río Amazonas* and *M/V Arca* leave Iquitos on Sunday, usually with a complement of passengers who arrived from Miami on the previous Saturday flight. They spend three days sailing downriver to Leticia/Tabatinga and three days returning to Iquitos. Stops are made at jungle towns, Indian villages (dancing and crafts sales), and almost a day is spent looking around the colorful Colombian port of Leticia and neighboring Tabatinga in Brazil. Short side trips are made to lagoons and up tributaries, and hikes in the jungle lasting from one to a few hours are offered. This trip is on a well-traveled and long-settled part of the Amazon and gives a good look at the river and its inhabitants today. Wildlife enthusiasts will see dozens of bird species, pink dolphins and beautiful butterflies and other insects, but you aren't guaranteed to see monkeys or other mammals. A similar trip is offered on the 16-passenger air-conditioned *M/V Amazon Explorer* leaving Iquitos on some Wednesdays.

US tour agencies such as International Journeys (☎ 813-466-6525, 1-800-622-6525, fax 813-466-7685), 17849, San Carlos Blvd, Fort Myers Beach, FL 33931, and Explorations (☎ 813-992-9660, 1-800-446-9600, fax 813-992-7666), 27655 Kent Rd, Bonita Springs, FL 33923, sell complete one-week packages on these two boats. They cost around US$1800 to US$2000 including airfare from Miami, an American biologist guide who accompanies you from Miami and throughout the trip (in addition to the on-board local naturalist guide), pre-departure information, all meals and hotel nights at either end. If you book direct with Amazon Tours & Cruises, you'll get the tour for a little less than half the price (without air from Miami, hotels, US guide) but some dates are unavailable if they have been blocked out by US tour groups. If you just show up in Iquitos, you can go even more cheaply on a space available basis but, with boats leaving once a week, you might have to wait for a week or two for space to become available. One-way passages for travelers wanting to continue into or arrive from Brazil or Colombia are also sold on a space available basis – these are open to bargaining.

The smaller *M/V Delfin* has scheduled departures for trips south to the Nauta area of the Río Marañón and to other areas. The smaller boats have a variety of destinations to various other rivers. All of these are available for charter from Amazon Tours & Cruises.

A new boat, operated by International Expeditions and Explorama (see Jungle Lodges, above, for addresses) began cruising in late 1994. The *M/V La Esmeralda* is an attractive small vessel carrying 16 passengers in air-conditioned double cabins. The small size of the boat enables it to navigate south of Iquitos along the Río Ucayali and the minor tributary of the Río Tapiche. Villages visited are unjaded by tourism. There are much greater opportunities to see

more wildlife, particularly various monkey species, than there are on the Amazon. Pink dolphin sightings occur several times a day and there are plenty of birds for the bird-watcher. Although the boat has only been operating for a short while I have received enthusiastic recommendations about it.

Roughing It
Various jungle guides can be found in Iquitos. They'll approach you at the airport, in restaurants or on the street. Their quality and reliability varies considerably and you should try to get references for any guide and proceed with caution. The better jungle lodge companies can provide reputable guides. Amazon Tours & Cruises arranges trips using thatch roofed, open sided expedition boats in which you sling a hammock or camp on shore. These trips are complete with guide, crew and cook and last from one to six nights. Rates depend on how many people are in a group and the longer tours are more economical. A six-night tour with about seven passengers might be around US$320 per person – you can try bargaining for a better rate if you just show up.

Moisés Torres Viena, on Brasil near Próspero, has been organizing trips for many years and is probably reliable, though not cheap. His jungle expeditions include camping, overnights in Indian villages, long walks in the jungle and catching your own food. Some river travel is involved. Moisés doesn't speak English. Tours reportedly last from a couple of days to over a month.

Adventure Tours Amazonia, Lores 267, has recently been recommended for adventure tours of varying lengths and difficulties. They reportedly start by charging the 'official' price of US$80 per day, but soon come down to under US$30 a day if there is a serious group of you. Another recent recommendation is for Arturo Díaz Ruiz, Soledad 1226 (follow Abtao six blocks west of Moore), who charges US$60 per person for a three-night expedition, meeting local people, building shelters to sleep in, fishing and canoeing. But the mosquitoes are pretty bad!

THE TRI-BORDER

Before leaving Peru, you need to get an exit stamp in your passport and you can't get an exit stamp if your entry stamp has expired. However, don't think that just because you are in the middle of the Amazon jungle nobody will bother to check. On the contrary, border officials have very little to do other than refuse you passage if your documents are not in order, so make sure you have enough days left on your visa or tourist card before attempting the trip.

Exit formalities change frequently. When I last left Peru for Brazil, I received my exit stamp at a Peruvian guard post just before the border (the boat stopped there long enough for travelers to do this, though make sure that the captain agrees to this before you leave Iquitos).

There are several ports at the three-way border that are several kilometers apart and connected by public ferries. They are reached by air or boat, but not road. The biggest town, Leticia in Colombia, boasts by far the best hotels, restaurants and a hospital. If you want to enter Colombia from Leticia, you can take one of the infrequent boats to Puerto Asis on the Río Putumayo – the trip can take almost two weeks. From Puerto Asis, you can catch a bus further into Colombia. Alternatively, you can fly from Leticia to Bogotá on almost daily commercial flights.

There are two small ports in the Brazilian section: Tabatinga and Benjamin Constant. Both have basic hotels. Tabatinga has an airport with flights to Manaus and Iquitos. Tabatinga is a continuation of Leticia and you can easily walk or take a taxi between the two with no immigration hassles, unless you are planning on traveling further into Brazil or Colombia. Boats leave from Tabatinga down river, usually stopping in Benjamin Constant for a night, then continuing on to Manaus, Brazil, a week away. Brazilian entry formalities are in Tabatinga. It takes about an hour to reach Benjamin Constant by public ferry.

Peru is on the south side of the river and currents here create a constantly shifting bank. The old ports of Ramón Castilla and Islandia are now disused. Most boats from Iquitos will drop you at Santa Rosa, where there are Peruvian immigration facilities and from where a motor canoe can take you to Leticia in about 15 minutes. If you are heading for Colombia or Brazil, Lonely Planet has guidebooks available for both countries.

If you are arriving from Colombia or Brazil, you'll find boats in Tabatinga and Leticia for Iquitos, US$20 or less for the three-day trip on a cargo river boat, US$50 for an expreso (12-14 hours) leaving three times a week. The cruise ships leave on Wednesdays and arrive in Iquitos on Saturday morning.

Bear in mind that the border hotels and restaurants (with the exception of Leticia) are fairly basic and slightly more expensive than other parts of Peru. Also remember that however disorganized things may appear you can always get meals, beds, money changed, boats and other services simply by asking around. The locals are used to the different way of doing things on the river, so ask them. As my Polish mother used to tell me, 'Koniec języka za przewodnika' – which, perhaps, is an appropriate way to finish this book. Roughly translated, it means 'Use your tongue as your guide.'

Appendix I: Climate Charts

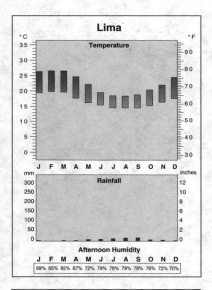

Lima

°C / °F — Temperature

mm / inches — Rainfall

Afternoon Humidity

J	F	M	A	M	J	J	A	S	O	N	D
69%	65%	65%	67%	72%	79%	78%	79%	78%	76%	72%	70%

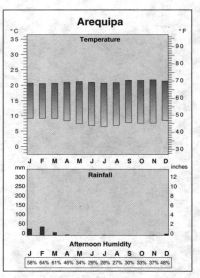

Arequipa

°C / °F — Temperature

mm / inches — Rainfall

Afternoon Humidity

J	F	M	A	M	J	J	A	S	O	N	D
58%	64%	61%	46%	34%	29%	28%	27%	30%	33%	37%	48%

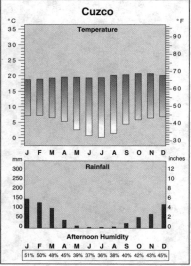

Cuzco

°C / °F — Temperature

mm / inches — Rainfall

Afternoon Humidity

J	F	M	A	M	J	J	A	S	O	N	D
51%	50%	48%	45%	39%	37%	36%	38%	40%	42%	43%	45%

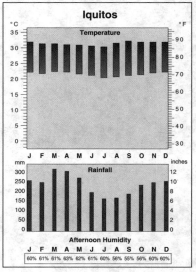

Iquitos

°C / °F — Temperature

mm / inches — Rainfall

Afternoon Humidity

J	F	M	A	M	J	J	A	S	O	N	D
60%	61%	61%	63%	62%	61%	60%	56%	55%	56%	60%	60%

Index

MAPS

TEXT

Thanks

Thanks to all the following travelers and
others (appologies if we have misspelled
your name) who took time to write to us
about their experiences in Peru.

Hal & Pat Amens
Peter Bolger
Lisette Boot
Matthew D Briggs
Jim Clements
Mike Clulow
Paul R Cripps
Susi Deterding
Mr M Drews
Kenneth Dreyfuss
Patricia Edmisten
Julian & Angie Fletcher
Patrick Francis
Emma Friers
Massimo Giannini
Edith Bellota Guzman
Ann Hertsens & Fico Aleman Arevalo
Pat Hickey

Ann Jones
Colleen Kelly
John Jose Kevin & Clare Langford
Gwenda Lansbury
Robie Loomer
Ian Macmillan
Bruce & Cheryl McLaren
Christina Maile
Charles Mays
Carolina Miranda
Matt Oliver
Susan Paven
Arne Ragossnig
Jan Rensen
Charles Thuaire
DrThuro
Helen Trott
Dvan der Laag
M Daeleman & P van Rompaey
Mrs B Wearne
Kathy Wiles
Mike Wilson
Niko Wolswijk

LONELY PLANET PHRASEBOOKS

Building bridges,
Breaking barriers,
Beyond babble-on

Listen for the gems

Speak your own words

Ask your own questions

Master of your own image

- handy pocket-sized books
- easy to understand Pronunciation chapter
- clear and comprehensive Grammar chapter
- romanisation alongside script to allow ease of pronunciation
- script throughout so users can point to phrases
- extensive vocabulary sections, words and phrases for every situation
- full of cultural information and tips for the traveller

'...vital for a real DIY spirit and attitude in language learning' – Backpacker

'the phrasebooks have good cultural backgrounders and offer solid advice for challenging situations in remote locations' – San Francisco Examiner

'...they are unbeatable for their coverage of the world's more obscure languages' – The Geographical Magazine

---

Arabic (Egyptian)
Arabic (Moroccan)
Australia
   Australian English, Aboriginal and Torres Strait languages
Baltic States
   Estonian, Latvian, Lithuanian
Bengali
Brazilian
Burmese
Cantonese
Central Asia
Central Europe
   Czech, French, German, Hungarian, Italian and Slovak
Eastern Europe
   Bulgarian, Czech, Hungarian, Polish, Romanian and Slovak
Ethiopian (Amharic)
Fijian
French
German
Greek

Hindi/Urdu
Indonesian
Italian
Japanese
Korean
Lao
Latin American Spanish
Malay
Mandarin
Mediterranean Europe
   Albanian, Croatian, Greek, Italian, Macedonian, Maltese, Serbian and Slovene
Mongolian
Nepali
Papua New Guinea
Pilipino (Tagalog)
Quechua
Russian
Scandinavian Europe
   Danish, Finnish, Icelandic, Norwegian and Swedish

South-East Asia
   Burmese, Indonesian, Khmer, Lao, Malay, Tagalog (Pilipino), Thai and Vietnamese
Spanish (Castilian)
   Basque, Catalan and Galician
Sri Lanka
Swahili
Thai
Thai Hill Tribes
Tibetan
Turkish
Ukrainian
USA
   US English, Vernacular, Native American languages and Hawaiian
Vietnamese
Western Europe
   Basque, Catalan, Dutch, French, German, Irish, Italian, Portuguese, Scottish Gaelic, Spanish (Castilian) and Welsh

---

LONELY PLANET JOURNEYS

JOURNEYS is a unique collection of travel writing – published by the company that understands travel better than anyone else. It is a series for anyone who has ever experienced – or dreamed of – the magical moment when they encountered a strange culture or saw a place for the first time. They are tales to read while you're planning a trip, while you're on the road or while you're in an armchair, in front of a fire.

JOURNEYS books catch the spirit of a place, illuminate a culture, recount a crazy adventure, or introduce a fascinating way of life. They always entertain, and always enrich the experience of travel.

'Idiosyncratic, entertainingly diverse and unexpected . . . from an international writership'
– The Australian

'Books which offer a closer look at the people and culture of a destination, and enrich travel experiences'
– American Bookseller

FULL CIRCLE
A South American Journey
Luis Sepúlveda
Translated by Chris Andrews

Full Circle invites us to accompany Chilean writer Luis Sepúlveda on 'a journey without a fixed itinerary'. Whatever his subject – brutalities suffered under Pinochet's dictatorship, sleepy tropical towns visited in exile, or the landscapes of legendary Patagonia – Sepúlveda is an unflinchingly honest yet lyrical storyteller. Extravagant characters and extraordinary situations are memorably evoked: gauchos organising a tournament of lies, a scheming heiress on the lookout for a husband, a pilot with a corpse on board his plane . . . Part autobiography, part travel memoir, *Full Circle* brings us the distinctive voice of one of South America's most compelling writers.

Luis Sepúlveda was born in Chile in 1949. Imprisoned by the Pinochet dictatorship for his socialist beliefs, he was for many years a political exile. He has written novels, short stories, plays and essays. His work has attracted many awards and has been translated into numerous languages.

'Detachment, humour and vibrant prose' **– El País**

'an absolute cracker' **– The Bookseller**

This project has been assisted by the Commonwealth Government through the Australia Council, its arts funding and advisory body.

LONELY PLANET TRAVEL ATLASES

Lonely Planet has long been famous for the number and quality of its guidebook maps. Now we've gone one step further and produced a handy companion series: Lonely Planet travel atlases – maps of a country produced in book form.

Unlike other maps, which look good but lead travellers astray, our travel atlases have been researched on the road by Lonely Planet's experienced team of writers. All details are carefully checked to ensure the atlas corresponds with the equivalent Lonely Planet guidebook.

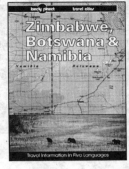

The handy atlas format means no holes, wrinkles, torn sections or constant folding and unfolding. These atlases can survive long periods on the road, unlike cumbersome fold-out maps. The comprehensive index ensures easy reference.

- full-colour throughout
- maps researched and checked by Lonely Planet authors
- place names correspond with Lonely Planet guidebooks
  – no confusing spelling differences
- legend and travelling information in English, French, German,
  Japanese and Spanish
- size: 230 x 160 mm

Available now:
Chile & Easter Island • Egypt • India & Bangladesh • Israel & the Palestinian Territories •Jordan, Syria & Lebanon • Kenya • Laos • Portugal • South Africa, Lesotho & Swaziland • Thailand • Turkey • Vietnam • Zimbabwe, Botswana & Namibia

---

LONELY PLANET TV SERIES & VIDEOS

Lonely Planet travel guides have been brought to life on television screens around the world. Like our guides, the programmes are based on the joy of independent travel, and look honestly at some of the most exciting, picturesque and frustrating places in the world. Each show is presented by one of three travellers from Australia, England or the USA and combines an innovative mixture of video, Super-8 film, atmospheric soundscapes and original music.

Videos of each episode – containing additional footage not shown on television – are available from good book and video shops, but the availability of individual videos varies with regional screening schedules.

Video destinations include: Alaska • American Rockies • Australia – The South-East • Baja California & the Copper Canyon • Brazil • Central Asia • Chile & Easter Island • Corsica, Sicily & Sardinia – The Mediterranean Islands • East Africa (Tanzania & Zanzibar) • Ecuador & the Galapagos Islands • Greenland & Iceland • Indonesia • Israel & the Sinai Desert • Jamaica • Japan • La Ruta Maya • Morocco • New York • North India • Pacific Islands (Fiji, Solomon Islands & Vanuatu) • South India • South West China • Turkey • Vietnam • West Africa • Zimbabwe, Botswana & Namibia

The Lonely Planet TV series is produced by:
Pilot Productions
The Old Studio
18 Middle Row
London W10 5AT UK

For video availability and ordering information contact your nearest Lonely Planet office.

Music from the TV series is available on CD & cassette.

PLANET TALK

Lonely Planet's FREE quarterly newsletter

We love hearing from you and think you'd like to hear from us.

When...is the right time to see reindeer in Finland?
Where...can you hear the best palm-wine music in Ghana?
How...do you get from Asunción to Areguá by steam train?
What...is the best way to see India?

For the answer to these and many other questions read PLANET TALK.

Every issue is packed with up-to-date travel news and advice including:

* a letter from Lonely Planet co-founders Tony and Maureen Wheeler
* go behind the scenes on the road with a Lonely Planet author
* feature article on an important and topical travel issue
* a selection of recent letters from travellers
* details on forthcoming Lonely Planet promotions
* complete list of Lonely Planet products

To join our mailing list contact any Lonely Planet office.

Also available: Lonely Planet T-shirts. 100% heavyweight cotton.

LONELY PLANET ONLINE

Get the latest travel information before you leave or while you're on the road

Whether you've just begun planning your next trip, or you're chasing down specific info on currency regulations or visa requirements, check out Lonely Planet Online for up-to-the minute travel information.

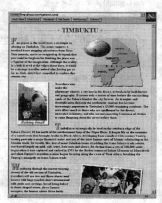

As well as travel profiles of your favourite destinations (including maps and photos), you'll find current reports from our researchers and other travellers, updates on health and visas, travel advisories, and discussion of the ecological and political issues you need to be aware of as you travel.

There's also an online travellers' forum where you can share your experience of life on the road, meet travel companions and ask other travellers for their recommendations and advice. We also have plenty of links to other online sites useful to independent travellers.

And of course we have a complete and up-to-date list of all Lonely Planet travel products including guides, phrasebooks, atlases, Journeys and videos and a simple online ordering facility if you can't find the book you want elsewhere.

www.lonelyplanet.com
or
AOL keyword: lp

LONELY PLANET PRODUCTS

Lonely Planet is known worldwide for publishing practical, reliable and no-nonsense travel information in our guides and on our web site. The Lonely Planet list covers just about every accessible part of the world. Currently there are nine series: *travel guides, shoestring guides, walking guides, city guides, phrasebooks, audio packs, travel atlases, Journeys – a unique collection of travel writing and Pisces Books - diving and snorkeling guides.*

EUROPE

Amsterdam • Andalucia • Austria • Baltic States phrasebook • Berlin • Britain • Canary Islands • Central Europe on a shoestring • Central Europe phrasebook • Czech & Slovak Republics • Denmark • Dublin • Eastern Europe on a shoestring • Eastern Europe phrasebook • Estonia, Latvia & Lithuania • Finland • France • French phrasebook • Germany • German phrasebook • Greece • Greek phrasebook • Hungary • Iceland, Greenland & the Faroe Islands • Ireland • Italian phrasebook • Italy • Lisbon • London • Mediterranean Europe on a shoestring • Mediterranean Europe phrasebook • Paris • Poland • Portugal • Portugal travel atlas • Prague • Romania & Moldova • Russia, Ukraine & Belarus • Russian phrasebook • Scandinavian & Baltic Europe on a shoestring • Scandinavian Europe phrasebook • Slovenia • Spain • Spanish phrasebook • St Petersburg • Switzerland • Trekking in Spain • Ukrainian phrasebook • Vienna • Walking in Britain • Walking in Italy • Walking in Switzerland • Western Europe on a shoestring • Western Europe phrasebook
Travel Literature: The Olive Grove: Travels in Greece

NORTH AMERICA

Alaska • Backpacking in Alaska • Baja California • California & Nevada • Canada • Chicago • Deep South • Florida • Hawaii • Honolulu • Los Angeles • Mexico • Mexico City • Miami • New England • New Orleans • New York City • New York, New Jersey & Pennsylvania • Pacific Northwest USA • Rocky Mountain States • San Francisco • Seattle • Southwest USA • USA phrasebook • Washington, DC & the Capital Region
Travel Literature: Drive thru America

CENTRAL AMERICA & THE CARIBBEAN

• Bahamas and Turks & Caicos • Bermuda • Central America on a shoestring • Costa Rica • Cuba • Eastern Caribbean • Guatemala, Belize & Yucatán: La Ruta Maya • Jamaica
Travel Literature Green Dreams: Travels in Central America

SOUTH AMERICA

Argentina, Uruguay & Paraguay • Bolivia • Brazil • Brazilian phrasebook • Buenos Aires • Chile & Easter Island • Chile & Easter Island travel atlas • Colombia • Ecuador & the Galápagos Islands • Latin American Spanish phrasebook • Peru • Quechua phrasebook • Rio de Janeiro • South America on a shoestring • Trekking in the Patagonian Andes • Venezuela
Travel Literature: Full Circle: A South American Journey

ISLANDS OF THE INDIAN OCEAN

Madagascar & Comoros • Maldives • Mauritius, Réunion & Seychelles

AFRICA

Africa - the South • Africa on a shoestring • Arabic (Moroccan) phrasebook • Cairo • Cape Town • Central Africa • East Africa • Egypt • Egypt travel atlas • Ethiopian (Amharic) phrasebook • The Gambia & Senegal • Kenya • Kenya travel atlas • Malawi, Mozambique & Zambia • Morocco • North Africa • South Africa, Lesotho & Swaziland • South Africa, Lesotho & Swaziland travel atlas • Swahili phrasebook • Tunisia • Trekking in East Africa • West Africa • Zimbabwe, Botswana & Namibia • Zimbabwe, Botswana & Namibia travel atlas
Travel Literature: Mali Blues • The Rainbird: A Central African Journey • Songs to an African Sunset: A Zimbabwean Story

MAIL ORDER

Lonely Planet products are distributed worldwide.They are also available by mail order from Lonely Planet, so if you have difficulty finding a title please write to us. North American and South American residents should write to 150 Linden St, Oakland CA 94607, USA; European and African residents should write to 10a Spring Place, London NW5 3BH; and residents of other countries to PO Box 617, Hawthorn, Victoria 3122, Australia.

NORTH-EAST ASIA

Beijing • Cantonese phrasebook • China • Hong Kong • Hong Kong, Macau & Guangzhou • Japan • Japanese phrasebook • Japanese audio pack • Korea • Korean phrasebook • Kyoto • Mandarin phrasebook • Mongolia • Mongolian phrasebook • North-East Asia on a shoestring • Seoul • Taiwan • Tibet • Tibet phrasebook • Tokyo
Travel Literature: Lost Japan

INDIAN SUBCONTINENT

Bangladesh • Bengali phrasebook • Bhutan • Delhi • Goa • Hindi/Urdu phrasebook • India • India & Bangladesh travel atlas • Indian Himalaya • Karakoram Highway • Nepal • Nepali phrasebook • Pakistan • Rajasthan • South India • Sri Lanka • Sri Lanka phrasebook • Trekking in the Indian Himalaya • Trekking in the Karakoram & Hindukush • Trekking in the Nepal Himalaya
Travel Literature: In Rajasthan • Shopping for Buddhas

SOUTH-EAST ASIA

Bali & Lombok • Bangkok • Burmese phrasebook • Cambodia • Ho Chi Minh City • Indonesia • Indonesian phrasebook • Indonesian audio pack • Indonesia's Eastern Islands • Jakarta • Java • Laos • Lao phrasebook • Laos travel atlas • Malay phrasebook • Malaysia, Singapore & Brunei • Myanmar (Burma) • Philippines • Pilipino phrasebook • Singapore • South-East Asia on a shoestring • South-East Asia phrasebook • South-West China • Thailand • Thailand's Islands & Beaches • Thailand travel atlas • Thai phrasebook • Thai audio pack • Thai Hill Tribes phrasebook • Vietnam • Vietnamese phrasebook • Vietnam travel atlas

AUSTRALIA & THE PACIFIC

Australia • Australian phrasebook • Bushwalking in Australia • Bushwalking in Papua New Guinea • Fiji • Fijian phrasebook • Islands of Australia's Great Barrier Reef • Melbourne • Micronesia • New Caledonia • New South Wales • New Zealand • Northern Territory • Outback Australia • Papua New Guinea • Papua New Guinea phrasebook • Queensland • Rarotonga & the Cook Islands • Samoa • Solomon Islands • South Australia • Sydney • Tahiti & French Polynesia • Tasmania • Tonga • Tramping in New Zealand • Vanuatu • Victoria • Western Australia
Travel Literature: Islands in the Clouds • Sean & David's Long Drive

MIDDLE EAST & CENTRAL ASIA

Arab Gulf States • Arabic (Egyptian) phrasebook • Central Asia • Central Asia phrasebook • Iran • Israel & the Palestinian Territories • Israel & the Palestinian Territories travel atlas • Istanbul • Jerusalem • Jordan & Syria • Jordan, Syria & Lebanon travel atlas • Lebanon • Middle East • Turkey • Turkish phrasebook • Turkey travel atlas • Yemen
Travel Literature: The Gates of Damascus • Kingdom of the Film Stars: Journey into Jordan

ALSO AVAILABLE:

Brief Encounters • Travel with Children • Traveller's Tales • Not the Only Planet

ANTARCTICA

Antarctica

THE LONELY PLANET STORY

Lonely Planet published its first book in 1973 in response to the numerous 'How did you do it?' questions Maureen and Tony Wheeler were asked after driving, busing, hitching, sailing and railing their way from England to Australia.

Written at a kitchen table and hand collated, trimmed and stapled, *Across Asia on the Cheap* became an instant local bestseller, inspiring thoughts of another book.

Eighteen months in South-East Asia resulted in their second guide, *South-East Asia on a shoestring*, which they put together in a backstreet Chinese hotel in Singapore in 1975. The 'yellow bible', as it quickly became known to backpackers around the world, soon became *the* guide to the region. It has sold well over half a million copies and is now in its 9th edition, still retaining its familiar yellow cover.

Today there are over 350 titles, including travel guides, walking guides, language kits & phrasebooks, travel atlases and travel literature. The company is the largest independent travel publisher in the world. Although Lonely Planet initially specialised in guides to Asia, today there are few corners of the globe that have not been covered.

The emphasis continues to be on travel for independent travellers. Tony and Maureen still travel for several months of each year and play an active part in the writing, updating and quality control of Lonely Planet's guides.

They have been joined by over 80 authors and 200 staff at our offices in Melbourne (Australia), Oakland (USA), London (UK) and Paris (France). Travellers themselves also make a valuable contribution to the guides through the feedback we receive in thousands of letters each year and on our web site.

The people at Lonely Planet strongly believe that travellers can make a positive contribution to the countries they visit, both through their appreciation of the countries' culture, wildlife and natural features, and through the money they spend. In addition, the company makes a direct contribution to the countries and regions it covers. Since 1986 a percentage of the income from each book has been donated to ventures such as famine relief in Africa; aid projects in India; agricultural projects in Central America; Greenpeace's efforts to halt French nuclear testing in the Pacific; and Amnesty International.

'I hope we send people out with the right attitude about travel. You realise when you travel that there are so many different perspectives about the world, so we hope these books will make people more interested in what they see. Guidebooks can't really guide people. All you can do is point them in the right direction.'

– Tony Wheeler

LONELY PLANET PUBLICATIONS

Australia
PO Box 617, Hawthorn 3122, Victoria
tel: (03) 9819 1877 fax: (03) 9819 6459
e-mail: talk2us@lonelyplanet.com.au

USA
150 Linden St
Oakland, CA 94607
tel: (510) 893 8555 TOLL FREE: 800 275-8555
fax: (510) 893 8572
e-mail: info@lonelyplanet.com

UK
10a Spring Place,
London NW5 3BH
tel: (0171) 428 4800 fax: (0171) 428 4828
e-mail: go@lonelyplanet.co.uk

France:
1 rue du Dahomey, 75011 Paris
tel: 01 55 25 33 00 fax: 01 55 25 33 01
e-mail: bip@lonelyplanet.fr

**World Wide Web: http://www.lonelyplanet.com
or *AOL keyword: lp***